CENSUS OF INDIA 1931

CENSUS OF INDIA, 1931

BOOK - 6: VOLUME - III

ASSAM

PART II - TABLES
PART III - ADMINISTRATIVE REPORT

C. S. MULLAN

GYAN

Published by

Gyan Publishing House
5, Ansari Road
Daryaganj, New Delhi-110002
Phone: 011-47034999, 9811692060
E-mail: books@gyanbooks.com

Distribution Network
gyanbooks.com
India, USA, Canada, UK, Australia

ISBN: 978-81-212-7123-3 (Set) 28 Vols. In 52 Bindings

ISBN: 978-81-212-7603-0 (PB) Vol. III, Pt. II, III

First Published, 1932

2nd Impression 2024

Printed at: Gyan Press, Delhi.

CENSUS OF INDIA 1931

Census of India, 1931

VOLUME III

ASSAM

PART II.—TABLES

By

C. S. MULLAN, M.A., I.C.S.

SHILLONG
PRINTED BY THE SUPERINTENDENT, ASSAM GOVERNMENT PRESS,
AND PUBLISHED BY THE GOVERNMENT OF INDIA
CENTRAL PUBLICATION BRANCH, CALCUTTA.
1932

Government of India Publications are obtainable from the Government of India Central Publication Branch, 3, Government Place, West, Calcutta, and from the following Agents :—

EUROPE.

OFFICE OF THE HIGH COMMISSIONER FOR INDIA, INDIA HOUSE, ALDWYCH, LONDON, W.C. 2.

And at all Booksellers.

INDIA AND CEYLON: Provincial Book Depôts.

MADRAS:—Superintendent, Government Press, Mount Road, Madras.
BOMBAY:—Superintendent, Government Printing and Stationery, Queen's Road, Bombay.
SIND:—Library attached to the Office of the Commissioner in Sind, Karachi.
BENGAL:—Bengal Secretariat Book Depôt, Writers' Buildings, Room No. 1, Ground Floor, Calcutta.
UNITED PROVINCES OF AGRA AND OUDH:—Superintendent of Government Press, United Provinces of Agra and Oudh, Allahabad.
PUNJAB:—Superintendent, Government Printing, Punjab, Lahore.
BURMA:—Superintendent, Government Printing, Burma, Rangoon.
CENTRAL PROVINCES AND BERAR:—Superintendent, Government Printing, Central Provinces, Nagpur.
ASSAM:—Superintendent, Assam Secretariat Press, Shillong.
BIHAR AND ORISSA:—Superintendent, Government Printing, Bihar and Orissa, P.O. Gulzarbagh, Patna.
NORTH-WEST FRONTIER PROVINCE:—Manager, Government Printing and Stationery, Peshawar.

Thacker Spink & Co., Calcutta and Simla.
W. Newman & Co., Ltd., Calcutta.
S. K. Lahiri & Co., Calcutta.
The Indian School Supply Depôt, 309, Bow Bazar Street, Calcutta.
Butterworth & Co. (India), Ltd., Calcutta.
M. C. Sarcar & Sons, 15, College Square, Calcutta.
Standard Literature Company, Limited, Calcutta.
Association Press, Calcutta.
Chukervertty, Chatterjee & Co., Ltd., 13, College Square, Calcutta.
The Book Company, Calcutta.
James Murray & Co., 12, Government Place, Calcutta. (For Meteorological Publications only.)
Ray, Chaudhury & Co., 68-5, Ashutosh Mukherji Road, Calcutta.
Scientific Publishing Co., 9, Taltolla Lane, Calcutta.
Chatterjee & Co., 3-1, Bacharam Chatterjee Lane, Calcutta.
Standard Law Book Society, 8-2, Hastings Street, Calcutta.
The Hindu Library, 3, Nandalal Mallick Lane, Calcutta.
Kamala Book Depôt, Ltd., 15, College Square, Calcutta.
* Bengal Flying Club, Dum Dum Cantt.
Kali Charan and Co., Municipal Market, Calcutta.
B. C. Basak, Esq., Proprietor, Albert Library, Dacca.
Higginbothams, Madras.
Rochouse & Sons, Madras.
G. A. Nateson & Co., Publishers, George Town, Madras.
P. Varadachary & Co., Madras.
City Book Co., Madras.
Law Publishing Co., Mylapore, Madras.
The Booklover's Resort, Taikad, Trivandrum, South India.
E. M. Gopalakrishna Kone, Pudumandapam, Madura.
Central Book Depôt, Madura.
Vijapur & Co., Vizagapatam.
Thacker & Co., Ltd., Bombay.
D. B. Taraporevala Sons & Co., Bombay.
Ram Chandra Govind & Sons, Kalbadevi Road, Bombay.
N. M. Tripathi & Co., Booksellers, Princess Street, Kalbadevi Road, Bombay.
New and Secondhand Bookshop, Kalbadevi Road, Bombay.
J. M. Pandia & Co., Bombay.
A. H. Wheeler & Co., Allahabad, Calcutta and Bombay.
Bombay Book Depôt, Girgaon, Bombay.
Bennett Coleman and Co., Ltd., The Times of India Press, Bombay.
The Manager, Oriental Book Supplying Agency, 15, Shukrawar, Poona City.
Rama Krishna Bros., Opposite Vishrambag, Poona City.
S. P. Bookstall, 21, Budhwar, Poona.
Mangaldas & Sons, Booksellers and Publishers, Bhaga Talao, Surat.
The Standard Book and Stationery Co., 32-33, Arbab Road, Peshawar.
The Students Own Book Depôt, Dharwar.
Shri Shankar Karnataka Pustaka Bhandara, Malamuddi, Dharwar.
The Standard Bookstall, Karachi, Quetta, Delhi, Murree and Rawalpindi.
*Hossenbhoy Karimji and Sons, Karachi.
The English Bookstall, Karachi.
The Standard Bookstall, Quetta.
U. P. Malhotra & Co., Quetta.
J. Ray & Sons, 43 K. & L., Edwardes Road, Rawalpindi, Murree and Lahore.
The Standard Book Depôt, Lahore, Nainital, Mussoorie, Dalhousie, Ambala Cantonment and Delhi.
The North India Christian Tract and Book Society, 18, Clive Road, Allahabad.
Ram Narain Lal, Katra, Allahabad.
The Indian Army Book Depôt, Dayalbagh, Agra.
Narayan & Co., Meston Road, Cawnpore.
The Indian Army Book Depôt, Jullundur City—Daryaganj, Delhi.
Manager, Newal Kishore Press, Lucknow.
The Upper India Publishing House, Ltd., Literature Palace, Ammuddaula Park, Lucknow.
Rai Sahib M. Gulab Singh & Sons, Mufid-i-Am Press, Lahore and Allahabad.
Rama Krishna & Sons, Booksellers, Anarkali, Lahore.
Student Popular Depôt, Anarkali, Lahore.
The Standard Bookstall, Lahore.
The Proprietor, Punjab Sanskrit Book Depôt, Saidmitha Street, Lahore.
The Insurance Publicity Co., Ltd., Lahore.
The Punjab Religious Book Society, Lahore.
The Commercial Book Co., Lahore.
The University Book Agency, Kachari Road, Lahore.
Manager of the Imperial Book Depôt, 63, Chandni Chowk Street, Delhi.
J. M. Jaina and Bros., Delhi.
Fono Book Agency, New Delhi and Simla.
Oxford Book and Stationery Company, Delhi, Lahore, Simla, Meerut and Calcutta.
Supdt., American Baptist Mission Press, Rangoon.
Burma Book Club, Ltd., Rangoon.
S. C. Talukdar, Proprietor, Students & Co., Cooch Behar.
The Manager, The Indian Book Shop, Benares City.
Nandkishore & Bros., Chowk, Benares City.
The Srivilliputtur Co-operative Trading Union, Ltd., Srivilliputtur (S. I. R.).
Raghunath Prasad & Sons, Patna City.
The Students' Emporium, Patna.
K. L. Mathur & Bros., Guzri, Patna City.
Kamala Book Stores, Bankipore, Patna.
G. Banarjea and Bros., Ranchi.
M. C. Kothari, Raipura Road, Baroda.
The Hyderabad Book Depôt, Chaderghat, Hyderabad (Deccan).
S. Krishnaswamy & Co., Teppakulam P. O., Trichinopoly Fort.
Karnataka Publishing House, Bangalore City.
Bheema Sons, Fort, Bangalore City.
Superintendent, Bangalore Press, Lake View, Mysore Road, Bangalore City.

AGENT IN PALESTINE:—Steimatzky, Jerusalem.

* Agents for publications on aviation only.

TABLE OF CONTENTS.

IMPERIAL TABLES.

Table.		Page.
I	Area, houses and population	1
II	Variation in population since 1881	3
III	Towns and villages classified by population	5
IV	Towns classified by population with variations since 1881 ...	7
V	Towns arranged territorially with population by religion ...	9
VI	Birthplace	13
VII	Age, sex and civil condition	35
	Part A.—Provincial Summary	36
	Part B.—Details for districts and States	43
VIII	Civil condition by age for selected castes...	63
IX	Infirmities	65
	Part I.—Distribution by age	66
	Part II.—Distribution by districts and States	67
X	Occupation or means of livelihood	69
	Part I.—Provincial Summary	70
	Part II.—Details for districts and States	86
XIII	Literacy by religion and age	211
	Part I.—Provincial Summary	212
	Part II.—Details for districts and States	214
XIV	Literacy by selected castes, tribes or races	223
XV	Language	225
	Part I.—Language	226
	Part II.—Bilingualism	252
XVI	Religion	255
XVII	Caste, tribe or race	259
	Appendix I.—Kuki (details)	262
	II.—Lushei-Kuki (details)	263
	III.—Naga (details)	264
	IV.—Nepalis (details)	265
	V.—Hindu "exterior" castes	266
XVIII	Variation of population of selected tribes and castes	267
XIX	Europeans by race and age	271
	Part I.—European and Allied Races	272
	Part II.—Anglo-Indians	274

PROVINCIAL TABLES.

Table.		Page.
I	Area and population of thanas, mauzas and other local units ...	275
II	Population of Districts, Subdivisions and Thanas by Religion and Literacy	291
III	Tea Garden Population by Sex and Religion	311

Imperial Table XI—Occupation of selected castes—has not been compiled for Assam. Imperial Table XII—Unemployment of educated persons—is not printed as an Imperial Table but has been shown as a Subsidiary Table in Chapter VIII—Occupation—of the Report Volume.

TABLE I.

AREA, HOUSES AND POPULATION.

This table shows for each district and for the State of Manipur and the Khasi States the area, the number of towns and villages, the number of occupied houses and the total urban and rural population, male and female.

The areas of the various districts in the table have been calculated by the Survey Department from modern maps. A large amount of topographical survey work has been done in the province during the last ten years and the areas given in previous Census Reports, which were calculated from old maps, are mostly inaccurate.

Although the exact area of the whole of the Khasi and Jaintia Hills is known, the exact area of the British portion of the district and the area of the Khasi States portion are not known as the boundaries between the two have never been precisely defined. The separate areas of the Khasi States and the British portion of the Khasi and Jaintia Hills as given in these tables must therefore be considered as approximate only.

The area of the Sadiya Frontier Tract is the administered (and censused) area as calculated by the Political Officer from up-to-date maps.

The areas added to the province since 1921 as the result of the incorporation into British India of previously unadministered tracts are as follows :—

	Area in square miles.	Population.
1. The Melomi Primi area in the Kohima Subdivision of the Naga Hills	396	4,620
2. Six villages east of Mokokchung...	32	2,200
3. The Zongling area to the south of the Lungleh Subdivision, Lushai Hills	160	1,696
4. Various Abor and Naga villages in the Sadiya Frontier Tract	320 (approximately).	7,195

The total area added to British territory in Assam since 1921 is thus approximately 908 square miles with a population of 15,711.

The total mapped areas of the Sadiya and Balipara Frontier Tracts amount to 18,473 and 9,537 square miles respectively. The areas of these Tracts as given in the table are the administered areas only.

At Imphal in Manipur State there is a small British administered area known as the "British Reserve." This "reserve" is not British Territory though it is administered by the Political Agent ; it has an area of ·7 of a square mile and a population of 3,625 of whom 2,212 are males and 1,413 females.

TABLE I.

Area, Houses and Population.

District or State.	Area in square miles.	Towns.	Villages.	Occupied Houses. Total.	Occupied Houses. In towns.	Occupied Houses. In villages.	Population. Persons. Total.	Persons. Urban.	Persons. Rural.	Males. Total.	Males. Urban.	Males. Rural.	Females. Total.	Females. Urban.	Females. Rural.
1	2	3	4	5	6	7	8	9	10	11	12	13	14	15	16
ASSAM	*67,334*	*30*	*35,726*	*1,898,734*	*64,489*	*1,834,245*	*9,247,857*	*315,917*	*8,931,940*	*4,844,133*	*184,456*	*4,659,677*	*4,403,724*	*131,461*	*4,272,263*
(1) British Territory	*55,014*	*29*	*32,879*	*1,771,295*	*43,646*	*1,727,649*	*8,622,251*	*213,421*	*8,408,830*	*4,537,206*	*135,320*	*4,401,886*	*4,085,045*	*78,101*	*4,006,944*
SURMA VALLEY AND HILL DIVISION	24,170	10	15,280	763,397	13,687	749,710	3,706,047	72,017	3,636,030	1,913,164	45,934	1,867,210	1,794,883	26,083	1,768,800
Cachar	3,862	1	1,607	122,963	2,962	120,001	570,531	15,071	555,460	301,338	9,707	291,631	269,193	5,364	263,829
Sylhet	5,478	5	11,717	548,541	8,036	540,505	2,724,342	44,543	2,679,799	1,407,645	27,573	1,379,770	1,316,697	16,468	1,300,229
Khasi and Jaintia Hills (British) ...	2,445	2*	934	22,061	1,929	20,132	109,926	9,841*	100,083	55,439	6,655	48,784	54,487	3,159	51,298
Naga Hills	4,289	1	461	47,598	760	46,838	178,844	2,769	176,075	89,536	1,697	87,839	89,308	1,062	88,246
Lushai Hills	8,000	...	540	22,334	...	22,334	124,404	...	124,404	59,186	...	59,186	65,218	...	65,218
ASSAM VALLEY DIVISION	27,094	18	17,169	996,193	28,996	967,297	4,855,711	137,034	4,718,677	2,592,144	86,712	2,505,432	2,263,567	50,322	2,213,245
Goalpara	3,985	3	3,188	157,961	4,298	153,669	862,748	21,442	841,306	470,273	13,141	457,132	412,475	8,301	404,174
Kamrup	3,844	3	2,738	189,035	8,127	180,908	976,746	39,028	937,718	513,345	23,403	489,942	463,401	15,625	447,776
Darrang	3,463	3	1,978	129,188	2,520	126,668	584,817	11,964	573,853	317,103	8,569	308,534	267,714	3,395	264,319
Nowgong	3,996	3	2,323	104,196	3,133	101,063	569,581	13,511	549,070	296,585	8,761	289,824	262,996	4,750	259,244
Sibsagar	5,131	4	2,364	204,036	4,948	199,088	933,326	23,175	910,151	496,288	14,173	482,115	437,038	9,002	428,036
Lakhimpur	4,996	4	2,498	172,229	5,966	166,263	724,583	27,914	696,669	399,108	18,665	380,443	325,475	9,249	316,226
Garo Hills	3,152	...	3,160	39,565	...	39,565	190,911	...	190,911	97,442	...	97,442	93,469	...	93,469
SADIYA FRONTIER TRACT	3,300	1	373	10,097	373	9,724	52,345	4,270	48,075	28,686	2,674	26,012	24,659	1,696	22,963
BALIPARA FRONTIER TRACT ...	500	...	33	1,096	...	1,096	5,148	...	5,148	3,232	...	3,232	1,916	...	1,916
(2) Assam States	*12,320*	*1*	*2,847*	*127,439*	*20,843*	*106,596*	*625,606*	*102,496*	*523,110*	*306,927*	*49,136*	*257,791*	*318,679*	*53,360*	*265,319*
Manipur State	8,620	1	1,372	89,151	17,463	71,688	445,606	85,804	359,802	215,815	40,157	175,658	229,791	45,647	184,144
Khasi States	3,700	*	1,475	38,288	3,380	34,908	180,000	16,692*	163,308	91,112	8,979	83,133	88,888	7,713	81,175

* The two towns shown under the Khasi and Jaintia Hills district are the Shillong Municipality and the Shillong Cantonment. The former lies partly in British territory and partly in the Khasi States.

TABLE II.

VARIATION IN POPULATION SINCE 1881.

The figures for 1921 and earlier years differ in several cases from those shown in the Census Tables of 1921. This is due to various inter-district transfers which have taken place during the last decade. The effect of these changes on the population of the districts concerned has been calculated and the figures adjusted accordingly. The 1921 population of thanas and mauzas given in Provincial Table I has been revised in a similar fashion.

2. The districts affected by transfer of areas were Cachar, the Naga Hills, Kamrup, Darrang, Balipara, Nowgong, Lakhimpur and the Sadiya Frontier Tract, but the only transfers worth mentioning are the transfer of one mauza from the Naga Hills to the North Cachar Hills, certain mutual transfers between Kamrup and Darrang following the declaration of the Jiya Bornadi as the boundary between these two districts and the transfer of some Abor villages from Lakhimpur to the Sadiya Frontier Tract.

3. The population censused for the first time amounts to 15,711. The distribution of this population is given in the fly-leaf of Table I. As it is quite impossible to estimate what this newly censused population would have amounted to at previous censuses no attempt has been made to effect any adjustments on this account in the previous population figures of the districts concerned.

4. In columns 11 and 12 the variations shown against the province do not agree with the totals of the British districts and States. This is due to the fact that the census papers of Manipur State were destroyed in the insurrection of 1891. Hence no variation of the population between 1881-1891 and 1891 to 1901 can be given for Manipur State or for the total of the Assam States. The Lushai Hills was not censused in 1881 and the figure given for 1891 is only an estimate of the population of the northern portion which was, at that time, the only part of the Lushai Hills within the province.

5. At all previous censuses the Khasi States were included in the Khasi and Jaintia Hills district of which only a part is British territory. The population of these States at previous censuses has now been calculated by adding the previous population figures of the Jowai subdivision (all British) to figures which, on the basis of the proportion as ascertained at this census, represent the population of the British portion of the sadr subdivision and then deducting these figures from the total population of the district as given at previous censuses.

TABLE II.—VARIATION IN POPULATION DURING LAST FIFTY YEARS.

DISTRICT OR STATE.	PERSONS. 1931.	1921.	1911.	1901.	1891.	1881.	VARIATION; INCREASE (+), DECREASE (—). 1921-1931.	1911-1921.	1901-1911.	1891-1901.	1881-1891.	NET VARIATION IN PERIOD 1881-1931.
1	2	3	4	5	6	7	8	9	10	11	12	13
ASSAM	*9,247,857*	*7,990,246*	*7,060,521*	*6,126,945*	*5,477,880*	*5,129,391*	*+1,257,611*	*+929,725*	*+933,576*	*+649,065*	*+348,489*	*+4,118,466*
(1) British Territory	*8,622,251*	*7,459,128*	*6,578,768*	*5,725,871*	*5,363,777*	*4,811,572*	*+1,163,123*	*+880,360*	*+852,897*	*+362,094*	*+552,205*	*+3,810,679*
SURMA VALLEY AND HILL DIVISION ...	**3,708,047**	**3,424,010**	**3,312,590**	**2,969,497**	**2,766,645**	**2,450,931**	+ **284,037**	+ **111,420**	+ **343,093**	+ **202,852**	+ **315,714**	+ **1,257,116**
Cachar ...	570,531	529,301	499,475	457,422	388,225	315,558	+ 41,230	+ 29,826	+ 42,053	+ 69,197	+ 72,667	+ 254,973
Sylhet ...	2,724,342	2,541,341	2,473,335	2,242,450	2,155,171	1,969,538	+ 183,001	+ 68,006	+ 230,885	+ 87,279	+ 185,633	+ 754,804
Khasi and Jaintia Hills (British) ...	109,926	96,161	99,538	85,641	83,801	71,055	+ 13,765	— 3,377	+ 13,897	+ 1,840	+ 12,746	+ 38,871
Naga Hills ...	178,844	158,801	149,038	101,550	95,414	94,780	+ 20,043	+ 9,763	+ 47,488	+ 6,136	+ 634	+ 84,064
Lushai Hills ...	124,404	98,406	91,204	82,434	43,634	...	+ 25,998	+ 7,202	+ 8,770	+ 38,800	...	...
ASSAM VALLEY DIVISION ...	**4,855,711**	**3,990,203**	**3,246,773**	**2,740,616**	**2,585,682**	**2,351,949**	+ **865,508**	+ **743,430**	+ **506,157**	+ **154,934**	+ **233,733**	+ **2,503,762**
Goalpara ...	882,748	762,523	600,685	462,089	452,812	446,741	+ 120,225	+ 161,838	+ 138,596	+ 9,277	+ 6,071	+ 436,007
Kamrup ...	976,746	763,571	668,646	590,010	635,079	645,779	+ 213,175	+ 94,925	+ 78,636	— 45,069	— 10,700	+ 330,967
Darrang ...	584,817	477,188	375,381	335,684	305,878	271,529	+ 107,629	+ 101,807	+ 39,697	+ 29,806	+ 34,349	+ 313,288
Nowgong ...	560,561	398,007	301,655	260,411	346,423	314,119	+ 162,554	+ 96,352	+ 41,244	— 86,012	+ 32,304	+ 246,442
Sibsagar ...	933,326	823,197	691,402	598,251	481,033	392,742	+ 110,129	+ 131,795	+ 93,151	+ 117,218	+ 88,291	+ 540,584
Lakhimpur ...	724,582	586,577	449,858	355,897	242,896	171,491	+ 138,005	+ 136,719	+ 93,961	+ 113,001	+ 71,405	+ 553,091
Garo Hills ...	190,911	179,140	158,836	138,274	121,570	109,548	+ 11,771	+ 20,304	+ 20,562	+ 16,704	+ 12,022	+ 81,363
SADIYA FRONTIER TRACT ...	**53,345**	**41,249**	**18,542**	**14,989**	**10,748**	**8,069**	+ **12,096**	+ **22,707**	+ **3,553**	+ **4,241**	+ **2,679**	+ **45,276**
BALIPARA FRONTIER TRACT ...	**5,148**	**3,666**	**863**	**769**	**702**	**623**	+ **1,482**	+ **2,803**	+ **94**	+ **67**	+ **79**	+ **4,525**
(2) Assam States	*625,606*	*531,118*	*481,753*	*401,074*	...	*317,819*	+ *94,488*	+ *49,365*	+ *80,679*	...	...	+ *307,787*
Manipur State ...	445,606	384,016	346,222	284,465	...	221,070	+ 61,590	+ 37,794	+ 61,757	...	...	+ 224,536
Khasi States ...	180,000	147,102	135,531	116,609	114,103	96,749	+ 32,898	+ 11,571	+ 18,922	+ 2,506	+ 17,354	+ 83,251

DISTRICT OR STATE.	MALES. 1931.	1921.	1911.	1901.	1891.	1881.	FEMALES. 1931.	1921.	1911.	1901.	1891.	1881.
	14	15	16	17	18	19	20	21	22	23	24	25
ASSAM	*4,844,133*	*4,149,228*	*3,638,646*	*3,144,017*	*2,820,248*	*2,626,728*	*4,403,724*	*3,841,018*	*3,421,875*	*2,982,928*	*2,657,632*	*2,502,663*
(1) British Territory	*4,537,206*	*3,887,880*	*3,401,309*	*2,948,331*	*2,765,702*	*2,471,182*	*4,085,045*	*3,571,248*	*3,177,459*	*2,777,540*	*2,598,075*	*2,340,390*
SURMA VALLEY AND HILL DIVISION ...	**1,913,164**	**1,758,423**	**1,696,821**	**1,518,057**	**1,417,555**	**1,249,866**	**1,794,883**	**1,665,587**	**1,615,769**	**1,451,440**	**1,349,090**	**1,201,065**
Cachar ...	301,338	276,778	261,398	245,038	204,505	167,736	269,193	252,523	238,077	212,384	183,720	147,822
Sylhet ...	1,407,645	1,308,734	1,268,828	1,141,385	1,101,350	1,000,071	1,316,697	1,232,607	1,204,507	1,101,065	1,053,821	969,467
Khasi and Jaintia Hills (British) ...	55,439	46,521	47,771	41,167	40,060	33,776	54,487	49,640	51,767	44,474	43,741	37,279
Naga Hills ...	89,536	79,738	74,796	51,473	48,501	48,283	89,308	79,063	74,242	50,077	46,913	46,497
Lushai Hills ...	59,186	46,653	43,034	39,004	22,838	...	65,218	51,753	48,170	43,430	20,796	...
ASSAM VALLEY DIVISION ...	**2,502,144**	**2,104,033**	**1,694,448**	**1,421,327**	**1,341,667**	**1,216,419**	**2,353,567**	**1,886,170**	**1,552,325**	**1,319,289**	**1,244,015**	**1,135,530**
Goalpara ...	470,273	406,628	318,506	242,712	236,892	229,413	412,475	355,895	282,179	219,377	215,920	217,328
Kamrup ...	513,345	397,736	339,797	293,272	321,430	329,461	463,401	365,835	328,849	296,738	313,649	316,318
Darrang ...	317,103	252,716	197,443	175,148	160,376	141,460	267,714	224,472	177,938	160,536	145,502	130,069
Nowgong ...	296,565	208,731	153,938	132,605	178,914	152,434	263,996	189,276	147,717	127,806	167,509	161,685
Sibsagar ...	496,278	433,913	365,131	316,968	252,726	206,274	437,048	389,284	326,271	281,283	228,307	186,468
Lakhimpur ...	389,108	312,843	238,169	190,587	130,116	91,624	335,474	273,734	211,689	165,310	112,780	79,867
Garo Hills ...	97,442	91,466	81,364	70,044	61,213	55,951	93,469	87,674	77,472	68,230	60,357	53,597
SADIYA FRONTIER TRACT ...	**29,095**	**22,887**	**10,532**	**8,495**	**6,086**	**4,530**	**24,250**	**18,362**	**8,010**	**6,494**	**4,662**	**3,539**
BALIPARA FRONTIER TRACT ...	**3,232**	**2,537**	**508**	**452**	**414**	**367**	**1,916**	**1,129**	**355**	**317**	**288**	**256**
(2) Assam States	*306,927*	*261,348*	*237,337*	*195,686*	...	*155,546*	*318,679*	*269,770*	*244,416*	*205,388*	...	*162,273*
Manipur State ...	225,815	188,119	170,666	139,632	...	109,552	219,791	195,897	175,556	144,833	...	111,518
Khasi States ...	91,113	73,229	66,671	56,054	54,546	45,989	88,888	73,873	68,860	60,555	59,557	50,760

TABLE III.

TOWNS AND VILLAGES CLASSIFIED BY POPULATION.

In this table the population enumerated in encampments, boats, trains, etc., has been excluded from the village and urban population and shown in a separate column.

In the temporarily settled districts of Assam the village corresponds to the cadastral village. In the hills and the permanently settled portion of the province the village is the residential village or group of houses bearing a separate name, small outlying hamlets being treated as parts of the nearest village.

TABLE III.

Towns and Villages classified by Population.

District or State.	Total number of inhabited towns and villages.	Population.	Under 500. Number.	Under 500. Population.	500—1,000. Number.	500—1,000. Population.	1,000—2,000. Number.	1,000—2,000. Population.	2,000—5,000. Number.	2,000—5,000. Population.	5,000—10,000. Number.	5,000—10,000. Population.	10,000—20,000. Number.	10,000—20,000. Population.	20,000—50,000. Number.	20,000—50,000. Population.	50,000—100,000. Number.	50,000—100,000. Population.	Encampments, boat and railway population unclassed.
1	2	3	4	5	6	7	8	9	10	11	12	13	14	15	16	17	18	19	20
ASSAM	*35,756*	*9,247,857*	*31,287*	*5,094,446*	*3,470*	*2,351,552*	*836*	*1,124,236*	*143*	*373,098*	*18*	*87,716*	*4*	*72,574*	*2*	*49,505*	*1*	*85,804*	*15,926*
(1) British Territory	*32,908*	*8,622,251*	*28,662*	*4,799,228*	*3,303*	*2,239,458*	*787*	*1,059,545*	*138*	*360,108*	*17*	*82,637*	*4*	*55,882*	*2*	*49,505*	...	...	*12,888*
SURMA VALLEY AND HILL DIVISION.	15,309	3,708,067	12,254	2,107,887	1,608	1,120,831	241	313,702	42	103,200	4	23,226	1	12,958	1	21,400	...	...	5,524
Cachar	1,600	570,531	1,124	206,162	453	310,737	20	36,226	1	2,088	...	...	1	12,958	...	...	...	...	2,944
Sylhet	11,723	2,724,342	10,427	1,662,681	1,077	715,125	175	229,859	39	93,231	3	18,000	...	...	1	21,400	...	...	2,247
Khasi and Jaintia Hills (British)	956	100,926	940	90,904	13	7,954	1	1,124	1*	4,008	1	5,226	...	...	...	...	...	...	...
Naga Hills	483	178,844	371	76,479	78	50,206	33	48,794	1	2,750	...	...	...	...	...	...	...	...	516
Lushai Hills	540	124,404	492	80,771	45	30,040	3	3,659	...	...	...	...	...	...	...	...	...	...	325
ASSAM VALLEY DIVISION ...	17,187	4,855,711	14,908	2,618,002	1,628	1,111,485	544	743,582	95	252,538	8	59,311	3	42,924	1	21,006	...	...	6,823
Goalpara	3,191	902,746	2,867	557,071	236	163,457	66	88,905	18	44,903	4	26,563	...	...	...	...	...	...	1,869
Kamrup	2,741	976,746	2,343	487,296	370	250,810	105	145,416	21	55,853	...	...	1	12,777	1	21,006	...	...	2,406
Darrang	1,980	586,817	1,703	224,530	190	127,743	80	107,977	6	13,551	1	9,961	...	...	...	...	...	...	1,046
Nowgong	2,325	560,581	2,004	228,128	253	173,160	64	90,194	4	10,309	...	...	1	10,413	...	...	...	...	286
Sibsagar	3,258	933,326	1,602	300,164	450	306,852	127	170,946	17	48,295	2	15,083	...	...	...	...	...	...	704
Lakhimpur	2,002	794,582	2,210	380,678	123	83,105	100	147,704	28	77,200	1	7,704	1	18,734	...	...	...	...	388
Garo Hills	2,160	190,911	2,150	181,116	7	4,280	3	3,138	1	2,358	...	...	...	...	...	...	...	...	...
SADIYA FRONTIER TRACT ...	374	53,345	363	39,974	8	6,046	2	2,961	1	4,370	...	...	...	...	...	...	...	...	694
BALIPARA FRONTIER TRACT	38	5,188	37	4,185	1	946	...	...	...	...	...	...	...	...	...	...	...	...	57
(2) Assam States ...	*2,848*	*625,606*	*2,625*	*295,218*	*167*	*112,094*	*49*	*64,691*	*5*	*12,990*	*1*	*5,079*	*	*16,692*	...	...	*1*	*85,804*	*3,038*
Manipur State	1,373	445,606	1,182	134,426	138	95,471	46	61,505	5	12,990	1	5,079	...	...	...	...	1	85,804	331
Khasi States	1,475	180,000	1,443	160,792	29	16,623	3	3,186	...	...	...	...	*	16,692	...	...	...	...	2,707

* The Municipality of Shillong falls both in British and non-British Territory.

TABLE IV.

POPULATION OF TOWNS WITH VARIATIONS SINCE 1881.

This table shows the population of all municipalities and 'small towns' constituted under the Assam Municipal Act (I of 1923), of the Shillong Cantonment and also of certain other places (3 district headquarters and one railway centre) which may be considered of an urban character. The total number of towns in Assam is now 30 as against 29 in 1921. The difference is due to the fact that the Shillong Cantonment has now been shown as a separate town, whereas in 1921 it was included in Shillong. No adjustment has been made in this table for the numerous small extensions of municipal boundaries which have taken place in the last decade. Persons enumerated in railway stations, boats and encampments within town limits have been included in the population of the towns in which they were enumerated.

TABLE IV.—Towns Classified by Population, with Variation for Fifty Years.

Name of Town.	District or State.	Description of town (Municipality, Cantonment, "Small town", etc.).	Population. 1931.	1921.	1911.	1901.	1891.	1881.	Variation: Increase (+), Decrease (−). 1921 to 1931.	1911 to 1921.	1901 to 1911.	1891 to 1901.	1881 to 1891.	Variation in period 1881 to 1931. Increase (+) Decrease (−).	Males. 1931.	1921.	1911.	Females. 1931.	1921.	1911.
1	2	3	4	5	6	7	8	9	10	11	12	13	14	15	16	17	18	19	20	21
TOTAL URBAN POPULATION		*30 Towns*	*315,917*	*258,148*	*211,318*	*187,162*	*100,730*	*92,047*	*+57,769*	*+46,830*	*+24,156*	*+86,496*	*+8,689*	*+223,870*	*184,456*	*147,960*	*119,893*	*131,461*	*110,888*	*91,425*
CLASS II—50,000—100,000		*1 Town*	*85,804*	*80,003*	*74,650*	*72,234*	...	...	*+5,801*	*+5,358*	*+2,416*			...	*40,157*	*38,268*	*36,393*	*45,647*	*41,735*	*38,257*
*Imphal	Manipur	...	85,804	80,003	74,650	72,234	...	...	+5,801	+5,353	+2,416	...	...	...	40,157	38,268	36,393	45,647	41,735	38,257
CLASS III—20,000—50,000		*3 Towns*	*64,532*	*48,861*	*38,066*	*32,984*	*28,220*	*30,390*	*+15,671*	*+10,795*	*+5,082*	*+4,764*	*−2,170*	*+34,142*	*39,693*	*29,485*	*22,553*	*24,839*	*19,376*	*15,513*
Gauhati	Kamrup	Municipality	21,797	16,480	12,481	11,661	8,343	11,695	+ 5,317	+ 3,999	+ 820	+ 3,318	− 3,412	+ 10,102	14,506	10,786	8,138	7,291	5,694	4,343
Sylhet	Sylhet	Ditto	21,435	16,912	14,457	13,523	14,027	14,407	+ 4,523	+ 2,455	+ 934	− 134	− 290	+ 7,028	13,100	10,032	8,314	8,335	6,880	6,143
†Shillong	Khasi and Jaintia Hills	Ditto	21,300	15,460	11,128	7,430	5,910	4,288	+ 5,831	+ 4,341	+ 3,698	+ 1,520	+ 1,612	+ 17,012	12,087	8,667	6,101	9,213	6,803	5,027
CLASS IV—10,000—20,000		*5 Towns*	*66,261*	*52,167*	*44,875*	*38,727*	*35,583*	*32,222*	*+14,094*	*+7,292*	*+6,148*	*+3,144*	*+3,361*	*+34,039*	*41,494*	*31,403*	*26,961*	*24,767*	*20,764*	*17,914*
Dibrugarh	Lakhimpur	Municipality	18,734	16,007	14,563	11,227	9,876	7,153	+ 2,727	+ 1,444	+ 3,336	+ 1,351	+ 2,723	+ 11,581	12,181	9,952	8,806	6,553	6,055	5,667
Barpeta	Kamrup	Ditto	13,777	11,730	10,739	8,747	9,312	11,332	+ 2,047	+ 991	+ 1,992	− 593	− 1,990	+ 2,445	6,939	5,692	5,261	6,838	6,038	5,478
Silchar	Cachar	Ditto	13,069	10,204	8,785	9,256	7,523	6,567	+ 2,865	+ 1,419	− 471	+ 1,733	+ 956	+ 6,502	8,417	6,570	5,900	4,652	3,634	2,885
Nowgong	Nowgong	Ditto	10,413	6,886	5,433	4,430	4,815	4,248	+ 3,527	+ 1,453	+ 1,003	− 385	+ 567	+ 6,165	6,660	4,120	3,145	3,753	2,766	2,288
Tezpur	Darrang	Ditto	10,268	7,341	5,355	5,067	4,027	2,922	+ 2,927	+ 1,986	+ 288	+ 1,040	+ 1,105	+ 7,346	7,297	5,060	3,759	2,971	2,281	1,596
CLASS V—5,000—10,000		*10 Towns*	*65,435*	*49,350*	*42,654*	*35,284*	*30,312*	*24,057*	*+16,085*	*+6,696*	*+7,370*	*+4,972*	*+6,255*	*+41,378*	*41,609*	*30,573*	*26,849*	*23,826*	*18,777*	*15,805*
Dhubri	Goalpara	Municipality	9,435	6,707	5,808	3,737	4,825	2,892	+ 2,728	+ 899	+ 2,071	− 1,088	+ 1,933	+ 6,543	6,107	4,310	3,910	3,328	2,397	1,898
Jorhat	Sibsagar	Ditto	8,334	6,626	5,231	2,849	2,109	1,984	+ 1,708	+ 1,395	+ 2,382	+ 740	+ 175	+ 6,350	5,236	4,094	3,225	3,098	2,532	2,006
Habiganj	Sylhet	Ditto	7,577	5,918	6,244	5,236	4,161	4,061	+ 1,659	− 333	+ 1,008	+ 1,075	+ 100	+ 3,516	4,776	3,754	3,912	2,801	2,164	2,332
Sibsagar	Sibsagar	Ditto	6,669	5,329	5,764	5,713	5,249	4,653	+ 1,340	− 435	+ 51	+ 463	+ 596	+ 2,086	3,922	2,997	3,228	2,747	2,332	2,536
Goalpara	Goalpara	Ditto	6,415	6,212	5,964	6,297	5,440	6,697	+ 203	+ 248	− 333	+ 847	− 1,257	− 282	3,869	3,760	3,602	2,546	2,452	2,362
Karimganj	Sylhet	Ditto	5,691	4,552	6,512	5,692	3,349	2,819	+ 1,139	− 1,960	+ 820	+ 2,343	+ 530	+ 2,872	3,909	3,216	4,027	1,782	1,336	2,485
Gauripur	Goalpara	"Small town"	5,592	4,311	...	...	...	...	+ 1,281	...	...	...	...	...	3,165	2,530	...	2,427	1,781	...
Sunamganj	Sylhet	Municipality	5,326	4,881	4,620	3,530	3,139	1,020	+ 444	+ 261	+ 1,090	+ 391	+ 2,119	+ 4,206	3,429	3,098	3,084	1,897	1,783	1,536
Shillong Cantonment	Khasi and Jaintia Hills	Cantonment	5,236	1,734	2,511	2,191	1,990	...	+ 3,502	− 777	+ 320	+ 201	...	...	3,547	845	1,661	1,689	889	850
Tinsukia	Lakhimpur	"Small town"	5,160	3,080	...	...	...	...	+ 2,080	...	...	...	...	...	3,649	1,969	...	1,511	1,111	...
CLASS VI—UNDER 5,000		*11 Towns*	*33,885*	*27,767*	*11,073*	*7,933*	*6,621*	*5,318*	*+6,118*	*+16,694*	*+3,140*	*+1,312*	*+1,303*	*+28,567*	*21,503*	*17,531*	*7,137*	*12,382*	*10,236*	*3,936*
Golaghat	Sibsagar	Municipality	4,688	3,655	2,236	2,359	2,211	2,141	+ 1,033	+ 1,419	− 123	+ 148	+ 70	+ 2,547	2,943	2,195	1,360	1,745	1,460	876
*Sadiya	Sadiya Frontier Tract	......	4,370	3,490	...	...	...	...	+ 780	...	...	...	...	...	2,674	2,209	...	1,696	1,281	...
Maulvi Bazar	Sylhet	Municipality	4,314	3,334	2,369	2,481	2,629	1,857	+ 980	+ 965	− 112	− 148	+ 772	+ 2,457	2,661	2,109	1,597	1,653	1,225	773
Nazira	Sibsagar	"Small town"	3,484	2,632	2,583	...	...	...	+ 852	+ 49	...	...	...	...	2,072	1,533	1,501	1,412	1,004	1,082
Palasbari	Kamrup	Ditto	3,454	2,733	...	...	...	...	+ 721	...	...	...	...	...	1,958	1,542	...	1,496	1,191	...
*Lumding	Nowgong	......	3,098	2,654	...	...	...	...	+ 444	...	...	...	...	...	2,101	1,832	...	997	822	...
*Kohima	Naga Hills	......	2,759	2,790	2,423	3,093	1,781	1,380	− 31	+ 367	− 670	+ 1,312	+ 401	+ 1,379	1,697	1,692	1,001	1,062	1,098	732
North Lakhimpur	Lakhimpur	"Small town"	2,120	1,966	...	...	...	...	+ 154	...	...	...	...	...	1,411	1,204	...	709	762	...
Hailakandi	Cachar	Ditto	2,002	2,228	1,462	...	...	...	− 226	+ 766	...	...	...	...	1,290	1,595	968	712	633	474
Doom Dooma	Lakhimpur	Ditto	1,900	1,162	...	...	...	...	+ 738	...	...	...	...	...	1,424	818	...	476	344	...
Mangaldai	Darrang	Ditto	1,696	1,023	...	...	...	...	+ 673	...	...	...	...	...	1,272	737	...	424	286	

* Treated as a town for Census purposes although neither a municipality nor a "small town" under the Assam Municipal Act, 1923, nor a cantonment.

† The figures for Shillong are exclusive of the Shillong Cantonment except for the year 1881, for which year they cannot be separated.

TABLE V.

TOWNS ARRANGED TERRITORIALLY WITH POPULATION BY RELIGION.

1. Shillong Municipality lies partly in British Territory and partly in the Khasi State of Mylliem. In this table the population of the British portion of the town has been shown separately from the non-British portion.

2. The Shillong Cantonment—the only cantonment in the province—has a total population of 5,236 persons of whom 3,447 (1,758 males and 1,689 females) constitute the "Civil" population and 1,789 (all males) the "Military" population.

3. The column "Others" includes the following :—

Town.	Religion.	Persons.	Males.	Females.
Silchar ...	... Nil	2	2	...
Sylhet	... Nil	5	3	2
Kohima	... 'Indefinite'	12	4	8
Dibrugarh ...	Parsi	6	5	1
	'Freethinker'	3	3	...
Shillong ...	Parsi	2	1	1
	Nil	7	5	2
	Total ...	37	23	14

TABLE

TOWNS ARRANGED TERRITORIALLY

Serial No.	DISTRICT OR STATE.	TOWN, MUNICIPALITY, CANTONMENT, ETC.	POPULATION.			HINDU.						SIKH.		
						BRAHMO.			OTHER HINDUS.					
			Persons.	Males.	Females.	Persons.	Males.	Females.	Persons.	Males.	Females.	Persons.	Males.	Females.
	1	2	3	4	5	6	7	8	9	10	11	12	13	14
1	**ASSAM** ...	...	*315,917*	*184,456*	*131,461*	*219*	*108*	*111*	*240,339*	*139,381*	*100,958*	*625*	*458*	*167*
2	**(1) British Territory**	...	*213,491*	*135,390*	*78,101*	*152*	*74*	*78*	*153,521*	*97,905*	*55,616*	*432*	*307*	*125*
3	**Surma Valley and Hill Division.**		*72,017*	*45,934*	*26,083*	*53*	*23*	*30*	*46,922*	*30,618*	*16,304*	*101*	*75*	*26*
4	Cachar ...	Silchar	12,869	8,417	4,452	1	1	...	9,873	6,318	3,555	...	...	...
5	Ditto ...	Hailakandi ...	2,002	1,290	712	...	...	...	1,532	958	574	...	...	...
6	Sylhet... ...	Sylhet	21,425	13,100	8,325	27	16	11	11,208	7,271	3,987	22	17	5
7	Ditto ...	Habiganj... ...	7,577	4,776	2,801	3	1	2	5,358	3,313	2,045	7	5	2
8	Ditto ...	Sunamganj ...	5,336	3,429	1,907	...	...	...	2,803	1,940	863	...	...	...
9	Ditto ...	Karimganj ...	5,631	3,909	1,722	1	1	...	3,972	2,674	1,298	10	7	3
10	Ditto ...	Maulvibazar ...	4,314	2,661	1,653	...	...	...	2,130	1,395	735	...	...	...
11	Khasi and Jaintia Hills.	Shillong* (British portion).	4,988	3,108	1,880	11	4	7	3,650	2,476	1,174	44	32	12
12	Ditto ...	Shillong Cantonment	5,236	3,547	1,689	...	...	...	4,806	3,366	1,430	16	12	4
13	Naga Hills ...	Kohima	2,750	1,697	1,053	...	...	...	1,591	1,007	584	2	2	...
14	**Assam Valley Division** ...		*137,034*	*86,719*	*50,322*	*99*	*51*	*48*	*102,869*	*65,032*	*37,839*	*314*	*223*	*91*
15	Goalpara ...	Dhubri	9,435	6,107	3,328	4	2	2	6,431	4,125	2,306	13	7	6
16	Ditto ...	Gauripur	5,592	3,165	2,427	11	3	8	3,992	2,274	1,718	...	...	...
17	Ditto ...	Goalpara... ...	6,415	3,869	2,546	8	5	3	3,832	2,330	1,502	9	5	4
18	Kamrup ...	Gauhati	21,797	14,506	7,291	35	19	16	16,777	11,337	5,440	64	47	17
19	Ditto ...	Palasbari	3,454	1,968	1,486	...	...	...	3,123	1,733	1,390	...	...	...
20	Ditto ...	Barpeta	13,777	6,930	6,838	...	...	...	13,404	6,657	6,747	...	...	...
21	Darrang ...	Tezpur	10,268	7,297	2,971	13	9	4	7,908	5,620	2,288	2	2	...
22	Ditto ...	Mangaldai ...	1,696	1,272	424	...	...	...	1,176	858	318	1	...	1
23	Nowgong ...	Nowgong	10,413	6,660	3,753	5	4	1	7,117	4,666	2,451	30	17	13
24	Ditto ...	Lumding	3,098	2,101	997	...	...	...	2,094	1,336	758	74	48	26
25	Sibsagar ...	Jorhat	8,324	5,226	3,098	...	...	...	6,235	4,011	2,224	21	15	6
26	Ditto ...	Sibsagar	6,669	3,922	2,747	...	...	...	4,489	2,726	1,763	1	1	...
27	Ditto ...	Golaghat... ...	4,693	2,948	1,745	...	...	...	3,161	2,041	1,120	4	2	2
28	Ditto ...	Nazira	3,484	2,072	1,412	...	...	...	2,562	1,521	1,041	9	7	2
29	Lakhimpur ...	Dibrugarh... ...	18,736	12,181	6,555	23	9	1	13,507	8,742	4,765	40	31	9
30	Ditto ...	Doom Dooma ...	1,900	1,424	476	...	...	...	1,322	1,087	235	3	3	...
31	Ditto ...	Tinsukia	5,160	3,649	1,511	...	...	...	4,125	2,878	1,247	45	36	9
32	Ditto ...	North Lakhimpur ...	2,120	1,411	709	...	...	...	1,406	920	486	...	...	...
33	**Sadiya Frontier Tract.**	**Sadiya** ...	*4,370*	*2,674*	*1,696*	...	...	...	*3,737*	*2,254*	*1,483*	*17*	*9*	*8*
34	**(2) Assam States**	...	*102,426*	*49,136*	*53,360*	*67*	*34*	*33*	*86,818*	*41,476*	*45,342*	*193*	*151*	*42*
35	Manipur State ...	Imphal	85,804	40,157	45,647	...	...	...	81,612	38,060	43,552	30	21	9
36	Khasi States ...	Shillong (Khasi States portion).	16,622	8,979	7,713	67	34	33	5,206	3,416	1,790	163	130	33

* Shillong Municipality falls partly in British territory and partly in the Khasi States. The In other Hindus is included one Arya.

V.

WITH POPULATION BY RELIGION.

Jain Persons	Jain Males	Jain Females	Buddhist Persons	Buddhist Males	Buddhist Females	Muslim Persons	Muslim Males	Muslim Females	Christian Persons	Christian Males	Christian Females	Tribal Persons	Tribal Males	Tribal Females	Others Persons	Others Males	Others Females	Serial No.
15	16	17	18	19	20	21	22	23	24	25	26	27	28	29	30	31	32	
1,031	739	292	309	244	65	55,644	34,559	21,085	8,306	4,239	4,067	9,417	4,645	4,772	37	23	14	1
880	642	238	278	218	60	53,067	33,186	19,881	3,325	1,863	1,462	1,678	1,048	630	28	17	11	2
119	90	29	71	57	14	22,446	13,778	8,668	1,055	576	479	1,331	708	623	19	9	10	3
21	16	5	7	5	2	2,956	1,956	1,000	202	116	86	7	3	4	2	2	—	4
1	1	—	—	—	—	468	330	138	1	1	—	—	—	—	—	—	—	5
36	26	10	2	1	1	9,882	5,678	4,204	139	85	54	6	5	1	5	3	2	6
—	—	—	—	—	—	2,167	1,443	724	36	8	28	6	6	—	—	—	—	7
9	8	1	—	—	—	2,698	1,670	1,028	14	9	5	2	2	—	—	—	—	8
17	14	3	—	—	—	1,624	1,183	441	67	30	37	—	—	—	—	—	—	9
30	20	10	4	1	3	2,128	1,322	806	22	12	10	—	—	—	—	—	—	10
—	—	—	54	47	7	421	322	99	265	140	125	163	87	76	—	—	—	11
—	—	—	4	3	1	145	126	19	112	64	48	154	76	78	—	—	—	12
7	7	—	—	—	—	57	37	20	197	111	86	803	539	264	12	4	8	13
734	538	196	187	102	85	30,339	19,232	11,107	2,909	1,979	930	341	256	85	9	8	1	14
37	35	2	1	1	—	2,912	1,914	998	33	20	13	3	3	—	—	—	—	15
77	63	14	6	2	4	1,497	817	680	9	6	3	—	—	—	—	—	—	16
67	63	4	—	—	—	2,496	1,416	1,080	53	51	2	20	9	11	—	—	—	17
89	82	7	10	10	—	4,166	2,688	1,478	689	331	358	97	37	60	—	—	—	18
282	185	97	—	—	—	75	66	9	4	4	—	—	—	—	—	—	—	19
—	—	—	—	—	—	372	281	91	1	1	—	—	—	—	—	—	—	20
39	36	3	18	13	5	2,111	1,612	499	129	80	49	48	34	14	—	—	—	21
—	—	—	2	2	—	516	411	105	1	1	—	—	—	—	—	—	—	22
56	34	22	—	—	—	2,877	1,803	1,074	281	130	151	7	7	—	—	—	—	23
—	—	—	5	5	—	605	428	177	140	83	57	10	7	3	—	—	—	24
2	2	—	2	2	—	2,001	1,153	848	56	28	28	10	10	—	—	—	—	25
1	1	—	—	—	—	2,012	1,095	917	152	84	68	12	12	—	—	—	—	26
2	2	—	6	5	1	1,210	746	464	286	138	148	9	9	—	—	—	—	27
—	—	—	—	—	—	905	644	261	3	—	3	—	—	—	—	—	—	28
135	88	47	66	47	19	4,521	2,839	1,682	335	266	69	108	92	16	9	8	1	29
1	1	—	12	6	6	506	376	130	14	9	5	—	—	—	—	—	—	30
—	—	—	9	9	—	957	708	249	23	18	5	3	2	1	—	—	—	31
6	6	—	—	—	—	687	385	302	37	36	1	4	4	—	—	—	—	32
37	24	13	70	59	11	392	196	196	121	68	53	106	84	22	—	—	—	33
141	97	44	31	26	5	3,577	1,873	1,704	4,922	2,376	2,546	7,780	3,597	4,183	9	6	3	34
130	86	44	5	5	—	1,730	885	845	157	73	84	2,171	1,065	1,106	—	—	—	35
2	2	—	26	21	5	857	535	322	4,734	2,303	2,431	5,588	2,532	3,056	9	6	3	36

total population of the Shillong Municipality is 21,300.
male enumerated in Dhubri.

TABLE VI.

BIRTHPLACE.

This table corresponds to table XI of the 1921 Census but for reasons of economy sorting was not done for birthplace by districts except in the case of Manipur State and certain contiguous Bengal districts. The statistics, therefore, of persons born in Assam (except Manipur) show only the total number of persons enumerated in each district who were born anywhere in Assam. Persons born outside Assam have been arranged under the following heads :—

A II(*a*)—Adjacent provinces, *i.e.*, Bengal and Burma.
A II(*b*)—Other provinces and States in India.
A II(*c*)—India unspecified.
A II(*d*)—French and Portuguese Settlements in India.
B —Other Asiatic countries.
C —Europe.
D —Africa.
E —America.
F —Australia.
G —At sea.

For the purpose of this table the Khasi States have been included in the British district of the Khasi and Jaintia Hills as it was found impossible to separate the figures of the Khasi States from those of the rest of the district.

TABLE VI

Birthplace.—Districts and States.

Birthplace.	Districts or States where enumerated.											
	Province.			Cachar.			Sylhet.			Khasi and Jaintia Hills.		
	Persons.	Males.	Females.	Persons.	Males.	Females.	Persons.	Males.	Females.	Persons.	Males.	Females.
1	2	3	4	5	6	7	8	9	10	11	12	13
TOTAL POPULATION	9,247,857	4,844,133	4,403,724	570,531	301,338	269,193	2,724,349	1,407,645	1,316,697	289,926	146,551	143,375
A.—Born in India	9,153,141	4,780,385	4,372,756	569,287	300,402	268,885	2,723,097	1,406,660	1,316,437	277,164	136,800	140,355
I.—BORN IN ASSAM	7,839,094	4,025,412	3,813,682	527,686	276,411	251,275	2,585,171	1,331,163	1,254,008	272,686	133,580	139,106
(1) British Territory	7,396,359	3,810,298	3,586,061	526,300	275,484	250,816	2,584,985	1,331,004	1,253,981	272,487	133,458	139,029
(2) Manipur State	442,735	215,114	227,621	1,386	927	459	186	159	27	199	122	77
II.—BORN IN OTHER PARTS OF INDIA	1,314,047	754,973	559,074	41,601	23,991	17,610	137,926	75,497	62,429	4,478	3,229	1,249
II(a).—Provinces and States adjacent to Assam	582,986	331,086	251,900	7,143	4,468	2,675	60,195	33,822	26,373	1,822	1,161	661
1. *Bengal (British Territory)*	572,756	325,965	246,791	7,109	4,453	2,656	59,594	33,563	26,031	1,721	1,157	564
(i) CONTIGUOUS DISTRICTS	402,707	220,815	181,892	1,361	874	487	43,606	22,230	21,376	477	391	136
Jalpaiguri	14,342	7,960	6,382	2	2	...	10	7	3	6	4	2
Rangpur	23,136	12,739	10,397	5	2	3	21	14	7	14	8	6
Mymensingh	337,572	185,400	152,172	266	163	103	21,178	11,340	9,838	259	148	111
Tippera	27,657	14,716	12,941	1,088	707	381	22,397	10,869	11,528	198	161	37
(ii) OTHER DISTRICTS	170,049	105,150	64,899	5,748	3,579	2,169	15,988	11,333	4,655	1,244	836	408
2. *Bengal States*	2,443	1,182	1,261	23	10	13	551	534	317	92	...	92
3. *Burma*	7,787	3,939	3,848	11	5	6	50	25	25	9	4	5

TABLE VI.

BIRTHPLACE.—DISTRICTS AND STATES—*contd.*

Birthplace.	Naga Hills.			Lushai Hills.			Goalpara.			Kamrup.		
	Persons.	Males.	Females.	Persons.	Males.	Females.	Persons.	Males.	Females.	Persons.	Males.	Females.
1	14	15	16	17	18	19	20	21	22	23	24	25
TOTAL POPULATION	178,844	89,536	89,308	124,404	59,186	65,218	882,748	470,273	412,475	976,746	513,345	463,401
A.—Born in India	177,317	88,312	89,005	123,514	58,574	64,940	873,235	464,152	409,083	965,789	505,982	459,807
I.—BORN IN ASSAM	175,952	87,267	88,685	115,761	54,580	61,181	658,121	339,422	318,699	807,677	412,959	394,718
(1) British Territory	175,034	86,639	88,395	114,929	54,162	60,767	658,109	339,417	318,692	807,597	412,909	394,688
(2) Manipur State	918	628	290	832	418	414	12	5	7	80	50	30
II.—BORN IN OTHER PARTS OF INDIA	1,365	1,045	320	7,753	3,994	3,759	215,114	124,730	90,384	158,112	93,023	65,089
II(a).—PROVINCES AND STATES ADJACENT TO ASSAM	310	206	104	7,546	3,795	3,751	172,161	96,385	75,776	134,002	75,589	58,413
1. Bengal (British Territory)	297	195	102	1,587	856	731	170,421	95,479	74,942	133,946	75,554	58,392
(i) CONTIGUOUS DISTRICTS	34	24	10	224	110	114	111,849	61,989	49,860	94,944	52,963	41,981
Jalpaiguri	...	...	...	...	...	...	13,665	7,586	6,079	520	275	245
Rangpur	7	2	5	...	...	...	17,870	9,498	8,372	2,178	1,004	1,174
Mymensingh	5	3	2	2	1	1	79,890	44,535	35,355	90,774	50,363	40,411
Tippera	22	19	3	213	100	113	424	380	44	482	331	151
(ii) OTHER DISTRICTS	263	171	92	1,363	746	617	58,572	33,490	25,082	39,002	22,591	16,411
2. Bengal States	2	1	1	1	...	1	1,690	875	815	43	29	14
3. Burma	11	10	1	5,958	2,939	3,019	50	31	19	13	6	7

TABLE VI.

BIRTHPLACE.—DISTRICTS AND STATES—*contd.*

BIRTHPLACE.	DISTRICTS OR STATES WHERE ENUMERATED.											
	DARRANG.			NOWGONG.			SIBSAGAR.			LAKHIMPUR.		
	Persons.	Males.	Females.	Persons.	Males.	Females.	Persons.	Males.	Females.	Persons.	Males.	Females.
1	26	27	28	29	30	31	32	33	34	35	36	37
TOTAL POPULATION	*644,817*	*377,103*	*267,714*	*562,581*	*298,585*	*263,996*	*933,326*	*496,288*	*437,038*	*724,582*	*399,108*	*325,474*
A.—Born in India	*559,103*	*302,188*	*256,915*	*558,743*	*296,080*	*262,663*	*926,900*	*491,896*	*435,004*	*711,199*	*389,204*	*321,995*
I.—BORN IN ASSAM	*381,561*	*199,693*	*181,868*	*405,967*	*209,810*	*196,157*	*757,948*	*397,272*	*360,676*	*476,104*	*251,412*	*224,692*
(1) British Territory	*381,408*	*199,563*	*181,845*	*405,816*	*209,672*	*196,144*	*756,894*	*396,281*	*360,613*	*475,091*	*250,452*	*224,639*
(2) Manipur State	*153*	*130*	*23*	*151*	*138*	*13*	*1,054*	*991*	*63*	*1,013*	*960*	*53*
II.—BORN IN OTHER PARTS OF INDIA	*177,542*	*102,495*	*75,047*	*152,776*	*86,270*	*66,506*	*168,952*	*94,624*	*74,328*	*235,095*	*137,799*	*97,332*
II(a).—PROVINCES AND STATES ADJACENT TO ASSAM	*41,223*	*23,992*	*17,231*	*120,461*	*66,884*	*53,577*	*11,716*	*7,412*	*4,304*	*19,170*	*13,371*	*5,799*
1. Bengal (British Territory)	*41,195*	*23,969*	*17,226*	*120,438*	*66,873*	*53,565*	*11,690*	*7,393*	*4,297*	*19,042*	*13,275*	*5,767*
(i) CONTIGUOUS DISTRICTS	*32,002*	*17,553*	*14,449*	*100,755*	*50,800*	*49,955*	*635*	*471*	*164*	*3,511*	*2,326*	*1,185*
Jalpaiguri	99	64	35	*6*	2	4	3	...	3	23	14	9
Rangpur	1,439	834	605	72	63	4	44	35	9	45	26	19
Mymensingh	30,264	16,498	13,766	108,453	58,861	49,592	265	187	78	2,431	1,462	969
Tippera	200	157	43	1,224	869	355	323	249	74	1,012	834	188
(ii) OTHER DISTRICTS...	9,193	*6,416*	*2,777*	*10,683*	*7,073*	*3,610*	*11,055*	*6,922*	*4,133*	*15,531*	*10,949*	*4,582*
2. Bengal States	*19*	*10*	*9*	*6*	*5*	*1*	*11*	*7*	*4*	*10*	*9*	*1*
3. Burma	*16*	*13*	*3*	*17*	*6*	*11*	*15*	*12*	*3*	*118*	*87*	*31*

TABLE VI.

BIRTHPLACE.—DISTRICTS AND STATES—*contd.*

BIRTHPLACE.	DISTRICTS OR STATES WHERE ENUMERATED.											
	GARO HILLS.			SADIYA FRONTIER TRACT.			BALIPARA FRONTIER TRACT.			MANIPUR STATE.		
	Persons.	Males.	Females.	Persons.	Males.	Females.	Persons.	Males.	Females.	Persons.	Males.	Females.
	38	39	40	41	42	43	44	45	46	47	48	49
TOTAL POPULATION	190,911	97,442	93,469	53,345	28,686	24,659	5,148	3,232	1,916	445,606	215,815	229,791
A.—Born in India	189,343	96,382	92,961	49,992	26,345	23,647	4,350	2,594	1,756	444,178	214,805	229,373
I.—BORN IN ASSAM	183,766	93,157	90,609	45,389	23,285	22,104	3,506	1,978	1,528	441,799	213,423	228,376
(1) British Territory	183,681	93,113	90,568	45,295	23,216	22,079	3,487	1,967	1,520	5,246	2,961	2,285
(2) Manipur State	85	44	41	94	69	25	19	11	8	436,553	210,462	226,091
II.—BORN IN OTHER PARTS OF INDIA	5,577	3,225	2,352	4,603	3,060	1,543	844	616	228	2,379	1,382	997
II(a).—PROVINCES AND STATES ADJACENT TO ASSAM ...	5,019	2,729	2,290	456	309	147	81	71	10	1,688	899	789
1. Bengal (British Territory)	4,997	2,707	2,290	453	308	145	80	70	10	186	113	73
(i) CONTIGUOUS DISTRICTS	4,219	2,089	2,130	57	45	12	10	9	1	23	11	12
Jalpaiguri	3	2	1	...	...	...	5	4	1	...	...	...
Rangpur	443	251	192	8	7	1	...	...	.	...	...	...
Mymensingh	3,762	1,830	1,932	15	14	1	5	5	...	3	...	3
Tippera	11	6	5	34	24	10	...	...	...	20	11	9
(ii) OTHER DISTRICTS	778	618	160	396	263	133	70	61	9	163	102	61
2. Bengal States	2	2	...	...	...	...	...	...	...	...	...	...
3. Burma	13	13	...	3	1	2	1	1	...	1,502	786	716

TABLE VI.

Birthplace.—Districts and States—*contd.*

Birthplace.	Districts or States where enumerated.											
	Province.			Cachar.			Sylhet.			Khasi and Jaintia Hills.		
	Persons.	Males.	Females.	Persons.	Males.	Females.	Persons.	Males.	Females.	Persons.	Males.	Females.
1	2	3	4	5	6	7	8	9	10	11	12	13
II(*b*).—Other provinces and states in India ...	*730,864*	*423,738*	*307,126*	*34,450*	*19,523*	*14,927*	*77,708*	*41,661*	*36,047*	*2,656*	*2,068*	*588*
(*I*) *British Territory*	*652,561*	*378,005*	*274,556*	*32,673*	*18,533*	*14,140*	*75,855*	*40,537*	*35,318*	*2,426*	*1,929*	*497*
Ajmer-Merwara	77	57	20	2	2	...	7	5	2	...	...	...
Andamans and Nicobars	4	3	1	...	...	...	2	2	...	...	...	...
Baluchistan (Districts and Administered Territories):	245	212	33	8	8	...	2	2	...	6	6	...
Bihar and Orissa	443,597	256,348	187,249	17,634	9,902	7,732	30,271	16,528	13,743	898	784	114
Bombay	6,400	3,797	2,603	329	203	126	587	323	264	23	14	9
Central Provinces and Berar	70,192	37,648	32,544	4,733	2,745	1,988	8,239	4,275	3,964	88	39	49
Coorg	1	...	1	...	...	...	...	...	...	1	...	1
Delhi	107	84	23	6	6	...	9	8	1	...	...	...
Madras	57,448	31,023	26,425	1,832	968	864	11,325	5,309	6,016	76	46	30
North-West Frontier Province (Districts and Administered Territories).	583	562	21	43	41	2	49	46	3	45	38	7
Punjab	5,355	4,061	1,294	231	178	53	220	175	45	470	362	108
United Provinces of Agra and Oudh	67,942	43,610	24,332	7,870	4,485	3,385	24,944	13,664	11,280	819	640	179

TABLE VI.

BIRTHPLACE.—DISTRICTS AND STATES—*contd.*

BIRTHPLACE.	DISTRICTS OR STATES WHERE ENUMERATED.											
	NAGA HILLS.			LUSHAI HILLS.			GOALPARA.			KAMRUP.		
	Persons.	Males.	Females.	Persons.	Males.	Females.	Persons.	Males.	Females.	Persons.	Males.	Females.
1	14	15	16	17	18	19	20	21	22	23	24	25
II(b).—OTHER PROVINCES AND STATES IN INDIA ...	*1,050*	*838*	*212*	*207*	*199*	*8*	*42,949*	*28,341*	*14,608*	*24,007*	*17,335*	*6,672*
(1) British Territory	*801*	*636*	*165*	*205*	*197*	*8*	*40,976*	*26,917*	*14,059*	*21,703*	*15,756*	*5,947*
Ajmer-Merwara	...	...	...	...	...	...	17	13	4	8	8	...
Andamans and Nicobars	...	...	...	...	...	...	...	...	...	...	...	...
Baluchistan (Districts and Administered Territories)	6	4	2	...	...	...	1	1	...	7	7	...
Bihar and Orissa	355	287	68	125	125	...	33,408	21,079	12,329	15,000	11,174	3,826
Bombay	27	20	7	...	...	...	86	53	33	212	125	87
Central Provinces and Berar	71	42	29	...	...	...	994	569	425	1,903	1,095	808
Coorg	...	...	...	...	...	...	...	...	...	...	...	...
Delhi	1	1	...	...	...	...	7	4	3	12	8	4
Madras	15	12	3	...	...	...	100	69	31	499	312	187
North-West Frontier Province (Districts and Administered Territories.)	100	95	5	...	...	...	15	15	...	25	23	2
Punjab	82	56	26	12	10	2	106	82	24	315	266	49
United Provinces of Agra and Oudh	144	119	25	68	62	6	5,840	4,532	1,308	3,692	2,728	964

TABLE VI.

Birthplace—Districts and States—*contd.*

Birthplace.	Darrang. Persons.	Darrang. Males.	Darrang. Females.	Nowgong. Persons.	Nowgong. Males.	Nowgong. Females.	Sibsagar. Persons.	Sibsagar. Males.	Sibsagar. Females.	Lakhimpur. Persons.	Lakhimpur. Males.	Lakhimpur. Females.
	Districts or States where enumerated.											
1	26	27	28	29	30	31	32	33	34	35	36	37
II (b).—Other Provinces and States in India ...	*136,806*	*78,496*	*57,810*	*39,812*	*19,883*	*19,929*	*157,296*	*87,302*	*70,094*	*215,897*	*124,450*	*91,437*
(1) British Territory	*119,947*	*69,767*	*50,180*	*29,452*	*17,463*	*11,989*	*143,861*	*79,345*	*64,516*	*179,375*	*103,232*	*76,143*
Ajmer-Merwara	...	...	...	11	9	2	5	4	1	26	15	11
Andamans and Nicobars	1	1	...	...	...	...	...	...	...	1	...	1
Baluchistan (District and Administered Territories)	...	...	...	1	1	...	5	3	2	212	184	28
Bihar and Orissa	95,469	60,161	35,308	17,670	10,643	7,028	110,480	69,883	40,597	163,225	79,027	84,198
Bombay	1,181	647	534	409	258	151	1,499	853	646	2,095	1,366	729
Central Provinces and Berar	13,886	7,392	6,494	6,707	3,419	3,288	13,102	7,136	5,966	20,237	10,824	9,413
Coorg	...	...	...	...	...	...	...	...	...	...	...	...
Delhi	7	5	2	13	9	4	6	2	4	45	40	5
Madras	15,080	8,773	6,307	1,152	616	536	12,088	6,411	5,677	14,532	8,097	6,435
North-West Frontier Province (Districts and Administered Territories).	25	25	...	22	22	...	11	11	...	257	245	12
Punjab	304	222	82	256	190	66	764	612	152	3,857	3,374	483
United Provinces of Agra and Oudh	3,894	2,531	1,363	3,181	2,267	914	5,921	3,730	2,191	10,788	8,160	2,628

TABLE VI.

Birthplace.—Districts and States—*contd.*

Birthplace.	Districts or States where enumerated.											
	Garo Hills.			Sadiya Frontier Tract.			Balipara Frontier Tract.			Manipur State.		
	Persons.	Males.	Females.	Persons.	Males.	Females.	Persons.	Males.	Females.	Persons.	Males.	Females.
1	38	39	40	41	42	43	44	45	46	47	48	49
II (b)—Other Provinces and States in India ...	*565*	*503*	*62*	*4,147*	*2,751*	*1,396*	*763*	*545*	*218*	*691*	*483*	*208*
(1) British Territory	*541*	*482*	*59*	*3,662*	*2,434*	*1,228*	*647*	*487*	*160*	*437*	*290*	*147*
Ajmer-Merwara	...	...	...	1	1	...	...	...	...	...	...	...
Andamans and Nicobars	...	...	...	...	...	...	...	...	...	...	...	...
Baluchistan (Districts and Administered Territories)	...	...	...	...	...	...	2	1	1	...	...	...
Bihar and Orissa	394	379	15	2,659	1,759	900	464	346	118	185	102	83
Bombay	1	...	1	3	1	2	3	2	1	5	2	3
Central Provinces and Berar	...	...	...	90	51	39	77	57	20	5	4	1
Coorg	...	...	...	...	...	...	...	...	...	...	...	...
Delhi	...	...	...	...	...	...	...	...	...	1	1	...
Madras	1	1	...	351	244	107	31	21	10	6	4	2
North-West Frontier Province (Districts and Administered Territories).	...	...	...	...	...	...	...	...	...	1	1	...
Punjab	12	11	1	63	52	11	4	4	...	77	57	20
United Provinces of Agra and Oudh	133	91	42	495	416	79	66	56	10	157	119	38

TABLE VI.

Birthplace.—Districts and States—*contd.*

Birthplace.	Province. Persons.	Province. Males.	Province. Females.	Cachar. Persons.	Cachar. Males.	Cachar. Females.	Sylhet. Persons.	Sylhet. Males.	Sylhet. Females.	Khasi and Jaintia Hills. Persons.	Khasi and Jaintia Hills. Males.	Khasi and Jaintia Hills. Females.
1	2	3	4	5	6	7	8	9	10	11	12	13
(2) Feudatory States ...	*73,303*	*43,733*	*29,570*	*1,777*	*990*	*787*	*1,853*	*1,124*	*729*	*230*	*139*	*91*
Baluchistan Agency Tracts ...	...	...	...	...	...	...	...	...	...	...	...	...
Baroda ...	232	107	125	...	...	...	29	17	12	...	...	...
Bihar and Orissa States ...	28,189	14,015	14,174	146	78	68	326	188	138	...	...	...
Bombay States ...	153	106	47	...	...	...	4	2	2	1	1	...
Central India Agency ...	14,887	8,258	6,629	1,271	692	579	786	364	422	3	3	...
Central Provinces States ...	11,853	6,788	5,065	43	6	37	209	154	55	...	...	...
Gwalior ...	262	183	79	3	2	1	32	22	10	...	...	...
Hyderabad ...	389	223	166	11	5	6	17	12	5	6	6	...
Kashmir ...	24	17	7	...	...	...	4	3	1	8	5	3
Madras States (including Cochin and Travancore) ...	23	7	16	...	...	...	...	...	...	...	...	...
Cochin ...	*1*	*1*	...	...	...	...	...	...	...	...	...	...
Travancore ...	*1*	*1*	...	...	...	...	...	...	...	...	...	...
Mysore ...	85	54	31	1	1	...	13	8	5	8	8	...
North-West Frontier Province (Agencies and Tribal areas).	...	...	...	...	...	...	...	...	...	...	...	...
Punjab States ...	179	131	48	43	24	19	10	8	2	1	1	...
Rajputana Agency ...	21,780	15,679	6,101	255	178	77	423	346	77	200	112	88
Sikkim ...	64	46	18	...	...	...	...	...	...	3	3	...
United Provinces States ...	184	120	64	4	4	...	...	...	...	...	...	...
Western India Agency ...	...	...	...	...	...	...	...	...	...	...	...	...
II(c)—Indian unspecified ...	*178*	*134*	*42*	*7*	...	*7*	*10*	*7*	*3*	...	...	...
II(d)—French and Portuguese Settlements ...	*22*	*15*	*7*	*1*	...	*1*	*13*	*7*	*6*	...	...	...

TABLE VI.

Birthplace.—Districts and States—*contd.*

Birthplace.	Naga Hills. Persons.	Naga Hills. Males.	Naga Hills. Females.	Lushai Hills. Persons.	Lushai Hills. Males.	Lushai Hills. Females.	Goalpara. Persons.	Goalpara. Males.	Goalpara. Females.	Kamrup. Persons.	Kamrup. Males.	Kamrup. Females.
1	14	15	16	17	18	19	20	21	22	23	24	25
(9) Feudatory States	*249*	*202*	*47*	*2*	*2*	...	*1,973*	*1,424*	*549*	*2,304*	*1,579*	*725*
Baluchistan Agency Tracts	...	...	...	...	...	...	...	...	...	...	...	...
Baroda	7	3	4	...	...	...	...	...	...	...	...	...
Bihar and Orissa States	8	8	...	...	...	...	104	61	43	56	34	22
Bombay States	1	1	...	...	...	...	7	6	1	...	...	...
Central India Agency	39	30	9	...	...	...	270	156	114	211	131	80
Central Provinces States	4	3	1	...	...	...	70	36	34	23	13	10
Gwalior	2	2	...	...	...	...	4	4	...	...	...	...
Hyderabad	2	2	...	...	...	...	...	...	...	...	...	...
Kashmir	...	...	...	...	...	...	1	1	...	2	2	...
Madras States (including Cochin and Travancore) ...	...	...	...	...	...	...	1	1	...	1	1	...
Cochin	...	...	...	...	...	...	...	...	...	...	...	...
Travancore	...	...	...	...	...	...	...	...	...	...	...	...
Mysore	1	...	1	2	2	...	1	1	...	15	6	9
North-West Frontier Province (Agencies and Tribal areas).	...	...	...	...	...	...	...	...	...	...	...	...
Punjab States	...	...	...	...	...	...	7	4	3	12	9	3
Rajputana Agency	182	150	32	...	...	...	1,465	1,127	338	1,974	1,381	593
Sikkim	3	3	...	...	...	...	38	25	13	1	...	1
United Provinces States	...	...	...	...	...	...	5	2	3	9	2	7
Western India Agency	...	...	...	...	...	...	...	...	...	...	...	...
II(c).—Indian unspecified	*5*	*1*	*4*	...	...	...	*4*	*4*	...	*99*	*95*	*4*
II(d).—French and Portuguese Settlements ...	...	...	...	...	...	...	...	...	...	*4*	*4*	...

TABLE VI.

Birthplace—Districts and States.—*contd.*

Birthplace.	Darrang. Persons.	Darrang. Males.	Darrang. Females.	Nowgong. Persons.	Nowgong. Males.	Nowgong. Females.	Sibsagar. Persons.	Sibsagar. Males.	Sibsagar. Females.	Lakhimpur. Persons.	Lakhimpur. Males.	Lakhimpur. Females.
	Districts or States where enumerated.											
1	26	27	28	29	30	31	32	33	34	35	36	37
(2) *Feudatory States* ...	*16,359*	*8,729*	*7,630*	*2,860*	*1,920*	*940*	*13,345*	*7,837*	*5,508*	*36,452*	*21,178*	*15,274*
Baluchistan Agency Tracts	...	...	...	...	...	...	...	...	...	...	...	...
Baroda ...	20	9	11	3	3	...	144	61	83	29	14	15
Bihar and Orissa States	7,154	2,833	4,321	244	119	125	4,265	2,120	2,145	15,849	8,572	7,277
Bombay States ...	26	19	7	...	...	...	97	70	27	16	6	10
Central India Agency	4,797	2,838	1,959	843	470	373	2,631	1,420	1,212	4,021	2,136	1,885
Central Provinces States	1,304	627	677	218	112	106	2,342	1,265	1,077	7,616	4,565	3,051
Gwalior ...	119	95	24	1	...	1	12	9	3	89	49	40
Hyderabad ...	42	34	8	2	2	...	13	10	3	296	152	144
Kashmir ...	...	...	...	...	...	...	3	1	2	4	3	1
Madras States (including Cochin and Travancore) ...	6	3	3	5	1	4	1	1	...	9	...	9
Cochin ...	...	...	...	...	...	...	*1*	*1*	...	...	...	...
Travancore ...	...	...	...	*1*	*1*	...	...	...	...	...	...	...
Mysore ...	17	12	5	1	1	...	9	6	3	13	5	8
North-West Frontier Province (Agencies and Tribal areas).	...	...	...	...	...	...	...	...	...	...	...	...
Punjab States ...	2	2	...	5	3	2	11	8	3	84	[illegible]	16
Rajputana Agency ...	2,865	2,253	612	1,531	1,204	327	3,828	2,872	956	8,271	5,501	2,770
Sikkim ...	6	4	2	3	2	1	1	1	...	2	2	...
United Provinces States	1	...	1	4	3	1	8	4	4	153	105	48
Western India Agency	...	...	...	...	...	...	...	...	...	...	...	...
II(c).—Indian unspecified ...	*12*	*6*	*6*	*2*	*2*	...	*10*	*10*	...	*26*	*9*	*17*
II(d).—French and Portuguese Settlements	*1*	*1*	...	*1*	*1*	...	...	...	...	2	2	...

TABLE VI.

BIRTHPLACE.—DISTRICTS AND STATES—*contd.*

BIRTHPLACE.	DISTRICTS OR STATES WHERE ENUMERATED.											
	GARO HILLS.			SADIYA FRONTIER TRACT.			BALIPARA FRONTIER TRACT.			MANIPUR STATE.		
	Persons.	Males.	Females.	Persons.	Males.	Females.	Persons.	Males.	Females.	Persons.	Males.	Females.
1	38	39	40	41	42	43	44	45	46	47	48	49
(9) *Feudatory States*	*24*	*21*	*3*	*485*	*317*	*168*	*116*	*58*	*58*	*254*	*193*	*61*
Baluchistan Agency Tracts	...	...	...	...	...	...	...	...	...	...	...	...
Baroda	...	...	...	...	...	...	...	...	...	...	...	...
Bihar and Orissa States	...	...	...	37	2	35	...	...	...	...	...	...
Bombay States	...	...	...	...	...	...	...	...	...	...	...	...
Central India Agency...	...	...	...	11	6	5	1	1	...	3	2	1
Central Provinces States	...	...	...	24	7	17	...	...	...	...	...	...
Gwalior	...	...	...	...	...	...	...	...	...	...	...	...
Hyderabad	...	...	...	...	...	...	...	...	...	...	...	...
Kashmir	...	...	...	1	1	...	...	...	...	1	1	...
Madras States (including Cochin and Travancore) ...	...	...	...	...	...	...	...	...	...	...	...	...
Cochin	...	...	...	...	...	...	...	...	...	...	...	...
Travancore	...	...	...	...	...	...	...	...	...	...	...	...
Mysore	...	...	...	4	4	...	...	...	...	...	...	...
North-West Frontier Province (Agencies and Tribal areas).	...	...	...	...	...	...	...	...	...	...	...	...
Punjab States	...	...	...	...	...	...	...	...	...	...	...	...
Rajputana Agency	24	21	3	404	293	111	115	57	58	4	4	...
Sikkim	...	...	...	4	4	...	...	...	...	243	184	59
United Provinces States	...	...	...	...	...	...	...	...	...	3	2	1
Western India Agency	...	...	...	...	...	...	...	...	...	...	...	...
II(c).—INDIAN UNSPECIFIED	...	...	...	...	...	...	...	...	...	...	...	...
II(d).—FRENCH AND PORTUGUESE SETTLEMENTS ...	...	...	...	...	...	...	...	...	...	...	...	...

TABLE VI.

BIRTHPLACE.—DISTRICTS AND STATES—*contd.*

BIRTHPLACE.	DISTRICTS OR STATES WHERE ENUMERATED.											
	PROVINCE.			CACHAR.			SYLHET.			KHASI AND JAINTIA HILLS.		
	Persons.	Males.	Females.	Persons.	Males.	Females.	Persons.	Males.	Females.	Persons.	Males.	Females.
1	2	3	4	5	6	7	8	9	10	11	12	13
B.—Born in other Asiatic Countries	*91,972*	*61,750*	*30,222*	*976*	*736*	*240*	*836*	*683*	*153*	*12,504*	*9,580*	*2,924*
(i) WITHIN BRITISH DOMINIONS	*28*	*15*	*13*	...	...	...	*12*	*4*	*8*	*2*	*1*	*1*
Ceylon	12	8	4	...	...	...	1	1	...	2	1	1
Straits Settlements and Malaya	15	6	9	...	...	...	11	3	8	...	...	...
Elsewhere	1	1	...	...	...	...	...	...	...	...	...	...
(ii) OUTSIDE BRITISH DOMINIONS	*91,943*	*61,734*	*30,209*	*976*	*736*	*240*	*824*	*679*	*145*	*12,502*	*9,579*	*2,923*
Afghanistan	1,346	1,316	30	154	148	6	225	223	2	70	64	6
China	540	480	60	4	4	...	22	21	1	36	32	4
Nepal	88,306	58,600	29,706	816	583	233	560	421	139	12,396	9,483	2,913
Elsewhere	1,651	1,238	413	2	1	1	17	14	3	...	...	...
(iii) ASIA UNSPECIFIED	*1*	*1*	...	...	...	...	...	...	...	...	...	...
C.—Born in Europe	*2,528*	*1,864*	*664*	*250*	*187*	*63*	*357*	*265*	*92*	*247*	*158*	*89*
(i) UNITED KINGDOM AND IRELAND ...	*2,341*	*1,722*	*619*	*243*	*183*	*60*	*322*	*244*	*78*	*152*	*74*	*78*
(ii) BRITISH POSSESSIONS IN EUROPE ...	...	...	...	...	...	...	...	...	...	...	...	...
(iii) CONTINENTAL EUROPE	*176*	*134*	*42*	*7*	*4*	*3*	*35*	*21*	*14*	*95*	*84*	*11*
(iv) EUROPE UNSPECIFIED	*11*	*8*	*3*	...	...	...	...	...	...	...	...	...

TABLE VI.

BIRTHPLACE—DISTRICT AND STATES—*contd.*

BIRTHPLACE.	DISTRICTS OR STATES WHERE ENUMERATED.											
	NAGA HILLS.			LUSHAI HILLS.			GOALPARA.			KAMRUP.		
	Persons.	Males.	Females.	Persons.	Males.	Females.	Persons.	Males.	Females.	Persons.	Males.	Females.
1	14	15	16	17	18	19	20	21	22	23	24	25
B.—Born in other Asiatic Countries ...	*1,510*	*1,915*	*295*	*864*	*599*	*265*	*9,484*	*6,103*	*3,381*	*10,877*	*7,307*	*3,570*
(*i*) WITHIN BRITISH DOMINIONS	...	...	...	...	...	...	*2*	*1*	*1*	*3*	*2*	*1*
Ceylon	...	...	...	...	...	...	1	1	...	2	1	1
Straits Settlements and Malaya	...	...	...	...	...	...	1	...	1	...	...	...
Elsewhere	...	...	...	...	...	...	...	...	...	1	1	...
(*ii*) OUTSIDE BRITISH DOMINIONS	*1,510*	*1,915*	*295*	*864*	*599*	*265*	*9,481*	*6,101*	*3,380*	*10,874*	*7,305*	*3,569*
Afghanistan	21	21	...	...	...	...	177	175	2	43	42	1
China	4	3	1	...	...	...	...	...	...	3	1	2
Nepal	1,483	1,890	293	861	596	265	8,827	5,583	3,344	10,101	6,724	3,397
Elsewhere	2	1	1	3	3	...	477	343	134	727	538	190
(*iii*) ASIA UNSPECIFIED	...	...	...	...	...	...	1	1	...	...	...	...
C.—Born in Europe	*13*	*7*	*6*	*23*	*11*	*12*	*25*	*16*	*9*	*64*	*50*	*14*
(*i*) UNITED KINGDOM AND IRELAND ...	*13*	*7*	*6*	*23*	*11*	*12*	*9*	*8*	*1*	*51*	*41*	*10*
(*ii*) BRITISH POSSESSIONS IN EUROPE ...	...	...	...	...	...	...	...	...	...	...	...	...
(*iii*) CONTINENTAL EUROPE	...	...	...	...	...	...	*16*	*8*	*8*	*13*	*9*	*4*
(*iv*) EUROPE UNSPECIFIED	...	...	...	...	...	...	...	...	...	...	...	...

TABLE VI.

BIRTHPLACE.—DISTRICTS AND STATES—*contd.*

BIRTHPLACE.	DISTRICTS OR STATES WHERE ENUMERATED.											
	DARRANG.			NOWGONG.			SIBSAGAR.			LAKHIMPUR.		
	Persons.	Males.	Females.	Persons.	Males.	Females.	Persons.	Males.	Females.	Persons.	Males.	Females.
1	26	27	28	29	30	31	32	33	34	35	36	37
B.—Born in other Asiatic Countries	*25,443*	*14,712*	*10,731*	*3,757*	*2,448*	*1,309*	*6,024*	*4,101*	*1,923*	*12,600*	*9,245*	*3,355*
(i) WITHIN BRITISH DOMINIONS	*2*	*2*	...	...	...	...	*2*	*1*	*1*	*4*	*3*	*1*
Ceylon...	...	...	...	...	...	...	2	1	1	4	3	1
Straits Settlements and Malaya	2	2	...	...	...	...	...	...	...	...	...	...
Elsewhere	...	...	...	...	...	...	...	...	...	...	...	...
(ii) OUTSIDE BRITISH DOMINIONS	*25,441*	*14,710*	*10,731*	*3,757*	*2,448*	*1,309*	*6,022*	*4,100*	*1,922*	*12,596*	*9,242*	*3,354*
Afghanistan	140	140	...	89	89	...	174	173	1	233	221	12
China	116	102	14	22	19	3	61	54	7	372	344	28
Nepal	24,862	14,198	10,664	3,620	2,323	1,297	5,780	3,866	1,914	11,951	8,644	3,307
Elsewhere	314	261	53	26	17	9	7	7	...	40	33	7
(iii) ASIA UNSPECIFIED	...	...	...	...	...	...	...	...	...	...	...	
C.—Born in Europe	*265*	*200*	*65*	*67*	*50*	*17*	*382*	*273*	*109*	*798*	*623*	*175*
(i) UNITED KINGDOM AND IRELAND ...	*261*	*197*	*64*	*67*	*50*	*17*	*377*	*269*	*108*	*787*	*615*	*172*
(ii) BRITISH POSSESSIONS IN EUROPE ...	...	...	...	...	...	...	...	...	...	...	...	...
(iii) CONTINENTAL EUROPE	*4*	*3*	*1*	...	...	...	*5*	*4*	*1*	...	...	...
(iv) EUROPE UNSPECIFIED	...	...	...	...	...	...	...	...	...	*11*	*8*	*3*

TABLE VI.

BIRTHPLACE.—DISTRICTS AND STATES—*contd.*

BIRTHPLACE.	DISTRICTS OR STATES WHERE ENUMERATED.											
	GARO HILLS.			SADIYA FRONTIER TRACT.			BALIPARA FRONTIER TRACT.			MANIPUR STATE.		
	Persons.	Males.	Females.	Persons.	Males.	Females.	Persons.	Males.	Females.	Persons.	Males.	Females.
1	38	39	40	41	42	43	44	45	46	47	48	49
B.—Born in other Asiatic Countries ...	*1,558*	*1,057*	*501*	*3,333*	*2,396*	*1,006*	*796*	*636*	*160*	*1,411*	*1,002*	*409*
(i) WITHIN BRITISH DOMINIONS	...	...	...	...	...	...	...	...	...	*1*	*1*	...
Ceylon	...	...	...	...	...	...	...	...	...	...	...	...
Straits Settlements and Malaya	...	...	...	...	...	...	...	...	...	1	1	...
Elsewhere	...	...	...	...	...	...	...	...	...	...	...	...
(ii) OUTSIDE BRITISH DOMINIONS	*1,553*	*1,057*	*501*	*3,339*	*2,396*	*1,006*	*796*	*636*	*160*	*1,410*	*1,001*	*409*
Afghanistan	1	1	...	10	10	...	...	...	...	...	...	...
China	...	...	...	...	...	...	...	...	...	...	...	...
Nepal	1,554	1,054	500	3,308	2,296	1,006	784	628	156	1,409	1,001	408
Elsewhere	3	2	1	20	20	...	12	8	4	1	...	1
(iii) ASIA UNSPECIFIED	...	...	...	...	...	...	...	...	...	...	...	...
C.—Born in Europe	*3*	*2*	*1*	*18*	*13*	*5*	*2*	*2*	...	*14*	*7*	*7*
(i) UNITED KINGDOM AND IRELAND ...	*2*	*1*	*1*	*18*	*13*	*5*	*2*	*2*	...	*14*	*7*	*7*
(ii) BRITISH POSSESSIONS IN EUROPE ...	...	...	...	...	...	...	...	...	...	...	...	...
(iii) CONTINENTAL EUROPE	*1*	*1*	...	...	...	...	...	...	...	...	...	...
(iv) EUROPE UNSPECIFIED .	...	...	...	...	...	...	...	...	...	...	...	...

TABLE VI.

Birthplace.—Districts and States—*contd.*

Birthplace.	Province. Persons.	Province. Males.	Province. Females.	Cachar. Persons.	Cachar. Males.	Cachar. Females.	Sylhet. Persons.	Sylhet. Males.	Sylhet. Females.	Khasi and Jaintia Hills. Persons.	Khasi and Jaintia Hills. Males.	Khasi and Jaintia Hills. Females.
1	2	3	4	5	6	7	8	9	10	11	12	13
D.—Born in Africa	76	57	19	5	4	1	30	23	7	3	3	...
(i) WITHIN BRITISH DOMINIONS	21	15	6	1	1	...	19	13	6	...	...	...
Natal	6	3	3	...	...	...	6	3	3	...	...	...
Transvaal	15	12	3	1	1	...	13	10	3	...	...	...
(ii) OUTSIDE BRITISH DOMINIONS	3	2	1	...	...	...	...	...	...	...	...	...
Mozambique	...	...	...	...	...	...	...	...	...	...	...	...
Elsewhere	3	2	1	...	...	...	...	...	...	...	...	...
(iii) AFRICA UNSPECIFIED	52	40	12	4	3	1	13	12	1	3	3	...
E.—Born in America	110	64	46	13	9	4	15	10	5	3	1	2
(i) WITHIN BRITISH DOMINIONS	3	3	...	...	...	...	1	1	...	...	...	...
British Guiana	2	2	...	...	...	...	1	1	...	...	...	...
Elsewhere	1	1	...	...	...	...	...	...	...	...	...	...
(ii) OUTSIDE BRITISH DOMINIONS	76	41	35	...	...	...	...	...	...	...	...	...
United States	76	41	35	...	...	...	...	...	...	...	...	
(iii) AMERICA UNSPECIFIED	31	20	11	13	9	4	14	9	5	3	1	2
F.—Born in Australasia	28	12	16	...	...	...	5	2	3	5	...	5
(i) WITHIN BRITISH DOMINIONS	28	12	16	...	...	...	5	2	3	5	...	5
Australia	16	6	10	...	...	...	...	...	...	2	...	2
Fiji Islands	7	4	3	...	...	...	5	2	3	...	...	...
New Zealand	5	2	3	...	...	...	...	...	...	3	...	3
G.—Born at Sea	3	2	1	...	...	...	...	...	...	...	...	...

TABLE VI.

Birthplace—Districts and States—*contd.*

Birthplace	Naga Hills. Persons.	Naga Hills. Males.	Naga Hills. Females.	Lushai Hills. Persons.	Lushai Hills. Males.	Lushai Hills. Females.	Goalpara. Persons.	Goalpara. Males.	Goalpara. Females.	Kamrup. Persons.	Kamrup. Males.	Kamrup. Females.
1	14	15	16	17	18	19	20	21	22	23	24	25
D.—Born in Africa	...	...	...	1	...	1	...	...	...	1	1	...
(i) WITHIN BRITISH DOMINIONS	...	...	...	...	...	...	...	...	...	1	1	...
Natal	...	...	...	...	...	...	...	...	...	...	...	...
Transvaal	...	...	...	...	...	...	...	...	...	1	1	...
(ii) OUTSIDE BRITISH DOMINIONS	...	...	...	...	...	...	...	...	...	...	...	...
Mozambique	...	...	...	...	...	...	...	...	...	...	...	...
Elsewhere	...	...	...	...	...	...	...	...	...	...	...	...
(iii) AFRICA UNSPECIFIED	...	...	...	1	...	1	...	...	...	...	...	...
E.—Born in America	4	2	2	2	2	...	3	2	1	15	5	10
(i) WITHIN BRITISH DOMINIONS	...	...	...	...	...	...	...	...	...	...	...	...
British Guiana	...	...	...	...	...	...	...	...	...	...	...	...
Elsewhere	...	...	...	...	...	...	...	...	...	...	...	...
(ii) OUTSIDE BRITISH DOMINIONS	4	2	2	2	2	...	2	1	1	15	5	10
United States	4	2	2	2	2	...	2	1	1	15	5	10
(iii) AMERICA UNSPECIFIED...	...	...	...	...	...	...	1	1	...	...	...	...
F.—Born in Australasia	...	...	...	...	...	...	...	...	...	...	...	...
(i) WITHIN BRITISH DOMINIONS	...	...	...	...	...	...	...	...	...	...	...	...
Australia	...	...	...	...	...	...	...	...	...	...	...	...
Fiji Islands	...	...	...	...	...	...	...	...	...	...	...	...
New Zealand	...	...	...	...	...	...	...	...	...	...	...	...
G.—Born at Sea	...	...	...	...	...	...	1	...	1	...	...	...

Column group heading: Districts or States where enumerated.

TABLE VI.

Birthplace—Districts and States—contd.

Birthplace.	Darrang. Persons.	Darrang. Males.	Darrang. Females.	Nowgong. Persons.	Nowgong. Males.	Nowgong. Females.	Sibsagar. Persons.	Sibsagar. Males.	Sibsagar. Females.	Lakhimpur. Persons.	Lakhimpur. Males.	Lakhimpur. Females.
	Districts or States where enumerated.											
1	26	27	28	29	30	31	32	33	34	35	36	37
D.—Born in Africa	2	1	1	2	1	1	8	8	...	22	14	8
(i) WITHIN BRITISH DOMINIONS	...	...	...	...	...	...	...	...	...	...	...	...
Natal	...	...	...	...	...	...	...	...	...	...	...	...
Transvaal	...	...	...	...	...	...	...	...	...	...	...	...
(ii) OUTSIDE BRITISH DOMINIONS	1	...	1	...	...	...	2	2	...	...	...	...
Mozambique	...	...	...	...	...	...	...	...	...	...	...	...
Elsewhere	1	...	1	...	...	...	2	2	...	...	...	...
(iii) AFRICA UNSPECIFIED	1	1	...	2	1	1	6	6	...	22	14	8
E.—Born in America	1	1	...	11	5	6	10	8	2	21	16	5
(i) WITHIN BRITISH DOMINIONS	...	...	...	...	...	...	1	1	...	1	1	...
British Guiana...	...	...	...	...	...	...	1	1	...	...	...	...
Elsewhere	...	...	...	...	...	...	...	...	...	1	1	...
(ii) OUTSIDE BRITISH DOMINIONS	1	1	...	11	5	6	9	7	2	20	15	5
United States	1	1	...	11	5	6	9	7	2	20	15	5
(iii) AMERICA UNSPECIFIED	...	...	...	...	...	...	...	...	...	...	...	...
F.—Born in Australasia	2	...	2	1	1	...	2	2	...	12	6	6
(i) WITHIN BRITISH DOMINIONS	2	...	2	1	1	...	2	2	...	12	6	6
Australia	2	...	2	1	1	...	1	1	...	10	4	6
Fiji Islands	...	...	...	...	...	...	...	...	...	2	2	...
New Zealand	...	...	...	...	...	...	1	1	...	...	...	...
G.—Born at sea	1	1	...	...	...	...	...	...	...	...	...	...

TABLE VI.

BIRTHPLACE.—DISTRICTS AND STATES—*concld.*

BIRTHPLACE.	DISTRICTS OR STATES WHERE ENUMERATED.											
	GARO HILLS.			SADIYA FRONTIER TRACT.			BALIPARA FRONTIER TRACT.			MANIPUR STATE.		
	Persons.	Males.	Females.	Persons.	Males.	Females.	Persons.	Males.	Females.	Persons.	Males.	Females.
1	38	39	40	41	42	43	44	45	46	47	48	49
D.—Born in Africa	...	...	...	...	...	...	...	...	...	...	...	...
(i) WITHIN BRITISH DOMINIONS	...	...	...	...	...	...	...	...	...	...	...	...
Natal	...	...	...	...	...	...	...	...	...	...	...	...
Transvaal	...	...	...	...	...	...	...	...	...	...	...	...
(ii) OUTSIDE BRITISH DOMINIONS	...	...	...	...	...	...	...	...	...	...	...	...
Mozambique	...	...	...	...	...	...	...	...	...	...	...	...
Elsewhere	...	...	...	...	...	...	...	...	...	...	...	...
(iii) AFRICA UNSPECIFIED	...	...	...	...	...	...	...	...	...	...	...	...
E.—Born in America	7	1	6	2	1	1	...	...	...	3	1	2
(i) WITHIN BRITISH DOMINIONS	...	...	...	...	...	...	...	...	...	...	...	...
British Guiana	...	...	...	...	...	...	...	...	...	...	...	...
Elsewhere	...	...	...	...	...	...	...	...	...	...	...	...
(ii) OUTSIDE BRITISH DOMINIONS	7	1	6	2	1	1	...	...	...	3	1	2
United States	7	1	6	2	1	1	...	...	...	3	1	2
(iii) AMERICA UNSPECIFIED...	...	...	...	...	...	...	...	...	...	...	...	...
F.—Born in Australasia	...	...	...	1	1	...	...	...	...	...	...	...
(i) WITHIN BRITISH DOMINIONS	...	...	...	1	1	...	...	...	...	...	...	...
Australia	...	...	...	...	...	...	...	...	...	...	...	...
Fiji Islands	...	...	...	...	...	...	...	...	...	...	...	...
New Zealand	...	...	...	1	1	...	...	...	...	...	...	...
G.—Born at Sea	...	...	...	...	...	...	...	...	...	...	...	...

TABLE VII.

Age, Sex and Civil Condition.

This table consists of two parts ; Part A gives the provincial summary of the whole population by religion, age, sex and civil condition and Part B contains the distribution by districts.

This table corresponds with Table VII of 1921 but the method of compiling the quinary age groups differs from that employed at the 1921 census. The method used at the present census is, briefly, as follows :—The ages returned were first grouped in alternate groups of 3 and 7, *e.g.*, 4-6 and 7-13 and then regrouped into quinary groups by halving each group and adding half the subsequent or preceding group.

TABLE VII.

Age, Sex and Civil Condition. Part A.—Provincial Summary.

Religion.	Age.	Population.			Unmarried.			Married.			Widowed.		
		Persons.	Males.	Females.	Persons.	Males.	Females.	Persons.	Males.	Females.	Persons.	Males.	Females.
	1	2	3	4	5	6	7	8	9	10	11	12	13
ALL RELIGIONS.	0—1	314,645	156,904	157,741	314,634	156,903	157,721	25	5	20	...	...	...
	1—2	356,555	[illegible]	[illegible]	356,401	161,588	194,813	153	35	118	1	1	...
	2—3	335,270	163,384	[illegible]	334,621	163,480	171,141	649	101	548	9	2	7
	3—4	326,817	160,467	165,350	324,063	160,580	163,463	2,131	285	1,846	43	2	41
	4—5	311,677	156,047	155,330	308,226	155,301	152,435	3,321	477	2,844	130	19	111
	Total 0—5	*1,596,177*	*789,069*	*807,108*	*1,589,715*	*788,142*	*801,573*	*6,279*	*903*	*5,376*	*183*	*24*	*159*
	5—10	1,249,517	653,574	595,943	1,177,980	641,753	536,231	69,894	11,448	58,376	1,703	367	1,336
	10—15	1,156,770	615,602	540,554	887,830	529,917	357,913	164,015	25,174	138,842	4,933	583	4,101
	15—20	850,615	403,681	447,451	366,680	295,565	70,815	461,161	111,997	349,164	23,494	5,019	18,405
	20—25	881,834	423,087	458,877	241,321	208,043	33,278	603,258	295,796	307,443	38,315	10,224	28,087
	25—30	813,548	433,695	380,852	81,882	74,024	7,859	666,306	338,515	327,883	65,257	20,157	45,100
	30—35	723,333	401,473	321,873	41,757	36,845	4,912	604,111	341,715	197,306	77,470	22,803	54,667
	35—40	546,665	313,761	232,904	14,656	11,790	2,866	434,682	277,064	157,618	97,917	24,007	73,310
	40—45	452,704	261,391	191,403	9,275	7,566	1,709	343,632	229,571	114,061	99,867	24,254	75,633
	45—50	331,654	191,513	139,801	4,940	3,917	1,023	222,523	163,496	59,027	103,991	24,150	79,841
	50—55	268,829	[illegible]	124,450	3,587	2,772	818	169,553	127,454	42,099	93,679	22,146	71,533
	55—60	172,068	[illegible]	75,708	1,975	1,441	534	94,778	76,482	18,296	75,255	18,382	56,873
	60—65	130,225	[illegible]	[illegible]	1,517	1,096	421	71,199	53,058	18,141	63,509	15,526	48,043
	65—70	[illegible]	[illegible]	[illegible]	749	510	239	29,953	25,204	4,749	30,888	8,438	22,450
	70 and over	107,345	[illegible]	[illegible]	1,440	949	491	47,277	40,765	6,512	58,668	17,806	40,802
	Total	*9,247,857*	*4,844,133*	*4,403,724*	*4,424,135*	*2,595,453*	*1,828,682*	*3,988,643*	*2,033,641*	*1,955,002*	*835,079*	*215,039*	*620,040*
HINDU (OTHER THAN BRAHMO AND ARYA).	0—1	175,429	87,763	87,666	175,427	87,765	87,662	2	...	2	...	...	...
	1—2	167,834	82,863	84,991	167,823	82,847	84,976	11	6	5	...	...	...
	2—3	179,409	87,874	91,625	179,432	87,853	91,579	63	20	43	4	1	3
	3—4	175,404	[illegible]	[illegible]	174,796	[illegible]	[illegible]	272	64	208	16	1	15
	4—5	167,844	84,432	83,413	167,335	84,311	83,024	404	116	288	45	6	39
	Total 0—5	*865,710*	*429,545*	*436,165*	*864,833*	*429,332*	*435,501*	*819*	*205*	*607*	*65*	*8*	*57*
	5—10	674,390	351,400	322,991	649,006	348,112	300,894	24,540	3,085	21,455	844	212	632
	10—15	568,861	290,131	278,730	406,009	200,172	206,037	169,613	8,107	61,546	2,639	492	2,147
	15—20	464,347	230,071	234,276	216,190	171,720	44,470	233,993	51,427	182,566	14,156	2,615	11,541
	20—25	489,313	241,306	248,007	146,575	131,868	14,707	316,899	102,719	214,180	23,839	6,119	17,720
	25—30	472,153	353,505	118,648	55,273	51,371	3,903	374,451	188,713	185,708	42,399	13,221	29,178
	30—35	467,296	278,076	189,220	29,202	26,706	2,496	347,349	185,703	161,646	50,675	15,507	35,078
	35—40	336,165	188,824	147,341	9,906	8,770	1,136	252,707	161,799	90,908	63,462	18,055	45,437
	40—45	279,619	166,462	114,157	6,583	5,623	960	201,572	135,006	66,566	64,524	17,833	46,691
	45—50	201,589	117,348	84,244	3,475	2,928	547	130,617	96,275	34,342	67,497	18,182	49,315
	50—55	164,949	95,100	69,849	2,529	2,094	435	100,841	76,186	24,655	61,578	16,830	44,748
	55—60	104,538	55,813	48,725	1,292	1,061	231	54,056	44,162	9,894	49,190	13,600	35,590
	60—65	81,374	44,772	36,602	966	786	180	39,427	32,667	6,760	40,961	11,319	29,642
	65—70	34,600	19,108	15,501	441	364	77	15,193	13,016	2,177	18,975	5,728	13,247
	70 and over	56,348	30,977	25,371	746	607	149	21,938	19,282	2,656	33,664	11,096	22,568
	Total	*5,204,190*	*2,751,414*	*2,452,776*	*2,485,645*	*1,471,903*	*1,013,742*	*2,184,037*	*1,128,319*	*1,055,718*	*534,508*	*151,199*	*383,309*

TABLE VII.

AGE, SEX AND CIVIL CONDITION. PART A.—PROVINCIAL SUMMARY—*contd.*

RELIGION.	AGE.	POPULATION.			UNMARRIED.			MARRIED.			WIDOWED.		
		Persons.	Males.	Females.	Persons.	Males.	Females.	Persons.	Males.	Females.	Persons.	Males.	Females.
	1	2	3	4	5	6	7	8	9	10	11	12	13
HINDU (Brahmo).	0—1	18	13	5	18	13	5	...	...	...	...	...	...
	1—2	14	7	7	14	7	7	...	...	...	...	...	...
	2—3	13	4	9	13	4	9	...	...	...	...	...	...
	3—4	9	4	5	9	4	5	...	...	...	...	...	...
	4—5	26	13	13	26	13	13	...	...	...	...	...	...
	Total 0—5	*80*	*41*	*39*	*80*	*41*	*39*	...	...	...	...	...	...
	5—10	54	31	23	53	31	23	1	...	1	...	...	...
	10—15	45	23	22	45	23	22	...	...	...	...	...	...
	15—20	38	17	21	29	14	15	8	2	6	1	1	...
	20—25	41	20	21	24	13	11	15	6	9	2	1	1
	25—30	36	14	20	12	8	4	22	8	14	2	...	2
	30—35	28	10	16	6	8	3	18	6	12	2	1	1
	35—40	27	12	13	5	1	4	21	11	10	1	...	1
	40—45	27	16	11	4	1	3	22	14	8	1	1	...
	45—50	22	15	7	...	...	...	18	13	5	4	2	2
	50—55	13	10	3	1	1	...	8	7	1	4	2	2
	55—60	14	8	8	...	...	...	9	5	4	5	1	4
	60—65	8	4	4	...	...	...	5	4	1	3	...	3
	65—70	7	4	3	...	...	...	2	1	1	5	3	2
	70 and over	10	7	3	...	...	...	5	4	1	5	3	2
	Total	*448*	*232*	*216*	*259*	*136*	*123*	*154*	*81*	*73*	*35*	*15*	*20*
HINDU (Arya).	0—1	...	...	...	...	...	...	...	...	...	...	...	...
	1—2	1	1	...	1	1	...	...	...	...	...	...	...
	2—3	...	...	...	...	...	...	...	...	...	...	...	...
	3—4	...	...	...	...	...	...	...	...	...	...	...	...
	4—5	...	...	...	...	...	...	...	...	...	...	...	...
	Total 0—5	*1*	*1*	...	*1*	*1*	...	...	...	...	...	...	...
	5—10	...	...	...	...	...	...	...	...	...	...	...	...
	10—15	1	1	...	1	1	...	...	...	...	...	...	...
	15—20	1	...	1	...	...	...	1	...	1	...	...	...
	20—25	1	1	...	...	...	...	1	1	...	...	...	...
	25—30	2	3	...	2	2	...	...	...	...	...	...	...
	30—35	2	2	...	2	2	...	...	...	...	...	...	...
	35—40	1	1	...	...	...	...	1	1	...	...	...	...
	40—45	1	1	...	1	1	...	...	...	...	...	...	...
	45—50	1	1	...	1	1	...	...	...	...	...	...	...
	50—55	1	1	...	...	...	...	1	1	...	...	...	...
	55—60	...	...	...	...	...	...	...	...	...	...	...	...
	60—65	...	...	...	...	...	...	...	...	...	...	...	...
	65—70	...	...	...	...	...	...	...	...	...	...	...	...
	70 and over	...	...	...	...	...	...	...	...	...	...	...	...
	Total	*19*	*11*	*1*	*8*	*8*	...	*4*	*3*	*1*	...	...	...

TABLE VII.

AGE, SEX AND CIVIL CONDITION. PART A.—PROVINCIAL SUMMARY—*contd.*

Religion.	Age.	Population. Persons.	Population. Males.	Population. Females.	Unmarried. Persons.	Unmarried. Males.	Unmarried. Females.	Married. Persons.	Married. Males.	Married. Females.	Widowed. Persons.	Widowed. Males.	Widowed. Females.
	1	2	3	4	5	6	7	8	9	10	11	12	13
SIKH.	0—1	58	26	33	58	26	33	...	...	...	...	...	...
	1—2	64	29	35	64	29	35	...	...	...	...	...	...
	2—3	64	29	35	64	29	35	...	...	...	...	...	...
	3—4	58	23	35	58	23	35	...	...	...	...	...	...
	4—5	97	35	62	95	34	61	2	1	1	...	...	...
	Total 0—5	*341*	*142*	*199*	*339*	*141*	*198*	2	1	1	...	...	...
	5—10	201	111	90	194	109	85	7	2	5	...	...	...
	10—15	158	108	50	135	100	35	23	8	15	...	...	...
	15—20	287	188	99	125	114	11	160	72	88	2	2	...
	20—25	360	246	114	114	108	6	250	143	107	5	4	1
	25—30	389	303	86	55	55	...	319	237	82	15	11	4
	30—35	348	285	63	33	33	...	304	245	59	11	7	4
	35—40	220	183	37	13	13	...	181	150	31	16	11	5
	40—45	151	124	27	3	3	...	133	113	20	15	8	7
	45—50	118	104	14	1	1	...	100	94	6	17	9	8
	50—55	81	69	12	2	1	1	67	61	6	12	6	6
	55—60	32	23	9	1	...	1	21	19	2	10	4	6
	60—65	16	10	6	...	...	...	10	9	1	6	1	5
	65—70	6	6	...	...	...	...	5	5	...	1	1	...
	70 and over	12	7	5	...	...	...	6	6	...	6	1	5
	Total	*2,729*	*1,918*	*811*	*1,015*	*678*	*337*	*1,508*	*1,175*	*493*	*116*	*65*	*51*
BUDDHIST.	0—1	463	232	231	463	232	231	...	...	...	...	...	...
	1—2	423	211	213	423	211	213	...	...	...	...	...	...
	2—3	475	239	236	475	239	236	...	...	...	...	...	...
	3—4	438	227	211	437	226	211	1	1	...	...	...	...
	4—5	409	213	196	401	209	193	6	3	3	2	1	1
	Total 0—5	*2,208*	*1,122*	*1,086*	*2,199*	*1,117*	*1,082*	7	4	3	2	1	1
	5—10	1,650	872	778	1,621	862	759	27	10	17	2	...	2
	10—15	1,472	780	692	1,376	718	658	91	21	70	5	1	4
	15—20	1,418	764	654	822	562	260	569	179	390	27	13	14
	20—25	1,538	865	673	627	489	138	860	341	518	41	24	17
	25—30	1,566	944	622	275	244	31	1,191	643	548	100	57	43
	30—35	1,405	872	533	158	139	19	1,129	665	464	118	68	50
	35—40	1,043	662	381	69	57	12	832	536	296	142	69	73
	40—45	877	558	319	48	43	5	689	449	240	140	66	74
	45—50	610	397	213	26	24	2	434	317	117	150	56	94
	50—55	493	311	182	11	11	...	345	252	93	137	48	89
	55—60	294	190	104	9	6	3	173	138	35	112	46	66
	60—65	223	139	84	4	2	2	124	102	22	95	35	60
	65—70	97	66	31	3	2	1	51	45	6	43	19	24
	70 and over	161	100	61	2	2	...	66	59	7	93	39	54
	Total	*15,045*	*8,622*	*6,423*	*7,250*	*4,318*	*2,932*	*6,588*	*3,762*	*2,826*	*1,207*	*542*	*665*

TABLE VII.

Age, Sex and Civil Condition. Part A.—Provincial Summary—*contd.*

Religion.	Age.	Population. Persons.	Population. Males.	Population. Females.	Unmarried. Persons.	Unmarried. Males.	Unmarried. Females.	Married. Persons.	Married. Males.	Married. Females.	Widowed. Persons.	Widowed. Males.	Widowed. Females.
	1	2	3	4	5	6	7	8	9	10	11	12	13
Jain.	0—1	53	25	28	53	25	28	...	...	...	...	...	...
	1—2	48	22	26	48	22	26	...	...	...	...	...	...
	2—3	47	25	22	47	25	22	...	...	...	...	...	...
	3—4	40	20	20	40	20	20	...	...	...	...	...	...
	4—5	61	28	33	60	28	32	1	...	1	...	...	...
	Total 0—5	*249*	*120*	*129*	*248*	*120*	*128*	*1*	...	*1*	...	...	...
	5—10	242	153	89	222	143	79	20	10	10	...	...	...
	10—15	278	201	77	217	175	42	59	26	33	2	...	2
	15—20	370	281	89	176	171	5	190	109	81	4	1	3
	20—25	394	316	78	147	143	4	238	168	70	9	5	4
	25—30	328	274	54	72	70	2	237	190	47	19	14	5
	30—35	261	218	43	41	41	...	206	167	39	14	10	4
	35—40	206	170	36	21	21	...	168	141	27	17	8	9
	40—45	179	148	31	14	14	...	137	116	21	28	18	10
	45—50	126	100	26	6	6	...	92	78	14	28	16	12
	50—55	88	73	15	4	4	...	62	53	9	22	16	[illegible]
	55—60	40	32	8	4	4	...	24	20	4	12	8	4
	60—65	20	14	6	2	2	...	9	8	1	9	4	5
	65—70	17	12	5	1	1	...	10	8	2	6	3	3
	70 and over	5	4	1	1	1	...	3	2	1	1	1	...
	Total	*2,803*	*2,116*	*687*	*1,176*	*916*	*260*	*1,458*	*1,098*	*360*	*169*	*102*	*67*
Confucian.	0—1	1	1	...	1	1	...	...	...	...	...	...	...
	1—2	...	...	...	...	...	...	...	...	...	...	...	...
	2—3	2	1	1	2	1	1	...	...	...	...	...	...
	3—4	1	1	...	1	1	...	...	...	...	...	...	...
	4—5	2	1	1	2	1	1	...	...	...	...	...	...
	Total 0—5	*7*	*4*	*3*	*7*	*4*	*3*	...	...	...	...	...	...
	5—10	2	1	1	2	1	1	...	...	...	...	...	...
	10—15	1	...	1	1	...	1	...	...	...	...	...	...
	15—20	4	3	1	2	1	1	2	2	...	...	...	...
	20—25	9	7	2	4	4	...	5	3	2	...	...	...
	25—30	13	12	1	5	5	...	8	7	1	...	...	...
	30—35	11	11	...	3	3	...	8	8	...	...	...	...
	35—40	11	10	1	...	...	...	10	9	1	1	1	...
	40—45	3	3	...	...	...	...	3	3	...	...	...	...
	45—50	1	1	...	...	...	...	1	1	...	...	...	...
	50—55	1	1	...	...	...	...	1	1	...	...	...	...
	55—60	...	...	...	...	...	...	...	...	...	...	...	...
	60—65	...	...	...	...	...	...	...	...	...	...	...	...
	65—70	...	...	...	...	...	...	...	...	...	...	...	...
	70 and over	...	...	...	...	...	...	...	...	...	...	...	...
	Total	*63*	*53*	*10*	*24*	*18*	*6*	*38*	*34*	*4*	*1*	*1*	...

TABLE VII.

Age, Sex and Civil Condition. Part A.—Provincial Summary—*contd.*

Religion.	Age.	Population. Persons.	Population. Males.	Population. Females.	Unmarried. Persons.	Unmarried. Males.	Unmarried. Females.	Married. Persons.	Married. Males.	Married. Females.	Widowed. Persons.	Widowed. Males.	Widowed. Females.
	1	2	3	4	5	6	7	8	9	10	11	12	13
MUSLIM.	0—1	93,117	46,240	46,877	93,099	46,238	46,861	18	2	16	...	...	...
	1—2	95,731	46,661	49,070	95,606	46,636	48,970	125	25	100	...	...	...
	2—3	106,991	51,833	55,158	106,442	51,763	54,679	545	70	475	4	...	4
	3—4	104,285	51,141	53,144	102,494	50,947	51,547	1,765	193	1,572	26	1	25
	4—5	99,509	49,742	49,767	96,775	49,437	47,338	2,674	297	2,377	60	8	53
	Total 0—5	*499,633*	*245,617*	*254,016*	*494,416*	*245,021*	*249,395*	*5,127*	*587*	*4,540*	*90*	*9*	*81*
	5—10	405,758	216,128	189,630	361,532	208,090	153,443	43,473	7,010	36,463	753	129	624
	10—15	345,938	184,848	161,090	257,111	168,324	88,787	86,916	15,767	71,149	1,911	257	1,654
	15—20	272,957	125,589	147,368	83,365	75,600	7,769	183,594	48,772	134,822	5,998	1,251	4,747
	20—25	281,774	132,357	149,417	51,885	49,573	2,312	220,773	80,360	140,413	9,116	2,484	6,653
	25—30	236,051	126,918	109,133	14,331	13,570	761	206,882	100,333	97,549	14,838	4,015	10,823
	30—35	201,989	114,512	67,157	5,986	5,443	543	177,491	105,274	72,287	18,492	4,165	14,327
	35—40	146,765	86,121	60,644	1,606	1,306	300	120,473	80,924	39,549	24,596	3,891	20,705
	40—45	117,368	69,631	47,737	1,051	843	208	90,950	65,257	25,693	25,367	3,531	21,836
	45—50	86,015	50,535	35,080	542	431	111	59,238	47,103	12,135	26,235	3,401	22,834
	50—55	65,675	38,445	27,230	354	264	90	42,841	35,214	7,627	22,480	2,967	19,513
	55—60	42,927	24,783	18,044	210	147	63	25,013	21,928	3,085	17,604	2,711	14,893
	60—65	33,996	19,236	14,761	160	118	43	18,888	16,727	2,161	14,950	2,391	12,559
	65—70	15,688	9,398	6,290	78	56	22	8,526	7,828	698	7,084	1,214	5,870
	70 and over	28,096	16,944	11,154	138	105	33	14,631	13,132	959	13,929	3,707	10,222
	Total	*2,780,514*	*1,461,762*	*1,318,752*	*1,272,855*	*769,446*	*503,409*	*1,304,916*	*655,983*	*648,933*	*203,443*	*36,333*	*167,110*
CHRISTIAN.	0—1	8,546	4,279	4,267	8,545	4,278	4,267	1	1	...	...	...	...
	1—2	8,084	3,969	4,115	8,080	3,966	4,114	3	2	1	1	1	...
	2—3	8,872	4,357	4,515	8,866	4,353	4,513	5	3	2	1	1	...
	3—4	8,658	4,301	4,357	8,645	4,299	4,346	13	2	11	...	...	...
	4—5	8,216	4,084	4,132	8,179	4,075	4,104	33	9	24	4	...	4
	Total 0—5	*42,376*	*20,990*	*21,386*	*42,315*	*20,971*	*21,344*	*55*	*17*	*38*	*6*	*2*	*4*
	5—10	34,576	17,426	17,150	34,290	17,354	16,936	270	66	204	16	6	10
	10—15	30,973	15,066	15,507	29,850	15,423	14,427	1,065	223	842	58	20	38
	15—20	25,125	11,557	13,568	16,567	9,537	7,030	7,985	1,833	6,152	573	138	455
	20—25	24,069	10,951	13,118	10,451	6,683	3,768	12,660	3,978	8,682	958	240	684
	25—30	21,402	10,942	10,460	3,217	2,474	743	16,728	7,124	8,604	1,457	544	913
	30—35	18,758	9,943	8,815	1,823	1,386	437	15,408	8,013	7,395	1,527	544	983
	35—40	13,637	7,214	6,423	769	563	206	11,056	6,174	4,882	1,812	477	1,335
	40—45	11,482	5,978	5,504	578	415	163	9,040	5,120	3,910	1,864	433	1,431
	45—50	7,800	4,097	3,703	310	222	88	5,659	3,515	2,144	1,831	360	1,471
	50—55	6,310	3,297	3,013	242	168	74	4,370	2,791	1,579	1,698	338	1,360
	55—60	4,150	2,046	2,104	155	93	62	2,443	1,651	792	1,552	302	1,250
	60—65	3,426	1,634	1,792	130	77	53	1,898	1,208	690	1,398	249	1,149
	65—70	1,793	790	1,003	78	40	38	854	604	250	861	146	715
	70 and over	3,369	1,514	1,855	135	67	68	1,448	1,100	318	1,786	347	1,439
	Total	*249,246*	*124,045*	*125,201*	*140,910*	*75,473*	*65,437*	*90,939*	*44,376*	*46,563*	*17,397*	*4,196*	*13,201*

TABLE VII.

Age, Sex and Civil Condition. . Part A.—Provincial Summary—*contd.*

Religion.	Age.	Population. Persons.	Population. Males.	Population. Females.	Unmarried. Persons.	Unmarried. Males.	Unmarried. Females.	Married. Persons.	Married. Males.	Married. Females.	Widowed. Persons.	Widowed. Males.	Widowed. Females.
	1	2	3	4	5	6	7	8	9	10	11	12	13
TRIBAL.	0—1	36,953	18,324	18,629	36,949	18,322	18,627	4	2	2	...	...	...
	1—2	36,331	17,847	18,484	36,317	17,846	18,473	14	2	12	...	...	...
	2—3	39,303	19,214	20,089	39,267	19,206	20,061	36	8	28	...	...	...
	3—4	37,634	18,547	19,087	37,553	18,522	19,031	80	25	55	1	...	1
	4—5	35,296	17,535	17,761	35,137	17,479	17,658	140	52	88	19	4	15
	Total 0—5	*185,517*	*91,467*	*94,050*	*185,223*	*91,374*	*93,849*	*274*	*89*	*185*	*20*	*4*	*16*
	5—10	133,224	67,434	65,790	131,652	67,050	64,602	1,484	364	1,120	88	20	68
	10—15	107,045	55,153	51,892	100,462	54,031	46,431	6,256	1,060	5,196	317	61	256
	15—20	86,078	39,103	46,975	48,768	28,856	19,912	34,650	9,551	25,099	2,660	696	1,964
	20—25	85,350	38,576	46,774	29,473	19,148	10,325	51,534	18,128	33,406	4,343	1,300	3,043
	25—30	81,559	39,955	41,604	8,639	6,217	2,422	66,498	31,445	35,053	6,422	2,293	4,129
	30—35	73,296	37,283	36,013	4,479	3,166	1,313	62,173	31,689	30,484	6,694	2,408	4,316
	35—40	58,560	30,754	27,806	1,515	968	547	49,209	27,302	21,907	7,836	2,484	5,352
	40—45	50,069	26,463	23,606	1,053	623	430	41,072	23,475	17,597	7,944	2,365	5,579
	45—50	35,146	18,512	16,634	578	303	275	26,345	16,088	10,257	8,223	2,121	6,102
	50—55	29,199	15,061	14,138	454	236	218	21,003	12,879	8,124	7,742	1,946	5,796
	55—60	20,098	10,404	9,694	293	139	154	13,031	8,557	4,474	6,774	1,708	5,066
	60—65	17,209	8,865	8,344	255	111	144	10,831	7,228	3,603	6,123	1,526	4,597
	65—70	9,366	4,774	4,592	148	57	91	5,308	3,694	1,614	3,910	1,023	2,887
	70 and over	19,296	9,853	9,443	416	177	239	9,763	7,169	2,594	9,117	2,507	6,610
	Total	*992,390*	*493,755*	*498,635*	*514,827*	*272,475*	*242,352*	*399,420*	*198,717*	*200,703*	*78,143*	*22,563*	*55,580*
ZOROASTRIAN (PARSI).	0—1	...	...	...	...	...	...	...	...	...	...	...	...
	1—2	...	...	...	...	...	...	...	...	...	...	...	...
	2—3	...	...	...	...	...	...	...	...	...	...	...	...
	3—4	...	...	...	...	...	...	...	...	...	...	...	...
	4—5	...	...	...	...	...	...	...	...	...	...	...	...
	Total 0—5	...	...	...	...	...	...	...	...	...	...	...	...
	5—10	1	...	1	1	...	1	...	...	...	...	...	...
	10—15	...	...	...	...	...	...	...	...	...	...	...	...
	15—20	1	1	...	1	1	...	...	...	...	...	...	...
	20—25	2	2	...	2	2	...	...	...	...	...	...	...
	25—30	1	1	...	1	1	...	1	1	...	...	...	...
	30—35	...	...	...	...	...	...	...	...	...	...	...	...
	35—40	1	1	...	...	...	...	1	1	...	...	...	...
	40—45	...	...	...	...	...	...	...	...	...	...	...	...
	45—50	2	1	1	...	...	...	2	1	1	...	...	...
	50—55	...	...	...	...	...	...	...	...	...	...	...	...
	55—60	...	...	...	...	...	...	...	...	...	...	...	...
	60—65	...	...	...	...	...	...	...	...	...	...	...	...
	65—70	...	...	...	...	...	...	...	...	...	...	...	...
	70 and over	...	...	...	...	...	...	...	...	...	...	...	...
	Total	*9*	*7*	*2*	*5*	*4*	*1*	*4*	*3*	*1*	...	...	...

TABLE VII.

Age, Sex and Civil Condition. Part A.—Provincial Summary—*concld.*

Religion.	Age.	Population. Persons.	Population. Males.	Population. Females.	Unmarried. Persons.	Unmarried. Males.	Unmarried. Females.	Married. Persons.	Married. Males.	Married. Females.	Widowed. Persons.	Widowed. Males.	Widowed. Females.
	1	2	3	4	5	6	7	8	9	10	11	12	13
JEW.	0—1	1	...	1	1	...	1	...	...	...	...	...	...
	1—2	...	...	...	...	...	...	...	...	...	...	...	...
	2—3	2	1	1	2	1	1	...	...	...	...	...	...
	3—4	...	...	...	...	...	...	...	...	...	...	...	...
	4—5	2	1	1	2	1	1	...	...	...	...	...	...
	Total 0—5	*5*	*2*	*3*	*5*	*2*	*3*	...	...	...	...	...	...
	5—10	2	1	1	2	1	1	...	...	...	...	...	...
	10—15	2	1	1	2	1	1	...	...	...	...	...	...
	15—20	3	3	...	3	3	...	...	...	...	...	...	...
	20—25	2	2	...	2	2	...	...	...	...	...	...	...
	25—30	1	...	1	...	...	...	1	...	1	...	...	...
	30—35	...	...	...	...	...	...	...	...	...	...	...	...
	35—40	2	1	1	...	...	...	2	1	1	...	...	...
	40—45	1	1	...	...	...	...	1	1	...	...	...	...
	45—50	...	...	...	...	...	...	...	...	...	...	...	...
	50—55	...	...	...	...	...	...	...	...	...	...	...	...
	55—60	...	...	...	...	...	...	...	...	...	...	...	...
	60—65	...	...	...	...	...	...	...	...	...	...	...	...
	65—70	...	...	...	...	...	...	...	...	...	...	...	...
	70 and over	...	...	...	...	...	...	...	...	...	...	...	...
	Total	*18*	*11*	*7*	*14*	*9*	*5*	*4*	*2*	*2*	...	...	...
INDEFINITE BELIEF.	0—1	10	3	7	10	3	7	...	...	...	...	...	...
	1—2	5	4	1	5	4	1	...	...	...	...	...	...
	2—3	10	6	4	10	6	4	...	...	...	...	...	...
	3—4	10	2	8	10	2	8	...	...	...	...	...	...
	4—5	15	3	12	14	3	11	1	...	1	...	...	...
	Total 0—5	*50*	*18*	*32*	*49*	*18*	*31*	*1*	...	*1*	...	...	...
	5—10	17	8	9	15	7	8	2	1	1	...	...	...
	10—15	24	10	14	21	9	12	2	1	1	1	...	1
	15—20	27	15	12	26	12	13	10	1	9	2	2	1
	20—25	41	18	23	17	10	7	22	7	15	2	1	1
	25—30	47	24	23	11	7	4	31	16	16	5	2	3
	30—35	36	21	15	4	3	1	25	15	10	7	3	4
	35—40	17	8	9	2	1	1	11	6	5	4	1	3
	40—45	17	6	11	...	...	...	11	5	6	6	1	5
	45—50	24	15	9	1	1	...	17	11	6	6	3	3
	50—55	20	11	9	...	...	...	14	8	6	6	3	3
	55—60	15	8	7	1	1	...	8	5	3	6	2	4
	60—65	11	6	5	...	...	...	7	5	2	4	1	3
	65—70	7	4	3	...	...	...	6	3	1	2	1	2
	70 and over	27	15	12	2	...	2	18	12	6	7	3	4
	Total	*390*	*187*	*203*	*147*	*69*	*78*	*183*	*95*	*88*	*60*	*23*	*37*

TABLE VII.

Age, Sex and Civil Condition. Part B.—Details for districts.

District.	Age.	Population. Persons.	Population. Males.	Population. Females.	Unmarried. Persons.	Unmarried. Males.	Unmarried. Females.	Married. Persons.	Married. Males.	Married. Females.	Widowed. Persons.	Widowed. Males.	Widowed. Females.
	1	2	3	4	5	6	7	8	9	10	11	12	13
GOALPARA.	ALL RELIGIONS ...	*882,748*	*470,273*	*412,475*	*315,341*	*163,982*	*151,359*	*495,429*	*290,877*	*204,552*	*71,978*	*15,414*	*56,564*
	0—1 ...	30,915	15,533	15,382	30,915	15,533	15,382	...	...	...	...	...	...
	1—2 ...	31,043	15,433	15,610	31,010	15,429	15,581	33	4	29	...	...	...
	2—3 ...	34,378	16,683	17,695	34,132	16,665	17,467	242	18	224	4	...	4
	3—4 ...	33,472	16,468	17,004	32,772	16,399	16,373	686	68	618	14	1	13
	4—5 ...	31,003	15,812	15,191	30,010	15,698	14,312	965	110	855	28	4	24
	Total 0—5 ...	*160,810*	*79,928*	*80,882*	*158,838*	*79,723*	*79,115*	*1,926*	*200*	*1,726*	*46*	*5*	*41*
	5—10 ...	126,048	67,392	58,656	106,551	63,404	43,147	19,131	3,918	15,213	366	70	296
	10—15 ...	104,829	55,162	49,667	71,442	47,652	23,790	32,640	7,387	25,253	747	123	624
	15—20 ...	81,792	38,158	43,634	22,962	19,834	3,128	56,558	17,891	38,667	2,272	433	1,839
	20—30 ...	160,000	82,879	77,121	20,570	19,045	1,525	1,30,459	61,701	68,758	8,971	2,133	6,838
	30—40 ...	117,599	69,752	47,847	4,062	3,712	350	96,057	62,586	33,471	15,480	3,454	12,026
	40—50 ...	67,600	40,760	26,840	1,142	979	163	49,485	36,515	12,970	16,973	3,266	13,707
	50—60 ...	37,106	21,484	15,624	460	380	80	22,839	18,423	4,416	13,800	2,673	11,128
	60 and over ...	27,963	15,789	12,174	305	244	61	16,394	12,348	3,046	13,322	3,256	10,066
	HINDU ...	*385,877*	*208,362*	*177,515*	*177,689*	*107,946*	*69,743*	*169,017*	*91,120*	*77,897*	*39,171*	*9,296*	*29,875*
	0—1 ...	12,900	6,483	6,417	12,900	6,483	6,417	...	...	...	...	...	...
	1—2 ...	12,605	6,294	6,311	12,605	6,294	6,311	...	...	...	...	...	...
	2—3 ...	13,691	6,616	7,075	13,677	6,613	7,064	13	3	10	1	...	1
	3—4 ...	13,412	6,561	6,851	13,367	6,553	6,814	43	8	35	2	...	2
	4—5 ...	12,608	6,374	6,234	12,541	6,362	6,179	63	13	50	5	...	5
	Total 0—5 ...	*65,316*	*32,428*	*32,888*	*65,190*	*32,405*	*32,785*	*118*	*23*	*95*	*8*	...	*8*
	5—10 ...	51,335	27,032	24,303	47,679	26,666	21,013	3,544	353	3,191	112	14	98
	10—15 ...	43,196	22,748	20,448	34,671	21,738	12,933	8,209	978	7,231	316	32	284
	15—20 ...	35,039	16,832	18,207	13,301	11,515	1,786	20,395	5,134	15,261	1,343	183	1,160
	20—30 ...	71,739	38,327	33,412	13,341	12,475	866	53,052	24,762	28,290	5,346	1,090	4,256
	30—40 ...	54,767	32,944	21,823	3,589	3,408	181	43,528	28,483	15,045	7,650	1,053	6,597
	40—50 ...	32,638	19,781	12,857	557	467	90	22,969	17,186	5,783	9,112	2,128	6,984
	50—60 ...	18,232	10,618	7,614	233	182	51	10,735	8,661	2,074	7,264	1,775	5,489
	60 and over ...	13,615	7,652	5,963	128	90	38	6,467	5,541	926	7,020	2,021	4,999
	MUSLIM ...	*387,709*	*205,386*	*182,323*	*148,986*	*92,969*	*56,017*	*212,076*	*108,250*	*103,826*	*26,647*	*4,167*	*22,480*
	0—1 ...	13,908	6,927	6,981	13,908	6,927	6,981	...	...	...	...	...	...
	1—2 ...	14,279	7,084	7,195	14,248	7,081	7,167	31	3	28	...	...	...
	2—3 ...	16,070	7,832	8,238	15,848	7,819	8,029	219	13	206	3	...	3
	3—4 ...	15,472	7,644	7,828	14,838	7,592	7,246	622	51	571	12	1	11
	4—5 ...	13,953	7,188	6,765	13,063	7,103	5,960	871	83	788	19	2	17
	Total 0—5 ...	*73,682*	*36,675*	*37,007*	*71,905*	*36,523*	*35,382*	*1,743*	*149*	*1,594*	*34*	*3*	*31*
	5—10 ...	56,680	30,464	26,216	41,306	26,952	14,354	15,138	3,462	11,676	236	50	186
	10—15 ...	48,237	25,443	22,794	24,798	19,204	5,594	23,047	6,158	16,889	392	81	311
	15—20 ...	37,673	17,240	20,433	6,008	5,615	393	30,900	11,426	19,474	765	199	566
	20—30 ...	70,272	35,785	34,487	4,238	4,004	234	63,112	31,013	32,099	2,922	768	2,154
	30—40 ...	49,128	29,158	19,970	582	486	96	42,868	27,688	15,180	5,678	984	4,694
	40—50 ...	26,925	16,300	10,625	157	120	37	20,285	15,439	4,846	6,483	741	5,742
	50—60 ...	14,425	8,317	6,108	51	36	15	9,066	7,718	1,348	5,308	563	4,745
	60 and over ...	10,687	6,004	4,683	41	28	13	5,818	5,198	620	4,829	778	4,051

TABLE VII.

AGE, SEX AND CIVIL CONDITION. PART B.—DETAILS FOR DISTRICTS—*contd.*

District.	Age.	Population. Persons.	Population. Males.	Population. Females.	Unmarried. Persons.	Unmarried. Males.	Unmarried. Females.	Married. Persons.	Married. Males.	Married. Females.	Widowed. Persons.	Widowed. Males.	Widowed. Females.
	1	2	3	4	5	6	7	8	9	10	11	12	13
GOALPARA—*concld.*	TRIBAL ...	*89,389*	*45,912*	*43,477*	*46,854*	*25,569*	*21,285*	*37,192*	*18,531*	*18,661*	*5,343*	*1,812*	*3,531*
	0-1 ...	3,405	1,730	1,675	3,405	1,730	1,675	...	...	...	...	...	...
	1-2 ...	3,522	1,739	1,783	3,520	1,738	1,782	2	1	1	...	...	...
	2-3 ...	3,903	1,881	2,022	3,893	1,878	2,015	10	3	7	...	...	...
	3-4 ...	3,898	1,917	1,981	3,878	1,908	1,970	20	9	11	...	...	...
	4-5 ...	3,760	1,915	1,845	3,729	1,899	1,830	27	14	13	4	2	2
	Total 0-5 ...	*18,488*	*9,182*	*9,306*	*18,425*	*9,153*	*9,272*	*59*	*27*	*32*	*4*	*2*	*2*
	5-10 ...	14,148	7,346	6,802	13,753	7,256	6,497	377	84	293	18	6	12
	10-15 ...	10,820	5,521	5,299	9,621	5,323	4,298	1,162	188	974	37	10	27
	15-20 ...	7,120	3,129	3,991	2,683	1,900	783	4,295	1,181	3,114	142	48	94
	20-30 ...	14,371	6,899	7,472	1,880	1,554	326	11,892	5,101	6,791	599	244	355
	30-40 ...	11,134	6,171	4,963	332	274	58	9,807	5,520	4,287	995	377	618
	40-50 ...	6,551	3,778	2,773	94	64	30	5,259	3,344	1,915	1,198	370	828
	50-60 ...	3,667	2,089	1,578	40	26	14	2,571	1,745	826	1,056	318	738
	60 and over ...	3,090	1,797	1,293	26	19	7	1,770	1,341	429	1,294	437	857
KAMRUP.	ALL RELIGIONS ...	*976,746*	*513,345*	*463,401*	*467,276*	*275,002*	*192,274*	*429,869*	*220,717*	*209,152*	*79,601*	*17,626*	*61,975*
	0-1 ...	37,599	18,654	18,945	37,586	18,653	18,933	13	1	12	...	...	...
	1-2 ...	35,601	17,450	18,151	35,537	17,430	18,107	64	20	44	...	...	...
	2-3 ...	38,476	18,776	19,700	38,234	18,721	19,513	240	54	186	2	1	1
	3-4 ...	37,182	18,448	18,734	36,486	18,346	18,140	689	101	588	7	1	6
	4-5 ...	35,212	17,780	17,432	34,187	17,644	16,543	1,009	133	876	16	3	13
	Total 0-5 ...	*184,070*	*91,108*	*92,962*	*182,030*	*90,794*	*91,236*	*2,015*	*309*	*1,706*	*25*	*5*	*20*
	5-10 ...	138,653	72,886	65,767	126,364	70,406	55,958	11,996	2,384	9,612	293	96	197
	10-15 ...	113,473	60,472	53,001	90,770	55,979	34,791	22,105	4,316	17,789	598	177	421
	15-20 ...	87,220	42,064	45,156	33,689	27,991	5,698	51,718	13,600	38,118	1,813	473	1,340
	20-30 ...	169,131	85,489	83,642	28,036	24,890	3,146	133,114	58,540	74,574	7,981	2,059	5,922
	30-40 ...	126,948	71,258	55,690	4,338	3,513	825	107,093	64,475	42,618	15,517	3,270	12,247
	40-50 ...	78,136	45,199	32,937	1,214	853	361	57,660	40,729	16,931	19,262	3,617	15,645
	50-60 ...	47,694	27,036	20,658	538	365	173	28,805	22,934	5,871	18,351	3,737	14,614
	60 and over ...	31,491	17,833	13,658	297	211	86	15,363	13,430	1,933	15,831	4,192	11,639
	HINDU ...	*709,960*	*370,669*	*339,291*	*351,359*	*205,839*	*145,520*	*293,849*	*150,408*	*143,441*	*64,752*	*14,422*	*50,330*
	0-1 ...	27,329	13,614	13,715	27,328	13,614	13,714	1	...	1	...	...	...
	1-2 ...	24,868	12,235	12,633	24,862	12,233	12,629	6	2	4	...	...	...
	2-3 ...	26,794	13,046	13,748	26,770	13,040	13,730	23	5	18	1	1	...
	3-4 ...	26,183	12,948	13,235	26,116	12,933	13,183	63	14	49	4	1	3
	4-5 ...	25,150	12,662	12,488	25,048	12,637	12,411	94	23	71	8	2	6
	Total 0-5 ...	*130,334*	*64,515*	*65,819*	*130,134*	*64,467*	*65,667*	*187*	*44*	*143*	*13*	*4*	*9*
	5-10 ...	99,638	52,040	47,598	94,933	51,392	43,541	4,521	584	3,937	184	64	120
	10-15 ...	81,588	43,442	38,146	70,008	42,030	27,978	11,185	1,295	9,890	395	117	278
	15-20 ...	62,337	30,485	31,852	27,577	22,890	4,687	33,398	7,276	26,122	1,362	319	1,043
	20-30 ...	121,911	61,163	60,748	23,375	20,873	2,502	92,116	38,768	53,348	6,420	1,522	4,898
	30-40 ...	93,870	51,513	42,357	3,668	3,001	667	77,387	45,880	31,507	12,815	2,632	10,183
	40-50 ...	59,239	33,511	25,728	994	708	286	42,511	29,764	12,747	15,734	3,039	12,695
	50-60 ...	37,110	20,760	16,350	434	303	131	21,638	17,231	4,407	15,038	3,226	11,812
	60 and over ...	23,933	13,231	10,702	236	175	61	10,906	9,567	1,339	12,791	3,489	9,302

TABLE VII.

Age, Sex and Civil Condition.—Part B.—Details for Districts—*contd.*

District.	Age.	Population. Persons.	Population. Males.	Population. Females.	Unmarried. Persons.	Unmarried. Males.	Unmarried. Females.	Married. Persons.	Married. Males.	Married. Females.	Widowed. Persons.	Widowed. Males.	Widowed. Females.
	1	2	3	4	5	6	7	8	9	10	11	12	13
KAMRUP—*concld.*	**MUSLIM**	*240,422*	*128,785*	*111,637*	*101,812*	*61,445*	*40,367*	*125,602*	*64,813*	*60,789*	*13,008*	*2,527*	*10,481*
	0—1	9,269	4,611	4,738	9,257	4,510	4,747	12	1	11	...	...	...
	1—2	9,707	4,721	4,986	9,649	4,703	4,946	58	18	40	...	...	...
	2—3	10,600	5,2 3	5,307	10,382	5,154	5,228	217	49	168	1	...	1
	3—4	9,991	4,94	5,006	9,366	4,900	4,466	622	55	567	3	...	3
	4—5	9,101	4,632	4,469	8,189	4,525	3,664	905	106	719	7	1	6
	Total 0—5	*48,668*	*24,052*	*24,616*	*46,843*	*23,792*	*23,051*	*1,814*	*239*	*1,555*	*11*	*1*	*10*
	5—10	35,332	18,897	16,435	27,821	17,100	10,721	7,404	1,767	5,637	107	30	77
	10—15	28,805	15,400	13,306	17,915	12,380	5,535	10,696	2,973	7,723	194	36	158
	15—20	22,536	10,479	12,057	4,807	4,306	501	17,329	6,037	11,292	400	136	264
	20—30	42,722	22,045	20,677	3,625	3,291	333	37,755	18,314	19,441	1,342	439	903
	30—40	29,504	17,775	11,729	503	393	110	26,664	16,903	9,763	2,337	490	1,847
	40—50	16,774	10,445	6,329	170	115	55	13,519	9,906	3,613	3,085	424	2,661
	50—60	9,279	5,535	3,744	77	46	31	6,370	5,111	1,259	2,832	378	2,454
	60 and over	6,802	4,148	2,651	51	31	20	4,051	3,541	507	2,700	573	2,127
DARRANG	**ALL RELIGIONS**	*584,817*	*317,103*	*267,714*	*271,795*	*158,134*	*113,661*	*263,016*	*140,287*	*122,729*	*50,006*	*18,682*	*31,324*
	0—1	19,792	9,819	9,973	19,789	9,818	9,971	3	1	2	...	...	...
	1—2	19,672	9,726	9,946	19,658	9,723	9,935	14	3	11	...	...	...
	2—3	20,287	10,011	10,276	20,241	10,004	10,337	46	7	39	—	...	...
	3—4	19,834	9,806	10,016	19,689	9,777	9,912	134	29	106	1	...	1
	4—5	18,937	9,488	9,440	18,723	9,434	9,289	206	52	154	8	2	6
	Total 0—5	*98,019*	*48,850*	*49,769*	*98,200*	*48,756*	*49,444*	*403*	*92*	*311*	*9*	*2*	*7*
	5—10	75,269	39,040	36,229	71,731	38,137	33,594	3,446	871	2,575	92	61	31
	10—15	62,517	32,036	30,481	53,913	31,051	22,862	8,253	1,606	6,647	251	79	172
	15—20	49,829	24,454	25,375	21,479	16,763	4,716	27,156	7,120	19,036	1,192	471	721
	20—30	110,639	58,298	52,341	20,468	18,212	2,256	84,130	37,107	47,023	6,041	2,979	3,062
	30—40	92,105	55,007	37,098	4,400	3,921	483	76,395	46,233	30,162	11,307	4,853	6,454
	40—50	53,486	33,345	20,141	1,073	887	186	39,578	28,023	11,555	12,835	4,435	8,400
	50—60	28,021	16,934	11,087	354	277	77	16,848	13,265	3,583	10,819	3,392	7,427
	60 and over	14,339	8,230	6,109	174	130	44	6,705	5,670	1,035	7,460	2,430	5,030
	HINDU	*455,623*	*246,526*	*209,097*	*213,440*	*124,018*	*89,422*	*200,725*	*106,827*	*93,898*	*41,458*	*15,681*	*25,777*
	0—1	15,257	7,623	7,634	15,257	7,623	7,634	...	...	...	...	...	...
	1—2	15,232	7,577	7,655	15,232	7,577	7,655	...	...	...	...	...	...
	2—3	15,607	7,675	7,932	15,603	7,674	7,929	4	1	3	...	...	...
	3—4	15,106	7,476	7,630	15,077	7,468	7,609	28	8	20	1	...	1
	4—5	14,482	7,243	7,239	14,426	7,224	7,202	52	18	34	4	1	3
	Total 0—5	*75,684*	*37,594*	*38,090*	*75,595*	*37,566*	*38,029*	*84*	*27*	*57*	*5*	*1*	*4*
	5—10	57,871	29,938	27,933	56,179	29,517	26,662	1,644	402	1,242	48	19	29
	10—15	48,190	25,396	22,794	42,880	24,385	18,454	5,146	994	4,152	165	47	118
	15—20	38,206	18,807	19,305	17,288	13,605	3,623	19,905	6,011	14,894	960	281	668
	20—30	85,794	41,947	40,847	16,574	14,770	1,804	64,186	27,708	36,478	5,034	2,489	2,545
	30—40	73,056	43,182	29,874	3,633	3,335	298	59,996	35,873	24,123	9,427	4,074	5,353
	40—50	42,928	26,549	16,379	890	787	153	31,332	22,008	9,314	10,656	3,344	6,912
	50—60	22,594	13,566	9,028	293	230	63	13,304	10,466	2,838	8,997	2,890	6,107
	60 and over	11,372	6,437	4,935	139	103	36	5,076	4,278	798	6,157	2,056	4,101

TABLE VII.

Age, Sex and Civil Condition. Part B.—Details for Districts—contd.

District.	Age.	Population. Persons.	Population. Males.	Population. Females.	Unmarried. Persons.	Unmarried. Males.	Unmarried. Females.	Married. Persons.	Married. Males.	Married. Females.	Widowed. Persons.	Widowed. Males.	Widowed. Females.
	1	2	3	4	5	6	7	8	9	10	11	12	13
DARRANG—contd.	MUSLIM	*67,503*	*37,529*	*29,974*	*28,015*	*17,149*	*10,866*	*35,099*	*19,135*	*15,964*	*4,389*	*1,245*	*3,144*
	0—1	2,262	1,077	1,185	2,249	1,096	1,153	3	1	2	...	...	...
	1—2	2,133	1,035	1,098	2,120	1,032	1,088	13	3	10	...	...	...
	2—3	2,401	1,164	1,237	2,362	1,161	1,201	39	3	36	...	...	...
	3—4	2,450	1,201	1,249	2,349	1,184	1,165	101	17	84	...	...	...
	4—5	2,278	1,148	1,130	2,130	1,118	1,012	146	30	116	2	...	2
	Total 0—5	*11,514*	*5,645*	*5,869*	*11,210*	*5,591*	*5,619*	*309*	*54*	*248*	*2*	...	*2*
	5—10	9,221	4,879	4,342	7,525	4,424	3,101	1,657	435	1,222	39	20	19
	10—15	7,971	4,229	3,742	5,227	3,472	1,755	2,674	729	1,945	70	28	42
	15—20	6,746	3,303	3,443	1,322	1,090	232	4,693	1,570	3,123	131	43	88
	20—30	12,944	7,365	5,579	1,758	1,646	112	10,807	5,400	5,407	490	220	270
	30—40	9,277	5,986	3,291	275	248	27	8,088	5,444	2,644	914	294	620
	40—50	5,064	3,337	1,727	67	55	12	3,922	3,035	887	1,075	247	828
	50—60	2,799	1,744	1,055	21	15	6	1,832	1,531	301	939	198	741
	60 and over	1,674	1,041	633	10	8	2	944	847	97	720	186	534
	TRIBAL	*44,370*	*23,469*	*20,901*	*21,993*	*12,147*	*9,846*	*19,281*	*9,996*	*9,285*	*3,096*	*1,326*	*1,770*
	0—1	1,635	793	842	1,635	793	842	...	...	...	...	...	...
	1—2	1,718	825	893	1,717	825	892	1	...	1	...	...	...
	2—3	1,788	876	912	1,785	873	912	3	3	...	...	...	...
	3—4	1,703	847	856	1,698	843	855	5	4	1	...	...	...
	4—5	1,597	805	792	1,588	800	788	8	4	4	1	1	...
	Total 0—5	*8,441*	*4,146*	*4,295*	*8,423*	*4,134*	*4,289*	*17*	*11*	*6*	*1*	*1*	...
	5—10	5,987	3,076	2,911	5,890	3,064	2,826	104	21	83	3	1	2
	10—15	4,669	2,372	2,297	4,278	2,316	1,962	378	53	325	13	3	10
	15—20	3,401	1,527	1,874	1,566	1,087	479	1,770	410	1,360	65	30	35
	20—30	8,037	4,011	4,026	1,436	1,200	236	6,225	2,609	3,616	376	202	174
	30—40	6,983	4,122	2,861	302	270	32	5,958	3,478	2,480	723	374	349
	40—50	3,956	2,492	1,464	64	53	11	3,090	2,108	982	802	331	471
	50—60	1,903	1,148	755	25	19	6	1,231	897	334	657	232	425
	60 and over	993	575	418	19	14	5	509	400	109	456	153	304
NOWGONG.	ALL RELIGIONS	*562,581*	*298,585*	*263,996*	*277,683*	*159,856*	*117,827*	*244,236*	*127,965*	*116,271*	*40,662*	*11,464*	*29,198*
	0—1	21,319	10,681	10,638	21,319	10,681	10,638	...	...	...	...	...	...
	1—2	21,794	10,753	11,041	21,794	10,753	11,041	...	...	...	...	...	...
	2—3	23,361	11,513	11,848	23,361	11,513	11,848	...	...	...	...	...	...
	3—4	22,564	11,205	11,359	22,511	11,197	11,314	52	8	44	1	...	1
	4—5	21,324	10,699	10,625	21,207	10,679	10,528	112	20	92	5	...	5
	Total 0—5	*110,362*	*54,851*	*55,511*	*110,192*	*54,823*	*55,369*	*164*	*28*	*136*	*6*	...	*6*
	5—10	79,017	41,265	37,752	73,429	40,157	33,272	5,501	1,088	4,413	87	20	67
	10—15	63,699	33,255	30,444	51,609	30,693	20,916	11,849	2,516	9,333	241	46	195
	15—20	51,625	24,343	27,282	20,817	15,575	6,242	29,796	8,400	21,396	1,013	269	744
	20—30	100,397	52,026	48,371	18,035	15,531	2,504	77,860	34,936	42,924	4,502	1,559	2,943
	30—40	70,871	41,229	29,642	2,768	2,442	326	60,308	36,430	23,878	7,795	2,357	5,438
	40—50	44,055	26,715	17,340	547	435	112	33,626	23,660	9,966	9,882	2,620	7,262
	50—60	25,022	14,816	10,206	198	142	56	15,928	12,415	3,513	8,896	2,259	6,637
	60 and over	17,533	10,085	7,448	88	58	30	9,205	7,693	1,512	8,240	2,334	5,906

TABLE VII.

Age, Sex and Civil Condition. Part B.—Details for Districts—*contd.*

District.	Age.	Population. Persons.	Population. Males.	Population. Females.	Unmarried. Persons.	Unmarried. Males.	Unmarried. Females.	Married. Persons.	Married. Males.	Married. Females.	Widowed. Persons.	Widowed. Males.	Widowed. Females.
	1	2	3	4	5	6	7	8	9	10	11	12	13
NOWGONG—*contd.*	HINDU	*325,710*	*172,659*	*153,051*	*164,508*	*93,923*	*70,585*	*139,449*	*70,061*	*69,388*	*28,453*	*8,375*	*20,078*
	0—1	12,140	6,059	6,081	12,140	6,059	6,081	...	...	...	...	...	...
	1—2	12,041	5,965	6,076	12,041	5,965	6,076	...	...	...	...	...	...
	2—3	12,632	6,261	6,371	12,632	6,261	6,371	...	...	...	...	...	...
	3—4	12,244	6,071	6,173	12,233	6,067	6,166	10	4	6	1	...	1
	4—5	11,671	5,856	5,815	11,647	5,847	5,800	23	9	14	1	...	1
	Total 0—5	*60,728*	*30,212*	*30,516*	*60,693*	*30,199*	*30,494*	*33*	*13*	*20*	*2*	...	*2*
	5—10	43,928	22,806	21,122	42,906	22,612	20,294	991	184	807	31	10	21
	10—15	35,466	18,514	16,952	32,115	18,037	14,078	3,245	453	2,792	106	24	82
	15—20	28,417	13,644	14,773	14,162	10,423	3,730	13,636	3,067	10,569	619	154	465
	20—30	57,835	30,026	27,809	12,413	10,753	1,660	42,376	18,266	24,110	3,046	1,007	2,039
	30—40	43,709	25,150	18,559	1,937	1,737	200	36,299	21,692	14,607	5,473	1,721	3,752
	40—50	28,396	16,863	11,533	382	315	67	20,868	14,505	6,363	7,145	2,043	5,103
	50—60	16,451	9,475	6,976	144	106	38	9,881	7,623	2,258	6,426	1,746	4,680
	60 and over	10,781	5,969	4,812	56	41	15	5,190	4,328	862	5,535	1,070	3,935
	MUSLIM	*177,762*	*95,597*	*82,165*	*80,821*	*48,428*	*32,393*	*88,294*	*45,133*	*43,161*	*8,647*	*2,036*	*6,611*
	0—1	7,286	3,670	3,616	7,286	3,670	3,616	...	...	...	...	...	...
	1—2	7,486	3,675	3,811	7,486	3,675	3,811	...	...	...	...	...	...
	2—3	8,162	4,016	4,146	8,162	4,016	4,146	...	...	...	...	...	...
	3—4	7,804	3,920	3,884	7,765	3,917	3,848	39	3	36	...	...	...
	4—5	7,244	3,672	3,572	7,161	3,664	3,497	81	8	73	2	...	2
	Total 0—5	*37,982*	*18,953*	*19,029*	*37,860*	*18,942*	*18,918*	*120*	*11*	*109*	*2*	...	*2*
	5—10	26,680	14,170	12,510	22,238	13,295	8,943	4,396	869	3,527	46	6	40
	10—15	21,487	11,266	10,221	13,229	9,288	3,941	8,146	1,963	6,183	112	15	97
	15—20	17,762	8,183	9,579	3,710	3,347	363	13,748	4,739	9,009	304	97	207
	20—30	32,412	16,955	15,457	3,277	3,104	173	28,095	13,438	14,657	1,040	413	627
	30—40	19,925	12,190	7,726	406	371	35	17,879	11,423	6,456	1,640	406	1,235
	40—50	11,086	7,202	3,884	68	55	13	9,031	6,796	2,235	1,987	351	1,636
	50—60	5,900	3,770	2,130	22	18	4	4,119	3,433	686	1,759	319	1,440
	60 and over	4,528	2,899	1,629	11	8	3	2,760	2,461	299	1,757	430	1,327
	TRIBAL	*53,094*	*27,094*	*26,000*	*28,899*	*15,483*	*13,416*	*21,003*	*10,698*	*10,305*	*3,192*	*913*	*2,279*
	0—1	1,700	846	854	1,700	846	854	...	...	...	...	...	...
	1—2	2,064	1,004	1,060	2,064	1,004	1,060	...	...	...	...	...	...
	2—3	2,350	1,133	1,217	2,350	1,133	1,217	...	...	...	...	...	...
	3—4	2,295	1,111	1,184	2,293	1,111	1,182	2	...	2	...	...	...
	4—5	2,171	1,066	1,105	2,164	1,064	1,100	6	2	4	1	...	1
	Total 0—5	*10,570*	*5,160*	*5,410*	*10,561*	*5,158*	*5,403*	*8*	*2*	*6*	*1*	...	*1*
	5—10	7,622	3,898	3,724	7,512	3,864	3,648	103	31	72	7	3	4
	10—15	6,105	3,153	2,952	5,668	3,057	2,611	417	90	327	20	6	14
	15—20	4,903	2,258	2,645	2,645	1,611	1,034	2,177	632	1,545	81	15	66
	20—30	8,984	4,390	4,594	2,037	1,438	599	6,582	2,852	3,730	365	100	265
	30—40	6,355	3,357	2,998	366	288	78	5,389	2,880	2,509	600	189	411
	40—50	4,092	2,339	1,753	74	49	25	3,344	2,086	1,258	674	204	470
	50—60	2,420	1,410	1,010	20	11	9	1,760	1,227	533	640	172	468
	60 and over	2,043	1,120	923	16	7	9	1,223	898	325	804	215	589

TABLE VII.

Age, Sex and Civil Condition. Part B.—Details for Districts—*contd.*

District.	Age.	Population. Persons.	Population. Males.	Population. Females.	Unmarried. Persons.	Unmarried. Males.	Unmarried. Females.	Married. Persons.	Married. Males.	Married. Females.	Widowed. Persons.	Widowed. Males.	Widowed. Females.
	1	2	3	4	5	6	7	8	9	10	11	12	13
SIBSAGAR.	**ALL RELIGIONS**	*933,326*	*496,288*	*437,038*	*486,207*	*275,798*	*210,409*	*370,649*	*190,092*	*180,557*	*76,470*	*30,392*	*46,078*
	0—1	34,606	17,448	17,158	34,604	17,447	17,157	2	1	1	...	...	...
	1—2	34,189	17,078	17,111	34,179	17,074	17,105	9	3	6	1	1	...
	2—3	35,086	17,266	17,820	35,072	17,260	17,812	13	5	8	1	1	...
	3—4	33,622	16,644	16,978	33,586	16,632	16,954	36	12	24	...	...	...
	4—5	32,632	16,537	16,095	32,558	16,511	16,047	69	25	44	5	1	4
	Total 0—5	*170,135*	*84,973*	*85,162*	*169,999*	*84,924*	*85,075*	*129*	*46*	*83*	*7*	*3*	*4*
	5—10	126,934	66,004	60,930	124,969	65,451	59,518	1,884	518	1,366	81	35	46
	10—15	105,264	55,235	50,029	98,197	53,856	44,341	6,796	1,276	5,520	271	103	168
	15—20	80,565	39,923	40,642	45,184	31,649	13,535	33,853	7,676	26,177	1,528	598	930
	20—30	163,749	84,097	79,652	38,111	31,799	6,312	117,143	48,104	69,039	8,495	4,194	4,301
	30—40	130,875	73,724	57,151	6,731	5,727	1,004	108,127	60,993	47,134	16,017	7,004	9,013
	40—50	82,399	48,491	33,908	1,847	1,481	366	60,874	39,715	21,159	19,678	7,295	12,383
	50—60	47,524	28,409	19,115	761	588	173	29,277	21,581	7,696	17,486	6,240	11,246
	60 and over	25,891	15,442	10,449	408	323	85	12,576	10,193	2,383	12,907	4,926	7,981
	HINDU	*841,035*	*445,658*	*395,377*	*436,892*	*247,669*	*189,223*	*333,543*	*169,053*	*163,590*	*70,600*	*28,036*	*42,564*
	0—1	31,624	15,972	15,652	31,623	15,972	15,651	1	...	1	...	...	...
	1—2	30,931	15,456	15,475	30,930	15,456	15,474	1	...	1	...	...	...
	2—3	31,555	15,528	16,027	31,553	15,527	16,026	2	1	1	...	...	...
	3—4	30,274	14,974	15,300	30,252	14,968	15,284	22	6	16	...	...	...
	4—5	29,373	14,869	14,504	29,329	14,858	14,471	43	11	32	1	...	1
	Total 0—5	*153,757*	*76,799*	*76,958*	*153,687*	*76,781*	*76,906*	*69*	*18*	*51*	*1*	...	*1*
	5—10	114,154	59,334	54,820	112,438	58,870	53,568	1,652	433	1,219	64	31	33
	10—15	94,549	49,548	45,001	88,193	48,303	39,890	6,117	1,150	4,967	239	95	144
	15—20	72,106	35,499	36,607	40,247	28,191	12,056	30,470	6,760	23,710	1,389	548	841
	20—30	147,089	74,961	72,128	33,703	28,309	5,394	105,607	42,821	62,786	7,779	3,831	3,948
	30—40	118,506	66,373	52,133	5,924	5,072	852	97,748	54,865	42,883	14,834	6,436	8,398
	40—50	74,730	43,786	30,944	1,649	1,329	320	54,759	35,671	19,088	18,322	6,784	11,538
	50—60	43,241	25,790	17,451	686	529	157	26,271	19,440	6,831	16,284	5,821	10,463
	60 and over	22,903	13,608	9,295	365	295	70	10,850	8,825	2,025	11,688	4,488	7,200
	MUSLIM	*43,907*	*24,916*	*18,991*	*23,537*	*13,813*	*9,724*	*17,333*	*9,940*	*7,393*	*3,037*	*1,163*	*1,874*
	0—1	1,507	751	756	1,507	751	756	...	...	...	...	...	...
	1—2	1,521	765	756	1,517	764	753	4	1	3	...	...	...
	2—3	1,604	791	813	1,599	789	810	5	2	3	...	...	...
	3—4	1,562	775	787	1,557	773	784	5	2	3	...	...	...
	4—5	1,535	778	757	1,525	773	752	8	4	4	2	1	1
	Total 0—5	*7,729*	*3,860*	*3,869*	*7,705*	*3,850*	*3,855*	*22*	*9*	*13*	*2*	*1*	*1*
	5—10	6,219	3,252	2,967	6,091	3,211	2,880	122	40	82	6	1	5
	10—15	5,348	2,858	2,490	4,929	2,777	2,152	401	78	323	18	3	15
	15—20	4,209	2,283	1,926	2,326	1,778	548	1,798	480	1,318	85	25	60
	20—30	8,106	4,757	3,349	2,005	1,793	212	5,701	2,786	2,915	400	178	222
	30—40	5,774	3,651	2,123	342	294	48	4,774	3,082	1,692	658	275	383
	40—50	3,473	2,270	1,203	86	68	18	2,650	1,945	705	737	257	480
	50—60	1,921	1,247	674	37	30	7	1,267	1,001	266	617	216	401
	60 and over	1,128	738	390	16	12	4	598	519	79	514	207	307

TABLE VII.

Age, Sex and Civil Condition. Part B.—Details for Districts—*contd.*

District.	Age.	Population. Persons.	Population. Males.	Population. Females.	Unmarried. Persons.	Unmarried. Males.	Unmarried. Females.	Married. Persons.	Married. Males.	Married. Females.	Widowed. Persons.	Widowed. Males.	Widowed. Females.
	1	2	3	4	5	6	7	8	9	10	11	12	13
SIBSAGAR—*contd.*	TRIBAL	*32,034*	*16,744*	*15,290*	*17,448*	*9,540*	*7,908*	*12,920*	*6,585*	*6,335*	*1,666*	*619*	*1,047*
	0—1	906	450	456	906	460	446	...	...	...	...	...	...
	1—2	1,181	581	600	1,179	581	598	2	...	2	...	...	...
	2—3	1,390	674	716	1,385	674	711	5	...	5	...	...	...
	3—4	1,278	638	640	1,271	635	636	7	3	4	...	...	...
	4—5	1,226	636	589	1,212	628	584	12	8	4	2	...	2
	Total 0—5	*5,980*	*2,979*	*3,001*	*5,953*	*2,968*	*2,985*	*25*	*11*	*14*	*2*	...	*2*
	5—10	4,487	2,368	2,119	4,419	2,340	2,079	68	27	35	6	1	5
	10—15	3,550	1,912	1,638	3,400	1,872	1,528	148	34	104	8	2	6
	15—20	2,794	1,403	1,391	1,775	1,096	679	993	296	696	27	11	16
	20—30	5,245	2,517	2,728	1,548	1,013	535	3,488	1,379	2,109	156	75	81
	30—40	4,130	2,207	1,923	204	192	12	3,615	1,879	1,736	260	136	124
	40—50	2,749	1,548	1,201	53	38	15	2,351	1,375	976	345	135	210
	50—60	1,594	896	698	21	15	6	1,234	781	453	339	100	239
	60 and over	1,400	814	586	15	6	9	871	649	222	523	159	364
LAKHIMPUR.	ALL RELIGIONS	*724,582*	*389,108*	*335,474*	*350,879*	*203,013*	*147,866*	*316,135*	*170,630*	*145,505*	*57,568*	*25,465*	*32,103*
	0—1	24,138	12,060	12,078	24,138	12,060	12,078	...	...	...	...	...	...
	1—2	24,342	12,029	12,313	24,341	12,029	12,312	1	...	1	...	...	...
	2—3	25,616	12,726	12,890	25,611	12,725	12,886	5	1	4	...	...	...
	3—4	24,714	12,428	12,286	24,688	12,426	12,262	26	2	24	...	...	...
	4—5	23,697	12,027	11,670	23,638	12,016	11,622	56	10	46	3	1	2
	Total 0—5	*122,507*	*61,270*	*61,237*	*122,416*	*61,256*	*61,160*	*88*	*13*	*75*	*3*	*1*	*2*
	5—10	91,339	47,777	43,562	89,421	47,290	42,131	1,830	447	1,383	78	40	38
	10—15	74,265	39,455	34,810	68,228	38,147	30,081	5,811	1,208	4,603	249	103	146
	15—20	59,817	30,547	29,270	30,904	22,206	8,698	27,567	7,681	19,846	1,336	600	736
	20—30	139,572	76,433	63,139	30,933	26,263	4,670	101,129	46,004	55,125	7,511	4,176	3,335
	30—40	116,788	69,846	46,942	6,702	5,974	728	96,549	57,073	39,477	13,537	6,800	6,737
	40—50	68,595	42,430	26,165	1,539	1,274	265	51,908	34,859	17,103	15,103	6,297	8,806
	50—60	34,280	20,956	13,324	489	390	99	22,836	16,140	6,696	11,745	4,426	7,319
	60 and over	17,466	10,301	7,165	197	143	54	9,233	7,226	2,007	8,016	3,022	4,994
	HINDU	*661,680*	*360,756*	*300,924*	*321,574*	*184,429*	*137,145*	*286,904*	*152,881*	*134,023*	*53,202*	*23,446*	*29,756*
	0—1	22,586	11,286	11,300	22,586	11,286	11,300	...	...	...	...	...	...
	1—2	22,701	11,185	11,516	22,701	11,185	11,516	...	...	...	...	...	...
	2—3	23,814	11,805	12,009	23,812	11,805	12,007	2	...	2	...	...	...
	3—4	22,951	11,540	11,411	22,935	11,539	11,396	16	1	15	...	...	...
	4—5	22,004	11,180	10,824	21,971	11,177	10,794	31	3	28	2	...	2
	Total 0—5	*113,998*	*56,938*	*57,060*	*113,947*	*56,934*	*57,013*	*49*	*4*	*45*	*2*	...	*2*
	5—10	84,443	44,152	40,291	82,729	43,706	39,023	1,643	410	1,233	71	36	35
	10—15	68,297	36,144	32,153	62,737	34,939	27,798	5,330	1,109	4,221	230	96	134
	15—20	53,773	26,928	26,845	27,635	19,619	8,016	24,932	6,771	18,161	1,206	538	668
	20—30	125,240	67,150	58,090	26,874	22,602	4,272	91,491	40,758	50,733	6,875	3,790	3,094
	30—40	105,706	62,333	43,373	5,715	5,063	652	87,483	51,021	36,462	12,510	6,249	6,261
	40—50	62,690	38,458	24,232	1,320	1,097	223	47,355	31,319	15,836	14,066	5,942	8,104
	50—60	31,486	19,129	12,357	433	343	90	20,167	14,681	5,486	10,906	4,105	6,801
	60 and over	16,036	9,525	6,511	175	136	40	8,476	6,608	1,868	7,387	2,791	4,596

TABLE VII.

AGE, SEX AND CIVIL CONDITION. PART B.—DETAILS FOR DISTRICTS—*contd.*

District.	Age.	Population. Persons.	Population. Males.	Population. Females.	Unmarried. Persons.	Unmarried. Males.	Unmarried. Females.	Married. Persons.	Married. Males.	Married. Females.	Widowed. Persons.	Widowed. Males.	Widowed. Females.
	1	2	3	4	5	6	7	8	9	10	11	12	13
GARO HILLS.	**ALL RELIGIONS**	*191,911*	*97,742*	*94,169*	*93,806*	*51,846*	*41,960*	*90,134*	*43,953*	*46,181*	*7,971*	*1,943*	*6,028*
	0—1	8,070	4,106	3,964	8,063	4,104	3,959	7	2	5	...	...	...
	1—2	7,338	3,699	3,639	7,326	3,698	3,628	12	1	11	...	...	...
	2—3	7,754	3,895	3,859	7,734	3,893	3,841	20	2	18	...	...	...
	3—4	7,327	3,681	3,646	7,294	3,679	3,615	33	2	31	...	...	...
	4—5	6,781	3,394	3,387	6,726	3,388	3,338	52	5	47	3	1	2
	Total 0—5	*37,290*	*18,775*	*18,515*	*37,263*	*18,762*	*18,401*	*124*	*12*	*112*	*3*	*1*	*2*
	5—10	24,917	12,905	12,012	24,030	12,764	11,266	864	137	727	23	4	19
	10—15	21,186	10,571	10,615	17,900	10,087	7,813	3,216	474	2,743	70	10	60
	15—20	18,541	7,959	10,582	7,374	5,040	2,334	10,894	2,868	8,026	273	51	222
	20—30	35,245	16,977	18,268	5,132	4,040	1,092	28,923	12,566	16,357	1,190	371	819
	30—40	24,585	13,595	10,990	773	599	174	22,210	12,601	9,609	1,602	395	1,207
	40—50	13,851	7,817	6,034	199	131	68	12,022	7,316	4,706	1,629	371	1,258
	50—60	7,563	4,292	3,271	93	50	43	6,126	3,951	2,175	1,344	291	1,053
	60 and over	7,833	4,651	3,182	142	73	69	5,754	4,029	1,725	1,937	549	1,388
	HINDU	*27,946*	*15,086*	*12,860*	*14,178*	*8,239*	*5,939*	*11,254*	*6,079*	*5,175*	*2,514*	*768*	*1,746*
	0—1	1,153	603	550	1,153	603	550	...	...	...	...	...	...
	1—2	1,032	527	505	1,032	527	505	...	...	...	...	...	...
	2—3	1,034	529	505	1,033	529	504	1	...	1	...	...	...
	3—4	983	499	484	981	499	482	2	...	2	...	...	...
	4—5	936	463	473	933	463	470	3	...	3	...	...	...
	Total 0—5	*5,138*	*2,621*	*2,517*	*5,132*	*2,621*	*2,511*	*6*	...	*6*	...	...	...
	5—10	3,721	1,916	1,805	3,616	1,901	1,715	102	14	88	3	1	2
	10—15	3,090	1,579	1,511	2,755	1,545	1,210	326	33	293	9	1	8
	15—20	2,396	1,102	1,294	1,104	800	304	1,236	291	945	56	11	45
	20—30	5,151	2,744	2,407	1,129	978	151	3,711	1,673	2,038	311	93	218
	30—40	3,881	2,405	1,476	265	237	28	3,183	2,009	1,174	483	109	374
	40—50	2,189	1,373	816	57	46	11	1,557	1,145	412	575	182	393
	50—60	1,183	701	482	23	17	6	700	549	151	460	135	325
	60 and over	1,087	655	432	17	16	3	433	365	68	557	176	381
	CHRISTIAN	*15,950*	*8,564*	*7,386*	*8,608*	*5,080*	*3,528*	*6,766*	*3,400*	*3,366*	*576*	*84*	*492*
	0—1	639	336	303	639	336	303	...	...	...	...	...	...
	1—2	563	296	267	563	296	267	...	...	...	...	...	...
	2—3	605	318	287	605	318	287	...	...	...	...	...	...
	3—4	565	295	270	565	295	270	...	...	...	...	...	...
	4—5	500	256	244	500	256	244	...	...	...	...	...	...
	Total 0—5	*2,872*	*1,501*	*1,371*	*2,872*	*1,501*	*1,371*	...	...	...	...	...	...
	5—10	2,102	1,132	970	2,091	1,132	959	11	...	11	...	...	...
	10—15	1,969	1,070	899	1,843	1,058	785	124	13	111	3	...	3
	15—20	1,802	902	900	982	705	277	800	193	607	20	4	16
	20—30	3,313	1,731	1,582	725	613	112	2,513	1,100	1,413	75	18	57
	30—40	1,880	1,167	713	80	65	15	1,697	1,080	617	103	22	81
	40—50	1,006	530	476	14	6	8	857	513	344	135	11	124
	50—60	489	273	216	...	...	...	389	265	124	100	8	92
	60 and over	457	268	189	1	...	1	316	247	69	140	21	119

TABLE VII.

AGE, SEX AND CIVIL CONDITION. PART B.—DETAILS FOR DISTRICTS—*contd.*

District.	Age.	Population. Persons.	Population. Males.	Population. Females.	Unmarried. Persons.	Unmarried. Males.	Unmarried. Females.	Married. Persons.	Married. Males.	Married. Females.	Widowed. Persons.	Widowed. Males.	Widowed. Females.
	1	2	3	4	5	6	7	8	9	10	11	12	13
GARO HILLS—concld.	TRIBAL ...	*136,707*	*68,194*	*68,513*	*66,235*	*35,756*	*30,479*	*66,502*	*31,527*	*34,975*	*3,970*	*911*	*3,059*
	0—1 ...	5,890	2,965	2,924	5,895	2,963	2,932	4	2	2	...	...	...
	1—2 ...	5,412	2,717	2,695	5,406	2,716	2,690	6	1	5	...	...	...
	2—3 ...	5,773	2,878	2,895	5,762	2,878	2,884	11	...	11	...	...	...
	3—4 ...	5,440	2,711	2,729	5,426	2,711	2,715	14	...	14	...	...	...
	4—5 ...	5,000	2,492	2,508	4,980	2,400	2,400	18	2	16	2	...	2
	Total 0—5 ...	*27,524*	*13,763*	*13,761*	*27,469*	*13,758*	*13,711*	*53*	*5*	*48*	*2*	...	*2*
	5—10 ...	17,990	9,106	8,884	17,298	9,036	8,262	691	40	[illegible]	11	1	10
	10—15 ...	14,902	7,277	7,625	12,604	6,906	5,698	2,256	314	1,920	42	5	37
	15—20 ...	13,237	5,607	7,630	5,003	3,258	1,745	8,062	2,120	5,943	172	29	143
	20—30 ...	24,721	11,347	13,374	3,128	2,305	823	20,984	8,914	12,070	609	128	481
	30—40 ...	17,241	9,118	8,123	408	278	130	16,084	8,676	7,408	749	164	585
	40—50 ...	9,824	5,413	4,411	122	76	46	9,013	5,197	3,816	688	141	547
	50—60 ...	5,476	3,078	2,398	68	31	37	4,795	2,926	1,869	613	121	492
	60 and over ...	6,082	3,685	2,407	124	59	65	4,884	3,304	1,580	1,064	323	762
CACHAR.	ALL RELIGIONS ...	*570,531*	*301,338*	*269,193*	*267,599*	*159,085*	*108,514*	*248,159*	*126,757*	*121,395*	*54,780*	*15,496*	*39,284*
	0—1 ...	18,475	9,296	9,179	18,475	9,296	9,179	...	...	...	...	...	...
	1—2 ...	17,911	8,811	9,100	17,910	8,810	9,100	1	1	...	...	...	...
	2—3 ...	19,834	9,643	10,191	19,828	9,639	10,189	5	4	1	1	...	1
	3—4 ...	19,636	9,689	9,947	19,608	9,679	9,929	27	10	17	1	...	1
	4—5 ...	18,912	9,541	9,371	18,854	9,522	9,332	53	18	35	5	1	4
	Total 0—5 ...	*94,768*	*46,980*	*47,788*	*94,675*	*46,946*	*47,729*	*86*	*33*	*53*	*7*	*1*	*6*
	5—10 ...	76,093	40,098	35,995	73,064	39,720	33,334	2,876	277	2,599	83	11	72
	10—15 ...	64,821	34,370	30,853	55,196	33,349	21,787	9,300	896	8,404	295	33	262
	15—20 ...	53,501	25,187	28,214	21,965	18,338	3,627	30,215	6,736	23,479	1,421	313	1,108
	20—30 ...	105,893	53,920	51,973	18,949	17,341	1,608	80,624	34,437	46,187	6,320	2,143	4,178
	30—40 ...	77,823	44,454	33,469	2,948	2,593	355	63,877	38,352	25,525	11,198	3,509	7,689
	40—50 ...	40,653	20,201	20,452	677	579	98	35,391	24,982	10,409	12,585	3,640	8,945
	50—60 ...	27,606	15,865	11,743	229	183	46	16,278	12,859	3,419	11,091	2,813	8,278
	60 and over ...	20,261	11,255	9,006	186	136	40	9,415	8,195	1,220	10,780	3,034	7,746
	HINDU ...	*359,936*	*189,906*	*169,829*	*163,106*	*97,842*	*65,265*	*156,778*	*80,103*	*76,675*	*39,354*	*11,963*	*27,392*
	0—1 ...	10,840	5,416	5,424	10,840	5,416	5,424	...	...	...	...	...	...
	1—2 ...	10,642	5,212	5,430	10,641	5,211	5,430	1	1	...	...	...	...
	2—3 ...	11,636	5,678	5,958	11,631	5,675	5,956	4	3	1	1	...	1
	3—4 ...	11,405	5,675	5,730	11,384	5,669	5,715	20	6	14	1	...	1
	4—5 ...	10,870	5,532	5,348	10,832	5,513	5,319	35	9	26	3	...	3
	Total 0—5 ...	*55,393*	*27,503*	*27,890*	*55,328*	*27,484*	*27,844*	*60*	*19*	*41*	*5*	...	*5*
	5—10 ...	44,892	23,457	21,435	42,916	23,229	19,687	1,922	222	1,700	54	6	48
	10—15 ...	39,123	20,460	19,663	33,351	19,816	13,535	5,596	618	4,978	183	22	161
	15—20 ...	32,863	15,662	17,201	14,701	11,996	2,705	17,261	3,783	13,479	901	204	697
	20—30 ...	67,554	34,670	32,884	12,795	12,617	1,178	49,448	20,626	28,837	4,607	1,518	3,089
	30—40 ...	52,193	29,617	22,576	2,243	2,069	174	41,806	24,819	16,987	8,144	2,729	5,415
	40—50 ...	34,063	19,977	14,046	547	480	67	23,617	16,553	7,064	9,859	2,944	6,915
	50—60 ...	19,062	10,795	8,267	187	164	33	10,749	8,374	2,375	8,126	2,257	5,869
	60 and over ...	13,726	7,455	6,271	126	96	32	5,983	5,097	886	7,675	2,272	5,403

TABLE VII.

Age, Sex and Civil Condition. Part B.—Details for Districts—*contd.*

District.	Age.	Population. Persons.	Population. Males.	Population. Females.	Unmarried. Persons.	Unmarried. Males.	Unmarried. Females.	Married. Persons.	Married. Males.	Married. Females.	Widowed. Persons.	Widowed. Males.	Widowed. Females.
	1	2	3	4	5	6	7	8	9	10	11	12	13
CACHAR—concld.	MUSLIM	*196,196*	*103,718*	*92,478*	*96,696*	*50,982*	*39,714*	*85,365*	*43,573*	*41,792*	*14,135*	*3,163*	*10,972*
	0–1	7,092	3,623	3,469	7,092	3,623	3,469	...	...	...	...	...	...
	1–2	6,715	3,327	3,388	6,715	3,327	3,388	...	...	...	...	...	...
	2–3	7,570	3,665	3,905	7,569	3,664	3,905	1	1	...	...	...	...
	3–4	7,631	3,720	3,911	7,624	3,716	3,908	7	4	3	...	...	...
	4–5	7,498	3,736	3,762	7,481	3,728	3,753	15	7	8	2	1	1
	Total 0–5	*36,506*	*18,071*	*18,435*	*36,481*	*18,058*	*18,423*	*23*	*12*	*11*	*2*	*1*	*1*
	5–10	29,214	15,555	13,659	28,257	15,500	12,757	930	50	880	27	5	22
	10–15	24,174	13,039	11,135	20,369	12,769	7,600	3,638	200	3,438	107	10	97
	15–20	18,223	8,080	10,143	6,414	5,778	636	11,993	2,850	9,143	486	102	384
	20–30	35,244	17,783	17,461	4,550	4,322	228	29,074	12,965	16,109	1,720	556	1,164
	30–40	23,636	13,730	9,906	467	425	42	20,479	12,618	7,861	2,700	657	2,043
	40–50	14,427	8,522	5,905	96	77	19	10,369	7,321	3,048	3,462	624	2,838
	50–60	7,897	4,707	3,190	35	28	7	5,112	4,185	927	2,740	404	2,336
	60 and over	6,085	3,631	2,454	27	25	2	3,257	2,922	335	2,811	654	2,157
	TRIBAL	*10,319*	*5,160*	*5,159*	*5,281*	*2,840*	*2,441*	*4,060*	*2,043*	*2,017*	*978*	*277*	*701*
	0–1	405	196	209	405	196	209	...	...	...	...	...	...
	1–2	407	201	206	407	201	206	...	...	...	...	...	...
	2–3	461	220	241	461	220	241	...	...	...	...	...	...
	3–4	443	215	228	443	215	228	...	...	...	...	...	...
	4–5	392	207	185	391	206	185	1	1	...	...	...	...
	Total 0–5	*2,108*	*1,039*	*1,069*	*2,107*	*1,038*	*1,069*	*1*	*1*	...	...	...	...
	5–10	1,332	703	629	1,313	700	613	18	3	15	1	...	1
	10–15	1,032	529	503	955	519	436	73	9	64	4	1	3
	15–20	927	391	536	440	250	190	441	106	335	26	5	21
	20–30	1,938	901	1,037	369	258	111	1,416	594	822	153	49	104
	30–40	1,310	690	620	53	37	16	1,057	587	470	200	66	134
	40–50	825	472	353	11	4	7	611	411	200	203	57	146
	50–60	461	246	215	8	3	5	282	203	79	171	40	131
	60 and over	386	189	197	5	1	4	162	129	33	220	59	161
SYLHET.	ALL RELIGIONS	*2,724,342*	*1,407,645*	*1,316,697*	*1,247,635*	*771,359*	*476,976*	*1,184,897*	*583,565*	*601,332*	*291,810*	*52,721*	*239,089*
	0–1	78,771	39,008	39,763	78,771	39,008	39,763	...	...	...	...	...	...
	1–2	81,152	39,221	41,931	81,137	39,218	41,919	15	3	12	...	...	...
	2–3	91,039	43,824	47,215	90,969	43,817	47,153	69	7	62	1	...	1
	3–4	88,938	43,329	45,609	88,509	43,287	45,222	412	42	370	17	...	17
	4–5	86,831	42,964	43,867	86,076	42,883	43,194	717	78	639	38	4	34
	Total 0–5	*426,731*	*208,346*	*218,385*	*425,462*	*208,212*	*217,250*	*1,213*	*130*	*1,083*	*56*	*4*	*52*
	5–10	368,340	194,862	173,478	346,287	193,231	153,056	21,545	1,583	19,962	508	38	470
	10–15	332,329	172,300	160,029	261,752	167,584	94,168	59,775	4,621	55,154	1,702	95	1,607
	15–20	265,006	122,046	142,960	99,091	91,408	7,683	158,175	29,788	128,387	7,830	850	6,980
	20–30	520,729	253,913	266,816	92,979	90,192	2,787	391,202	157,418	233,784	36,548	6,303	30,245
	30–40	358,948	193,063	165,885	15,578	14,817	761	289,013	177,549	111,464	54,357	10,697	43,660
	40–50	233,660	132,042	101,618	3,978	3,473	505	154,767	116,283	38,484	74,935	12,104	62,829
	50–60	127,857	71,284	56,573	1,519	1,362	157	69,473	59,340	10,133	56,865	10,583	46,282
	60 and over	80,732	40,769	39,963	989	880	109	39,734	36,843	2,891	40,009	12,046	27,963

TABLE VII.

Age, Sex and Civil Condition. Part B.—Details for districts—*contd.*

District.	Age.	Population. Persons.	Population. Males.	Population. Females.	Unmarried. Persons.	Unmarried. Males.	Unmarried. Females.	Married. Persons.	Married. Males.	Married. Females.	Widowed. Persons.	Widowed. Males.	Widowed. Females.
	1	2	3	4	5	6	7	8	9	10	11	12	13
SYLHET—concld.	HINDU ...	*1,113,354*	*575,624*	*537,730*	*480,966*	*309,234*	*171,732*	*470,443*	*234,477*	*235,966*	*161,945*	*31,013*	*130,032*
	0—1 ...	28,891	14,319	14,572	28,891	14,319	14,572	...	...	...	...	...	...
	1—2 ...	28,830	13,950	14,880	28,827	13,947	14,880	3	3	...	...	...	...
	2—3 ...	32,170	15,525	16,645	32,155	15,518	16,637	14	7	7	1	...	1
	3—4 ...	31,353	15,333	16,020	31,287	15,318	15,969	60	15	45	6	...	6
	4—5 ...	30,636	15,226	15,410	30,524	15,200	15,324	98	24	74	14	2	12
	Total 0—5 ...	*151,880*	*74,363*	*77,517*	*151,684*	*74,312*	*77,372*	*175*	*49*	*126*	*21*	*2*	*19*
	5—10 ...	132,895	69,625	63,270	124,498	69,213	55,285	8,169	387	7,782	228	25	203
	10—15 ...	119,417	63,062	56,355	96,228	61,791	34,437	22,460	1,228	21,232	729	43	686
	15—20 ...	125,650	60,013	65,637	63,454	50,635	12,819	58,011	9,178	48,833	4,185	200	3,985
	20—30 ...	217,276	107,413	109,863	48,990	47,821	1,169	147,179	56,946	90,233	21,108	2,646	18,462
	30—40 ...	165,966	90,512	75,454	10,983	10,673	310	118,922	73,682	45,240	36,061	6,157	29,904
	40—50 ...	112,394	62,435	49,959	3,117	2,971	146	68,908	51,409	16,799	40,099	8,058	32,041
	50—60 ...	63,673	34,710	28,963	1,230	1,153	77	30,833	26,314	4,519	31,610	7,243	24,367
	60 and over ...	44,273	23,488	20,785	783	725	58	16,486	15,284	1,202	27,004	7,479	19,525
	MUSLIM ...	*1,603,805*	*828,123*	*775,689*	*763,199*	*460,059*	*303,140*	*711,301*	*347,491*	*363,840*	*129,359*	*20,650*	*108,709*
	0—1 ...	49,649	24,563	25,086	49,649	24,563	25,086	...	...	...	...	...	...
	1—2 ...	52,590	26,153	26,437	52,578	26,153	26,425	12	...	12	...	...	...
	2—3 ...	56,613	26,176	30,437	56,558	26,176	30,382	55	...	55	...	...	...
	3—4 ...	57,334	27,874	29,460	57,004	27,847	29,157	319	27	292	11	...	11
	4—5 ...	55,960	27,614	28,346	55,324	27,558	27,766	612	54	558	24	2	22
	Total 0—5 ...	*272,146*	*132,380*	*139,766*	*271,113*	*132,297*	*138,816*	*1,023*	*81*	*947*	*35*	*2*	*33*
	5—10 ...	234,602	124,792	109,810	220,874	123,576	97,298	13,349	1,203	12,146	279	13	266
	10—15 ...	203,835	108,915	94,920	164,917	106,452	58,465	37,946	2,381	35,565	972	82	890
	15—20 ...	158,786	71,709	87,077	55,316	50,597	4,719	99,840	20,525	79,315	3,630	587	3,043
	20—30 ...	301,902	145,686	156,216	43,598	42,044	1,554	242,933	100,008	142,925	15,371	3,634	11,737
	30—40 ...	201,866	111,882	89,984	4,483	4,048	435	169,200	103,337	65,863	28,183	4,497	23,686
	40—50 ...	120,716	69,225	51,491	833	679	154	86,068	64,532	21,536	33,815	4,014	29,801
	50—60 ...	63,856	36,371	27,485	283	205	78	38,425	32,857	5,568	25,148	3,309	21,839
	60 and over ...	45,276	26,173	19,103	205	154	51	23,152	21,477	1,675	21,919	4,542	17,377
KHASI AND JAINTIA HILLS (BRITISH).	ALL RELIGIONS ...	*109,926*	*55,439*	*54,487*	*56,457*	*30,613*	*25,844*	*42,939*	*22,179*	*20,760*	*10,530*	*2,647*	*7,883*
	0—1 ...	4,462	2,178	2,284	4,462	2,178	2,284	...	...	...	...	...	...
	1—2 ...	3,853	1,861	1,992	3,853	1,861	1,992	...	...	...	...	...	...
	2—3 ...	4,161	2,025	2,136	4,161	2,025	2,136	...	...	...	...	...	...
	3—4 ...	3,869	1,901	1,968	3,869	1,901	1,968	...	...	...	...	...	...
	4—5 ...	3,474	1,704	1,770	3,473	1,703	1,770	1	1	...	...	...	...
	Total 0—5 ...	*19,819*	*9,669*	*10,150*	*19,818*	*9,668*	*10,150*	*1*	*1*	...	...	...	...
	5—10 ...	13,594	6,853	6,741	13,558	6,846	6,712	33	7	26	3	...	3
	10—15 ...	11,983	6,105	5,878	11,428	6,013	5,415	491	84	407	64	8	56
	15—20 ...	11,225	5,500	5,725	6,059	3,856	2,203	4,613	1,518	3,095	553	126	427
	20—30 ...	21,082	10,707	10,375	4,607	3,480	1,127	14,617	6,664	7,953	1,858	563	1,295
	30—40 ...	14,542	7,803	6,739	686	550	136	11,809	6,654	5,155	2,047	599	1,448
	40—50 ...	8,853	4,543	4,310	179	125	54	6,547	3,910	2,637	2,127	508	1,619
	50—60 ...	4,820	2,419	2,401	66	48	18	2,986	1,980	1,006	1,768	391	1,377
	60 and over ...	3,988	1,830	2,158	56	37	19	1,822	1,341	481	2,110	452	1,658

TABLE VII.

Age, Sex and Civil Condition. Part B.—Details for Districts—*contd.*

District.	Age.	Population. Persons.	Population. Males.	Population. Females.	Unmarried. Persons.	Unmarried. Males.	Unmarried. Females.	Married. Persons.	Married. Males.	Married. Females.	Widowed. Persons.	Widowed. Males.	Widowed. Females.
	1	2	3	4	5	6	7	8	9	10	11	12	13
KHASI AND JAINTIA HILLS (BRITISH)—concld.	TRIBAL ...	*74,768*	*36,039*	*38,736*	*38,448*	*20,141*	*18,307*	*28,366*	*13,897*	*14,460*	*7,954*	*1,994*	*5,960*
	0—1 ...	3,143	1,522	1,621	3,143	1,522	1,621	...	...	...	...	...	...
	1—2 ...	2,789	1,334	1,455	2,789	1,334	1,455	...	...	...	...	...	...
	2—3 ...	3,065	1,493	1,572	3,065	1,493	1,572	...	...	...	...	...	...
	3—4 ...	2,850	1,391	1,459	2,850	1,391	1,459	...	...	...	...	...	...
	4—5 ...	2,528	1,228	1,300	2,527	1,227	1,300	1	1	...	...	...	...
	Total 0—5 ...	*14,355*	*6,968*	*7,387*	*14,354*	*6,967*	*7,387*	*1*	*1*	...	...	...	...
	5—10 ...	9,582	4,795	4,787	9,561	4,792	4,769	18	3	15	3	...	3
	10—15 ...	8,228	4,177	4,051	7,877	4,112	3,765	298	59	239	53	6	47
	15—20 ...	7,163	3,258	3,905	3,662	2,170	1,492	3,053	987	2,066	448	101	347
	20—30 ...	13,386	6,125	7,261	2,414	1,674	740	9,483	4,006	5,477	1,489	445	1,044
	30—40 ...	9,547	4,724	4,823	331	246	85	7,675	4,031	3,644	1,541	447	1,094
	40—50 ...	6,174	3,031	3,143	106	70	36	4,496	2,585	1,911	1,572	376	1,196
	50—60 ...	3,374	1,628	1,746	40	29	11	2,038	1,316	722	1,296	283	1,013
	60 and over ...	2,929	1,326	1,603	43	21	22	1,334	969	365	1,552	336	1,216
	CHRISTIAN ...	*23,314*	*11,207*	*12,107*	*12,771*	*6,731*	*6,040*	*8,427*	*4,067*	*4,360*	*2,116*	*418*	*1,698*
	0—1 ...	888	439	449	888	439	449	...	...	...	...	...	...
	1—2 ...	747	349	398	747	349	398	...	...	...	...	...	...
	2—3 ...	800	388	412	800	388	412	...	...	...	...	...	...
	3—4 ...	768	390	378	768	390	378	...	...	...	...	...	...
	4—5 ...	739	356	383	739	356	383	...	...	...	...	...	...
	Total 0—5 ...	*3,993*	*1,994*	*1,999*	*3,993*	*1,994*	*1,999*	...	...	...	...	...	...
	5—10 ...	3,142	1,583	1,559	3,139	1,583	1,556	3	...	3	...	...	...
	10—15 ...	2,915	1,461	1,454	2,845	1,455	1,390	64	6	58	6	...	6
	15—20 ...	2,418	1,080	1,338	1,545	884	661	781	176	605	92	20	72
	20—30 ...	4,133	1,915	2,218	1,104	738	366	2,725	1,095	1,630	304	82	222
	30—40 ...	2,909	1,437	1,472	142	95	47	2,379	1,258	1,121	388	84	304
	40—50 ...	1,879	897	982	45	28	17	1,381	791	590	453	78	375
	50—60 ...	1,080	510	570	16	9	7	689	441	248	375	60	315
	60 and over ...	915	400	515	12	6	6	405	300	105	498	94	404
NAGA HILLS.	ALL RELIGIONS ...	*178,844*	*89,536*	*89,308*	*93,648*	*48,944*	*44,704*	*68,624*	*34,666*	*33,958*	*16,572*	*5,926*	*10,646*
	0—1 ...	4,557	2,244	2,313	4,557	2,244	2,313	...	...	...	...	...	...
	1—2 ...	5,180	2,544	2,636	5,177	2,544	2,633	3	...	3	...	...	...
	2—3 ...	5,878	2,870	3,008	5,874	2,868	3,006	4	2	2	...	...	...
	3—4 ...	5,927	2,907	3,020	5,910	2,899	3,011	17	8	9	...	...	...
	4—5 ...	5,844	2,894	2,950	5,811	2,883	2,928	29	10	19	4	1	3
	Total 0—5 ...	*27,386*	*13,459*	*13,927*	*27,329*	*13,438*	*13,891*	*53*	*20*	*33*	*4*	*1*	*3*
	5—10 ...	24,013	12,100	11,913	23,823	12,026	11,797	173	69	104	17	5	12
	10—15 ...	20,867	10,651	10,216	20,521	10,547	9,974	315	93	222	31	11	20
	15—20 ...	14,444	7,215	7,229	11,234	6,306	4,928	2,866	784	2,082	344	125	219
	20—30 ...	26,681	13,044	13,637	8,681	5,385	3,296	16,015	6,768	9,247	1,985	891	1,094
	30—40 ...	24,595	12,401	12,194	1,250	850	401	20,405	10,333	10,072	2,930	1,299	1,631
	40—50 ...	17,717	9,096	8,621	385	222	163	14,061	7,718	6,343	3,271	1,156	2,115
	50—60 ...	10,747	5,284	5,463	151	83	68	7,571	4,292	3,279	3,025	909	2,116
	60 and over ...	12,304	6,196	6,108	174	78	96	7,165	4,589	2,576	4,965	1,530	3,435

TABLE VII.

Age, Sex and Civil condition. Part B.—Details for Districts—*contd.*

District.	Age.	Population. Persons.	Population. Males.	Population. Females.	Unmarried. Persons.	Unmarried. Males.	Unmarried. Females.	Married. Persons.	Married. Males.	Married. Females	Widowed. Persons.	Widowed. Males.	Widowed. Females.
	1	2	3	4	5	6	7	8	9	10	11	12	13
NAGA HILLS—contd.	TRIBAL	*148,289*	*73,182*	*75,107*	*77,978*	*40,299*	*37,679*	*56,038*	*27,744*	*28,294*	*14,273*	*5,139*	*9,134*
	0—1	3,901	1,908	1,993	3,901	1,908	1,993	...	...	...	...	...	...
	1—2	4,461	2,176	2,285	4,459	2,176	2,283	2	...	2	...	...	...
	2—3	4,996	2,436	2,562	4,992	2,433	2,561	4	2	2	...	...	...
	3—4	5,012	2,459	2,553	4,988	2,442	2,546	14	7	7	...	...	...
	4—5	4,950	2,442	2,488	4,924	2,451	2,473	24	10	14	2	1	1
	Total 0—5	*23,292*	*11,410*	*11,882*	*23,245*	*11,390*	*11,855*	*44*	*19*	*25*	*3*	*1*	*2*
	5—10	20,174	10,173	10,001	20,024	10,111	9,913	138	58	78	14	4	10
	10—15	17,379	8,876	8,503	17,127	8,793	8,334	229	73	154	23	10	13
	15—20	11,673	5,706	5,967	9,144	5,023	4,121	2,216	573	1,643	313	110	203
	20—30	21,370	9,997	11,373	6,841	4,067	2,774	12,788	5,166	7,622	1,741	764	977
	30—40	20,304	9,975	10,329	1,027	614	413	16,758	8,340	8,418	2,519	1,121	1,398
	40—50	14,797	7,503	7,294	295	165	130	11,624	6,329	5,295	2,809	1,009	1,800
	50—60	8,979	4,324	4,655	119	65	54	6,255	3,463	2,773	2,605	777	1,828
	60 and over	10,381	5,218	5,163	147	71	76	5,988	3,804	2,184	4,246	1,343	2,903
	CHRISTIAN	*22,908*	*11,324*	*11,584*	*12,149*	*6,297*	*5,852*	*8,962*	*4,491*	*4,471*	*1,797*	*536*	*1,261*
	0—1	456	244	212	456	244	212	...	...	...	...	...	...
	1—2	516	253	264	515	252	263	1	...	1	...	...	...
	2—3	684	333	351	684	333	351	...	...	...	...	...	...
	3—4	727	358	369	725	358	367	2	...	2	...	...	...
	4—5	723	361	362	720	361	359	2	...	2	1	...	1
	Total 0—5	*3,106*	*1,548*	*1,558*	*3,100*	*1,548*	*1,552*	*5*	...	*5*	*1*	...	*1*
	5—10	3,126	1,550	1,676	3,112	1,531	1,581	20	7	13	2	1	1
	10—15	2,871	1,447	1,424	2,837	1,435	1,402	32	12	20	2	...	2
	15—20	1,968	997	971	1,649	916	733	302	73	229	17	8	9
	20—30	3,286	1,575	1,711	1,203	726	477	1,909	766	1,143	175	84	91
	30—40	2,912	1,459	1,453	158	88	70	2,553	1,236	1,307	201	115	136
	40—50	2,369	1,149	1,220	45	21	24	1,975	1,035	940	349	93	256
	50—60	1,460	754	706	23	9	14	1,127	686	441	310	79	231
	60 and over	1,701	836	865	22	4	18	1,039	676	363	640	156	484
LUSHAI HILLS.	ALL RELIGIONS	*124,404*	*59,186*	*65,218*	*70,330*	*35,504*	*34,826*	*43,044*	*21,730*	*21,314*	*11,030*	*1,952*	*9,078*
	0—1	4,053	2,007	2,046	4,053	2,007	2,046	...	...	...	...	...	...
	1—2	3,926	1,897	2,029	3,926	1,897	2,029	...	...	...	...	...	...
	2—3	4,616	2,202	2,414	4,615	2,202	2,413	1	...	1	...	...	...
	3—4	4,578	2,226	2,352	4,576	2,226	2,350	2	...	2	...	...	...
	4—5	4,201	2,069	2,134	4,190	2,065	2,125	8	4	4	3	...	3
	Total 0—5	*21,374*	*10,401*	*10,973*	*21,360*	*10,397*	*10,963*	*11*	*4*	*7*	*3*	...	*3*
	5—10	17,020	8,378	8,642	16,991	8,344	8,637	25	14	11	4	...	4
	10—15	14,652	7,245	7,307	14,444	7,178	7,266	180	94	86	28	13	15
	15—20	11,975	5,505	6,470	8,465	4,451	3,914	3,097	854	2,229	413	86	327
	20—30	21,572	9,897	11,675	6,927	4,103	2,824	12,970	5,356	7,614	1,675	428	1,247
	30—40	15,752	7,646	8,106	1,124	588	536	12,675	6,624	6,052	1,953	425	1,528
	40—50	9,922	4,796	5,126	421	154	267	7,503	4,328	3,174	1,996	314	1,686
	50—60	6,085	2,726	3,359	282	94	188	3,800	2,386	1,414	2,003	246	1,757
	60 and over	6,052	2,562	3,490	216	65	251	2,784	2,057	727	2,952	440	2,512

TABLE VII.

Age, Sex and Civil Condition. Part B.—Details for Districts—*contd.*

District.	Age.	Population.			Unmarried.			Married.			Widowed.		
		Persons.	Males.	Females.	Persons.	Males.	Females.	Persons.	Males.	Females.	Persons.	Males.	Females.
	1	2	3	4	5	6	7	8	9	10	11	12	13
LUSHAI HILLS—*contd.*	TRIBAL	*60,155*	*29,513*	*30,649*	*30,774*	*16,136*	*14,638*	*23,000*	*12,174*	*10,826*	*6,381*	*1,203*	*5,178*
	0—1	1,941	949	992	1,941	949	992	...	...	...	...	...	...
	1—2	1,840	895	945	1,840	895	945	...	...	...	...	...	...
	2—3	2,182	1,036	1,146	2,181	1,036	1,145	1	...	1	...	...	...
	3—4	2,147	1,038	1,109	2,145	1,038	1,107	2	...	2	...	...	...
	4—5	1,953	963	990	1,935	961	974	6	2	4	2	...	2
	Total 0—5	*10,053*	*4,881*	*5,179*	*10,049*	*4,879*	*5,163*	*9*	*2*	*7*	*2*	...	*2*
	5—10	7,301	3,706	3,595	7,278	3,696	3,582	19	10	9	4	...	4
	10—15	5,905	3,108	2,797	5,829	3,088	2,741	66	19	47	10	1	9
	15—20	5,084	2,561	2,523	3,404	2,048	1,356	1,450	460	990	240	63	177
	20—30	10,255	4,947	5,308	3,041	1,943	1,098	6,269	2,760	3,509	945	244	701
	30—40	8,099	3,921	4,178	579	295	284	6,409	3,398	3,011	1,111	228	883
	40—50	5,630	2,716	2,914	240	83	157	4,257	2,850	1,407	1,133	183	950
	50—60	3,781	1,752	2,029	168	61	107	2,445	1,523	922	1,168	168	1,000
	60 and over	4,047	1,911	2,136	193	43	150	2,076	1,552	524	1,778	326	1,452
	CHRISTIAN	*59,123*	*26,676*	*32,447*	*36,873*	*17,778*	*19,095*	*17,839*	*8,260*	*9,579*	*4,411*	*638*	*3,773*
	0—1	1,923	976	947	1,923	976	947	...	...	...	...	...	...
	1—2	1,915	911	904	1,915	911	904	...	...	...	...	...	...
	2—3	2,252	1,075	1,177	2,252	1,075	1,177	...	...	...	...	...	...
	3—4	2,263	1,101	1,162	2,263	1,101	1,162	...	...	...	...	...	...
	4—5	2,094	1,019	1,075	2,092	1,017	1,075	2	2	...	...	...	...
	Total 0—5	*10,447*	*5,092*	*5,355*	*10,445*	*5,090*	*5,355*	*2*	*2*	...	...	...	...
	5—10	9,085	4,345	4,740	9,082	4,342	4,740	3	3	...	...	...	...
	10—15	8,222	3,913	4,309	8,120	3,831	4,289	86	70	16	16	12	4
	15—20	6,354	2,641	3,713	4,780	2,288	2,492	1,399	323	1,076	175	30	145
	20—30	10,262	4,303	5,959	3,599	1,903	1,696	5,984	2,241	3,743	689	169	520
	30—40	6,981	3,274	3,707	476	237	239	5,711	2,869	2,842	794	168	626
	40—50	3,891	1,891	2,000	157	50	107	2,913	1,643	1,270	821	108	713
	50—60	2,052	794	1,258	105	27	78	1,150	705	445	797	64	733
	60 and over	1,829	511	1,318	119	29	90	591	404	187	1,119	87	1,033
SADIYA FRONTIER TRACT.	ALL RELIGIONS	*53,345*	*28,686*	*24,659*	*27,789*	*15,833*	*11,956*	*21,343*	*11,292*	*10,051*	*4,213*	*1,561*	*2,652*
	0—1	1,815	896	919	1,815	896	919	...	...	...	...	...	...
	1—2	1,777	883	894	1,776	883	893	1	...	1	...	...	...
	2—3	1,870	924	946	1,868	923	945	2	1	1	...	...	...
	3—4	1,801	925	876	1,798	924	874	3	1	2	...	...	...
	4—5	1,725	907	818	1,716	904	812	8	3	5	1	...	1
	Total 0—5	*8,988*	*4,524*	*4,464*	*8,973*	*4,519*	*4,454*	*14*	*5*	*9*	*1*	...	*1*
	5—10	6,517	3,490	3,027	6,432	3,476	2,956	77	11	66	8	3	5
	10—15	5,342	2,793	2,549	5,037	2,724	2,313	294	65	229	11	4	7
	15—20	5,002	2,425	2,577	3,086	1,907	1,179	1,832	484	1,348	84	34	50
	20—30	10,712	5,758	4,954	3,264	2,408	856	6,961	3,134	3,827	487	216	271
	30—40	8,069	4,768	3,301	768	650	118	6,410	3,737	2,673	891	381	510
	40—50	4,825	2,797	2,028	228	184	44	3,518	2,235	1,283	1,079	378	701
	50—60	2,530	1,401	1,129	68	49	19	1,522	1,059	463	940	293	647
	60 and over	1,360	720	640	33	26	7	615	452	163	712	242	470

TABLE VII.

Age, Sex and Civil Condition. Part B.—Details for Districts—*contd.*

District.	Age.	Population. Persons.	Population. Males.	Population. Females.	Unmarried. Persons.	Unmarried. Males.	Unmarried. Females.	Married. Persons.	Married. Males.	Married. Females.	Widowed. Persons.	Widowed. Males.	Widowed. Females.
	1	2	3	4	5	6	7	8	9	10	11	12	13
SADIYA FRONTIER TRACT—*concld.*	TRIBAL	*23,486*	*11,677*	*11,809*	*12,531*	*6,739*	*5,792*	*8,954*	*4,421*	*4,533*	*2,001*	*517*	*1,484*
	0—1	778	379	399	778	379	399	...	...	...	...	...	...
	1—2	819	397	422	818	397	421	1	...	1	...	...	...
	2—3	875	421	454	874	421	453	1	...	1	...	...	...
	3—4	827	422	405	826	422	404	1	...	1	...	...	...
	4—5	769	407	362	766	406	360	3	1	2	...	...	...
	Total 0—5	*4,068*	*2,026*	*2,042*	*4,062*	*2,025*	*2,037*	*6*	*1*	*5*	...	...	...
	5—10	2,858	1,546	1,312	2,834	1,539	1,295	22	7	15	2	...	2
	10—15	2,345	1,213	1,132	2,247	1,184	1,063	95	29	66	3	...	3
	15—20	2,192	957	1,235	1,446	738	708	720	211	509	26	8	18
	20—30	4,511	2,153	2,358	1,494	933	561	2,811	1,159	1,652	206	61	145
	30—40	3,477	1,794	1,683	292	221	71	2,776	1,446	1,330	409	127	282
	40—50	2,238	1,148	1,090	99	63	36	1,587	948	639	552	137	415
	50—60	1,146	542	606	40	24	16	644	422	222	464	96	368
	60 and over	649	298	351	17	13	5	293	198	95	339	88	251
	HINDU	*26,009*	*14,809*	*11,193*	*13,319*	*7,921*	*5,398*	*10,799*	*5,981*	*4,818*	*1,884*	*907*	*977*
	0—1	932	451	481	932	451	481	...	...	...	...	...	...
	1—2	852	433	419	852	433	419	...	...	...	...	...	...
	2—3	872	440	432	872	440	432	...	...	...	...	...	...
	3—4	858	440	418	857	440	417	1	...	1	...	...	...
	4—5	845	440	405	841	439	402	3	1	2	1	...	1
	Total 0—5	*4,359*	*2,204*	*2,155*	*4,354*	*2,203*	*2,151*	*4*	*1*	*3*	*1*	...	1
	5—10	3,205	1,703	1,502	3,148	1,687	1,461	51	13	38	6	3	3
	10—15	2,601	1,367	1,234	2,410	1,329	1,081	183	34	149	8	4	4
	15—20	2,459	1,281	1,178	1,334	922	412	1,075	336	739	50	23	27
	20—30	5,441	3,160	2,281	1,527	1,277	250	3,672	1,748	1,924	242	135	107
	30—40	3,975	2,596	1,379	401	367	34	3,162	1,997	1,165	412	232	180
	40—50	2,205	1,413	792	108	102	6	1,642	1,099	543	455	212	243
	50—60	1,184	740	444	26	24	2	747	546	201	411	170	241
	60 and over	578	345	233	11	10	1	263	207	56	299	128	171
BALIPARA FRONTIER TRACT.	ALL RELIGIONS	*5,148*	*3,232*	*1,916*	*2,445*	*1,620*	*825*	*2,376*	*1,432*	*944*	*327*	*180*	*147*
	0—1	185	94	91	185	94	91	...	...	...	...	...	...
	1—2	152	78	74	152	78	74	...	...	...	...	...	...
	2—3	157	87	70	157	87	70	...	...	...	...	...	...
	3—4	144	81	63	144	81	63	...	...	...	...	...	...
	4—5	147	81	66	146	81	65	1	...	1	...	...	...
	Total 0—5	*785*	*421*	*364*	*784*	*421*	*363*	*1*	...	*1*	...	...	...
	5—10	510	279	231	499	276	223	11	3	8	...	...	...
	10—15	401	209	192	361	204	157	39	5	34	1	...	1
	15—20	502	311	191	268	221	47	225	84	141	9	6	3
	20—30	1,286	860	426	421	394	27	817	434	383	48	32	16
	30—40	919	644	275	98	92	6	752	506	246	69	46	23
	40—50	467	330	137	11	11	...	368	269	99	88	50	38
	50—60	207	135	72	2	1	1	129	102	27	76	32	44
	60 and over	71	43	28	1	...	1	34	29	5	36	14	22

TABLE VII.

AGE, SEX AND CIVIL CONDITION. PART B.—DETAILS FOR DISTRICTS—*contd.*

District.	Age.	Population. Persons.	Population. Males.	Population. Females.	Unmarried. Persons.	Unmarried. Males.	Unmarried. Females.	Married. Persons.	Married. Males.	Married. Females.	Widowed. Persons.	Widowed. Males.	Widowed. Females.
	1	2	3	4	5	6	7	8	9	10	11	12	13
BALIPARA FRONTIER TRACT—*concld.*	HINDU ...	*3,811*	*2,487*	*1,324*	*1,843*	*1,249*	*594*	*1,726*	*1,099*	*627*	*242*	*139*	*103*
	0—1 ...	137	69	68	137	69	68	...	...	...	...	...	...
	1—2 ...	113	60	53	113	60	53	...	...	...	...	...	...
	2—3 ...	117	65	52	117	65	52	...	...	...	...	...	...
	3—4 ...	114	62	52	114	62	52	...	...	...	...	...	...
	4—5 ...	106	58	48	105	58	47	1	...	1	...	...	...
	Total 0—5 ...	*587*	*314*	*273*	*586*	*314*	*272*	*1*	...	*1*	...	...	...
	5—10 ...	362	198	164	355	196	159	7	2	5	...	...	...
	10—15 ...	273	141	132	247	138	109	25	3	22	1	...	1
	15—20 ...	384	251	133	210	178	32	167	65	102	7	5	2
	20—30 ...	981	704	277	354	336	18	591	342	249	36	26	10
	30—40 ...	677	500	177	81	78	3	549	389	160	47	33	14
	40—50 ...	341	243	98	8	8	...	266	197	69	67	38	29
	50—60 ...	154	104	50	2	1	1	97	79	18	55	24	31
	60 and over ...	53	33	20	...	...	...	23	19	4	29	13	16
	TRIBAL ...	*813*	*439*	*374*	*344*	*218*	*196*	*405*	*187*	*218*	*64*	*34*	*30*
	0—1 ...	19	11	8	19	11	8	...	...	...	...	...	...
	1—2 ...	19	9	10	19	9	10	...	...	...	...	...	...
	2—3 ...	20	10	10	20	10	10	...	...	...	...	...	...
	3—4 ...	16	10	6	16	10	6	...	...	...	...	...	...
	4—5 ...	18	10	8	18	10	8	...	...	...	...	...	...
	Total 0—5 ...	*99*	*50*	*49*	*99*	*50*	*49*	...	...	...	...	...	...
	5—10 ...	86	49	37	83	48	35	3	1	2	...	...	...
	10—15 ...	82	45	37	73	44	29	9	1	8	...	...	...
	15—20 ...	69	31	38	38	27	11	30	4	26	1	...	1
	20—30 ...	194	87	107	46	38	8	138	44	94	10	5	5
	30—40 ...	169	96	73	10	9	1	141	75	66	18	12	6
	40—50 ...	84	59	25	2	2	...	64	46	18	18	11	7
	50—60 ...	27	17	10	...	...	...	15	12	3	12	5	7
	60 and over ...	10	5	5	...	...	...	5	4	1	5	1	4
KHASI STATES.	ALL RELIGIONS ...	*180,000*	*91,112*	*88,888*	*95,068*	*51,758*	*44,310*	*66,320*	*34,483*	*31,837*	*17,712*	*4,871*	*12,841*
	0—1 ...	7,462	3,730	3,732	7,462	3,730	3,732	...	...	...	...	...	...
	1—2 ...	6,400	3,161	3,239	6,400	3,161	3,239	...	...	...	...	...	...
	2—3 ...	6,366	3,144	3,222	6,366	3,144	3,222	...	...	...	...	...	...
	3—4 ...	6,021	2,959	3,062	6,021	2,959	3,062	...	...	...	...	...	...
	4—5 ...	5,764	2,811	2,953	5,761	2,811	2,950	3	...	3	...	...	...
	Total 0—5 ...	*32,013*	*15,805*	*16,208*	*32,010*	*15,805*	*16,205*	*3*	...	*3*	...	...	...
	5—10 ...	23,105	11,596	11,509	23,037	11,587	11,450	59	9	50	9	...	9
	10—15 ...	20,341	10,273	10,066	19,590	10,161	9,429	660	100	560	91	14	77
	15—20 ...	18,221	8,493	9,728	10,733	6,442	4,291	6,475	1,814	4,661	1,013	237	776
	20—25 ...	18,451	8,820	9,631	6,702	4,616	2,086	10,207	3,709	6,498	1,542	495	1,047
	25—30 ...	14,886	7,879	7,007	1,998	1,671	327	11,253	5,670	5,583	1,635	538	1,097
	30—35 ...	12,836	6,907	5,929	1,026	859	167	10,163	5,583	4,580	1,647	465	1,182
	35—40 ...	10,266	5,502	4,764	346	264	83	8,143	4,730	3,413	1,777	518	1,259
	40—45 ...	8,696	4,600	4,096	206	143	63	6,680	3,983	2,697	1,810	474	1,336
	45—50 ...	6,268	3,315	2,953	98	68	30	4,354	2,799	1,555	1,816	448	1,368
	50—55 ...	4,967	2,613	2,354	70	48	22	3,277	2,157	1,120	1,620	408	1,212
	55—60 ...	3,263	1,758	1,505	43	27	16	1,940	1,386	554	1,280	345	935
	60—65 ...	2,652	1,413	1,239	41	27	14	1,480	1,084	396	1,131	302	829
	65—70 ...	1,429	705	724	19	12	7	669	506	163	741	187	554
	70 and over ...	2,626	1,261	1,365	49	28	21	1,007	793	214	1,570	440	1,130

TABLE VII.

Age, Sex and Civil Condition. Part B.—Details for Districts—contd.

District.	Age.	Population. Persons.	Population. Males.	Population. Females.	Unmarried. Persons.	Unmarried. Males.	Unmarried. Females.	Married. Persons.	Married. Males.	Married. Females.	Widowed. Persons.	Widowed. Males.	Widowed. Females.
	1	2	3	4	5	6	7	8	9	10	11	12	13
KHASI STATES—concld.	TRIBAL ...	*126,154*	*61,613*	*64,541*	*66,408*	*34,828*	*31,580*	*45,993*	*23,060*	*22,933*	*13,753*	*3,725*	*10,028*
	0—1 ...	5,404	2,719	2,685	5,404	2,719	2,685	...	...	...	...	...	...
	1—2 ...	4,768	2,360	2,408	4,768	2,360	2,408	...	...	...	...	...	...
	2—3 ...	4,655	2,306	2,349	4,655	2,306	2,349	...	...	...	...	...	...
	3—4 ...	4,385	2,159	2,226	4,385	2,159	2,226	...	...	...	...	...	...
	4—5 ...	4,205	2,037	2,168	4,205	2,037	2,168	...	...	...	...	...	...
	Total 0—5 ...	*23,417*	*11,581*	*11,836*	*23,417*	*11,581*	*11,836*	...	...	...	...	...	...
	5—10 ...	16,548	8,229	8,319	16,508	8,226	8,282	34	3	31	6	...	6
	10—15 ...	14,393	7,175	7,218	13,830	7,092	6,738	483	70	413	80	13	67
	15—20 ...	12,370	6,490	5,880	6,960	4,921	2,039	4,553	1,272	3,281	857	197	660
	20—25 ...	12,222	6,341	5,881	3,851	2,511	1,340	7,070	2,488	4,582	1,271	321	950
	25—30 ...	9,734	4,682	5,052	913	721	193	7,512	3,567	3,945	1,309	394	915
	30—35 ...	8,587	4,359	4,228	456	359	97	6,845	3,588	3,257	1,286	412	874
	35—40 ...	7,193	3,692	3,501	171	122	49	5,659	3,484	2,175	1,363	386	977
	40—45 ...	6,133	3,108	3,025	104	69	35	4,653	2,686	1,967	1,376	353	1,023
	45—50 ...	4,545	2,324	2,221	58	38	20	3,088	1,939	1,149	1,399	347	1,052
	50—55 ...	3,629	1,854	1,775	37	24	13	2,346	1,517	829	1,246	313	933
	55—60 ...	2,368	1,269	1,099	16	10	6	1,407	996	411	945	263	682
	60—65 ...	1,913	1,016	897	15	10	5	1,072	775	297	826	231	595
	65—70 ...	1,060	522	538	9	6	3	494	372	122	557	144	413
	70 and over ...	2,042	971	1,071	33	17	16	777	603	174	1,232	351	881
	CHRISTIAN ...	*36,259*	*17,295*	*18,964*	*21,273*	*11,032*	*10,241*	*11,959*	*5,638*	*6,321*	*3,028*	*626*	*2,402*
	0—1 ...	1,534	742	792	1,534	742	792	...	...	...	...	...	...
	1—2 ...	1,203	591	612	1,203	591	612	...	...	...	...	...	...
	2—3 ...	1,253	615	638	1,253	615	638	...	...	...	...	...	...
	3—4 ...	1,221	597	624	1,221	597	624	...	...	...	...	...	...
	4—5 ...	1,172	580	592	1,170	580	590	2	...	2	...	...	...
	Total 0—5 ...	*6,383*	*3,125*	*3,258*	*6,381*	*3,125*	*3,256*	*2*	...	*2*	...	...	...
	5—10 ...	5,062	2,557	2,505	5,052	2,554	2,498	9	3	6	1	..	1
	10—15 ...	4,676	2,359	2,317	4,599	2,351	2,248	69	7	62	8	1	7
	15—20 ...	3,972	1,792	2,180	2,771	1,513	1,258	1,074	254	820	127	25	102
	20—25 ...	3,680	1,592	2,088	1,700	1,001	699	1,768	541	1,227	212	50	162
	25—30 ...	2,624	1,224	1,400	377	251	126	2,003	905	1,098	244	68	176
	30—35 ...	2,248	1,079	1,169	183	121	62	1,819	896	923	246	62	184
	35—40 ...	1,836	834	1,002	74	45	29	1,465	735	730	297	54	243
	40—45 ...	1,613	739	874	47	25	22	1,244	660	584	322	54	268
	45—50 ...	1,188	571	617	20	12	8	839	503	336	329	56	273
	50—55 ...	950	460	490	17	9	8	643	395	248	290	56	234
	55—60 ...	671	327	344	17	7	10	391	265	126	263	55	208
	60—65 ...	567	272	295	15	7	8	303	216	87	249	49	200
	65—70 ...	299	138	161	7	3	4	141	106	35	151	29	122
	70 and over ...	490	226	264	12	7	5	189	152	37	289	67	222

TABLE VII.

Age, Sex and Civil Condition. Part B.—Details for districts—*contd.*

District.	Age.	Population. Persons.	Population. Males.	Population. Females.	Unmarried. Persons.	Unmarried. Males.	Unmarried. Females.	Married. Persons.	Married. Males.	Married. Females.	Widowed. Persons.	Widowed. Males.	Widowed. Females.
	1	2	3	4	5	6	7	8	9	10	11	12	13
MANIPUR.	ALL RELIGIONS ...	*445,606*	*215,815*	*229,791*	*230,977*	*123,406*	*106,871*	*171,480*	*83,716*	*87,764*	*43,849*	*8,693*	*35,156*
	0–1 ...	18,410	9,164	9,246	18,410	9,164	9,246	...	...	...	...	...	...
	1–2 ...	14,226	7,002	7,224	14,226	7,002	7,224	...	...	...	...	...	...
	2–3 ...	16,300	7,994	8,306	16,298	7,994	8,304	2	...	2	...	...	...
	3–4 ...	16,598	8,170	8,428	16,582	8,168	8,414	14	2	12	2	...	2
	4–5 ...	14,993	7,379	7,614	14,950	7,370	7,580	32	8	24	11	1	10
	Total 0–5 ...	*80,597*	*39,709*	*40,818*	*80,466*	*39,698*	*40,768*	*48*	*10*	*38*	*13*	*1*	*12*
	5–10 ...	59,248	29,730	29,518	58,824	29,634	29,190	373	92	281	51	4	47
	10–15 ...	49,916	24,987	24,929	47,522	24,692	22,830	2,111	282	1,829	283	13	270
	15–20 ...	41,310	19,251	22,059	22,890	14,598	8,292	16,080	4,306	11,774	2,340	347	1,993
	20–25 ...	40,204	18,582	21,622	13,830	10,030	3,790	23,183	7,929	15,254	3,201	623	2,578
	25–30 ...	36,333	17,314	19,019	3,582	2,677	905	29,099	13,764	15,335	3,652	873	2,779
	30–35 ...	32,174	13,612	18,562	1,746	1,274	472	26,887	13,544	13,343	3,541	794	2,747
	35–40 ...	24,106	11,823	12,283	466	291	175	19,920	10,788	9,132	3,722	744	2,978
	40–45 ...	20,949	10,208	10,741	319	196	123	16,853	9,294	7,559	3,777	718	3,059
	45–50 ...	15,076	7,229	7,847	161	88	73	10,886	6,430	4,456	4,029	711	3,318
	50–55 ...	13,493	6,453	7,040	129	63	66	9,387	5,649	3,738	3,977	741	3,236
	55–60 ...	10,138	4,819	5,319	101	51	50	6,119	4,017	2,102	3,918	751	3,167
	60–65 ...	8,777	4,142	4,635	86	43	43	4,975	3,392	1,583	3,716	707	3,009
	65–70 ...	5,270	2,437	2,833	59	30	29	2,506	1,855	651	2,705	552	2,153
	70 and over ...	8,083	3,519	4,564	106	41	65	3,053	2,364	689	4,924	1,114	3,810
	HINDU ...	*257,255*	*124,343*	*132,912*	*129,142*	*71,409*	*57,740*	*99,001*	*47,645*	*51,356*	*29,119*	*5,296*	*23,816*
	0–1 ...	10,358	5,193	5,165	10,358	5,193	5,165	...	...	...	...	...	...
	1–2 ...	6,966	3,441	3,525	6,966	3,441	3,525	...	...	...	...	...	...
	2–3 ...	8,573	4,211	4,362	8,573	4,211	4,362	...	...	...	...	...	...
	3–4 ...	9,294	4,578	4,716	9,286	4,576	4,710	7	2	5	1	...	1
	4–5 ...	8,318	4,107	4,211	8,296	4,101	4,195	17	5	12	5	1	4
	Total 0–5 ...	*43,509*	*21,530*	*21,979*	*43,479*	*21,522*	*21,957*	*24*	*7*	*17*	*6*	*1*	*5*
	5–10 ...	34,682	17,464	17,108	34,269	17,395	16,974	253	66	187	40	3	37
	10–15 ...	30,330	15,224	15,106	28,536	15,043	13,493	1,547	172	1,375	247	9	238
	15–20 ...	26,014	12,230	13,784	12,908	9,116	3,792	11,092	2,851	8,241	2,014	263	1,751
	20–25 ...	24,955	11,656	13,299	7,124	6,066	1,058	15,170	5,128	10,042	2,661	462	2,199
	25–30 ...	20,317	9,653	10,664	1,409	1,248	161	16,256	7,839	8,417	2,652	566	2,086
	30–35 ...	17,659	8,445	9,214	690	577	113	14,488	7,380	7,108	2,481	488	1,993
	35–40 ...	12,956	6,195	6,761	217	158	59	10,411	5,635	4,776	2,328	402	1,926
	40–45 ...	11,285	5,364	5,921	146	108	38	8,828	4,872	3,956	2,311	384	1,927
	45–50 ...	8,394	3,951	4,443	75	54	21	5,929	3,489	2,440	2,390	408	1,982
	50–55 ...	7,723	3,674	4,049	55	34	21	5,273	3,207	2,066	2,395	433	1,963
	55–60 ...	6,098	2,879	3,210	41	28	13	3,608	2,418	1,190	2,449	433	2,016
	60–65 ...	5,283	2,485	2,798	36	27	9	2,892	2,036	856	2,355	422	1,933
	65–70 ...	3,342	1,561	1,781	28	14	14	1,561	1,195	366	1,755	352	1,403
	70 and over ...	4,728	2,032	2,696	31	12	19	1,669	1,350	319	3,028	670	2,358

TABLE VII.

Age, Sex and Civil Condition. Part B.—Details for districts—*concld.*

District.	Age.	Population.			Unmarried.			Married.			Widowed.		
		Persons.	Males.	Females.	Persons.	Males.	Females.	Persons.	Males.	Females.	Persons.	Males.	Females.
	1	2	3	4	5	6	7	8	9	10	11	12	13
MANIPUR—concld.	TRIBAL	*154,804*	*74,850*	*79,954*	*89,432*	*49,117*	*40,315*	*59,955*	*29,837*	*30,118*	*12,417*	*9,896*	*2,521*
	0—1	6,501	3,194	3,307	6,501	3,194	3,307	...	...	...	...	...	...
	1—2	5,961	2,925	3,036	5,961	2,925	3,036	...	...	...	...	...	...
	2—3	6,328	3,108	3,220	6,326	3,108	3,218	2	...	2	...	...	...
	3—4	5,894	2,898	2,996	5,886	2,898	2,988	7	...	7	1	...	1
	4—5	5,390	2,631	2,759	5,373	2,629	2,744	13	2	11	4	...	4
	Total 0—5	*30,064*	*14,756*	*15,308*	*30,037*	*14,754*	*15,283*	*22*	*2*	*20*	*5*	...	*5*
	5—10	19,658	9,739	9,919	19,566	9,721	9,845	84	17	67	8	1	7
	10—15	15,444	7,631	7,813	15,106	7,573	7,533	324	57	267	14	1	13
	15—20	12,023	5,506	6,517	8,313	4,477	3,836	3,515	974	2,541	195	55	140
	20—25	12,003	5,398	6,605	5,801	3,378	2,423	5,838	1,906	3,932	364	114	250
	25—30	13,203	6,367	6,836	1,947	1,271	676	10,463	4,746	5,717	793	350	443
	30—35	12,160	5,960	6,200	947	624	323	10,352	5,076	5,276	861	260	601
	35—40	9,596	4,810	4,786	214	111	103	8,209	4,400	3,809	1,173	299	874
	40—45	8,385	4,180	4,205	150	74	76	6,996	3,816	3,180	1,239	290	949
	45—50	5,861	2,881	2,980	81	33	48	4,370	2,584	1,786	1,410	265	1,145
	50—55	5,067	2,437	2,630	68	27	41	3,630	2,141	1,489	1,369	269	1,100
	55—60	3,514	1,680	1,834	55	20	35	2,185	1,284	901	1,274	376	898
	60—65	3,069	1,447	1,622	49	16	33	1,836	1,183	653	1,184	248	936
	65—70	1,687	756	932	28	13	15	824	567	257	835	175	660
	70 and over	2,980	1,313	1,667	70	26	44	1,217	894	323	1,693	393	1,300

TABLE VIII.

Civil Condition by Age for Selected Castes.

This table, like Table XIV, deals only with certain selected castes and tribes in certain districts or areas where they are specially numerous.

The figures for the various castes differ in certain instances from those shown in Table XVII. This is due to the fact that the figures in Table XVII include entries sorted under other heads which were afterwards added in the course of compilation.

TABLE VIII.

CIVIL CONDITION BY AGE FOR SELECTED CASTES.

Caste, Tribe or Race.	Locality.	Sex.	Population dealt with.	UNMARRIED.							MARRIED.							WIDOWED.						
				Total.	0–6	7–13	14–16	17–23	24–43	44 and over.	Total	0–6	7–13	14–16	17–23	24–43	44 and over	Total.	0–6	7–13	14–16	17–23	24–43	44 and over.
1	2	3	4	5	6	7	8	9	10	11	12	13	14	15	16	17	18	19	20	21	22	23	24	25
AHOM (Hindu) ...	Brahmaputra Valley.	Male ...	120,021	79,705	31,460	23,291	7,411	11,478	6,528	353	42,864	4	150	174	2,793	26,667	13,076	7,058	...	12	18	144	3,580	4,289
		Female ...	119,236	63,251	31,181	10,398	6,618	4,333	821	111	43,390	8	320	1,430	10,996	24,704	5,803	12,615	1	6	22	496	4,023	8,060
BAIDYA (Hindu) ...	Sylhet and Cachar Plains.	Male ...	3,405	2,130	654	686	210	348	226	17	1,160	...	3	14	40	597	507	117	...	...	...	3	39	88
		Female ...	2,993	1,479	656	613	128	29	65	...	1,058	1	14	66	274	674	131	461	...	2	3	16	157	284
BRAHMAN (Hindu) ...	Plains districts	Male ...	96,557	46,340	16,709	14,094	6,017	7,300	3,508	512	36,905	12	330	418	3,400	21,390	10,474	4,012	1	31	48	127	1,362	2,589
		Female ...	70,025	26,076	15,306	9,556	507	284	287	134	31,542	30	2,034	3,718	9,200	13,413	2,438	12,607	6	61	134	632	5,006	6,940
BANIA (Brittal Bania) (Hindu).	Brahmaputra Valley.	Male ...	7,465	4,503	1,707	1,435	443	580	307	23	2,694	3	16	22	296	1,638	737	338	...	...	2	16	148	172
		Female ...	6,496	3,048	1,587	1,065	304	116	48	10	2,535	4	46	229	746	1,206	104	913	...	1	4	45	320	536
GARO (Hindu) ...	Garo Hills and Goalpara.	Male ...	1,381	748	311	219	73	80	26	3	613	...	2	4	47	376	184	26	...	1	...	...	6	19
		Female ...	1,278	506	328	106	27	38	7	3	631	1	19	41	174	310	76	91	...	...	1	5	29	56
GARO (Tribal) ...	Garo Hills ...	Male ...	67,905	35,860	17,496	10,589	3,290	3,109	993	134	31,476	7	68	494	3,728	18,122	9,057	569	...	1	7	46	308	504
		Female ...	68,349	30,413	17,440	9,013	2,294	1,167	271	119	34,911	70	600	3,221	8,625	17,015	5,353	3,025	3	13	53	219	1,170	1,568
KACHARI (Hindu) ...	Brahmaputra Valley.	Male ...	101,281	55,652	26,342	16,996	4,217	5,006	2,843	200	38,780	14	307	896	4,004	23,672	9,907	6,849	...	8	41	310	2,707	3,783
		Female ...	95,645	47,513	26,315	15,064	3,364	2,036	630	104	37,507	35	918	2,850	9,267	20,173	4,335	10,425	1	27	72	361	3,757	6,317
KACHARI (Tribal) ...	Brahmaputra Valley.	Male ...	10,458	5,871	2,866	1,853	364	506	243	15	4,048	3	20	60	461	2,560	635	530	...	1	...	17	218	306
		Female ...	10,390	5,107	2,983	1,706	286	158	63	14	4,105	13	96	319	1,121	2,310	366	1,018	...	...	9	43	391	876
KHASI (Tribal) ...	Khasi and Jaintia Hills.	Male ...	68,958	35,048	14,631	10,548	3,974	4,806	1,930	107	28,237	1	8	119	9,318	13,738	7,068	4,067	...	1	22	363	1,776	1,906
		Female ...	66,136	32,161	15,016	10,410	3,505	2,047	510	73	23,139	3	50	644	5,763	13,155	3,514	10,846	...	8	115	1,341	4,093	5,236
KHASI (Christian) ...	Khasi and Jaintia Hills.	Male ...	18,391	11,391	4,163	3,534	1,338	1,760	570	27	6,275	4	7	12	978	3,371	1,903	725	...	1	2	81	280	411
		Female	19,685	10,618	4,100	3,333	1,440	1,356	303	26	6,063	4	5	119	1,666	3,753	1,046	2,804	...	1	16	203	876	1,548
MANIPURI (Hindu) ...	Manipur State ...	Male ...	190,540	69,318	27,081	21,031	7,413	10,311	2,409	183	66,140	11	108	312	5,337	36,044	14,420	5,082	...	5	13	507	2,738	1,889
		Female ...	130,257	56,856	25,047	30,246	6,460	3,136	1,248	219	60,890	31	470	3,827	13,575	33,344	8,730	23,511	4	63	533	3,016	8,335	11,571
NADIYAL (Kaibartta) (Hindu).	Brahmaputra Valley.	Male ...	60,528	30,225	12,135	9,274	2,981	4,064	1,735	104	17,784	5	65	74	1,386	11,360	6,036	2,519	...	16	4	80	925	1,405
		Female ...	46,405	22,903	12,361	7,940	1,601	726	230	35	17,779	17	220	1,003	6,400	9,348	1,853	5,633	...	12	30	323	3,316	3,148
NAMASUDRA (Hindu) ...	Sylhet and Cachar Plains.	Male ...	71,925	35,973	10,821	10,834	4,195	6,002	3,000	533	31,734	22	130	708	3,466	17,831	9,614	4,218	4	44	90	297	1,332	3,461
		Female ...	67,016	18,447	11,044	5,908	193	173	126	119	31,428	43	12,815	4,300	9,323	13,091	1,648	17,141	3	91	256	815	7,380	8,077
TANTI (Hindu) ...	Sibsagar and Lakhimpur.	Male ...	29,046	13,790	6,114	3,961	1,187	1,832	1,116	82	12,774	...	71	163	808	9,406	3,313	2,292	3	7	30	186	1,348	834
		Female ...	28,133	10,906	6,104	3,467	737	373	218	20	13,714	6	195	644	3,090	5,886	1,194	3,420	...	5	23	140	1,633	1,682
YOGI (Hindu) ...	Sylhet ...	Male ...	27,061	13,894	5,006	5,435	2,290	3,364	2,306	493	15,768	27	328	354	1,093	8,635	4,022	2,459	...	29	61	80	706	1,094
		Female ...	23,963	9,480	5,616	3,283	90	40	123	138	14,026	13	1,206	2,173	4,404	5,963	846	9,937	6	73	114	649	4,304	4,708

TABLE IX.

INFIRMITIES.

The infirmities recorded at the Census were insanity, deaf-mutism, blindness and leprosy.

The Table is divided into two parts—Part I shows the distribution of the persons afflicted according to age, and Part II their distribution by districts.

Some unfortunate persons were returned as suffering from more than one infirmity. In the table they have been shown under each. This explains why the total number of afflicted persons shown in columns 2, 3 and 4 does not agree with the total of the figures for each separate infirmity. The following is a list of these double entries :—

—	Total.	Males.	Females.
1	2	3	4
Insane and blind	19	5	14
Insane and leper	2	2	...
Insane and deaf-mute	163	80	83
Deaf-mute and blind	20	11	9
Deaf-mute and leper	11	9	2
Blind and leper	29	21	8
Total	244	128	116

TABLE IX.

INFIRMITIES. PART I.—DISTRIBUTION BY AGE.

AGE.	POPULATION AFFLICTED.			INSANE.			DEAF-MUTES.			BLIND.			LEPERS.		
	Persons.	Males.	Females.	Persons.	Males.	Females.	Persons.	Males.	Females.	Persons.	Males.	Females.	Persons.	Males.	Females.
1	2	3	4	5	6	7	8	9	10	11	12	13	14	15	16
Total ...	*27,506*	*15,940*	*11,566*	*5,426*	*3,138*	*2,288*	*6,978*	*3,984*	*2,994*	*9,926*	*4,914*	*5,012*	*5,420*	*4,032*	*1,388*
0–1	42	23	19	...	...	...	3	1	2	39	23	16	1	...	1
1–2	87	42	45	4	2	2	29	12	17	51	26	25	4	2	2
2–3	185	87	98	9	3	6	100	44	56	73	37	36	5	3	2
3–4	301	158	143	19	10	9	189	98	91	85	46	39	8	4	4
4–5	359	202	157	30	18	12	238	134	104	85	50	35	16	8	8
Total 0–5	*974*	*512*	*462*	*69*	*33*	*29*	*559*	*289*	*270*	*333*	*182*	*151*	*34*	*17*	*17*
5–10	1,978	1,175	803	233	133	100	1,239	733	506	407	243	164	129	81	48
10–15	2,074	1,195	879	314	161	153	1,204	695	509	401	238	163	184	117	67
15–20	1,890	1,036	854	436	224	212	814	444	370	386	210	176	286	175	111
20–25	1,974	1,140	825	506	284	222	731	420	311	404	216	188	354	239	115
25–30	2,285	1,407	878	691	417	274	581	343	238	449	227	222	581	428	153
30–35	2,321	1,438	883	727	445	282	457	250	207	455	218	237	662	496	166
35–40	2,256	1,395	861	630	393	237	391	214	177	562	261	301	696	539	157
40–45	2,145	1,307	838	552	337	215	318	172	146	635	296	339	654	500	143
45–50	1,965	1,151	814	416	229	187	212	133	79	817	385	432	535	411	124
50–55	1,798	1,040	758	342	189	153	164	106	58	835	396	439	465	355	110
55–60	1,585	845	740	202	118	84	102	56	46	869	424	445	317	250	67
60–65	1,272	712	560	146	80	66	81	45	36	914	406	508	235	183	52
65–70	805	431	374	73	39	34	28	15	13	610	302	308	103	81	22
70 and over	2,081	1,144	937	96	56	40	57	30	27	1,740	910	830	185	151	34

TABLE IX.

INFIRMITIES. PART II.—DISTRIBUTION BY DISTRICTS.

DISTRICT OR STATE.	POPULATION AFFLICTED.			INSANE.			DEAF-MUTES.			BLIND.			LEPERS.		
	Persons.	Males.	Females.	Persons.	Males.	Females.	Persons.	Males.	Females.	Persons.	Males.	Females.	Persons.	Males.	Females.
1	2	3	4	5	6	7	8	9	10	11	12	13	14	15	16
ASSAM	*27,506*	*15,940*	*11,566*	*5,426*	*3,138*	*2,288*	*6,978*	*3,984*	*2,994*	*9,926*	*4,914*	*5,012*	*5,420*	*4,032*	*1,388*
(1) British territory ...	*25,960*	*15,080*	*10,880*	*5,037*	*2,929*	*2,108*	*6,780*	*3,859*	*2,921*	*9,222*	*4,556*	*4,666*	*5,164*	*3,864*	*1,300*
SURMA VALLEY AND HILL DIVISION.	12,225	6,859	5,366	2,435	1,289	1,146	3,101	1,721	1,380	4,730	2,233	2,497	2,108	1,691	417
Cachar	1,887	1,033	854	395	211	184	422	248	174	769	333	436	316	255	69
Sylhet	8,473	4,994	3,479	1,475	830	645	2,027	1,160	867	3,332	1,063	1,009	1,687	1,373	314
Khasi and Jaintia Hills (British territory).	307	161	146	73	32	41	50	29	21	140	63	77	51	40	11
Naga Hills	581	273	308	62	26	36	261	132	129	204	82	122	54	23	31
Lushai Hills	978	398	580	430	190	240	341	153	180	285	92	193	2	...	2
ASSAM VALLEY DIVISION ...	13,405	8,029	5,376	2,577	1,629	948	3,454	2,008	1,446	4,431	2,289	2,142	3,037	2,156	881
Goalpara...	2,867	1,720	1,147	677	384	293	555	343	212	1,047	543	504	638	475	163
Kamrup	2,149	1,274	875	346	208	138	587	341	246	782	422	360	446	311	135
Darrang	2,155	1,387	768	693	523	170	569	338	231	486	274	212	419	262	157
Nowgong	1,431	867	564	203	124	79	577	339	233	360	173	187	302	237	65
Sibsagar	2,397	1,444	953	352	228	124	598	317	281	798	408	390	653	463	190
Lakhimpur	1,599	913	686	207	107	100	541	285	256	452	234	218	403	289	114
Garo Hills	807	424	383	99	53	44	27	15	12	506	235	271	177	120	57
SADIYA FRONTIER TRACT ...	317	188	129	24	11	13	219	128	91	57	34	23	17	15	2
BALIPARA FRONTIER TRACT ...	13	4	9	1	...	1	6	2	4	4		4	2	2	...
(2) Assam states ...	*1,546*	*860*	*686*	*389*	*209*	*180*	*198*	*125*	*73*	*704*	*358*	*346*	*256*	*168*	*88*
Manipur State	1,207	701	506	242	100	142	143	91	63	504	272	232	218	148	70
Khasi States	339	159	180	47	19	28	55	34	21	200	86	114	33	20	15

TABLE X.

OCCUPATION OR MEANS OF LIVELIHOOD.

This table consists of two parts—Part I gives the summary for the Province and Part II the details for districts.

Occupations have been divided into four main classes :—A.—Production of Raw Materials, B.—Preparation and Supply of Material Substances, C.—Public Administration and Liberal Arts and D.—Miscellaneous. These four main classes have been further subdivided into twelve sub-classes, 55 orders and 195 groups.

The groups which are blank for Assam have been omitted from the table. These, groups with their numbers are :—9—Cinchona, 10—Cocoanut, 14—Rubber, 20—Collectors of lac, 29—Gold, 30—Iron, 32—Manganese, 33—Tin and wolfram, 34—Other metallic minerals, 38—Mica, 41—Other non-metallic minerals, 48—Hair (horse-hair), 52—Furriers, 62—Workers in mints, 79—Manufacturers of opium, 80—Manufacturers of *ganja*, 101—Persons connected with aerodromes and aeroplanes, 155—Navy, and 156—Air Force.

TABLE X.—Occupation or Means of Livelihood.

ASSAM.

Total earners	...	...	...	... 3,098,590
,, working dependants	...	...	...	... 1,082,119
,, non-working dependants	...	...	...	... 5,067,148
,, population	...	...	...	... 9,247,857

Group Number.	Occupation.	Total following occupation.	As principal occupation.		As working dependants.		As subsidiary to other occupation.	
			Males.	Females.	Males.	Females.	Males.	Females.
1	2	3	4	5	6	7	8	9
	TOTAL OF ALL CLASSES.	4,738,642	2,534,693	563,897	429,249	652,870	457,697	100,236
	A.—PRODUCTION OF RAW MATERIALS ...	3,874,268	2,198,691	488,470	405,029	419,681	292,758	68,629
	I.—EXPLOITATION OF ANIMALS AND VEGETATION.	3,857,246	2,183,877	487,350	405,477	419,642	292,287	68,613
	1.—Pasture and Agriculture	3,772,014	2,147,885	485,257	400,164	418,690	251,660	68,348
	(a) Cultivation	2,920,828	1,735,634	193,397	293,308	398,493	194,480	55,516
1	Non-cultivating proprietors taking rent in money or kind	44,627	20,421	4,387	873	443	17,776	727
2	Estate Agents and Managers of owners ...	239	140	...	3	...	96	...
3	Estate Agents and Managers of Government	41	32	...	...	...	9	...
4	Rent collectors, clerks, etc.	4,167	2,812	19	98	11	1,209	18
5	Cultivating owners	1,307,219	995,810	99,304	33,856	80,701	68,496	29,022
6	Tenant cultivators	735,543	583,165	30,419	7,015	6,318	90,862	17,764
7	Agricultural labourers	92,462	54,176	5,149	6,980	8,001	13,417	4,739
7A	Helpers in Agricultural work	469,031	...	...	230,900	238,131	...	...
8	Cultivators of *jhum*, *taungya* and shifting areas.	267,499	129,048	54,119	13,583	64,888	2,615	3,246
	(b) Cultivation of special crops, fruit, etc. (Planters, Managers, clerks and labourers).	708,781	343,804	290,770	5,823	13,912	42,611	11,861
11	Coffee	43	7	9	4	9	13	1
12	*Ganja*	6	4	...	...	...	2	...
13	Pan-Vine	9,147	4,732	1,485	257	341	1,847	436
15	Tea	680,476	333,979	285,585	4,479	12,828	33,613	9,992
16	Market gardeners, flower and fruit growers ...	19,109	5,032	3,691	1,083	734	7,136	1,433
	(c) Forestry	7,860	2,728	214	413	184	4,214	107
17	Forest officers, rangers, guards, etc. ...	1,275	1,005	...	30	...	231	...
18	Wood cutters and charcoal burners ...	5,070	1,249	184	283	150	3,175	79
19	Collectors of forest produce	1,515	474	30	141	34	808	28
	(d) Stock raising	130,294	15,534	855	100,294	6,024	7,110	477
21	Cattle and buffalo breeders and keepers ...	129,711	15,388	849	100,049	5,951	7,060	414
22	Breeders of transport animals	17	15	...	...	...	2	...
23	Herdsmen, shepherds and breeders of other animals.	566	131	15	245	73	39	63
	(e) Raising of small animals and insects ...	4,251	185	31	326	77	3,245	387
24	Birds, bees, etc.	80	30	9	2	1	33	5
25	Silkworms	285	19	...	10	38	214	4
26	Lac cultivation	3,886	136	22	314	38	2,998	378
	2. Fishing and Hunting	85,232	35,992	2,083	5,313	952	40,627	265
27	Fishing and pearling	84,624	35,799	2,057	5,303	948	40,252	265
28	Hunting	608	193	26	10	4	376	...

Part I—Provincial Summary.

BRITISH TERRITORY.			ASSAM STATES.		
Total earners ...	...	... 2,900,365	Total earners ...	...	... 198,225
" working dependants	...	... 976,393	" working dependants	...	... 105,726
" non-working dependants	...	... 4,745,493	" non-working dependants	...	... 321,655
" population ...	...	... 8,622,251	" population ...	...	... 625,606

Total following occupation.	As principal occupation.		As working dependants.		As subsidiary to other occupation.		Total following occupation.	As principal occupation.		As working dependants.		As subsidiary to other occupation.	
	Males.	Females.	Males.	Females.	Males.	Females.		Males.	Females.	Males.	Females.	Males.	Females.
10	11	12	13	14	15	16	17	18	19	20	21	22	23
4,393,229	2,399,646	500,719	398,600	577,793	432,789	83,682	345,413	135,047	63,178	30,649	75,077	24,908	16,554
3,603,385	2,035,554	441,421	377,232	364,062	276,071	59,045	270,883	113,137	47,049	28,797	55,619	16,697	9,584
3,586,760	2,070,810	440,473	376,808	364,025	275,615	59,029	270,436	113,067	46,877	28,669	55,617	16,672	9,584
3,504,879	2,036,034	437,606	371,653	363,380	235,382	58,824	267,135	111,851	45,651	28,511	55,310	16,278	9,524
2,679,226	1,680,879	151,642	263,556	344,788	186,125	47,235	241,602	104,755	41,755	24,752	53,705	8,355	8,280
41,451	18,802	3,380	755	257	17,317	680	3,176	1,619	807	118	156	429	47
239	140	...	3	...	96	...	...	..	...	..	...	...	...
41	32	...	...	...	9	..	...	...	...	...	...	...	...
4,158	2,804	19	98	11	1,208	18	9	8	...	...	...	1	...
1,171,495	926,647	70,541	22,371	19,130	65,573	26,733	135,724	69,393	28,763	11,485	21,271	3,623	3,280
710,565	571,796	24,858	5,172	2,934	89,948	15,857	24,978	11,363	5,561	1,843	3,384	914	1,907
80,284	62,137	3,094	6,773	7,292	9,710	1,278	12,178	2,039	2,056	207	709	3,707	3,461
456,436	...	...	226,438	229,998	...	...	12,595	...	...	4,462	8,133	...	...
214,557	108,631	49,550	6,946	44,836	1,934	2,670	52,912	20,427	4,569	6,637	20,052	681	576
690,958	338,821	287,253	4,668	13,202	36,105	10,909	17,823	4,983	3,517	1,155	710	6,506	952
9	1	2	1	...	5	...	34	6	7	3	9	8	1
6	4	...	...	...	2	...	...	...	...	...	...	...	...
4,993	2,522	915	72	133	1,186	165	4,154	2,260	570	185	208	661	270
680,476	333,979	285,585	4,479	12,828	33,613	9,992	...	...	..	...	...	...	...
5,474	2,315	761	116	241	1,299	732	13,635	2,717	2,940	967	493	6,537	681
6,799	2,593	102	253	100	3,667	84	1,051	125	112	160	84	547	23
1,274	1,004	...	39	...	231	...	1	1	...	...	...	...	...
4,059	1,126	72	89	66	2,689	56	1,011	123	112	153	84	616	23
1,466	463	30	134	34	777	28	49	11	...	7	...	31	...
124,310	13,573	581	97,850	5,213	6,815	273	5,984	1,961	274	2,444	811	295	199
123,989	13,464	570	97,684	5,197	6,796	278	5,722	1,924	270	2,365	754	273	136
17	15	...	...	...	2	...	...	...	...	...	...	...	...
304	94	11	166	16	17	...	262	37	4	79	57	22	63
3,586	168	28	326	77	2,670	317	665	17	3	...	...	575	70
65	20	9	2	1	28	5	15	10	...	...	...	5	...
285	19	...	10	38	214	4	...	...	...	...	...	...	...
3,236	129	19	314	33	2,428	308	650	7	3	...	...	570	70
81,881	34,776	867	5,155	645	40,233	205	3,351	1,216	1,216	158	307	394	60
81,278	34,584	841	5,145	641	39,862	205	3,346	1,215	1,216	158	307	390	60
603	192	26	10	4	371	...	5	1	...	...	...	4	...

TABLE X.—Occupation or Means of Livelihood.

Group Number.	Occupation.	Total following occupation.	ASSAM. As principal occupation. Males.	Females.	As working dependants. Males.	Females.	As subsidiary to other occupation Males.	Females.
1	2	3	4	5	6	7	8	9
	II.—EXPLOITATION OF MINERALS ...	17,022	14,814	1,120	552	39	481	16
	3. Metallic Minerals	4	1	...	...	...	3	...
31	Lead, silver and zinc	4	1	...	...	...	3	...
	4. Non-Metallic Minerals	17,018	14,813	1,120	552	39	478	16
35	Coal	7,464	6,376	681	237	31	135	4
36	Petroleum	9,165	8,377	264	187	4	321	12
37	Building materials (including stone, materials for cement-manufacture and clays).	46	34	...	4	...	8	...
39	Precious and semi-precious stones ...	12	...	3	...	2	7	...
40	Salt, saltpetre and other saline substances ...	331	26	172	124	2	7	...
	B.—PREPARATION AND SUPPLY OF MATERIAL SUBSTANCES.	653,030	212,805	47,578	13,096	226,192	125,143	28,216
	III.—INDUSTRY	390,957	71,240	27,462	6,418	218,829	43,702	23,306
	5. Textiles	255,144	2,169	15,620	1,993	211,792	2,831	20,739
42	Cotton ginning, cleaning and pressing ...	361	176	169	...	...	10	6
43	Cotton spinning, seizing and weaving ...	248,169	1,236	13,770	1,812	208,716	2,252	20,383
44	Jute pressing, spinning and weaving ...	763	501	88	6	48	111	9
45	Rope, twine, string and other fibres ...	3,424	125	758	72	1,922	337	210
46	Wool carding, spinning and weaving ...	2	1	...	...	1	...	...
47	Silk spinning and weaving	1,476	101	176	103	941	120	35
49	Dyeing, bleaching, printing, preparation and sponging of textiles.	21	20	...	...	...	1	...
50	Lace, crepe, embroideries, fringes, etc., and insufficiently described textile industries.	928	9	659	...	164	...	96
	6. Hides, skins and hard materials from the animal kingdom.	1,066	695	17	55	13	280	6
51	Working in leather	1,028	666	17	54	13	276	2
53	Bone, ivory, horn, shell, etc., workers (except buttons).	37	29	...	1	...	4	3
	7. Wood	52,573	24,418	1,712	1,901	1,914	21,858	770
54	Sawyers	11,382	6,285	360	195	24	4,511	7
55	Carpenters, turners and joiners, etc. ...	20,045	12,332	65	657	40	6,939	12
56	Basket makers and other industries of woody materials, including leaves and thatchers and builders working with bamboo, reeds or similar materials.	21,146	5,801	1,287	1,049	1,850	10,408	751
	8. Metals	8,123	5,330	78	227	67	2,413	8
57	Smelting, forging and rolling of iron and other metals.	14	6	...	...	...	8	...
58	Makers of arms, guns, etc.	32	22	...	2	...	8	...
59	Blacksmiths, other workers in iron, makers of implements.	5,547	3,426	53	171	17	1,877	3
60	Workers in brass, copper and bell metal ...	2,279	1,663	25	48	50	488	5
61	Workers in other metals (except precious metals)	251	213	...	6	...	32	...

PART I—PROVINCIAL SUMMARY—*contd.*

BRITISH TERRITORY.							ASSAM STATES.						
Total following occupation.	As principal occupation.		As working dependants.		As subsidiary to other occupation.		Total following occupation.	As principal occupation.		As working dependants.		As subsidiary to other occupation.	
	Males.	Females.	Males.	Females.	Males.	Females.		Males.	Females.	Males.	Females.	Males.	Females.
10	11	12	13	14	15	16	17	18	19	20	21	22	23
16,625	14,744	948	424	37	456	16	397	70	172	128	2	25	...
4	1	...	...	...	3	...	...	...	...	...	...	...	...
4	1	...	...	...	3	...	...	...	...	...	...	...	...
16,621	14,743	948	424	37	453	16	397	70	172	128	2	25	...
7,43[illegible]	6,363	621	237	31	120	4	28	13	...	...	...	15	...
9,165	8,377	284	187	4	321	12	...	..	...	...	...	...	...
...	...	...	...	...	...	...	46	34	...	4	...	8	...
12	...	3	...	2	7	...	...	...	...	...	...	...	...
8	3	...	...	...	5	...	323	23	172	134	2	2	...
596,240	201,344	33,876	12,023	207,266	119,387	22,339	56,790	11,461	13,702	1,068	18,926	5,756	5,877
354,646	65,790	19,458	5,872	201,360	42,512	19,654	35,311	5 450	8,004	546	17,469	1,150	3,652
227,954	2,023	8,760	1,849	194,957	2,777	17,538	27,190	146	6,860	144	16,835	54	3,151
361	176	169	...	...	10	6	...	...	...	...	...	...	...
221,941	1,104	7,580	1,672	192,086	2,201	17,348	26 228	132	6,190	140	16,680	51	3,035
763	501	88	6	48	111	9	...	...	...	...	...	...	...
3,374	116	748	68	1,915	334	193	50	9	10	4	7	3	17
2	1	...	...	1	...	...	...	...	...	...	...	...	...
1,456	101	103	103	937	120	32	20	...	13	...	4	...	3
29	19	...	...	...	1	...	1	1	...	...	...	...	...
37	5	12	...	20	...	...	891	4	647	...	144	...	96
1,056	693	17	54	13	274	5	9	2	...	1	...	6	...
1,019	661	17	53	13	270	2	9	2	...	1	...	6	...
37	29	...	1	...	4	3	...	...	...	...	...	...	...
48,939	22,196	1,609	1,714	1,843	21,098	479	3,634	2,222	301	187	71	760	291
11,313	6,172	360	195	24	4,455	7	169	113	...	...	...	56	...
17,759	10,469	61	562	28	6,619	10	2,286	1,863	4	95	2	320	2
19,967	5,555	1,188	957	1,781	10,024	462	1,179	246	99	92	69	384	289
7,718	5,057	33	198	61	2,364	5	405	273	45	29	6	49	3
14	6	...	...	...	8	...	...	...	...	...	...	...	...
32	22	...	2	...	8	...	...	...	...	...	...	.	.
5,165	3,164	15	144	11	1,831	...	382	262	38	27	6	46	3
2,259	1,655	18	46	50	485	5	20	8	7	2	...	3	...
248	210	...	6	...	32	...	3	3	...	...	...	...	...

TABLE X.—Occupation or means of livelihood.

Group Number.	Occupation.	ASSAM. Total following occupation.	As principal occupation. Males.	As principal occupation. Females.	As working dependants. Males.	As working dependants. Females.	As subsidiary to other occupation. Males.	As subsidiary to other occupation. Females.
1	2	3	4	5	6	7	8	9
	9.—Ceramics	11,590	3 867	1,438	381	2,875	2,836	192
63	Potters and makers of earthenware ...	8,669	2,076	1,322	314	2,855	1,917	185
64	Brick and tile makers	2,361	1,524	84	29	13	707	4
65	Other workers in ceramics	560	267	32	38	8	213	3
	10.—Chemical products properly so-called and analogous.	1,836	967	45	33	27	751	13
66	Manufacture of matches, fireworks and other explosives.	263	236	...	6	...	21	...
67	Manufacture of aerated and mineral waters and ice.	27	21	...	...	...	6	...
68	Manufacture and refining of vegetable oils ...	1,492	670	38	27	25	723	9
70	Others	54	40	7	...	2	1	4
	11.—Food Industries	13,517	3,585	6,411	222	1,430	673	1,196
71	Rice pounders and huskers and flour grinders	7,304	394	4,897	106	923	61	923
72	Grain parchers, etc.	1,883	357	850	13	374	108	181
73	Butchers	333	205	...	1	...	117	...
74	Makers of sugar, molasses and gur ...	127	49	5	1	3	57	12
75	Sweetmeat and condiment makers ...	2,254	1,803	129	46	33	233	10
76	Toddy drawers	20	20	...	...	...	...	...
77	Brewers and distillers	746	99	480	9	84	13	61
78	Manufacturers of tobacco	15	9	3	...	1	2	...
81	Others	845	649	47	46	12	82	9
	12.—Industries of dress and the toilet ...	23.747	14,482	1 245	862	591	6,227	340
82	Boot, shoe, sandal and clog makers ...	1,716	1,168	47	58	17	422	4
83	Tailors, milliners, dressmakers and darners ...	9,823	6,631	622	409	410	1,536	225
84	Embroiderers, hat makers and makers of other articles of wear.	540	293	83	7	36	83	38
85	Washing and cleaning	3,978	1,983	483	102	111	1,328	71
86	Barbers, hair dressers and wig makers ...	7,63 9	4,380	10	286	5	2,956	2
87	Other industries connected with the toilet ...	51	37	...	...	12	2	...
	13.—Furniture Industries	190	124	31	1	7	13	14
88	Cabinet makers, carriage painters, etc. ...	57	45	2	1	...	9	...
89	Upholsterers, tent makers, etc.	133	79	29	...	7	4	14
	14.—Building Industries	6,582	4,902	125	98	21	1,431	5
90	Lime burners, cement workers; Excavators and well sinkers; Stone cutters and dressers; Brick layers and masons; builders (other than buildings made of bamboo or similar materials), painters, decorators of houses, tilers, plumbers, etc.	6,582	4,902	125	98	21	1,431	5
	15.—Construction of means of transport	2,108	956	1	78	1	1,068	4
91	Persons engaged in making, assembling or repairing motor vehicles or cycles.	623	555	...	13	...	55	...
92	Carriage, cart, palki, etc., makers and wheel wrights.	280	220	1	7	...	52	...
93	Ship, boat, aeroplane builders	1,205	181	...	58	1	961	4

PART I—PROVINCIAL SUMMARY—*contd*

BRITISH TERRITORY.							ASSAM STATES						
Total following occupation.	As principal occupation.		As working dependants.		As subsidiary to other occupation.		Total following occupation.	As principal occupation.		As working dependants.		As subsidiary to other occupation.	
	Males.	Females.	Males.	Females.	Males.	Females.		Males.	Females.	Males.	Females.	Males.	Females.
10	11	12	13	14	15	16	17	18	19	20	21	22	23
10,864	3,627	1 273	377	2,582	2,820	180	726	24[illegible]	160	4	2[illegible]4	16	12
8,121	2,000	1,162	314	2,561	1,911	173	548	76	160	...	294	6	12
2,231	1,397	84	29	18	704	4	130	127	...	...	...	3	...
512	2[illegible]0	32	24	8	205	3	48	37	...	4	...	7	...
1,803	943	3[illegible]	33	25	751	11	33	24	6	..	1	...	2
268	236	...	6	...	21	...	...	...	...	...	...	...	...
25	19	...	...	...	6	...	2	2	...	...	...	...	...
1,490	668	88	27	25	723	9	2	2	...	..	...	...	...
25	20	1	...	1	1	2	29	20	6	...	1	...	2
12,619	3,375	5,988	211	1,314	592	1,139	898	210	423	11	116	81	57
7,194	394	4,826	105	889	61	919	110	...	71	1	34	...	4
1,860	354	8[illegible]0	13	374	108	181	3	3	...	...	...	...	...
207	157	...	1	...	49	...	116	48	...	...	...	68	...
84	6	5	1	3	57	12	43	43	...	...	...	...	...
2,254	1,803	129	46	33	233	10	...	...	...	...	...	...	...
20	20	...	...	...	...	...	...	...	...	...	...	...	...
187	13	150	...	4	4	16	559	86	330	9	80	9	45
15	9	3	...	1	2	...	..	...	...	...	...	...	...
778	619	25	45	10	78	1	67	30	22	1	2	4	8
22,124	13,569	930	770	489	6,146	220	1,623	913	315	92	102	81	120
1,646	1,111	40	54	17	420	4	70	57	7	4	...	2	...
8,438	5,918	318	323	321	1,459	106	1,385	708	304	87	89	77	120
520	273	83	7	36	83	38	20	20	...	...	...	...	...
3,928	1,[illegible]39	479	101	110	1,228	71	50	44	4	1	1	...	...
7,574	4,316	10	286	5	2,958	2	65	64	...	...	...	1	...
18	17	...	...	...	1	...	33	20	...	...	12	1	...
140	124	2	1	...	13	...	50	...	29	...	7	...	14
57	45	2	1	...	9	...	...	...	...	...	...	...	...
83	79	...	...	...	4	...	50	...	29	...	7	...	14
6,055	4 474	124	87	21	1,344	5	527	428	1	11	...	87	...
6,055	4,474	124	87	21	1,344	5	527	428	1	11	...	87	...
2,029	905	..	75	1	1,043	4	79	50	1	3	...	25	...
601	533	...	13	...	55	...	22	22	...	...	...	...	...
252	201	...	4	...	47	...	28	19	1	3	...	5	...
1,176	172	...	58	1	941	4	29	9	...	...	...	20	...

TABLE X.—Occupation or means of livelihood.

Group Number.	Occupation.	ASSAM. Total following occupation.	As principal occupation. Males.	As principal occupation. Females.	As working dependants. Males.	As working dependants. Females.	As subsidiary to other occupation. Males.	As subsidiary to other occupation. Females.
1	2	3	4	5	6	7	8	9
	16.—Production and transmission of physical force	213	202	...	2	...	9	...
94	Heat, light, electricity, motive power, etc., gas works and electric light and power.	213	202	...	2	...	9	...
	17.—Miscellaneous and undefined industries ...	14,269	9,543	739	565	90	3,312	20
95	Printers, engravers, book binders, etc. ...	614	532	5	17	...	60	...
96	Makers of musical instruments	157	97	2	5	...	53	...
97	Makers of clocks and surgical or scientific instruments, etc.	141	102	...	4	...	35	...
98	Makers of jewellery and ornaments ...	9,829	6,492	81	507	45	2,695	9
99	Other miscellaneous and undefined industries (toy making, taxidermy, etc.).	326	131	17	14	7	157	...
100	Scavenging	3,202	2,189	634	18	38	312	11
	IV.—TRANSPORT	82,072	50,379	2,549	1,711	335	26,243	855
	19.—Transport by water	20,046	12,287	11	645	4	7,084	15
102	Ship-owners, boat-owners and their employees, officers, mariners, etc. Ships brokers, boatmen and tow men.	19,668	11,917	11	645	4	7,076	15
103	Persons (other than labourers) employed in harbours, docks, rivers and canals, including pilots.	117	112	...	...	...	5	...
104	Labourers employed on harbours, docks, rivers and canals.	261	258	...	...	...	3	...
	20.—Transport by road	45,871	24,153	1,919	928	299	17,735	837
105	Persons (other than labourers) employed on the construction and maintenance of roads and bridges.	1,260	996	5	13	...	246	...
106	Labourers employed on roads and bridges ...	25,634	13,325	1,617	376	206	9,733	377
107	Owners, managers and employees (including personal servants) connected with mechanically driven vehicles (including trams).	2,419	2,213	...	45	...	160	1
108	Owners, managers and employees (excluding personal servants) connected with other vehicles.	13,288	6,479	282	421	89	5,765	252
109	Palki, etc., bearers and owners	2,780	769	13	63	8	1,725	207
110	Pack elephant, camel, mule, ass and bullock, owners and drivers.	184	109	...	6	...	69	...
111	Porters and messengers	306	262	2	4	1	37	...
	21.—Transport by rail	13,251	11,442	619	91	31	1,066	2
112	Railway employees of all kinds other than coolies.	6,356	5,900	12	69	...	475	...
113	Labourers employed on railway construction and maintenance and coolies and porters employed on railway premises.	6,895	5,642	607	22	31	591	2
	22.—Post office, telegraph and telephone services	2,904	2,477	...	47	1	358	1
114	Post office, telegraph and telephone services ...	2,904	2,497	...	47	1	358	1
	V.—TRADE	180,001	91,186	17,567	4,967	7,028	55,198	4,055
	23.—Banks, establishments of credit exchange and insurance.	4,519	2,219	309	64	19	1,805	103
115	Bank managers, money lenders, exchange and insurance agents, money changers and brokers and their employees.	4,519	2,219	309	64	19	1,805	103

Part I—Provincial Summary—*contd.*

BRITISH TERRITORY.							ASSAM STATES.						
Total following occupation.	As principal occupation.		As working dependants.		As subsidiary to other occupation.		Total following occupation.	As principal occupation.		As working dependants.		As subsidiary to other occupation.	
	Males.	Females.	Males.	Females.	Males.	Females.		Males.	Females.	Males.	Females.	Males.	Females.
10	11	12	13	14	15	16	17	18	19	20	21	22	23
203	192	...	2	...	9	...	10	10	...	...	...	...	...
203	192	...	2	..	9	...	10	10	...	...	...	...	...
13,142	8,611	678	501	53	3,281	18	1,127	932	61	64	37	31	2
459	379	3	17	...	60	...	155	153	2	...	...	...	...
148	91	2	4	...	51	...	9	6	...	1	...	2	...
126	91	...	1	...	34	...	15	11	...	3	...	1	...
9,132	5,960	28	452	9	2,676	7	697	532	63	55	36	19	2
313	125	17	9	7	154	...	14	6	...	5	...	3	...
2,965	1,965	628	18	37	306	11	237	224	6	...	1	6	...
77,245	47,865	2,159	1,497	225	24,987	12	4,827	2,514	390	214	110	1,256	343
19,829	12,247	11	644	4	6,908	15	217	40	...	1	...	176	...
19,451	11,877	11	644	4	6,900	15	217	40	...	1	...	176	...
117	112	...	...	...	5	...	...	...	...	...	...	...	...
261	258	...	...	...	3	...	...	...	...	...	...	...	...
41,367	21,782	1,529	715	190	16,657	494	4,504	2,371	390	213	109	1,078	343
1,096	840	4	6	...	246	...	164	156	1	7	...	...	...
23,260	12,338	1,304	237	126	9,104	251	2,374	1,087	313	139	80	629	126
1,967	1,789	...	25	—	152	1	453	424	...	20	...	8	...
12,171	5,904	219	378	63	5,365	242	1,117	575	63	43	26	400	10
2,432	679	...	69	...	1,684	...	358	90	13	4	3	41	207
164	89	...	6	...	69	...	20	20	...	...	...	...	...
287	243	2	4	1	37	...	19	19	...	...	...	...	...
13,251	11,442	619	91	31	1,066	2	...	...	...	...	...	...	...
6,356	5,900	12	69	...	475	...	...	...	...	...	...	...	...
6,895	5,642	607	22	31	591	2	...	...	...	...	...	...	...
2,738	2,334	...	47	...	356	1	105	103	...	...	1	2	...
2,798	2,391	...	47	...	356	1	106	103	...	...	1	2	...
164,349	87,689	12,259	4,659	5,681	51,838	2,173	15,652	3,497	5,308	308	1,347	3,310	1,882
4,377	2,155	287	63	16	1,789	87	122	64	22	1	3	16	16
4,397	2,155	287	63	16	1,789	87	122	64	22	1	3	16	16

TABLE X.—Occupation or means of Livelihood.

Occup. Number.	Occupation.	ASSAM. Total following occupation	As principal occupation. Males.	As principal occupation. Females.	As working dependants. Males.	As working dependants. Females.	As subsidiary to other occupation. Males.	As subsidiary to other occupation. Females.
1	2	3	4	5	6	7	8	9
	24.—Brokerage commission and export ...	240	143	4	7	...	84	2
116	Brokers, commission agents, commercial travellers, warehouse owners and employees.	240	143	4	7	...	84	2
	25.—Trade in textiles	8,089	4,097	1,499	202	274	1,867	150
117	Trade in piece-goods, wool, cotton, silk, hair and other textiles.	8,089	4,097	1,499	302	274	1,867	150
	26.—Trade in skins, leather and furs ...	2,800	1,693	23	107	33	925	19
118	Trade in skins, leather, furs, feathers, horn, etc., and the articles made from these.	2,800	1,693	23	107	33	925	19
	27.—Trade in Wood	10,110	2,660	93	241	14	7,050	52
119	Trade in wood (not firewood)	2,680	1,345	28	61	4	1,229	13
120	Trade in barks	9	7	...	...	...	2	...
121	Trade in bamboos and canes	5,178	779	60	139	10	4,155	35
122	Trade in thatches and other forest produce ...	2,243	539	5	41	...	1,664	4
	28.—Trade in metals	792	566	20	10	2	188	6
123	Trade in metals, machinery, knives, tools, etc.	792	666	20	10	2	188	6
	29.—Trade in pottery, bricks and tiles ...	338	174	18	1	8	133	4
124	Trade in pottery, bricks and tiles ...	338	174	18	1	8	133	4
	30.—Trade in chemical products	1,139	603	53	38	7	424	14
125	Drugs, dyes, paints, petroleum, explosives, etc.	1,139	603	53	38	7	424	14
	31.—Hotels, cafes, restaurants, etc. ...	2,586	1,720	381	30	106	258	91
126	Vendors of wine, liquors, aerated waters and ice	688	341	237	9	37	53	11
127	Owners and Managers of hotels, cookshops, serais, etc. (and employees).	1,746	1,302	129	21	64	155	75
128	Hawkers of drink and foodstuffs ...	152	77	15	...	5	50	5
	32.—Other trade in foodstuffs	108,188	52,175	12,504	[illegible],029	5,551	32,258	2,671
129	Grain and pulse dealers	21,467	9,169	4,018	304	1,153	6,100	723
130	Dealers in sweetmeats, sugar and spices ...	5,826	2,708	456	259	116	1,877	410
131	Dealers in dairy products, eggs and poultry ...	7,579	3,967	328	167	72	3,055	90
132	Dealers in animals for food	248	73	36	4	17	114	5
133	Dealers in fodder for animals	151	80	16	5	13	26	11
134	Dealers in other foodstuffs	70,461	34,671	7,6[illegible]	3,211	4,113	20,475	1,385
135	Dealers in tobacco	1,748	947	143	66	67	478	47
136	Dealers in opium	487	380	...	12	...	95	...
137	Dealers in *ganja*	221	181	1	1	...	38	...
	33.—Trade in clothing and toilet articles ...	8,361	6,712	537	202	91	708	111
138	Trade in ready-made clothing and other articles of dress and the toilet (hats, umbrellas, socks, ready-made shoes, perfumes, etc.).	8,361	6,712	537	202	91	708	111
	34.—Trade in furniture	4,882	2,399	434	129	302	1,435	183
139	Trade in furniture, carpets, curtains and beddings.	666	281	56	24	21	187	97
140	Hardware, cooking utensils, porcelain, crockery, glassware, bottles, articles for gardening, etc.	4,216	2,118	373	105	281	1,248	86

Part I—Provincial Summary—*contd.*

BRITISH TERRITORY.							ASSAM STATES.						
Total following occupation.	As principal occupation.		As working dependants.		As subsidiary to other occupation.		Total following occupation.	As principal occupation.		As working dependants.		As subsidiary to other occupation.	
	Males.	Females.	Males.	Females.	Males.	Females.		Males.	Females.	Males.	Females.	Males.	Females.
10	11	12	13	14	15	16	17	18	19	20	21	22	23
237	141	4	7	...	83	2	3	2	...	...	...	1	...
237	141	4	7	...	83	2	3	2	...	...	...	1	...
5,428	3,296	199	149	17	1,750	17	2,661	801	1,300	53	257	117	133
5,428	3,296	199	119	17	1,750	17	2,661	801	1,300	53	257	117	133
2,793	1,690	21	107	33	925	17	7	3	2	...	...	...	2
2,793	1,690	21	107	33	925	17	7	3	2	...	...	...	2
9,806	2,553	85	238	13	6,871	46	304	107	8	3	1	179	6
2,468	1,259	25	58	4	,1110	12	212	86	8	3	...	119	1
9	7	...	...	...	2	...	...	...	...	...	...	...	...
5,086	758	55	132	9	4,095	30	92	21	5	...	1	60	5
2,243	539	5	41	...	1,664	4	...	...	...	...	...	...	...
773	564	19	10	1	175	4	19	2	1	...	1	13	2
773	564	19	10	1	175	4	19	2	1	...	1	13	2
318	155	18	...	8	133	4	20	19	...	1	...	...	...
318	155	18	...	8	133	4	20	19	...	1	...	...	...
910	568	50	34	6	238	14	229	35	3	4	1	186	...
910	568	50	34	6	238	14	229	35	3	4	1	186	...
2,248	1,694	184	26	61	252	31	338	26	197	4	45	6	60
459	323	76	5	1	49	5	229	18	161	4	36	4	6
1,642	1,294	96	21	57	153	21	104	8	33	...	7	2	54
147	77	12	..	3	50	5	5	...	3	...	2	...	...
99,035	50,681	9,309	2,858	4,649	29,966	1,572	9,153	1,494	3,195	171	902	2,292	1,039
19,755	8,758	3,194	291	895	5,971	646	1,712	411	824	13	258	129	77
4,329	2,474	267	174	36	1,300	78	1,407	234	189	85	80	577	233
7,288	3,867	195	157	53	2,915	71	291	100	33	10	19	110	19
165	54	1	3	4	102	1	83	18	35	1	13	12	4
118	75	12	4	6	10	11	33	5	4	1	7	16	...
65,122	33,979	5,583	2,155	3,609	19,039	757	5,339	692	2,023	56	504	1,436	628
1,562	915	56	61	46	466	8	196	32	87	5	21	12	39
485	378	...	12	...	95	...	2	2	...	...	...	...	...
221	181	1	1	...	38	...	...	...	...	...	...	...	...
8,063	6,660	411	200	70	694	28	298	52	126	2	21	14	83
8,063	6,660	411	200	70	694	28	298	52	126	2	21	14	83
4,642	2,323	371	124	290	1,429	105	240	76	63	5	12	6	78
548	280	19	24	18	186	21	118	1	37	...	3	1	76
4,094	2,043	352	100	272	1,243	84	122	75	26	5	9	5	2

TABLE X.—Occupation or means of livelihood.

Group Number.	Occupation.	ASSAM. Total following occupation.	As principal occupation. Males.	As principal occupation. Females.	As working dependants. Males.	As working dependants. Females.	As subsidiary to other occupation. Males.	As subsidiary to other occupation. Females.
1	2	3	4	5	6	7	8	9
	35.—Trade in building materials	714	399	10	18	11	275	...
141	Trade in building materials (other than bricks, tiles and woody materials).	714	399	10	18	11	276	...
	36.—Trade in means of transport	2,725	1,136	88	30	5	1,453	13
142	Dealers and hirers, in mechanical transport, motors, cycles, etc.	92	86	1	...	...	5	...
143	Dealers and hirers in other carriages, carts, boats, etc.	968	373	1	10	1	580	3
144	Dealers and hirers of elephants, camels, horses, cattle, asses, mules, etc.	1,665	677	86	20	4	868	10
	37.—Trade in fuel	4,623	1,142	521	141	356	1,977	486
145	Dealers in firewood, charcoal, coal, cowdung, etc.	4,623	1,142	521	141	356	1,977	486
	38.—Trade in articles of luxury and those pertaining to letters and the art and sciences.	9,166	6,317	555	250	116	1,891	37
146	Dealers in precious stones, jewellery (real and imitation), clocks, optical instruments, etc.	373	236	17	20	...	96	4
147	Dealers in common bangles, bead necklaces, fans, small articles, toys, hunting and fishing tackle, flowers, etc.	3,700	2,909	302	59	83	349	7
148	Publishers, book sellers, stationers, dealers in music, pictures, musical instruments and curiosities.	5,084	3,172	236	171	33	1,446	26
	39.—Trade of other sorts	10,729	7,031	518	463	133	2,466	113
149	Dealers in rags, stable refuse, etc. ...	1	...	...	...	...	1	...
150	General storekeepers and shopkeepers otherwise unspecified.	9,857	6,505	488	439	137	2,187	111
151	Itinerant traders, pedlars and hawkers (of other than food, etc.).	43	16	19	...	5	2	1
152	Other trades (including farmers of pound, tolls and markets).	828	610	11	29	1	276	1
	C.—PUBLIC ADMINISTRATION AND LIBERAL ARTS.	87,011	59,319	2,502	2,682	420	21,818	270
	VI.—PUBLIC FORCE	14,344	10,940	...	155	...	3,248	1
	40.—Army	1,932	1,932	...	...	...	...	...
153	Army (Imperial)	1,836	1,836	...	...	...	...	...
154	Army (Indian States)	96	96	...	...	...	...	...
	43.—Police	12,412	9,008	...	155	...	3,248	1
157	Police	7,647	7,566	...	9	...	73	...
158	Village watchmen	4,765	1,442	...	146	...	3,176	1
	VII.—PUBLIC ADMINISTRATION ...	14,283	10,467	120	130	2	3,562	2
	44.—Public Administration	14,283	10,467	120	130	2	3,562	2
159	Service of the state	8,385	7,541	11	37	2	794	...
160	Service of Indian and foreign states ...	714	667	18	1	...	28	...
161	Municipal and other local (not village) service	1,119	864	85	5	...	164	1
162	Village officials and servants other than watchmen.	4,065	1,395	6	87	...	2,576	1

PART I—PROVINCIAL SUMMARY—*contd.*

BRITISH TERRITORY.							ASSAM STATES.						
Total following occupation.	As principal occupation.		As working dependants.		As subsidiary to other occupation.		Total following occupation.	As principal occupation.		As working dependants.		As subsidiary to other occupation.	
	Males.	Females.	Males.	Females.	Males.	Females.		Males.	Females.	Males	Females.	Males.	Females.
10	11	12	13	14	15	16	17	18	19	20	21	22	23
688	385	9	18	11	265	...	26	14	1	...	...	11	...
688	385	9	18	11	265	...	26	14	1	...	...	11	...
2,461	998	84	27	5	1,334	13	264	138	4	3	...	119	...
86	81	1	...	...	4	...	6	5	...	...	...	1	...
947	355	1	10	1	577	3	21	18	...	...	...	3	...
1,428	562	82	17	4	753	10	237	115	4	3	...	115	...
3,698	1,047	425	122	289	1,701	114	925	95	96	19	67	276	372
3,698	1,047	425	122	289	1,701	114	925	95	96	19	67	276	372
8,762	6,088	467	220	103	1,852	32	404	229	88	30	13	39	5
365	236	11	20	...	96	2	8	...	6	...	...	...	2
3,394	2,862	281	44	80	320	7	115	47	21	15	3	29	...
4,803	2,990	175	156	23	1,436	23	281	182	61	15	10	10	3
10,090	6,691	316	456	109	2,431	87	639	340	202	12	24	35	26
1	...	...	...	...	1	...	...	...	...	...	...	...	...
9,219	6,165	286	427	103	2,153	85	638	340	202	12	24	34	26
43	16	19	...	5	2	1	...	...	...	...	...	...	...
827	510	11	29	1	275	1	1	...	...	...	...	1	...
80,354	54,011	2,233	2,313	349	21,204	244	6,657	5,308	269	369	71	614	25
13,241	9,863	...	152	...	3,225	1	1,103	1,077	...	3	...	23	...
1,836	1,836	...	...	...	...	...	96	96	...	...	...	...	...
1,836	1,836	...	...	...	...	...	...	...	...	...	...	...	...
...	...	...	...	...	...	...	96	96	...	...	...	...	...
11,405	8,027	...	152	...	3,225	1	1,007	981	...	3	...	23	...
6,752	6,672	...	8	...	72	...	895	894	...	1	...	...	...
4,653	1,356	...	144	...	3,153	1	112	87	...	2	...	23	...
12,778	9,034	101	128	2	3,511	2	1,505	1,433	19	2	...	51	...
12,778	9,034	101	128	2	3,511	2	1,505	1,433	19	2	...	51	...
7,662	6,824	11	37	2	788	...	723	717	...	...	...	6	...
2	2	...	...	...	...	...	712	665	18	1	...	28	...
1,093	841	84	5	...	163	1	26	23	1	...	...	2	...
4,021	1,367	6	86	...	2,561	1	44	28	...	1	...	15	...

TABLE X.—Occupation or means of Livelihood.

Group Number.	Occupation.	Total following occupation.	As principal occupation.		As working dependants.		As subsidiary to other occupation.	
			Males.	Females.	Males.	Females.	Males.	Females.
1	2	3	4	5	6	7	8	9
	VIII.—PROFESSIONS AND LIBERAL ARTS	58,384	37,912	2,382	2,397	418	15,008	267
	45.—Religion	25,383	15,827	804	1,630	167	6,842	113
163	Priests, ministers, etc.	19,462	12,245	322	1,359	48	5,451	37
164	Monks, nuns, religious mendicants ...	1,230	568	314	57	52	216	23
165	Other religious workers	3,548	2,294	143	159	46	855	51
166	Servants in religious edifices, burial and burning grounds, pilgrim conductors, circumcisers, etc.	1,143	720	25	55	21	320	2
	46.—Law	3,314	2,649	...	49	...	616	...
167	Lawyers of all kinds including Qazis, Law Agents and Mukhtiars.	1,096	1,006	...	...	...	90	...
168	Lawyers' clerks, petition-writers, etc. ..	2,218	1,643	...	49	...	526	...
	47.—Medicine	9,839	6,402	653	156	173	2,441	74
169	Registered medical practitioners including oculists.	2,033	1,776	23	14	...	218	2
170	Other persons practising the healing arts without being registered.	5,689	3,209	149	133	53	2,113	32
171	Dentists	12	11	1	...	...	...	...
172	Midwives, vaccinators, compounders, nurses, masseurs, etc.	2,043	1,298	480	8	120	97	40
173	Veterinary surgeons	122	108	...	1	...	13	...
	48.—Instruction	14,176	10,056	799	260	50	2,951	60
174	Professors and teachers of all kinds ...	13,515	9,579	685	257	40	2,901	53
175	Clerks and servants connected with education	661	477	114	3	10	50	7
	49.—Letters, arts and sciences (other than 44)...	5,612	2,978	126	302	28	2,158	20
176	Public scribes, stenographers, etc. ...	15	15	...	...	...	...	...
177	Architects, surveyors, engineers and their employees (not being State servants).	401	355	1	2	...	43	...
178	Authors, editors, journalists and photographers	155	103	...	1	...	51	...
179	Artists, sculptors and image makers ...	141	109	1	10	...	20	1
180	Scientists (astronomers, botanists, etc.) ...	59	45	...	...	...	14	...
181	Horoscope casters, astrologers, fortune-tellers, wizards, witches and mediums.	586	355	2	27	3	198	1
182	Musicians (composers and performers other than military), actors, dancers, etc.	3,666	1,560	77	269	12	1,746	12
183	Managers and employees of places of public entertainments, race courses, societies, clubs.	194	150	...	3	...	41	...
184	Conjurors, acrobats, recitors, exhibitors of curiosities and wild animals, etc.	395	286	45	...	13	45	6
	D.—MISCELLANEOUS	124,333	63,878	25,347	7,442	6,577	17,968	3,121
	IX.—PERSONS LIVING ON THEIR INCOME.	2,254	1,311	171	45	45	669	13
	50.—Persons living principally on their income	2,254	1,311	171	45	45	669	13
185	Proprietors (other than of agricultural land), fund and scholarship holders and pensioners.	2,254	1,311	171	45	45	669	13
	X.—DOMESTIC SERVICE	36,332	24,161	3,604	2,358	3,614	2,293	302
	51.—Domestic service	36,332	24,161	3,604	2,358	3,614	2,293	302
186	Private motor-drivers and cleaners ...	754	673	...	13	...	69	...
187	Other domestic service	35,578	23,488	3,604	2,346	3,614	2,224	302

PART I—PROVINCIAL SUMMARY—*contd.*

BRITISH TERRITORY.							ASSAM STATES.						
Total following occupation.	As principal occupation.		As working dependants.		As subsidiary to other occupation.		Total following occupation.	As principal occupation.		As working dependants.		As subsidiary to other occupation.	
	Males.	Females.	Males.	Females.	Males.	Females.		Males.	Females.	Males.	Females.	Males.	Females.
10	11	12	13	14	15	16	17	18	19	20	21	22	23
54,335	35,114	2,132	2,033	347	14,468	241	4,049	2,798	250	364	71	540	26
23,834	14,804	754	1,392	115	6,661	108	1,549	1,023	50	238	52	181	5
18,186	11,363	293	1,170	28	5,296	36	1,276	882	29	189	20	156	1
1,185	567	295	57	31	216	19	45	1	19	...	21	...	4
3,321	2,155	141	110	35	839	51	227	139	2	49	11	26	...
1,142	719	25	55	21	320	2	1	1	...	...	...	...	...
3,255	2,590	...	49	...	616	...	59	59	...	...	...	...	...
1,077	987	...	...	...	90	...	19	19	...	...	...	...	...
2,178	1,603	...	49	...	526	...	40	40	...	...	...	...	...
9,027	5,887	550	111	160	2,251	68	872	515	103	45	13	190	6
1,950	1,707	22	13	...	207	1	83	69	1	1	...	11	1
5,069	2,826	135	89	52	1,935	32	620	383	14	44	1	178	...
9	9	...	...	...	...	...	3	2	1	...	...	...	...
1,891	1,251	393	8	108	96	35	152	47	87	...	12	1	5
108	94	...	1	...	13	...	14	14	...	...	...	...	...
13,347	9,351	732	254	47	2,917	46	829	705	67	6	3	34	14
12,716	8,897	621	251	37	2,871	39	799	682	64	6	3	30	14
631	454	111	3	10	46	7	30	23	3	...	...	4	...
4,872	2,482	96	227	25	2,023	19	740	496	30	75	3	135	1
12	12	...	...	...	...	...	3	3	...	...	...	...	...
372	328	1	2	...	41	...	29	27	...	...	...	2	...
151	100	...	...	...	51	...	4	3	...	1	...	...	...
84	54	1	9	...	19	1	57	55	...	1	...	1	...
59	45	...	...	...	14	...	...	...	...	...	...	...	...
550	334	2	24	3	186	1	36	21	...	3	...	12	...
3,063	1,181	47	189	9	1,626	11	608	379	30	70	3	120	1
192	148	...	3	...	41	...	2	2	...	...	...	...	...
389	280	45	...	13	45	6	6	6	...	...	...	...	...
113,250	58,737	23,189	7,027	6,116	16,127	2,054	11,083	5,141	2,158	415	461	1,841	1,067
2,059	1,141	152	42	44	667	13	195	170	19	3	1	2	...
2,059	1,141	152	42	44	667	13	195	170	19	3	1	2	...
2,059	1,141	152	42	44	667	13	195	170	19	3	1	2	...
33,698	22,123	3,297	2,295	3,440	2,279	264	2,634	2,038	307	63	174	14	38
33,698	22,123	3,297	2,295	3,440	2,279	264	2,634	2,038	307	63	174	14	38
740	659	...	12	...	69	...	14	14	...	...	...	...	...
32,958	21,464	3,297	2,283	3,440	2,210	264	2,620	2,024	307	63	174	14	38

TABLE X.—Occupation or means of Livelihood.

Group Number.	Occupation	ASSAM. Total following occupation.	As principal occupation. Males.	As principal occupation. Females.	As working dependants. Males.	As working dependants. Females.	As subsidiary to other occupation. Males.	As subsidiary to other occupation. Females.
1	2	3	4	5	6	7	8	9
	XI.—INSUFFICIENTLY DESCRIBED OCCUPATION.	52,511	27,089	8,100	1,312	1,099	13,027	1,884
	52.—General terms which do not indicate a definite occupation.	52,511	27,089	8,100	1,312	1,099	13,027	1,884
188	Manufacturers, businessmen and contractors otherwise unspecified.	2,834	1,973	21	73	1	764	2
189	Cashiers, accountants, book-keepers, clerks and other employees in unspecified offices and ware-houses and shops.	6,045	4,768	65	256	36	919	1
190	Mechanics otherwise unspecified	315	265	...	21	...	29	...
191	Labourers and workmen otherwise unspecified...	43,317	20,083	8,014	962	1,062	11,315	1,881
	XII.—UNPRODUCTIVE	33,236	11,317	13,472	3,727	1,819	1,979	922
	53.—Inmates of Jails, asylums and alms houses.	3,116	...	...	3,075	41	...	...
192	Inmates of jails, asylums and alms houses ...	3,116	...	...	3,075	41	...	...
	54.—Beggars, vagrants, prostitutes ...	30,102	11,312	13,472	652	1,778	1,966	922
193	Beggars and vagrants	29,559	11,312	12,933	652	1,777	1,966	919
194	Procurers and prostitutes	543	...	539	...	1	...	3
	55.—Other unclassified non-productive industries.	18	5	...	...	...	13	...
195	Other unclassified non-productive industries ...	18	5	...	...	...	13	...

PART I.—PROVINCIAL SUMMARY—*concld.*

BRITISH TERRITORY.							ASSAM STATES.						
Total following occupation.	As principal occupation.		As working dependants.		As subsidiary to other occupation.		Total following occupation.	As principal occupation.		As working dependants.		As subsidiary to other occupation.	
	Males.	Females.	Males.	Females.	Males.	Females.		Males.	Females.	Males.	Females.	Males.	Females.
10	11	12	13	14	15	16	17	18	19	20	21	22	23
44,637	24,255	6,368	1,129	827	11,203	855	7,874	2,834	1,73[illegible]	183	272	1,824	1,029
44,637	24,255	6,368	1,129	827	11,203	855	7,874	2,834	1,732	183	272	1,824	1,029
2,642	1,787	19	72	1	761	2	192	186	2	1	...	3	...
5,928	4,661	56	255	36	919	1	117	107	9	1	...	...	...
255	205	...	21	...	29	...	60	60	...	...	...	...	...
35,812	17,602	6,293	781	790	9,494	852	7,505	2,481	1,721	181	272	1,821	1,029
32,856	11,218	13,372	3,561	1,805	1,978	922	380	99	100	166	14	1	...
2,971	...	...	2,930	41	...	...	145	...	...	145	...	...	...
2,971	...	...	2,930	41	...	...	145	...	...	145	...	...	...
29,869	11,215	13,372	631	1,764	1,965	922	233	97	100	21	14	1	...
29,326	11,215	12,833	631	1,763	1,965	919	233	97	100	21	14	1	...
543	...	539	...	1	...	3	...	...	...	...	...	...	...
16	3	...	...	...	13	...	2	2	...	...	...	...	...
16	3	...	...	...	13	...	2	2	...	...	...	...	...

TABLE X.—OCCUPATION OR MEANS OF LIVELIHOOD. PART II.—DETAILS FOR DISTRICTS.

DISTRICT OR STATE.	Total population.		Total of all classes. Total population. Total earners (principal occupation).		Total working dependants.		Total non-working dependant population.		Total earners with subsidiary occupation.	
	Males.	Females.	Males.	Females.	Males.	Females.	Males.	Females.	Males.	Females.
1	2	3	4	5	6	7	8	9	10	11
ASSAM	*4,844,183*	*4,403,724*	*2,534,693*	*563,897*	*439,349*	*659,870*	*1,880,191*	*3,186,957*	*457,697*	*100,936*
(1) British Territory	*4,537,906*	*4,085,045*	*2,399,646*	*500,719*	*398,600*	*577,793*	*1,738,960*	*3,006,533*	*439,789*	*83,689*
SURMA VALLEY AND HILL DIVISION ...	**1,913,144**	**1,794,903**	**960,912**	**198,470**	**162,001**	**63,288**	**790,230**	**1,533,145**	**252,034**	**22,790**
Cachar ...	301,339	269,198	146,631	60,083	26,341	8,153	128,206	210,957	42,253	5,858
Sylhet ...	1,407,645	1,316,097	708,121	85,008	119,712	10,896	579,812	1,220,703	197,441	8,248
Khasi and Jaintia Hills (British) ...	55,439	54,487	31,037	19,826	3,468	6,945	20,934	27,716	7,943	5,108
Naga Hills ...	89,536	89,206	43,016	13,962	11,812	35,615	34,700	39,731	1,828	3,746
Lushai Hills ...	59,166	65,318	32,059	29,501	648	1,079	26,479	34,038	2,559	265
ASSAM VALLEY DIVISION ...	**2,592,144**	**2,263,567**	**1,419,450**	**292,685**	**235,331**	**510,344**	**937,363**	**1,460,538**	**178,857**	**56,590**
Goalpara ...	470,373	412,475	214,756	12,791	77,254	54,636	178,263	345,048	18,867	1,369
Kamrup ...	513,345	463,401	274,559	18,450	38,381	125,432	200,405	319,510	23,964	3,517
Darrang ...	317,103	267,714	194,644	46,983	23,565	78,659	98,874	142,043	22,212	7,601
Nowgong ...	298,585	263,996	159,706	17,331	26,485	56,598	112,396	190,067	12,751	3,097
Sibsagar ...	496,388	437,036	269,640	88,919	42,691	98,002	184,058	250,117	55,001	20,491
Lakhimpur ...	399,106	325,474	249,075	106,096	24,081	58,732	125,352	161,046	41,778	19,706
Garo Hills ...	97,443	93,469	57,163	2,516	2,264	38,265	38,016	52,698	4,294	153
SADIYA FRONTIER TRACT ...	**28,696**	**24,650**	**16,999**	**9,201**	**1,010**	**3,654**	**10,687**	**11,904**	**1,496**	**4,422**
BALIPARA FRONTIER TRACT ...	**3,233**	**1,916**	**2,294**	**363**	**258**	**507**	**680**	**1,046**	**402**	**16**
(2) Manipur State ...	*215,815*	*229,791*	*86,500*	*25,415*	*25,610*	*67,458*	*103,705*	*136,918*	*10,595*	*3,719*
(3) Khasi States ...	*91,112*	*88,888*	*48,547*	*37,763*	*5,039*	*7,619*	*37,526*	*43,506*	*14,318*	*12,849*

TABLE X.—Occupation or means of livelihood. Part II.—Details for Districts—*contd.*

DISTRICT OR STATE.	Class A.—Production of raw materials.											
	Total of class A.						Sub-class I.—Exploitation of animals and vegetation. Total of sub-class I.—Exploitation of animals and vegetation.					
	Total earners (principal occupation).		Total working dependants.		Total following occupation as subsidiary to other.		Total earners (principal occupation).		Total working dependants.		Total following occupation as subsidiary to other.	
	Males.	Females.	Males.	Females.	Males.	Females.	Males.	Females.	Males.	Females.	Males.	Females.
	12	13	14	15	16	17	18	19	20	21	22	23
ASSAM	*2,198,691*	*488,470*	*406,089*	*419,681*	*292,768*	*68,629*	*2,183,877*	*487,350*	*405,477*	*419,643*	*292,287*	*68,613*
(1) British Territory	*2,085,554*	*441,421*	*377,939*	*364,069*	*276,071*	*59,045*	*2,070,010*	*440,473*	*376,808*	*364,025*	*275,615*	*59,029*
SURMA VALLEY AND HILL DIVISION	839,016	169,797	151,966	42,076	157,967	14,724	837,081	169,650	151,930	42,074	157,962	14,716
Cachar	125,079	44,198	38,133	2,033	32,911	3,516	124,756	44,055	25,120	2,032	33,742	3,506
Sylhet	620,447	68,074	112,231	2,612	117,003	4,784	620,306	68,973	112,220	2,612	116,975	4,784
Khasi and Jaintia Hills (British)	22,793	14,480	3,084	3,004	5,811	3,168	22,791	14,460	3,084	3,004	5,810	3,168
Naga Hills	40,300	13,640	11,479	34,214	1,003	3,147	40,350	13,608	11,448	34,213	996	3,147
Lushai Hills	20,769	28,506	40	123	539	109	20,759	28,506	40	123	539	109
ASSAM VALLEY DIVISION	1,233,341	262,075	224,034	318,758	117,995	44,148	1,219,582	261,874	223,646	318,723	117,764	44,160
Goalpara	182,191	6,228	74,911	33,790	7,971	209	182,166	6,225	74,810	33,790	7,967	209
Kamrup	227,530	8,274	35,286	25,614	9,293	673	227,536	8,274	35,786	25,514	9,288	673
Darrang	179,963	43,613	22,451	65,030	15,954	6,733	170,946	43,513	22,451	65,020	15,954	6,132
Nowgong	140,982	14,528	25,524	33,627	6,171	1,463	140,879	14,826	25,524	32,635	6,169	1,869
Sibsagar	240,553	85,484	40,644	79,835	42,080	17,421	240,834	85,484	40,643	79,833	42,070	17,421
Lakhimpur...	215,627	102,237	23,168	45,205	35,031	17,397	202,936	101,428	22,803	45,173	34,601	17,379
Garo Hills	84,308	2,121	2,130	36,758	1,405	74	84,305	2,121	2,130	36,758	1,195	74
SADIYA FRONTIER TRACT	13,037	8,704	975	2,965	681	106	12,987	8,704	975	2,965	681	106
BALIPARA FRONTIER TRACT	1,160	945	257	263	128	7	1,160	945	257	263	128	7
(2) Manipur State	*75,719*	*13,783*	*24,314*	*49,325*	*7,387*	*545*	*75,687*	*13,611*	*24,190*	*49,393*	*7,385*	*545*
(3) Khasi States	*37,425*	*33,266*	*4,483*	*6,994*	*9,310*	*8,739*	*37,380*	*33,266*	*4,479*	*6,994*	*9,287*	*8,739*

TABLE X.—Occupation or means of livelihood. Part II.—Details for Districts—*contd.*

Class A.—Production of raw materials. Sub-class I.—Exploitation of animals and vegetation. Order 1.—Pasture and Agriculture.

District or State.	Total of order 1.—Pasture and Agriculture. Total earners (principal occupation). Males.	Females.	Total working dependants. Males.	Females.	Total following occupation as subsidiary to other. Males.	Females.	Total of sub-order 1(a)—Cultivation. Total earners (principal occupation). Males.	Females.	Total working dependants. Males.	Females.	Total following occupation as subsidiary to other. Males.	Females.
	24	25	26	27	28	29	30	31	32	33	34	35
ASSAM	*2,147,885*	*485,967*	*400,164*	*418,690*	*251,660*	*68,348*	*1,785,634*	*193,397*	*293,308*	*398,493*	*194,480*	*55,516*
(1) British Territory	*2,036,034*	*439,606*	*371,053*	*363,380*	*235,389*	*58,894*	*1,680,879*	*151,649*	*268,556*	*344,788*	*186,195*	*47,936*
SURMA VALLEY AND HILL DIVISION	**810,606**	**168,937**	**147,323**	**41,616**	**121,282**	**14,553**	**716,891**	**82,350**	**143,694**	**40,385**	**110,624**	**12,724**
Cachar	123,610	44,040	21,944	2,029	30,268	3,501	67,540	8,246	23,609	1,925	27,343	3,238
Sylhet	596,067	68,295	107,798	2,168	83,709	4,628	549,140	18,979	107,207	1,901	79,600	4,334
Khasi and Jaintia Hills (British)	22,743	14,480	3,064	3,093	5,791	3,108	18,553	13,069	1,686	2,601	2,369	1,027
Naga Hills...	39,390	13,008	11,448	34,213	973	3,147	38,974	13,391	11,006	33,036	608	3,140
Lushai Hills	29,788	28,606	49	123	531	109	29,665	28,465	37	122	385	85
ASSAM VALLEY DIVISION	**1,211,368**	**261,720**	**223,009**	**318,536**	**113,323**	**44,098**	**950,981**	**60,984**	**124,015**	**301,239**	**75,139**	**34,383**
Goalpara	170,734	6,169	74,617	33,796	7,727	299	176,252	4,700	53,266	33,250	6,090	289
Kamrup	224,523	8,222	35,166	25,427	8,367	670	218,443	5,813	17,304	24,324	6,294	544
Darrang	170,129	43,484	22,435	65,019	17,667	6,723	116,165	4,062	8,404	63,650	10,203	6,306
Nowgong	140,568	14,836	25,407	32,625	5,537	1,550	130,637	7,365	12,993	31,771	3,822	1,380
Sibsagar	239,901	85,483	40,539	79,769	40,271	17,416	153,460	13,607	24,070	74,670	29,107	15,149
Lakhimpur...	202,008	101,415	22,715	45,140	33,941	17,357	102,230	23,337	10,890	38,326	18,622	10,773
Garo Hills	64,305	2,131	2,130	36,758	1,493	74	53,404	2,100	1,103	36,739	1,301	73
SADIYA FRONTIER TRACT	**12,890**	**8,704**	**974**	**2,965**	**670**	**166**	**12,155**	**8,276**	**701**	**2,906**	**253**	**183**
BALIPARA FRONTIER TRACT	**1,150**	**245**	**257**	**263**	**127**	**7**	**982**	**32**	**146**	**256**	**100**	**6**
(2) Manipur State	*74,493*	*19,495*	*24,039*	*49,018*	*7,002*	*785*	*73,454*	*19,900*	*22,638*	*48,749*	*1,410*	*739*
(3) Khasi States	*37,358*	*33,166*	*4,479*	*6,292*	*9,276*	*8,739*	*31,301*	*29,555*	*2,114*	*4,956*	*6,945*	*7,541*

TABLE X.—OCCUPATION OR MEANS OF LIVELIHOOD. PART II.—DETAILS FOR DISTRICTS—*contd.*

DISTRICT OR STATE.	Class A.—Production of raw materials. Sub-class I.—Exploitation of animals and vegetation. Order 1.—Pasture and Agriculture. Sub-order 1(a).—Cultivation.											
	Group (1).—Non-cultivating proprietors taking rent in money or kind.						Group (2).—Estate Agents and Managers of owners.					
	Total earners (principal occupation).		Total working dependants.		Total following occupation as subsidiary to other.		Total earners (principal occupation).		Total working dependants.		Total following occupation as subsidiary to other.	
	Males.	Females.	Males.	Females.	Males.	Females.	Males.	Females.	Males.	Females.	Males.	Females.
	36	37	38	39	40	41	42	43	44	45	46	47
ASSAM	*20,491*	*4,887*	*873*	*443*	*17,776*	*797*	*140*	...	*3*	...	*96*	...
(1) British Territory	*18,809*	*3,580*	*755*	*287*	*17,347*	*680*	*140*	...	*3*	...	*96*	...
SURMA VALLEY AND HILL DIVISION	16,100	1,805	525	184	13,327	338	54	...	...	...	76	...
Cachar	1,288	318	9	10	2,048	74	1	...	...	...	1	...
Sylhet	14,476	1,367	514	145	10,626	216	53	...	...	...	75	...
Khasi and Jaintia Hills (British)	44	78	2	20	49	40	...	...	...	...	...	...
Naga Hills	...	...	...	...	1	...	...	...	...	...	...	...
Lushai Hills	292	42	...	...	3	...	...	...	...	...	...	...
ASSAM VALLEY DIVISION	2,702	1,775	230	103	4,019	341	86	...	3	...	20	...
Goalpara	671	200	123	21	1,090	95	83	...	3	...	3	...
Kamrup	1,150	742	78	33	963	52	3	...	...	...	16	...
Darrang	251	317	...	2	333	15	...	...	...	...	1	...
Nowgong	70	39	1	9	193	6	...	...	...	...	...	...
Sibsagar	369	377	18	20	507	151	...	...	...	...	...	...
Lakhimpur	74	35	2	9	179	6	...	...	...	...	...	...
Garo Hills	117	165	7	9	163	16	...	...	...	...	...	...
SADIYA FRONTIER TRACT	...	...	...	...	1	1	...	...	...	...	...	...
BALIPARA FRONTIER TRACT	...	...	...	...	...	...	...	...	...	...	...	...
(2) Manipur State	*1,000*	*748*	*118*	*137*	*421*	*34*	...	...	...	...	...	...
(3) Khasi States	*19*	*59*	...	*19*	*8*	*13*	...	...	...	...	...	...

TABLE X.—OCCUPATION OR MEANS OF LIVELIHOOD. PART II.—DETAILS FOR DISTRICTS—*contd.*

DISTRICT OR STATE.	Class A.—Production of raw materials. Sub-class I.—Exploitation of animals and vegetation. Order 1.—Pasture and Agriculture. Sub order 1(a)—Cultivation.											
	Group (3).—Estate Agents and Managers of Government.						Group (4).—Rent collectors, clerks, etc.					
	Total earners (principal occupation).		Total working dependants.		Total following occupation as subsidiary to other.		Total earners (principal occupation).		Total working dependants.		Total following occupation as subsidiary to other.	
	Males.	Females.	Males.	Females.	Males.	Females.	Males.	Females.	Males.	Females.	Males.	Females.
	48	49	50	51	52	53	54	55	56	57	58	59
ASSAM	*32*	...	...	...	*9*	...	*2,812*	*19*	*98*	*11*	*1,209*	*18*
(1) British Territory	*32*	...	...	...	*9*	...	*2,804*	*19*	*98*	*11*	*1,208*	*18*
SURMA VALLEY AND HILL DIVISION	6	...	...		1	...	1,098	18	45	11	888	17
Cachar	3	...	...	...	1	...	22	...	...	...	13	...
Sylhet	...	...	...	...	...	...	1,070	18	45	11	875	17
Khasi and Jaintia Hills (British)	1	...	...	...	...	...	2	...	...	...	...	...
Naga Hills	...	...	...	...	...	...	4	...	...	...	...	...
Lushai Hills	2	...	...	...	...	...	...	...	...	...	...	...
ASSAM VALLEY DIVISION	25	...	...	...	8		1,700	1	53	...	314	1
Goalpara	9	...	...	...	6	...	1,090	1	41	...	113	...
Kamrup	5	...	...	...	2	...	168	...	4	...	54	...
Darrang	4	...	...	...	...	...	118	...	...	...	30	...
Nowgong	1	...	...	...	...	...	103	...	3	...	15	...
Sibsagar	3	...	...	...	...	...	115	...	3	...	65	...
Lakhimpur	3	...	...	...	...	...	85	...	2	...	35	1
Garo Hills	...	...	...	...	...	...	21	...	...	...	2	...
SADIYA FRONTIER TRACT	1	...	...	...	...	...	3	...	...	...	5	...
BALIPARA FRONTIER TRACT	...	...	...	...	...	...	3	...	...	...	1	...
(2) Manipur State	...	...	...	...	...	...	*8*	...	...	...	*1*	...
(3) Khasi States	...	...	...	...	...	...	...	...	...	...	...	...

TABLE X.—OCCUPATION OR MEANS OF LIVELIHOOD: PART II.—DETAILS FOR DISTRICTS—*contd.*

DISTRICT OR STATE.	Class A.—Production of raw materials. Sub-class I.—Exploitation of animals and vegetation. Order 1.—Pasture and Agriculture. Sub-order 1(a).—Cultivation.											
	Group (5).—Cultivating owners.						Group (6).—Tenant cultivators.					
	Total earners (principal occupation).		Total working dependants.		Total following occupation as subsidiary to other.		Total earners (principal occupation).		Total working dependants.		Total following occupation as subsidiary to other.	
	Males.	Females.	Males.	Females.	Males.	Females.	Males.	Females.	Males.	Females.	Males.	Females.
	60	61	62	63	64	65	66	67	68	69	70	71
ASSAM	*995,840*	*99,704*	*33,856*	*80,701*	*68,496*	*99,099*	*583,165*	*30,419*	*7,015*	*6,318*	*90,869*	*17,764*
(1) British Territory	*936,547*	*70,541*	*22,371*	*59,430*	*65,873*	*96,733*	*571,796*	*24,858*	*5,179*	*2,034*	*89,948*	*15,857*
SURMA VALLEY AND HILL DIVISION	206,726	18,217	5,974	16,303	19,377	1,897	413,551	18,568	4,365	1,145	67,583	6,953
Cachar	49,260	1,927	302	30	3,765	65	33,520	2,503	125	156	21,253	3,017
Sylhet	131,644	3,494	2,109	60	14,929	257	377,076	13,730	4,143	503	45,908	3,718
Khasi and Jaintia Hills (British)	8,409	5,557	973	1,206	978	736	2,902	2,294	89	458	411	218
Naga Hills	18,409	7,236	2,500	14,007	706	789	7	3	...	...	...	...
Lushai Hills	4	8	...	1	...	...	46	18	8	28	11	...
ASSAM VALLEY DIVISION	712,480	49,071	16,369	43,077	46,147	94,729	156,218	6,287	807	1,789	22,362	8,904
Goalpara	63,790	1,096	6,953	8,184	1,098	120	114,063	3,033	233	134	1,875	88
Kamrup	192,780	3,021	3,311	6,179	14,234	250	15,152	567	118	1,001	624	70
Darrang	100,868	2,896	792	3,979	6,094	3,400	9,161	502	59	16	4,606	3,083
Nowgong	120,279	7,011	1,054	1,256	1,763	1,113	6,471	214	236	203	1,431	218
Sibsagar	137,614	12,095	2,115	10,406	21,294	12,847	8,035	930	55	142	6,971	3,028
Lakhimpur	97,414	22,124	1,940	9,789	11,409	6,906	3,327	994	106	160	6,458	3,847
Garo Hills	10,036	228	214	2,984	310	5	2,946	27	...	35	107	1
SADIYA FRONTIER TRACT	6,596	3,224	28	50	241	101	2	2	...	...	3	...
BALIPARA FRONTIER TRACT	743	29	...	...	108	6	25	1	...	...	...	...
(2) Manipur State	*47,773*	*8,595*	*10,620*	*18,707*	*454*	*383*	*6,451*	*479*	*985*	*1,801*	*96*	*21*
(3) Khasi States	*21,520*	*20,168*	*865*	*2,564*	*2,169*	*1,906*	*4,918*	*5,082*	*858*	*1,583*	*818*	*1,886*

TABLE X.—OCCUPATION OR MEANS OF LIVELIHOOD. PART II.—DETAILS FOR DISTRICTS—*contd.*

DISTRICT OR STATE.	Class A.—Production of raw materials.											
	Sub-class I.—Exploitation of animals and vegetation.											
	Order 1.—Pasture and Agriculture.											
	Sub-order 1(a).—Cultivation.											
	Group (7).—Agricultural labourers.						Group (7A).—Helpers in agricultural work.					
	Total earners (principal occupation).		Total working dependants.		Total following occupation as subsidiary to other.		Total earners (principal occupation).		Total working dependants.		Total following occupation as subsidiary to other.	
	Males.	Females.	Males.	Females.	Males.	Females.	Males.	Females.	Males.	Females.	Males.	Females.
	72	73	74	75	76	77	78	79	80	81	82	83
ASSAM	*54,176*	*5,149*	*6,980*	*8,001*	*13,417*	*4,739*	...	...	*230,900*	*238,131*	...	...
(1) British Territory	*53,137*	*3,094*	*6,773*	*7,399*	*9,710*	*1,278*	...	...	*226,438*	*229,998*	...	...
SURMA VALLEY AND HILL DIVISION	**20,274**	**814**	**1,549**	**369**	**8,186**	**873**	...	...	*124,098*	*6,891*	...	...
Cachar	2,175	108	111	30	444	65	...	...	22,613	667	...	...
Sylhet	17,576	222	1,327	44	7,156	85	...	...	99,050	1,024	...	...
Khasi and Jaintia Hills (British)	519	480	110	279	586	721	...	...	...	65	...	...
Naga Hills	4	4	1	16	...	1	...	...	3,797	5,135	...	...
Lushai Hills	...	...	...	...	...	...	...	...	8	...	...	...
ASSAM VALLEY DIVISION	**31,681**	**2,280**	**5,216**	**6,644**	**1,524**	**401**	...	...	**100,663**	**220,296**	...	...
Goalpara	6,487	339	2,877	1,571	416	16	...	...	43,036	23,047	...	...
Kamrup	9,141	883	1,281	2,443	351	142	...	...	7,512	12,028	...	...
Darrang	6,073	347	194	280	115	40	...	...	7,450	58,403	...	...
Nowgong	4,712	97	120	140	131	14	...	...	11,574	29,581	...	...
Sibsagar	3,157	235	310	1,603	242	122	...	...	22,436	62,207	...	...
Lakhimpur	1,421	124	433	230	258	21	...	...	8,406	29,143	...	...
Garo Hills	454	155	11	18	21	46	...	...	210	5,075	...	...
SADIYA FRONTIER TRACT	**182**	...	**7**	**279**	...	**4**	...	...	**632**	**2,555**	...	...
BALIPARA FRONTIER TRACT	...	...	**1**	...	...	...	...	...	**145**	**256**	...	...
(2) Manipur State	*179*	*165*	*46*	*208*	*75*	*30*	...	...	*4,420*	*8,133*	...	...
(3) Khasi States	*1,860*	*1,890*	*161*	*501*	*3,632*	*3,429*	...	...	*42*	...	...	...

TABLE X.—OCCUPATION OR MEANS OF LIVELIHOOD. PART II.—DETAILS FOR DISTRICTS—*contd.*

DISTRICT OR STATE.	Class A.—Production of raw materials.											
	Sub-class I.—Exploitation of animals and vegetation.											
	Order 1.—Pasture and Agriculture.											
	Sub-order 1(a).—Cultivation.						Sub-order 1(b).—Cultivation of special crops, fruit, etc.					
	Group (8).—Cultivators of *jhum*, *taungya* and shifting areas.						Total of sub-order 1(b).—Cultivation of special crops, fruit, etc.					
	Total earners (principal occupation)		Total working dependants.		Total following occupation as subsidiary to other.		Total earners (principal occupation).		Total working dependants.		Total following occupation as subsidiary to other.	
	Males.	Females.	Males.	Females.	Males.	Females.	Males.	Females.	Males.	Females.	Males.	Females.
	84	85	86	87	88	89	90	91	92	93	94	95
ASSAM	*139,048*	*54,119*	*13,583*	*64,888*	*2,615*	*3,246*	*343,804*	*390,770*	*5,823*	*13,912*	*42,611*	*11,861*
(1) British Territory	*108,621*	*49,550*	*6,946*	*44,836*	*1,934*	*2,670*	*338,821*	*387,953*	*4,068*	*13,909*	*36,105*	*10,909*
SURMA VALLEY AND HILL DIVISION	**59,072**	**42,928**	**6,238**	**15,482**	**1,186**	**2,046**	**90,457**	**86,357**	**535**	**630**	**6,032**	**1,386**
Cachar	2,271	3,395	339	923	2 8	16	35,664	35,743	109	91	2,365	330
Sylhet	234	138	19	114	40	11	51,612	49,254	336	236	2,674	378
Khasi and Jaintia Hills (British)	6,676	4,560	612	474	363	184	3,137	1,307	86	302	919	850
Naga Hills	20,670	6,348	5,207	13,878	193	2,350	21	2	...	...	...	...
Lushai Hills	29,321	28,397	21	93	371	85	23	21	5	1	86	19
ASSAM VALLEY DIVISION	**44,089**	**1,570**	**674**	**29,330**	**745**	**7**	**247,620**	**300,258**	**4,133**	**12,568**	**30,051**	**9,522**
Goalpara	40	11	...	...	...	...	1,867	1,458	25	11	63	1
Kamrup	9	..	...	...	...	...	3,146	2,311	102	436	1,029	114
Darrang	..	...	...	...	4	...	50,801	39,284	408	1,346	4,306	501
Nowgong	...	4	...	...	...	...	8,633	7,415	157	1,021	1,683	193
Sibsagar	4,144	70	33	9	35	...	84,857	71,770	1,285	3,672	8,896	2,171
Lakhimpur	6	..	...	...	34	2	97,882	78,018	3,156	6,082	14,074	6,542
Garo Hills	39,800	1,465	641	29,321	669	5	4	...	...	...	2	...
SADIYA FRONTIER TRACT	**5,360**	**5,050**	**34**	**24**	**3**	**17**	**477**	**425**	...	**4**	**18**	...
BALIPARA FRONTIER TRACT	**81**	**2**	...	...	...	...	**267**	**213**	...	...	**4**	**1**
(2) Manipur State	*17,443*	*2,913*	*6,449*	*19,763*	*363*	*269*	*574*	*140*	*804*	*147*	*5,044*	*31*
(3) Khasi States	*2,984*	*2,356*	*188*	*289*	*318*	*314*	*4,409*	*3,377*	*351*	*563*	*1,462*	*921*

TABLE X.—OCCUPATION OR MEANS OF LIVELIHOOD. PART II.—DETAILS FOR DISTRICTS—*contd.*

Class A.—Production of raw materials.

Sub-class I.—Exploitation of animals and vegetation.

Order I.—Pasture and Agriculture.

Sub-order 1(b).—Cultivation of special crops, fruits, etc. (planters, managers, clerks and labourers).

DISTRICT OR STATE.	Group (11).—Coffee.						Group (12).—Ganja.						Group (13).—Pan-vine.					
	Total earners (principal occupation.		Total working dependants.		Total following occupation as subsidiary to other.		Total earners (principal occupation).		Total working dependants.		Total following occupation as subsidiary to other.		Total earners (principal occupation).		Total working dependants.		Total following occupation as subsidiary to other.	
	Males.	Females.	Males.	Females.	Males.	Females.	Males.	Females.	Males.	Females.	Males.	Females.	Males.	Females.	Males.	Females.	Males.	Females.
	96	97	98	99	100	101	102	103	104	105	106	107	108	109	110	111	112	113
ASSAM	*7*	*9*	*4*	*9*	*13*	*1*	*4*	...	...	...	*2*	...	*4,782*	*1,485*	*257*	*341*	*1,847*	*435*
(1) British Territory	*1*	*2*	*1*	...	*5*	...	*4*	...	...	...	*2*	...	*2,522*	*915*	*72*	*133*	*1,186*	*165*
SURMA VALLEY AND HILL DIVISION	1	2	1	...	5	...	...	...	...	...	...	...	2,519	915	71	133	1,159	165
Cachar	...	...	...	...	...	...	...	...	...	...	...	...	310	89	19	4	101	2
Sylhet	...	...	...	...	...	...	...	...	...	...	...	...	232	57	25	...	718	2
Khasi and Jaintia Hills (British)	1	2	1	...	5	...	...	...	...	...	...	...	1,977	769	27	129	340	161
Naga Hills	...	...	...	...	...	...	...	...	...	...	...	...	...	...	...	...	...	...
Lushai Hills	...	...	...	...	...	...	...	...	...	...	...	...	...	...	...	...	...	...
ASSAM VALLEY DIVISION	...	...	...	...	...	...	4	...	...	...	2	...	3	...	1	...	27	...
Goalpara	...	...	...	...	...	...	4	...	...	...	2	...	2	...	1	...	4	...
Kamrup	...	...	...	...	...	...	...	...	...	...	...	...	...	...	...	...	...	...
Darrang	...	...	...	...	...	...	...	...	...	...	...	...	1	...	...	...	...	...
Nowgong	...	...	...	...	...	...	...	...	...	...	...	...	...	...	...	...	...	...
Sibsagar	...	...	...	...	...	...	...	...	...	...	...	...	...	...	...	...	...	...
Lakhimpur	...	...	...	...	...	...	...	...	...	...	...	...	...	...	...	...	23	...
Garo Hills	...	...	...	...	...	...	...	...	...	...	...	...	...	...	...	...	...	...
SADIYA FRONTIER TRACT	...	...	...	...	...	...	...	...	...	...	...	...	...	...	...	...	...	...
BALIPARA FRONTIER TRACT	...	...	...	...	...	...	...	...	...	...	...	...	...	...	...	...	...	...
(2) Manipur State	...	...	...	...	...	...	...	...	...	...	...	...	...	...	...	...	...	...
(3) Khasi States	*6*	*7*	*3*	*9*	*8*	*1*	...	...	...	...	...	...	*2,260*	*570*	*185*	*208*	*661*	*270*

TABLE X—Occupation or means of livelihood. Part II.—Details for Districts—*contd.*

District or State.	Class A.—Production of raw materials. Sub-class I.—Exploitation of animals and vegetation. Order I.—Pasture and Agriculture. Sub-order 1(b).—Cultivation of special crops, fruits, etc. (planters, managers, clerks and labourers). Group (15).—Tea. Total earners (principal occupation). Males.	Group (15).—Tea. Total earners (principal occupation). Females.	Group (15).—Tea. Total working dependants. Males.	Group (15).—Tea. Total working dependants. Females.	Group (15).—Tea. Total following occupation as subsidiary to other. Males.	Group (15).—Tea. Total following occupation as subsidiary to other. Females.	Group (16).—Market gardeners, flower and fruit growers. Total earners (principal occupation). Males.	Group (16). Total earners (principal occupation). Females.	Group (16). Total working dependants. Males.	Group (16). Total working dependants. Females.	Group (16). Total following occupation as subsidiary to other. Males.	Group (16). Total following occupation as subsidiary to other. Females.
	114	115	116	117	118	119	120	121	122	123	124	125
ASSAM	*333,979*	*285,585*	*4,479*	*12,898*	*33,613*	*9,999*	*5,032*	*3,691*	*1,083*	*734*	*7,136*	*1,483*
(1) British Territory	*333,979*	*285,585*	*4,479*	*12,898*	*33,613*	*9,999*	*2,315*	*751*	*116*	*241*	*1,399*	*759*
SURMA VALLEY AND HILL DIVISION	**86,691**	**84,872**	**397**	**383**	**3,914**	**504**	**1,246**	**568**	**66**	**176**	**964**	**717**
Cachar...	35,338	35,044	90	87	2,109	228	16	10	...	...	63	...
Sylhet...	51,347	49,227	307	296	1,805	276	13	...	3	...	151	...
Khasi and Jaintia Hills (British)	2	...	...	...	...	...	1,177	536	58	173	664	699
Naga Hills	4	1	...	...	...	...	17	1	...	...	...	...
Lushai Hills	...	...	...	...	...	...	23	21	6	1	86	19
ASSAM VALLEY DIVISION	**246,638**	**200,077**	**4,082**	**12,508**	**29,677**	**9,487**	**975**	**181**	**50**	**66**	**345**	**85**
Goalpara	1,827	1,441	12	11	34	1	34	17	12	...	33	...
Kamrup	3,461	2,301	89	635	965	114	35	10	13	1	64	...
Darrang	50,755	39,379	408	1,366	4,234	434	45	7	...	...	23	17
Nowgong	8,466	7,413	155	1,021	1,652	193	78	2	2	...	30	...
Sibsagar	84,780	71,736	1,265	3,068	8,840	2,164	96	34	...	4	44	7
Lakhimpur	97,351	77,937	2,133	6,031	13,803	6,531	631	111	23	61	168	11
Garo Hills	...	...	...	...	...	...	4	...	...	...	2	...
SADIYA FRONTIER TRACT	**397**	**493**	...	**3**	**18**	...	**90**	**2**	...	**1**	...	...
BALIPARA FRONTIER TRACT	**363**	**213**	...	...	**4**	**1**	**6**	...	...	...	...	...
(2) Manipur State	...	...	...	...	...	...	*574*	*140*	*804*	*147*	*5,044*	*31*
(3) Khasi States	...	...	...	...	...	...	*2,143*	*2,800*	*163*	*346*	*793*	*650*

TABLE X—OCCUPATION OR MEANS OF LIVELIHOOD. PART II.—DETAILS FOR DISTRICTS—*contd.*

DISTRICT OR STATE.	Class A.—Production of raw materials. Sub-class I.—Exploitation of animals and vegetation. Order I.—Pasture and Agriculture. Sub-order 1(c)—Forestry. Total of sub-order 1(c)—Forestry. Total earners (principal occupation). Males.	Females.	Total working dependants. Males.	Females.	Total following occupation as subsidiary to other. Males.	Females.	Group (17).—Forest officers, rangers, guards, etc. Total earners (principal occupation). Males.	Females.	Total working dependants. Males.	Females.	Total following occupation as subsidiary to other. Males.	Females.
	126	127	128	129	130	131	132	133	134	135	136	137
ASSAM	*2,728*	*214*	*413*	*184*	*4,914*	*107*	*1,005*	...	*39*	...	*231*	...
(1) British Territory	*2,593*	*109*	*253*	*100*	*3,667*	*84*	*1,004*	...	*39*	...	*231*	...
SURMA VALLEY AND HILL DIVISION	711	30	39	19	1,171	35	220	...	...	...	38	...
Cachar	111	13	3	12	499	20	62	...	...	...	...	...
Sylhet	409	14	10	6	596	8	134	...	...	...	36	...
Khasi and Jaintia Hills (British)	42	...	...	...	5	...	2	...	...	...	...	...
Naga Hills	133	3	26	1	63	7	11	...	...	...	1	...
Lushai Hills	17	...	...	...	8	...	11	...	...	...	...	...
ASSAM VALLEY DIVISION	1,809	72	212	67	2,194	32	743	...	39	...	171	...
Goalpara	315	3	65	2	1,215	5	343	...	38	...	115	...
Kamrup	246	26	14	40	346	...	115	...	1	...	37	...
Darrang	161	3	9	1	29	...	48	...	...	...	3	...
Nowgong	152	1	...	...	15	...	82	...	...	...	6	...
Sibsagar	442	23	83	7	340	20	70	...	...	...	...	...
Lakhimpur	363	16	42	17	154	7	93	...	...	...	8	...
Garo Hills	90	...	...	...	214	...	63	...	...	...	2	...
SADIYA FRONTIER TRACT	63	...	2	14	305	17	36	...	...	...	19	...
BALIPARA FRONTIER TRACT	10	...	...	...	7	...	5	...	...	...	2	...
(2) Manipur State	*76*	*107*	*159*	*84*	*535*	*13*	...	...	...	...	...	...
(3) Kh i Staves	*59*	*5*	*1*	...	*12*	*10*	*1*	...	...	...	...	...

TABLE X.—Occupation or Means of Livelihood. Part II.—Details for Districts—*contd.*

Class A.—Production of raw materials. Sub-class I.—Exploitation of animals and vegetation. Order 1.—Pasture and Agriculture. Sub-order 1(e).—Forestry.

District or State.	Group (18).—Wood cutters and charcoal burners. Total earners (principal occupation). Males.	Females.	Total working dependants. Males.	Females.	Total following occupation as subsidiary to other. Males.	Females.	Group (19).—Collectors of forest produce. Total earners (principal occupation). Males.	Females.	Total working dependants. Males.	Females.	Total following occupation as subsidiary to other. Males.	Females.
	138	139	140	141	142	143	144	145	146	147	148	149
ASSAM	*2,349*	*184*	*233*	*150*	*3,175*	*79*	*474*	*30*	*141*	*34*	*808*	*98*
(1) British Territory	*1,196*	*72*	*80*	*66*	*2,659*	*56*	*463*	*30*	*134*	*34*	*777*	*98*
SURMA VALLEY AND HILL DIVISION	340	28	9	18	560	29	168	2	30	1	563	6
Cachar	14	13	...	13	8	20	35	...	3	...	401	...
Sylhet	263	14	8	6	544	8	10	...	2	...	16	...
Khasi and Jaintia Hills (British)	4	...	...	...	7	...	36	...	...	...	1	...
Naga Hills	63	1	1	...	7	1	55	2	25	1	85	6
Lushai Hills	3	...	...	...	3	...	3	...	...	...	...	...
ASSAM VALLEY DIVISION	756	44	71	48	1,744	27	310	28	108	19	200	5
Goalpara	72	3	27	2	1,100	5	...	...	...	...	...	...
Kamrup	182	26	13	40	211	...	19	...	...	...	...	...
Darrang	108	1	...	...	7	...	5	2	9	1	10	...
Nowgong	33	1	...	...	6	...	33	...	...	...	3	...
Sibsagar	254	13	26	4	300	19	109	11	87	3	40	1
Lakhimpur	131	1	6	3	42	3	139	15	36	15	104	4
Garo Hills	7	...	...	...	69	...	...	...	...	...	63	...
SADIYA FRONTIER TRACT	17	...	...	...	346	...	10	...	2	14	...	17
BALIPARA FRONTIER TRACT	4	...	...	...	...	...	1	...	...	...	5	...
(2) Manipur State	*69*	*107*	*153*	*84*	*504*	*13*	*7*	...	*6*	...	*31*	...
(3) Khasi States	*54*	*5*	...	...	*19*	*10*	*4*	...	*1*	...	...	...

TABLE X.—OCCUPATION OR MEANS OF LIVELIHOOD. PART II.—DETAILS FOR DISTRICTS—*contd.*

Class A.—Production of raw materials.
Sub-class I.—Exploitation of animals and vegetation.
Order 1.—Pasture and Agriculture.
Sub-order 1(d).—Stock raising.

DISTRICT OR STATE.	Total of sub-order 1(d).—Stock raising.						Group (21).—Cattle and buffalo breeders and keepers.					
	Total earners (principal occupation).		Total working dependants.		Total following occupation as subsidiary to other.		Total earners (principal occupation).		Total working dependants.		Total following occupation as subsidiary to other.	
	Males.	Females.	Males.	Females.	Males.	Females.	Males.	Females.	Males.	Females.	Males.	Females.
	150	151	152	153	154	155	156	157	158	159	160	161
ASSAM	*15,834*	*855*	*100,994*	*6,024*	*7,110*	*477*	*15,388*	*840*	*100,049*	*5,951*	*7,069*	*474*
(1) British Territory	*13,573*	*581*	*97,850*	*5,213*	*6,815*	*278*	*13,464*	*570*	*97,684*	*5,197*	*6,796*	*278*
SURMA VALLEY AND HILL DIVISION	2,417	172	2,760	546	981	96	2,347	170	2,505	543	975	96
Cachar	306	46	1,164	101	73	12	348	46	1,154	101	73	13
Sylhet	904	10	245	15	804	5	804	9	245	15	803	5
Khasi and Jaintia Hills (British)	940	85	907	132	47	74	948	84	806	151	45	76
Naga Hills	186	12	327	276	11	...	174	12	308	276	11	...
Lushai Hills	83	19	7	...	46	5	83	19	7	...	46	6
ASSAM VALLEY DIVISION	10,928	406	94,728	4,683	5,793	156	10,893	397	94,707	4,608	5,780	156
Goalpara	1,296	8	21,361	525	330	4	1,278	8	21,360	523	356	4
Kamrup	2,360	73	22,743	693	767	12	2,347	73	22,741	693	767	12
Darrang	3,001	133	13,524	1,031	1,129	15	3,097	127	13,511	1,009	1,137	15
Nowgong	1,161	45	12,352	333	617	16	1,130	43	12,358	333	617	16
Sibsagar	1,189	83	14,195	1,363	1,785	74	1,153	83	14,192	1,304	1,784	76
Lakhimpur	1,320	44	9,036	715	1,046	35	1,318	46	9,034	715	1,045	36
Garo Hills	717	21	1,037	14	71	...	717	21	1,087	14	64	...
SADIYA FRONTIER TRACT	206	2	271	20	34	96	206	2	271	20	34	96
BALIPARA FRONTIER TRACT	90	...	111	7	7	...	90	...	111	7	7	...
(2) Manipur State	*389*	*48*	*431*	*38*	*13*	*9*	*380*	*48*	*430*	*38*	*13*	*9*
(3) Khasi States	*1,872*	*226*	*2,013*	*778*	*282*	*197*	*1,544*	*222*	*1,935*	*716*	*260*	*234*

TABLE X.—Occupation or means of livelihood. Part II.—Details for Districts—*contd.*

District or State.	Group (22)—Breeders of transport animals. Total earners (principal occupation). Males.	Females.	Total working dependants. Males.	Females.	Total following occupation as subsidiary to other. Males.	Females.	Group (23).—Herdsmen, shepherds and breeders of other animals. Total earners (principal occupation). Males.	Females.	Total working dependants. Males.	Females.	Total following occupation as subsidiary to other. Males.	Females.
	Class A.—Production of raw materials. Sub-class I.—Exploitation of animals and vegetation. Order 1.—Pasture and Agriculture. Sub-order 1(d).—Stock raising.											
	163	163	164	165	166	167	168	169	170	171	172	173
ASSAM	*15*	...	...	...	*9*	...	*131*	*15*	*245*	*73*	*39*	*63*
(1) British territory	*15*	...	...	...	*9*	...	*84*	*11*	*176*	*16*	*17*	...
SURMA VALLEY AND HILL DIVISION	14	...	...	...	9	...	56	2	155	1	4	...
Cachar	4	...	...	...	...	...	43	...	10	...	1	...
Sylhet	10	...	...	...	...	...	...	1	...	...	...	...
Khasi and Jaintia Hills (British)	...	...	...	...	2	...	1	1	11	1	2	...
Naga Hills	...	...	...	...	...	...	12	...	134	...	1	...
Lushai Hills	...	...	...	...	...	...	...	...	...	...	...	...
ASSAM VALLEY DIVISION	1	...	...	...	...	...	28	9	21	15	13	...
Goalpara	...	...	...	...	...	...	14	...	1	3	3	...
Kamrup	...	...	...	...	...	...	1	...	2	...	...	...
Darrang	...	...	...	...	...	...	4	6	13	12	2	...
Nowgong	1	...	...	...	...	...	1	2	...	...	...	...
Sibsagar	...	...	...	...	...	...	6	...	3	...	1	...
Lakhimpur	...	...	...	...	...	...	2	1	2	...	...	...
Garo Hills	...	...	...	...	...	...	...	...	...	...	7	...
SADIYA FRONTIER TRACT	...	...	...	...	...	...	...	...	...	...	...	...
BALIPARA FRONTIER TRACT	...	...	...	...	...	...	...	...	...	...	...	...
(2) Manipur State	...	...	...	...	...	...	*9*	...	*2*	...	...	...
(3) Khasi States	...	...	...	...	...	...	*38*	*4*	*78*	*57*	*22*	*63*

TABLE X.—OCCUPATION OR MEANS OF LIVELIHOOD. PART II.—DETAILS FOR DISTRICTS—contd.

DISTRICT OR STATE.	Class A.—Production of raw materials. Sub-class I.—Exploitation of animals and vegetation. Order 1.—Pasture and Agriculture. Sub-order 1(c).—Raising of small animals and insects. Total of sub-order (c)—Raising of small animals and insects. Total earners (principal occupation). Males.	Females.	Total working dependants. Males.	Females.	Total following occupation as subsidiary to other. Males.	Females.	Group (24).—Birds, bees, etc. Total earners (principal occupation.) Males.	Females.	Total working dependants. Males.	Females.	Total following occupation as subsidiary to other. Males.	Females.
	174	175	176	177	178	179	180	181	182	183	184	185
ASSAM	185	31	396	77	3,945	387	30	9	9	1	33	5
(1) British Territory	168	28	396	77	3,670	317	20	9	9	1	28	5
SURMA VALLEY AND HILL DIVISION	168	28	315	38	2,454	318	14	9	1	...	28	4
Cachar	...	1	...	...	...	1	...	1	...	...	...	1
Sylhet	13	8	...	...	24	3	13	8	...	...	24	3
Khasi and Jaintia Hills (British)	62	19	315	38	2,438	308	1	...	1	...	2	...
Naga Hills	67	...	...	...	...	...	...	...	...	...	...	...
Lushai Hills...	...	...	...	...	2	...	...	...	...	...	2	...
ASSAM VALLEY DIVISION	26	...	11	30	216	5	6	...	1	1	...	1
Goalpara	4	...	...	1	...	...	4	...	...	...	...	...
Kamrup	...	...	3	4	30	...	...	...	...	1	...	...
Darrang	1	...	...	1	...	1	1	...	...	...	...	1
Nowgong	5	...	...	...	1	...	1	...	...	...	...	...
Sibsagar	13	...	7	23	135	3	...	...	...	...	...	...
Lakhimpur	3	...	1	...	44	...	...	...	1	...	...	...
Garo Hills	...	...	...	5	5	1	...	...	...	...	...	...
SADIYA FRONTIER TRACT	...	...	...	...	...	...	...	...	...	...	...	...
BALIPARA FRONTIER TRACT	...	...	...	...	...	...	...	...	...	...	...	...
(2) Manipur State	...	...	...	...	...	...	...	...	...	...	...	...
(3) Khasi States	17	3	...	...	575	70	10	...	...	...	5	...

TABLE X.—Occupation or means of livelihood. Part II.—Details for Districts—*contd.*

District or State.	Class A.—Production of raw materials.											
	Sub-class I.—Exploitation of animals and vegetation.											
	Order 1.—Pasture and Agriculture.											
	Sub-order 1(f).—Raising of small animals and insects.											
	Group (25).—Silk worms.						Group (26).—Lac cultivation.					
	Total earners (principal occupation).		Total working dependants.		Total following occupation as subsidiary to other.		Total earners (principal occupation).		Total working dependants.		Total following occupation as subsidiary to other.	
	Males.	Females.	Males.	Females.	Males.	Females.	Males.	Females.	Males.	Females.	Males.	Females.
	186	187	188	189	190	191	192	193	194	195	196	197
ASSAM	*19*	...	*10*	*38*	*214*	*4*	*136*	*22*	*314*	*38*	*2,998*	*378*
(1) British Territory ...	*19*		*10*	*38*	*214*	*4*	*129*	*19*	*314*	*38*	*2,428*	*308*
SURMA VALLEY AND HILL DIVISION ...	2	...	...		...	...	129	19	314	38	2,426	308
Cachar ...	...	...	...	...	...	...	...	...	...	...	...	...
Sylhet ...		...	...	...	...	...	...	...	...	...	...	...
Khasi and Jaintia Hills (British)	2	...	...	...	...	...	62	19	314	38	2,426	308
Naga Hills ...	...	...	...	...	...	...	67	...	...	...	...	...
Lushai Hills ...		...	...	...	...	...	...	...	...	...	...	...
ASSAM VALLEY DIVISION	17		10	38	214	4	3	...	...	...	2	...
Goalpara ...	...	...	...	1	...	...	...	...	...	...	...	...
Kamrup ...	...	...	3	3	28	...	...	...	...	...	1	...
Darrang ...	...	...	...	1	...	...	...	...	...	...	...	...
Nowgong ...	1	...	...	...	1	...	3	...	...	...	...	...
Sibsagar ...	13	...	7	28	134	3	...	...	...	...	...	...
Lakhimpur ...	3	...	...	...	46	...	...	...	...	...	1	...
Garo Hills ...	...	...	...	5	5	1	...	...	...	...	...	...
SADIYA FRONTIER TRACT ...	...	...	...	...	...	...	...	...	...	...	...	...
BALIPARA FRONTIER TRACT ...	...	...	...	...	...	...	...	...	...	...	...	...
(2) Manipur State ...	...	...	...	...	...	...	...	...	...	...	...	...
(3) Khasi States ...	...	...	...	...	...	...	*7*	*3*	...	...	*570*	*70*

TABLE X.—Occupation or means of livelihood. Part II—Details for Districts—*contd.*

DISTRICT OR STATE.	Class A.—Production of raw materials. Sub-class I.—Exploitation of animals and vegetation. Order 2.—Fishing and Hunting. Total of order 2.—Fishing and Hunting. Total earners (principal occupation). Males.	Females.	Total working dependants. Males.	Females.	Total following occupation as subsidiary to other. Males.	Females.	Group (77).—Fishing and Pearling. Total earners (principal occupation). Males.	Females.	Total working dependants. Males.	Females.	Total following occupation as subsidiary to other. Males.	Females.
	198	199	200	201	202	203	204	205	206	207	208	209
ASSAM	*35,999*	*9,083*	*5,313*	*959*	*40,697*	*965*	*35,799*	*9,057*	*5,303*	*948*	*40,359*	*965*
(1) British Territory	*34,776*	*867*	*5,155*	*645*	*40,333*	*905*	*34,584*	*841*	*5,145*	*641*	*39,869*	*905*
SURMA VALLEY AND HILL DIVISION	26,473	713	4,607	458	35,899	163	26,398	687	4,606	458	35,558	163
Cachar	1,146	36	185	3	3,474	7	1,117	19	155	3	3,345	7
Sylhet	25,279	677	4,423	454	33,306	156	25,233	668	4,421	454	32,256	156
Khasi and Jaintia Hills (British)	48	...	...	1	19	...	48	...	...	1	19	...
Naga Hills	...	...	...	...	23	...	...	...	...	...	22	...
Lushai Hills	...	...	...	...	18	...	...	...	...	...	16	...
ASSAM VALLEY DIVISION	8,214	154	547	187	4,421	42	8,000	154	538	183	4,301	42
Goalpara	2,433	59	193	1	340	...	2,374	59	192	1	236	...
Kamrup	3,003	53	120	87	901	3	2,957	52	119	85	877	3
Darrang	817	29	16	1	287	9	815	20	16	1	275	9
Nowgong	291	...	27	...	333	3	265	...	21	...	291	3
Sibsagar	843	1	104	66	1,799	5	818	1	103	64	1,783	5
Lakhimpur	828	13	87	32	800	23	630	13	87	32	837	22
Garo Hills	...	...	...	...	2	...	...	...	...	...	2	...
SADIYA FRONTIER TRACT	88	...	1	...	11	...	87	...	1	...	8	...
BALIPARA FRONTIER TRACT	1	...	...	...	1	...	...	...	...	...	...	...
(2) Manipur State	*1,194*	*1,116*	*158*	*305*	*383*	*60*	*1,193*	*1,116*	*158*	*305*	*379*	*60*
(3) Khasi States	*99*	*100*	...	*9*	*11*	...	*99*	*100*	...	*9*	*11*	...

TABLE X.—OCCUPATION OR MEANS OF LIVELIHOOD. PART II.—DETAILS FOR DISTRICTS—*contd.*

DISTRICT OR STATE.	Class A.—Production of raw materials.											
	Sub-class I.—Exploitation of animals and vegetation.						Sub-class II.—Exploitation of minerals.					
	Order 2.—Fishing and Hunting.						Total of sub-class II.—Exploitation of minerals.					
	Group (28).—Hunting.											
	Total earners (principal occupation).		Total working dependants.		Total following occupation as subsidiary to other.		Total earners (principal occupation).		Total working dependants.		Total following occupation as subsidiary to other.	
	Males.	Females.	Males.	Females.	Males.	Females.	Males.	Females.	Males.	Females.	Males.	Females.
	210	211	212	213	214	215	216	217	218	219	220	221
ASSAM	*193*	*96*	*10*	*4*	*375*	...	*14,814*	*1,190*	*559*	*39*	*481*	*16*
(1) British Territory	*199*	*96*	*10*	*4*	*371*	...	*14,744*	*948*	*494*	*37*	*456*	*16*
SURMA VALLEY AND HILL DIVISION	75	26	1	...	242	...	1,935	167	36	2	206	8
Cachar	29	17	...	...	220	...	923	113	4	1	160	8
Sylhet	46	9	1	...	10	...	81	2	1	...	28	...
Khasi and Jaintia Hills (British)	...	...	...	...	...	...	2	...	...	...	1	...
Naga Hills	...	...	...	...	1	...	929	33	31	1	7	...
Lushai Hills	...	...	...	...	2	...	...	...	...	...	...	...
ASSAM VALLEY DIVISION	115	...	9	4	120	...	12,750	801	388	35	251	8
Goalpara	58	...	1	...	4	...	15	...	1	...	4	...
Kamrup	16	...	1	2	24	...	4	...	...	...	5	...
Darrang	2	...	...	...	13	...	7	...	...	...	5	...
Nowgong	6	...	6	...	41	...	3	3	...	2	2	...
Sibsagar	25	...	1	2	16	...	19	...	1	...	10	...
Lakhimpur	8	...	...	...	23	...	12,701	790	336	33	230	8
Garo Hills	...	...	...	...	...	...	...	...	...	...	...	...
SADIYA FRONTIER TRACT	1	...	...	...	8	...	50	...	...	...	...	...
BALIPARA FRONTIER TRACT	1	...	...	...	1	...	...	...	...	...	...	...
(2) Manipur State	*1*	...	...	...	*4*	...	*25*	*179*	*124*	*9*	*9*	...
(3) Khasi States	...	...	...	...	...	...	*45*	...	*4*	...	*23*	...

TABLE X.—Occupation or means of livelihood. Part II—Details for Districts—*contd.*

DISTRICT OR STATE.	Class A.—Production of raw materials. Sub-class II.—Exploitation of minerals. Order 3.—Metallic minerals. Total of order 3.—Metallic Minerals. Total earners (principal occupation). Males.	Females.	Total working dependants. Males.	Females.	Total following occupation as subsidiary to other. Males.	Females.	Group (31).—Lead, silver and zinc. Total earners (principal occupation). Males.	Females.	Total working dependants. Males.	Females.	Total following occupation as subsidiary to other. Males.	Females.
	223	223	224	225	226	227	228	229	230	231	232	233
ASSAM	1	...			3		1	...	...		3	...
(1) British Territory	1		...	...	3		1		...	...	3	...
SURMA VALLEY AND HILL DIVISION	1		...	...	3		1		...	...	3	...
Cachar	...	...	...		...		...	...	...		...	...
Sylhet	1	...		...	3		1			...	3	...
Khasi and Jaintia Hills (British)	...	...	...	...	...	...	...	...	...	...	...	...
Naga Hills	...	...	...		...		...	...	...			...
Lushai Hills	...	...	...	...	...	...	...	...	...		...	...
ASSAM VALLEY DIVISION	...	...			...	...	...	...	...		...	...
Goalpara	...	...	...		...	...	...	...	...	...	...	...
Kamrup	...	...		...	...	...	...	...	...	...	...	...
Darrang	...	...	...	...	...	...	...	...	...	...	...	...
Nowgong	...	...	...	...	...	...		...	...	...	...	...
Sibsagar	...	...	...	...	...	...	...	...	...	...	...	...
Lakhimpur	...	...	...	...	...	...	...	...	...	...	...	...
Garo Hills	...	...	...	...	...	...	...	...	...	...	...	...
SADIYA FRONTIER TRACT		...		...	...	...	...	...	...	...	...	...
BALIPARA FRONTIER TRACT	...	...			...	...	...	...		...	...	...
(2) Manipur State	...	...	...	...	...	...	...	...	...	...	...	...
(3) Khasi States	...	...	...	...	...	...	...	...	...	...	...	...

TABLE X.—OCCUPATION OR MEANS OF LIVELIHOOD. PART II.—DETAILS FOR DISTRICTS—*contd.*

DISTRICT OR STATE.	Class A.—Production of raw materials. Sub-class II.—Exploitation of minerals. Order 4.—Non-metallic minerals.											
	Total of order 4.—Non-metallic minerals.						Group (35) Coal.					
	Total earners (principal occupation).		Total working dependants.		Total following occupation as subsidiary to other.		Total earners (principal occupation).		Total working dependants.		Total following occupation as subsidiary to other.	
	Males.	Females.	Males.	Females.	Males.	Females.	Males.	Females.	Males.	Females.	Males.	Females.
	234	235	236	237	238	239	240	241	242	243	244	245
ASSAM	*14,813*	*1,120*	*554*	*39*	*478*	*16*	*6,376*	*681*	*237*	*31*	*135*	*4*
(1) British Territory	*14,743*	*948*	*424*	*37*	*453*	*16*	*6,363*	*681*	*237*	*31*	*120*	*4*
SURMA VALLEY AND HILL DIVISION	1,934	147	36	2	202	6	939	33	31	1	8	...
Cachar	923	113	4	1	169	6	7	...	...	...	...	...
Sylhet	80	2	1	...	25	...	3	...	...	...	...	...
Khasi and Jaintia Hills (British)	2	...	...	...	1	...	2	...	...	...	1	...
Naga Hills	929	32	31	1	7	...	927	33	31	1	7	...
Lushai Hills	...	...	...	...	...	...	...	...	...	...	...	...
ASSAM VALLEY DIVISION	12,759	801	388	35	251	8	5,423	648	206	30	112	4
Goalpara	25	...	1	...	4	...	22	...	1	...	4	...
Kamrup	4	...	...	...	5	...	1	...	...	...	...	...
Darrang	7	...	...	...	...	...	4	...	...	...	...	...
Nowgong	3	2	...	2	2	...	...	...	...	...	...	...
Sibsagar	19	...	1	...	10	...	9	...	1	...	7	...
Lakhimpur	12,701	799	386	33	230	8	5,387	648	204	30	101	4
Garo Hills	...	...	...	...	...	...	...	...	...	...	...	...
SADIYA FRONTIER TRACT	50	...	...	...	...	...	1	...	...	...	...	...
BALIPARA FRONTIER TRACT	...	...	...	...	...	...	...	...	...	...	...	...
(2) Manipur State	*25*	*172*	*124*	*2*	*2*	...	...	...	...	...	...	...
(3) Khasi States	*45*	...	*6*	...	*23*	...	*13*	...	...	...	*15*	...

TABLE X.—OCCUPATION OR MEANS OF LIVELIHOOD. PART II.—DETAILS FOR DISTRICTS—*contd.*

DISTRICT OR STATE.	Class A.—Production of raw materials. Sub-class II.—Exploitation of minerals. Order 4.—Non-metallic minerals.											
	Group (36).—Petroleum.						Group (37).—Building materials (including stone materials for cement manufacture and clays).					
	Total earners (principal occupation).		Total working dependants.		Total following occupation as subsidiary to other.		Total earners (principal occupation).		Total working dependants.		Total following occupation as subsidiary to other.	
	Males.	Females.	Males.	Females.	Males.	Females.	Males.	Females.	Males.	Females.	Males.	Females.
	246	247	248	249	250	251	252	253	254	255	256	257
ASSAM	*8,377*	*964*	*187*	*4*	*391*	*19*	*34*	...	*4*	...	*8*	...
(1) British Territory	*8,377*	*964*	*187*	*4*	*391*	*19*	...	...	...	...	...	...
SURMA VALLEY AND HILL DIVISION	996	114	5	1	189	8	...	...	...	...	...	...
Cachar	916	112	4	1	164	8	...	...	...	...	...	...
Sylhet	77	2	1	...	25	...	...	...	...	...	...	...
Khasi and Jaintia Hills (British)	...	...	...	...	...	...	...	...	...	...	...	...
Naga Hills	3	...	...	...	...	...	...	...	...	...	...	...
Lushai Hills...	...	...	...	...	...	...	...	...	...	...	...	...
ASSAM VALLEY DIVISION	7,333	150	182	3	133	4	...	...	...	...	...	...
Goalpara	3	...	...	...	...	...	...	...	...	...	...	...
Kamrup	...	...	...	...	...	...	...	...	...	...	...	...
Darrang	8	...	...	...	...	...	...	...	...	...	...	...
Nowgong	8	...	...	...	...	...	...	...	...	...	...	...
Sibsagar	10	...	...	...	3	...	...	...	...	...	...	...
Lakhimpur	7,314	150	182	3	130	4	...	...	...	...	...	...
Garo Hills	...	...	...	...	...	...	...	...	...	...	...	...
SADIYA FRONTIER TRACT	40	...	...	...	...	...	...	...	...	...	...	...
BALIPARA FRONTIER TRACT	...	...	...	...	...	...	...	...	...	...	...	...
(2) Manipur State	...	...	...	...	...	...	2	...	...	...	...	...
(3) Khasi States	...	...	...	...	...	...	32	...	4	...	8	...

TABLE X.—Occupation or means of livelihood. Part II.—Details for Districts—*contd.*

DISTRICT OR STATE.	Class A.—Production of raw materials.											
	Sub-class II.—Exploitation of minerals.											
	Order 4.—Non-metallic minerals.											
	Group (39).—Precious and semi-precious stones.						Group (40).—Salt, saltpetre and other saline substances.					
	Total earners (principal occupation).		Total working dependants.		Total following occupation as subsidiary to other.		Total earners (principal occupation).		Total working dependants.		Total following occupation as subsidiary to other.	
	Males.	Females.	Males.	Females.	Males.	Females.	Males.	Females.	Males.	Females.	Males.	Females.
	258	259	260	261	262	263	264	265	266	267	268	269
ASSAM	...	3	...	2	7	...	26	179	194	2	7	...
(1) British Territory	...	3	...	2	7	...	3	...	...	...	5	...
SURMA VALLEY AND HILL DIVISION	...	1	...	...	5	...	...	...	...	...	...	...
Cachar	...	1	...	...	5	...	...	...	...	...	...	...
Sylhet	...	...	...	...	...	...	...	...	...	...	...	...
Khasi and Jaintia Hills (British)	...	...	...	...	...	...	...	...	...	...	...	...
Naga Hills	...	...	...	...	...	...	...	...	...	...	...	...
Lushai Hills	...	...	...	...	...	...	...	...	...	...	...	...
ASSAM VALLEY DIVISION	...	2	...	2	2	...	3	...	...	...	5	...
Goalpara	...	...	...	...	...	...	...	...	...	...	...	...
Kamrup	...	...	...	...	...	...	3	...	...	...	5	...
Darrang	...	...	...	...	...	...	...	...	...	...	...	...
Nowgong	...	2	...	2	2	...	...	...	...	...	...	...
Sibsagar	...	...	...	...	...	...	...	...	...	...	...	...
Lakhimpur	...	...	...	...	...	...	...	...	...	...	...	...
Garo Hills	...	...	...	...	...	...	...	...	...	...	...	...
SADIYA FRONTIER TRACT	...	...	...	...	...	...	...	...	...	...	...	...
BALIPARA FRONTIER TRACT	...	...	...	...	...	...	...	...	...	...	...	...
(2) Manipur State	...	...	...	...	...	...	23	179	194	2	2	...
(3) Khasi States	...	...	...	...	...	...	...	...	...	...	...	...

TABLE X.—OCCUPATION OR MEANS OF LIVELIHOOD. PART II.—DETAILS FOR DISTRICTS—*contd.*

DISTRICT OR STATE.	Class B.—Preparation and supply of material substances.											
	Total of class B.—Preparation and supply of material substances.						Sub-class III.—Industry. Total of sub-class III.—Industry.					
	Total earners (principal occupation).		Total working dependants.		Total following occupation as subsidiary to other.		Total earners (principal occupation).		Total working dependants.		Total following occupation as subsidiary to other.	
	Males.	Females.	Males.	Females.	Males.	Females.	Males.	Females.	Males.	Females.	Males.	Females.
	270	271	272	273	274	275	276	277	278	279	280	281
ASSAM	*219,805*	*47,578*	*13,096*	*226,192*	*125,143*	*28,216*	*71,240*	*27,462*	*6,418*	*218,829*	*43,709*	*23,306*
(1) British Territory	*201,344*	*33,876*	*12,028*	*207,966*	*119,387*	*22,339*	*65,790*	*19,458*	*5,873*	*201,360*	*42,512*	*19,654*
SURMA VALLEY AND HILL DIVISION	71,312	15,946	6,113	18,392	74,364	6,493	24,614	10,513	3,003	17,192	26,824	4,907
Cachar	12,443	4,177	676	5,913	6,885	1,663	4,234	1,766	292	5,550	3,068	1,298
Sylhet	54,716	9,616	4,915	7,376	64,138	2,605	18,700	7,605	2,336	7,026	23,579	2,229
Khasi and Jaintia Hills (British)	2,303	1,557	171	3,456	1,301	1,498	1,064	858	94	3,197	256	713
Naga Hills	1,031	146	134	1,210	484	592	317	67	110	1,157	260	583
Lushai Hills	819	450	217	847	1,556	115	299	137	163	202	671	85
ASSAM VALLEY DIVISION	127,563	17,558	5,897	188,056	44,427	11,596	39,950	8,636	2,850	183,293	15,454	10,497
Goalpara	22,220	4,118	1,310	20,401	6,665	948	6,180	1,525	467	19,529	2,094	707
Kamrup	30,923	6,077	1,812	98,818	10,571	2,630	10,323	4,218	1,339	97,·42	3,593	2,413
Darrang	16,082	1,523	296	18,914	4,639	700	4,457	676	129	18,002	1,400	834
Nowgong	12,516	1,513	640	23,300	4,910	2,080	2,902	637	226	22,978	1,855	1,944
Sibsagar	19,445	2,043	1,078	17,896	10,095	2,961	6,146	764	379	16,232	3,610	2,684
Lakhimpur	24,636	2,047	737	13,196	4,929	2,210	9,318	741	291	12,191	2,030	1,910
Garo Hills	1,741	239	25	1,429	2,618	68	543	73	8	1,419	703	46
SADIYA FRONTIER TRACT	2,152	355	18	606	465	4,255	1,014	296	10	633	107	4,248
BALIPARA FRONTIER TRACT	317	17	...	248	121	5	203	13	...	242	127	4
(2) Manipur State	*6,147*	*11,398*	*804*	*18,043*	*2,611*	*2,856*	*3,032*	*7,347*	*475*	*10,923*	*556*	*2,545*
(3) Khasi States	*5,314*	*2,304*	*264*	*883*	*3,145*	*3,091*	*2,416*	*657*	*71*	*546*	*634*	*1,107*

TABLE X.—OCCUPATION OR MEANS OF LIVELIHOOD. PART II.—DETAILS FOR DISTRICTS—*contd.*

Class B.—Preparation and supply of material substances. Sub-class III.—Industry. Order 5.—Textiles.

DISTRICT OR STATE.	Total of Order 5.—Textiles. Total earners (principal occupation). Males.	Females.	Total working dependants. Males.	Females.	Total following occupation as subsidiary to other. Males.	Females.	Group (43)—Cotton ginning, cleaning and pressing. Total earners (principal occupation). Males.	Females.	Total working dependants. Males.	Females.	Total following occupation as subsidiary to other. Males.	Females.
	282	283	284	285	286	287	288	289	290	291	292	293
ASSAM	*2,169*	*15,620*	*1,993*	*211,792*	*2,831*	*20,739*	*176*	*169*	...	...	*10*	*6*
(1) British Territory ...	*2,093*	*8,760*	*1,849*	*194,957*	*2,777*	*17,588*	*176*	*169*	...	...	*10*	*6*
SURMA VALLEY AND HILL DIVISION ...	880	3,627	308	14,210	1,990	3,567	3	...	...	...	1	...
Cachar ...	68	854	26	5,391	72	1,189	2	...	...	...	...	...
Sylhet ...	795	2,135	233	4,437	1,903	878	1	...	...	...	1	...
Khasi and Jaintia Hills (British) ...	2	499	37	3,090	5	855	...	...	...	...	...	...
Naga Hills ...	8	23	8	1,096	10	571	...	...	...	...	...	...
Lushai Hills ...	7	116	4	196	...	74	...	...	...	...	...	...
ASSAM VALLEY DIVISION ...	1,143	5,123	1,541	179,874	767	10,872	173	169	...	...	9	6
Goalpara ...	384	563	145	19,128	56	728	160	169	...	...	2	6
Kamrup ...	452	3,074	1,009	96,348	355	2,358	...	...	...	...	...	...
Darrang ...	49	151	48	12,816	30	836	...	...	...	...	...	...
Nowgong ...	205	811	134	23,074	29	1,923	5	...	...	...	3	...
Sibsagar ...	30	349	128	15,300	236	2,568	...	...	...	...	2	...
Lakhimpur ...	19	161	74	12,220	29	1,900	8	...	...	...	...	...
Garo Hills ...	3	14	3	1,345	2	35	...	...	...	...	1	...
SADIYA FRONTIER TRACT ...	...	8	...	631	30	4,366	...	...	...	...	...	...
BALIPARA FRONTIER TRACT ...	...	2	...	262	...	3	...	...	...	...	...	...
(2) Manipur State ...	*134*	*6,789*	*143*	*16,497*	*49*	*2,496*	...	...	...	...	...	...
(3) Khasi States ...	*19*	*71*	*1*	*408*	*5*	*655*	...	...	...	...	...	...

TABLE X.—OCCUPATION OR MEANS OF LIVELIHOOD. PART II.—DETAILS FOR DISTRICTS—*contd.*

DISTRICT OR STATE.	Class B.—Preparation and supply of material substances. Sub-class III.—Industry. Order 6.—Textiles. Group (43).—Cotton spinning, Sizing and weaving. Total earners (principal occupation). Males.	Females.	Total working dependants. Males.	Females.	Total following occupation as subsidiary to other. Males.	Females.	Group (44).—Jute pressing, spinning and weaving. Total earners (principal occupation). Males.	Females.	Total working dependants. Males.	Females.	Total following occupation as subsidiary to other. Males.	Females.
	294	295	296	297	298	299	300	301	302	303	304	305
ASSAM	*1,936*	*13,770*	*1,819*	*208,716*	*2,952*	*20,383*	*501*	*88*	*6*	*48*	*111*	*9*
(1) British Territory	*1,104*	*7,580*	*1,673*	*199,036*	*2,901*	*17,348*	*501*	*88*	*6*	*48*	*111*	*9*
SURMA VALLEY AND HILL DIVISION	791	2,874	262	13,694	1,727	3,121	1	39	...	...	2	9
Cachar	65	644	36	5,355	70	1,180	1	...	...	...	...	...
Sylhet	710	1,306	183	3,277	1,643	748	...	39	...	...	2	9
Khasi and Jaintia Hills (British)	2	494	37	3,000	5	553	...	...	...	...	...	...
Naga Hills	8	23	8	1,098	10	571	...	...	...	...	...	...
Lushai Hills	6	116	8	195	...	74	...	...	...	...	...	...
ASSAM VALLEY DIVISION	313	4,696	1,410	178,144	454	9,979	500	49	6	48	109	...
Goalpara	83	354	143	10,097	83	718	131	32	...	...	1	...
Kamrup	136	3,360	885	94,784	104	2,231	189	17	6	48	107	...
Darrang	24	147	46	12,768	28	535	25	...	...	...	1	...
Nowgong	37	302	134	23,647	20	1,914	154	...	...	...	...	...
Sibsagar	26	369	128	15,207	233	2,508	...	...	...	...	...	...
Lakhimpur	7	151	73	13,346	29	1,876	1	...	...	...	...	...
Garo Hills	...	14	2	1,315	1	36	...	...	...	...	...	...
SADIYA FRONTIER TRACT	...	8	...	631	20	4,246	...	...	...	...	...	...
BALIPARA FRONTIER TRACT	...	2	...	237	...	2	...	...	...	...	...	...
(2) Manipur State	*193*	*6,124*	*139*	*16,280*	*47*	*2,396*	...	...	...	...	...	...
(3) Khasi States	*10*	*66*	*1*	*400*	*4*	*639*	...	...	...	...	...	...

TABLE X.—OCCUPATION OR MEANS OF LIVELIHOOD. PART II.—DETAILS FOR DISTRICTS—*contd.*

DISTRICT OR STATE.	Class B.—Preparation and supply of material substances.											
	Sub-class III.—Industry.											
	Order 5.—Textiles.											
	Group (45).—Rope, Twine, String and other fibres.						Group (46).—Wool carding, spinning and weaving.					
	Total earners (principal occupation).		Total working dependants.		Total following occupation as subsidiary to other.		Total earners (Principal occupation).		Total working dependants.		Total following occupation as subsidiary to other.	
	Males.	Females.	Males.	Females.	Males.	Females.	Males.	Females.	Males.	Females.	Males.	Females.
	306	307	308	309	310	311	312	313	314	315	316	317
ASSAM	*125*	*758*	*72*	*1,922*	*337*	*210*	*1*	...	...	*1*	...	...
(1) British Territory	*116*	*748*	*68*	*1,915*	*334*	*193*	*1*	...	...	*1*	...	...
SURMA VALLEY AND HILL DIVISION	82	711	46	1,185	260	137	...	...	...	...	...	...
Cachar	...	8	...	36	2	9	...	...	...	...	...	...
Sylhet	82	697	45	1,149	258	126	...	...	...	...	...	...
Khasi and Jaintia Hills (British)	...	5	...	...	...	2	...	...	...	...	...	...
Naga Hills	...	1	...	...	...	...	...	...	...	...	...	...
Lushai Hills	...	...	1	...	...	...	...	...	...	...	...	...
ASSAM VALLEY DIVISION	34	37	22	725	74	55	1	...	...	1	...	...
Goalpara	5	4	3	25	20	3	1	...	...	...	...	...
Kamrup	17	31	16	690	53	52	...	...	...	...	...	...
Darrang	...	1	2	7	1	...	...	...	...	...	...	...
Nowgong	6	1	...	1	...	...	...	...	...	...	...	...
Sibsagar	2	...	...	1	...	...	...	...	...	1	...	...
Lakhimpur	2	...	...	1	...	...	...	...	...	...	...	...
Garo Hills	2	...	1	...	...	...	...	...	...	...	...	...
SADIYA FRONTIER TRACT	...	...	...	...	...	...	...	...	...	...	...	...
BALIPARA FRONTIER TRACT	...	...	...	5	...	1	...	...	...	...	...	...
(2) Manipur State	7	7	4	...	2	1	...	...	...	...	...	...
(3) Khasi States	2	3	...	7	1	16	...	...	...	...	...	...

TABLE X.—OCCUPATION OR MEANS OF LIVELIHOOD. PART II.—DETAILS FOR DISTRICTS—*contd.*

Class B.—Preparation and supply of material substances. Sub-class III.—Industry. Order 6.—Textiles.

DISTRICT OR STATE.	Group (67).—Silk spinning and weaving. Total earners (principal occupation). Males.	Females.	Total working dependants. Males.	Females.	Total following occupation as subsidiary to other. Males.	Females.	Group (69).—Dyeing, bleaching, printing, preparation and sponging of textiles. Total earners (Principal occupation). Males.	Females.	Total working dependants. Males.	Females.	Total following occupation as subsidiary to other. Males.	Females.
	318	319	320	321	322	323	324	325	326	327	328	329
ASSAM	*101*	*176*	*103*	*941*	*190*	*35*	*20*	...	...	...	*1*	...
(1) British Territory	*101*	*163*	*103*	*937*	*190*	*39*	*19*	...	...	...	*1*	...
SURMA VALLEY AND HILL DIVISION	...	...	...	...	...	...	1	...	...	...	...	...
Cachar	...	...	...	...	...	...	...	...	...	...	...	...
Sylhet	...	...	...	...	...	...	1	...	...	...	...	...
Khasi and Jaintia Hills (British)	...	...	...	...	...	...	...	...	...	...	...	...
Naga Hills	...	...	...	...	...	...	...	...	...	...	...	...
Lushai Hills	...	...	...	...	...	...	...	...	...	...	...	...
ASSAM VALLEY DIVISION	101	163	103	937	190	32	18	...	...	...	1	...
Goalpara	2	4	...	6	...	1	4	...	...	...	...	...
Kamrup	98	148	103	841	190	20	9	...	...	...	1	...
Darrang	...	3	...	41	...	1	...	...	...	...	...	...
Nowgong	...	8	...	36	...	9	3	...	...	...	...	...
Sibsagar	...	...	...	30	...	...	2	...	...	...	...	...
Lakhimpur	1	...	1	3	...	1	...	...	...	...	...	...
Garo Hills	...	...	...	...	...	...	...	...	...	...	...	...
SADIYA FRONTIER TRACT	...	...	...	...	...	...	...	...	...	...	...	...
BALIPARA FRONTIER TRACT	...	...	...	...	...	...	...	...	...	...	...	...
(2) Manipur State	...	*13*	...	*4*	...	*3*	*1*	...	...	...	...	...
(3) Khasi States	...	...	...	...	...	...	...	...	...	...	...	...

TABLE X.—Occupation or means of livelihood. Part II.—Details for Districts—*contd.*

District or State.	Class B.—Preparation and supply of material substances.											
	Sub-class III.—Industry.											
	Order 5.—Textiles.						Order 6.—Hides, skins and hard materials from the animal kingdom.					
	Group (50)—Lace, crepe, embroideries, fringes, etc., and insufficiently described textile industries.						Total of order 6.—Hides, skins, etc.					
	Total earners (principal occupation).		Total working dependants.		Total following occupation as subsidiary to other.		Total earners (principal occupation).		Total working dependants.		Total following occupation as subsidiary to other.	
	Males.	Females.	Males.	Females.	Males.	Females.	Males.	Females.	Males.	Females.	Males.	Females.
	330	331	332	333	334	335	336	337	338	339	340	341
ASSAM	*9*	*659*	...	*164*	...	*96*	*695*	*17*	*55*	*13*	*280*	*5*
(1) British Territory	*5*	*12*	...	*20*	...	...	*693*	*17*	*54*	*13*	*274*	*5*
SURMA VALLEY AND HILL DIVISION	2	3	...	1	...	...	292	12	35	1	100	1
Cachar	...	...	...	...	...	...	10	1	...	...	13	...
Sylhet	1	3	...	1	...	...	282	11	35	1	147	1
Khasi and Jaintia Hills (British)	...	...	...	...	...	...	...	...	...	...	...	...
Naga Hills	...	...	...	...	...	...	...	...	...	...	...	...
Lushai Hills	1	...	...	...	...	...	...	...	...	...	...	...
ASSAM VALLEY DIVISION	3	9	...	19	...	...	401	5	19	13	114	4
Goalpara	...	...	...	...	...	...	111	...	11	6	22	...
Kamrup	3	9	...	19	...	...	215	5	6	3	41	3
Darrang	...	...	...	...	...	...	33	...	...	...	9	...
Nowgong	...	...	...	...	...	...	38	...	1	4	38	1
Sibsagar	...	...	...	...	...	...	6	...	...	1	8	...
Lakhimpur	...	...	...	...	...	...	4	...	1	...	...	...
Garo Hills	...	...	...	...	...	...	...	...	...	...	...	...
SADIYA FRONTIER TRACT	...	...	...	...	...	...	...	...	...	...	...	...
BALIPARA FRONTIER TRACT	...	...	...	...	...	...	...	...	...	...	...	...
(2) Manipur State	*4*	*645*	...	*143*	...	*96*	*2*	...	*1*	...	...	...
(3) Khasi States	...	*2*	...	*1*	...	...	...	...	...	...	*6*	...

TABLE X.—OCCUPATION OR MEANS OF LIVELIHOOD. PART II.—DETAILS FOR DISTRICTS—*contd.*

Class B.—Preparation and supply of material substances. Sub-class III.—Industry. Order 6.—Hides, skins and hard materials from the animal kingdom.

DISTRICT OR STATE.	Group (51). Working in leather. Total earners (principal occupation). Males.	Females.	Total working dependants. Males.	Females.	Total following occupation as subsidiary to other. Males.	Females.	Group (53).—Bone, ivory, horn, shell, etc., workers (except buttons). Total earners (principal occupation). Males.	Females.	Total working dependants. Males.	Females.	Total following occupation as subsidiary to other. Males.	Females.
	342	343	344	345	346	347	348	349	350	351	352	353
ASSAM	*666*	*17*	*54*	*13*	*276*	*2*	*29*	...	*1*	...	*4*	*3*
(1) British Territory	*664*	*17*	*53*	*13*	*270*	*2*	*29*	...	*1*	...	*4*	*3*
SURMA VALLEY AND HILL DIVISION	281	12	34	1	160	1	11	...	1	...	...	...
Cachar	10	1	...	...	13	...	...	...	...	...	...	...
Sylhet	271	11	34	1	147	1	11	...	1	...	...	...
Khasi and Jaintia Hills (British)	...	...	...	...	...	...	...	...	...	...	...	...
Naga Hills	...	...	...	...	...	...	...	...	...	...	...	...
Lushai Hills	...	...	...	...	...	...	...	...	...	...	...	...
ASSAM VALLEY DIVISION	383	5	19	12	110	1	18	...	...	...	4	3
Goalpara	103	...	11	5	23	...	2	...	...	...	...	...
Kamrup	213	5	6	2	41	...	2	...	...	...	...	3
Darrang	20	...	...	...	9	...	12	...	...	...	...	...
Nowgong	33	...	1	4	33	1	...	...	...	...	...	...
Sibsagar	5	...	...	1	6	...	1	...	...	...	4	...
Lakhimpur	3	...	1	...	...	...	1	...	...	...	...	...
Garo Hills	...	...	...	...	...	...	...	...	...	...	...	...
SADIYA FRONTIER TRACT	...	...	...	...	...	...	...	...	...	...	...	...
BALIPARA FRONTIER TRACT	...	...	...	...	...	...	...	...	...	...	...	...
(2) Manipur State	*2*	...	*1*	...	...	...	...	...	...	...	...	...
(3) Khasi States	...	...	...	...	*6*	...	...	...	...	...	...	...

TABLE X.—Occupation or means of livelihood. Part II.—Details for Districts—*contd.*

DISTRICT OR STATE.	Class B.—Preparation and supply of material substances. Sub-class III.—Industry. Order 7.—Wood. Total of Order 7.—Wood. Total earners (principal occupation). Males.	Total earners (principal occupation). Females.	Total working dependants. Males.	Total working dependants. Females.	Total following occupation as subsidiary to other. Males.	Total following occupation as subsidiary to other. Females.	Group (54).—Sawyers. Total earners (principal occupation). Males.	Total earners (principal occupation). Females.	Total working dependants. Males.	Total working dependants. Females.	Total following occupation as subsidiary to other. Males.	Total following occupation as subsidiary to other. Females.
	354	355	356	357	358	359	360	361	362	363	364	365
ASSAM	*24,418*	*1,712*	*1,901*	*1,914*	*21,858*	*770*	*6,985*	*360*	*195*	*24*	*4,511*	*7*
(1) British Territory	*22,196*	*1,609*	*1,714*	*1,843*	*21,098*	*479*	*6,172*	*360*	*195*	*24*	*4,455*	*7*
SURMA VALLEY AND HILL DIVISION	8,143	908	1,360	1,476	14,306	343	1,350	1	181	...	2,202	2
Cachar	1,089	60	123	27	1,034	7	300	...	43	...	194	...
Sylhet	6,750	778	927	1,400	12,889	235	1,004	1	138	...	1,908	1
Khasi and Jaintia Hills (British)	179	64	34	49	183	101	30	...	...	...	80	1
Naga Hills	104	...	24	...	137	...	16	...	...	...	74	...
Lushai Hills	81	1	143	...	76	...	10	...	...	...	6	...
ASSAM VALLEY DIVISION	13,153	447	470	367	6,653	135	4,102	100	14	24	2,068	5
Goalpara	1,633	116	68	67	1,474	25	516	1	2	...	1,063	4
Kamrup	3,796	67	119	86	1,207	34	1,718	...	2	...	304	...
Darrang	1,263	30	18	9	463	23	245	...	1	...	109	...
Nowgong	709	11	22	14	485	21	94	4	1	...	16	...
Sibsagar	1,806	16	103	98	1,228	14	416	...	5	...	201	...
Lakhimpur	3,773	196	138	93	1,268	18	1,084	95	3	24	222	1
Garo Hills	213	...	2	...	156	...	29	...	...	...	83	...
SADIYA FRONTIER TRACT	700	200	4	...	13	...	641	259	...	...	6	...
BALIPARA FRONTIER TRACT	140	...	...	...	194	1	70	...	...	...	80	...
(2) Manipur State	*1,349*	*22*	*153*	*19*	*359*	*5*	*63*	...	...	...	*6*	...
(3) Khasi States	*880*	*81*	*34*	*59*	*401*	*286*	*50*	...	...	...	*50*	...

TABLE X.—OCCUPATION OR MEANS OF LIVELIHOOD. PART II.—DETAILS FOR DISTRICTS—*contd.*

DISTRICT OR STATE.	Class B.—Preparation and supply of material substances.											
	Sub-class III.—Industry.											
	Order 7.—Wood.											
	Group (55).—Carpenters, turners and joiners, etc.						Group (56).—Basket makers and other industries of woody materials, including leaves and thatchers and builders working with bamboo, reeds or similar materials.					
	Total earners (principal occupation).		Total working dependants.		Total following occupation as subsidiary to other.		Total earners (principal occupation).		Total working dependants.		Total following occupation as subsidiary to other.	
	Males.	Females.	Males.	Females.	Males.	Females.	Males.	Females.	Males.	Females.	Males.	Females.
	366	367	368	369	370	371	372	373	374	375	376	377
ASSAM	*13,332*	*65*	*657*	*40*	*6,939*	*13*	*5,801*	*1,287*	*1,049*	*1,850*	*10,408*	*751*
(1) British Territory	*10,469*	*61*	*567*	*38*	*6,619*	*10*	*5,555*	*1,188*	*957*	*1,781*	*10,094*	*469*
SURMA VALLEY AND HILL DIVISION	**4,112**	**4**	**385**	...	**4,052**	**2**	**2,672**	**897**	**674**	**1,476**	**7,904**	**330**
Cachar	643	1	36	...	406	...	255	58	43	37	434	7
Sylhet	3,327	3	323	...	3,579	2	2,329	774	466	1,400	7,403	233
Khasi and Jaintia Hills (British)	130	...	3	...	28	...	19	64	21	49	74	100
Naga Hills	40	...	23	...	29	...	45	...	1	...	24	...
Lushai Hills	60	...	...	...	10	...	21	1	143	...	60	...
ASSAM VALLEY DIVISION	**6,283**	**56**	**174**	**38**	**2,558**	**8**	**2,769**	**291**	**282**	**305**	**2,007**	**138**
Goalpara	668	37	41	11	340	...	149	78	25	68	83	21
Kamrup	1,683	9	45	13	761	4	406	65	72	73	443	39
Darrang	747	...	8	...	100	...	261	30	9	9	104	33
Nowgong	627	...	18	...	293	1	78	7	3	14	166	20
Sibsagar	1,033	4	28	10	654	3	217	12	60	88	343	11
Lakhimpur	1,175	6	23	4	285	...	1,514	97	113	65	760	17
Garo Hills	130	...	2	...	45	...	54	...	...	...	29	...
SADIYA FRONTIER TRACT	**61**	**1**	**3**	...	**7**	...	**58**	...	**1**	...	...	...
BALIPARA FRONTIER TRACT	**16**	...	...	...	**2**	...	**56**	...	...	...	**23**	**1**
(2) Manipur State	*975*	*3*	*81*	*1*	*164*	*1*	*204*	*19*	*72*	*11*	*180*	*4*
(3) Khasi States	*888*	*1*	*14*	*1*	*156*	*1*	*42*	*80*	*20*	*58*	*195*	*285*

TABLE X.—OCCUPATION OR MEANS OF LIVELIHOOD. PART II.—DETAILS FOR DISTRICTS—*contd.*

Class B.—Preparation and supply of material substances. Sub-class III.—Industry. Order 8.—Metals.

DISTRICT OR STATE.	Total of order 8.—Metals. Total earners (principal occupation). Males.	Females.	Total working dependants. Males.	Females.	Total following occupation as subsidiary to other. Males.	Females.	Group (57).—Smelting, forging and rolling of iron and other metals. Total earners (principal occupation). Males.	Females.	Total working dependants. Males.	Females.	Total following occupation as subsidiary to other. Males.	Females.
	378	379	380	381	382	383	384	385	386	387	388	389
ASSAM	*5,330*	*78*	*997*	*67*	*2,413*	*8*	*6*	...	...	...	*8*	...
(1) British Territory ...	*5,057*	*33*	*198*	*61*	*2,364*	*5*	*6*	...	...	...	*8*	...
SURMA VALLEY AND HILL DIVISION ...	1,578	...	102	2	996	...	6	...	...	...	8	...
Cachar ...	101	...	4	...	41	...	...	...	...	...	...	...
Sylhet ...	1,312	...	84	2	614	...	6	...	...	...	8	...
Khasi and Jaintia Hills (British) ...	44	...	1	...	23	...	...	...	...	...	...	...
Naga Hills ...	34	...	1	...	50	...	...	...	...	...	...	...
Lushai Hills ...	87	...	12	...	268	...	...	...	...	...	...	...
ASSAM VALLEY DIVISION ...	3,440	33	96	59	1,368	5	...	...	...	...	...	...
Goalpara ...	421	2	9	7	77	...	...	...	...	...	...	...
Kamrup ...	1,600	9	45	40	317	...	...	...	...	...	...	...
Darrang ...	340	6	8	...	142	...	...	...	...	...	...	...
Nowgong ...	256	2	6	3	190	1	...	...	...	...	...	...
Sibsagar ...	434	10	18	8	419	4	...	...	...	...	...	...
Lakhimpur ...	468	4	7	1	186	...	...	...	...	...	...	...
Garo Hills ...	63	...	...	...	29	...	...	...	...	...	...	...
SADIYA FRONTIER TRACT ...	38	...	...	...	...	...	...	...	...	...	...	...
BALIPARA FRONTIER TRACT ...	1	...	...	...	...	...	...	...	...	...	...	...
(2) Manipur State ...	*133*	*42*	*28*	*6*	*26*	*2*	...	...	...	...	...	...
(3) Khasi States ...	*140*	*3*	*1*	...	*23*	*1*	...	...	...	...	...	...

TABLE X.—OCCUPATION OR MEANS OF LIVELIHOOD. PART II.—DETAILS FOR DISTRICTS—*contd.*

DISTRICT OR STATE.	Class B.—Preparation and supply of material substances.											
	Sub-class III.—Industry.											
	Order 8.—Metals.											
	Group (58).—Makers of arms, guns, etc.						Group (59).—Blacksmiths, other workers in iron, makers of implements.					
	Total earners (principal occupation).		Total working dependants.		Total following occupation as subsidiary to other.		Total earners (principal occupation).		Total working dependants.		Total following occupation as subsidiary to other.	
	Males.	Females.	Males.	Females.	Males.	Females.	Males.	Females.	Males.	Females.	Males.	Females.
	390	391	392	393	394	395	396	397	398	399	400	401
ASSAM	*22*	...	*2*	...	*8*	...	*3,476*	*53*	*171*	*17*	*1,877*	*3*
(1) British Territory	*22*	...	*2*	...	*8*	...	*3,164*	*15*	*144*	*11*	*1,831*	...
SURMA VALLEY AND HILL DIVISION	7	...	...	...	3	...	1,280	...	95	1	953	...
Cachar	3	...	...	...	...	...	154	..	4	...	40	...
Sylhet	4	...	...	...	...	...	1,017	...	77	1	575	...
Khasi and Jaintia Hills (British)	...	...	...	...	...	...	38	...	1	...	23	...
Naga Hills	...	...	...	...	3	...	22	...	1	...	47	...
Lushai Hills	...	...	...	...	...	...	57	...	13	...	368	...
ASSAM VALLEY DIVISION	14	...	2	...	5	...	1,958	15	49	10	878	...
Goalpara	3	...	2	...	1	...	350	...	7	1	65	...
Kamrup	2	...	...	...	1	...	417	...	20	...	109	...
Darrang	4	...	...	...	2	...	218	3	3	...	116	...
Nowgong	3	...	...	...	...	...	157	2	3	2	73	...
Sibsagar	...	...	...	...	...	...	201	7	10	7	277	...
Lakhimpur	1	...	...	...	...	...	353	3	6	...	127	...
Garo Hills	1	...	...	...	1	...	62	...	...	...	28	...
SADIYA FRONTIER TRACT	1	...	...	...	...	...	25	...	...	...	...	...
BALIPARA FRONTIER TRACT	...	...	...	...	...	...	1	...	...	...	...	...
(2) Manipur State	...	...	...	...	...	...	*128*	*35*	*26*	*6*	*24*	*2*
(3) Khasi States	...	...	...	...	...	...	*134*	*3*	*1*	...	*22*	*1*

TABLE X.—Occupation or means of livelihood. Part II.—Details for Districts—*contd.*

DISTRICT OR STATE.	Class B.—Preparation and supply of material substances. Sub-class III.—Industry. Order 8.—Metals. Group (60).—Workers in brass, copper and bell metal. Total earners (principal occupation). Males.	Females.	Total working dependants. Males.	Females.	Total following occupation as subsidiary to other. Males.	Females.	Group (61).—Workers in other metals (except precious metals). Total earners (principal occupation). Males.	Females.	Total working dependants. Males.	Females.	Total following occupation as subsidiary to other. Males.	Females.
	402	403	404	405	406	407	408	409	410	411	412	413
ASSAM.	*1,663*	*25*	*48*	*50*	*488*	*5*	*913*	...	*6*	...	*39*	...
(1) British Territory	*1,655*	*18*	*46*	*50*	*485*	*5*	*910*	...	*6*	...	*39*	...
SURMA VALLEY AND HILL DIVISION	160	...	4	1	15	...	75	...	3	...	17	...
Cachar	22	...	...	...	...	...	10	...	...	...	1	...
Sylhet	136	...	4	1	15	...	59	...	3	...	16	...
Khasi and Jaintia Hills (British)...	...	...	...	...	...		6	...	...	...	...	...
Naga Hills	2	...	...	...	...	...	...	...	...	...	...	...
Lushai Hills	...	...	...	...	...	...	...	...	...	...	...	...
ASSAM VALLEY DIVISION	1,484	18	42	49	470	5	134	...	3	...	15	...
Goalpara	54	2	...	6	6	...	14	...	...	...	1	...
Kamrup	1,033	9	25	40	117	...	58	...	3	...	10	...
Darrang	106	3	5	...	23	...	13	...	...	...	1	...
Nowgong	85	...	8	1	125	1	10	...	...	...	1	...
Sibsagar	133	3	3	1	140	4	10	...	...	...	2	...
Lakhimpur	76	1	1	1	59	...	29	...	...	...	...	...
Garo Hills	...	...	...	...	...	...	...	...	...	...	...	...
SADIYA FRONTIER TRACT	11	...	...	...	...	...	1	...	...	...	...	...
BALIPARA FRONTIER TRACT	...	...	...	...	...	...	...	...	...	...	...	...
(2) Manipur State	*5*	*7*	*2*	...	*2*	...	...	...	...	...	...	...
(3) Khasi States	*3*	...	...	...	*2*	...	*3*	...	...	...	...	...

TABLE X.—Occupation or means of livelihood. Part II.—Details for Districts—*contd.*

Class B.—Preparation and supply of material substances. Sub-class III.—Industry. Order 9.—Ceramics.

DISTRICT OR STATE.	Total of order 9.—Ceramics. Total earners (principal occupation). Males.	Females.	Total working dependants. Males.	Females.	Total following occupation as subsidiary to other. Males.	Females.	Group (83).—Potters and makers of earthenware. Total earners (principal occupation). Males.	Females.	Total working dependants. Males.	Females.	Total following occupation as subsidiary to other. Males.	Females.
	414	415	416	417	418	419	420	421	422	423	424	425
ASSAM	*3,667*	*1,438*	*381*	*2,876*	*2,836*	*199*	*2,076*	*1,329*	*314*	*2,855*	*1,917*	*185*
(1) British Territory	*3,697*	*1,978*	*377*	*2,589*	*2,820*	*180*	*2,000*	*1,169*	*314*	*2,561*	*1,911*	*173*
SURMA VALLEY AND HILL DIVISION	1,256	309	266	271	1,803	54	927	283	226	264	1,260	52
Cachar	274	38	23	58	111	3	332	38	20	64	94	3
Sylhet	963	260	243	208	1,691	35	595	234	206	201	1,165	33
Khasi and Jaintia Hills (British)	...	11	...	1	...	5	...	11	...	1	...	5
Naga Hills	...	...	...	6	1	11	...	...	...	6	1	11
Lushai Hills	...	...	...	...	...	...	...	...	...	...	...	...
ASSAM VALLEY DIVISION	2,371	960	111	2,311	1,017	126	1,173	879	89	2,297	651	121
Goalpara	338	214	30	161	40	5	305	210	17	161	23	5
Kamrup	350	245	23	1,067	321	41	306	239	23	1,057	247	41
Darrang	151	193	3	86	30	3	100	103	3	85	10	3
Nowgong	136	187	7	196	103	23	84	157	7	196	101	23
Sibsagar	528	100	38	748	357	40	176	75	38	743	241	48
Lakhimpur	748	47	11	30	161	6	115	1	2	12	20	1
Garo Hills	90	4	...	45	6	3	83	4	...	44	1	2
SADIYA FRONTIER TRACT	...	...	...	...	...	...	...	...	...	...	...	...
BALIPARA FRONTIER TRACT	...	...	...	...	...	...	...	...	...	...	...	...
(2) Manipur State	*233*	*159*	*4*	*299*	*16*	*12*	*69*	*159*	...	*299*	*6*	*12*
(3) Khasi States	*7*	*1*	...	*9*	...	...	*7*	*1*	...	*9*	...	...

TABLE X.—OCCUPATION OR MEANS OF LIVELIHOOD. PART II.—DETAILS FOR DISTRICTS—*contd.*

DISTRICT OR STATE.	Class B.—Preparation and supply of material substances.											
	Sub-class III.—Industry.											
	Order 9.—Ceramics.											
	Group (64).—Brick and tile makers.						Group (65).—Other workers in ceramics.					
	Total earners (principal occupation).		Total working dependants.		Total following occupation as subsidiary to other.		Total earners (principal occupation).		Total working dependants.		Total following occupation as subsidiary to other.	
	Males.	Females.	Males.	Females.	Males.	Females.	Males.	Females.	Males.	Females.	Males.	Females.
	426	427	428	429	430	431	432	433	434	435	436	437
ASSAM	*1,524*	*84*	*29*	*13*	*707*	*4*	*267*	*32*	*38*	*8*	*212*	*3*
(1) British Territory	*1,397*	*84*	*29*	*13*	*704*	*4*	*230*	*32*	*34*	*8*	*205*	*3*
SURMA VALLEY AND HILL DIVISION	228	4	20	...	364	...	201	22	21	7	179	2
Cachar	4	...	1	...	6	...	38	...	2	...	12	...
Sylhet	224	4	19	...	330	...	163	22	19	7	167	2
Khasi and Jaintia Hills (British)	...	...	...	...	...	...	...	...	...	...	...	...
Naga Hills	...	...	...	...	...	...	...	...	...	...	...	...
Lushai Hills	...	...	...	...	...	...	...	...	...	...	...	...
ASSAM VALLEY DIVISION	1,169	80	9	13	340	4	29	10	13	1	26	1
Goalpara	15	...	...	...	11	...	18	4	13	...	7	...
Kamrup	37	...	...	...	64	...	8	6	...	...	10	...
Darrang	81	...	...	...	15	...	...	...	...	...	1	...
Nowgong	51	...	...	...	...	...	1	...	...	...	2	...
Sibsagar	332	31	...	5	115	...	...	...	...	...	1	1
Lakhimpur	633	45	9	8	132	4	...	...	...	...	...	...
Garo Hills	...	...	...	...	...	...	2	...	...	1	5	...
SADIYA FRONTIER TRACT	...		...	...	...	...	...	...	...	...	...	...
BALIPARA FRONTIER TRACT	...	...	...	...	...	...	...	...	...	...	...	...
(2) Manipur State	*127*	...	...	...	*3*	...	*37*	...	*4*	...	*7*	...
(3) Khasi States	...	...	...	...	...	...	...	...	...	...	...	...

TABLE X.—Occupation or means of livelihood. Part II.—Details for Districts—contd.

District or State.	Class B.—Preparation and supply of material substances. Sub-class III.—Industry. Order 10.—Chemical products properly so-called and analogous. Total of order 10.—Chemical products properly so-called and analogous. Total earners (principal occupation). Males.	Females.	Total working dependants. Males.	Females.	Total following occupation as subsidiary to other. Males.	Females.	Group (66).—Manufacture of matches, fire-works and other explosives. Total earners (principal occupation). Males.	Females.	Total working dependants. Males.	Females.	Total following occupation as subsidiary to other. Males.	Females.
	438	439	440	441	442	443	444	445	446	447	448	449
ASSAM	*967*	*45*	*33*	*27*	*751*	*13*	*236*	...	*6*	...	*21*	...
(1) British Territory	*943*	*39*	*33*	*26*	*751*	*11*	*236*	...	*6*	...	*21*	...
SURMA VALLEY AND HILL DIVISION	118	7	15	4	213	8	4	...	...	...	4	...
Cachar	77	...	3	...	40	...	2	...	...	...	...	...
Sylhet	37	7	12	4	172	8	2	...	...	...	4	...
Khasi and Jaintia Hills (British)	...	...	...	...	...	...	...	...	...	...	...	...
Naga Hills	4	...	...	...	1	...	...	...	...	...	...	...
Lushai Hills	...	...	...	...	...	...	...	...	...	...	...	...
ASSAM VALLEY DIVISION	824	32	18	22	538	3	232	...	6	...	17	...
Goalpara	315	16	11	10	448	1	224	...	6	...	7	...
Kamrup	192	4	2	1	33	...	7	...	...	...	9	...
Darrang	77	1	3	1	11	...	...	...	...	...	...	...
Nowgong	55	1	1	1	13	...	1	...	...	...	1	...
Sibsagar	82	4	...	...	2	1	...	...	...	...	...	...
Lakhimpur	88	3	...	...	3	...	...	...	...	...	...	...
Garo Hills	15	3	1	...	29	1	...	...	...	...	...	...
SADIYA FRONTIER TRACT	1	...	...	...	...	...	...	...	...	...	...	...
BALIPARA FRONTIER TRACT	...	...	...	...	...	...	...	...	...	...	...	...
(2) Manipur State	*9*	*6*	...	*1*	...	*2*	...	...	...	...	...	...
(3) Khasi States	*22*	...	...	...	...	...	...	...	...	...	...	...

TABLE X.—OCCUPATION OR MEANS OF LIVELIHOOD. PART II.—DETAILS FOR DISTRICTS—*contd.*

DISTRICT OR STATE.	Class B.—Preparation and supply of material substances. Sub-class III.—Industry. Order 10.—Chemical products properly so-called and analogous. Group (67).—Manufacture of aerated and mineral waters and ice. Total earners (principal occupation). Males.	Females.	Total working dependants. Males.	Females.	Total following occupation as subsidiary to other. Males.	Females.	Group (68).—Manufacture and refining of vegetable oils. Total earners (principal occupation). Males.	Females.	Total working dependants. Males.	Females.	Total following occupation as subsidiary to other. Males.	Females.
	450	451	452	453	454	455	456	457	458	459	460	461
ASSAM	*21*	...	...	...	*6*	...	*670*	*38*	*27*	*25*	*723*	*9*
(1) British Territory	*19*	...	...	...	*6*	...	*668*	*38*	*27*	*25*	*723*	*9*
SURMA VALLEY AND HILL DIVISION	...	...	...	...	2	...	111	7	15	4	207	6
Cachar	...	...	...	...	...	...	75	...	3	...	40	...
Sylhet	...	...	...	...	1	...	32	7	12	4	167	6
Khasi and Jaintia Hills (British)	...	...	...	...	...	...	...	...	...	...	...	...
Naga Hills	...	...	...	...	1	...	4	...	...	...	...	...
Lushai Hills	...	...	...	...	...	...	...	...	...	...	...	...
ASSAM VALLEY DIVISION	19	...	...	...	4	...	556	31	13	21	516	3
Goalpara	...	...	...	...	...	...	91	18	6	19	441	1
Kamrup	6	...	...	...	2	...	174	4	2	1	22	...
Darrang	2	...	...	...	1	...	75	1	3	...	10	...
Nowgong	...	...	...	...	...	...	54	1	1	1	11	...
Sibsagar	4	...	...	...	1	...	73	2	...	...	1	1
Lakhimpur	7	...	...	...	...	...	74	2	...	...	2	...
Garo Hills	...	...	...	...	...	...	15	3	1	...	29	1
SADIYA FRONTIER TRACT	...	...	...	...	...	...	1	...	...	...	...	...
BALIPARA FRONTIER TRACT	...	...	...	...	...	...	...	...	...	...	...	...
(2) Manipur State	...	...	...	...	...	...	*2*	...	...	...	...	...
(3) Khasi States	*2*	...	...	...	...	...	...	...	...	...	...	...

TABLE X.—OCCUPATION OR MEANS OF LIVELIHOOD. PART II.—DETAILS FOR DISTRICTS—*contd.*

DISTRICT OR STATE.	Class B.—Preparation and supply of material substances.											
	Sub-class III.—Industry.											
	Order 10.—Chemical products properly so-called and analogous.						Order 11.—Food Industries.					
	Group (70).—Others.						Total of order 11.—Food Industries.					
	Total earners (principal occupation).		Total working dependants.		Total following occupation as subsidiary to other.		Total earners (principal occupation).		Total working dependants.		Total following occupation as subsidiary to other.	
	Males.	Females.	Males.	Females.	Males.	Females.	Males.	Females.	Males.	Females.	Males.	Females.
	462	463	464	465	466	467	468	469	470	471	472	473
ASSAM	*20*	*7*	...	*2*	*1*	*4*	*3,585*	*6,411*	*222*	*1,430*	*673*	*1,196*
(1) British Territory	*20*	*1*	...	*1*	*1*	*2*	*3,376*	*5,988*	*211*	*1,314*	*592*	*1,139*
SURMA VALLEY AND HILL DIVISION	3	...	...	...	...	2	631	4,844	152	975	328	1,045
Cachar	...	...	...	...	...	...	108	574	...	81	114	98
Sylhet	3	...	...	...	...	2	480	4,087	65	865	198	926
Khasi and Jaintia Hills (British)	...	...	...	...	...	...	39	162	3	6	9	17
Naga Hills	...	...	...	...	...	...	7	14	84	77	3	...
Lushai Hills	...	...	...	...	...	...	...	7	...	6	5	10
ASSAM VALLEY DIVISION	17	1	...	1	1	...	2,796	1,142	59	338	215	94
Goalpara	...	...	...	...	...	...	548	853	23	114	60	29
Kamrup	5	...	...	...	...	...	440	174	5	50	55	8
Darrang	...	...	...	1	...	...	453	193	4	55	29	27
Nowgong	...	...	...	...	...	...	274	64	2	51	13	16
Sibsagar	5	1	...	...	...	...	443	59	11	31	23	7
Lakhimpur	7	...	...	...	1	...	581	56	6	23	33	3
Garo Hills	...	...	...	...	...	...	7	40	...	24	3	4
SADIYA FRONTIER TRACT	...	...	...	...	...	...	13	2	...	1	49	...
BALIPARA FRONTIER TRACT	...	...	...	...	...	...	2	...	...	...	...	...
(2) Manipur State	...	*6*	...	*1*	...	*2*	*51*	*198*	*5*	*103*	*1*	*10*
(3) Khasi States	*20*	...	...	...	...	...	*159*	*225*	*6*	*13*	*80*	*47*

TABLE X.—OCCUPATION OR MEANS OF LIVELIHOOD. PART II.—DETAILS FOR DISTRICTS—*contd.*

DISTRICT OR STATE.	Class B.—Preparation and supply of material substances. Sub-class III.—Industry. Order 11.—Food Industries. Group (71).—Rice pounders and huskers and flour grinders. Total earners (principal occupation). Males.	Group (71). Total earners (principal occupation). Females.	Group (71). Total working dependants. Males.	Group (71). Total working dependants. Females.	Group (71). Total following occupation as subsidiary to other. Males.	Group (71). Total following occupation as subsidiary to other. Females.	Group (72).—Grain parchers, etc. Total earners (principal occupation). Males.	Group (72). Total earners (principal occupation). Females.	Group (72). Total working dependants. Males.	Group (72). Total working dependants. Females.	Group (72). Total following occupation as subsidiary to other. Males.	Group (72). Total following occupation as subsidiary to other. Females.
	474	475	476	477	478	479	480	481	482	483	484	485
ASSAM	*394*	*4,897*	*106*	*923*	*61*	*923*	*357*	*850*	*13*	*374*	*108*	*181*
(1) British Territory	*394*	*4,826*	*105*	*889*	*61*	*919*	*354*	*850*	*13*	*374*	*108*	*181*
SURMA VALLEY AND HILL DIVISION	32	4,372	99	811	45	893	182	293	5	149	53	123
Cachar	6	411	...	30	7	63	41	162	...	51	6	30
Sylhet	26	3,946	15	704	38	830	141	131	5	98	47	93
Khasi and Jaintia Hills (British)	...	...	...	...	...	...	...	...	...	...	...	...
Naga Hills	1	13	84	77	...	...	...	...	...	...	...	...
Lushai Hills	...	2	...	...	...	...	...	...	...	...	...	...
ASSAM VALLEY DIVISION	362	452	6	78	16	26	169	557	8	224	53	58
Goalpara	16	269	3	39	...	11	121	253	3	73	33	18
Kamrup	122	97	1	18	7	7	22	70	...	22	3	...
Darrang	84	58	1	3	2	6	6	72	1	44	11	19
Nowgong	80	14	1	8	6	...	...	45	...	43	...	16
Sibsagar	25	10	...	2	1	1	10	29	4	11	6	3
Lakhimpur	35	4	...	7	...	...	10	16	...	8	...	...
Garo Hills	...	...	...	1	...	1	...	40	...	23	...	2
SADIYA FRONTIER TRACT	...	2	...	...	...	...	3	...	...	1	2	...
BALIPARA FRONTIER TRACT	...	...	...	...	...	...	...	...	...	...	...	...
(2) Manipur State	...	*69*	*1*	*34*	...	*3*	*3*	...	...	...	...	...
(3) Khasi States	...	*2*	...	...	...	*1*	...	...	...	...	...	...

TABLE X.—OCCUPATION OR MEANS OF LIVELIHOOD. PART II.—DETAILS FOR DISTRICTS—*contd.*

DISTRICT OR STATE.	Class B.—Preparation and supply of material substances. Sub-class III.—Industry. Order 11.—Food Industries. Group (73).—Butchers. Total earners (principal occupation). Males.	Females.	Total working dependants. Males.	Females.	Total following occupation as subsidiary to other. Males.	Females.	Group (74).—Makers of sugar, molasses and gur. Total earners (principal occupation). Males.	Females.	Total working dependants. Males.	Females.	Total following occupation as subsidiary to other. Males.	Females.
	486	487	488	489	490	491	492	493	494	495	496	497
ASSAM	*205*	...	*1*	...	*117*	...	*49*	*5*	*1*	*3*	*57*	*12*
(1) British Territory	*157*	...	*1*	...	*49*	...	*6*	*5*	*1*	*3*	*57*	*12*
SURMA VALLEY AND HILL DIVISION ...	**49**	...	**1**	...	**44**	...	**6**	**5**	...	**2**	**53**	**12**
Cachar	19	...	...	...	36	...	6	...	...	...	48	...
Sylhet	10	...	...	...	1	...	...	...	...	2	...	2
Khasi and Jaintia Hills (British)	14	...	1	...	6	...	...	...	...	...	...	...
Naga Hills	6	...	...	...	1	...	...	...	...	...	5	10
Lushai Hills	...	...	...	...	...	...	...	5	...	...	...	...
ASSAM VALLEY DIVISION	**106**	...	...	...	**5**	...	...	...	**1**	**1**	**4**	...
Goalpara	1	...	...	...	1	...	...	...	...	...	...	...
Kamrup	23	...	...	...	...	...	...	...	...	...	...	...
Darrang	26	...	...	...	...	...	...	...	...	...	...	...
Nowgong	7	...	...	...	...	...	...	...	...	...	...	...
Sibsagar	30	...	...	...	1	...	...	...	...	...	...	...
Lakhimpur	17	...	...	...	3	...	...	...	1	1	2	...
Garo Hills	2	...	...	...	...	...	...	...	...	...	2	...
SADIYA FRONTIER TRACT	...	...	...	...	...	...	...	...	...	...	...	...
BALIPARA FRONTIER TRACT	**2**	...	...	...	...	...	...	...	...	...	...	...
(2) Manipur State	...	...	...	...	...	...	*43*	...	...	...	...	...
(3) Khasi States	*48*	...	...	...	*68*	...	...	...	...	...	...	...

TABLE X.—OCCUPATION OR MEANS OF LIVELIHOOD. PART II.—DETAILS FOR DISTRICTS—*contd.*

DISTRICT OR STATE.	Class B.—Preparation and supply of material substances. Sub-class III.—Industry. Order 11.—Food Industries. Group (75).—Sweetmeat and condiment makers. Total earners (principal occupation). Males.	Females.	Total working dependants. Males.	Females.	Total following occupation as subsidiary to other. Males.	Females.	Group (76).—Toddy drawers. Total earners (principal occupation). Males.	Females.	Total working dependants. Males.	Females.	Total following occupation as subsidiary to other. Males.	Females.
	498	499	500	501	502	503	504	505	506	507	508	509
ASSAM	*1,803*	*199*	*46*	*33*	*233*	*10*	*20*	...	...	...	...	...
(1) British Territory	*1,803*	*199*	*46*	*33*	*233*	*10*	*20*	...	...	...	...	...
SURMA VALLEY AND HILL DIVISION.	222	7	4	...	61	...	...	...	...	...	...	...
Cachar	6	...	...	...	...	...	...	...	...	...	...	...
Sylhet	216	7	4	...	60	...	...	...	...	...	...	...
Khasi and Jaintia Hills (British)	...	...	...	...	...	...	...	...	...	...	...	...
Naga Hills	...	...	...	...	1	...	...	...	...	...	...	...
Lushai Hills	...	...	...	...	...	...	...	...	...	...	...	...
ASSAM VALLEY DIVISION	1,571	192	42	33	125	10	20	...	...	...	...	...
Goalpara	335	3	22	2	24	...	5	...	...	...	...	...
Kamrup	203	7	3	10	45	1	14	...	...	...	...	...
Darrang	200	60	2	8	14	2	...	...	...	...	...	...
Nowgong	143	4	1	1	4	...	...	...	...	...	...	...
Sibsagar	275	19	9	8	12	4	...	...	...	...	...	...
Lakhimpur	335	30	5	4	26	3	1	...	...	...	...	...
Garo Hills	...	...	...	...	...	...	...	...	...	...	...	...
SADIYA FRONTIER TRACT	10	...	...	...	67	...	...	...	...	...	...	...
BALIPARA FRONTIER TRACT	...	...	...	...	...	...	...	...	...	...	...	...
(2) Manipur State	...	...	...	...	...	...	...	...	...	...	...	...
(3) Khasi States	...	...	...	...	...	...	...	...	...	...	...	...

TABLE X.—OCCUPATION OR MEANS OF LIVELIHOOD. PART II.—DETAILS FOR DISTRICTS—*contd.*

Class B.—Preparation and supply of material substances.
Sub-class III.—Industry.
Order 11.—Food Industries.

DISTRICT OR STATE.	Group (77).—Brewers and distillers.						Group (78).—Manufacturers of Tobacco.					
	Total earners (principal occupation).		Total working dependants.		Total following occupation as subsidiary to other.		Total earners (principal occupation).		Total working dependants.		Total following occupation as subsidiary to other.	
	Males.	Females.	Males.	Females.	Males.	Females.	Males.	Females.	Males.	Females.	Males.	Females.
	510	511	512	513	514	515	516	517	518	519	520	521
ASSAM	*99*	*480*	*9*	*84*	*13*	*61*	*9*	*3*	...	*1*	*2*	...
(1) British Territory	*13*	*150*	...	*4*	*4*	*16*	*9*	*3*	...	*1*	*2*	...
SURMA VALLEY AND HILL DIVISION	12	150	...	4	3	16	...	3	...	1	...	...
Cachar	...	...	...	...	...	...	...	...	...	...	...	...
Sylhet	...	...	...	...	...	...	...	1	...	...	...	...
Khasi and Jaintia Hills (British)	12	150	...	4	3	16	...	2	...	1	...	...
Naga Hills	...	...	...	...	...	...	...	...	...	...	...	...
Lushai Hills	...	...	...	...	...	...	...	...	...	...	...	...
ASSAM VALLEY DIVISION	1	...	...	...	1	...	9	...	...	...	2	...
Goalpara	...	...	...	...	...	...	...	...	...	...	...	...
Kamrup	...	...	...	...	...	...	...	...	...	...	...	...
Darrang	...	...	...	...	...	...	9	...	...	...	...	...
Nowgong	...	...	...	...	1	...	...	...	...	...	2	...
Sibsagar	...	...	...	...	...	...	...	...	...	...	...	...
Lakhimpur	...	...	...	...	...	...	...	...	...	...	...	...
Garo Hills	1	...	...	...	...	...	...	...	...	...	...	...
SADIYA FRONTIER TRACT	...	...	...	...	...	...	...	...	...	...	...	...
BALIPARA FRONTIER TRACT	...	...	...	...	...	...	...	...	...	...	...	...
(2) Manipur State	*5*	*120*	*4*	*69*	*1*	*7*	...	...	...	...	...	...
(3) Khasi States	*81*	*201*	*5*	*11*	*8*	*38*	...	...	...	...	...	...

TABLE X.—OCCUPATION OR MEANS OF LIVELIHOOD. PART II.—DETAILS FOR DISTRICTS—*contd.*

DISTRICT OR STATE.	Class B.—Preparation and supply of material substances. — Sub-class III.—Industry. — Order 11.—Food Industries. — Group (81).—Others.						Order 12.—Industries of dress and the toilet. — Total of Order 12.—Industries of dress and the toilet.					
	Total earners (principal occupation).		Total working dependants.		Total following occupation as subsidiary to other.		Total earners (principal occupation).		Total working dependants.		Total following occupation as subsidiary to other.	
	Males.	Females.	Males.	Females.	Males.	Females.	Males.	Females.	Males.	Females.	Males.	Females.
	532	533	534	535	536	537	538	539	530	531	532	533
ASSAM	*649*	*47*	*46*	*13*	*89*	*9*	*14,483*	*1,245*	*863*	*591*	*6,227*	*340*
(1) British Territory	*619*	*25*	*45*	*10*	*78*	*1*	*13,569*	*930*	*770*	*489*	*6,146*	*220*
SURMA VALLEY AND HILL DIVISION	131	14	43	8	69	1	5,905	548	551	235	4,518	185
Cachar	31	...	...	...	17	...	1,274	126	85	34	332	6
Sylhet	87	1	42	...	52	...	4,096	307	440	156	4,128	144
Khasi and Jaintia Hills (British)...	13	13	1	3	...	1	406	107	25	41	24	35
Naga Hills	...	1	...	...	...	...	79	6	1	3	7	...
Lushai Hills	...	...	...	6	...	...	50	2	...	1	27	...
ASSAM VALLEY DIVISION	488	11	2	2	9	...	7,534	369	215	254	1,618	35
Goalpara	50	...	...	...	2	...	1,218	20	54	13	165	1
Kamrup	47	...	1	...	...	...	1,242	46	41	57	453	2
Darrang	77	3	...	...	2	...	1,179	53	26	22	236	5
Nowgong	24	2	...	...	...	...	705	21	16	28	134	...
Sibsagar	103	...	1	...	3	...	1,560	100	40	60	449	8
Lakhimpur	183	6	...	2	2	...	1,566	128	36	93	175	19
Garo Hills	4	...	...	...	...	...	64	1	1	3	6	...
SADIYA FRONTIER TRACT	...	...	...	...	...	...	96	11	6	...	10	...
BALIPARA FRONTIER TRACT	...	...	...	...	...	...	31	2	...	...	...	...
(2) Manipur State	...	...	...	...	...	...	*516*	*49*	*74*	*39*	*56*	*9*
(3) Khasi States	*30*	*22*	*1*	*2*	*4*	*8*	*397*	*266*	*18*	*63*	*25*	*118*

TABLE X.—OCCUPATION OR MEANS OF LIVELIHOOD. PART II.—DETAILS FOR DISTRICTS—*contd.*

DISTRICT OR STATE.	Class B.—Preparation and supply of material substances. Sub-class III.—Industry. Order 12.—Industries of dress and the toilet.											
	Group (82).—Boot, shoe, sandal and clog makers.						Group (83).—Tailors, milliners, dress makers and darners.					
	Total earners (principal occupation).		Total working dependants.		Total following occupation as subsidiary to other.		Total earners (principal occupation).		Total working dependants.		Total following occupation as subsidiary to other.	
	Males.	Females.	Males.	Females.	Males.	Females.	Males.	Females.	Males.	Females.	Males.	Females.
	534	535	536	537	538	539	540	541	542	543	544	545
ASSAM	*1,168*	*47*	*58*	*17*	*422*	*4*	*6,621*	*622*	*409*	*410*	*1,536*	*225*
(1) British Territory	*1,111*	*40*	*54*	*17*	*420*	*4*	*5,913*	*318*	*322*	*321*	*1,459*	*105*
SURMA VALLEY AND HILL DIVISION	**271**	**17**	**18**	**6**	**101**	**2**	**2,246**	**208**	**219**	**111**	**578**	**86**
Cachar	71	10	6	...	24	...	379	31	27	18	90	5
Sylhet	156	7	12	5	73	2	1,511	66	167	51	437	47
Khasi and Jaintia Hills (British)	24	...	...	1	1	...	280	103	25	40	23	34
Naga Hills	12	...	...	...	2	...	39	6	...	1	2	...
Lushai Hills	8	...	...	...	1	...	37	2	...	1	26	...
ASSAM VALLEY DIVISION	**839**	**23**	**36**	**11**	**319**	**2**	**3,604**	**108**	**99**	**210**	**873**	**19**
Goalpara	151	3	12	...	88	...	454	6	17	11	43	1
Kamrup	182	5	1	...	41	...	582	19	25	45	198	2
Darrang	88	1	...	4	59	2	663	28	18	21	187	3
Nowgong	124	1	3	3	46	...	323	6	10	14	80	...
Sibsagar	134	8	8	3	68	...	753	19	18	33	324	1
Lakhimpur	146	5	11	1	13	...	830	29	11	85	130	12
Garo Hills	14	...	1	...	4	...	19	1	...	1	2	...
SADIYA FRONTIER TRACT	1	...	...	...	...	...	52	1	4	...	8	...
BALIPARA FRONTIER TRACT	...	...	...	...	...	...	11	1	...	...	...	...
(2) Manipur State	*39*	*6*	*4*	...	*2*	...	*423*	*43*	*70*	*27*	*53*	*2*
(3) Khasi States	*95*	*1*	...	...	...	...	*285*	*261*	*17*	*62*	*24*	*118*

TABLE X.—Occupation or means of livelihood. Part II.—Details for Districts—*contd.*

Class B.—Preparation and supply of material substances. Sub-class III.—Industry. Order 12.—Industries of dress and the toilet.

District or State.	Group (84).—Embroiderers, hat-makers and makers of other articles of wear. Total earners (principal occupation). Males.	Females.	Total working dependants. Males.	Females.	Total following occupation as subsidiary to other. Males.	Females.	Group (85).—Washing and cleaning. Total earners (principal occupation). Males.	Females.	Total working dependants. Males.	Females.	Total following occupation as subsidiary to other. Males.	Females.
	546	547	548	549	550	551	552	553	554	555	556	557
ASSAM	*293*	*83*	*7*	*36*	*83*	*38*	*1,983*	*483*	*102*	*111*	*1,228*	*72*
(1) British Territory	*273*	*83*	*7*	*36*	*83*	*38*	*1,939*	*479*	*101*	*110*	*1,228*	*72*
SURMA VALLEY AND HILL DIVISION	146	82	5	30	53	38	1,006	236	86	75	1,155	57
Cachar	28	...	...	...	6	...	223	83	20	6	41	1
Sylhet	115	82	5	30	47	38	680	149	66	67	1,111	55
Khasi and Jaintia Hills (British)	2	...	...	...	...	...	73	4	...	...	...	1
Naga Hills	1	...	...	...	...	...	17	...	...	2	1	...
Lushai Hills	...	...	...	...	...	...	6	...	...	...	...	...
ASSAM VALLEY DIVISION	127	1	2	6	30	...	898	232	15	35	72	14
Goalpara	4	1	...	...	2	...	93	9	...	1	4	...
Kamrup	16	...	...	...	4	...	113	19	3	11	36	...
Darrang	21	...	...	3	1	...	113	24	6	5	6	...
Nowgong	26	...	...	...	4	...	73	14	1	11	7	...
Sibsagar	42	...	2	...	11	...	235	73	2	4	10	7
Lakhimpur	18	...	...	2	8	...	263	93	1	3	9	7
Garo Hills	...	...	...	1	...	...	8	...	...	...	...	...
SADIYA FRONTIER TRACT	...	...	...	...	...	...	23	10	...	...	5	...
BALIPARA FRONTIER TRACT	...	...	...	...	...	...	13	1	...	...	...	...
(2) Manipur State	*15*	...	...	...	...	...	*7*	...	...	...	...	...
(3) Khasi States	*5*	...	...	...	...	...	*37*	*4*	*1*	*1*	...	...

TABLE X.—Occupation or means of livelihood. Part II.—Details for Districts—*contd.*

DISTRICT OR STATE.	Class B.—Preparation and supply of material substances. Sub-class III.—Industry. Order 12.—Industries of dress and the toilet.											
	Group (86).—Barbers, hair-dressers and wig-makers.						Group (87).—Other industries connected with the toilet.					
	Total earners (principal occupation).		Total working dependants.		Total following occupation as subsidiary to other.		Total earners (principal occupation).		Total working dependants.		Total following occupation as subsidiary to other.	
	Males.	Females.	Males.	Females.	Males.	Females.	Males.	Females.	Males.	Females.	Males.	Females.
	558	559	560	561	562	563	564	565	566	567	568	569
ASSAM	*4,380*	*10*	*286*	*5*	*2,956*	*2*	*37*	...	...	*19*	*2*	...
(1) British Territory	*4,316*	*10*	*286*	*5*	*2,955*	*2*	*17*	...	...	...	*1*	...
SURMA VALLEY AND HILL DIVISION	2,225	5	223	3	2,630	2	16	...	...	...	1	...
Cachar	573	2	33	...	171	...	...	...	...	...	...	...
Sylhet	1,606	3	190	3	2,459	2	14	...	...	...	1	...
Khasi and Jaintia Hills (British)	28	...	...	...	...	...	...	...	...	...	...	...
Naga Hills	10	...	1	...	...	...	...	...	...	...	...	...
Lushai Hills...	8	...	...	...	...	...	...	...	...	...	...	...
ASSAM VALLEY DIVISION	2,063	5	63	2	326	...	3	...	...	...	...	...
Goalpara	514	1	25	...	30	...	...	...	...	...	...	...
Kamrup	378	3	13	1	184	...	3	...	...	...	...	...
Darrang	291	...	...	...	23	...	...	...	...	...	...	...
Nowgong	189	...	3	...	17	...	1	...	...	...	...	...
Sibsagar	293	...	19	...	37	...	...	...	...	...	...	...
Lakhimpur	302	1	3	1	35	...	...	...	...	...	...	...
Garo Hills	26	...	...	...	...	...	...	...	...	...	...	...
SADIYA FRONTIER TRACT	20	...	...	...	...	...	...	...	...	...	...	...
BALIPARA FRONTIER TRACT	8	...	...	...	...	...	...	...	...	...	...	...
(2) Manipur State	*19*	...	...	...	*1*	...	*20*	...	...	*19*	...	...
(3) Khasi States	*45*	...	...	...	...	...	...	...	...	...	*1*	...

TABLE X.—OCCUPATION OR MEANS OF LIVELIHOOD. PART II.—DETAILS FOR DISTRICTS—*contd.*

DISTRICT OR STATE.	Class B.—Preparation and supply of material substances.											
	Sub-class III.—Industry.											
	Order 13.—Furniture industries.											
	Total of Order 13.—Furniture Industries.						Group (85).—Cabinet-makers, carriage painters, etc.					
	Total earners (principal occupation).		Total working dependants.		Total following occupation as subsidiary to other.		Total earners (principal occupation).		Total working dependants.		Total following occupation as subsidiary to other.	
	Males.	Females.	Males.	Females.	Males.	Females.	Males.	Females.	Males.	Females.	Males.	Females.
	570	571	572	573	574	575	576	577	578	579	580	581
ASSAM	194	31	1	7	13	14	45	2	1	...	3	...
(1) British Territory	194	2	1	...	13	...	45	2	1	...	3	...
SURMA VALLEY AND HILL DIVISION	30	2	...	...	3	...	3	2	...	...	...	...
Cachar	8	...	...	...	1	...	...	...	...	...	...	...
Sylhet	22	2	...	...	2	...	3	2	...	...	...	...
Khasi and Jaintia Hills (British)	...	...	...	...	...	...	...	...	...	...	...	...
Naga Hills	...	...	...	...	...	...	...	...	...	...	...	...
Lushai Hills	...	...	...	...	...	...	...	...	...	...	...	...
ASSAM VALLEY DIVISION	94	...	1	...	10	...	42	...	1	...	3	...
Goalpara	12	...	...	...	1	...	1	...	...	...	...	...
Kamrup	14	...	...	...	...	...	...	...	...	...	...	...
Darrang	12	...	...	...	...	...	12	...	...	...	...	...
Nowgong	1	...	...	...	...	...	...	...	...	...	...	...
Sibsagar	21	...	1	...	9	...	7	...	1	...	3	...
Lakhimpur	34	...	...	...	...	...	22	...	...	...	...	...
Garo Hills	...	...	...	...	...	...	...	...	...	...	...	...
SADIYA FRONTIER TRACT	...	...	...	...	...	...	...	...	...	...	...	...
BALIPARA FRONTIER TRACT	...	...	...	...	...	...	...	...	...	...	...	...
(2) Manipur State	...	29	...	7	...	14	...	...	...	...	...	...
(3) Khasi States	...	...	...	...	...	...	...	...	...	...	...	...

TABLE X.—Occupation or means of livelihood. Part II.—Details for Districts—*contd.*

DISTRICT OR STATE.	Class B.—Preparation and supply of material substances.											
	Sub-class III.—Industry.											
	Order 13.—Furniture Industries.						Order 14.—Building Industries.					
	Group (89).—Upholsterers, tent-makers, etc.						Total of Order 14.—Building Industries.					
	Total earners (principal occupation).		Total working dependants.		Total following occupation as subsidiary to other.		Total earners (principal occupation).		Total working dependants.		Total following occupation as subsidiary to other.	
	Males.	Females.	Males.	Females.	Males.	Females.	Males.	Females.	Males.	Females.	Males.	Females.
	582	583	584	585	586	587	588	589	590	591	592	593
ASSAM	*79*	*99*	...	*7*	*4*	*14*	*4,909*	*195*	*98*	*21*	*1,431*	*5*
(1) British Territory	*79*	...	...	...	*4*	...	*4,474*	*184*	*87*	*21*	*1,344*	*5*
SURMA VALLEY AND HILL DIVISION	27	...	...	...	3	...	1,975	13	46	2	930	...
Cachar	8	...	...	...	1	...	675	9	3	...	170	...
Sylhet	19	...	...	...	2	...	1,173	3	41	2	714	...
Khasi and Jaintia Hills (British)	...	...	...	...	...	...	91	1	2	...	6	...
Naga Hills	...	...	...	...	...	...	12	...	...	...	33	...
Lushai Hills	...	...	...	...	...	...	24	...	...	...	8	...
ASSAM VALLEY DIVISION	52	...	...	...	1	...	2,482	111	41	19	406	5
Goalpara	11	...	...	...	1	...	383	3	26	4	54	...
Kamrup...	14	...	...	...	...	...	269	8	3	4	62	1
Darrang	...	...	...	...	...	...	296	1	3	2	47	...
Nowgong	1	...	...	...	...	...	109	8	...	7	27	...
Sibsagar	14	...	...	...	...	...	204	57	...	1	118	...
Lakhimpur	12	...	...	...	...	...	817	34	9	1	83	4
Garo Hills	...	...	...	...	...	...	15	...	...	...	15	...
SADIYA FRONTIER TRACT	...	...	...	...	...	...	7	...	...	...	5	...
BALIPARA FRONTIER TRACT	...	...	...	...	...	...	10	...	...	...	3	...
(2) Manipur State	...	*99*	...	*7*	...	*14*	*143*	...	*5*	...	*11*	...
(3) Khasi States	...	...	...	...	...	...	*285*	*1*	*6*	...	*76*	...

TABLE X.—Occupation or means of livelihood. Part II.—Details for Districts—*contd.*

Class B.—Preparation and supply of material substances. Sub-class III.—Industry.

DISTRICT OR STATE.	Order 14.—Building Industries. Group (90).—Lime burners, cement workers; Excavators and well sinkers; Stone cutters and dressers; Brick layers and masons; Builders (other than buildings made of bamboo or similar materials), painters, decorators of houses, tilers, plumbers, etc. — Total earners (principal occupation). Males.	Females.	Total working dependants. Males.	Females.	Total following occupation as subsidiary to other. Males.	Females.	Order 15.—Construction of means of transport. Total of Order 15.—Construction of means of transport. — Total earners (principal occupation). Males.	Females.	Total working dependants. Males.	Females.	Total following occupation as subsidiary to other. Males.	Females.
	594	595	596	597	598	599	600	601	602	603	604	605
ASSAM	*4,909*	*135*	*98*	*91*	*1,431*	*5*	*956*	*1*	*78*	*1*	*1,068*	*4*
(1) British Territory	*4,474*	*134*	*87*	*91*	*1,344*	*5*	*906*	...	*75*	*1*	*1,043*	*4*
SURMA VALLEY AND HILL DIVISION	1,975	13	46	2	930	...	200	...	61	1	280	...
Cachar	675	9	2	...	170	...	3	...	...	...	...	...
Sylhet	1,173	3	41	2	714	...	179	...	59	1	247	...
Khasi and Jaintia Hills (British)	91	1	3	...	6	...	6	...	...	...	...	...
Naga Hills	12	...	...	...	32	...	9	...	...	...	1	...
Lushai Hills	24	...	...	...	8	...	3	...	2	...	32	...
ASSAM VALLEY DIVISION	2,482	111	41	19	406	5	694	...	14	...	760	4
Goalpara	362	3	26	4	54	...	56	...	2	...	4	...
Kamrup	359	8	3	4	62	1	125	...	2	...	210	...
Darrang	196	1	3	2	47	...	103	...	...	...	18	...
Nowgong	109	8	...	7	37	...	118	...	6	...	8	...
Sibsagar	504	57	...	1	113	...	101	...	2	...	49	...
Lakhimpur	817	34	9	1	83	4	190	...	2	...	18	...
Garo Hills	15	...	...	...	16	...	1	...	...	...	453	4
SADIYA FRONTIER TRACT	7	...	...	...	5	...	12	...	...	...	3	...
BALIPARA FRONTIER TRACT	10	...	...	...	3	...	...	...	...	...	...	...
(2) Manipur State	*143*	...	*5*	...	*11*	...	*26*	...	...	...	*9*	...
(3) Khasi States	*292*	*1*	*6*	...	*76*	...	*24*	*1*	*3*	...	*16*	...

TABLE X.—OCCUPATION OR MEANS OF LIVELIHOOD. PART II.—DETAILS FOR DISTRICTS—contd.

DISTRICT OR STATE.	Class B.—Preparation and supply of material substances.											
	Sub-class III.—Industry.											
	Order 15.—Construction of means of transport.											
	Group (91).—Persons engaged in making, assembling or repairing motor vehicles or cycles.						Group (92).—Carriage, cart, palki, etc., makers and wheel-wrights.					
	Total earners (principal occupation).		Total working dependants.		Total following occupation as subsidiary to other.		Total earners (principal occupation).		Total working dependants.		Total following occupation as subsidiary to other.	
	Males.	Females.	Males.	Females.	Males.	Females.	Males.	Females.	Males.	Females.	Males.	Females.
	606	607	608	609	610	611	612	613	614	615	616	617
ASSAM	*555*	...	*13*	...	*55*	...	*220*	*1*	*7*	...	*52*	...
(1) British Territory	*533*	...	*13*	...	*55*	...	*201*	...	*4*	...	*47*	...
SURMA VALLEY AND HILL DIVISION	57	...	2	...	9	...	13	...	2	...	...	...
Cachar	3	...	...	...	...	...	...	...	...	...	...	...
Sylhet	45	...	2	...	8	...	7	...	2	...	...	...
Khasi and Jaintia Hills (British)	6	...	...	...	...	...	...	...	...	...	...	...
Naga Hills	3	...	...	...	1	...	6	...	...	...	...	...
Lushai Hills...	...	...	...	...	...	...	...	...	...	...	...	...
ASSAM VALLEY DIVISION	473	...	11	...	46	...	188	...	2	...	45	...
Goalpara	13	...	1	...	...	...	38	...	1	...	4	...
Kamrup	73	...	...	...	2	...	46	...	1	...	13	...
Darrang	38	...	...	...	8	...	64	...	...	...	7	...
Nowgong	90	...	6	...	8	...	17	...	...	...	...	...
Sibsagar	82	...	2	...	15	...	17	...	...	...	18	...
Lakhimpur	169	...	2	...	12	...	6	...	...	...	3	...
Garo Hills	1	...	...	...	1	...	...	...	...	...	...	...
SADIYA FRONTIER TRACT	3	...	...	...	...	...	...	...	...	...	2	...
BALIPARA FRONTIER TRACT	...	...	...	...	...	...	...	...	...	...	...	...
(2) Manipur State	*10*	...	...	...	...	...	*9*	...	...	...	...	...
(3) Khasi States	*12*	...	...	...	...	...	*10*	*1*	*3*	...	*5*	...

TABLE X.—OCCUPATION OR MEANS OF LIVELIHOOD. PART II.—DETAILS FOR DISTRICTS—*contd.*

DISTRICT OR STATE.	Class B.—Preparation and supply of material substances. Sub-class III.—Industry. Order 15.—Construction of means of transport. Group (93).—Ship, boat, aeroplane builders.						Order 16.—Production and transmission of physical force. Total of Order 16.—Production and transmission of physical force.					
	Total earners (principal occupation).		Total working dependants.		Total following occupation as subsidiary to other.		Total earners (principal occupation).		Total working dependants.		Total following occupation as subsidiary to other.	
	Males.	Females.	Males.	Females.	Males.	Females.	Males.	Females.	Males.	Females.	Males.	Females.
	618	619	620	621	622	623	624	625	626	627	628	629
ASSAM	*181*	...	*58*	*1*	*961*	*4*	*199*	...	*2*	...	*9*	...
(1) British Territory	*172*	...	*58*	*1*	*941*	*4*	*192*	...	*2*	...	*9*	...
SURMA VALLEY AND HILL DIVISION	130	...	57	1	271	...	20	...	1	...	6	...
Cachar	...	...	...	...	...	...	11	...	1	...	6	...
Sylhet	127	...	55	1	238	...	4	...	...	...	...	...
Khasi and Jaintia Hills (British)	...	...	...	...	...	...	5	...	...	...	...	...
Naga Hills	...	...	...	...	...	...	...	...	...	...	...	...
Lushai Hills	3	...	2	...	33	...	...	...	...	...	...	...
ASSAM VALLEY DIVISION	33	...	1	...	669	4	172	...	1	...	3	...
Goalpara	5	...	...	...	...	...	4	...	...	...	...	...
Kamrup	7	...	1	...	195	...	29	...	...	...	...	...
Darrang	1	...	...	...	3	...	22	...	...	...	...	...
Nowgong	2	...	...	...	...	...	...	...	...	...	...	...
Sibsagar	2	...	...	...	16	...	54	...	...	...	3	...
Lakhimpur	16	...	...	...	3	...	63	...	1	...	...	...
Garo Hills	...	...	...	...	453	4	...	...	...	...	...	...
SADIYA FRONTIER TRACT	9	...	...	...	1	...	...	...	...	...	...	...
BALIPARA FRONTIER TRACT	...	...	...	...	...	...	...	...	...	...	...	...
(2) Manipur State	*7*	...	...	...	*9*	...	*2*	...	...	...	...	...
(3) Khasi States	*2*	...	...	...	*11*	...	*5*	...	...	...	...	...

TABLE X.—Occupation or Means of Livelihood. Part IV.—Details for Districts—*contd.*

District or State.	Class B.—Preparation and supply of material substances.											
	Sub-class III.—Industry.											
	Order 16.—Production and transmission of physical force.						Order 17.—Miscellaneous and undefined industries.					
	Group (94).—Heat, light, electricity, motive power, etc., Gas works and electric light and power.						Total of Order 17.—Miscellaneous and undefined industries.					
	Total earners (principal occupation).		Total working dependants.		Total following occupation as subsidiary to other.		Total earners (principal occupation).		Total working dependants.		Total following occupation as subsidiary to other.	
	Males.	Females.	Males.	Females.	Males.	Females.	Males.	Females.	Males.	Females	Males.	Females.
	630	631	632	633	634	635	636	637	638	639	640	641
ASSAM	*209*	...	*2*	...	*9*	...	*9,543*	*739*	*565*	*90*	*3,319*	*20*
(1) British Territory	*199*	...	*2*	...	*9*	...	*8,611*	*678*	*501*	*53*	*3,281*	*18*
SURMA VALLEY AND HILL DIVISION	20	...	1	...	6	...	3,630	249	226	25	1,299	4
Cachar	11	...	1	...	6	...	506	105	25	1	134	...
Sylhet	4	...	...	...	...	...	2,004	105	196	20	874	3
Khasi and Jaintia Hills (British)	5	...	...	...	...	...	292	14	3	1	7	...
Naga Hills	...	...	...	...	...	...	70	14	1	3	29	...
Lushai Hills	...	...	...	...	...	...	68	11	1	...	255	1
ASSAM VALLEY DIVISION	172	...	1	...	3	...	4,875	405	273	27	1,605	14
Goalpara	4	...	...	...	...	...	736	33	103	2	201	8
Kamrup	29	...	...	...	...	...	1,680	86	81	3	209	1
Darrang	21	...	...	...	...	...	400	30	17	2	306	1
Nowgong	...	...	...	...	...	...	333	88	31	...	313	...
Sibsagar	54	...	...	...	3	...	627	51	28	6	637	3
Lakhimpur	63	...	1	...	...	...	977	130	14	12	134	1
Garo Hills	...	...	...	...	...	...	73	13	1	2	5	...
SADIYA FRONTIER TRACT	...	...	...	...	...	...	87	15	2	1	7	...
BALIPARA FRONTIER TRACT	...	...	...	...	...	...	19	9	...	...	...	...
(2) Manipur State	*2*	...	...	...	...	...	*548*	*53*	*62*	*36*	*29*	*2*
(3) Khasi States	*8*	...	...	...	...	...	*384*	*8*	*2*	*1*	*9*	...

TABLE X.—OCCUPATION OR MEANS OF LIVELIHOOD. PART II.—DETAILS FOR DISTRICTS—*contd.*

DISTRICT OR STATE.	Class B.—Preparation and supply of material substances. Sub-class III.—Industry. Order 17.—Miscellaneous and undefined industries.											
	Group (95).—Printers, engravers, book-binders, etc.						Group (96).—Makers of musical instruments.					
	Total earners (principal occupation).		Total working dependants.		Total following occupation as subsidiary to other.		Total earners (principal occupation).		Total working dependants.		Total following occupation as subsidiary to other.	
	Males.	Females.	Males.	Females.	Males.	Females.	Males.	Females.	Males.	Females.	Males.	Females.
	642	643	644	645	646	647	648	649	650	651	652	653
ASSAM	*539*	*5*	*17*	...	*60*	...	*97*	*2*	*5*	...	*53*	...
(1) British Territory	*379*	*3*	*17*	...	*60*	...	*91*	*2*	*4*	...	*51*	...
SURMA VALLEY AND HILL DIVSION	149	1	6	...	22	...	20	...	2	...	18	...
Cachar	33	...	3	...	14	...	5	...	...	...	8	...
Sylhet	94	1	3	...	5	...	15	...	2	...	6	...
Khasi and Jaintia Hills (British)	12	...	...	...	2	...	...	...	...	...	...	...
Naga Hills	...	...	...	...	...	...	...	...	...	...	4	...
Lushai Hills	10	...	...	...	1	...	...	...	...	...	...	...
ASSAM VALLEY DIVISION	229	2	11	...	38	...	71	2	2	...	33	...
Goalpara	22	...	2	...	3	...	13	...	1	...	13	...
Kamrup	66	...	...	...	5	...	16	...	...	...	...	...
Darrang	10	...	...	...	...	...	3	...	...	...	10	...
Nowgong	7	...	...	...	1	...	1	...	...	...	2	...
Sibsagar	70	1	...	...	19	...	14	1	...	...	6	...
Lakhimpur	63	1	8	...	10	...	24	1	1	...	2	...
Garo Hills	1	...	1	...	...	...	...	...	...	...	...	...
SADIYA FRONTIER TRACT	1	...	...	...	...	...	...	...	...	...	...	...
BALIPARA FRONTIER TRACT	...	...	...	...	...	...	...	...	...	...	...	...
(2) Manipur State	*11*	...	...	...	...	...	*6*	...	*1*	...	*2*	...
(3) Khasi States	*149*	*2*	...	...	...	...	...	...	...	...	...	...

TABLE X.—OCCUPATION OR MEANS OF LIVELIHOOD. PART II.—DETAILS FOR DISTRICTS—*contd.*

DISTRICT OR STATE.	Class B.—Preparation and supply of material substances. Sub-class III.—Industry. Order 17.—Miscellaneous and undefined Industries.											
	Group (97).—makers of clocks, etc., and surgical or scientific instruments.						Group (98).—makers of jewellery and ornaments.					
	Total earners (principal occupation).		Total working dependants.		Total following occupation as subsidiary to other.		Total earners (principal occupation).		Total working dependants.		Total following occupation as subsidiary to other.	
	Males.	Females.	Males.	Females.	Males.	Females.	Males.	Females.	Males.	Females.	Males.	Females.
	654	655	656	657	658	659	660	661	662	663	664	665
ASSAM	*102*	...	*4*	...	*35*	...	*6,492*	*81*	*507*	*45*	*2,695*	*9*
(1) British Territory	*91*	...	*1*	...	*34*	...	*5,960*	*28*	*452*	*9*	*2,676*	*7*
SURMA VALLEY AND HILL DIVISION	41	...	1	...	28	...	2,575	4	202	...	790	2
Cachar	5	...	...	...	3	...	298	...	17	...	98	...
Sylhet	34	...	1	...	25	...	2,129	3	181	...	668	2
Khasi and Jaintia Hills (British)	2	...	...	...	...	...	125	...	3	...	6	...
Naga Hills	...	...	...	...	...	...	31	1	1	...	17	...
Lushai Hills	...	...	...	...	...	...	2	...	...	...	4	...
ASSAM VALLEY DIVISION	49	...	...	...	6	...	3,355	24	240	9	1,879	5
Goalpara	3	...	...	...	1	...	551	4	23	...	267	...
Kamrup	6	...	...	...	1	...	1,372	7	61	2	203	1
Darrang	2	...	...	...	1	...	346	4	13	1	384	1
Nowgong	3	...	...	...	2	...	234	1	31	...	308	...
Sibsagar	12	...	...	...	...	...	297	4	26	1	612	2
Lakhimpur	22	...	...	...	1	...	411	3	5	3	104	...
Garo Hills	1	...	...	...	...	...	44	1	...	2	1	...
SADIYA FRONTIER TRACT	1	...	...	...	...	...	28	...	1	...	7	...
BALIPARA FRONTIER TRACT	...	...	...	...	...	...	4	...	...	...	...	...
(2) Manipur State	*21*	...	*3*	...	*1*	...	*426*	*53*	*53*	*36*	*17*	*2*
(3) Khasi States	...	...	...	...	...	...	*106*	...	*2*	...	*2*	...

TABLE X.—OCCUPATION OR MEANS OF LIVELIHOOD. PART II.—DETAILS FOR DISTRICTS—*contd.*

DISTRICT OR STATE.	Class B.—Preparation and supply of material substances. Sub-class III.—Industry. Order 17.—Miscellaneous and undefined Industries. Group (99).—Other miscellaneous and undefined industries (toy-making, taxidermy, etc.). Total earners (principal occupation).		Total working dependants.		Total following occupation as subsidiary to other.		Group (100).—Scavenging. Total earners (principal occupation).		Total working dependants.		Total following occupation as subsidiary to other.	
	Males.	Females.	Males.	Females.	Males.	Females.	Males.	Females.	Males.	Females.	Males.	Females.
	666	667	668	669	670	671	672	673	674	675	676	677
ASSAM	*131*	*17*	*14*	*7*	*157*	...	*2,180*	*634*	*18*	*38*	*319*	*11*
(1) British Territory	*125*	*17*	*9*	*7*	*154*	...	*1,905*	*628*	*18*	*37*	*306*	*11*
SURMA VALLEY AND HILL DIVISION	121	17	9	7	153	...	734	227	6	18	278	2
Cachar	1	2	...	...	2	...	164	103	5	1	1	...
Sylhet	120	15	9	7	143	...	303	86	...	13	27	1
Khasi and Jaintia Hills (British)	...	...	...	...	...	...	143	14	...	1	...	...
Naga Hills	...	...	...	...	8	...	40	13	...	3	...	...
Lushai Hills...	...	...	...	...	...	...	56	11	1	...	250	1
ASSAM VALLEY DIVISION	4	...	...	...	1	...	1,167	377	11	18	28	9
Goalpara	2	...	...	...	1	...	145	34	7	2	6	8
Kamrup		...	...	...	...	...	120	79	...	1	...	...
Darrang	...	...	...	...	...	...	99	35	4	1	1	...
Nowgong	...	...	...	...	...	...	77	57	...	...	...	...
Sibsagar	1	...	...	...	...	...	133	46	...	4	...	...
Lakhimpur	1	...	...	...	...	...	406	115	...	9	17	1
Garo Hills	...	...	...	...	...	...	27	12	...	...	4	...
SADIYA FRONTIER TRACT	...	...	...	...	...	...	59	15	1	1	...	...
BALIPARA FRONTIER TRACT	...	...	...	...	...	...	15	9	...	...	...	...
(2) Manipur State	*6*	...	*5*	...	*3*	...	*88*	...	...	...	*6*	...
(3) Khasi States	...	...	...	...	...	...	*186*	*6*	...	*1*	...	...

TABLE X.—OCCUPATION OR MEANS OF LIVELIHOOD. PART II.—DETAILS FOR DISTRICTS—*contd.*

DISTRICT OR STATE.	Class B.—Preparation and supply of material substances.											
	Sub-class IV.—Transport.											
							Order 19.—Transport by water.					
	Total of Sub-class IV.—Transport.						Total of Order 19.—Transport by water.					
	Total earners (principal occupation).		Total working dependants.		Total following occupation as subsidiary to other.		Total earners (principal occupation).		Total working dependants.		Total following occupation as subsidiary to other.	
	Males.	Females.	Males.	Females.	Males.	Females.	Males.	Females.	Males.	Females.	Males.	Females.
	678	679	680	681	682	683	684	685	686	687	688	689
ASSAM	*50,379*	*2,549*	*1,711*	*335*	*26,243*	*855*	*12 287*	*11*	*645*	*4*	*7,084*	*15*
(1) British Territory	*47,865*	*2,150*	*1,497*	*225*	*24,987*	*519*	*12,247*	*11*	*644*	*4*	*6,908*	*15*
SURMA VALLEY AND HILL DIVISION	15,338	1,107	816	112	16,394	415	6,012	3	496	3	6,227	14
Cachar	3,182	600	70	17	906	27	623	...	80	...	227	1
Sylhet	10,920	168	665	15	13,691	33	5,371	3	416	3	5,964	13
Khasi and Jaintia Hills (British)	549	271	51	78	806	350	13	...	...	...	23	...
Naga Hills	450	8	2	2	144	1	...	...	...	...	...	...
Lushai Hills	237	...	19	...	757	4	1	...	...	...	73	...
ASSAM VALLEY DIVISION	31,811	1,047	677	113	8,380	96	6,047	8	147	1	546	1
Goalpara	5,610	110	217	5	1,215	5	1,805	6	98	...	132	...
Kamrup	7,093	293	39	40	2,279	23	1,320	1	9	1	112	1
Darrang	4,728	147	31	...	1,129	8	953	...	4	...	67	...
Nowgong	3,863	161	42	15	874	7	196	...	9	...	30	...
Sibsagar	4,476	113	161	20	2,019	16	606	...	6	...	175	...
Lakhimpur	5,611	196	131	28	840	35	979	...	21	...	60	...
Garo Hills	430	27	2	1	104	2	2	1	...	...	11	...
SADIYA FRONTIER TRACT	640	5	4	...	231	1	188	...	1	...	135	...
BALIPARA FRONTIER TRACT	76	...	...	...	2	...	...	...	...	...	...	...
(2) Manipur State	*787*	*2*	*59*	...	*270*	...	*23*	...	...	...	*13*	...
(3) Khasi States	*1,727*	*388*	*155*	*110*	*986*	*343*	*17*	...	*1*	...	*163*	...

TABLE X.—OCCUPATION OR MEANS OF LIVELIHOOD. PART II.—DETAILS FOR DISTRICTS—*contd.*

Class B.—Preparation and supply of material substances.

Sub-class IV.—Transport.

Order 19.—Transport by water.

DISTRICT OR STATE.	Group (102).—Ship-owners, boat-owners and their employees, officers, mariners, etc. Ships brokers, boatmen and tow men.						Group (103).—Persons (other than labourers) employed in harbours, docks, rivers, and canals, including pilots.					
	Total earners (principal occupation).		Total working dependants.		Total following occupation as subsidiary to other.		Total earners (principal occupation).		Total working dependants.		Total following occupation as subsidiary to other.	
	Males.	Females.	Males.	Females.	Males.	Females.	Males.	Females.	Males.	Females.	Males.	Females.
	690	691	692	693	694	695	696	697	698	699	700	701
ASSAM	*11,917*	*11*	*645*	*4*	*7,076*	*15*	*119*	...	...	...	*5*	...
(1) British Territory	*11,877*	*11*	*644*	*4*	*6,900*	*15*	*119*	...	...	...	*5*	...
SURMA VALLEY AND HILL DIVISION	5,986	3	496	3	6,225	14	26	...	...	...	1	...
Cachar	633	...	50	...	267	1	...	...	...	...	...	...
Sylhet	5,340	3	446	3	5,863	13	26	...	...	...	1	...
Khasi and Jaintia Hills (British)	13	...	...	...	23	...	...	...	...	...	...	...
Naga Hills	...	...	...	...	...	...	...	...	...	...	...	...
Lushai Hills	1	...	...	...	73	...	...	...	...	...	...	...
ASSAM VALLEY DIVISION	5,704	8	147	1	540	1	85	...	...	...	4	...
Goalpara	1,894	6	98	...	133	...	1	...	...	...	...	...
Kamrup	1,311	1	9	1	112	1	18	...	...	...	...	...
Darrang	796	...	4	...	61	...	27	...	...	...	4	...
Nowgong	196	...	9	...	30	...	1	...	...	...	...	...
Sibsagar	643	...	6	...	125	...	36	...	...	...	...	...
Lakhimpur	963	...	21	...	69	...	3	...	...	...	...	...
Garo Hills	2	1	...	...	11	...	...	...	...	...	...	...
SADIYA FRONTIER TRACT	187	...	1	...	135	...	1	...	...	...	...	...
BALIPARA FRONTIER TRACT	...	...	...	...	...	...	...	...	...	...	...	...
(2) Manipur State	*23*	...	...	...	*13*	...	...	...	...	...	...	...
(3) Khasi States	*17*	...	*1*	...	*163*	...	...	...	...	...	...	...

TABLE X.—OCCUPATION OR MEANS OF LIVELIHOOD. PART II.—DETAILS FOR DISTRICTS—*contd.*

DISTRICT OR STATE.	Class B.—Preparation and supply of material substances.											
	Sub-class IV.—Transport.											
	Order 19.—Transport by water.						Order 20.—Transport by road.					
	Group (104).—Labourers employed on harbours, docks, rivers and canals.						Total of Order 20.—Transport by road.					
	Total earners (principal occupation).		Total working dependants.		Total following occupation as subsidiary to other.		Total earners (principal occupation).		Total working dependants.		Total following occupation as subsidiary to other.	
	Males.	Females.	Males.	Females.	Males.	Females.	Males.	Females.	Males.	Females.	Males.	Females.
	702	703	704	705	706	707	708	709	710	711	712	713
ASSAM	*258*	...	...	...	*3*	...	*24,153*	*1,919*	*928*	*299*	*17,735*	*887*
(1) British Territory	*258*	...	...	...	*3*	...	*21,789*	*1,529*	*715*	*190*	*16,657*	*494*
SURMA VALLEY AND HILL DIVISION	...	...	...	...	1	...	5,584	863	273	107	9,662	398
Cachar	...	...	...	...	...	...	731	433	21	17	643	25
Sylhet	...	...	...	...	1	...	3,774	152	180	10	7,636	19
Khasi and Jaintia Hills (British)	...	...	...	...	...	...	636	271	61	78	783	340
Naga Hills	...	...	...	...	...	...	369	8	2	2	131	1
Lushai Hills	...	...	...	...	...	...	164	...	19	...	609	4
ASSAM VALLEY DIVISION	258	...	...	...	2	...	15,723	685	430	83	6,897	95
Goalpara	...	...	...	...	...	...	2,803	101	113	5	1,044	5
Kamrup	97	...	...	...	...	...	3,753	130	68	26	2,027	23
Darrang	130	...	...	...	2	...	2,637	90	53	...	860	8
Nowgong	...	...	...	...	...	...	1,026	87	30	2	687	7
Sibsagar	18	...	...	...	...	...	1,955	98	148	29	1,519	16
Lakhimpur	13	...	...	...	...	...	3,296	133	60	17	684	36
Garo Hills	...	...	...	...	...	...	303	36	3	1	176	2
SADIYA FRONTIER TRACT	...	...	...	...	...	...	401	1	8	...	96	1
BALIPARA FRONTIER TRACT	...	...	...	...	...	...	74	...	...	...	2	...
(2) Manipur State	...	...	...	...	...	...	*713*	*9*	*59*	...	*955*	...
(3) Khasi States	...	...	...	...	...	...	*1,658*	*388*	*154*	*109*	*823*	*343*

TABLE X.—OCCUPATION OR MEANS OF LIVELIHOOD. PART II.—DETAILS FOR DISTRICTS—*contd.*

DISTRICT OR STATE.	Class B.—Preparation and supply of material substances. Sub-class IV.—Transport. Order 20.—Transport by road. Group (105).—Persons (other than labourers) employed on the construction and maintenance of roads and bridges.						Group (106).—Labourers employed on roads and bridges.					
	Total earners (principal occupation).		Total working dependants.		Total following occupation as subsidiary to other.		Total earners (principal occupation).		Total working dependants.		Total following occupation as subsidiary to other.	
	Males.	Females.	Males.	Females.	Males.	Females.	Males.	Females.	Males.	Females.	Males.	Females.
	714	715	716	717	718	719	720	721	722	723	724	725
ASSAM	*996*	*5*	*13*	...	*246*	...	*13,395*	*1,617*	*374*	*206*	*9,733*	*377*
(1) British Territory	*840*	*4*	*6*	...	*246*	...	*12,238*	*1,304*	*237*	*126*	*9,104*	*251*
SURMA VALLEY AND HILL DIVISION	128	1	...	...	80	...	3,496	660	153	48	6,862	181
Cachar	9	...	...	...	...	...	414	431	11	16	480	35
Sylhet	37	1	...	...	15	...	2,784	149	107	10	5,407	19
Khasi and Jaintia Hills (British)	5	...	...	...	1	...	80	74	16	20	324	132
Naga Hills	72	...	...	...	23	...	93	6	...	2	19	1
Lushai Hills	5	...	...	...	36	...	116	...	19	...	632	4
ASSAM VALLEY DIVISION	653	3	4	...	161	...	8,468	644	84	78	2,190	70
Goalpara	31	...	...	...	7	...	1,508	98	22	5	224	1
Kamrup	189	...	1	...	45	...	2,012	124	9	27	740	17
Darrang	77	...	...	...	12	...	1,705	90	4	...	207	...
Nowgong	96	...	1	...	16	...	849	84	6	3	374	7
Sibsagar	30	...	2	...	11	...	1,128	94	28	26	306	8
Lakhimpur	179	...	...	...	64	...	1,014	131	14	16	140	35
Garo Hills	43	3	...	...	4	...	252	23	1	1	100	2
SADIYA FRONTIER TRACT	53	...	2	...	5	...	217	...	...	...	52	...
BALIPARA FRONTIER TRACT	6	...	...	...	...	...	57	...	...	...	...	...
(2) Manipur State	*86*	*1*	*6*	...	...	...	*108*	*2*	*3*	...	*20*	...
(3) Khasi States	*70*	...	*1*	...	...	...	*981*	*312*	*136*	*80*	*609*	*126*

TABLE X.—OCCUPATION OR MEANS OF LIVELIHOOD. PART II.—DETAILS FOR DISTRICTS—*contd.*

DISTRICT OR STATE.	Class B.—Preparation and supply of material substances.											
	Sub-class IV.—Transport.											
	Order 20.—Transport by road.											
	Group (107).—Owners, managers and employees (excluding personal servants) connected with mechanically driven vehicles (including trams).						Group (108).—Owners, managers and employees (excluding personal servants) connected with other vehicles.					
	Total earners (principal occupation).		Total working dependants.		Total following occupation as subsidiary to other.		Total earners (principal occupation).		Total working dependants.		Total following occupation as subsidiary to other.	
	Males.	Females.	Males.	Females.	Males.	Females.	Males.	Females.	Males.	Females.	Males.	Females.
	726	727	728	729	730	731	732	733	734	735	736	737
ASSAM	*2,913*	...	*45*	...	*160*	*1*	*5,479*	*282*	*421*	*89*	*5,705*	*259*
(1) British Territory	*1,789*	...	*25*	...	*152*	*1*	*5,904*	*219*	*378*	*63*	*5,365*	*249*
SURMA VALLEY AND HILL DIVISION	**676**	...	**18**	...	**69**	...	**658**	**202**	**38**	**59**	**956**	**217**
Cachar	91	...	5	...	11	...	109	1	6	1	161	...
Sylhet	376		13	...	40	...	145	2	8	...	340	...
Khasi and Jaintia Hills (British)...	111	...	...	...	1	...	177	197	23	58	390	217
Naga Hills	98	...	...	...	8	...	101	2	2	...	74	...
Lushai Hills	...	...	...	...	...	...	36	...	...	...	1	...
ASSAM VALLEY DIVISION	**1,308**	.	**7**	...	**83**	**1**	**5,116**	**16**	**339**	**4**	**4,370**	**24**
Goalpara	23	...	...	...	...	.	1,274	5	90	...	804	4
Kamrup	464	...	4	...	11	1	890	5	60	...	1,163	4
Darrang	60	...	...	...	1	...	941	...	19	...	550	8
Nowgong	15	...	...	...	...	...	738	2	23	...	240	...
Sibsagar	242	...	...	...	28	.	542	4	113	3	1,169	8
Lakhimpur	393	...	3	...	41	...	676	1	43	1	388	...
Garo Hills	74	...	...	...	2	...	75	...	1	...	87	...
SADIYA FRONTIER TRACT	**11**	...	...	...	...	...	**119**	**1**	**1**	...	**37**	**1**
BALIPARA FRONTIER TRACT	...	...	...	...	...	...	**11**	...	...	...	**2**	...
(2) Manipur State	*197*	...	*20*	...	*1*	...	*289*	...	*30*	...	*233*	...
(3) Khasi States	*239*	...	...	...	*7*	...	*286*	*63*	*13*	*26*	*167*	*10*

TABLE X.—OCCUPATION OR MEANS OF LIVELIHOOD. PART II.—DETAILS FOR DISTRICTS—*contd.*

DISTRICT OR STATE.	Class B.—Preparation and supply of material substances. Sub-class IV.—Transport. Order 20.—Transport by road. Group (109).—Palki, etc., bearers and owners. Total earners (principal occupation). Males.	Females.	Total working dependants. Males.	Females.	Total following occupation as subsidiary to other. Males.	Females.	Group (110).—Pack elephants, camel, mule, ass and bullock, owners and drivers. Total earners (principal occupation). Males.	Females.	Total working dependants. Males.	Females.	Total following occupation as subsidiary to other. Males.	Females.
	738	739	740	741	742	743	744	745	746	747	748	749
ASSAM.	*769*	*13*	*63*	*3*	*1,723*	*207*	*109*	...	*6*	...	*69*	...
(1) British Territory ...	*679*	...	*59*	...	*1,684*	...	*89*	...	*6*	...	*69*	...
SURMA VALLEY AND HILL DIVISION ...	603	...	58	...	1,614	...	89	...	6	...	69	...
Cachar ...	13	...	...	...	1	...	5	...	...	...	...	...
Sylhet ...	440	...	46	...	1,546	...	77	...	6	...	69	...
Khasi and Jaintia Hills (British)...	141	...	12	...	67	...	...	...	...	...	...	...
Naga Hills ...	...	...	...	...	...	...	...	...	...	...	...	...
Lushai Hills ...	...	...	...	...	...	...	7	...	...	...	...	...
ASSAM VALLEY DIVISION ...	76	...	1	...	70	...	...	...	...	...	...	...
Goalpara ...	11	...	1	...	8	...	...	...	...	...	...	...
Kamrup ...	65	...	...	...	48	...	...	...	...	...	...	...
Darrang ...	...	...	...	...	...	...	...	...	...	...	...	...
Nowgong ...	...	...	...	...	7	...	...	...	...	...	...	...
Sibsagar ...	...	...	...	...	4	...	...	...	...	...	...	...
Lakhimpur ...	...	...	...	...	...	...	...	...	...	...	...	...
Garo Hills ...	...	...	...	...	3	...	...	...	...	...	...	...
SADIYA FRONTIER TRACT ...	...	...	...	...	...	...	...	...	...	...	...	...
BALIPARA FRONTIER TRACT ...	...	...	...	...	...	...	...	...	...	...	...	...
(2) Manipur State ...	*2*	...	...	...	*1*	...	*20*	...	...	...	...	...
(3) Khasi States ...	*88*	*13*	*4*	*3*	*40*	*207*	...	...	...	...	...	...

TABLE X.—Occupation or means of livelihood. Part II.—Details for Districts—*contd.*

DISTRICT OR STATE.	Class B.—Preparation and supply of material substances. Sub-class IV.—Transport. Order 20.—Transport by road. Group (111)—Porters and messengers. Total earners (principal occupation). Males.	Females.	Total working dependants. Males.	Females.	Total following occupation as subsidiary to other. Males.	Females.	Order 21.—Transport by rail. Total of Order 21.—Transport by rail. Total earners (principal occupation). Males.	Females.	Total working dependants. Males.	Females.	Total following occupation as subsidiary to other. Males.	Females.
	750	751	752	753	754	755	756	757	758	759	760	761
ASSAM	*969*	*9*	*4*	*1*	*37*	...	*11,449*	*619*	*91*	*31*	*1,066*	*9*
(1) British Territory	*943*	*9*	*4*	*1*	*37*	...	*11,449*	*619*	*91*	*31*	*1,066*	*9*
SURMA VALLEY AND HILL DIVISION	**34**	...	...	...	**12**	...	**2,831**	**241**	**27**	**2**	**309**	**2**
Cachar	30	...	...	...	...	...	1,541	228	3	...	70	1
Sylhet	6	...	...	...	10	...	1,260	13	24	2	237	1
Khasi and Jaintia Hills (British)	3	...	...	...	...	...	...	...	...	...	...	...
Naga Hills	5	...	...	...	2	...	30	...	...	...	2	...
Lushai Hills	...	...	...	...	...	...	...	...	...	...	...	...
ASSAM VALLEY DIVISION	**208**	**2**	**4**	**1**	**23**	...	**8,593**	**374**	**64**	**29**	**757**	...
Goalpara	6	...	...	...	...	...	667	3	3	...	8	...
Kamrup	148	1	4	1	20	...	1,720	162	10	11	74	...
Darrang	4	...	...	...	...	...	611	57	3	...	66	...
Nowgong	...	...	...	...	...	...	1,580	74	3	12	151	...
Sibsagar	4	...	...	...	2	...	1,512	15	7	...	324	...
Lakhimpur	46	1	...	...	1	...	1,003	63	35	6	113	...
Garo Hills	...	...	...	...	...	...	...	...	...	...	...	...
SADIYA FRONTIER TRACT	**1**	...	...	...	**2**	...	**18**	**4**	...	...	...	...
BALIPARA FRONTIER TRACT	...	...	...	...	...	...	...	...	...	...	...	...
(2) Manipur State	*18*	...	...	...	...	...	...	...	...	...	...	...
(3) Khasi States	*1*	...	...	...	...	...	...	...	...	...	...	...

TABLE X.—Occupation or means of livelihood. Part II.—Details for Districts—*contd.*

Class B.—Preparation and supply of material substances. Sub-class IV.—Transport. Order 21.—Transport by rail.

DISTRICT OR STATE.	Group (112).—Railway employees of all kinds other than coolies.						Group (113).—Labourers employed on railway construction and maintenance and coolies and porters employed on railway premises.					
	Total earners (principal occupation).		Total working dependants.		Total following occupation as subsidiary to other.		Total earners (principal occupation).		Total working dependants.		Total following occupation as subsidiary to other.	
	Males.	Females.	Males.	Females.	Males.	Females.	Males.	Females.	Males.	Females.	Males.	Females.
	763	763	764	765	766	767	768	769	770	771	772	773
ASSAM	*5,800*	*12*	*69*	...	*475*	...	*5,642*	*607*	*22*	*31*	*591*	*2*
(1) British Territory	*5,800*	*12*	*69*	...	*475*	...	*5,642*	*607*	*22*	*31*	*591*	*2*
SURMA VALLEY AND HILL DIVISION	1,047	...	26	...	139	...	1,784	241	2	2	170	2
Cachar	584	...	3	...	53	...	937	228	...	...	17	1
Sylhet	440	...	23	...	84	...	840	13	2	2	153	1
Khasi and Jaintia Hills (British)	...	...	...	...	...	...	...	...	...	...	...	...
Naga Hills	23	...	...	...	2	...	7	...	...	...	...	...
Lushai Hills	...	...	...	...	...	...	...	...	...	...	...	...
ASSAM VALLEY DIVISION	4,730	12	44	...	336	...	3,854	362	20	29	421	...
Goalpara	151	...	...	...	2	...	516	3	3	...	6	...
Kamrup	833	1	1	...	33	...	587	161	8	11	43	...
Darrang	335	...	3	...	8	...	486	57	1	...	77	...
Nowgong	1,125	2	1	...	20	...	725	72	3	12	122	...
Sibsagar	834	1	2	...	196	...	718	14	5	...	128	...
Lakhimpur	1,471	8	37	...	68	...	523	55	1	6	43	...
Garo Hills	...	...	...	...	...	...	...	...	...	...	...	...
SADIYA FRONTIER TRACT	14	...	...	...	...	...	4	4	...	...	...	...
BALIPARA FRONTIER TRACT	...	...	...	...	...	...	...	...	...	...	...	...
(2) Manipur State	...	...	...	...	...	...	...	...	...	...	...	...
(3) Khasi States	...	...	...	...	...	...	...	...	...	...	...	...

TABLE X—Occupation or means of livelihood. Part II.—Details for Districts—*contd.*

Class B.—Preparation and supply of material substances. Sub-class IV—Transport. Order 22.—Post office, Telegraph and Telephone services.

DISTRICT OR STATE.	Total of Order 22.—Post Office, Telegraph and Telephone Services. Total earners (principal occupation). Males.	Females.	Total working dependants. Males.	Females.	Total following occupation as subsidiary to other. Males.	Females.	Group (116).—Post Office, Telegraph and Telephone services. Total earners (principal occupation). Males.	Females.	Total working dependants. Males.	Females.	Total following occupation as subsidiary to other. Males.	Females.
	774	775	776	777	778	779	780	781	782	783	784	785
ASSAM	*2,497*	...	*47*	*1*	*358*	*1*	*2,497*	...	*47*	*1*	*358*	*1*
(1) British Territory ...	*2,394*	...	*47*	...	*356*	*1*	*2,394*	...	*47*	...	*356*	*1*
BURMA VALLEY AND HILL DIVISION ...	911	...	20	...	196	1	911	...	20	...	196	1
Cachar ...	237	...	6	...	16	...	237	...	5	...	16	...
Sylhet ...	401	...	15	...	154	...	401	...	15	...	154	...
Khasi and Jaintia Hills (British) ...	10	...	...	...	...	1	10	...	...	...	...	1
Naga Hills ...	51	...	...	...	11	...	51	...	...	...	11	...
Lushai Hills ...	122	...	...	...	15		122	...	...	...	15	...
ASSAM VALLEY DIVISION ...	1,448	...	27	...	160	...	1,448	...	27	...	160	...
Goalpara ...	246	...	3	...	31	...	246		3	...	31	...
Kamrup ...	205	...	2	...	14	...	205	...	2	...	14	...
Darrang ...	137	...	1	...	17	...	137	...	1	...	17	...
Nowgong ...	122	...	...	...	16	...	122	...	...	...	16	...
Sibsagar ...	273	...	6	...	51	...	273	...	5	...	51	...
Lakhimpur ...	341	...	16	...	24	...	341	...	16	...	24	...
Garo Hills ...	33	...	...	...	7	...	33	...	...	...	7	...
SADIYA FRONTIER TRACT ...	33	...	...	...	...	...	33	...	...	...	...	...
BALIPARA FRONTIER TRACT ...	2	...	...	...	...	...	2	...	...	...	...	...
(2) Manipur State ...	*51*	...	...	...	*2*	...	*51*	...	...	...	*2*	...
(3) Khasi States ...	*52*	...	...	*1*	...	...	*52*	...	...	*1*	...	...

TABLE X.—OCCUPATION OR MEANS OF LIVELIHOOD. PART II.—DETAILS FOR DISTRICTS—contd.

DISTRICT OR STATE.	Class B.—Preparation and supply of material substances. Sub-class V.—Trade. Total of sub-class V.—Trade. Total earners (principal occupation).		Total working dependants.		Total following occupation as subsidiary to other.		Order 23.—Banks, establishments of credit, exchange and insurance. Total of Order 23.—Banks, establishments of credit, etc. Total earners (principal occupation).		Total working dependants.		Total following occupation as subsidiary to other.	
	Males.	Females.	Males.	Females.	Males.	Females.	Males.	Females.	Males.	Females.	Males.	Females.
	786	787	788	789	790	791	792	793	794	795	796	797
ASSAM	*91,186*	*17,567*	*4,967*	*7,098*	*55,198*	*4,055*	*2,919*	*309*	*64*	*19*	*1,805*	*103*
(1) British Territory	*87,089*	*12,259*	*4,659*	*5,681*	*51,888*	*2,173*	*2,155*	*287*	*63*	*16*	*1,789*	*87*
SURMA VALLEY AND HILL DIVISION	31,380	4,326	2,294	998	31,146	1,171	858	232	27	11	1,126	58
Cachar	4,077	1,751	305	816	3,831	358	78	22	1	...	76	9
Sylhet	25,006	1,753	1,914	333	26,908	343	765	199	26	8	1,044	43
Khasi and Jaintia Hills (British)	690	428	26	161	239	435	11	12	...	3	6	7
Naga Hills	264	81	13	21	80	9	4	...	...	...	...	...
Lushai Hills	333	313	36	145	128	26	...	...	...	...	...	...
ASSAM VALLEY DIVISION	55,783	7,875	2,361	4,650	20,612	993	1,297	55	36	5	663	29
Goalpara	10,430	2,183	606	867	2,756	146	651	22	30	...	383	20
Kamrup	13,507	1,566	384	1,136	4,749	154	228	21	4	1	130	8
Darrang	6,807	660	135	218	2,310	98	91	5	1	...	29	...
Nowgong	5,661	715	372	307	2,721	78	213	1	1	...	46	1
Sibsagar	8,823	1,168	338	1,435	4,467	261	34	1	...	...	17	...
Lakhimpur...	9,707	1,110	311	884	1,909	236	37	8	...	4	9	...
Garo Hills	769	137	15	9	1,721	20	23	1	...	...	40	...
SADIYA FRONTIER TRACT	498	54	4	23	127	8	...	...	...	...	...	...
BALIPARA FRONTIER TRACT	38	4	...	...	2	1	...	...	...	...	...	...
(2) Manipur State	*2,328*	*4,049*	*270*	*1,190*	*1,785*	*311*	*49*	*2*	*1*	*1*	*6*	...
(3) Khasi States	*1,169*	*1,259*	*38*	*227*	*1,525*	*1,571*	*15*	*20*	...	*2*	*19*	*16*

TABLE X.—OCCUPATION OR MEANS OF LIVELIHOOD. PART II.—DETAILS FOR DISTRICTS—*contd.*

DISTRICT OR STATE.	Class B.—Preparation and supply of material substances.											
	Sub-class V.—Trade.											
	Order 23.—Banks, establishments of credit, exchange and insurance.						Order 24.—Brokerage, commission and export.					
	Group (115).—Bank managers, money lenders, exchange and insurance agents, money changers and brokers and their employees.						Total of Order 24.—Brokerage, commission and export.					
	Total earners (principal occupation).		Total working dependants.		Total following occupation as subsidiary to other.		Total earners (principal occupation).		Total working dependants.		Total following occupation as subsidiary to other.	
	Males.	Females.	Males.	Females.	Males.	Females.	Males.	Females.	Males.	Females.	Males.	Females.
	798	799	800	801	802	803	804	805	806	807	808	809
ASSAM	*2,219*	*309*	*64*	*19*	*1,805*	*103*	*142*	*4*	*7*	...	*84*	*2*
(1) British Territory ...	*2,155*	*287*	*63*	*16*	*1,789*	*87*	*141*	*4*	*7*	...	*83*	*2*
SURMA VALLEY AND HILL DIVISION ...	858	232	27	11	1,126	58	45	2	7	...	61	2
Cachar ...	78	22	1	...	76	9	1	...	...	...	...	...
Sylhet ...	765	198	26	8	1,044	42	33	2	7	...	61	2
Khasi and Jaintia Hills (British) ...	11	12	...	3	6	7	10	...	...	...	...	...
Naga Hills ...	4	...	...	...	...	...	1	...	...	...	...	...
Lushai Hills ...	...	...	...	...	...	...	...	...	...	...	...	...
ASSAM VALLEY DIVISION ...	1,297	55	36	5	663	29	96	2	...	...	22	...
Goalpara ...	631	23	30	...	333	20	8	...	...	...	3	...
Kamrup ...	228	21	4	1	130	8	36	2	...	...	14	...
Darrang ...	91	5	1	...	39	...	17	...	...	...	...	...
Nowgong ...	213	1	1	...	48	1	1	...	...	...	...	...
Sibsagar ...	24	1	...	...	17	...	10	...	...	...	1	...
Lakhimpur ...	37	3	...	4	9	...	16	...	...	...	...	...
Garo Hills ...	23	1	...	...	40	...	8	...	...	...	4	...
SADIYA FRONTIER TRACT ...	...	...	...	...	...	...	...	...	...	...	...	...
BALIPARA FRONTIER TRACT ...	...	...	...	...	...	...	...	...	...	...	...	...
(2) Manipur State ...	*49*	*2*	*1*	*1*	*4*	...	*2*	...	...	...	*1*	...
(3) Khasi States ...	*15*	*20*	...	*2*	*19*	*16*	...	...	...	...	...	...

TABLE X—Occupation or means of livelihood. Part II.—Details for Districts—*contd.*

DISTRICT OR STATE.	Class B.—Preparation and supply of material substances.											
	Sub-class V.—Trade.											
	Order 24.—Brokerage commission and export.						Order 25.—Trade in textiles.					
	Group (116).—Brokers, commission agents, commercial travellers, warehouse owners and employees.						Total of Order 25.—Trade in textiles.					
	Total earners (principal occupation).		Total working dependants.		Total following occupation as subsidiary to other.		Total earners (principal occupation).		Total working dependants.		Total following occupation as subsidiary to other.	
	Males.	Females.	Males.	Females.	Males.	Females.	Males.	Females.	Males.	Females.	Males.	Females.
	810	811	812	[illegible]	814	815	816	817	818	819	[illegible]	821
ASSAM	*143*	*4*	*7*	...	*84*	*2*	*4,097*	*1,499*	*202*	*274*	*1,867*	*150*
(1) British Territory	*141*	*4*	*7*	...	*83*	*2*	*3,396*	*199*	*149*	*17*	*1,750*	*17*
SURMA VALLEY AND HILL DIVISION	45	2	7	...	61	2	2,092	166	124	12	1,314	13
Cachar	1	...	...	...	...	...	327	136	8	5	125	7
Sylhet	33	2	7	...	61	2	1,734	24	116	4	1,167	3
Khasi and Jaintia Hills (British)	10	...	...	...	...	...	21	16	...	2	2	3
Naga Hills	1	...	...	...	...	...	10	...	...	1	19	...
Lushai Hills	...	...	...	...	...	...	...	...	...	...	...	...
ASSAM VALLEY DIVISION	96	2	...	...	22	...	1,140	31	25	5	437	4
Goalpara	8	...		...	3	...	370	20	13	2	102	2
Kamrup	36	2		...	14	...	257	6	9	3	122	1
Darrang	17	...	...	...	...	...	123	...	...	...	24	1
Nowgong	1	...	...	...	...	...	152	...	1	...	52	...
Sibsagar	10	...	...	...	1	...	73	2	1	...	34	...
Lakhimpur	16	...	...	...	...	...	25	3	...	...	3	...
Garo Hills	9	...	...	...	4	...	30	...	1	...	99	...
SADIYA FRONTIER TRACT	...	...	...	...	...	...	64	2	...	...	...	...
BALIPARA FRONTIER TRACT	...	...	...	...	...	...	...	...	...	...	...	...
(2) Manipur State	*2*	...	...	...	*1*	...	*661*	*1,197*	*47*	*239*	*54*	*70*
(3) Khasi States	...	...	...	...	...	...	*140*	*103*	*6*	*18*	*63*	*63*

TABLE X.—OCCUPATION OR MEANS OF LIVELIHOOD. PART II.—DETAILS FOR DISTRICTS—*contd.*

DISTRICT OR STATE.	Class B.—Preparation and supply of material substances. Sub-class V.—Trade. Order 25.—Trade in textiles. Group (117).—Trade in piece-goods, wool, cotton, silk, hair and other textiles. Total earners (principal occupation). Males.	Females.	Total working dependants. Males.	Females.	Total following occupation as subsidiary to other. Males.	Females.	Order 26.—Trade in skins, leather and furs. Total of Order 26.—Trade in skins, leather and furs. Total earners (principal occupation). Males.	Females.	Total working dependants. Males.	Females.	Total following occupation as subsidiary to other. Males.	Females.
	822	823	824	825	826	827	828	829	830	831	832	833
ASSAM	*4,097*	*1,499*	*202*	*274*	*1,867*	*150*	*1,693*	*93*	*107*	*33*	*925*	*19*
(1) British Territory	*3,296*	*199*	*149*	*17*	*1,750*	*17*	*1,690*	*91*	*107*	*33*	*925*	*17*
SURMA VALLEY AND HILL DIVISION	**2,092**	**166**	**124**	**12**	**1,313**	**13**	**882**	**16**	**76**	**29**	**683**	**15**
Cachar	327	126	8	5	125	7	74	4	...	...	73	...
Sylhet	1,734	24	116	4	1,167	3	808	12	76	29	609	15
Khasi and Jaintia Hills (British)	21	16	...	2	2	3	...	...	...	...	1	...
Naga Hills	10	...	...	1	19	...	...	...	...	...	...	...
Lushai Hills	...	...	...	...	...	...	...	...	...	...	...	...
ASSAM VALLEY DIVISION	**1,140**	**31**	**25**	**5**	**437**	**4**	**808**	**5**	**31**	**4**	**242**	**2**
Goalpara	369	20	13	2	102	2	250	1	21	4	58	...
Kamrup	257	6	9	3	123	1	237	1	5	...	71	...
Darrang	225	...	...	...	24	1	91	...	...	...	30	...
Nowgong	152	...	1	...	53	...	160	...	3	...	42	2
Sibsagar	73	2	1	...	34	...	43	3	...	...	28	...
Lakhimpur	25	3	...	...	3	...	9	...	...	...	13	...
Garo Hills	39	...	1	...	98	...	12	...	...	...	...	...
SADIYA FRONTIER TRACT	**64**	**2**	...	...	...	...	...	...	...	...	...	...
BALIPARA FRONTIER TRACT	...	...	...	...	...	...	...	...	...	...	...	...
(2) Manipur State	*661*	*1,197*	*47*	*239*	*54*	*70*	*1*	...	...	...	...	...
(3) Khasi States	*140*	*103*	*6*	*18*	*63*	*63*	*2*	*2*	...	...	...	*2*

TABLE X.—Occupation or means of livelihood. Part II.—Details for districts—*contd.*

District or State.	Class B.—Preparation and supply of material substances.											
	Sub-class V.—Trade.											
	Order 26.—Trade in skins, leather and furs.						Order 27.—Trade in wood.					
	Group (115).—Trade in skins, leather, furs, feathers, horn, etc., and the articles made from these.						Total of Order 27.—Trade in wood.					
	Total earners (principal occupation).		Total working dependants.		Total following occupation as subsidiary to other.		Total earners (principal occupation).		Total working dependants.		Total following occupation as subsidiary to other.	
	Males.	Females.	Males.	Females.	Males.	Females.	Males.	Females.	Males.	Females.	Males.	Females.
	834	835	836	837	838	839	840	841	842	843	844	845
ASSAM	*1,693*	*93*	*107*	*33*	*925*	*19*	*2,660*	*93*	*241*	*14*	*7,050*	*52*
(1) British Territory ...	*1,690*	*91*	*107*	*33*	*925*	*17*	*2,553*	*83*	*238*	*13*	*6,871*	*46*
SURMA VALLEY AND HILL DIVISION ...	882	16	76	29	683	15	1,743	78	211	1	5,294	20
Cachar ...	74	4	...	...	73	...	415	67	13	...	1,077	14
Sylhet ...	808	12	76	29	609	15	1,296	11	198	1	4,209	5
Khasi and Jaintia Hills (British) ...	...	...	...	...	1	...	3	...	...	...	2	...
Naga Hills ...	...	...	...	...	...	...	22	...	...	...	...	...
Lushai Hills ...	...	...	...	...	...	...	7	...	...	...	6	1
ASSAM VALLEY DIVISION ...	808	5	31	4	242	2	808	7	27	12	1,577	26
Goalpara ...	250	1	24	4	54	...	243	...	9	...	363	...
Kamrup ...	237	1	5	...	71	...	188	1	11	...	151	1
Darrang ...	91	...	...	...	30	...	98	...	...	...	30	1
Nowgong ...	180	...	2	...	42	2	40	1	...	...	8	...
Sibsagar ...	40	3	...	...	28	...	131	5	5	12	80	...
Lakhimpur ...	9	...	...	...	13	...	85	...	...	...	53	20
Garo Hills ...	12	...	...	...	...	...	14	...	2	...	893	4
SADIYA FRONTIER TRACT ...	...	...	...	...	...	...	1	...	...	...	...	...
BALIPARA FRONTIER TRACT ...	...	...	...	...	...	...	1	...	...	...	...	...
(2) Manipur State ...	*1*	...	...	...	...	...	*63*	*2*	*3*	*1*	*6*	...
(3) Khasi States ...	*2*	*2*	...	...	...	*2*	*44*	*6*	...	...	*173*	*6*

TABLE X—Occupation or means of livelihood. Part II.—Details for Districts—*contd.*

DISTRICT OR STATE.	Class B.—Preparation and supply of material substances. Sub-class V.—Trade. Order 27.—Trade in wood. Group (119).—Trade in wood (not fire wood). Total earners (principal occupation). Males.	Females.	Total working dependants. Males.	Females.	Total following occupation as subsidiary to other. Males.	Females.	Group (120).—Trade in barks. Total earners (principal occupation). Males.	Females.	Total working dependants. Males.	Females.	Total following occupation as subsidiary to other. Males.	Females.
	846	847	848	849	850	851	852	853	854	855	856	857
ASSAM	*1,345*	*28*	*61*	*4*	*1,229*	*13*	*7*	...	...	...	*2*	...
(1) British Territory ...	*1,259*	*25*	*58*	*4*	*1,110*	*12*	*7*	...	...	...	*2*	...
SURMA VALLEY AND HILL DIVISION ...	**634**	**23**	**35**	**1**	**521**	**11**	**1**	...	...	...	**1**	...
Cachar ...	265	19	8	...	116	11	...	...	...	...	...	...
Sylhet ...	340	4	27	1	405	...	...	...	...	...	1	...
Khasi and Jaintia Hills (British) ...	3	...	...	...	1	...	...	...	...	...	...	...
Naga Hills ...	19	...	...	...	...	...	1	...	...	...	...	...
Lushai Hills ...	7	...	...	...	1	...	...	...	...	...	...	...
ASSAM VALLEY DIVISION ...	**623**	**2**	**23**	**3**	**589**	**1**	**6**	...	...	...	**1**	...
Goalpara ...	239	...	9	...	339	...	...	...	...	...	...	...
Kamrup ...	179	1	9	...	114	1	...	...	...	...	...	...
Darrang ...	46	...	...	...	17	...	1	...	...	...	...	...
Nowgong ...	36	1	...	...	6	...	2	...	...	...	1	...
Sibsagar ...	46	...	5	3	38	...	...	...	...	...	...	...
Lakhimpur ...	63	...	...	...	5	...	3	...	...	...	...	...
Garo Hills ...	13	...	...	...	66	...	...	...	...	...	...	...
SADIYA FRONTIER TRACT ...	1	...	...	...	...	...	...	...	...	...	...	...
BALIPARA FRONTIER TRACT ...	1	...	...	...	...	...	...	...	...	...	...	...
(2) Manipur State ...	*50*	...	*3*	...	*3*	...	...	...	...	...	...	...
(3) Khasi States ...	*36*	*3*	...	...	*116*	*1*	...	...	...	...	...	...

TABLE X.—Occupation or means of livelihood. Part II.—Details for Districts—*contd.*

Class B.—Preparation and supply of material substances. Sub-class V.—Trade. Order 27.—Trade in wood.

District or State.	Group (121).—Trade in bamboos and canes. Total earners (principal occupation). Males.	Females.	Total working dependants. Males.	Females.	Total following occupation as subsidiary to other. Males.	Females.	Group (122).—Trade in thatches and other forest produce. Total earners (Principal occupation). Males.	Females.	Total working dependants. Males.	Females.	Total following occupation as subsidiary to other. Males.	Females.
	858	859	860	861	862	863	864	865	866	867	868	869
ASSAM	*779*	*60*	*139*	*10*	*4,155*	*35*	*529*	*5*	*41*	...	*1,664*	*4*
(1) British Territory	*758*	*55*	*139*	*9*	*4,095*	*30*	*529*	*5*	*41*	...	*1,664*	*4*
SURMA VALLEY AND HILL DIVISION	700	55	136	...	3,175	6	408	...	40	...	1,597	3
Cachar	80	48	...	...	745	2	70	...	5	...	218	...
Sylhet	620	7	136	...	2,424	3	336	...	35	...	1,379	3
Khasi and Jaintia Hills (British)	...	...	...	...	1	...	...	...	...	...	...	...
Naga Hills	...	...	...	...	...	...	2	...	...	...	...	...
Lushai Hills	...	...	...	...	5	1	...	...	...	...	...	...
ASSAM VALLEY DIVISION	58	...	3	9	920	24	121	5	1	...	67	1
Goalpara	2	...	...	...	4	...	2	...	...	...	19	...
Kamrup	5	...	2	...	26	...	4	...	...	...	7	...
Darrang	1	...	...	...	4	...	48	...	...	...	9	1
Nowgong	3	...	...	...	...	...	8	...	...	...	1	...
Sibsagar	38	...	...	9	27	...	47	5	...	...	15	...
Lakhimpur	9	...	...	...	43	20	11	...	...	...	5	...
Garo Hills	...	...	1	...	816	4	1	...	1	...	11	...
SADIYA FRONTIER TRACT	...	...	...	...	...	...	...	...	...	...	...	...
BALIPARA FRONTIER TRACT	...	...	...	...	...	...	...	...	...	...	...	...
(2) Manipur State	*13*	*2*	...	*1*	*3*	...	...	...	...	...	...	...
(3) Khasi States	*8*	*3*	...	...	*57*	*5*	...	...	...	...	...	...

TABLE X.—Occupation or Means of Livelihood. Part II.—Details for Districts—*contd.*

District or State.	Class B.—Preparation and supply of material substances. Sub-class V.—Trade. Order 28.—Trade in metals. Total of Order 28.—Trade in minerals. Total earners (principal occupation).		Total working dependants.		Total following occupation as subsidiary to other.		Group (123).—Trade in metals, machinery, knives, tools, etc. Total earners (principal occupation).		Total working dependants.		Total following occupation as subsidiary to other.	
	Males.	Females.	Males.	Females.	Males.	Females.	Males.	Females.	Males.	Females.	Males.	Females.
	870	871	872	873	874	875	876	877	878	879	880	881
ASSAM	*566*	*20*	*10*	*2*	*188*	*6*	*566*	*20*	*10*	*2*	*188*	*6*
(1) British Territory	*564*	*19*	*10*	*1*	*175*	*4*	*564*	*19*	*10*	*1*	*175*	*4*
SURMA VALLEY AND HILL DIVISION	175	10	2	1	96	1	175	10	2	1	96	1
Cachar	40	...	...	...	21	...	59	...	...	...	1	...
Sylhet	112	10	2	1	75	...	112	10	2	1	75	...
Khasi and Jaintia Hills (British)	1	...	...	...	...	...	1	...	...	...	...	...
Naga Hills...	2	...	...	...	...	...	2	...	...	...	...	...
Lushai Hills	1	...	...	...	...	1	1	...	...	...	...	1
ASSAM VALLEY DIVISION	388	8	8	...	79	3	388	8	8	...	79	3
Goalpara	39	...	1	...	18	...	39	...	1	...	16	...
Kamrup	151	8	4	...	28	...	151	3	4	...	28	...
Darrang	38	2	...	...	3	...	35	2	...	...	3	...
Nowgong	22	...	...	...	4	...	22	...	...	...	4	...
Sibsagar	75	2	...	...	21	...	75	2	...	...	21	...
Lakhimpur	54	1	3	...	5	3	54	1	3	...	5	3
Garo Hills	9	...	...	...	...	...	9	...	...	...	...	...
SADIYA FRONTIER TRACT	1	1	...	...	...	...	1	1	...	...	...	...
BALIPARA FRONTIER TRACT	...	...	...	...	...	...	...	...	...	...	...	...
(2) Manipur State	...	...	...	...	...	...	...	...	...	...	...	...
(3) Khasi States	*2*	*1*	...	*1*	*13*	*2*	*2*	*1*	...	*1*	*13*	*2*

TABLE X.—OCCUPATION OR MEANS OF LIVELIHOOD. PART II.—DETAILS FOR DISTRICTS—*contd.*

DISTRICT OR STATE.	Class B.—Preparation and supply of material substances. Sub-class V.—Trade. Order 29.—Trade in pottery, bricks and tiles.											
	Total of Order 29—Trade in pottery, bricks and tiles.						Group (124).—Trade in pottery, bricks and tiles.					
	Total earners (principal occupation).		Total working dependants.		Total following occupation as subsidiary to other.		Total earners (principal occupation).		Total working dependants.		Total following occupation as subsidiary to other.	
	Males.	Females.	Males.	Females.	Males.	Females.	Males.	Females.	Males.	Females.	Males.	Females.
	882	883	884	885	886	887	888	889	890	891	892	893
ASSAM	*174*	*18*	*1*	*8*	*133*	*4*	*174*	*18*	*1*	*8*	*133*	*4*
(1) British Territory	*155*	*18*	...	*8*	*133*	*4*	*155*	*18*	...	*8*	*133*	*4*
SURMA VALLEY AND HILL DIVISION	**62**	...	...	...	**89**	...	**62**	...	...	...	**89**	...
Cachar	...	...	...	...	...	...	...	...	...	...	...	...
Sylhet	58	...	...	...	89	...	58	...	...	...	89	...
Khasi and Jaintia Hills (British)	...	...	...	...	...	...	...	...	...	...	...	...
Naga Hills	4	...	...	...	...	...	4	...	...	...	...	...
Lushai Hills	...	...	...	...	...	...	...	...	...	...	...	...
ASSAM VALLEY DIVISION	**93**	**18**	...	**8**	**44**	**4**	**93**	**18**	...	**8**	**44**	**4**
Goalpara	7	18	...	8	1	4	7	18	...	8	1	4
Kamrup	3	...	...	...	2	...	3	...	...	...	2	...
Darrang	61	...	...	...	27	...	61	...	...	...	27	...
Nowgong	...	...	...	...	1	...	...	...	...	...	1	...
Sibsagar	9	...	...	...	...	...	9	...	...	...	...	...
Lakhimpur	13	...	...	...	13	...	13	...	...	...	13	...
Garo Hills	...	...	...	...	...	...	...	...	...	...	...	...
SADIYA FRONTIER TRACT	...	...	...	...	...	...	...	...	...	...	...	...
BALIPARA FRONTIER TRACT	...	...	...	...	...	...	...	...	...	...	...	...
(2) Manipur State	*19*	...	*1*	...	...	...	*19*	...	*1*	...	...	...
(3) Khasi States	...	...	...	...	...	...	...	...	...	...	...	...

TABLE X.—OCCUPATION OR MEANS OF LIVELIHOOD. PART II.—DETAILS FOR DISTRICTS—*contd.*

DISTRICT OR STATE.	Class B.—Preparation and supply of material substances.											
	Sub-class V.—Trade.											
	Order 30.—Trade in chemical products.											
	Total of Order 30.—Trade in chemical products.						Group (135).—Drugs, dyes, paints, petroleum, explosives, etc.					
	Total earners (principal occupation).		Total working dependants.		Total following occupation as subsidiary to other.		Total earners (principal occupation).		Total working dependants.		Total following occupation as subsidiary to other.	
	Males.	Females.	Males.	Females.	Males.	Females.	Males.	Females.	Males.	Females	Males.	Females.
	894	895	896	897	898	899	900	901	902	903	904	905
ASSAM	*603*	*53*	*38*	*7*	*494*	*14*	*603*	*53*	*38*	*7*	*494*	*14*
(1) British Territory	*568*	*50*	*34*	*6*	*238*	*14*	*568*	*50*	*34*	*6*	*238*	*14*
SURMA VALLEY AND HILL DIVISION	258	39	27	4	121	7	258	39	27	4	121	7
Cachar	14	...	...	...	7	...	14	...	...	...	7	...
Sylhet	151	15	12	2	107	1	151	15	12	2	107	1
Khasi and Jaintia Hills (British)	89	24	7	2	6	6	89	24	7	2	6	6
Naga Hills	4	...	...	...	...	...	4	...	...	...	...	...
Lushai Hills...	...	...	8	...	1	...	...	...	8	...	1	...
ASSAM VALLEY DIVISION	310	11	7	2	117	7	310	11	7	2	117	7
Goalpara	66	...	3	...	13	1	66	...	3	...	13	1
Kamrup	42	4	2	2	44	6	42	4	2	2	44	6
Darrang	33	2	...	...	1	...	33	2	...	...	1	...
Nowgong	56	...	...	...	18	...	56	...	...	...	18	...
Sibsagar	77	5	...	...	5	...	77	5	...	...	5	...
Lakhimpur	34	...	1	...	2	...	34	...	1	...	2	...
Garo Hills	2	...	1	...	34	...	2	...	1	...	34	...
SADIYA FRONTIER TRACT	...	...	...	...	...	...	...	...	...	...	...	...
BALIPARA FRONTIER TRACT	...	...	...	...	...	...	...	...	...	...	...	...
(2) Manipur State	...	...	...	...	...	...	...	...	...	...	...	...
(3) Khasi States	*35*	*3*	*4*	*1*	*186*	...	*35*	*3*	*4*	*1*	*186*	...

TABLE X.—OCCUPATION OR MEANS OF LIVELIHOOD. PART II.—DETAILS FOR DISTRICTS—*contd.*

DISTRICT OR STATE.	Class B.—Preparation and supply of material substances.											
	Sub-class V.—Trade.											
	Order 31.—Hotels, cafes, restaurants, etc.											
	Total of Order 31.—Hotels, cafes, etc.						Group (126).—Vendors of wine, liquors, aerated waters and ice.					
	Total earners (principal occupation).		Total working dependants.		Total following occupation as subsidiary to other.		Total earners (principal occupation.).		Total working dependants.		Total following occupation as subsidiary to other.	
	Males.	Females.	Males.	Females.	Males.	Females.	Males.	Females.	Males.	Females.	Males.	Females.
	906	907	908	909	910	911	912	913	914	915	916	917
ASSAM	*1,720*	*344*	*30*	*106*	*258*	*91*	*341*	*237*	*9*	*37*	*53*	*11*
(1) British Territory	*1,694*	*184*	*26*	*61*	*252*	*31*	*323*	*76*	*5*	*1*	*49*	*5*
SURMA VALLEY AND HILL DIVISION	400	110	4	6	129	28	67	73	...	...	14	5
Cachar	23	3	...	...	8	...	16	...	...	...	7	...
Sylhet	354	13	4	1	118	4	33	...	...	...	5	1
Khasi and Jaintia Hills (British)	7	22	...	5	1	21	3	3	...	...	...	1
Naga Hills	10	2	...	...	...	...	4	...	...	...	...	...
Lushai Hills	7	70	...	...	2	3	7	70	...	...	2	3
ASSAM VALLEY DIVISION	1,284	71	22	50	123	2	254	3	5	1	35	...
Goalpara	257	14	5	1	10	1	44	2	1	...	2	...
Kamrup	240	5	7	2	33	...	28	...	1	...	18	...
Darrang	167	30	3	21	19	...	29	...	...	...	1	...
Nowgong	37	1	...	...	8	...	14	...	...	...	5	...
Sibsagar...	341	4	5	...	28	...	78	1	3	...	6	...
Lakhimpur	237	17	2	26	24	1	57	...	...	1	3	...
Garo Hills	5	...	...	...	1	...	4	...	...	...	...	...
SADIYA FRONTIER TRACT	10	3	...	5	...	1	2	...	...	...	...	...
BALIPARA FRONTIER TRACT	...	...	...	...	...	...	...	...	...	...	...	...
(2) Manipur State	*17*	*161*	*4*	*36*	*2*	*6*	*12*	*161*	*4*	*36*	*2*	*6*
(3) Khasi States...	*9*	*36*	...	*9*	*4*	*54*	*6*	...	...	...	*2*	...

TABLE X.—Occupation or means of livelihood. Part II.—Details for Districts—contd.

Class B.—Preparation and supply of material substances. Sub-class V.—Trade. Order 31.—Hotels, cafes, restaurants, etc.

DISTRICT OR STATE.	Group (127).—Owners and Managers of hotels, cook shops, serais, etc. (and employees). Total earners (principal occupation). Males.	Females.	Total working dependants. Males.	Females.	Total following occupation as subsidiary to other. Males.	Females.	Group (128).—Hawkers of drink and food stuffs. Total earners (principal occupation). Males.	Females.	Total working dependants. Males.	Females.	Total following occupation as subsidiary to other. Males.	Females.
	918	919	920	921	922	923	924	925	926	927	928	929
ASSAM	*1,302*	*129*	*21*	*64*	*155*	*75*	*77*	*15*	...	*5*	*50*	*5*
(1) British Territory	*1,294*	*96*	*21*	*57*	*153*	*21*	*77*	*12*	...	*3*	*50*	*5*
BURMA VALLEY AND HILL DIVISION	324	29	4	5	72	19	9	8	...	1	43	4
Cachar	6	3	...	...	1	...	...	...	...	...	...	...
Sylhet	307	5	4	...	70	...	9	8	...	1	43	3
Khasi and Jaintia Hills (British)	5	19	...	5	1	19	...	...	...	...	...	1
Naga Hills	6	2	...	...	...	...	...	...	...	...	...	...
Lushai Hills	...	...	...	...	...	...	...	...	...	...	...	...
ASSAM VALLEY DIVISION	962	64	17	47	81	2	68	4	...	2	7	...
Goalpara	194	9	4	1	8	1	19	3	...	...	...	...
Kamrup	190	5	6	3	13	...	22	...	...	...	2	...
Darrang	136	30	3	21	13	...	3	...	...	...	...	...
Nowgong	23	1	...	...	3	...	...	...	...	...	...	...
Sibsagar	153	2	2	...	21	...	10	1	...	...	1	...
Lakhimpur	265	17	3	23	17	1	15	...	...	2	4	...
Garo Hills	1	...	...	...	1	...	...	...	...	...	...	...
SADIYA FRONTIER TRACT	8	3	...	5	...	...	...	...	...	...	...	1
BALIPARA FRONTIER TRACT	...	...	...	...	...	...	...	...	...	...	...	...
(2) Manipur State	*5*	...	...	...	...	...	...	...	...	...	...	...
(3) Khasi States...	*3*	*33*	...	*7*	*2*	*54*	...	*3*	...	*2*	...	...

TABLE X.—Occupation or means of livelihood. Part II.—Details for Districts—*contd.*

District or State.	Class B.—Preparation and supply of material substances. — Sub-class V.—Trade. — Order 32.—Other trade in food stuffs. — Total of Order 32.—Other trade in food stuffs. — Total earners (principal occupation). Males.	Total earners (principal occupation). Females.	Total working dependants. Males.	Total working dependants. Females.	Total following occupation as subsidiary to other. Males.	Total following occupation as subsidiary to other. Females.	Group (129).—Grain and pulse dealers. — Total earners (principal occupation). Males.	Total earners (principal occupation). Females.	Total working dependants. Males.	Total working dependants. Females.	Total following occupation as subsidiary to other. Males.	Total following occupation as subsidiary to other. Females.
	930	931	932	933	934	935	936	937	938	939	940	941
ASSAM	*52,175*	*17,504*	*3,079*	*5,351*	*32,958*	*9,671*	*9,169*	*4,018*	*304*	*1,153*	*6,100*	*793*
(1) British Territory	*50,681*	*9,309*	*2,858*	*4,649*	*29,966*	*1,572*	*8,758*	*3,194*	*291*	*895*	*5,071*	*646*
SURMA VALLEY AND HILL DIVISION	**16,398**	**2,619**	**1,276**	**544**	**16,878**	**783**	**2,404**	**1,304**	**165**	**354**	**3,733**	**419**
Cachar	2,601	1,268	193	237	1,988	307	330	891	35	257	580	214
Sylhet	13,592	1,006	1,072	187	14,288	211	1,930	368	129	79	3,154	85
Khasi and Jaintia Hills (British)	209	181	4	50	93	256	74	26	1	8	9	118
Naga Hills	129	63	2	20	25	9	9	19	...	10	...	2
Lushai Hills	7	9	4	...	4	...	1	...	...	...	1	...
ASSAM VALLEY DIVISION	**34,038**	**6,638**	**1,581**	**4,077**	**13,468**	**781**	**6,320**	**1,879**	**126**	**535**	**2,929**	**227**
Goalpara	3,553	2,179	319	736	1,391	106	727	1,071	12	231	136	50
Kamrup	9,147	1,171	253	936	3,243	97	3,719	84	60	27	1,106	3
Darrang	4,316	560	100	167	1,624	86	303	163	8	21	104	48
Nowgong	3,756	637	349	270	2,183	67	559	160	15	83	249	19
Sibsagar	6,108	1,029	345	1,319	3,333	234	470	176	9	104	330	50
Lakhimpur	6,856	984	200	649	1,461	185	531	155	20	65	135	87
Garo Hills	373	110	1	9	238	7	11	80	1	2	20	2
SADIYA FRONTIER TRACT	**216**	**48**	**1**	**28**	**124**	**7**	**29**	**11**	...	**6**	**9**	...
BALIPARA FRONTIER TRACT	**29**	**4**	...	...	**2**	**1**	**5**	...	...	...	...	...
(2) Manipur State	*1,009*	*7,497*	*166*	*800*	*1,603*	*226*	*235*	*738*	*13*	*248*	*59*	*49*
(3) Khasi States	*485*	*698*	*5*	*102*	*600*	*873*	*156*	*86*	...	*10*	*77*	*35*

TABLE X.—OCCUPATION OR MEANS OF LIVELIHOOD. PART II.—DETAILS FOR DISTRICTS—*contd.*

DISTRICT OR STATE.	Class B.—Preparation and supply of material substances. Sub-class V.—Trade. Order 32.—Other trade in food stuffs.											
	Group (130).—Dealers in sweetmeats, sugar and spices.						Group (131).—Dealers in dairy product, eggs and poultry.					
	Total earners (principal occupation).		Total working dependants.		Total following occupation as subsidiary to other.		Total earners (principal occupation).		Total working dependants.		Total following occupation as subsidiary to other.	
	Males.	Females.	Males.	Females.	Males.	Females.	Males.	Females.	Males.	Females.	Males.	Females.
	942	943	944	945	946	947	948	949	950	951	952	953
ASSAM	*2,708*	*456*	*259*	*116*	*1,877*	*410*	*3,967*	*298*	*167*	*72*	*3,055*	*90*
(1) British Territory	*2,474*	*267*	*174*	*36*	*1,300*	*78*	*3,867*	*195*	*157*	*53*	*2,945*	*71*
SURMA VALLEY AND HILL DIVISION	**1,873**	**143**	**159**	**13**	**1,156**	**63**	**1,337**	**98**	**64**	**10**	**1,462**	**27**
Cachar	376	82	31	8	100	48	133	28	7	...	133	7
Sylhet	1,464	56	127	5	1,050	13	1,184	60	57	8	1,298	13
Khasi and Jaintia Hills (British)	20	2	1	...	5	...	18	1	...	1	30	6
Naga Hills	14	1	...	...	...	1	1	1	...	1	1	1
Lushai Hills...	...	...	...	...	1	...	1	8	...	...	...	...
ASSAM VALLEY DIVISION	**597**	**124**	**15**	**22**	**143**	**16**	**2,517**	**102**	**92**	**43**	**1,470**	**42**
Goalpara	108	25	1	6	16	2	528	34	45	5	167	6
Kamrup	56	11	...	2	6	1	521	16	7	13	323	5
Darrang	74	13	...	...	42	...	616	14	6	3	303	13
Nowgong	41	8	...	...	4	...	60	4	...	...	36	1
Sibsagar	179	20	13	3	21	2	420	12	14	7	331	8
Lakhimpur	87	47	1	11	15	10	316	22	17	15	186	10
Garo Hills	53	...	...	...	37	1	3	...	...	...	4	...
SADIYA FRONTIER TRACT	**4**	...	...	**1**	**1**	...	**13**	...	**1**	...	**13**	...
BALIPARA FRONTIER TRACT	...	...	...	...	...	...	...	**1**	...	...	...	**1**
(2) Manipur State	*189*	*189*	*85*	*79*	*316*	*96*	*60*	*14*	*9*	*17*	*99*	*1*
(3) Khasi States	*45*	*7*	...	*1*	*261*	*306*	*40*	*19*	*1*	*9*	*18*	*18*

TABLE X.—Occupation or means of livelihood. Part II. Details for Districts—*contd.*

DISTRICT OR STATE.	Class B.—Preparation and supply of material substances. Sub-class V.—Trade. Order 32.—Other trade in food stuffs. Group (132).—Dealers in animals for food. Total earners (principal occupation).		Total working dependants.		Total following occupation as subsidiary to other.		Group (133).—Dealers in fodder for animals. Total earners (principal occupation).		Total working dependants.		Total following occupation as subsidiary to other.	
	Males.	Females.	Males.	Females.	Males.	Females.	Males.	Females.	Males.	Females.	Males.	Females.
	954	955	956	957	958	959	960	961	962	963	964	965
ASSAM	*72*	*36*	*4*	*17*	*114*	*5*	*80*	*16*	*5*	*13*	*26*	*11*
(1) British Territory ...	*54*	*1*	*3*	*4*	*102*	*1*	*75*	*12*	*4*	*6*	*10*	*11*
SURMA VALLEY AND HILL DIVISON ...	14	1	...	1	36	1	52	11	2	3	10	11
Cachar ...	5	...	...	...	11	1	5	6	...	...	2	2
Sylhet ...	8	1	...	1	25	...	46	3	2	3	7	2
Khasi and Jaintia Hills (British) ...	...	.	...	...	...	...	1	2	...	...	1	7
Naga Hills ...	1	...	...	...	...	...	.	...	...	...	...	...
Lushai Hills ...	...	...	...	...	...	...	...	...	...	...	...	...
ASSAM VALLEY DIVISION ...	39	...	3	3	65	...	23	1	2	3	...	...
Goalpara ...	1		...	...	2	...	1	...	...	...	...	...
Kamrup ...	4		1	...	17	...	20	1	2	...	...	...
Darrang ...	8	..	...	...	17	...	...	...	...	...	...	...
Nowgong ...	...	...	...	...	3	...	...	...	...	...	...	...
Sibsagar ...	1	...	2	...	2	.	2	...	...	3	...	...
Lakhimpur ...	23	...	...	3	1	...	...	...	...	...	...	...
Garo Hills ...	3	...	...	...	23	...	...	...	...	...	...	...
SADIYA FRONTIER TRACT ...	1	...	...	...	1	...	...	...	...	...	...	...
BALIPARA FRONTIER TRACT ...	...	...	...	...	...	...	...	...	...	...	...	...
(2) Manipur State ...	*14*	*34*	*1*	*13*	*6*	*2*	...	*1*	...	...	...	...
(3) Khasi States ...	*4*	*1*	...	...	*6*	*2*	*5*	*3*	*1*	*7*	*16*	...

TABLE X.—OCCUPATION OR MEANS OF LIVELIHOOD. PART II.—DETAILS FOR DISTRICTS—*contd.*

DISTRICT OR STATE.	Class II.—Preparation and supply of material substances.											
	Sub-class V.—Trade.											
	Order 32.—Other trade in food stuffs.											
	Group (134).—Dealers in other food stuffs.						Group (135).—Dealers in tobacco.					
	Total earners (principal occupation).		Total working dependants.		Total following occupation as subsidiary to other.		Total earners (principal occupation).		Total working dependants.		Total following occupation as subsidiary to other.	
	Males.	Females.	Males.	Females.	Males.	Females.	Males.	Females.	Males.	Females.	Males.	Females.
	966	967	968	969	970	971	972	973	974	975	976	977
ASSAM	*34,671*	*7,606*	*2,911*	*4,113*	*20,475*	*1,385*	*947*	*143*	*66*	*67*	*478*	*47*
(1) British Territory ...	*33,979*	*5,583*	*2,155*	*3,600*	*19,039*	*757*	*915*	*56*	*61*	*46*	*466*	*8*
SURMA VALLEY AND HILL DIVISION ...	10,292	1,054	841	163	9,707	260	355	13	44	...	262	3
Cachar ...	1,711	260	119	22	1,163	35	15	1	1	...	18	...
Sylhet ...	8,394	603	714	91	8,472	98	334	5	43	...	243	...
Khasi and Jaintia Hills (British) ...	80	143	2	41	47	122	3	7	...	...	1	3
Naga Hills ...	102	42	2	9	24	5	...	...	...	...	...	...
Lushai Hills ...	5	6	4	...	2	...	...	...	...	...	...	...
ASSAM VALLEY DIVISION ...	23,502	4,459	1,314	3,425	9,230	490	554	43	17	46	204	5
Goalpara ...	3,972	956	252	491	1,033	30	191	13	6	3	31	...
Kamrup ...	4,684	1,057	180	893	1,579	88	81	2	2	1	61	...
Darrang ...	3,135	374	92	143	934	74	70	5	2	...	50	...
Nowgong ...	2,974	471	328	171	1,871	46	43	4	1	14	11	1
Sibsagar ...	3,819	814	301	1,176	2,593	101	50	7	2	26	26	4
Lakhimpur ...	4,631	748	161	544	1,083	128	94	12	4	2	8	...
Garo Hills ...	287	39	...	7	137	4	16	...	...	...	17	...
SADIYA FRONTIER TRACT ...	161	37	...	21	100	7	6	...	...	...	...	...
BALIPARA FRONTIER TRACT ...	24	3	...	...	2	...	...	...	...	...	...	...
(2) Manipur State ...	*462*	*1,458*	*53*	*428*	*1,131*	*152*	*29*	*70*	*5*	*15*	*5*	*3*
(3) Khasi States ...	*230*	*565*	*3*	*76*	*305*	*476*	*3*	*17*	...	*6*	*7*	*36*

TABLE X.—OCCUPATION OR MEANS OF LIVELIHOOD. PART II.—DETAILS FOR DISTRICTS—*contd.*

DISTRICT OR STATE.	Class B.—Preparation and supply of material substances.											
	Sub-class V.—Trade.											
	Order 22.—Other trade in food stuffs.											
	Group (136).—Dealers in opium.						Group (137).—Dealers in *ganja*.					
	Total earners (principal occupation).		Total working dependants.		Total following occupation as subsidiary to other.		Total earners (principal occupation).		Total working dependants.		Total following occupation as subsidiary to other.	
	Males.	Females.	Males.	Females.	Males.	Females.	Males.	Females.	Males.	Females.	Males.	Females.
	978	979	980	981	982	983	984	985	986	987	988	989
ASSAM	*380*	...	*19*	...	*95*	...	*181*	*1*	*1*	...	*38*	...
(1) British Territory	*378*	...	*19*	...	*95*	...	*181*	*1*	*1*	...	*38*	...
SURMA VALLEY AND HILL DIVISION	10	...	...	...	1	...	61	1	1	...	11	...
Cachar	4	...	...	...	1	...	19	...	...	...	2	...
Sylhet	...	...	...	...	...	...	42	1	1	...	9	...
Khasi and Jaintia Hills (British)...	4	...	...	...	...	...	...	...	...	...	...	...
Naga Hills	2	...	...	...	...	...	...	...	...	...	...	...
Lushai Hills	...	...	...	...	...	...	...	...	...	...	...	...
ASSAM VALLEY DIVISION	306	...	12	...	94	...	120	...	...	...	27	...
Goalpara	3	...	...	...	1	...	22	...	...	...	5	...
Kamrup	45	...	...	...	11	...	15	...	...	...	7	...
Darrang	35	...	1	...	22	...	6	...	...	...	3	...
Nowgong	74	...	4	...	10	...	5	...	...	...	...	...
Sibsagar	120	...	4	...	24	...	29	...	...	...	6	...
Lakhimpur	89	...	3	...	26	...	43	...	...	...	7	...
Garo Hills	...	...	...	...	...	...	...	...	...	...	...	...
SADIYA FRONTIER TRACT	8	...	...	...	...	...	...	...	...	...	...	...
BALIPARA FRONTIER TRACT	...	...	...	...	...	...	...	...	...	...	...	...
(2) Manipur State	...	...	...	...	...	...	...	...	...	...	...	...
(3) Khasi States		...	...	...	...	...	...	...	...	...	...	...

TABLE X.—OCCUPATION OR MEANS OF LIVELIHOOD. PART II.—DETAILS FOR DISTRICTS—*contd.*

DISTRICT OR STATE.	Class B.—Preparation and supply of material substances. Sub-class V.—Trade. Order 23.—Trade in clothing and toilet articles.											
	Total of Order 23.—Trade in clothing and toilet articles.						Group (138).—Trade in ready-made clothing and other articles of dress and the toilet (hats, umbrellas, socks, ready-made shoes, perfumes, etc.)					
	Total earners (principal occupation).		Total working dependants.		Total following occupation as subsidiary to other.		Total earners (principal occupation).		Total working dependants.		Total following occupation as subsidiary to other.	
	Males.	Females.	Males.	Females.	Males.	Females.	Males.	Females.	Males.	Females.	Males.	Females.
	990	991	992	993	994	995	996	997	998	999	1000	1001
ASSAM	*6,712*	*537*	*909*	*91*	*708*	*111*	*6,712*	*537*	*909*	*91*	*708*	*111*
(1) British Territory	*6,660*	*411*	*900*	*70*	*694*	*98*	*6,660*	*411*	*900*	*70*	*694*	*98*
SURMA VALLEY AND HILL DIVISION	885	233	36	34	236	8	885	233	36	34	236	8
Cachar	311	143	15	10	77	5	311	143	15	10	77	5
Sylhet	476	45	14	8	103	...	476	45	14	8	103	...
Khasi and Jaintia Hills (British)	84	40	7	16	55	3	84	40	7	16	55	3
Naga Hills	12	...	...	...	1	...	12	...	...	...	1	...
Lushai Hills	2	5	...	...	...	...	2	5	...	...	...	...
ASSAM VALLEY DIVISION	5,748	178	162	36	458	20	5,748	178	162	36	458	20
Goalpara	939	2	39	...	88	...	939	2	39	...	88	...
Kamrup	518	91	16	22	83	15	518	91	16	22	83	15
Darrang	639	2	5	...	18	1	639	2	5	...	18	1
Nowgong	407	15	6	6	34	1	407	15	6	6	34	1
Sibsagar	1,572	7	35	...	130	...	1,572	7	35	...	130	...
Lakhimpur	1,524	61	61	8	112	3	1,524	61	61	8	112	3
Garo Hills	59	...	...	...	3	...	59	...	...	...	3	...
SADIYA FRONTIER TRACT	20	...	2	...	...	...	20	...	2	...	...	...
BALIPARA FRONTIER TRACT	7	...	...	...	...	...	7	...	...	...	...	...
(2) Manipur State	*39*	*7*	*9*	*2*	*12*	*2*	*39*	*7*	*9*	*2*	*12*	*2*
(3) Khasi States	*13*	*119*	...	*19*	*2*	*83*	*13*	*119*	...	*19*	*2*	*83*

TABLE X.—OCCUPATION OR MEANS OF LIVELIHOOD. PART II.—DETAILS FOR DISTRICTS—*contd.*

DISTRICT OR STATE.	Class B.—Preparation and supply of material substances. Sub-class V.—Trade. Order 34.—Trade in furniture. Total of Order 34.—Trade in furniture. Total earners (principal occupation). Males.	Females.	Total working dependants. Males.	Females.	Total following occupation as subsidiary to other. Males.	Females.	Group (139).—Trade in furniture, carpets, curtains and bedding. Total earners (principal occupation). Males.	Females.	Total working dependants. Males.	Females.	Total following occupation as subsidiary to other. Males.	Females.
	1002	1003	1004	1005	1006	1007	1008	1009	1010	1011	1012	1013
ASSAM	*2,390*	*434*	*120*	*302*	*1,435*	*183*	*281*	*56*	*24*	*21*	*187*	*97*
(1) British Territory	*2,393*	*371*	*194*	*290*	*1,429*	*105*	*280*	*19*	*24*	*18*	*186*	*92*
SURMA VALLEY AND HILL DIVISION	483	129	20	61	296	49	96	4	13	...	92	7
Cachar	71	3	10	...	81	...	36	3	10	...	33	...
Sylhet	340	136	10	60	213	43	40	1	3	...	60	1
Khasi and Jaintia Hills (British)	3	...	...	1	...	6	...	...	...	...	...	6
Naga Hills	1	...	...	...	2	...	1	...	...	...	...	...
Lushai Hills	...		...	...	...	...	...	...	...	...	...	...
ASSAM VALLEY DIVISION	1,897	942	103	299	1,133	56	193	15	10	18	94	14
Goalpara	357	33	57	6	54	6	8	...	1	2	...	...
Kamrup...	646	126	24	194	297	11	13	...	1	...	33	...
Darrang...	375	11	3	16	166	...	138	11	3	16	7	...
Nowgong	114	35	3	...	117	5	23	3	2	...	4	5
Sibsagar...	207	30	12	81	410	25	1	...	...	...	...	...
Lakhimpur	116	2	3	2	79	9	6	1	3	...	56	9
Garo Hills	3	...	...	...	4	...	3	...	...	...	4	...
SADIYA FRONTIER TRACT	3	...	1	...	...	...	1	...	1	...	...	...
BALIPARA FRONTIER TRACT	...	...	...	...	...	...	...	...	...	...	...	...
(2) Manipur State	*74*	*29*	*5*	*11*	*5*	*2*	...	*7*	...	*2*	...	...
(3) Khasi States	*2*	*34*	...	*1*	*1*	*76*	*1*	*30*	...	*1*	*1*	*76*

TABLE X.—OCCUPATION OR MEANS OF LIVELIHOOD. PART II.—DETAILS FOR DISTRICTS—*contd.*

DISTRICT OR STATE.	Class B.—Preparation and supply of material substances.											
	Sub-class V.—Trade.											
	Order 34.—Trade in furniture.						Order 35.—Trade in building materials.					
	Group 140.—Hardware, cooking utensils, porcelain, crockery, glassware, bottles, articles for gardening, etc.						Total of order 35.—Trade in building materials.					
	Total earners (principal occupation).		Total working dependants.		Total following occupation as subsidiary to other.		Total earners (principal occupation).		Total working dependants.		Total following occupation as subsidiary to other.	
	Males.	Females.	Males.	Females.	Males.	Females.	Males.	Females.	Males.	Females.	Males.	Females.
	1014	1015	1016	1017	1018	1019	1020	1021	1022	1023	1024	1025
ASSAM	*2,118*	*378*	*105*	*281*	*1,948*	*86*	*399*	*10*	*18*	*11*	*276*	...
(1) British Territory	*2,043*	*359*	*100*	*279*	*1,943*	*84*	*385*	*9*	*18*	*11*	*265*	...
SURMA VALLEY AND HILL DIVISION	337	135	7	81	204	42	264	1	17	...	218	...
Cachar	35	...	...	...	49	...	14	1	1	...	11	...
Sylhet	300	135	7	80	153	42	246	...	16	...	207	...
Khasi and Jaintia Hills (British)	2	...	...	1	...	...	4	...	...	...	...	...
Naga Hills	...	...	...	...	2	...	...	...	...	...	...	...
Lushai Hills	...	...	...	...	...	...	...	...	...	...	...	...
ASSAM VALLEY DIVISION	1,704	227	93	211	1,039	42	121	8	1	11	47	...
Goalpara	340	33	56	4	54	6	19	2	1	3	...	...
Kamrup	673	126	24	134	274	11	44	...	...	...	34	...
Darrang...	187	...	...	...	150	...	16	3	...	...	4	...
Nowgong	89	33	1	...	113	...	9	3	...	8	1	...
Sibsagar	296	36	13	81	416	25	20	...	...	...	1	...
Lakhimpur	100	1	...	2	23	...	13	...	...	...	7	...
Garo Hills	1	...	...	...	...	...	1	...	...	...	...	...
SADIYA FRONTIER TRACT	2	...	...	...	...	...	...	...	...	...	...	...
BALIPARA FRONTIER TRACT	...	...	...	...	...	...	...	...	...	...	...	...
(2) Manipur State	*74*	*22*	*5*	*2*	*5*	*2*	*9*	...	...	...	*5*	...
(3) Khasi States	*1*	*4*	...	...	...	...	*5*	*1*	...	...	*6*	...

TABLE X.—Occupation or means of livelihood. Part II.—Details for Districts—*contd.*

Class B.—Preparation and supply of material substances. Sub-class V.—Trade.

District or State.	Order 35.—Trade in building materials. Group (141).—Trade in building materials (other than bricks, tiles and woody materials). Total earners (principal occupation). Males.	Females.	Total working dependants. Males.	Females.	Total following occupation as subsidiary to other. Males.	Females.	Order 36. Trade in means of transport. Total of Order 36.—Trade in means of Transport. Total earners (principal occupation). Males.	Females.	Total working dependants. Males.	Females.	Total following occupation as subsidiary to other. Males.	Females.
	1026	1027	1028	1029	1030	1031	1032	1033	1034	1035	1036	1037
ASSAM	*390*	*10*	*18*	*11*	*276*	...	*1,136*	*88*	*30*	*5*	*1,453*	*13*
(1) British Territory	*385*	*9*	*18*	*11*	*265*	...	*998*	*84*	*27*	*5*	*1,334*	*13*
SURMA VALLEY AND HILL DIVISION	264	1	17	...	218	...	249	7	8	1	408	1
Cachar	14	1	1	...	11	...	19	3	4	...	43	...
Sylhet	246	...	16	...	207	...	162	...	4	1	310	1
Khasi and Jaintia Hills (British)	4	...	...	...	...	...	64	4	...	...	39	...
Naga Hills	...	...	...	...	...	...	4	...	...	...	17	...
Lushai Hills	...	...	...	...	...	...	...	...	...	...	...	...
ASSAM VALLEY DIVISION...	121	8	1	11	47	...	742	77	19	4	861	12
Goalpara	19	3	1	3	...	...	167	4	7	1	92	2
Kamrup	44	...	...	...	34	...	161	36	5	...	108	4
Darrang	16	3	...	...	4	...	84	22	...	3	34	3
Nowgong	9	2	...	8	1	...	43	3	1	...	126	...
Sibsagar	20	...	...	...	1	...	126	10	5	...	163	1
Lakhimpur	12	...	...	...	7	...	141	2	1	...	83	...
Garo Hills	1	...	...	...	...	...	20	...	...	...	273	3
SADIYA FRONTIER TRACT	...	...	...	...	...	...	6	...	...	...	1	...
BALIPARA FRONTIER TRACT	...	...	...	...	...	...	1	...	...	...	...	...
(2) Manipur State	*9*	...	...	...	*5*	...	*79*	*4*	*2*	...	*31*	...
(3) Khasi States	*5*	*1*	...	...	*6*	...	*59*	...	*1*	...	*88*	...

TABLE X.—OCCUPATION OR MEANS OF LIVELIHOOD. PART II.—DETAILS FOR DISTRICTS—*contd.*

DISTRICT OR STATE.	Class B.—Preparation and supply of material substances. Sub-class V.—Trade. Order 36.—Trade in means of transport. Group (142).—Dealers and hirers, in mechanical transport motors, cycles, etc.						Group (143).—Dealers and hirers in other carriages, carts, boats, etc.					
	Total earners (principal occupation).		Total working dependants.		Total following occupation as subsidiary to other.		Total earners (principal occupation.)		Total working dependants.		Total following occupation as subsidiary to other.	
	Males.	Females.	Males.	Females.	Males.	Females.	Males.	Females.	Males.	Females.	Males.	Females.
	1038	1039	1040	1041	1042	1043	1044	1045	1046	1047	1048	1049
ASSAM	*86*	*1*	...	...	*5*	...	*373*	*1*	*10*	*1*	*680*	*3*
(1) British Territory	*81*	*1*	...	...	*4*	...	*355*	*1*	10	*1*	*577*	*3*
SURMA VALLEY AND HILL DIVISION	14	...	...	...	...	...	65	1	3	1	110	...
Cachar	...	...	...	...	...	...	2	1	...	...	...	...
Sylhet	14	...	...	...	...	...	62	...	3	1	100	...
Khasi and Jaintia Hills (British)	...	...	...	...	...	...	...	...	...	...	...	...
Naga Hills	...	...	...	...	...	...	1	...	...	...	1	...
Lushai Hills	...	...	...	...	...	...	...	...	...	...	...	...
ASSAM VALLEY DIVISION	66	1	...	...	4	...	289	...	7	...	467	3
Goalpara	8	...	...	...	...	...	96	...	1	...	51	1
Kamrup	6	...	...	...	...	...	88		3	...	71	...
Darrang	7	...	...	...	...	...	34	...	...	...	12	...
Nowgong	9	1	...	...	1	...	18	...	1	...	41	...
Sibsagar	15	...	...	...	2	...	10	...	2	...	15	...
Lakhimpur	21	...	...	...	1	...	47	...	...	...	5	...
Garo Hills	...	...	...	...	...	...	7	...	...	...	273	2
SADIYA FRONTIER TRACT	1	...	...	...	...	...	1	...	...	...	...	...
BALIPARA FRONTIER TRACT	...	...	...	...	...	...	...	...	...	...	...	...
(2) Manipur State	*5*	...	...	...	...	...	*18*	...	...	...	*3*	...
(3) Khasi States	...	...	...	...	*1*	...	...	...	...	...	...	...

TABLE X.—Occupation or means of livelihood. Part II.—Details for Districts—*contd.*

District or State.	Class B.—Preparation and supply of material substances.											
	Sub-class V.—Trade.											
	Order 36.—Trade in means of transport.						Order 37.—Trade in fuel.					
	Group (144).—Dealers and hirers of elephants, camels, horses, cattle, asses, mules, etc.						Total of Order 37.—Trade in fuel.					
	Total earners (principal occupation).		Total working dependants.		Total following occupation as subsidiary to other.		Total earners (principal occupation).		Total working dependants.		Total following occupation as subsidiary to other.	
	Males.	Females.	Males.	Females.	Males.	Females.	Males.	Females.	Males.	Females.	Males.	Females.
	1050	1051	1052	1053	1054	1055	1056	1057	1058	1059	1060	1061
ASSAM	*677*	*86*	*20*	*4*	*868*	*10*	*1,149*	*521*	*141*	*356*	*1,977*	*486*
(1) British Territory	*563*	*82*	*17*	*4*	*753*	*10*	*1,047*	*425*	*122*	*289*	*1,701*	*114*
SURMA VALLEY AND HILL DIVISION	170	6	5	...	292	1	674	298	87	215	1,440	86
Cachar	17	2	4	...	43	...	73	35	5	9	73	6
Sylhet	86	.	1	...	201	1	598	37	59	10	1,294	3
Khasi and Jaintia Hills (British)	64	4	...	...	33	...	...	14	...	60	6	59
Naga Hills	3		...	...	16	...	1	3	...	...	...	...
Lushai Hills		...	...	...	...	...	2	206	23	136	67	19
ASSAM VALLEY DIVISION	357	76	12	4	460	9	373	127	35	74	261	28
Goalpara	64	4	6	1	41	1	21	22	8	23	21	3
Kamrup	67	34	2	...	122	4	163	71	16	40	52	15
Darrang	63	22	...	3	22	3	30	1	...	1	21	...
Nowgong	16	2	...	...	83	...	16	3	...	...	10	1
Sibsagar	101	19	3	...	145	1	31	16	1	...	14	...
Lakhimpur	73	2	1	...	46	...	112	13	9	4	39	3
Garo Hills	13	...	...	...	1	...	10	1	1	...	104	7
SADIYA FRONTIER TRACT	4	...	...	...	1	...	...	...	...	...	...	...
BALIPARA FRONTIER TRACT	1	...	...	...	...	...	...	...	...	...	...	...
(2) Manipur State	*56*	*4*	*2*	...	*28*	...	*14*	*36*	*3*	*14*	*20*	*1*
(3) Khasi States	*59*	...	*1*	...	*87*	...	*81*	*60*	*16*	*53*	*256*	*371*

TABLE X.—Occupation or means of livelihood. Part II.—Details for Districts—*contd.*

District or State.	Class B.—Preparation and supply of material substances. Sub-class V.—Trade. Order 37.—Trade in fuel. Group (145).—Dealers in firewood, charcoal, coal, cowdung, etc. Total earners (principal occupation). Males.	Total earners (principal occupation). Females.	Total working dependants. Males.	Total working dependants. Females.	Total following occupation as subsidiary to other. Males.	Total following occupation as subsidiary to other. Females.	Order 38.—Trade in articles of luxury and those pertaining to letters and the arts and sciences. Total of Order 38.—Trade in articles of luxury, etc. Total earners (principal occupation). Males.	Total earners (principal occupation). Females.	Total working dependants. Males.	Total working dependants. Females.	Total following occupation as subsidiary to other. Males.	Total following occupation as subsidiary to other. Females.
	1062	1063	1064	1065	1066	1067	1068	1069	1070	1071	1072	1073
ASSAM	*1,149*	*521*	*141*	*356*	*1,977*	*486*	*6,317*	*555*	*250*	*116*	*1,891*	*37*
(1) British Territory	*1,047*	*425*	*129*	*289*	*1,701*	*114*	*6,088*	*467*	*220*	*103*	*1,859*	*39*
SURMA VALLEY AND HILL DIVISION	676	298	87	215	1,446	96	2,350	143	144	17	1,331	19
Cachar	73	38	5	9	73	6	304	14	25	2	109	...
Sylhet	608	37	19	10	1,294	2	1,807	90	117	10	1,213	9
Khasi and Jaintia Hills (British)...	...	14	...	80	6	59	12	15	1	5	6	10
Naga Hills	1	3	...	...	...	...	37	13	1	...	4	...
Lushai Hills	2	206	23	136	67	19	10	3	...	...	...	...
ASSAM VALLEY DIVISION	373	127	35	74	261	28	3,721	324	76	86	521	13
Goalpara	21	23	8	29	21	3	906	202	28	70	73	1
Kamrup	153	71	16	40	89	15	398	21	2	3	94	5
Darrang	30	1	...	1	21	...	440	43	4	4	61	2
Nowgong	16	3	...	...	10	1	328	10	8	4	42	1
Sibsagar	31	16	1	...	14	...	619	19	11	3	160	1
Lakhimpur	112	13	9	4	30	2	984	18	23	...	78	3
Garo Hills	10	1	1	...	104	7	47	13	...	...	4	...
SADIYA FRONTIER TRACT	...	...	...	...	...	...	17	...	...	...	...	...
BALIPARA FRONTIER TRACT	...	...	...	...	...	...	...	...	...	...	...	...
(2) Manipur State	*14*	*36*	*3*	*14*	*90*	*1*	*202*	*77*	*30*	*12*	*36*	*9*
(3) Khasi States	*81*	*60*	*16*	*53*	*256*	*371*	*27*	*11*	...	*1*	*3*	*3*

TABLE X.—Occupation or means of livelihood. Part II.—Details for Districts—*contd.*

Class B.—Preparation and supply of material substances. Sub-class V.—Trade. Order 38.—Trade in articles of luxury and those pertaining to letters and the arts and sciences.

District or State.	Group (146).—Dealers in precious stones, jewellery (real and imitation), clocks, optical instruments, etc.						Group (147).—Dealers in common bangles, bead necklaces, fans, small articles, toys, hunting and fishing tackle, flowers, etc.					
	Total earners (principal occupation).		Total working dependants.		Total following occupation as subsidiary to other.		Total earners (principal occupation).		Total working dependants.		Total following occupation as subsidiary to other.	
	Males.	Females.	Males.	Females.	Males.	Females.	Males.	Females.	Males.	Females.	Males.	Females.
	1074	1075	1076	1077	1078	1079	1080	1081	1082	1083	1084	1085
ASSAM	*236*	*17*	*20*	...	*86*	*4*	*2,909*	*302*	*59*	*83*	*349*	*7*
(1) British Territory	*236*	*11*	*20*	...	*86*	*2*	*2,862*	*281*	*44*	*80*	*320*	*7*
SURMA VALLEY AND HILL DIVISION	94	1	14	...	28	...	48	27	5	2	16	1
Cachar ...	77	...	14	...	3	...	1	3	...	...	...	...
Sylhet ...	17	1	...	...	25	...	46	11	5	2	16	1
Khasi and Jaintia Hills (British) ...	...	...	...	...	...	...	...	...	...	...	...	...
Naga Hills ...	...	...	...	...	...	...	1	13	...	...	...	...
Lushai Hills ...	...	...	...	...	...	...	...	...	...	...	...	...
ASSAM VALLEY DIVISION ...	138	10	6	...	58	2	2,801	254	39	78	304	6
Goalpara ...	28	2	4	...	13	1	812	197	15	70	45	...
Kamrup ...	33	...	...	...	6	...	236	13	1	4	36	6
Darrang ...	2	...	...	...	1	1	243	7	2	...	37	...
Nowgong ...	6	...	...	...	2	...	221	...	5	1	6	1
Sibsagar ...	25	3	...	...	6	...	483	15	11	3	163	1
Lakhimpur ...	44	5	2	...	30	...	709	10	5	...	17	...
Garo Hills ...	...	...	...	...	...	...	38	12	...	...	...	...
SADIYA FRONTIER TRACT ...	4	...	...	...	...	...	13	...	...	...	...	...
BALIPARA FRONTIER TRACT ...	...	...	...	...	...	...	...	...	...	...	...	...
(2) Manipur State	...	...	...	...	...	...	*43*	*20*	*15*	*2*	*27*	...
(3) Khasi States	...	*6*	...	...	...	*2*	*4*	*1*	...	*1*	*2*	...

TABLE X.—Occupation or means of livelihood. Part II.—Details for Districts—*contd.*

DISTRICT OR STATE.	Class B.—Preparation and supply of material substances. Sub-class V.—Trade. Order 38.—Trade in articles of luxury and those pertaining to letters and the arts and sciences. Group (148).—Publishers, book-sellers, stationers, dealers in music, pictures, musical instruments, and curiosities. Total earners (principal occupation). Males.	Females.	Total working dependants. Males.	Females.	Total following occupation as subsidiary to other. Males.	Females.	Order 39.—Trade of other sorts. Total of Order 39.—Trade of other sorts. Total earners (principal occupation). Males.	Females.	Total working dependants. Males.	Females.	Total following occupation as subsidiary to other. Males.	Females.
	1086	1087	1088	1089	1090	1091	1092	1093	1094	1095	1096	1097
ASSAM	*3,172*	*236*	*171*	*33*	*1,446*	*26*	*7,031*	*518*	*468*	*133*	*2,466*	*113*
(1) British Territory	*2,990*	*175*	*156*	*23*	*1,436*	*23*	*6,691*	*316*	*456*	*109*	*2,431*	*87*
SURMA VALLEY AND HILL DIVISION	2,208	115	125	15	1,277	18	3,602	243	228	62	1,933	81
Cachar	[illegible]	11	11	2	106	...	544	59	30	3	63	10
Sylhet	[illegible]	87	112	8	1,161	8	2,663	63	180	13	1,703	5
Khasi and Jaintia Hills (British)	13	15	1	5	6	10	173	100	7	37	28	64
Naga Hills	[illegible]	...	1	...	4	...	23	...	10	...	12	...
Lushai Hills	10	2	...	...	...	...	107	21	1	9	48	2
ASSAM VALLEY DIVISION	782	60	31	8	159	5	2,929	73	228	47	496	6
Goalpara	76	3	9	...	4	...	548	13	63	7	57	...
Kamrup	129	8	1	1	62	1	1,015	8	56	1	150	1
Darrang	194	38	2	4	23	1	276	9	10	...	119	5
Nowgong	102	10	3	3	35	...	206	6	1	19	30	...
Sibsagar	111	...	...	...	...	...	362	27	118	20	29	...
Lakhimpur	171	3	16	...	31	3	354	6	2	...	49	...
Garo Hills	9	...	...	...	4	...	143	4	9	...	24	...
SADIYA FRONTIER TRACT	...	...	...	...	...	...	166	...	...	...	2	...
BALIPARA FRONTIER TRACT	...	...	...	...	...	...	...	...	...	...	...	...
(2) Manipur State	*159*	*57*	*15*	*10*	*9*	*2*	*90*	*37*	*6*	*4*	*7*	*3*
(3) Khasi States	*23*	*4*	...	...	*1*	*1*	*250*	*165*	*6*	*20*	*28*	*23*

TABLE X.—OCCUPATION OR MEANS OF LIVELIHOOD. PART II.—DETAILS FOR DISTRICTS—*contd.*

DISTRICT OR STATE.	Class B.—Preparation and supply of material substances. Sub-class V.—Trade. Order 39.—Trade of other sorts. Group (149).—Dealers in rags, stable refuse, etc.						Group (150).—General store-keepers and shop-keepers otherwise unspecified.					
	Total earners (principal occupation).		Total working dependants.		Total following occupation as subsidiary to other.		Total earners (principal occupation).		Total working dependants.		Total following occupation as subsidiary to other.	
	Males.	Females.	Males.	Females.	Males.	Females.	Males.	Females.	Males.	Females.	Males.	Females.
	1098	1099	1100	1101	1102	1103	1104	1105	1106	1107	1108	1109
ASSAM	...	...	...	...	*1*	...	*6,505*	*488*	*439*	*137*	*2,187*	*111*
(1) British Territory	...	...	...	...	*1*	...	*6,165*	*286*	*427*	*103*	*2,153*	*85*
SURMA VALLEY AND HILL DIVISION	...	...	...	...	...	...	3,413	223	204	59	1,817	79
Cachar	...	...	...	...	...	...	400	54	9	1	73	9
Sylhet	...	...	...	...	...	...	2,568	51	177	13	1,659	5
Khasi and Jaintia Hills (British)	...	...	...	...	...	...	173	97	7	36	27	63
Naga Hills	...	...	...	...	...	...	19	...	10	...	11	...
Lushai Hills	...	...	...	...	...	...	194	21	1	9	48	2
ASSAM VALLEY DIVISION	...	...	...	...	1	...	2,504	63	223	44	336	6
Goalpara	...	...	...	...	...	...	401	8	60	4	71	...
Kamrup	...	...	...	...	...	...	901	3	24	1	84	1
Darrang	...	...	...	...	...	...	256	9	10	...	102	5
Nowgong	...	...	...	...	...	...	170	6	1	19	13	...
Sibsagar	...	...	...	...	...	...	318	27	117	20	12	...
Lakhimpur	...	...	...	...	...	...	320	6	2	...	35	...
Garo Hills	...	...	...	...	1	...	138	4	9	...	19	...
SADIYA FRONTIER TRACT	...	...	...	...	...	...	158	...	...	...	...	...
BALIPARA FRONTIER TRACT	...	...	...	...	...	...	...	...	...	...	...	...
(2) Manipur State	...	...	...	...	...	...	*90*	*37*	*6*	*4*	*6*	*3*
(3) Khasi States	...	...	...	...	...	...	*250*	*165*	*6*	*20*	*28*	*23*

TABLE X.—OCCUPATION OR MEANS OF LIVELIHOOD. PART II.—DETAILS FOR DISTRICTS—*contd.*

DISTRICT OR STATE.	Class B.—Preparation and supply of material substances. Sub-class V.—Trade. Order 30.—Trade of other sorts. Group (151).—Itinerant traders, pedlars, and hawkers (of other than food, etc.). Total earners (principal occupation).		Total working dependants.		Total following occupation as subsidiary to other.		Group (152).—Other trades (including farmers of pounds, tolls and markets). Total earners (principal occupation).		Total working dependants.		Total following occupation as subsidiary to other.	
	Males.	Females.	Males.	Females.	Males.	Females.	Males.	Females.	Males.	Females.	Males.	Females.
	1110	1111	1112	1113	1114	1115	1116	1117	1118	1119	1120	1121
ASSAM	*16*	*19*	...	*5*	*2*	*1*	*510*	*11*	*99*	*1*	*276*	*1*
(1) British Territory	*16*	*10*	...	*5*	*9*	*1*	*510*	*11*	*99*	*1*	*273*	*1*
SURMA VALLEY AND HILL DIVISION	5	15	...	3	...	1	181	5	24	...	116	1
Cachar	4	1	...	2	...	...	80	4	21	...	11	1
Sylhet	1	11	...	...	...	...	90	1	3	...	103	...
Khasi and Jaintia Hills (British)	...	3	...	1	...	1	...	...	...	...	1	...
Naga Hills	...	...	...	...	...	...	5	...	...	...	1	...
Lushai Hills	...	...	...	...	...	...	3	...	...	...	...	...
ASSAM VALLEY DIVISION	11	4	...	2	2	...	321	6	5	1	157	...
Goalpara	1	3	...	2	1	...	56	2	3	1	15	...
Kamrup	7	1	...	...	1	...	110	4	2	...	65	...
Darrang	3	...	...	...	...	...	37	...	...	...	17	...
Nowgong	...	...	...	...	...	...	35	...	...	...	20	...
Sibsagar	...	...	...	...	...	...	44	...	1	...	16	...
Lakhimpur	...	...	...	...	...	...	34	...	...	...	14	...
Garo Hills	...	...	...	...	...	...	5	...	...	...	4	...
SADIYA FRONTIER TRACT	...	...	...	...	...	...	2	...	...	...	2	...
BALIPARA FRONTIER TRACT	...	...	...	...	...	...	...	...	...	...	...	...
(2) Manipur State	...	...	...	...	—	...	...	...	...	...	1	...
(3) Khasi States	...	...	...	...	...	...	...	...	...	...	...	...

TABLE X.—OCCUPATION OR MEANS OF LIVELIHOOD. PART II.—DETAILS FOR DISTRICTS—*contd.*

DISTRICT OR STATE.	Class C.—Public administration and liberal arts.											
	Total of Class C—Public administration and liberal arts.						Sub-class VI.—Public force. Total of sub-class VI.—Public force.					
	Total earners (principal occupation).		Total working dependants.		Total following occupation as subsidiary to other.		Total earners (principal occupation).		Total working dependants.		Total following occupation as subsidiary to other.	
	Males.	Females.	Males.	Females.	Males.	Females.	Males.	Females.	Males.	Females.	Males.	Females.
	1122	1123	1124	1125	1126	1127	1128	1129	1130	1131	1132	1133
ASSAM	*59,319*	*2,502*	*2,682*	*490*	*21,818*	*270*	*10,940*	...	*155*	...	*3,248*	*1*
(1) British Territory	*54,011*	*2,233*	*2,313*	*349*	*21,204*	*244*	*9,863*	...	*152*	...	*3,225*	*1*
SURMA VALLEY AND HILL DIVISION	**28,155**	**1,364**	**1,151**	**151**	**12,386**	**185**	**5,919**	...	**143**	...	**2,885**	**1**
Cachar	4,088	356	87	31	1,099	27	845	...	11	...	200	...
Sylhet	18,980	877	1,010	103	10,550	147	1,987	...	128	...	2,522	1
Khasi and Jaintia Hills (British)	2,900	72	4	15	44	6	2,006	...	...	...	...	...
Naga Hills	1,043	6	2	2	361	5	646	...	...	...	1	...
Lushai Hills	1,082	53	48	...	332	...	435	...	4	...	162	...
ASSAM VALLEY DIVISION	**23,903**	**850**	**1,161**	**198**	**8,800**	**58**	**2,732**	...	**9**	...	**340**	...
Goalpara	3,503	137	625	29	1,330	13	601	...	6	...	317	...
Kamrup	8,063	203	296	67	2,103	18	487	...	...	...	4	...
Darrang	2,487	87	24	9	987	...	352	...	...	...	3	...
Nowgong	2,004	60	49	11	909	9	253	...	...	...	3	...
Sibsagar	4,183	171	120	23	1,513	6	409	...	3	...	11	...
Lakhimpur	2,857	143	55	18	1,014	6	450	...	...	...	1	...
Garo Hills	586	50	2	41	114	6	180	...	...	...	1	...
SADIYA FRONTIER TRACT	**1,218**	**18**	...	...	**13**	**1**	**786**	...	...	...	...	...
BALIPARA FRONTIER TRACT	**735**	**1**	**1**	...	**5**	...	**426**	...	...	...	...	...
(2) Manipur State	*3,878*	*103*	*314*	*63*	*561*	*6*	*914*	...	*2*	...	*23*	...
(3) Khasi States	*1,430*	*166*	*55*	*8*	*53*	*20*	*163*	...	*1*	...	...	...

TABLE X.—OCCUPATION OR MEANS OF LIVELIHOOD. PART II.—DETAILS FOR DISTRICTS—*contd.*

DISTRICT OR STATE.	Class C.—Public administration and liberal arts. Sub-class VI.—Public force. Order 40.—Army.											
	Total of Order 40.—Army.						Group (153).—Army (Imperial).					
	Total earners (principal occupation).		Total working dependants.		Total following occupation as subsidiary to other.		Total earners (principal occupation).		Total working dependants.		Total following occupation as subsidiary to other.	
	Males.	Females.	Males.	Females.	Males.	Females.	Males.	Females.	Males.	Females.	Males.	Females.
	1134	1135	1136	1137	1138	1139	1140	1141	1142	1143	1144	1145
ASSAM	*1,932*	...	...	...	...	...	*1,836*	...	...	...	...	...
(1) British Territory	*1,836*	...	...	...	...	...	*1,836*	...	...	...	...	...
SURMA VALLEY AND HILL DIVISION	**1,815**	...	...	...	...	...	**1,815**	...	...	...	...	...
Cachar	1	...	...	...	...	...	1	...	...	...	...	...
Sylhet	...	...	...	...	...	...	...	...	...	...	...	...
Khasi and Jaintia Hills (British)	1,807	...	...	...	...	...	1,807	...	...	...	...	...
Naga Hills	4	...	...	...	...	...	4	...	...	...	...	...
Lushai Hills	3	...	...	...	...	...	3	...	...	...	...	...
ASSAM VALLEY DIVISION	**12**	...	...	...	...	...	**12**	...	...	...	...	...
Goalpara	...	...	...	...	...	...	...	...	...	...	...	...
Kamrup	...	...	...	...	...	...	...	...	...	...	...	...
Darrang	1	...	...	...	...	...	1	...	...	...	...	...
Nowgong	...	...	...	...	...	...	...	...	...	...	...	...
Sibsagar	...	...	...	...	...	...	...	...	...	...	...	...
Lakhimpur	11	...	...	...	...	...	11	...	...	...	...	...
Garo Hills	...	...	...	...	...	...	...	...	...	...	...	...
SADIYA FRONTIER TRACT	**7**	...	...	...	...	...	**7**	...	...	...	...	...
BALIPARA FRONTIER TRACT	**2**	...	...	...	...	...	**2**	...	...	...	...	...
(2) Manipur State	*96*	...	...	...	...	...	...	...	...	...	...	...
(3) Khasi States	...	...	...	...	...	...	...	...	...	...	...	...

TABLE X.—Occupation or means of livelihood. Part II.—Details for Districts—*contd.*

DISTRICT OR STATE.	Class C.—Public administration and liberal arts.											
	Sub-class VI.—Public force.											
	Order 40.—Army.						Order 43.—Police.					
	Group (151).—Army (Indian states).						Total of Order 43.—Police.					
	Total earners (principal occupation).		Total working dependants.		Total following occupation as subsidiary to other.		Total earners (principal occupation).		Total working dependants.		Total following occupation as subsidiary to other.	
	Males.	Females.	Males.	Females.	Males.	Females.	Males.	Females.	Males.	Females.	Males.	Females.
	1146	1147	1148	1149	1150	1151	1152	1153	1154	1155	1156	1157
ASSAM	*96*	...	...	...	...	...	*9,008*	...	*155*	...	*3,318*	*1*
(1) British Territory	...	...	...	...	...	...	*8,097*	...	*152*	...	*3,225*	*1*
SURMA VALLEY AND HILL DIVISION	...	...	...	...	...	...	**4,104**	...	**143**	...	**2,885**	**1**
Cachar	...	...	...	...	...	...	844	...	11	...	260	...
Sylhet		...	...	...	...	...	1,867	...	128	...	2,522	1
Khasi and Jaintia Hills (British)	...	...	...	...	...		190	...	...	...	...	...
Naga Hills	...	...	...		...	...	642		...	...	1	...
Lushai Hills	...	...	...	...	...	...	532		4	...	102	...
ASSAM VALLEY DIVISION	...		...	...	...	...	**2,720**	...	**9**	...	**340**	...
Goalpara	...	...	...	...	...	...	601	...	6	...	317	...
Kamrup	...	...		...	...	...	487	...	...	...	4	...
Darrang	...	...	...	...	...	...	341	...		...	3	...
Nowgong	...	...	...	...	...	...	283	...	...	...	3	...
Sibsagar		...		...	...	...	409	...	3	...	11	...
Lakhimpur	...	...	...	...	...	...	430	...	...	...	1	...
Garo Hills	...	...	...	...	...	...	150	...	...	...	1	...
SADIYA FRONTIER TRACT	...	...	...	...	...	...	**779**	...	...	...	...	...
BALIPARA FRONTIER TRACT	...	...	...	...	...	...	**494**	...	...	...	...	...
(2) Manipur State	*96*	...	...	...	...	...	*818*	...	*2*	...	*93*	...
(3) Khasi States	...	...	...	...	...	...	*103*	...	*1*	...	...	...

TABLE X.—OCCUPATION OR MEANS OF LIVELIHOOD. PART II.—DETAILS FOR DISTRICTS—*contd.*

DISTRICT OR STATE.	Class C.—Public administration and liberal arts.											
	Sub-class VI—Public force.											
	Order 43.—Police.											
	Group (157).—Police.						Group (158).—Village Watchmen.					
	Total earners (principal occupation).		Total working dependants.		Total following occupation as subsidiary to other.		Total earners (principal occupation).		Total working dependants.		Total following occupation as subsidiary to other.	
	Males.	Females.	Males.	Females.	Males.	Females.	Males.	Females.	Males.	Females.	Males.	Females.
	1158	1159	1160	1161	1162	1163	1164	1165	1166	1167	1168	1169
ASSAM	7,566	...	9	...	79	...	1,442	...	146	...	3,176	1
(1) British Territory	6,672	...	8	...	79	...	1,355	...	144	...	3,153	1
SURMA VALLEY AND HILL DIVISION	2,977	...	4	...	37	...	1,127	...	139	...	2,848	1
Cachar	603	...	3	...	2	...	241	...	8	...	258	...
Sylhet	1,406	...	1	...	33	...	881	...	127	...	2,489	1
Khasi and Jaintia Hills (British)	199	...	...	...	...	...	...	...	...	...	...	...
Naga Hills	642	...	...	...	1	...	...	...	...	...	...	...
Lushai Hills	127	...	...	...	1	...	5	...	4	...	101	...
ASSAM VALLEY DIVISION	2,403	...	4	...	35	...	228	...	5	...	305	...
Goalpara	374	...	1	...	13	...	227	...	5	...	304	...
Kamrup	457	...	...	...	4	...	...	...	...	...	...	...
Darrang	351	...	...	...	3	...	...	...	...	...	...	...
Nowgong	233	...	...	...	3	...	...	...	...	...	...	...
Sibsagar	409	...	3	...	11	...	...	...	...	...	...	...
Lakhimpur	439	...	...	...	1	...	...	...	...	...	...	...
Garo Hills	140	...	...	...	...	...	1	...	...	...	1	...
SADIYA FRONTIER TRACT	779	...	...	...	...	...	...	...	...	...	...	...
BALIPARA FRONTIER TRACT	494	...	...	...	...	...	...	...	...	...	...	...
(2) Manipur State	731	...	...	...	...	...	87	...	2	...	23	...
(3) Khasi States	163	...	1	...	...	...	...	...	...	...	...	...

TABLE X.—Occupation or means of livelihood. Part II.—Details for Districts—contd.

District or State.	Class C.—Public administration and liberal arts. Sub-class VII.—Public administration. Total of sub-class VII.—Public Administration. Total earners (principal occupation). Males.	Females.	Total working dependants. Males.	Females.	Total following occupation as subsidiary to other. Males.	Females.	Order 44.—Public Administration. Total of Order 44.—Public Administration. Total earners (principal occupation). Males.	Females.	Total working dependants. Males.	Females.	Total following occupation as subsidiary to other. Males.	Females.
	1170	1171	1172	1173	1174	1175	1176	1177	1178	1179	1180	1181
ASSAM	*10,467*	*120*	*130*	*2*	*3,562*	*2*	*10,467*	*120*	*130*	*2*	*3,562*	*2*
(1) British Territory	*9,034*	*101*	*128*	*2*	*3,511*	*2*	*9,034*	*101*	*128*	*2*	*3,511*	*2*
SURMA VALLEY AND HILL DIVISION	4,013	54	18	2	880	1	4,013	54	18	2	880	1
Cachar	701	2	3	...	95	1	701	2	3	...	95	1
Sylhet	2,275	46	12	...	465	...	2,275	46	12	...	465	...
Khasi and Jaintia Hills (British)	600	...	1	...	13	...	600	...	1	...	13	...
Naga Hills	173	...	2	2	262	...	173	...	2	2	262	...
Lushai Hills	264	6	...	...	45	...	264	6	...	...	45	...
ASSAM VALLEY DIVISION	4,338	47	109	...	2,546	...	4,338	47	109	...	2,546	...
Goalpara	614	20	8	...	159	...	614	20	8	...	159	...
Kamrup	1,196	14	20	...	538	...	1,196	14	20	...	538	...
Darrang	645	8	4	...	411	...	645	8	4	...	411	...
Nowgong	407	...	18	...	334	...	407	...	18	...	334	...
Sibsagar	721	3	35	...	550	...	721	3	35	...	550	...
Lakhimpur	654	1	24	...	494	...	654	1	24	...	494	...
Garo Hills	101	1	...	...	60	...	101	1	...	...	60	...
SADIYA FRONTIER TRACT	392	...	...	...	80	1	392	...	...	...	80	1
BALIPARA FRONTIER TRACT	291	...	1	...	5	...	291	...	1	...	5	...
(2) Manipur State	*715*	*19*	*2*	...	*27*	...	*715*	*19*	*2*	...	*27*	...
(3) Khasi States	*718*	...	...	...	*24*	...	*718*	...	...	...	*24*	...

TABLE X.—OCCUPATION OR MEANS OF LIVELIHOOD. PART II.—DETAILS FOR DISTRICTS—*contd.*

DISTRICT OR STATE.	Class C.—Public Administration and liberal arts. Sub-class VII.—Public Administration. Order 44.—Public Administration. Group (159).—Service of the State.						Group (160).—Service of Indian and Foreign States.					
	Total earners (principal occupation).		Total working dependants.		Total following occupation as subsidiary to other.		Total earners (principal occupation).		Total working dependants.		Total following occupation as subsidiary to other.	
	Males.	Females.	Males.	Females.	Males.	Females.	Males.	Females.	Males.	Females.	Males.	Females.
	1182	1183	1184	1185	1186	1187	1188	1189	1190	1191	1192	1193
ASSAM	*7,541*	*11*	*37*	*2*	*794*		*667*	*18*	*1*	...	*28*	...
(1) British Territory ...	*6,824*	*11*	*37*	*2*	*788*	.	*2*	...	...	...	...	...
SURMA VALLEY AND HILL DIVISION	**3,778**	**4**	**15**	**2**	**542**	...	...	...	...	...	...	...
Cachar ...	631	1	3	...	84	...	...	...	...	...	...	...
Sylhet ...	2,134	3	11	...	391	...	...	...	...	...	...	...
Khasi and Jaintia Hills (British)	474	...	1	...	...	...	...	...	...	...	...	...
Naga Hills ...	107	...	1	2	23	...	...	...	...	...	...	...
Lushai Hills	252	...	...	...	44	...	...	...	...	...	...	...
ASSAM VALLEY DIVISION	**2,374**	**7**	**22**	...	**237**	...	**2**	...	...	...	...	...
Goalpara	375	...	4	...	51	...	...	...	...	...	...	...
Kamrup	643	1	8	...	50	...	2	...	...	...	...	...
Darrang	270	1	...	...	32	...	...	...	...	...	...	...
Nowgong	105	...	4	...	12	...	...	...	...	...	...	...
Sibsagar	429	3	4	...	54	...	...	...	...	...	...	...
Lakhimpur	384	1	2	...	33	...	...	...	...	...	...	...
Garo Hills	73	1	...	...	5	...	...	...	...	...	...	...
SADIYA FRONTIER TRACT ...	**381**	...	...	...	8	...	...	...	...	...	...	...
BALIPARA FRONTIER TRACT ...	**291**	...	...	...	1	...	...	...	...	...	...	...
(2) Manipur State ...	*61*	...	...	...	*5*	...	*609*	*18*	*1*	...	*11*	...
(3) Khasi States ...	*656*	...	...	...	*1*	...	*56*	...	...	...	*17*	...

TABLE X.—Occupation or means of livelihood. Part II.—Details for Districts—*contd.*

Class C.—Public administration and liberal arts.
Sub-class VII.—Public administration.
Order 44.—Public administration.

District or State.	Group (161).—Municipal and other local (not village) service. Total earners (principal occupation). Males.	Total earners (principal occupation). Females.	Total working dependants. Males.	Total working dependants. Females.	Total following occupation as subsidiary to other. Males.	Total following occupation as subsidiary to other. Females.	Group (162).—Village officials and servants other than watchmen. Total earners (principal occupation). Males.	Total earners (principal occupation). Females.	Total working dependants. Males.	Total working dependants. Females.	Total following occupation as subsidiary to other. Males.	Total following occupation as subsidiary to other. Females.
	1194	1195	1196	1197	1198	1199	1200	1201	1202	1203	1204	1205
ASSAM	*864*	*85*	*5*	...	*164*	*1*	*1,395*	*6*	*87*	...	*2,576*	*1*
(1) British Territory	*841*	*84*	*5*	...	*169*	*1*	*1,367*	*6*	*86*	...	*2,561*	*1*
SURMA VALLEY AND HILL DIVISION	173	44	...	...	26	1	63	6	3	...	312	...
Cachar	41	1	...	...	7	1	9	...	1	...	4	...
Sylhet	130	43	...	...	19	...	11	...	1	...	54	...
Khasi and Jaintia Hills (British)	2	...	...	...	...	...	24	...	...	...	13	...
Naga Hills	...	...	...	...	...	...	6	...	1	...	240	...
Lushai Hills	...	...	...	...	...	...	13	6	...	...	1	...
ASSAM VALLEY DIVISION	667	40	5	...	138	...	1,295	...	82	...	2,173	...
Goalpara	207	20	1	...	70	...	31	...	3	...	38	...
Kamrup	118	13	1	...	4	...	323	...	11	...	454	...
Darrang	65	7	...	...	5	...	274	...	4	...	374	...
Nowgong	86	...	1	...	16	...	246	...	13	...	305	...
Sibsagar	119	...	1	...	35	...	174	...	30	...	441	...
Lakhimpur	70	...	1	...	8	...	230	...	21	...	453	...
Garo Hills	2	...	...	...	...	...	26	...	...	...	65	...
SADIYA FRONTIER TRACT	1	...	...	...	...	...	10	...	...	...	72	1
BALIPARA FRONTIER TRACT	...	...	...	...	...	...	...	...	1	...	4	...
(2) Manipur State	*20*	*1*	...	...	*2*	...	*25*	...	*1*	...	*9*	...
(3) Khasi States	*3*	...	...	...	...	...	*3*	...	...	...	*6*	...

TABLE X.—OCCUPATION OR MEANS OF LIVELIHOOD. PART II.—DETAILS FOR DISTRICTS—*contd.*

DISTRICT OR STATE.	Class C.—Public administration and liberal arts.											
	Sub-class VIII.—Professions and liberal arts.											
	Total of sub-class VIII.—Professions and liberal arts.						Order 45.—Religion.					
							Total of Order 45.—Religion					
	Total earners (principal occupation).		Total working dependants.		Total following occupation as subsidiary to other.		Total earners (principal occupation).		Total working dependants.		Total following occupation as subsidiary to other.	
	Males.	Females.	Males.	Females.	Males.	Females.	Males.	Females.	Males.	Females.	Males.	Females.
	1206	1207	1208	1209	1210	1211	1212	1213	1214	1215	1216	1217
ASSAM	*37,919*	*2,349*	*2,397*	*418*	*15,008*	*267*	*15,897*	*804*	*1,630*	*167*	*6,849*	*113*
(1) British Territory	*35,114*	*2,132*	*2,033*	*347*	*14,468*	*241*	*14,804*	*754*	*1,399*	*115*	*6,661*	*108*
SURMA VALLEY AND HILL DIVISION	**18,223**	**1,310**	**990**	**149**	**8,541**	**183**	**8,506**	**638**	**592**	**90**	**3,658**	**94**
Cachar	2,543	354	73	31	744	26	1,105	177	48	9	322	9
Sylhet	14,818	831	870	103	7,563	148	7,222	423	400	71	3,180	83
Khasi and Jaintia Hills (British)	364	72	3	15	31	4	43	17	...	10	9	2
Naga Hills	226	6	...	...	18	5	38	1	...	...	4	...
Lushai Hills	283	47	44	...	186	...	80	20	44	...	143	...
ASSAM VALLEY DIVISION	**16,733**	**803**	**1,043**	**198**	**5,914**	**58**	**6,237**	**107**	**810**	**25**	**2,904**	**14**
Goalpara	2,378	117	611	29	854	13	809	9	541	4	180	1
Kamrup	6,470	150	266	67	2,391	18	3,410	51	198	9	1,342	7
Darrang	1,490	79	30	9	573	...	386	4	6	2	344	...
Nowgong	1,234	60	31	11	572	9	370	7	14	4	379	5
Sibsagar	3,053	168	63	23	963	6	873	17	48	4	544	1
Lakhimpur	1,793	141	31	19	519	6	318	4	13	...	174	...
Garo Hills	335	49	2	41	43	6	62	15	3	2	22	...
SADIYA FRONTIER TRACT	**160**	**18**	...	...	**18**	...	**57**	**9**	...	...	**9**	...
BALIPARA FRONTIER TRACT	**18**	**1**	...	...	...	...	**4**	...	...	...	...	...
(2) Manipur State	*2,249*	*84*	*310*	*63*	*511*	*6*	*971*	*25*	*199*	*51*	*181*	*4*
(3) Khasi States	*549*	*166*	*54*	*8*	*29*	*20*	*53*	*25*	*46*	*1*	...	*1*

TABLE X.—OCCUPATION OR MEANS OF LIVELIHOOD. PART II.—DETAILS FOR DISTRICTS—*contd.*

DISTRICT OR STATE.	Class C.—Public administration and liberal arts. Sub-class VIII.—Professions and liberal arts. Order 45.—Religion. Group (163).—Priests, ministers, etc. Total earners (principal occupation). Males.	Females.	Total working dependants. Males.	Females.	Total following occupation as subsidiary to other. Males.	Females.	Group (164).—Monks, nuns, religious mendicants. Total earners (principal occupation). Males.	Females.	Total working dependants. Males.	Females.	Total following occupation as subsidiary to other. Males.	Females.
	1218	1219	1220	1221	1222	1223	1224	1225	1226	1227	1228	1229
ASSAM	*12,245*	*399*	*1,359*	*48*	*5,451*	*37*	*568*	*314*	*57*	*52*	*916*	*23*
(1) British Territory	*11,363*	*293*	*1,170*	*28*	*5,296*	*36*	*567*	*295*	*57*	*31*	*916*	*19*
SURMA VALLEY AND HILL DIVISION	6,389	227	453	22	2,800	27	322	286	35	23	138	15
Cachar	776	36	37	5	263	6	71	139	...	...	16	...
Sylhet	5,412	160	372	17	2,391	20	251	143	35	23	122	15
Khasi and Jaintia Hills (British)	44	11	...	...	3	1	...	5	...	...	...	...
Naga Hills	18	1	...	...	1	...	...	...	...	...	...	...
Lushai Hills	60	20	44	...	143	...	...	...	...	...	...	...
ASSAM VALLEY DIVISION	4,931	57	717	6	2,487	9	230	9	22	8	78	4
Goalpara	654	3	531	3	145	...	44	4	4	...	18	1
Kamrup	2,946	19	166	1	1,113	4	39	2	7	3	7	2
Darrang	294	1	5	...	301	...	28	2	...	...	8	...
Nowgong	294	6	7	...	291	5	23	...	3	4	12	...
Sibsagar	129	11	21	...	468	...	71	...	5	1	26	1
Lakhimpur	197	3	5	...	183	...	24	...	3	...	2	...
Garo Hills	37	14	2	2	18	...	11	1	...	...	3	...
SADIYA FRONTIER TRACT	39	9	...	...	9	...	15	...	...	...	...	...
BALIPARA FRONTIER TRACT	4	...	...	...	...	...	...	...	...	...	...	...
(2) Manipur State	*834*	*9*	*143*	*19*	*165*	...	...	*14*	...	*21*	...	*4*
(3) Khasi States	*48*	*20*	*46*	*1*	...	*1*	*1*	*5*	...	...	...	...

TABLE X.—Occupation or means of livelihood. Part II.—Details for Districts—*contd.*

District or State.	Class C.—Public administration and liberal arts. Sub-class VIII.—Professions and liberal arts. Order 45.—Religion. Group (165).—Other religious workers. Total earners (principal occupation). Males.	Females.	Total working dependants. Males.	Females.	Total following occupation as subsidiary to other. Males.	Females.	Group (166).—Servants in religious edifices, burial and burning grounds, pilgrim conductors, circumcisers, etc. Total earners (principal occupation). Males.	Females.	Total working dependants. Males.	Females.	Total following occupation as subsidiary to other. Males.	Females.
	1230	1231	1232	1233	1234	1235	1236	1237	1238	1239	1240	1241
ASSAM	*2,294*	*143*	*159*	*46*	*855*	*51*	*720*	*25*	*55*	*21*	*320*	*2*
(1) British Territory	*2,155*	*141*	*110*	*35*	*829*	*51*	*719*	*25*	*55*	*21*	*320*	*2*
SURMA VALLEY AND HILL DIVISION	1,720	124	90	32	656	51	75	1	4	13	64	1
Cachar	226	12	11	4	40	3	2	...	...	...	4	...
Sylhet	1,464	111	79	27	614	48	65	1	4	4	53	...
Khasi and Jaintia Hills (British)	...	1	...	1	...	...	8	...	...	9	6	1
Naga Hills	30	...	...	...	2	...	...	...	...	...	1	...
Lushai Hills	...	...	...	...	...	...	...	...	...	...	...	...
ASSAM VALLEY DIVISION	434	17	20	3	173	...	642	24	51	8	256	1
Goalpara	31	2	2	...	4	...	80	...	14	1	22	...
Kamrup	107	9	7	...	90	...	207	21	16	5	123	1
Darrang	42	...	...	1	34	...	22	1	1	1	11	...
Nowgong	4	...	4	...	21	...	40	1	...	...	54	...
Sibsagar	69	5	6	2	13	...	274	1	16	1	40	...
Lakhimpur	83	1	1	...	13	...	14	...	4	...	6	...
Garo Hills	6	...	...	...	1	...	6	...	...	...	...	...
SADIYA FRONTIER TRACT	1	...	...	...	...	...	2	...	...	...	...	...
BALIPARA FRONTIER TRACT	...	...	...	...	...	...	...	...	...	...	...	...
(2) Manipur State	*136*	*9*	*49*	*11*	*26*	...	*1*	...	...	...	...	...
(3) Khasi States	*3*	...	...	...	...	...	...	...	...	...	...	...

TABLE X.—OCCUPATION OR MEANS OF LIVELIHOOD. PART II.—DETAILS FOR DISTRICTS—*contd.*

DISTRICT OR STATE.	Class C.—Public administration and liberal arts.											
	Sub-class VIII.—Professions and liberal arts.											
	Order 46.—Law.											
	Total of Order 46.—Law.						Group (167).—Lawyers of all kinds, including Qazis, Law Agents and Mukhtiars.					
	Total earners (Principal occupation).		Total working dependants.		Total following occupation as subsidiary to other.		Total earners (principal occupation).		Total working dependants.		Total following occupation as subsidiary to other.	
	Males.	Females.	Males.	Females.	Males.	Females.	Males.	Females.	Males.	Females.	Males.	Females.
	1242	1243	1244	1245	1246	1247	1248	1249	1250	1251	1252	1253
ASSAM	*2,649*	...	*49*	...	*616*	...	*1,006*	...	...	...	*90*	...
(1) British Territory	*2,590*		*49*	...	*616*	...	*987*	...	...	...	*90*	...
SURMA VALLEY AND HILL DIVISION	**1,684**	...	**43**	...	**490**	...	**611**	...	...	...	**75**	...
Cachar	179	...	1	...	51	...	97	...	...	...	11	...
Sylhet	1,497	...	42	...	403	...	510	...	...	...	64	...
Khasi and Jaintia Hills (British)	3	...	...	...	...	...	3	...	...	...	...	...
Naga Hills	1	...	...	...	1	...	1	...	...	...	...	...
Lushai Hills	4	...	...	...	35	...	...	...	...	...	...	...
ASSAM VALLEY DIVISION	**906**	...	**6**	...	**126**	...	**376**	...	...	...	**15**	...
Goalpara	161	...	3	...	10	...	61	...	...	...	4	...
Kamrup	303	...	1	...	20	...	114	...	...	...	3	...
Darrang	72	...	...	...	11	...	30	...	...	...	2	...
Nowgong	95	...	...	...	30	...	41	...	...	...	2	...
Sibsagar	176	...	2	...	39	...	88	...	...	...	4	...
Lakhimpur	95	...	...	...	16	...	42	...	...	...	...	...
Garo Hills	4	...	...	...	...	...	...	...	...	...	...	...
SADIYA FRONTIER TRACT	...	...	...	...	...	...	...	...	...	...	...	...
BALIPARA FRONTIER TRACT	...	...	...	...	...	...	...	...	...	...	...	...
(2) Manipur State	*41*	...	...	...	...	...	*3*	...	...	...	...	...
(3) Khasi States	*18*	...	...	...	...	...	*16*	...	...	...	...	...

TABLE X.—OCCUPATION OR MEANS OF LIVELIHOOD. PART II.—DETAILS FOR DISTRICTS—*contd.*

DISTRICT OR STATE.	Class C.—Public administration and liberal arts.											
	Sub-class VIII.—Professions and liberal arts.											
	Order 46.—Law.						Order 47.—Medicine.					
	Group (163).—Lawyers' clerks, petition-writers, etc.						Total of Order 47.—Medicine.					
	Total earners (principal occupation).		Total working dependants.		Total following occupation as subsidiary to other.		Total earners (principal occupation).		Total working dependants.		Total following occupation as subsidiary to other.	
	Males.	Females.	Males.	Females.	Males.	Females.	Males.	Females.	Males.	Females.	Males.	Females.
	1254	1255	1256	1257	1258	1259	1260	1261	1262	1263	1264	1265
ASSAM	*1,643*	...	*49*	...	*526*	...	*6,402*	*653*	*136*	*173*	*2,441*	*74*
(1) British Territory ...	*1,603*	...	*49*	...	*526*	...	*5,887*	*550*	*111*	*160*	*2,251*	*68*
SURMA VALLEY AND HILL DIVISION ...	1,073	...	43	...	415	...	2,468	253	44	34	993	33
Cachar ...	82	...	1	...	40	...	309	91	5	17	107	8
Sylhet ...	987	...	42	...	339	...	2,014	126	39	15	875	25
Khasi and Jaintia Hills (British)...	...	...	...	...	...	...	46	16	...	2	10	...
Naga Hills ...	...	...	...	...	1	...	48	3	...	...	1	...
Lushai Hills ...	4	...	...	...	35	...	51	17	...	...	...	...
ASSAM VALLEY DIVISION ...	530	...	6	...	111	...	3,382	289	67	126	1,258	35
Goalpara ...	100	...	3	...	6	...	408	36	16	12	363	13
Kamrup ...	189	...	1	...	17	...	981	67	35	46	689	11
Darrang ...	42	...	...	...	9	...	425	41	4	3	11	...
Nowgong ...	54	...	...	...	28	...	197	14	2	4	40	1
Sibsagar ...	88	...	2	...	35	...	700	47	7	10	86	4
Lakhimpur ...	43	...	...	...	16	...	550	69	3	13	61	1
Garo Hills ...	4	...	...	...	...	...	51	15	...	38	8	6
SADIYA FRONTIER TRACT ...	...	...	...	...	...	...	32	7	...	...	...	...
BALIPARA FRONTIER TRACT ...	...	...	...	...	...	...	5	1	...	...	...	...
(2) Manipur State ...	*38*	...	...	...	...	...	*394*	*25*	*30*	*9*	*178*	...
(3) Khasi States...	*2*	...	...	...	...	...	*121*	*78*	*6*	*4*	*19*	*6*

TABLE X.—OCCUPATION OR MEANS OF LIVELIHOOD. PART II.—DETAILS FOR DISTRICTS—*contd.*

DISTRICT OR STATE.	Class C.—Public administration and liberal arts.											
	Sub-class VIII.—Professions and liberal arts.											
	Order 47.—Medicine.											
	Group (169).—Registered medical practitioners including oculists.						Group (170).—Other persons practising the healing arts without being registered.					
	Total earners (principal occupation).		Total working dependants.		Total following occupation as subsidiary to other.		Total earners (principal occupation).		Total working dependants.		Total following occupation as subsidiary to other.	
	Males.	Females.	Males.	Females.	Males.	Females.	Males.	Females.	Males.	Females.	Males.	Females.
	1266	1267	1268	1269	1270	1271	1272	1273	1274	1275	1276	1277
ASSAM	*1,776*	*23*	*14*	...	*218*	*2*	*3,209*	*140*	*133*	*53*	*2,113*	*39*
(1) British Territory	*1,707*	*22*	*13*	...	*207*	*1*	*2,836*	*135*	*89*	*52*	*1,935*	*39*
SURMA VALLEY AND HILL DIVISION	**643**	**6**	**11**	...	**154**	...	**1,560**	**53**	**30**	**1**	**795**	**13**
Cachar	104	1	1	...	16	...	168	13	4	1	97	...
Sylhet	503	5	10	...	138	...	1,367	38	26	...	698	13
Khasi and Jaintia Hills (British)	13	...	...	...	...	...	25	2	...	...	10	...
Naga Hills	17	...	...	...	...	...	...	...	...	...	...	...
Lushai Hills	6	...	...	...	...	...	...	...	...	...	...	...
ASSAM VALLEY DIVISION	**1,045**	**16**	**2**	...	**53**	**1**	**1,264**	**82**	**59**	**51**	**1,140**	**19**
Goalpara	98	4	1	...	11	...	536	22	14	5	341	9
Kamrup	195	3	1	...	15	...	459	45	31	39	640	10
Darrang	150	2	...	...	...	...	[illegible]	6	3	2	3	...
Nowgong	100	2	...	...	5	1	56	4	...	3	31	...
Sibsagar	233	3	...	...	11	...	134	2	6	1	60	...
Lakhimpur	137	2	...	...	11	...	49	3	2	1	33	...
Garo Hills	20	...	...	...	...	...	6	...	...	...	8	...
SADIYA FRONTIER TRACT	**17**	...	...	...	...	...	**2**	...	...	...	...	...
BALIPARA FRONTIER TRACT	**2**	...	...	...	...	...	...	...	...	...	...	...
(2) Manipur State	*31*	...	*1*	...	*11*	...	*329*	*6*	*38*	*1*	*167*	...
(3) Khasi States	*38*	*1*	...	...	...	*1*	*61*	*8*	*6*	...	*11*	...

TABLE X.—OCCUPATION OR MEANS OF LIVELIHOOD. PART II.—DETAILS FOR DISTRICTS—*contd.*

DISTRICT OR STATE.	Class C.—Public administration and liberal arts. Sub-class VIII.—Professions and liberal arts. Order 47.—Medicine. Group (171).—Dentists. Total earners (principal occupation).		Total working dependants.		Total following occupation as subsidiary to other.		Group (172).—Midwives, Vaccinators, compounders, nurses, masseurs, etc. Total earners (principal occupation).		Total working dependants.		Total following occupation as subsidiary to other.	
	Males.	Females.	Males.	Females.	Males.	Females.	Males.	Females.	Males.	Females.	Males.	Females.
	1278	1279	1280	1281	1282	1283	1284	1285	1286	1287	1288	1289
ASSAM	*11*	*1*	...	...	...	...	*1,298*	*480*	*8*	*120*	*97*	*40*
(1) British Territory	*9*	...	...	...	...	...	*1,251*	*393*	*8*	*108*	*96*	*35*
BURMA VALLEY AND HILL DIVISION	2	—	...	...	...	...	250	194	3	33	42	20
Cachar	...	...	...	...	...	...	37	77	...	16	4	8
Sylhet	2	...	...	...	...	...	130	83	3	15	37	12
Khasi and Jaintia Hills (British)	...	...	...	...	...	...	8	14	...	2	...	...
Naga Hills	...	...	...	...	...	...	30	3	...	...	1	...
Lushai Hills	...	...	...	...	...	...	45	17	...	...	...	...
ASSAM VALLEY DIVISION	7	...	...	...	...	...	987	191	5	75	54	15
Goalpara	...	...	...	...	...	...	69	10	1	7	10	3
Kamrup	1	...	...	...	...	...	103	19	...	7	7	1
Darrang	2	...	...	...	...	...	154	33	...	1	8	...
Nowgong	...	...	...	...	...	...	35	8	2	1	2	...
Sibsagar	1	...	...	...	...	...	377	42	1	9	14	4
Lakhimpur	3	...	...	...	...	...	228	64	1	13	13	1
Garo Hills	...	...	...	...	...	...	21	15	...	28	...	6
SADIYA FRONTIER TRACT	...	...	...	...	...	...	11	7	...	...	...	...
BALIPARA FRONTIER TRACT...	...	...	...	...	...	...	3	1	...	...	...	...
(2) Manipur State	*2*	...	...	...	...	...	*28*	*19*	...	*8*	...	...
(3) Khasi States	...	*1*	...	...	...	...	*19*	*68*	...	*4*	*1*	*5*

TABLE X.—OCCUPATION OR MEANS OF LIVELIHOOD. PART II.—DETAILS FOR DISTRICTS—*contd.*

DISTRICT OR STATE.	Class C.—Public administration and liberal arts.											
	Sub-class VIII.—Professions and liberal arts.											
	Order 47.—Medicine.						Order 48.—Instruction.					
	Group (173).—Veterinary Surgeons.						Total of Order 48.—Instruction.					
	Total earners (principal occupation).		Total working dependants.		Total following occupation as subsidiary to other.		Total earners (principal occupation).		Total working dependants.		Total following occupation as subsidiary to other.	
	Males.	Females.	Males.	Females.	Males.	Females.	Males.	Females.	Males.	Females.	Males.	Females.
	1290	1291	1292	1293	1294	1295	1296	1297	1298	1299	1300	1301
ASSAM	*108*	...	*2*	...	*13*	...	*10,056*	*799*	*260*	*50*	*2,952*	*60*
(1) British Territory	*94*	...	*1*	...	*13*	...	*9,351*	*739*	*254*	*47*	*2,917*	*46*
SURMA VALLEY AND HILL DIVISION	13	...	...	...	2	...	4,243	390	138	24	1,836	43
Cachar	...	...	...	...	...	...	747	80	16	5	103	7
Sylhet	12	...	...	...	2	...	3,024	260	121	17	1,005	33
Khasi and Jaintia Hills (British)	...	...	...	...	...	...	227	39	1	2	11	3
Naga Hills	1	...	...	...	...	...	115	1	...	...	11	...
Lushai Hills	...	...	...	...	...	...	130	10	...	...	7	...
ASSAM VALLEY DIVISION	79	...	1	...	11	...	5,058	331	116	23	1,068	6
Goalpara	5	...	...	...	1	...	779	53	46	3	215	...
Kamrup	20	...	...	...	8	...	1,843	61	26	7	149	...
Darrang	6	...	1	...	...	...	503	33	7	2	166	...
Nowgong	6	...	...	...	1	...	518	36	14	3	109	5
Sibsagar	15	...	...	...	1	...	1,060	82	16	5	244	1
Lakhimpur	22	...	...	...	...	...	460	47	6	3	220	...
Garo Hills	5	...	...	...	...	...	188	19	...	1	7	...
SADIYA FRONTIER TRACT	2	...	...	...	...	...	44	2	...	...	8	...
BALIPARA FRONTIER TRACT	...	...	...	...	...	...	6	...	...	...	...	...
(2) Manipur State	*11*	...	...	...	...	...	*377*	*4*	*4*	...	*13*	*2*
(3) Khasi States	*3*	...	...	...	...	...	*398*	*63*	*9*	*3*	*16*	*13*

TABLE X.—Occupation or means of livelihood. Part II.—Details for Districts—*contd.*

DISTRICT OR STATE.	Class C.—Public administration and liberal arts. Sub-class VIII.—Professions and liberal arts. Order 46.—Instruction. Group (174).—Professors and teachers of all kinds. Total earners (principal occupation). Males.	Females.	Total working dependants. Males.	Females.	Total following occupation as subsidiary to other. Males.	Females.	Group (175).—Clerks and servants connected with education. Total earners (principal occupation). Males.	Females.	Total working dependants. Males.	Females.	Total following occupation as subsidiary to other. Males.	Females.
	1302	1303	1304	1305	1306	1307	1308	1309	1310	1311	1312	1313
ASSAM	*9,579*	*685*	*257*	*40*	*2,901*	*53*	*477*	*114*	*3*	*10*	*50*	*7*
(1) British Territory	*8,897*	*621*	*251*	*37*	*2,871*	*39*	*454*	*111*	*3*	*10*	*46*	*7*
SURMA VALLEY AND HILL DIVISION	4,001	347	138	23	1,816	36	153	53	...	1	10	6
Cachar	741	66	16	5	193	7	6	14	...	...	...	...
Sylhet	2,687	233	121	17	1,593	26	137	36	...	...	10	6
Khasi and Jaintia Hills (British)	237	37	1	1	12	3	...	3	...	1	...	...
Naga Hills	106	1	...	...	11	...	9	...	...	...	...	...
Lushai Hills	130	10	...	...	7	...	...	...	...	...	...	...
ASSAM VALLEY DIVISION	4,767	273	113	16	1,052	3	201	58	3	9	36	1
Goalpara	747	40	45	2	197	...	32	13	1	1	18	...
Kamrup	1,434	50	23	5	145	...	108	11	2	2	4	...
Darrang	478	28	7	1	139	...	25	5	...	1	5	...
Nowgong	480	28	14	...	105	3	28	5	...	3	4	...
Sibsagar	1,004	65	18	4	240	...	63	14	...	1	4	1
Lakhimpur	434	40	6	1	219	...	25	7	...	1	1	...
Garo Hills	190	19	...	1	7	...	8	...	...	...	...	...
SADIYA FRONTIER TRACT	37	1	...	...	3	...	7	1	...	...	...	...
BALIPARA FRONTIER TRACT	2	...	...	...	...	...	4	...	...	...	...	...
(2) Manipur State	*362*	*4*	*4*	...	*14*	*1*	*15*	...	...	...	*4*	...
(3) Khasi States	*320*	*60*	*2*	*3*	*16*	*13*	*8*	*3*	...	...	...	...

TABLE X.—OCCUPATION AND MEANS OF LIVELIHOOD. PART II.—DETAILS FOR DISTRICTS—*contd.*

Class C.—Public administration and liberal arts. Sub-class VIII.—Professions and liberal arts. Order 49.—Letters, arts and sciences (other than 44).

DISTRICT OR STATE.	Total of Order 49.—Letters, Arts, Sciences (other than 44). Total earners (principal occupation). Males.	Females.	Total working dependants. Males.	Females.	Total following occupation as subsidiary to other. Males.	Females.	Group (176).—Public scribes, stenographers, etc. Total earners (principal occupation). Males.	Females.	Total working dependants. Males.	Females.	Total following occupation as subsidiary to other. Males.	Females.
	1314	1315	1316	1317	1318	1319	1320	1321	1322	1323	1324	1325
ASSAM	*2,978*	*126*	*309*	*28*	*2,158*	*20*	*15*	...	...	...	...	...
(1) British Territory	*2,482*	*96*	*227*	*25*	*2,023*	*19*	*12*	...	...	...	...	...
SURMA VALLEY AND HILL DIVISION	1,332	20	183	1	1,574	14	2	...	...	...	...	...
Cachar	203	6	3	...	71	3	1	...	...	...	...	...
Sylhet	1,061	13	178	...	1,502	6	...	...	...	...	...	...
Khasi and Jaintia Hills (British)	26	...	2	1	...	1	...	...	...	...	...	...
Naga Hills	24	1	...	...	1	5	1	...	...	...	...	...
Lushai Hills	9	...	...	...	...	...	...	...	...	...	...	...
ASSAM VALLEY DIVISION	1,150	76	44	24	448	5	10	...	...	...	...	...
Goalpara	221	19	6	10	77	...	2	...	...	...	...	...
Kamrup	225	10	19	5	191	...	6	...	...	...	...	...
Darrang	104	1	3	2	63	...	2	...	...	...	...	...
Nowgong	44	3	1	...	16	...	...	...	...	...	...	...
Sibsagar	176	22	7	4	30	...	...	...	...	...	...	...
Lakhimpur	352	21	9	3	48	5	...	...	...	...	...	...
Garo Hills	29	...	...	...	16	...	...	...	...	...	...	...
SADIYA FRONTIER TRACT	7	...	...	...	1	...	...	...	...	...	...	...
BALIPARA FRONTIER TRACT	3	...	...	...	...	...	...	...	...	...	...	...
(2) Manipur State	*466*	*30*	*75*	*3*	*134*	*1*	*3*	...	...	...	...	...
(3) Khasi States	*30*	...	...	...	*1*	...	...	...	...	...	...	...

TABLE X.—Occupation or means of livelihood. Part II.—Details for Districts—*contd.*

DISTRICT OR STATE.	Class C.—Public administration and liberal arts. Sub-class VIII.—Professions and liberal arts. Order 49.—Letters, arts and sciences (other than 44). Group (177).—Architects, surveyors, engineers and their employees (not being state servants). Total earners (principal occupation). Males.	Females.	Total working dependants. Males.	Females.	Total following occupation as subsidiary to other. Males.	Females.	Group (178).—Authors, editors, journalists and photographers. Total earners (principal occupation). Males.	Females.	Total working dependants. Males.	Females.	Total following occupation as subsidiary to other. Males.	Females.
	1326	1327	1328	1329	1330	1331	1332	1333	1334	1335	1336	1337
ASSAM	*355*	*1*	*2*	...	*43*	...	*103*	...	*1*	...	*51*	...
(1) British Territory ...	*328*	*1*	*2*	...	*41*	...	*100*	...	...	...	*51*	...
SURMA VALLEY AND HILL DIVISION ...	110	1	...	...	25	...	60	...	...	...	21	...
Cachar ...	16	...	...	...	...	...	23	...	...	...	11	...
Sylhet ...	91	1	...	...	24	...	24	...	...	...	10	...
Khasi and Jaintia Hills (British) ...	...	...	...	...	...	...	6	...	...	...	...	...
Naga Hills ...	1	...	...	...	1	...	...	...	...	...	...	...
Lushai Hills ...	2	...	...	...	...	...	7	...	...	...	...	...
ASSAM VALLEY DIVISION ...	211	...	2	...	16	...	40	...	...	...	30	...
Goalpara ...	31	...	...	...	7	...	4	...	...	...	1	...
Kamrup ...	31	...	...	...	5	...	8	...	...	...	1	...
Darrang ...	20	...	2	...	3	...	6	...	...	...	1	...
Nowgong ...	4	...	...	...	...	...	2	...	...	...	1	...
Sibsagar ...	35	...	...	...	...	...	5	...	...	...	1	...
Lakhimpur ...	80	...	...	...	1	...	15	...	...	...	24	...
Garo Hills ...	10	...	...	...	...	...	...	...	...	...	1	...
SADIYA FRONTIER TRACT ...	5	...	...	...	...	...	...	...	...	...	...	...
BALIPARA FRONTIER TRACT ...	2	...	...	...	...	...	...	...	...	...	...	...
(2) Manipur State ...	*7*	...	...	...	*9*	...	*3*	...	*1*	...	...	...
(3) Khasi States ...	*20*	...	...	...	...	...	...	...	...	...	...	...

TABLE X.—OCCUPATION OR MEANS OF LIVELIHOOD. PART II.—DETAILS FOR DISTRICTS—*contd.*

DISTRICT OR STATE.	Class C.—Public administration and liberal arts.											
	Sub-class VIII.—Professions and liberal arts.											
	Order 49.—Letters, arts and sciences (other than 44).											
	Group (179).—Artists, sculptors, and image-makers.						Group (180).—Scientists (astronomers, botanists, etc.).					
	Total earners (principal occupation).		Total working dependants.		Total following occupation as subsidiary to other.		Total earners (principal occupation).		Total working dependants.		Total following occupation as subsidiary to other.	
	Males.	Females.	Males.	Females.	Males.	Females.	Males.	Females.	Males.	Females.	Males.	Females.
	1338	1339	1340	1341	1342	1343	1344	1345	1346	1347	1348	1349
ASSAM	*109*	*1*	*10*	...	*20*	*1*	*45*	...	...	...	*14*	...
(1) British Territory	*54*	*1*	*9*	...	*19*	*1*	*45*	...	...	...	*14*	...
SURMA VALLEY AND HILL DIVISION	22	1	...	...	13	1	30	...	...	...	14	...
Cachar	...	...	...	...	...	...	2	...	...	...	...	...
Sylhet	21	1	...	...	13	1	27	...	...	...	14	...
Khasi and Jaintia Hills (British)	1	...	...	...	...	...	1	...	...	...	...	...
Naga Hills	...	...	...	...	...	...	...	...	...	...	...	...
Lushai Hills	...	...	...	...	...	...	...	...	...	...	...	...
ASSAM VALLEY DIVISION	32	...	9	...	6	...	14	...	...	...	...	...
Goalpara	3	...	...	...	...	...	2	...	...	...	...	...
Kamrup	20	...	7	...	...	...	...	...	...	...	...	...
Darrang	3	...	...	...	4	...	2	...	...	...	...	...
Nowgong	2	...	...	...	2	...	...	...	...	...	...	...
Sibsagar	3	...	2	...	...	...	4	...	...	...	...	...
Lakhimpur	1	...	...	...	...	...	5	...	...	...	...	...
Garo Hills	...	...	...	...	...	...	1	...	...	...	...	...
SADIYA FRONTIER TRACT	...	...	...	...	...	...	1	...	...	...	...	...
BALIPARA FRONTIER TRACT	...	...	...	...	...	...	...	...	...	...	...	...
(2) Manipur State	*50*	...	*1*	...	*1*	...	...	...	...	...	...	...
(3) Khasi States	*5*	...	...	...	...	...	...	...	...	...	...	...

TABLE X.—OCCUPATION OR MEANS OF LIVELIHOOD. PART II.—DETAILS FOR DISTRICTS—*contd.*

Class C.—Public administration and liberal arts. Sub-class VIII.—Professions and liberal arts. Order 46.—Letters, arts and sciences (other than 44).

DISTRICT OR STATE.	Group (181).—Horoscope casters, astrologers, fortune-tellers, wizards, witches and mediums.						Group (182).—Musicians (composers and performers other than military), actors, dancers, etc.					
	Total earners (principal occupation).		Total working dependants.		Total following occupation as subsidiary to other.		Total earners (principal occupation).		Total working dependants.		Total following occupation as subsidiary to other.	
	Males.	Females.	Males.	Females.	Males.	Females.	Males.	Females.	Males.	Females.	Males.	Females.
	1350	1351	1352	1353	1354	1355	1356	1357	1358	1359	1360	1361
ASSAM	*355*	*2*	*27*	*3*	*198*	*1*	*1,560*	*77*	*259*	*12*	*1,746*	*19*
(1) British Territory	*334*	*2*	*24*	*3*	*186*	*1*	*1,181*	*47*	*189*	*9*	*1,696*	*11*
SURMA VALLEY AND HILL DIVISION	190	...	17	1	84	1	812	6	163	...	1,377	6
Cachar	35	...	...	...	5	...	74	1	3	...	51	2
Sylhet	155	...	17	...	79	...	704	5	160	...	1,336	4
Khasi and Jaintia Hills (British)	...	...	...	1	...	1	13	...	...	...	...	...
Naga Hills	...	...	...	...	...	...	21	...	...	...	...	...
Lushai Hills	...	...	...	...	...	...	...	...	...	...	...	...
ASSAM VALLEY DIVISION	144	2	7	2	102	...	367	41	26	9	248	5
Goalpara	13	...	1	...	2	...	107	4	4	1	40	...
Kamrup	70	2	1	2	57	...	61	5	11	3	124	...
Darrang	15	...	1	...	23	...	...	...	...	...	21	...
Nowgong	5	...	...	...	3	...	6	3	1	...	3	...
Sibsagar	16	...	2	...	9	...	61	13	3	2	22	...
Lakhimpur	31	...	2	...	9	...	119	16	7	3	12	5
Garo Hills	4	...	...	...	...	...	13	...	...	...	15	...
SADIYA FRONTIER TRACT	...	...	...	...	...	...	1	...	...	...	1	...
BALIPARA FRONTIER TRACT	...	...	...	...	...	...	1	...	...	...	...	...
(2) Manipur State	*19*	...	*3*	...	*11*	...	*378*	*30*	*70*	*3*	*190*	*7*
(3) Khasi States	*9*	...	...	...	*1*	...	*1*	...	...	...	...	...

TABLE X.—OCCUPATION OR MEANS OF LIVELIHOOD. PART II.—DETAILS FOR DISTRICTS—*contd.*

DISTRICT OR STATE.	Class C.—Public administration and liberal arts.											
	Sub-class VIII.—Professions and liberal arts.											
	Order 49.—Letters, arts and sciences (other than 44).											
	Group (183).—Managers and employees of places of public entertainments, race courses, societies, clubs.						Group (184).—Conjurors, acrobats, reciters, exhibitors of curiosities and wild animals, etc.					
	Total earners (principal occupation).		Total working dependants.		Total following occupation as subsidiary to other.		Total earners (principal occupation).		Total working dependants.		Total following occupation as subsidiary to other.	
	Males.	Females.	Males.	Females.	Males.	Females.	Males.	Females.	Males.	Females.	Males.	Females.
	1362	1363	1364	1365	1366	1367	1368	1369	1370	1371	1372	1373
ASSAM	*150*	...	*3*	...	*41*	...	*286*	*45*	...	*13*	*45*	*6*
(1) British Territory	*148*	...	*3*	...	*41*	...	*280*	*45*	...	*13*	*45*	*6*
SURMA VALLEY AND HILL DIVISION	21	...	3	...	27	...	75	12	...	...	13	6
Cachar	8	...	...	...	4	...	43	5	...	...	...	...
Sylhet	8	...	1	...	23	...	31	6	...	...	13	1
Khasi and Jaintia Hills (British)	5	...	2	...	...	...	1	...	...	...	...	...
Naga Hills	...	...	...	...	...	...	...	1	...	...	...	5
Lushai Hills	...	...	...	...	...	...	...	...	...	...	...	...
ASSAM VALLEY DIVISION	127	...	...	...	14	...	205	33	...	13	32	...
Goalpara	7	...	...	...	1	...	53	15	...	9	17	...
Kamrup	10	...	...	...	3	...	19	3	...	...	2	...
Darrang	9	...	...	...	...	...	47	1	...	2	11	...
Nowgong	20	...	...	...	4	...	5	...	...	...	...	...
Sibsagar	26	...	...	...	6	...	25	9	...	2	...	...
Lakhimpur	54	...	...	...	...	...	57	5	...	...	2	...
Garo Hills	1	...	...	...	...	...	...	...	...	...	...	...
SADIYA FRONTIER TRACT	...	...	...	...	...	...	...	...	...	...	...	...
BALIPARA FRONTIER TRACT	...	...	...	...	...	...	...	...	...	...	...	...
(2) Manipur State	...	...	...	...	...	...	*6*	...	...	...	...	...
(3) Khasi States	*2*	...	...	...	...	...	...	...	...	...	...	...

TABLE X.—OCCUPATION OR MEANS OF LIVELIHOOD PART II.—DETAILS FOR DISTRICTS—*contd.*

DISTRICT OR STATE.	Class D.—Miscellaneous.											
	Total of Class D.—Miscellaneous.						Sub-class IX.—Persons living on their income. Total of sub-class IX.—Persons living on their income.					
	Total earners (principal occupation).		Total working dependants.		Total following occupation as subsidiary to other.		Total earners (principal occupation).		Total working dependants.		Total following occupation as subsidiary to other.	
	Males.	Females.	Males.	Females.	Males.	Females.	Males.	Females.	Males.	Females.	Males.	Females.
	1374	1375	1376	1377	1378	1379	1380	1381	1382	1383	1384	1385
ASSAM	*63,878*	*25,347*	*7,443*	*6,577*	*17,968*	*3,191*	*1,311*	*171*	*45*	*45*	*669*	*13*
(1) British Territory	*58,737*	*23,180*	*7,037*	*6,116*	*16,197*	*2,054*	*1,141*	*159*	*42*	*44*	*667*	*13*
SURMA VALLEY AND HILL DIVISION	22,430	11,363	2,771	2,759	8,007	1,318	619	71	11	9	200	3
Cachar	4,471	1,353	465	176	1,358	133	74	16	3	...	37	1
Sylhet	13,978	5,631	1,566	805	5,750	707	234	38	8	7	117	2
Khasi and Jaintia Hills (British)	2,981	3,717	309	390	787	436	115	9	...	2	...	...
Naga Hills	630	170	197	189	70	2	94	5	...	...	17	...
Lushai Hills	370	493	334	1,209	132	41	96	3	...	...	30	...
ASSAM VALLEY DIVISION	35,743	11,008	4,239	3,332	7,635	732	496	78	28	35	387	10
Goalpara	6,733	2,308	508	407	2,901	109	79	14	5	2	85	4
Kamrup	8,043	3,896	997	1,083	1,067	196	137	16	9	7	126	4
Darrang	5,123	1,860	515	440	633	60	44	4	...	...	28	...
Nowgong	4,393	930	273	600	761	57	30	1	2	...	27	...
Sibsagar	5,068	1,272	830	448	1,403	103	114	23	8	24	43	...
Lakhimpur	5,955	1,290	701	311	804	193	70	20	4	2	67	2
Garo Hills	530	106	107	27	67	5	22	...	...	...	11	...
SADIYA FRONTIER TRACT	482	194	17	23	257	...	26	3	3	...	76	...
BALIPARA FRONTIER TRACT	82	100	...	2	128	4	...	...	...	...	4	...
(2) Manipur State	*763*	*131*	*178*	*27*	*36*	*5*	*28*	*9*	*3*	...	...	...
(3) Khasi States	*4,378*	*2,097*	*237*	*434*	*1,805*	*1,069*	*149*	*27*	...	*1*	*9*	...

TABLE X.—Occupation or means of livelihood. Part II.—Details for Districts—*contd.*

DISTRICT OR STATE.	Class D.—Miscellaneous. Sub-class IX.—Persons living on their income. Order 50.—Persons living principally on their income. Total of Order 50.—Persons living principally on their income.						Group (185).—Proprietors (other than of agricultural land), fund and scholarship holders and pensioners.					
	Total earners (principal occupation).		Total working dependants.		Total following occupation as subsidiary to other.		Total earners (principal occupation).		Total working dependants.		Total following occupation as subsidiary to other.	
	Males.	Females.	Males.	Females.	Males.	Females.	Males.	Females.	Males.	Females.	Males.	Females.
	1386	1387	1388	1389	1390	1391	1392	1393	1394	1395	1396	1397
ASSAM	*1,311*	*171*	*45*	*45*	*669*	*13*	*1,311*	*171*	*45*	*45*	*669*	*13*
(1) British Territory	*1,141*	*152*	*42*	*44*	*667*	*13*	*1,141*	*152*	*42*	*44*	*667*	*13*
SURMA VALLEY AND HILL DIVISION	619	71	11	9	200	3	619	71	11	9	200	3
Cachar	78	16	3	...	27	1	78	16	3	...	27	1
Sylhet	234	38	8	7	117	2	234	38	8	7	117	2
Khasi and Jaintia Hills (British)...	115	9	...	2	...	...	115	9	...	2	...	...
Naga Hills	94	5	...	...	17	...	94	5	...	...	17	...
Lushai Hills	98	3	...	...	39	...	98	3	...	...	39	...
ASSAM VALLEY DIVISION	496	78	28	35	387	10	496	78	28	35	387	10
Goalpara	79	14	5	3	85	4	79	14	5	3	85	4
Kamrup	137	16	9	7	136	4	137	16	9	7	136	4
Darrang	44	4	...	...	26	...	44	4	...	...	26	...
Nowgong	30	1	2	...	27	...	30	1	2	...	27	...
Sibsagar	114	23	8	24	43	...	114	23	8	24	43	...
Lakhimpur	70	20	4	2	67	2	70	20	4	2	67	2
Garo Hills	22	...	...	...	11	...	22	...	...	...	11	...
SADIYA FRONTIER TRACT	26	3	3	...	76	...	26	3	3	...	76	...
BALIPARA FRONTIER TRACT	...	...	...	...	6	...	...	...	...	...	6	...
(2) Manipur State	*28*	*2*	*3*	...	...	...	*28*	*2*	*3*	...	...	...
(3) Khasi States	*142*	*17*	...	*1*	*2*	...	*142*	*17*	...	*1*	*2*	...

TABLE X.—OCCUPATION OR MEANS OF LIVELIHOOD. PART II.—DETAILS FOR DISTRICTS—*contd.*

DISTRICT OR STATE.	Class D.—Miscellaneous. Sub-class X.—Domestic service. Total of sub-class X.—Domestic service. Total earners (principal occupation). Males.	Females.	Total working dependants. Males.	Females.	Total following occupation as subsidiary to other. Males.	Females.	Order 51.—Domestic service. Total of Order 51.—Domestic service. Total earners (principal occupation). Males.	Females.	Total working dependants. Males.	Females.	Total following occupation as subsidiary to other. Males.	Females.
	1398	1399	1400	1401	1402	1403	1404	1405	1406	1407	1408	1409
ASSAM	*24,161*	*3,604*	*2,358*	*3,614*	*2,293*	*302*	*24,161*	*3,604*	*2,358*	*3,614*	*2,293*	*302*
(1) British Territory	*22,123*	*3,297*	*2,295*	*3,440*	*2,279*	*264*	*22,123*	*3,297*	*2,295*	*3,440*	*2,279*	*264*
SURMA VALLEY AND HILL DIVISION	**6,000**	**1,290**	**698**	**1,716**	**961**	**120**	**6,000**	**1,290**	**698**	**1,716**	**961**	**120**
Cachar	1,313	123	48	101	305	5	1,313	123	48	101	305	5
Sylhet	3,330	650	185	226	567	71	3,330	650	185	226	567	71
Khasi and Jaintia Hills (British)	1,078	127	23	39	20	2	1,078	127	23	39	20	2
Naga Hills	128	37	114	144	3	1	128	37	114	144	3	1
Lushai Hills	151	463	329	1,206	66	41	151	463	329	1,206	66	41
ASSAM VALLEY DIVISION	**15,733**	**1,972**	**1,591**	**1,709**	**1,388**	**144**	**15,733**	**1,972**	**1,591**	**1,709**	**1,388**	**144**
Goalpara	2,532	223	224	246	163	9	2,532	223	224	246	163	9
Kamrup	3,779	365	306	344	273	22	3,779	365	306	344	273	22
Darrang	2,276	400	224	318	116	30	2,276	400	224	318	116	30
Nowgong	1,468	179	142	516	313	22	1,468	179	142	516	313	22
Sibsagar	2,419	315	290	150	288	9	2,419	315	290	150	288	9
Lakhimpur	2,954	394	363	131	226	51	2,954	394	363	131	226	51
Garo Hills	305	17	42	4	9	1	305	17	42	4	9	1
SADIYA FRONTIER TRACT	**230**	**23**	**6**	**15**	**13**	...	**230**	**23**	**6**	**15**	**13**	...
BALIPARA FRONTIER TRACT	**61**	**3**	...	...	**17**	...	**61**	**3**	...	...	**17**	...
(2) Manipur State	*309*	*10*	*12*	*4*	*6*	*2*	*309*	*10*	*12*	*4*	*6*	*2*
(3) Khasi States	*1,729*	*297*	*51*	*170*	*8*	*36*	*1,729*	*297*	*51*	*170*	*8*	*36*

TABLE X.—Occupation or means of livelihood. Part II.—Details for Districts—*contd.*

DISTRICT OR STATE.	Class D.—Miscellaneous. Sub-class X.—Domestic service. Order 51.—Domestic service. Group (186).—Private motor-drivers and cleaners. Total earners (principal occupation). Males.	Females.	Total working dependants. Males.	Females.	Total following occupation as subsidiary to other. Males.	Females.	Group (187).—Other domestic service. Total earners (principal occupation). Males.	Females.	Total working dependants. Males.	Females.	Total following occupation as subsidiary to other. Males.	Females.
	1410	1411	1412	1413	1414	1415	1416	1417	1418	1419	1420	1421
ASSAM	*673*	...	*12*	...	*69*	...	*23,488*	*3,604*	*2,346*	*3,614*	*2,224*	*302*
(1) British Territory	*659*	...	*12*	...	*69*	...	*21,464*	*3,397*	*2,283*	*3,440*	*2,210*	*264*
SURMA VALLEY AND HILL DIVISION	123	...	6	...	12	...	5,976	1,399	692	1,716	849	120
Cachar	23	...	...	...	...	...	1,189	122	47	101	205	5
Sylhet	83	...	5	...	10	...	3,247	650	180	226	557	71
Khasi and Jaintia Hills (British)	8	...	...	...	...	...	1,070	127	23	39	20	2
Naga Hills	8	...	1	...	1	...	320	37	113	144	2	1
Lushai Hills	1	...	...	...	1	...	150	463	329	1,206	65	41
ASSAM VALLEY DIVISION	527	...	6	...	57	...	15,206	1,972	1,585	1,709	1,331	144
Goalpara	41	...	3	...	10	...	2,401	293	221	246	153	8
Kamrup	54	...	1	...	1	...	3,725	365	363	344	273	23
Darrang	143	...	...	...	9	...	2,153	409	224	318	107	30
Nowgong	58	...	...	...	3	...	1,410	179	143	516	310	22
Sibsagar	156	...	1	...	20	...	2,353	318	290	150	266	9
Lakhimpur	71	...	...	...	14	...	2,863	394	303	131	213	51
Garo Hills	4	...	1	...	...	...	301	17	41	4	9	1
SADIYA FRONTIER TRACT	6	...	...	...	...	...	224	23	6	15	13	...
BALIPARA FRONTIER TRACT	3	...	...	...	...	...	58	3	...	...	17	...
(2) Manipur State	*10*	...	...	...	...	...	*299*	*10*	*12*	*4*	*6*	*2*
(3) Khasi States	*4*	...	...	...	...	...	*1,725*	*197*	*51*	*170*	*8*	*36*

TABLE X.—Occupation or means of livelihood. Part II.—Details for Districts—*contd.*

District or State.	Class D.—Miscellaneous.											
	Sub-class XI.—Insufficiently described occupations.											
	Total of sub-class XI.—Insufficiently described occupations.						Order 52.—General terms which do not indicate a definite occupation. Total of Order 52.—General terms, etc.					
	Total earners (principal occupation).		Total working dependants.		Total following occupation as subsidiary to other.		Total earners (principal occupation).		Total working dependants.		Total following occupation as subsidiary to other.	
	Males.	Females.	Males.	Females.	Males.	Females.	Males.	Females.	Males.	Females.	Males.	Females.
	1422	1423	1424	1425	1426	1427	1428	1429	1430	1431	1432	1433
ASSAM	*27,089*	*8,100*	*1,319*	*1,099*	*13,097*	*1,884*	*27,089*	*8,100*	*1,319*	*1,099*	*13,097*	*1,884*
(1) British Territory	*24,255*	*6,368*	*1,139*	*897*	*11,903*	*855*	*24,255*	*6,368*	*1,199*	*897*	*11,903*	*855*
SURMA VALLEY AND HILL DIVISION	10,157	4,490	647	438	5,461	588	10,157	4,490	647	438	5,461	588
Cachar	2,174	376	236	31	1,000	87	2,174	376	236	31	1,000	87
Sylhet	5,901	419	245	63	3,617	96	5,901	419	245	63	3,617	96
Khasi and Jaintia Hills (British)	1,782	3,577	113	239	767	434	1,782	3,577	113	239	767	434
Naga Hills	187	90	54	4	50	1	187	90	54	4	50	1
Lushai Hills	113	19	...	1	27	...	113	19	...	1	27	...
ASSAM VALLEY DIVISION	13,917	1,721	479	382	5,458	263	13,917	1,721	479	382	5,458	263
Goalpara	2,803	260	100	18	2,523	41	2,803	260	100	18	2,523	41
Kamrup	2,417	177	78	17	533	9	2,417	177	78	17	533	9
Darrang...	2,268	450	73	56	477	8	2,268	450	73	56	477	8
Nowgong	2,236	948	20	106	408	29	2,236	948	20	106	408	29
Sibsagar	1,613	165	126	100	1,021	38	1,613	165	126	100	1,021	38
Lakhimpur	2,383	417	70	83	458	136	2,383	417	70	83	458	136
Garo Hills	147	20	4	...	30	2	147	20	4	...	30	2
SADIYA FRONTIER TRACT	104	64	3	6	167	...	104	64	3	6	167	...
BALIPARA FRONTIER TRACT	17	93	...	1	117	4	17	93	...	1	117	4
(2) Manipur State	*338*	*38*	*5*	*10*	*29*	*3*	*338*	*38*	*5*	*10*	*99*	*3*
(3) Khasi States	*2,496*	*1,694*	*178*	*269*	*1,795*	*1,026*	*2,496*	*1,694*	*178*	*269*	*1,795*	*1,026*

TABLE X.—OCCUPATION OR MEANS OF LIVELIHOOD. PART II.—DETAILS FOR DISTRICTS—*contd.*

DISTRICT OR STATE.	Class D.—Miscellaneous. Sub-class XI.—Insufficiently described occupations. Order 53.—General terms which do not indicate a definite occupation.											
	Group (189).—Manufacturers, business men and contractors otherwise unspecified.						Group (190).—Cashiers, accountants, book-keepers, clerks and other employees in unspecified offices and warehouses and shops.					
	Total earners (principal occupation).		Total working dependants.		Total following occupation as subsidiary to other.		Total earners (principal occupation).		Total working dependants.		Total following occupation as subsidiary to other.	
	Males.	Females.	Males.	Females.	Males.	Females.	Males.	Females.	Males.	Females.	Males.	Females.
	1434	1435	1436	1437	1438	1439	1440	1441	1442	1443	1444	1445
ASSAM	*1,973*	*21*	*73*	*1*	*764*	*2*	*4,768*	*65*	*256*	*36*	*919*	*1*
(1) British Territory	*1,787*	*10*	*72*	*1*	*761*	*2*	*4,661*	*56*	*255*	*36*	*919*	*1*
SURMA VALLEY AND HILL DIVISION	841	9	26	...	208	1	2,563	30	115	2	758	...
Cachar	603	4	20	...	126	1	467	20	48	1	68	...
Sylhet	197	5	6	...	71	...	1,991	10	67	1	683	...
Khasi and Jaintia Hills (British)	24	...	...	...	3	...	68	...	...	...	...	...
Naga Hills	3	...	...	...	8	...	15	...	...	...	7	...
Lushai Hills	14	...	...	...	...	...	3	...	...	...	...	...
ASSAM VALLEY DIVISION	929	9	46	1	512	1	2,087	26	140	34	161	1
Goalpara	174	...	6	...	51	...	213	1	33	...	10	...
Kamrup	60	...	1	...	11	...	405	8	45	2	126	1
Darrang	147	2	8	...	63	...	435	2	14	7	5	...
Nowgong	24	...	...	...	16	...	325	9	6	...	5	...
Sibsagar	275	6	5	1	260	1	95	3	29	23	11	...
Lakhimpur	237	1	26	...	102	...	79	3	11	2	3	...
Garo Hills	3	...	...	...	...	...	43	...	2	...	1	...
SADIYA FRONTIER TRACT	17	1	...	...	40	...	12	...	...	...	...	...
BALIPARA FRONTIER TRACT	...	...	...	...	1	...	...	...	...	...	...	...
(2) Manipur State	*114*	...	*1*	...	...	...	*79*	*9*	*1*	...	...	...
(3) Khasi States	*79*	*2*	...	...	*3*	...	*28*	...	...	...	...	...

TABLE X.—OCCUPATION OR MEANS OF LIVELIHOOD. PART II.—DETAILS FOR DISTRICTS—*contd.*

DISTRICT OR STATE.	Class D.—Miscellaneous. Sub-class XI.—Insufficiently described occupations. Order 53.—General terms which do not indicate a definite occupation.											
	Group (190).—Mechanics otherwise unspecified.						Group (191).—Labourers and workmen otherwise unspecified.					
	Total earners (principal occupation).		Total working dependants.		Total following occupation as subsidiary to other.		Total earners (principal occupation).		Total working dependants.		Total following occupation as subsidiary to other.	
	Males.	Females.	Males.	Females.	Males.	Females.	Males.	Females.	Males.	Females.	Males.	Females.
	1446	1447	1448	1449	1450	1451	1452	1453	1454	1455	1456	1457
ASSAM	*965*	...	*21*	...	*29*	...	*20,083*	*8,014*	*969*	*1,069*	*11,315*	*1,881*
(1) British Territory	*905*	...	*21*	...	*29*	...	*17,609*	*6,293*	*781*	*790*	*9,494*	*853*
SURMA VALLEY AND HILL DIVISION	84	...	19	...	21	...	6,670	4,451	487	436	4,674	587
Cachar	73	...	19	...	21	...	1,113	352	149	30	785	56
Sylhet	10	...	...	...	...	...	3,603	404	173	63	3,063	96
Khasi and Jaintia Hills (British)	3	...	...	...	...	...	1,690	3,577	112	339	764	434
Naga Hills	...	...	...	...	...	...	160	90	54	4	35	1
Lushai Hills	...	...	...	...	...	...	96	19	...	1	27	...
ASSAM VALLEY DIVISION	131	...	2	...	8	...	10,780	1,696	291	347	4,777	261
Goalpara	35	...	...	...	1	...	2,451	240	70	18	2,480	41
Kamrup	15	...	...	...	...	...	1,338	160	32	15	396	8
Darrang	9	...	...	...	...	...	1,677	446	50	49	409	8
Nowgong	...	...	...	...	...	...	1,077	233	14	108	387	29
Sibsagar	73	...	3	...	7	...	1,171	156	90	76	734	37
Lakhimpur	...	...	...	...	...	...	2,067	413	33	81	363	136
Garo Hills	...	...	...	...	...	...	99	20	3	...	38	3
SADIYA FRONTIER TRACT	...	...	...	...	...	...	135	63	3	6	127	...
BALIPARA FRONTIER TRACT	...	...	...	...	...	...	17	93	...	1	116	4
(2) Manipur State	*58*	...	...	...	...	...	*87*	*29*	*3*	*10*	*29*	*3*
(3) Khasi States	*2*	...	...	...	...	...	*2,394*	*1,692*	*178*	*269*	*1,792*	*1,026*

TABLE X.—OCCUPATION OR MEANS OF LIVELIHOOD. PART II.—DETAILS FOR DISTRICTS—contd.

DISTRICT OR STATE.	Class D.—Miscellaneous. Sub-class XII.—Unproductive. Total of sub-class XII.—Unproductive.						Order 53.—Inmates of jails, asylums and alms houses. Total of Order 53.—Inmates of jails, etc.					
	Total earners (principal occupation).		Total working dependants.		Total following occupation as subsidiary to other.		Total earners (principal occupation).		Total working dependants.		Total following occupation as subsidiary to other.	
	Males.	Females.	Males.	Females.	Males.	Females.	Males.	Females.	Males.	Females.	Males.	Females.
	1458	1459	1460	1461	1462	1463	1464	1465	1466	1467	1468	1469
ASSAM	*11,617*	*13,472*	*3,727*	*1,919*	*1,979*	*922*	...	...	*3,075*	*41*	...	...
(1) British Territory	*11,518*	*13,372*	*3,561*	*1,885*	*1,978*	*922*	...	...	*2,930*	*41*	...	...
SURMA VALLEY AND HILL DIVISION	5,555	5,503	1,415	596	1,575	607	...	...	1,134	4	...	...
Cachar	1,007	837	179	44	135	69	...	...	123	1	...	...
Sylhet	4,513	4,624	1,133	509	1,440	538	...	...	912	1	...	...
Khasi and Jaintia Hills (British)	6	4	75	...	...	...	...	...	73	...	...	...
Naga Hills	21	29	20	41	...	...	...	...	21	2	...	...
Lushai Hills	8	9	5	2	...	...	...	...	5	...	...	...
ASSAM VALLEY DIVISION	5,897	7,831	2,141	1,286	402	315	...	...	1,798	37	...	...
Goalpara	1,278	1,751	170	141	131	55	...	...	116	1	...	...
Kamrup	1,710	3,038	604	685	135	161	...	...	455	1	...	...
Darrang	834	997	519	72	11	31	...	...	490	10	...	...
Nowgong	579	808	108	96	13	6	...	...	96	5	...	...
Sibsagar	922	719	415	174	51	56	...	...	352	10	...	...
Lakhimpur	518	449	264	95	53	4	...	...	226	7	...	...
Garo Hills	56	69	61	23	8	2	...	...	63	3	...	...
SADIYA FRONTIER TRACT	63	34	5	2	1	...	...	...	...	...	...	...
BALIPARA FRONTIER TRACT	4	4	...	1	...	...	...	...	...	...	...	...
(2) Manipur State	*88*	*81*	*158*	*13*	*1*	...	...	...	*140*	...	...	...
(3) Khasi States	*11*	*19*	*8*	*2*	...	...	...	...	*5*	...	...	...

TABLE X.—OCCUPATION OR MEANS OF LIVELIHOOD. PART II.—DETAILS FOR DISTRICTS—*contd.*

DISTRICT OR STATE.	Class D.—Miscellaneous. Sub-class XII.—Unproductive. Order 53.—Inmates of jails, asylums and alms houses. Group (191).—Inmates of jails, asylums and alms houses. Total earners (principal occupation).		Total working dependants.		* *Total non-working dependants*		Order 54.—Beggars, vagrants; prostitutes. Total of Order 54.—Beggars, vagrants, etc. Total earners (principal occupation).		Total working dependants.		Total following occupation as subsidiary to other.	
	Males.	Females.	Males.	Females.	Males.	Females.	Males.	Females.	Males.	Females.	Males.	Females.
	1470	1471	1472	1473	1474	1475	1476	1477	1478	1479	1480	1481
ASSAM	...	...	*3,075*	*41*	*527*	*122*	*11,319*	*13,472*	*659*	*1,778*	*1,966*	*999*
(1) British Territory	...	...	*2,930*	*41*	*527*	*122*	*11,213*	*13,372*	*631*	*1,764*	*1,965*	*999*
SURMA VALLEY AND HILL DIVISION	...	...	1,134	4	80	19	5,555	5,503	281	592	1,563	607
Cachar	...	...	123	1	...	...	1,007	837	55	43	126	69
Sylhet	...	...	912	1	67	7	4,513	4,624	216	508	1,437	538
Khasi and Jaintia Hills (British)	...	...	73	...	...	...	6	4	2	...	...	...
Naga Hills	...	...	21	2	13	12	21	29	8	39	...	...
Lushai Hills	...	...	5	...	...	...	8	9	...	2	...	...
ASSAM VALLEY DIVISION	...	...	1,796	37	447	103	5,594	7,831	345	1,169	401	315
Goalpara	...	...	116	1	...	...	1,278	1,751	84	140	131	55
Kamrup	...	...	455	1	...	...	1,705	3,338	140	664	134	161
Darrang	...	...	400	10	447	103	533	907	20	62	11	31
Nowgong	...	...	96	5	...	...	679	608	12	31	13	4
Sibsagar	...	...	353	10	...	...	923	719	63	104	51	56
Lakhimpur	...	...	326	7	...	...	518	440	38	88	63	4
Garo Hills	...	...	52	3	...	...	56	69	9	20	8	2
SADIYA FRONTIER TRACT	...	...	...	...	...	...	63	34	5	2	1	...
BALIPARA FRONTIER TRACT	...	...	...	...	...	...	4	4	...	1	...	...
(2) Manipur State	...	...	*140*	...	...	...	*86*	*81*	*18*	*13*	*1*	...
(3) Khasi States	...	...	*5*	...	...	...	*11*	*19*	*3*	*1*	...	...

* This column has been introduced to show the inmates of lunatic and leper asylums as such persons are neither earners nor working dependants. The column "Total following occupation as subsidiary to other" is blank for this group.

TABLE X.—Occupation or means of livelihood. Part II.—Details for Districts—contd.

Class D.—Miscellaneous. Sub-class XII.—Unproductive. Order 54.—Beggars, vagrants, prostitutes.

District or State.	Group (193).—Beggars and vagrants. Total earners (principal occupation). Males.	Females.	Total working dependants. Males.	Females.	Total following occupation as subsidiary to other. Males.	Females.	Group (194).—Procurers and prostitutes. Total earners (principal occupation). Males.	Females.	Total working dependants. Males.	Females.	Total following occupation as subsidiary to other. Males.	Females.
	1483	1483	1484	1485	1486	1487	1488	1489	1490	1491	1492	1493
ASSAM	*11,319*	*19,933*	*659*	*1,777*	*1,966*	*919*	...	*539*	...	*1*	...	*3*
(1) British Territory	*11,215*	*19,833*	*631*	*1,763*	*1,965*	*919*	...	*539*	...	*1*	...	*3*
SURMA VALLEY AND HILL DIVISION	5,555	5,319	231	588	1,563	604	...	184	...	...	...	3
Cachar	1,007	806	55	43	126	69	...	29	...	...	...	...
Sylhet	4,513	4,409	216	508	1,437	535	...	155	...	...	...	3
Khasi and Jaintia Hills (British)	6	4	2	...	...	...	...	...	...	...	...	...
Naga Hills	21	29	8	30	...	...	...	...	...	...	...	...
Lushai Hills	8	9	...	7	...	...	...	...	...	...	...	...
ASSAM VALLEY DIVISION	5,504	7,476	345	1,168	401	315	...	355	...	1	...	...
Goalpara	1,278	1,533	54	140	131	55	...	229	...	...	...	...
Kamrup	1,708	3,334	140	603	134	161	...	104	...	1	...	...
Darrang	633	994	30	62	11	31	...	3	...	...	...	...
Nowgong	579	608	13	81	13	6	...	...	...	...	...	...
Sibsagar	972	719	63	164	51	56	...	...	...	...	...	...
Lakhimpur	518	448	36	98	53	4	...	1	...	...	...	...
Garo Hills	56	51	9	20	8	2	...	18	...	...	...	...
SADIYA FRONTIER TRACT	63	34	5	9	1	...	...	...	...	...	...	...
BALIPARA FRONTIER TRACT	4	6	...	1	...	...	...	...	...	...	...	...
(2) Manipur State	*86*	*81*	*18*	*13*	*1*	...	...	...	...	...	...	...
(3) Khasi States	*11*	*19*	*3*	*1*	...	...	...	...	...	...	...	...

TABLE X.—OCCUPATION OR MEANS OF LIVELIHOOD. PART II.—DETAILS FOR DISTRICTS—*concld.*

DISTRICT OR STATE.	Class D.—Miscellaneous. Sub-class XII.—Unproductive. Order 56.—Other unclassified non-productive industries.											
	Total of Order 55.—Other unclassified non-productive industries.						Group (196).—Other unclassified non-productive industries.					
	Total earners (principal occupation).		Total working dependants.		Total following occupation as subsidiary to other.		Total earners (principal occupation).		Total working dependants.		Total following occupation as subsidiary to other.	
	Males.	Females.	Males.	Females.	Males.	Females.	Males.	Females.	Males.	Females.	Males.	Females.
	1494	1495	1496	1497	1498	1499	1500	1501	1502	1503	1504	1505
ASSAM	5	...	...	...	13	...	5	...	...	...	13	...
(1) British Territory	3	...	...	...	13	...	3	...	...	...	13	...
SURMA VALLEY AND HILL DIVISION	...	...	...	...	12		...	...	...	...	12	...
Cachar	...	...	...	...	...	...	...	...	...	...	...	...
Sylhet	...	...	...	...	12	...	...	...	...	...	12	...
Khasi and Jaintia Hills (British)	...	...	...	...	...	...	...	...	...	...	...	...
Naga Hills	...	...	...	...	...	...	...	...	...	...	...	...
Lushai Hills	...	...	...	...	...	...	...	...	...	...	...	...
ASSAM VALLEY DIVISION	3	...	...	...	1	...	3	...	...	...	1	...
Goalpara	...	...	...	...	...	...	...	...	...	...	...	...
Kamrup	2	...	...	...	1	...	2	...	...	...	1	...
Darrang	1	...	...	...	...	...	1	...	...	...	...	...
Nowgong	...	...	...	...	...	...	...	...	...	...	...	...
Sibsagar	...	...	...	...	...	...	...	...	...	...	...	...
Lakhimpur	...	...	...	...	...	...	...	...	...	...	...	...
Garo Hills	...	...	...	...	...	...	...	...	...	...	...	...
SADIYA FRONTIER TRACT	...	...	...	...	...	...	...	...	...	...	...	...
BALIPARA FRONTIER TRACT	...	...	...	...	...	...	...	...	...	...	...	...
(2) Manipur State	2	...	...	...	...	...	2	...	...	...	...	...
(3) Khasi States	...	...	...	...	...	...	...	...	...	...	...	...

TABLE XIII.

LITERACY BY RELIGION AND AGE.

1. Part I of this table gives the statistics for the Province as a whole under each religion and age group and Part II gives similar information for each district and for the Manipur and Khasi States.

2. The figures of Christians given in the table include Christians of all races and nationalities. The following statement shows the extent of literacy among Indian Christians and Christians who are not Indians :—

RACE.	Population.											
	Total.			Literate.			Illiterate.			Literate in English.		
	Persons.	Males.	Females.	Persons.	Males.	Females.	Persons.	Males.	Females.	Persons.	Males.	Females.
1	2	3	4	5	6	7	8	9	10	11	12	13
TOTAL CHRISTIANS ...	***249,246***	***124,045***	***125,201***	***40,376***	***28,563***	***11,813***	***208,870***	***95,482***	***113,388***	***8,677***	***6,586***	***2,091***
(1) Indian Christians ...	245,191	121,264	123,927	36,788	26,030	10,758	208,403	95,234	113,169	5,111	4,072	1,039
(2) Other Christians ...	4,055	2,781	1,274	3,588	2,533	1,055	467	248	219	3,566	2,514	1,052

TABLE XIII.—Literacy by religion and age. Part I.—Provincial Summary.

Religion and Age.	Population. Total. Persons	Total. Males.	Total. Females.	Literate. Persons.	Literate. Males.	Literate. Females.	Illiterate. Persons.	Illiterate. Males.	Illiterate. Females.	Literate in English. Persons.	Literate in English. Males.	Literate in English. Females.
1	2	3	4	5	6	7	8	9	10	11	12	13
ALL RELIGIONS ...	*9,947,857*	*4,844,133*	*4,403,794*	*697,498*	*616,365*	*81,133*	*8,550,359*	*4,297,768*	*4,322,591*	*94,835*	*89,389*	*5,446*
0—5 ...	1,596,177	789,069	807,108	...	...	...	1,596,177	789,069	807,108	...	...	...
5—10 ...	1,249,517	653,574	595,943	51,900	41,072	10,818	1,197,537	612,502	585,095	2,978	2,477	501
10—15 ...	1,056,778	555,928	500,846	77,733	62,749	14,984	979,045	493,173	485,872	7,416	6,509	907
15—20 ...	850,665	403,581	447,084	91,083	76,189	14,894	759,582	327,392	432,190	15,052	13,952	1,100
20 and over ...	4,494,720	2,441,987	2,052,733	476,692	436,355	40,337	4,018,028	2,005,632	2,012,396	69,389	66,451	2,938
HINDU (OTHER THAN BRAHMO AND ARYA) ...	*5,204,190*	*2,751,414*	*2,452,776*	*482,090*	*431,954*	*50,136*	*4,722,100*	*2,319,460*	*2,402,640*	*67,760*	*65,148*	*2,621*
0—5 ...	865,710	429,545	436,165	...	...	...	865,710	429,545	436,165	...	...	...
5—10 ...	674,390	351,409	322,981	35,085	28,270	6,815	639,305	323,139	316,166	2,031	1,707	324
10—15 ...	568,861	299,131	269,730	52,453	43,082	9,371	516,408	256,049	260,359	5,208	4,625	583
15—20 ...	464,347	226,071	238,276	61,740	52,899	8,841	402,607	173,172	229,435	10,848	10,235	613
20 and over ...	2,630,582	1,445,258	1,185,324	332,812	307,703	25,109	2,298,070	1,137,555	1,160,515	49,682	48,581	1,101
HINDU (BRAHMO) ...	*448*	*239*	*216*	*255*	*140*	*115*	*193*	*99*	*101*	*165*	*90*	*75*
0—5 ...	80	41	39	...	...	...	80	41	39	...	...	...
5—10 ...	54	31	23	25	15	10	29	16	13	7	5	2
10—15 ...	45	23	22	34	18	16	11	5	6	17	9	8
15—20 ...	38	17	21	30	13	17	8	4	4	20	9	11
20 and over ...	231	120	111	166	94	72	65	26	39	121	67	54
HINDU (ARYA) ...	*12*	*11*	*1*	*9*	*8*	*1*	*3*	*3*	...	*7*	*6*	*1*
0—5 ...	1	1	...	...	...	...	1	1	...	...	...	...
5—10 ...	...	...	...	...	...	...	...	...	...	...	...	...
10—15 ...	1	1	...	1	1	...	...	...	...	...	...	...
15—20 ...	1	...	1	1	...	1	...	...	...	1	...	1
20 and over ...	9	9	...	7	7	...	2	2	...	6	6	...
SIKH ...	*2,799*	*1,918*	*811*	*940*	*871*	*69*	*1,789*	*1,047*	*742*	*137*	*134*	*3*
0—5 ...	341	142	199	...	...	...	341	142	199	...	...	...
5—10 ...	201	111	90	20	18	2	181	93	88	2	1	1
10—15 ...	158	108	50	34	29	5	124	79	45	5	4	1
15—20 ...	287	188	99	114	95	19	173	93	80	18	18	...
20 and over ...	1,742	1,369	373	772	729	43	970	640	330	112	111	1
JAIN ...	*2,803*	*2,116*	*687*	*1,459*	*1,429*	*30*	*1,344*	*687*	*657*	*72*	*69*	*3*
0—5 ...	249	130	119	...	...	...	249	130	119	...	...	...
5—10 ...	242	153	89	48	47	1	194	106	88	2	2	...
10—15 ...	278	201	77	104	100	4	174	101	73	5	5	...
—20 ...	370	281	89	236	227	9	134	54	80	15	14	1
20 and over ...	1,664	1,361	303	1,071	1,055	16	593	306	287	50	48	2
BUDDHIST ...	*15,045*	*8,629*	*6,423*	*1,550*	*1,507*	*43*	*13,495*	*7,115*	*6,380*	*127*	*124*	*3*
0—5 ...	2,208	1,122	1,086	...	...	...	2,208	1,122	1,086	...	...	...
5—10 ...	1,650	872	778	54	51	3	1,596	821	775	2	2	...
10—15 ...	1,472	780	692	92	89	3	1,380	691	689	4	3	1
15—20 ...	1,418	754	664	173	164	9	1,245	590	655	16	15	1
20 and over ...	8,297	5,094	3,203	1,231	1,203	28	7,066	3,891	3,175	105	104	1

TABLE XIII.—LITERACY BY RELIGION AND AGE. PART I—PROVINCIAL SUMMARY.

RELIGION AND AGE.	POPULATION. Total. Persons.	Total. Males.	Total. Females.	Literate. Persons.	Literate. Males.	Literate. Females.	Illiterate. Persons.	Illiterate. Males.	Illiterate. Females.	LITERATE IN ENGLISH. Persons.	Males.	Females.
1	2	3	4	5	6	7	8	9	10	11	12	13
ZOROASTRIAN (PARSI)	*9*	*7*	*2*	*9*	*7*	*2*	...	...	...	*9*	*7*	*2*
0—5	...	...	...	...	...	...	...	...	...	...	...	...
5—10	1	...	1	1	...	1	...	...	...	1	...	1
10—15	...	...	...	...	...	...	...	...	...	...	...	...
15—20	1	1	...	1	1	...	...	...	...	1	1	...
20 and over	7	6	1	7	6	1	...	...	...	7	6	1
MUSLIM	*2,780,514*	*1,461,769*	*1,318,759*	*156,650*	*139,290*	*17,360*	*2,623,864*	*1,322,479*	*1,301,392*	*16,897*	*16,309*	*588*
0—5	499,633	245,617	254,016	...	...	...	499,633	245,617	254,016	...	...	...
5—10	405,758	216,128	189,630	13,664	10,618	3,046	392,094	206,510	185,584	659	592	67
10—15	325,938	164,848	161,090	19,290	15,578	3,712	326,648	169,270	157,378	1,566	1,441	125
15—20	272,957	125,689	147,368	19,939	16,723	3,216	253,018	108,964	144,152	2,794	2,647	147
20 and over	1,256,228	689,580	666,048	103,757	96,371	7,386	1,152,471	583,209	569,262	11,878	11,639	239
CHRISTIAN	*249,246*	*124,045*	*125,201*	*40,376*	*28,563*	*11,813*	*208,870*	*95,482*	*113,388*	*8,677*	*6,586*	*2,091*
0—5	42,376	20,990	21,386	...	...	...	42,376	20,990	21,386	...	...	...
5—10	34,576	17,426	17,150	2,330	1,452	878	32,246	15,974	16,273	251	151	100
10—15	30,973	15,666	15,307	4,412	2,774	1,638	26,561	12,892	13,669	543	363	180
15—20	25,125	11,557	13,568	6,699	4,228	2,471	18,426	7,329	11,097	1,173	860	313
20 and over	116,196	58,406	57,790	26,935	20,109	6,836	89,261	38,297	50,964	6,710	5,212	1,498
JEW	*18*	*11*	*7*	*11*	*8*	*3*	*7*	*3*	*4*	*9*	*6*	*3*
0—5	5	2	3	...	...	...	5	2	3	...	...	...
5—10	2	1	1	1	...	1	1	1	...	1	...	1
10—15	2	1	1	1	1	...	1	...	1	...	...	...
15—20	3	3	...	3	3	...	...	...	...	2	2	...
20 and over	6	4	2	6	4	2	...	...	...	6	4	2
TRIBAL	*992,390*	*493,755*	*498,635*	*14,094*	*12,538*	*1,556*	*978,296*	*481,217*	*497,079*	*956*	*900*	*56*
0—5	185,517	91,467	94,050	...	...	...	185,517	91,467	94,050	...	...	...
5—10	132,624	67,434	65,190	761	600	161	131,863	66,834	65,029	22	17	5
10—15	109,025	55,153	53,872	1,312	1,077	235	107,713	54,076	53,637	68	59	9
15—20	86,077	40,102	45,975	2,143	1,833	310	83,935	37,270	44,665	163	150	13
20 and over	479,147	240,599	238,548	9,879	9,029	850	469,268	231,570	237,698	703	674	29
INDEFINITE BELIEF	*390*	*187*	*203*	*27*	*22*	*5*	*363*	*165*	*198*	*7*	*7*	...
0—5	50	18	32	...	...	...	50	18	32	...	...	...
5—10	17	8	9	1	1	...	16	7	9	...	...	...
10—15	24	10	14	...	...	...	24	10	14	...	...	...
15—20	37	15	22	4	3	1	33	12	21	1	1	...
20 and over	262	136	126	22	18	4	240	118	122	6	6	...
CONFUCIAN	*63*	*53*	*10*	*28*	*28*	...	*35*	*25*	*10*	*3*	*3*	...
0—5	7	4	3	...	...	...	7	4	3	...	...	...
5—10	2	1	1	...	...	...	2	1	1	...	...	...
10—15	1	...	1	...	...	...	1	...	1	...	...	...
15—20	4	3	1	1	1	...	3	2	1	...	...	...
20 and over	49	45	4	27	27	...	22	18	4	3	3	...

TABLE XIII.—LITERACY BY RELIGION AND AGE. PART II—DETAILS FOR DISTRICTS.

District.	Age.	Population: Total: Persons.	Total: Males.	Total: Females.	Literate: Persons.	Literate: Males.	Literate: Females.	Illiterate: Persons.	Illiterate: Males.	Illiterate: Females.	Literate in English: Persons.	Literate in English: Males.	Literate in English: Females.
	1	2	3	4	5	6	7	8	9	10	11	12	13
CACHAR.	ALL RELIGIONS	*570,531*	*301,338*	*269,193*	*51,692*	*46,271*	*5,421*	*518,839*	*255,067*	*263,772*	*6,316*	*5,960*	*356*
	0—5	94,768	46,980	47,788	...	...	...	94,768	46,980	47,788	...	...	...
	5—10	76,003	40,008	35,995	3,556	2,781	775	72,447	37,227	35,220	195	163	32
	10—15	64,881	34,268	30,553	5,297	4,265	1,032	59,584	30,003	29,531	486	427	59
	15—20	53,501	25,287	28,214	6,394	5,415	979	47,107	19,872	27,235	935	863	72
	20 and over	281,428	154,795	126,643	36,445	33,810	2,635	244,983	120,985	124,008	4,700	4,507	193
	HINDU	*350,238*	*189,906*	*169,332*	*37,989*	*33,524*	*4,465*	*321,249*	*156,382*	*164,867*	*4,765*	*4,559*	*206*
	0—5	55,393	27,503	27,890	...	...	...	55,393	27,503	27,890	...	...	...
	5—10	44,892	23,457	21,435	2,561	1,919	642	42,331	21,538	20,793	148	122	26
	10—15	39,132	20,450	18,682	3,832	2,968	864	35,300	17,482	17,818	380	335	45
	15—20	33,263	15,982	17,281	4,756	3,956	800	28,507	12,026	16,481	731	682	49
	20 and over	186,558	102,514	84,044	26,840	24,081	2,159	159,718	77,833	81,885	3,506	3,430	56
	MUSLIM	*196,196*	*103,718*	*92,478*	*12,732*	*12,009*	*723*	*183,464*	*91,709*	*91,755*	*1,039*	*1,031*	*8*
	0—5	36,506	18,071	18,435	...	...	...	36,506	18,071	18,435	...	...	...
	5—10	29,214	15,555	13,659	971	845	126	28,243	14,710	13,533	41	39	2
	10—15	24,174	13,039	11,135	1,406	1,263	143	22,768	11,776	10,992	83	81	2
	15—20	18,823	8,680	10,143	1,508	1,376	132	17,315	7,304	10,011	145	143	2
	20 and over	87,479	48,373	39,106	8,847	8,525	322	78,632	39,848	38,784	760	758	2
	TRIBAL	*10,319*	*5,160*	*5,159*	*50*	*48*	*2*	*10,269*	*5,112*	*5,157*	*7*	*7*	...
	0—5	2,108	1,039	1,069	...	...	...	2,108	1,039	1,069	...	...	...
	5—10	1,332	703	629	...	...	...	1,332	703	629	...	...	...
	10—15	1,032	529	503	1	1	...	1,031	528	503	...	...	...
	15—20	927	391	536	4	4	...	923	387	536	...	...	...
	20 and over	4,920	2,498	2,422	45	43	2	4,875	2,455	2,420	7	7	...
SYLHET.	ALL RELIGIONS	*2,724,349*	*1,407,648*	*1,316,697*	*252,626*	*215,848*	*36,778*	*2,471,716*	*1,191,797*	*1,279,919*	*29,315*	*27,885*	*1,430*
	0—5	426,731	208,346	218,385	...	...	...	426,731	208,346	218,385	...	...	...
	5—10	368,340	194,862	173,478	22,146	16,677	5,469	346,194	178,185	168,009	1,026	879	147
	10—15	323,229	172,300	150,929	31,420	24,266	7,154	291,809	148,034	143,775	2,601	2,226	375
	15—20	265,096	122,046	143,050	32,394	25,875	6,519	232,702	96,171	136,531	4,991	4,664	327
	20 and over	1,340,946	710,091	630,855	166,666	149,030	17,636	1,174,280	561,061	613,219	20,697	20,016	681
	HINDU	*1,113,354*	*575,624*	*537,730*	*157,423*	*133,600*	*23,823*	*955,931*	*442,094*	*513,907*	*20,076*	*19,254*	*822*
	0—5	151,880	74,363	77,517	...	...	...	151,880	74,363	77,517	...	...	...
	5—10	132,895	69,625	63,270	13,085	9,880	3,205	119,810	59,745	60,065	625	528	97
	10—15	119,417	63,063	56,355	18,789	14,352	4,437	100,628	48,710	51,918	1,648	1,465	183
	15—20	105,650	50,013	55,637	19,993	15,837	4,156	85,657	34,176	51,481	3,362	3,167	196
	20 and over	603,512	318,561	284,951	105,556	93,531	12,025	497,956	225,030	272,926	14,441	14,094	347
	MUSLIM	*1,603,805*	*828,123*	*775,682*	*93,988*	*81,337*	*12,651*	*1,509,817*	*746,786*	*763,031*	*8,595*	*8,190*	*405*
	0—5	273,646	133,380	140,266	...	...	...	273,646	133,380	140,266	...	...	...
	5—10	234,602	124,792	109,810	9,014	6,765	2,249	225,588	118,027	107,561	389	344	45
	10—15	203,135	108,885	94,250	12,560	9,869	2,691	190,575	99,016	91,559	929	848	81
	15—20	158,786	71,709	87,077	12,258	9,940	2,318	146,528	61,769	84,759	1,559	1,463	106
	20 and over	733,636	389,357	344,279	60,156	54,763	5,393	673,480	334,594	338,886	5,648	5,475	173

TABLE XIII.—LITERACY BY RELIGION AND AGE. PART II—DETAILS FOR DISTRICTS.

District.	Age.	Population. Total. Persons.	Total. Males.	Total. Females.	Literate. Persons.	Literate. Males.	Literate. Females.	Illiterate. Persons.	Illiterate. Males.	Illiterate. Females.	Literate in English. Persons.	Literate in English. Males.	Literate in English. Females.
	1	2	3	4	5	6	7	8	9	10	11	12	13
KHASI AND JAINTIA HILLS (BRITISH).	ALL RELIGIONS ...	*109,926*	*55,439*	*54,487*	*10,106*	*7,355*	*2,751*	*99,820*	*48,084*	*51,736*	*1,734*	*1,398*	*336*
	0—5 ...	19,819	9,669	10,150	...	...	...	19,819	9,669	10,150	...	...	...
	5—10 ...	13,594	6,853	6,741	518	297	221	13,076	6,556	6,520	85	63	22
	10—15 ...	11,983	6,105	5,878	890	505	385	11,093	5,600	5,493	150	100	50
	15—20 ...	11,225	5,500	5,725	1,661	1,086	575	9,564	4,414	5,150	215	166	49
	20 and over	53,305	27,312	25,993	7,037	5,467	1,570	46,268	21,845	24,423	1,284	1,079	205
	TRIBAL ...	*74,768*	*36,032*	*38,736*	*1,202*	*948*	*254*	*73,566*	*35,084*	*38,482*	*75*	*66*	*9*
	0—5 ...	14,355	6,968	7,387	...	...	...	14,355	6,968	7,387	...	...	...
	5—10 ...	9,582	4,795	4,787	56	35	21	9,526	4,760	4,766	3	2	1
	10—15 ...	8,258	4,177	4,081	109	70	39	8,149	4,107	4,042	7	6	1
	15—20 ...	7,163	3,258	3,905	200	140	60	6,963	3,118	3,845	14	12	2
	20 and over	35,410	16,834	18,576	837	703	134	34,573	16,131	18,442	51	46	5
	CHRISTIAN ...	*23,314*	*11,207*	*12,107*	*4,760*	*2,769*	*1,991*	*18,554*	*8,438*	*10,116*	*698*	*463*	*235*
	0—5 ...	3,923	1,924	1,999	...	...	...	3,923	1,924	1,999	...	...	...
	5—10 ...	3,142	1,583	1,559	271	136	135	2,871	1,447	1,424	33	16	17
	10—15 ...	2,915	1,461	1,454	513	250	263	2,402	1,211	1,191	46	21	25
	15—20 ...	2,418	1,080	1,338	808	385	423	1,610	695	915	69	42	27
	20 and over	10,916	5,159	5,757	3,168	1,998	1,170	7,748	3,161	4,587	550	384	166
NAGA HILLS.	ALL RELIGIONS ...	*178,844*	*89,536*	*89,308*	*3,310*	*2,920*	*390*	*175,534*	*86,616*	*88,918*	*530*	*490*	*40*
	0—5 ...	27,386	13,459	13,927	...	...	...	27,386	13,459	13,927	...	...	...
	5—10 ...	24,013	12,100	11,913	202	164	38	23,811	11,936	11,875	10	6	4
	10—15 ...	20,867	10,651	10,216	335	277	58	20,532	10,374	10,158	18	15	3
	15—20 ...	14,444	7,215	7,229	517	431	86	13,927	6,784	7,143	57	49	8
	20 and over	92,134	46,111	46,023	2,256	2,048	208	89,878	44,063	45,815	445	420	25
	TRIBAL ...	*148,289*	*73,182*	*75,107*	*675*	*650*	*25*	*147,614*	*72,532*	*75,082*	*78*	*77*	*1*
	0—5 ...	23,292	11,410	11,882	...	...	...	23,292	11,410	11,882	...	...	...
	5—10 ...	20,174	10,173	10,001	63	59	4	20,111	10,114	9,997	1	1	...
	10—15 ...	17,379	8,876	8,503	106	102	4	17,273	8,774	8,499	4	4	...
	15—20 ...	11,673	5,706	5,967	120	117	3	11,553	5,589	5,964	11	10	1
	20 and over	75,771	37,017	38,754	386	372	14	75,385	36,645	38,740	62	62	...
	CHRISTIANS ...	*22,908*	*11,324*	*11,584*	*1,080*	*815*	*265*	*21,828*	*10,509*	*11,319*	*210*	*180*	*30*
	0—5 ...	3,106	1,548	1,558	...	...	...	3,106	1,548	1,558	...	...	...
	5—10 ...	3,135	1,559	1,576	85	63	22	3,050	1,496	1,554	5	3	2
	10—15 ...	2,871	1,447	1,424	143	103	40	2,728	1,344	1,384	9	8	1
	15—20 ...	1,968	997	971	201	135	66	1,767	862	905	27	21	6
	20 and over	11,828	5,773	6,055	651	514	137	11,177	5,259	5,918	169	148	21

TABLE XIII.—Literacy by religion and age. Part II—Details for Districts.

District.	Age.	Population. Total. Persons.	Total. Males.	Total. Females.	Literate. Persons.	Literate. Males.	Literate. Females.	Illiterate. Persons.	Illiterate. Males.	Illiterate. Females.	Literate in English. Persons.	Literate in English. Males.	Literate in English. Females.
	1	2	3	4	5	6	7	8	9	10	11	12	13
LUSHAI HILLS.	ALL RELIGIONS	*124,404*	*59,186*	*65,218*	*13,390*	*11,783*	*1,537*	*111,084*	*47,403*	*63,681*	*847*	*776*	*71*
	0—5	21,374	10,401	10,973	...	...	...	21,374	10,401	10,973	...	...	...
	5—10	17,020	8,378	8,642	429	354	75	16,591	8,024	8,567	10	7	3
	10—15	14 652	7,285	7,367	1,034	865	169	13 618	6,420	7,198	38	32	6
	15—20	11 975	5,505	6,470	2 267	1,883	385	9,708	3,623	6,085	165	147	18
	20 and over	59,383	27,617	31,766	9,590	8,683	908	49,793	18,935	30,858	634	600	44
	TRIBAL	*60,155*	*29,513*	*30,642*	*3,375*	*3,278*	*97*	*56,780*	*26,235*	*30,545*	*79*	*78*	*1*
	0—5	10,053	4,881	5,172	...	...	...	10,053	4,881	5,172	...	...	...
	5—10	7,301	3,706	3,595	32	30	2	7 269	3,676	3,593	...	...	...
	10—15	5,905	3,108	2,797	135	131	4	5,770	2,977	2,793	1	1	...
	15—20	5 084	2,561	2,523	547	528	19	4,537	2,033	2,504	15	14	1
	20 and over	31,812	15,257	16,555	2,661	2,589	72	29,151	12,668	16,483	63	63	...
	CHRISTIAN	*59,193*	*26,676*	*32,447*	*9,113*	*7,739*	*1,374*	*50,010*	*18,937*	*31,073*	*671*	*609*	*62*
	0—5	10,447	5,092	5,355	...	...	...	10,447	5,092	5,355	...	...	...
	5—10	9,085	4,345	4,740	369	307	62	8 716	4,038	4,678	6	4	2
	10—15	8,222	3,913	4,309	858	705	153	7,364	3,208	4,156	32	27	5
	15—20	6,354	2,641	3,713	1,602	1,251	351	4,752	1,390	3,362	137	132	15
	20 and over	25,015	10,685	14,330	6,284	5,476	808	18,731	5,209	13,522	496	456	40
GOALPARA.	ALL RELIGIONS	*882,748*	*470,273*	*412,475*	*55,044*	*50,285*	*4,759*	*827,704*	*419,988*	*407,716*	*6,369*	*6,024*	*345*
	0—5	160,810	79,928	80,882	...	...	...	160,810	79,928	80,882	...	...	...
	5—10	125,048	66,392	58,656	4,124	3,369	755	120,924	63,023	57,901	249	200	49
	10—15	104 829	55,132	49,697	6,020	5,033	987	98,809	50,099	48,710	582	496	86
	15—20	81,792	38,158	43,634	6,790	5,953	837	75,002	32,206	42,797	1,000	923	77
	20 and over	410,269	230,663	179,606	38,110	35,930	2,180	372,159	194,733	177,426	4,538	4,405	133
	HINDU	*385,877*	*208,369*	*177,515*	*35,997*	*32,920*	*3,077*	*349,880*	*175,442*	*174,438*	*4,933*	*4,031*	*902*
	0—5	65,316	32,428	32,888	...	...	...	65,316	32,428	32 888	...	...	...
	5—10	51,335	27,032	24,303	2,554	2,094	460	48,781	24,938	23,843	169	134	35
	10—15	43,196	22,748	20,448	3,754	3,151	603	39,442	19,597	19,845	388	325	63
	15—20	35,039	16,832	18,207	4 333	3,815	518	30,706	13,017	17,689	651	599	52
	20 and over	190,991	100,332	81,669	25,356	23,860	1,496	165,635	85,463	80,173	3,045	2,973	72
	MUSLIM	*387,709*	*205,386*	*182,323*	*13,829*	*12,821*	*1,008*	*373,880*	*192,565*	*181,315*	*1,358*	*1,348*	*10*
	0—5	73,682	36,675	37,007	...	...	...	73 682	36,675	37,007	...	...	...
	5—10	56,680	30,464	26,216	1,075	892	183	55,605	29,572	26,033	41	40	1
	10—15	48 237	25,443	22,794	1,525	1,287	238	46,712	24,156	22,556	106	105	1
	15—20	37,673	17,240	20,433	1,708	1 505	203	35,965	15,735	20,230	212	210	2
	20 and over	171,437	95,264	76,173	9,521	9,137	384	161,916	86,427	75,489	999	993	6
	TRIBAL	*89,389*	*45,912*	*43,477*	*2,827*	*2,661*	*166*	*86,562*	*43,251*	*43,311*	*192*	*188*	*4*
	0—5	18,488	9,182	9,306	...	...	...	18 488	9,182	9,306	...	...	...
	5—10	14,148	7,346	6,802	321	271	50	13,827	7,075	6,752	9	8	1
	10—15	10,820	5,521	5,299	436	386	50	10,384	5,135	5,249	20	19	1
	15—20	7,120	3,129	3,991	385	368	17	6,735	2,761	3,974	37	37	...
	20 and over	38,813	20,734	18,079	1,685	1,636	49	37,128	19,098	18,030	126	124	2

TABLE XIII.—Literacy by religion and age. Part II.—Details for Districts.

Districts.	Age.	Population. Total. Persons.	Population. Total. Males.	Population. Total. Females.	Population. Literate. Persons.	Population. Literate. Males.	Population. Literate. Females.	Population. Illiterate. Persons.	Population. Illiterate. Males.	Population. Illiterate. Females.	Literate in English. Persons.	Literate in English. Males.	Literate in English. Females.
	1	2	3	4	5	6	7	8	9	10	11	12	13
KAMRUP.	ALL RELIGIONS ...	*976,746*	*513,345*	*463,401*	*79,896*	*73,639*	*6,264*	*896,850*	*439,713*	*457,137*	*9,997*	*9,469*	*458*
	0—5 ...	184,070	91,108	92,962	...	...	...	184,070	91,108	92,962	...	...	...
	5—10 ...	138,653	72,886	65,767	6,199	5,363	836	132,454	67,523	64,931	361	314	47
	10—15 ...	113,473	60,472	53,001	9,372	8,218	1,154	104,101	52,254	51,847	915	833	82
	15—20 ...	87,220	42,064	45,156	10,716	9,579	1,137	76,504	32,485	44,019	1,886	1,781	105
	20 and over ...	453,330	246,815	206,515	53,609	50,472	3,137	399,721	196,343	203,378	6,765	6,542	223
	HINDU ...	*709,960*	*370,069*	*339,891*	*66,324*	*61,494*	*4,830*	*643,636*	*309,175*	*334,461*	*8,043*	*7,734*	*309*
	0—5 ...	130,334	64,515	65,819	...	...	...	130,334	64,515	65,819	...	...	...
	5—10 ...	99,638	52,049	47,589	5,116	4,468	638	94,522	47,581	46,961	274	238	36
	10—15 ...	81,588	42,442	39,146	7,786	6,912	874	73,802	35,530	37,272	739	672	67
	15—20 ...	62,337	30,485	31,852	8,949	8,077	872	53,388	22,408	30,980	1,559	1,483	76
	20 and over ...	336,063	180,178	155,885	44,473	42,017	2,456	291,590	138,161	153,429	5,471	5,341	130
	MUSLIM ...	*240,422*	*128,785*	*111,637*	*11,056*	*10,281*	*775*	*229,366*	*118,504*	*110,862*	*1,350*	*1,315*	*35*
	0—5 ...	48,668	24,052	24,616	...	...	...	48,668	24,052	24,616	...	...	...
	5—10 ...	35,332	18,847	16,485	828	718	110	34,504	18,129	16,375	47	43	4
	10—15 ...	28,805	15,409	13,396	1,202	1,051	151	27,603	14,358	13,245	104	96	8
	15—20 ...	22,536	10,479	12,057	1,367	1,218	149	21,169	9,261	11,908	229	220	9
	20 and over ...	105,081	59,948	45,133	7,659	7,294	365	97,422	52,654	44,768	970	966	14
DARRANG.	ALL RELIGIONS ...	*584,817*	*317,103*	*267,714*	*31,739*	*29,237*	*2,502*	*553,078*	*287,866*	*265,212*	*4,769*	*4,539*	*230*
	0—5 ...	98,612	48,850	49,762	...	...	...	98,612	48,850	49,762	...	...	...
	5—10 ...	75,309	39,040	36,220	1,973	1,628	345	73,336	37,461	35,875	99	80	19
	10—15 ...	63,117	33,936	29,181	3,063	2,605	458	59,454	30,331	28,123	257	227	30
	15—20 ...	49,829	24,454	25,375	3,912	3,420	484	45,916	20,966	24,921	656	634	22
	20 and over ...	298,590	171,814	126,776	22,830	21,585	1,245	275,760	150,229	125,531	3,757	3,608	149
	HINDU ...	*455,623*	*246,526*	*209,097*	*26,757*	*24,605*	*2,159*	*428,866*	*221,921*	*206,945*	*3,893*	*3,778*	*115*
	0—5 ...	75,684	37,594	38,090	...	...	...	75,684	37,594	38,090	...	...	...
	5—10 ...	57,871	29,938	27,933	1,683	1,377	306	56,188	28,561	27,627	87	71	16
	10—15 ...	48,120	25,396	22,724	2,673	2,259	414	45,447	23,137	22,310	232	206	26
	15—20 ...	38,202	18,897	19,305	3,358	2,953	405	34,844	15,944	18,900	579	545	34
	20 and over ...	235,746	134,701	101,045	19,043	18,016	1,027	216,703	116,685	100,018	3,004	2,956	49
	MUSLIM ...	*67,503*	*37,529*	*29,974*	*3,396*	*3,253*	*143*	*64,107*	*34,276*	*29,831*	*418*	*412*	*6*
	0—5 ...	11,514	5,645	5,869	...	...	...	11,514	5,645	5,869	...	...	...
	5—10 ...	9,221	4,879	4,342	183	160	23	9,038	4,719	4,319	5	5	...
	10—15 ...	7,971	4,229	3,742	287	260	27	7,684	3,969	3,715	15	14	1
	15—20 ...	6,746	3,303	3,443	372	350	22	6,374	2,953	3,421	52	51	1
	20 and over ...	32,051	19,473	12,578	2,554	2,483	71	29,497	16,990	12,507	346	342	4
	TRIBAL ...	*44,370*	*23,469*	*20,901*	*245*	*229*	*16*	*44,125*	*23,240*	*20,885*	*6*	*6*	...
	0—5 ...	8,441	4,146	4,295	...	...	...	8,441	4,146	4,295	...	...	...
	5—10 ...	5,987	3,076	2,911	16	14	2	5,971	3,062	2,909	...	...	...
	10—15 ...	4,669	2,372	2,297	25	24	1	4,644	2,348	2,296	...	...	...
	15—20 ...	3,401	1,527	1,874	36	33	3	3,365	1,494	1,871	1	1	...
	20 and over ...	21,872	12,344	9,524	168	158	10	21,704	12,190	9,514	5	5	...

TABLE XIII.—LITERACY BY RELIGION AND AGE. PART II—DETAILS FOR DISTRICTS.

District.	Age.	Population. Total. Persons.	Total. Males.	Total. Females.	Literate. Persons.	Literate. Males.	Literate. Females.	Illiterate. Persons.	Illiterate. Males.	Illiterate. Females.	Literate in English. Persons.	Literate in English. Males.	Literate in English. Females.
	1	2		4	5	6	7	8	9	10	11	12	13
NOWGONG.	ALL RELIGIONS	*562,581*	*298,585*	*263,996*	*36,111*	*32,973*	*3,138*	*526,470*	*265,612*	*260,858*	*3,957*	*3,779*	*178*
	0—5	110,362	54,851	54,811	...	...	...	110,362	54,851	55,511	...	...	...
	5—10	79,017	41,265	37,752	2,643	2,202	441	76,374	39,063	37,311	104	86	18
	10—15	63,[illegible]	33,365	30,444	3,929	3,300	629	59,770	29,965	29,815	261	231	30
	15—20	51,[illegible]	24,343	27,292	4,547	3,963	594	47,079	20,390	26,689	579	536	43
	20 and over	257,878	144,871	113,007	24,992	23,518	1,474	232,885	121,353	111,533	3,022	2,934	88
	HINDU	*325,710*	*172,659*	*153,051*	*27,245*	*25,113*	*2,132*	*298,465*	*147,546*	*150,919*	*2,888*	*2,820*	*68*
	0—5	60,729	30,213	30,516	...	...	...	60,729	30,213	30,516	...	...	...
	5—10	43,928	22,806	21,122	1,895	1,624	271	42,033	21,182	20,851	67	59	8
	10—15	35,446	18,514	16,932	2,898	2,494	404	32,548	16,020	16,548	190	172	18
	15—20	28,417	13,644	14,773	3,440	3,048	392	24,977	10,596	14,381	434	416	18
	20 and over	157,171	87,483	69,688	19,012	17,947	1,065	138,159	69,536	68,623	2,197	2,173	24
	MUSLIM	*177,762*	*95,597*	*82,165*	*7,532*	*6,804*	*728*	*170,230*	*88,793*	*81,437*	*784*	*759*	*25*
	0—5	37,982	18,953	19,029	...	...	...	37,982	18,953	19,029	...	...	...
	5—10	26,680	14,170	17,510	660	527	133	26,020	13,643	12,377	26	22	4
	10—15	21,487	11,266	10,221	903	730	173	20,584	10,536	10,048	57	52	5
	15—20	17,762	8,183	9,579	938	792	146	16,824	7,391	9,433	105	98	7
	20 and over	73,851	43,025	30,826	5,031	4,755	276	68,820	38,270	30,550	596	587	9
	TRIBAL	*53,094*	*27,094*	*26,000*	*368*	*339*	*9*	*52,726*	*26,735*	*25,991*	*26*	*25*	*1*
	0—5	10,570	5,160	5,410	...	...	...	10,570	5,160	5,410	...	...	...
	5—10	7,622	3,898	3,724	15	14	1	7,607	3,884	3,723	...	...	...
	10—15	6,105	3,153	2,962	24	23	1	6,081	3,130	2,951	1	1	...
	15—20	4,903	2,258	2,644	38	37	1	4,865	2,221	2,644	4	4	...
	20 and over	23,894	12,625	11,269	291	285	6	23,603	12,340	11,263	21	20	1
SIBSAGAR.	ALL RELIGIONS	*933,326*	*496,288*	*437,038*	*71,558*	*65,575*	*5,983*	*861,768*	*430,713*	*431,055*	*13,091*	*12,495*	*596*
	0—5	170,135	84,973	85,162	...	...	...	170,135	84,973	85,162	...	...	...
	5—10	126,934	66,004	60,930	5,033	4,164	870	121,901	61,840	60,061	406	340	67
	10—15	105,254	55,225	50,029	7,970	6,770	1,200	97,284	48,455	48,829	1,067	970	97
	15—20	80,565	39,923	40,642	9,371	8,349	1,022	71,194	31,574	39,620	2,070	1,978	93
	20 and over	450,438	250,163	200,275	49,184	46,291	2,893	401,254	203,871	197,383	9,548	9,198	350
	HINDU	*841,035*	*445,658*	*395,377*	*62,343*	*57,543*	*4,800*	*778,692*	*388,115*	*390,577*	*10,638*	*10,299*	*339*
	0—5	153,757	76,720	76,958	...	...	...	153,757	76,799	76,958	...	...	...
	5—10	114,154	59,334	54,830	4,387	3,699	698	109,767	55,635	54,142	338	293	45
	10—15	94,549	49,518	45,031	6,972	6,003	969	87,577	43,515	44,062	887	814	73
	15—20	72,106	35,499	36,607	8,191	7,353	838	63,915	28,146	35,769	1,750	1,686	64
	20 and over	406,469	224,518	181,951	42,793	40,488	2,306	363,676	184,030	179,646	7,683	7,526	157
	MUSLIM	*43,907*	*24,916*	*18,991*	*6,747*	*6,022*	*725*	*37,160*	*18,894*	*18,266*	*1,578*	*1,531*	*47*
	0—5	7,729	3,860	3,869	...	...	...	7,729	3,860	3,869	...	...	...
	5—10	6,219	3,252	2,967	530	394	136	5,689	2,858	2,831	51	46	5
	10—15	5,348	2,858	2,490	803	631	172	4,545	2,227	2,318	154	136	18
	15—20	4,209	2,283	1,921	873	750	123	3,336	1,533	1,803	249	241	8
	20 and over	20,402	12,663	7,739	4,541	4,247	294	15,861	8,416	7,445	1,124	1,108	16

TABLE XIII.—Literacy by Religion and Age. Part II.—Details for Districts.

District.	Age.	Population. Total. Persons.	Total. Males.	Total. Females.	Literate. Persons.	Literate. Males.	Literate. Females.	Illiterate. Persons.	Illiterate. Males.	Illiterate. Females.	Literate in English. Persons.	Literate in English. Males.	Literate in English. Females.
	1	2	3	4	5	6	7	8	9	10	11	12	13
SIBSAGAR—concld.	TRIBAL	32,034	16,744	15,290	304	289	15	31,730	16,455	15,275	15	15	...
	0—5	5,980	2,979	3,001	...	...	...	5,980	2,970	3,001	...	...	...
	5—10	4,487	2,368	2,119	7	7	...	4,480	2,361	2,119	...	...	...
	10—15	3,550	1,912	1,638	16	16	...	3,534	1,896	1,638	1	1	...
	15—20	2,794	1,403	1,391	38	36	2	2,756	1,367	1,379	2	2	...
	20 and over	15,233	8,082	7,151	243	230	13	14,990	7,853	7,138	13	12	...
LAKHIMPUR.	ALL RELIGIONS	794,582	399,108	395,474	59,407	48,396	4,011	679,175	350,719	391,463	11,945	11,347	598
	0—5	122,507	61,270	61,237	...	...	...	122,507	61,270	61,237	...	...	...
	5—10	91,289	47,777	43,552	3,096	2,621	475	88,293	45,216	43,077	264	236	28
	10—15	74,265	39,455	34,810	4,495	3,861	634	69,773	35,597	34,176	547	477	70
	15—20	59,817	30,547	29,270	6,367	5,655	712	53,450	24,892	28,558	1,506	1,403	103
	20 and over	376,661	220,056	156,005	38,509	36,319	2,190	338,152	183,737	154,415	9,646	9,263	383
	HINDU	661,680	360,756	300,924	44,058	40,850	3,208	617,622	319,906	297,716	9,492	9,177	315
	0—5	113,996	56,938	57,060	...	...	...	113,998	56,938	57,060	...	...	...
	5—10	84,443	44,152	40,291	2,678	2,296	382	81,765	41,872	39,893	197	168	29
	10—15	68,297	34,144	32,153	3,939	3,408	531	64,358	32,736	31,622	467	409	58
	15—20	53,773	26,928	26,845	5,414	4,825	589	48,359	22,103	26,256	1,257	1,174	83
	20 and over	341,169	196,594	144,575	32,927	30,337	1,690	309,142	166,257	142,985	7,571	7,426	145
GARO HILLS.	ALL RELIGIONS	190,911	97,442	93,469	5,059	4,218	841	185,852	93,224	92,628	516	451	65
	0—5	37,290	18,775	18,515	...	...	...	37,290	18,775	18,515	...	...	...
	5—10	24,917	12,905	12,012	203	153	50	24,714	12,752	11,962	8	5	3
	10—15	21,186	10,571	10,615	483	300	183	20,703	10,271	10,432	10	4	6
	15—20	18,541	7,969	10,552	768	569	199	17,773	7,390	10,383	62	48	14
	20 and over	88,977	47,232	41,745	3,665	3,196	469	85,312	44,036	41,276	436	394	42
	HINDU	27,946	15,086	12,860	1,245	1,186	59	26,701	13,900	12,801	140	134	6
	0—5	5,138	2,621	2,517	...	...	...	5,138	2,621	2,517	...	...	...
	5—10	3,721	1,914	1,805	36	28	8	3,685	1,886	1,797	4	2	2
	10—15	3,089	1,579	1,511	67	56	11	3,022	1,523	1,500	4	2	2
	15—20	2,496	1,192	1,294	134	124	10	2,352	1,068	1,284	16	15	1
	20 and over	13,511	7,778	5,733	1,006	976	30	12,505	6,800	5,703	116	115	1
	TRIBAL	136,707	68,194	68,513	565	505	60	136,142	67,689	68,453	36	32	4
	0—5	27,524	13,763	13,761	...	...	...	27,524	13,763	13,761	...	...	...
	5—10	17,690	9,106	8,584	29	25	4	17,661	9,081	8,580	1	1	...
	10—15	14,902	7,277	7,625	54	43	11	14,848	7,234	7,614	1	...	1
	15—20	13,237	5,407	7,830	78	63	15	13,159	5,344	7,815	4	2	1
	20 and over	63,354	32,641	30,713	404	374	30	62,950	32,267	30,683	30	28	2
	CHRISTIANS	15,950	8,564	7,386	2,873	2,163	710	13,077	6,401	6,676	282	227	55
	0—5	2,672	1,301	1,371	...	...	...	2,672	1,301	1,371	...	...	...
	5—10	2,102	1,132	970	124	96	28	1,978	1,046	932	1	...	1
	10—15	1,969	1,070	899	234	185	99	1,685	885	800	4	1	3
	15—20	1,862	902	960	511	341	170	1,351	561	790	35	23	12
	20 and over	7,145	3,959	3,186	1,964	1,361	603	5,181	2,408	2,783	242	203	39

TABLE XIII.—LITERACY BY RELIGION AND AGE. PART II.—DETAILS FOR DISTRICTS.

District.	Age.	Population. Total. Persons.	Population. Total. Males.	Population. Total. Females.	Population. Literate. Persons.	Population. Literate. Males.	Population. Literate. Females.	Population. Illiterate. Persons.	Population. Illiterate. Males.	Population. Illiterate. Females.	Literate in English. Persons.	Literate in English. Males.	Literate in English. Females.
	1	2	3	4	5	6	7	8	9	10	11	12	13
SADIYA FRONTIER TRACT.	ALL RELIGIONS	*53,345*	*28,686*	*24,659*	*2,964*	*2,738*	*226*	*50,381*	*25,948*	*24,433*	*249*	*223*	*26*
	0—5	8,988	4,524	4,464	...	...	...	8,988	4,524	4,464	...	...	...
	5—10	6,517	3,490	3,027	147	119	28	6,370	3,371	2,999	6	3	3
	10—15	5,342	2,793	2,549	207	171	36	5,135	2,622	2,513	11	8	3
	15—20	5,002	2,425	2,577	366	316	50	4,636	2,109	2,527	39	35	4
	20 and over	27,496	15,454	12,042	2,244	2,132	112	25,252	13,322	11,930	193	177	16
	HINDU	*26,002*	*14,809*	*11,193*	*2,360*	*2,192*	*168*	*23,642*	*12,617*	*11,025*	*169*	*162*	*7*
	0—5	4,359	2,204	2,155	...	...	...	4,359	2,204	2,155	...	...	...
	5—10	3,205	1,703	1,502	127	103	24	3,078	1,600	1,478	4	3	1
	10—15	2,601	1,367	1,234	170	140	30	2,431	1,227	1,204	8	7	1
	15—20	2,459	1,281	1,178	297	258	39	2,162	1,023	1,139	30	28	2
	20 and over	13,378	8,254	5,124	1,706	1,631	75	11,672	6,623	5,049	127	124	3
	TRIBAL	*23,486*	*11,677*	*11,809*	*13*	*12*	*1*	*23,473*	*11,665*	*11,808*	*1*	*1*	...
	0—5	4,068	2,026	2,042	...	...	...	4,068	2,026	2,042	...	...	...
	5—10	2,858	1,546	1,312	...	...	...	2,858	1,546	1,312	...	...	...
	10—15	2,345	1,213	1,132	2	1	1	2,343	1,212	1,131	...	...	...
	15—20	2,192	957	1,235	4	4	...	2,188	953	1,235	1	1	...
	20 and over	12,023	5,935	6,088	7	7	...	12,016	5,928	6,088	...	...	...
BALIPARA FRONTIER TRACT.	ALL RELIGIONS	*5,148*	*3,232*	*1,916*	*484*	*459*	*25*	*4,664*	*2,773*	*1,891*	*38*	*37*	*1*
	0—5	785	421	364	...	...	...	785	421	364	...	...	...
	5—10	510	279	231	11	8	3	499	271	228	...	...	...
	10—15	401	209	192	20	16	4	381	193	188	...	...	...
	15—20	502	311	191	72	66	6	430	245	185	5	4	1
	20 and over	2,950	2,012	938	381	369	12	2,569	1,643	926	33	33	...
	HINDU	*3,811*	*2,487*	*1,324*	*399*	*386*	*13*	*3,412*	*2,101*	*1,311*	*31*	*30*	*1*
	0—5	587	314	273	...	...	...	587	314	273	...	...	...
	5—10	362	198	164	7	7	...	355	191	164	...	...	...
	10—15	273	141	132	15	13	2	258	128	130	...	...	...
	15—20	384	251	133	61	58	3	323	193	130	4	3	1
	20 and over	2,205	1,583	622	216	208	8	1,989	1,375	614	27	27	...
	TRIBAL	*813*	*439*	*374*	*2*	*2*	...	*811*	*437*	*374*	...	...	...
	0—5	92	50	42	...	...	...	92	50	42	...	...	...
	5—10	86	49	37	...	...	...	86	49	37	...	...	...
	10—15	82	45	37	...	...	...	82	45	37	...	...	...
	15—20	66	31	35	1	1	...	65	30	35	...	...	...
	20 and over	484	264	220	1	1	...	483	263	220	...	...	...

TABLE XII.—LITERACY BY RELIGION AND AGE. PART I.—DETAILS FOR STATES.

District.	Age.	POPULATION. Total. Persons.	Total. Males.	Total. Females.	Literate. Persons.	Literate. Males.	Literate. Females.	Illiterate. Persons.	Illiterate. Males.	Illiterate. Females.	LITERATE IN ENGLISH. Persons.	Literate in English. Males.	Literate in English. Females.
	1	2	3	4	5	6	7	8	9	10	11	12	13
MANIPUR.	ALL RELIGIONS	*445,606*	*215,815*	*229,791*	*14,495*	*13,806*	*689*	*431,111*	*202,009*	*229,102*	*2,072*	*2,021*	*51*
	0—5	80,527	39,709	40,818	...	...	...	80,527	39,709	40,818	...	...	...
	5—10	59,248	29,730	29,518	750	673	77	58,498	29,057	29,441	61	59	2
	10—15	49,916	24,997	24,929	1,322	1,210	112	48,594	23,777	24,817	167	163	4
	15—20	41,310	19,261	22,060	2,146	2,023	123	39,164	17,238	21,926	316	308	8
	20 and over	214,605	103,138	112,467	10,277	9,900	377	204,328	93,238	112,090	1,478	1,441	37
	HINDU	*257,255*	*124,343*	*132,912*	*11,561*	*11,213*	*348*	*245,694*	*113,130*	*132,564*	*1,383*	*1,359*	*24*
	0—5	43,509	21,530	21,979	...	...	...	43,509	21,530	21,979	...	...	...
	5—10	34,662	17,464	17,198	564	520	44	34,098	16,944	17,154	31	29	2
	10—15	30,230	15,124	15,106	895	838	57	29,335	14,286	15,049	95	92	3
	15—20	26,014	12,230	13,784	1,665	1,616	49	24,349	10,614	13,735	248	244	4
	20 and over	122,760	57,895	64,865	8,337	8,150	186	114,423	49,755	64,647	1,009	994	15
	TRIBAL	*154,604*	*74,650*	*79,954*	*634*	*593*	*41*	*154,170*	*74,257*	*79,913*	*50*	*50*	...
	0—5	30,064	14,756	15,308	...	...	...	30,064	14,756	15,308	...	...	...
	5—10	19,658	9,739	9,919	20	15	5	19,638	9,724	9,914	...	...	...
	10—15	15,444	7,631	7,813	46	40	6	15,398	7,591	7,807	2	2	...
	15—20	12,023	5,506	6,517	99	93	6	11,924	5,413	6,511	6	6	...
	20 and over	77,615	37,218	40,397	469	445	24	77,146	36,773	40,373	42	42	...
KHASI STATES.	ALL RELIGIONS	*180,000*	*91,119*	*88,888*	*16,687*	*10,869*	*5,818*	*163,313*	*80,243*	*83,070*	*3,160*	*2,495*	*665*
	0—5	32,013	15,805	16,208	...	...	...	32,013	15,806	16,208	...	...	...
	5—10	23,105	11,596	11,509	1,060	599	461	22,045	10,997	11,048	114	68	46
	10—15	20,341	10,275	10,066	1,936	1,097	840	18,405	9,188	9,217	306	201	105
	15—20	18,221	8,593	9,628	2,794	1,578	1,216	15,427	7,015	8,412	527	382	145
	20 and over	86,320	44,843	41,477	10,897	7,605	3,292	75,428	37,238	38,185	2,213	1,844	369
	TRIBAL	*126,154*	*61,613*	*64,541*	*3,341*	*2,501*	*840*	*122,813*	*59,112*	*63,701*	*369*	*335*	*34*
	0—5	23,417	11,581	11,836	...	...	...	23,417	11,581	11,836	...	...	...
	5—10	16,548	8,229	8,319	169	100	69	16,379	8,129	8,250	8	5	3
	10—15	14,393	7,175	7,218	312	197	115	14,081	6,978	7,103	29	23	6
	15—20	12,370	5,490	6,880	533	354	179	11,837	5,136	6,701	63	56	7
	20 and over	59,426	29,138	30,288	2,327	1,850	477	57,099	27,288	29,811	263	244	19
	CHRISTIANS	*36,259*	*17,295*	*18,964*	*10,284*	*5,849*	*4,435*	*25,975*	*11,446*	*14,529*	*1,764*	*1,247*	*517*
	0—5	6,383	3,125	3,258	...	...	...	6,383	3,125	3,258	...	...	...
	5—10	5,062	2,557	2,505	722	400	322	4,340	2,157	2,183	68	30	38
	10—15	4,676	2,359	2,317	1,374	730	644	3,302	1,629	1,673	193	118	75
	15—20	3,972	1,792	2,180	1,925	967	958	2,047	825	1,222	333	223	110
	20 and over	16,166	7,462	8,704	6,263	3,752	2,511	9,903	3,710	6,193	1,170	867	303

TABLE XIV.

LITERACY BY SELECTED CASTES, TRIBES OR RACES.

This table gives the statistics of literacy for certain selected castes and tribes. The population figures for the various castes and tribes do not show the entire number of persons in each caste or tribe but only the number of persons of the age of 7 years and over who were enumerated in the localities mentioned in column 2. The localities mentioned in this column are the districts or areas where these particular castes and tribes are principally found.

The number of literates shown against each caste or tribe is the number of literates of the age of 7 and over.

TABLE XIV.—LITERACY BY SELECTED CASTES, TRIBES OR RACES.

Caste Tribe or Race.	Locality.	Population 7 years and over. Total. Persons.	Total. Males.	Total. Females.	Literate. Persons.	Literate. Males.	Literate. Females.	Illiterate. Persons.	Illiterate. Males.	Illiterate. Females.	Literate in English (7 years and over). Persons.	Males.	Females.
1	2	3	4	5	6	7	8	9	10	11	12	13	14
Ahom (Hindu) ...	Brahmaputra Valley ...	186,215	98,167	88,048	25,406	24,174	1,232	160,809	73,993	86,816	4,489	4,431	58
Baidya (Hindu) ...	Sylhet and Cachar plains...	5,106	2,771	2,335	3,943	2,405	1,538	1,163	366	797	1,585	1,389	196
Brahman (Hindu) ...	All plains districts ...	126,056	70,774	55,282	61,696	50,993	10,703	64,360	19,781	44,579	14,275	13,728	547
Bania (Brittial Bania) (Hindu). ...	Brahmaputra Valley ...	10,650	5,755	4,895	2,103	1,771	332	8,547	3,984	4,563	293	268	25
Garo (Tribal)	Garo Hills	101,329	50,502	50,827	565	505	60	100,764	49,997	50,767	36	32	4
Kachari (Hindu) ...	Brahmaputra Valley ...	144,319	75,025	69,294	5,893	5,657	236	138,426	69,368	69,058	824	814	10
Kachari (Tribal) ...	Brahmaputra Valley ...	14,898	7,567	7,331	492	468	24	14,406	7,099	7,307	41	41	...
Khasi (Tribal) ...	Khasi and Jaintia Hills (including Khasi States).	99,447	48,330	51,117	4,173	3,158	1,015	95,274	45,172	50,102	409	366	43
Khasi (Christian) ...	Khasi and Jaintia Hills (including Khasi States).	29,957	14,245	15,712	10,947	6,004	4,943	19,010	8,241	10,769	1,418	1,034	384
Lushai (Tribal) ...	Lushai Hills	42,171	20,868	21,303	3,110	3,017	93	39,061	17,851	21,210	75	74	1
Lushai (Christian) ...	Lushai Hills	44,998	19,779	25,219	8,906	7,569	1,337	36,092	12,210	23,882	620	577	43
Manipuri (Hindu) ...	Manipur State ...	198,123	93,448	104,675	10,605	10,307	298	187,518	83,141	104,377	1,226	1,210	16
Mikir (Tribal)	Sibsagar and Nowgong ...	49,865	26,129	23,736	354	349	5	49,511	25,780	23,731	15	15	...
Nadiyal (Kaibartta) (Hindu)	Brahmaputra Valley ...	72,412	38,388	34,024	7,600	7,032	568	64,812	31,356	33,456	750	725	25
Namasudra (Hindu) ...	Sylhet and Cachar plains ...	116,625	61,578	55,047	6,386	6,128	258	110,239	55,450	54,789	180	180	...
Tanti (Hindu)	Sibsagar and Lakhimpur ...	45,703	23,730	21,973	946	910	36	44,757	22,820	21,937	39	36	3
Yogi (Hindu)	Sylhet	60,265	31,939	28,326	9,237	8,496	741	51,028	23,443	27,585	363	357	6

TABLE XV.

LANGUAGE.

This table is divided into two parts: Part I gives the distribution by districts of the languages returned as their mother-tongue by the persons enumerated in Assam and Part II shows the extent of bi-lingualism in the province.

Part I falls into three groups, *viz* :—

A.—Vernaculars of India { (*i*) of Assam, (*ii*) of India outside Assam.

B.—Vernaculars of Asiatic countries beyond India.

C.—European languages.

Languages which have so few speakers that they are not worth a separate column are included in "Others" at the end of the table.

The vernaculars of Assam—unlike the languages in the rest of the table—have not been given in alphabetical order but follow generally the order of families, branches, groups, etc., given in the Linguistic Survey of India. This has the advantage of showing in close proximity languages which fall into the same sub-group, *e.g.*, all the Central Naga languages will be found next to each other in the table. In certain cases I have given details of languages which are really dialects of another language, *e.g.*, Changsen is a dialect of Thado though the Changsens are of different origin from the Thados. I have done this as certain district officers of hill districts have asked me to give as much detailed information as possible in this table.

"Kachha Naga" which appears in the tables of previous censuses and the Linguistic Survey as "Empeo or Kachha Naga" appears in this table under three heads, *viz.*, Kachha Naga, Liyengmai and Zemi. I am informed by Mr. J. P. Mills, I.C.S., Deputy Commissioner Naga Hills, that the term "Kachha Naga" (though in common use) is a meaningless term and that about half the Kachha Naga speakers in Manipur are really Liyengmai and half Zemi. As however "Kachha Naga" was returned as their tribe and language by the Liyengmai and Zemi of Manipur I have shown it as such. Part II of the table should be read in connection with the Linguistic Map in the Report Volume.

TABLE XV.

PART I—LANGUAGE.

DISTRICT OR STATE.	POPULATION.			A.—VERNACULARS OF INDIA (VERNACULARS OF ASSAM).								
				Khasi.			Aka.			Abor.		
	Persons.	Males.	Females.	Persons.	Males.	Females.	Persons.	Males.	Females.	Persons.	Males.	Females.
1	2	3	4	5	6	7	8	9	10	11	12	13
ASSAM	*9,247,857*	*4,844,133*	*4,403,724*	*233,879*	*113,690*	*120,189*	*33*	*28*	*5*	*13,880*	*6,846*	*7,034*
(1) British Territory	*8,622,951*	*4,537,906*	*4,085,045*	*80,946*	*39,946*	*41,000*	*33*	*28*	*5*	*13,874*	*6,845*	*7,029*
SURMA VALLEY AND HILL DIVISION	3,706,047	1,912,144	1,794,903	78,665	38,486	40,179	...	...	...	1	1	...
Cachar	570,531	301,338	269,193	1,737	937	800	...	...	...	...	...	...
Sylhet	2,724,252	1,407,645	1,316,607	2,417	1,260	1,157	...	...	...	...	...	...
Khasi and Jaintia Hills (British)	109,936	55,439	54,497	74,409	36,227	38,182	...	...	...	...	...	...
Naga Hills	178,844	89,536	89,308	20	9	11	...	...	...	1	1	...
Lushai Hills	124,404	59,186	65,218	82	53	29	...	...	...	...	...	...
ASSAM VALLEY DIVISION	4,855,711	2,502,144	2,353,567	1,564	754	810	33	28	5	254	201	53
Goalpara	882,748	470,273	412,475	2	1	1	...	...	...	...	...	...
Kamrup	976,746	513,345	463,401	636	353	283	...	...	...	...	...	...
Darrang	584,817	317,103	267,714	81	51	30	8	8	...	1	1	...
Nowgong	562,581	298,585	263,996	180	67	113	3	1	2	...	...	...
Sibsagar	933,296	496,258	437,038	111	26	85	...	...	...	...	...	...
Lakhimpur	724,582	399,108	325,474	237	94	143	22	19	3	253	200	53
Garo Hills	190,911	97,442	93,469	317	162	155	...	...	...	...	...	...
SADIYA FRONTIER TRACT	53,365	28,706	24,659	13	4	9	...	...	...	13,619	6,643	6,976
BALIPARA FRONTIER TRACT	5,168	3,252	1,916	4	2	2	...	...	...	...	...	...
(2) Manipur State	*445,606*	*215,815*	*229,791*	*2*	*2*	...	...	...	...	*6*	*1*	*5*
(3) Khasi States	*180,000*	*91,119*	*88,882*	*153,635*	*74,443*	*79,192*	...	...	...	...	...	...

TABLE XV.

PART I—LANGUAGE—*contd.*

DISTRICT OR STATE.	A.—VERNACULARS OF INDIA (VERNACULARS OF ASSAM)—*contd.*											
	Miri.			Dafla.			Mishmi.			Garo.		
	Persons.	Males.	Females.	Persons.	Males.	Females.	Persons.	Males.	Females.	Persons.	Males.	Females.
	14	15	16	17	18	19	20	21	22	23	24	25
ASSAM	*80,831*	*41,560*	*39,271*	*1,644*	*931*	*713*	*2,285*	*1,286*	*999*	*192,480*	*97,077*	*95,403*
(1) British Territory	*80,831*	*41,560*	*39,271*	*1,644*	*931*	*713*	*2,285*	*1,286*	*999*	*187,266*	*94,514*	*92,752*
SURMA VALLEY AND HILL DIVISION	9	9	...	...	...	...	...	...	...	4,346	2,208	2,138
Cachar	9	9	...	...	...	...	...	...	...	1	1	...
Sylhet	...	...	...	...	...	...	...	...	...	2,026	1,047	979
Khasi and Jaintia Hills (British)	...	...	...	...	...	...	...	...	...	2,230	1,112	1,118
Naga Hills...	...	...	...	...	...	...	...	...	...	90	49	41
Lushai Hills	...	...	...	...	...	...	...	...	...	...	...	...
ASSAM VALLEY DIVISION	75,073	38,603	36,470	943	565	378	335	230	105	182,663	92,175	90,488
Goalpara	4	3	1	...	...	...	...	...	...	20,906	10,654	10,252
Kamrup	5	2	3	2	1	1	...	...	...	7,918	4,081	3,837
Darrang	5,734	2,876	2,858	358	217	141	...	...	...	437	235	202
Nowgong	8	4	4	...	...	...	...	...	...	395	197	198
Sibsagar	33,068	16,819	16,249	1	1	...	98	58	40	659	347	312
Lakhimpur...	36,254	18,899	17,355	582	346	236	237	172	65	40	32	8
Garo Hills...	...	...	...	...	...	...	...	...	...	152,309	76,590	75,719
SADIYA FRONTIER TRACT	5,281	2,701	2,580	...	...	...	1,950	1,056	894	25	16	9
BALIPARA FRONTIER TRACT	468	247	221	701	366	335	...	...	...	232	115	117
(2) Manipur State	...	...	...	...	...	...	...	...	...	*14*	*8*	*6*
(3) Khasi States	...	...	...	...	...	...	...	...	...	*5,200*	*2,555*	*2,645*

TABLE XV.

Part I—Language—contd.

A.—VERNACULARS OF INDIA (VERNACULARS OF ASSAM)—contd.

District or State.	Rabha.			Chutiya.			Koch.			Bârâ, Bodo or Plains Kâchârî.		
	Persons.	Males.	Females.	Persons.	Males.	Females.	Persons.	Males.	Females.	Persons.	Males.	Females.
	26	27	28	29	30	31	32	33	34	35	36	37
ASSAM	*27,006*	*13,462*	*13,544*	*4,315*	*2,244*	*2,071*	*1,370*	*678*	*692*	*282,582*	*143,544*	*139,038*
(1) British Territory	*27,004*	*13,462*	*13,542*	*4,315*	*2,244*	*2,071*	*1,370*	*678*	*692*	*282,372*	*143,418*	*138,954*
SURMA VALLEY AND HILL DIVISION	11	11	...	2	2	...	47	25	22	9,931	5,106	4,825
Cachar	...	...	...	2	2	...	7	3	4	9,068	4,617	4,451
Sylhet	...	...	...	...	...	...	40	22	18	273	167	106
Khasi and Jaintia Hills (British)	...	...	..	...	...	..	...	...	...	72	38	34
Naga Hills	6	6	...	...	...	...	...	...	...	509	275	234
Lushai Hills	5	5	...	...	...	...	...	...	...	9	9	...
ASSAM VALLEY DIVISION	26,993	13,451	13,542	4,269	2,212	2,057	1,323	653	670	272,036	138,062	133,974
Goalpara	18,959	9,406	9,553	...	...	..	373	195	178	115,549	59,253	56,296
Kamrup	948	478	470	...	...	...	22	9	13	93,361	46,283	47,078
Darrang	348	184	164	...	...	...	...	...	...	50,915	26,201	24,714
Nowgong	11	3	8	...	...	...	...	...	...	9,388	4,733	4,655
Sibsagar	1	1	...	821	450	371	...	...	...	1,184	687	497
Lakhimpur	...	...	...	3,448	1,762	1,686	...	...	...	781	476	305
Garo Hills	6,726	3,379	3,347	...	...	...	928	449	479	858	429	429
SADIYA FRONTIER TRACT	...	...	...	14	11	3	...	...	...	51	31	20
BALIPARA FRONTIER TRACT	...	...	...	30	19	11	...	...	...	354	219	135
(2) Manipur State	...	...	...	...	...	...	...	...	...	9	7	2
(3) Khasi States	2	...	2	...	...	...	...	...	...	*201*	*119*	*82*

TABLE XV.

PART I—LANGUAGE—*contd.*

DISTRICT OR STATE.	A.—VERNACULARS OF INDIA (VERNACULARS OF ASSAM)—*contd.*											
	Dimasa or Hills Kachari.			Lalung.			*Tipura			Kachha Naga.		
	Persons.	Males.	Females.	Persons.	Males.	Females.	Persons.	Males.	Females.	Persons.	Males.	Females.
	38	39	40	41	42	43	44	45	46	47	48	49
ASSAM	*14,680*	*7,439*	*7,241*	*9,017*	*4,280*	*4,737*	*6,404*	*3,536*	*2,868*	*7,282*	*3,536*	*3,746*
(1) British Territory	*14,680*	*7,439*	*7,241*	*8,673*	*4,089*	*4,584*	*6,083*	*3,368*	*2,715*	...	...	...
SURMA VALLEY AND HILL DIVISION	14,088	7,144	6,944	3,105	1,354	1,751	6,082	3,367	2,715	...	...	...
Cachar	13,547	6,873	6,674	...	...	...	852	396	456	...	...	...
Sylhet	...	...	...	...	...	...	4,867	2,864	2,003	...	...	...
Khasi and Jaintia Hills (British)...	...	...	...	3,105	1,354	1,751	...	...	...	...	...	...
Naga Hills	541	271	270	...	...	...	...	...	...	...	...	...
Lushai Hills	...	...	...	...	...	...	363	107	256	...	...	...
ASSAM VALLEY DIVISION	602	296	307	5,568	2,735	2,833	1	1	...	...	...	...
Goalpara	6	3	3	...	...	...	...	...	...	...	...	...
Kamrup	...	...	...	744	365	379	...	...	...	...	...	...
Darrang	...	...	...	2	...	2	...	...	...	...	...	...
Nowgong	596	293	304	4,822	2,367	2,455	1	1	...	...	...	...
Sibsagar	...	...	...	...	...	...	...	...	...	...	...	...
Lakhimpur	...	...	...	...	...	...	...	...	...	...	...	...
Garo Hills	...	...	...	...	...	...	...	...	...	...	...	...
SADIYA FRONTIER TRACT	...	...	...	...	...	...	...	...	...	...	...	...
BALIPARA FRONTIER TRACT	...	...	...	...	...	...	...	...	...	...	...	...
(2) Manipur State	...	...	...	...	...	...	...	...	...	*7,282*	*3,536*	*3,746*
(3) Khasi States	...	...	...	*344*	*191*	*153*	*321*	*168*	*153*	...	...	...

* This is a Kuki language and corresponds to the Hallam of the Linguistic Survey. Some examples are given in the appendix to chapter X.

TABLE XV.

PART I—LANGUAGE—*contd.*

DISTRICT OR STATE.	A.—VERNACULARS OF INDIA (VERNACULARS OF ASSAM)—*contd.*											
	Liyengmai (Naga).			Nzemi or Zemi (Naga).			Kabui (Naga).			Khoirao (Naga).		
	Persons.	Males.	Females.	Persons.	Males.	Females.	Persons.	Males.	Females.	Persons.	Males.	Females.
	50	51	52	53	54	55	56	57	58	59	60	61
ASSAM	2,209	1,072	1,137	10,263	5,093	5,170	18,475	8,664	9,811	2,635	1,257	1,378
(1) British Territory	2,209	1,072	1,137	10,263	5,093	5,170	33	17	16	25	9	16
SURMA VALLEY AND HILL DIVISION	2,209	1,072	1,137	10,263	5,093	5,170	33	17	16	...	...	...
Cachar	...	...	...	5,213	2,572	2,641	...	...	...	...	...	...
Sylhet	...	...	...	...	...	...	...	...	...	...	...	...
Khasi and Jaintia Hills (British)	...	...	...	...	...	...	...	...	...	...	...	...
Naga Hills	2,209	1,072	1,137	5,050	2,521	2,529	33	17	16	...	...	...
Lushai Hills	...	...	...	...	...	...	...	...	...	...	...	...
ASSAM VALLEY DIVISION	...	...	...	...	...	...	...	...	...	25	9	16
Goalpara	...	...	...	...	...	...	...	...	...	...	...	...
Kamrup	...	...	...	...	...	...	...	...	...	25	9	16
Darrang	...	...	...	...	...	...	...	...	...	...	...	...
Nowgong	...	...	...	...	...	...	...	...	...	...	...	...
Sibsagar	...	...	...	...	...	...	...	...	...	...	...	...
Lakhimpur	...	...	...	...	...	...	...	...	...	...	...	...
Garo Hills	...	...	...	...	...	...	...	...	...	...	...	...
SADIYA FRONTIER TRACT	...	...	...	...	...	...	...	...	...	...	...	...
BALIPARA FRONTIER TRACT	...	...	...	...	...	...	...	...	...	...	...	...
(2) Manipur State	...	...	...	...	...	...	18,442	8,647	9,795	2,610	1,248	1,362
(3) Khasi States	...	...	...	...	...	...	...	...	...	...	...	...

TABLE XV.

PART I—LANGUAGE—*contd.*

DISTRICT OR STATE.	A.—VERNACULARS OF INDIA (VERNACULARS OF ASSAM)—*contd.*											
	Angami (Naga).			Kezhama (Chizomi).			Sema (Naga).			Rengma (Naga).		
	Persons.	Males.	Females.	Persons.	Males.	Females.	Persons.	Males.	Females.	Persons.	Males.	Females.
	62	63	64	65	66	67	68	69	70	71	72	73
ASSAM	*43,666*	*22,203*	*21,463*	*5,288*	*2,879*	*2,409*	*38,146*	*18,937*	*19,209*	*6,269*	*3,117*	*3,152*
(1) British Territory	*43,190*	*21,903*	*21,287*	*5,286*	*2,877*	*2,409*	*38,129*	*18,920*	*19,209*	*6,269*	*3,117*	*3,152*
SURMA VALLEY AND HILL DIVISION	43,105	21,894	21,211	5,284	2,875	2,409	38,012	18,808	19,204	6,269	3,117	3,152
Cachar	...	...	...	...	...	...	...	...	...	...	...	...
Sylhet	1	1	...	...	...	...	...	...	...	...	...	...
Khasi and Jaintia Hills (British)	...	...	...	...	...	...	...	...	...	...	...	...
Naga Hills	43,104	21,893	21,211	5,284	2,875	2,409	38,012	18,808	19,204	6,269	3,117	3,152
Lushai Hills	...	...	...	...	...	...	...	...	...	...	...	...
ASSAM VALLEY DIVISION	9	7	2	2	2	...	30	29	1	...	...	...
Goalpara	...	...	...	...	...	...	...	...	...	...	...	...
Kamrup	...	...	...	...	...	...	...	...	...	...	...	...
Darrang	...	...	...	...	...	...	...	...	...	...	...	...
Nowgong	...	...	...	...	...	...	...	...	...	...	...	...
Sibsagar	8	6	2	2	2	...	15	14	1	...	...	...
Lakhimpur	...	...	...	...	...	...	15	15	...	...	...	...
Garo Hills	1	1	...	...	...	...	...	...	...	...	...	...
SADIYA FRONTIER TRACT	6	2	4	...	...	...	87	83	4	...	...	...
BALIPARA FRONTIER TRACT	...	...	...	...	...	...	...	...	...	...	...	...
(2) Manipur State	*537*	*291*	*246*	*2*	*2*	...	*15*	*15*	...	...	...	...
(3) Khasi States	*9*	*9*	...	...	...	...	*2*	*2*	...	...	...	...

TABLE XV.

PART I—LANGUAGE—*contd.*

A.—VERNACULARS OF INDIA (VERNACULARS OF ASSAM)—*contd.*

DISTRICT OR STATE	Ao (Naga).			Lhota (Naga).			Sangtam (Naga).			Yachami (Yimsungr) (Naga).		
	Persons.	Males.	Females.	Persons.	Males.	Females.	Persons.	Males.	Females.	Persons.	Males.	Females.
	74	75	76	77	78	79	80	81	82	83	84	85
ASSAM	*33,117*	*15,323*	*17,794*	*18,254*	*8,970*	*9,284*	*4,362*	*2,179*	*2,183*	*115*	*55*	*60*
(1) British Territory	*33,117*	*15,323*	*17,794*	*18,249*	*8,968*	*9,281*	*4,362*	*2,179*	*2,183*	*115*	*55*	*60*
SURMA VALLEY AND HILL DIVISION	33,114	15,322	17,792	18,243	8,962	9,281	4,362	2,179	2,183	115	55	60
Cachar	...	...	...	...	...	...	...	...	...	...	...	...
Sylhet	...	...	...	...	...	...	...	...	...	...	...	...
Khasi and Jaintia Hills (British)	...	...	...	...	...	...	...	...	...	...	...	...
Naga Hills	33,114	15,322	17,792	18,243	8,962	9,281	4,362	2,179	2,183	115	55	60
Lushai Hills	...	...	...	...	...	...	...	...	...	...	...	...
ASSAM VALLEY DIVISION	3	3	...	...	...	...	...	...	...	...	...	...
Goalpara...	...	...	...	...	...	...	...	...	...	...	...	...
Kamrup	...	...	...	...	...	...	...	...	...	...	...	...
Darrang	...	...	...	...	...	...	...	...	...	...	...	...
Nowgong...	2	2	...	...	...	...	...	...	...	...	...	...
Sibsagar	1	1	...	...	...	...	...	...	...	...	...	...
Lakhimpur	...	...	...	...	...	...	...	...	...	...	...	...
Garo Hills	...	...	...	...	...	...	...	...	...	...	...	...
SADIYA FRONTIER TRACT	...	...	...	6	6	...	...	...	...	...	...	...
BALIPARA FRONTIER TRACT	...	...	...	...	...	...	...	...	...	...	...	...
(2) Manipur State	...	...	...	*5*	*2*	*3*	...	...	...	...	...	...
(3) Khasi States	...	...	...	...	...	...	...	...	...	...	...	...

TABLE XV.

Part I.—Language—*contd.*

District or State.	A.—Vernaculars of India (Vernaculars of Assam)—*contd.*											
	Kalyo-kengngu (Naga).			Konyak (Naga).			Rangpang (Naga).			Phom (Naga).		
	Persons.	Males.	Females.	Persons.	Males.	Females.	Persons.	Males.	Females.	Persons.	Males.	Females.
	86	87	88	89	90	91	92	93	94	95	96	97
ASSAM	580	312	268	9,476	4,560	4,916	11,079	5,710	5,369	854	446	408
(1) British Territory	580	312	268	9,471	4,557	4,914	11,079	5,710	5,369	854	446	408
SURMA VALLEY AND HILL DIVISION	580	312	268	9,471	4,557	4,914	...	...	...	854	446	408
Cachar	...	...	...	...	...	...	...	...	...	...	...	...
Sylhet	...	...	...	...	...	...	...	...	...	...	...	...
Khasi and Jaintia Hills (British)	...	...	...	...	...	...	...	...	...	...	...	...
Naga Hills	580	312	268	9,471	4,557	4,914	...	...	...	854	446	408
Lushai Hills	...	...	...	...	...	...	...	...	...	...	...	...
ASSAM VALLEY DIVISION	...	...	...	...	...	...	4,593	2,483	2,110	...	...	...
Goalpara	...	...	...	...	...	...	...	...	...	...	...	...
Kamrup...	...	...	...	...	...	...	...	...	...	...	...	...
Darrang...	...	...	...	...	...	...	...	...	...	...	...	...
Nowgong	...	...	...	...	...	...	...	...	...	...	...	...
Sibsagar...	...	...	...	...	...	...	...	...	...	...	...	...
Lakhimpur	...	...	...	...	...	...	4,593	2,483	2,110	...	...	...
Garo Hills	...	...	...	...	...	...	...	...	...	...	...	...
SADIYA FRONTIER TRACT	...	...	...	...	...	...	6,479	3,227	3,252	...	...	...
PALIPARA FRONTIER TRACT	...	...	...	...	...	...	...	...	...	...	...	...
(2) Manipur State	...	...	...	7	5	2	...	...	...	...	...	...
(3) Khasi States	...	...	...	...	...	...	...	...	...	...	...	...

TABLE XV.

PART I.—LANGUAGE—*contd.*

DISTRICT OR STATE.	A.—VERNACULARS OF INDIA (VERNACULARS OF ASSAM)—*contd.*											
	Naga (unspecified).			**Memi (Mao) (Naga).**			**Maram (Naga).**			**Kwoireng (Quoireng) (Naga).**		
	Persons.	Males.	Females.	Persons.	Males.	Females.	Persons.	Males.	Females.	Persons.	Males.	Females.
	98	99	100	101	102	103	104	105	106	107	108	109
ASSAM	*3,627*	*2,011*	*1,616*	*16,678*	*8,364*	*8,314*	*2,609*	*1,256*	*1,353*	*591*	*328*	*263*
(1) British Territory	*3,602*	*1,987*	*1,615*	*1,237*	*665*	*572*	*13*	*7*	*6*	...	...	...
SURMA VALLEY AND HILL DIVISION	1,765	808	957	1,237	665	572	13	7	6	...	...	...
Cachar	1,658	747	911	...	...	...	...	...	...	...	...	...
Sylhet	...	...	...	...	...	...	13	7	6	...	...	...
Khasi and Jaintia Hills (British)	10	7	3	...	...	...	...	...	...	...	...	...
Naga Hills	76	49	27	1,237	665	572	...	...	...	...	...	...
Lushai Hills	21	5	16	...	...	...	...	...	...	...	...	...
ASSAM VALLEY DIVISION	1,837	1,179	658	...	...	...	...	...	...	...	...	...
Goalpara	4	4	...	...	...	...	...	...	...	...	...	...
Kamrup	14	8	6	...	...	...	...	...	...	...	...	...
Darrang	21	16	5	...	...	...	...	...	...	...	...	...
Nowgong	9	4	5	...	...	...	...	...	...	...	...	...
Sibsagar	1,789	1,147	642	...	...	...	...	...	...	...	...	...
Lakhimpur	...	...	...	...	...	...	...	...	...	...	...	...
Garo Hills	...	...	...	...	...	...	...	...	...	...	...	...
SADIYA FRONTIER TRACT	...	...	...	...	...	...	...	...	...	...	...	...
BALIPARA FRONTIER TRACT	...	...	...	...	...	...	...	...	...	...	...	...
(2) Manipur State	...	...	...	*15,441*	*7,699*	*7,742*	*2,596*	*1,249*	*1,347*	*591*	*328*	*263*
(3) Khasi States	*25*	*24*	*1*	...	...	...	...	...	...	...	...	...

TABLE XV.

PART I.—LANGUAGE—*contd.*

DISTRICT OR STATE.	A.—VERNACULARS OF INDIA (VERNACULARS OF ASSAM)—*contd.*											
	Tangkhul (Naga).			Mikir.			Maring.			Manipuri (Meithei).		
	Persons.	Males.	Females.	Persons.	Males.	Females.	Persons.	Males.	Females.	Persons.	Males.	Females.
	110	111	112	113	114	115	116	117	118	119	120	121
ASSAM	*29,100*	*13,692*	*15,408*	*126,457*	*64,181*	*62,276*	*4,951*	*2,111*	*2,140*	*368,347*	*181,648*	*186,609*
(1) British Territory	*21*	*13*	*8*	*123,425*	*62,653*	*60,772*	*34*	*21*	*13*	*88,914*	*46,905*	*42,009*
SURMA VALLEY AND HILL DIVISION	21	13	8	21,947	10,019	11,928	34	21	13	85,180	43,904	41,276
Cachar	...	...	...	3,132	1,586	1,546	...	...	...	55,550	28,269	27,281
Sylhet	...	...	...	198	120	78	...	...	...	29,135	15,190	13,945
Khasi and Jaintia Hills (British)	...	...	...	16,709	7,707	9,002	...	...	...	20	16	4
Naga Hills	21	13	8	1,208	606	602	...	...	...	465	422	43
Lushai Hills	...	...	...	...	...	...	34	21	13	10	7	3
ASSAM VALLEY DIVISION	...	...	...	102,134	52,613	49,521	...	...	...	3,653	2,931	722
Goalpara	...	...	...	...	...	...	...	...	...	1	1	...
Kamrup	...	...	...	8,923	4,523	4,400	...	...	...	166	106	60
Darrang	...	...	...	4,269	2,296	1,973	...	...	...	158	146	12
Nowgong	...	...	...	57,064	29,245	27,819	...	...	...	881	514	367
Sibsagar	...	...	...	31,878	16,549	15,329	...	...	...	1,310	1,136	174
Lakhimpur	...	...	...	...	...	...	...	...	...	1,133	1,024	109
Garo Hills	...	...	...	...	...	...	...	...	...	4	4	...
SADIYA FRONTIER TRACT	...	...	...	...	...	...	...	...	...	77	67	10
BALIPARA FRONTIER TRACT	...	...	...	44	21	23	...	...	...	4	3	1
(2) Manipur State	*29,079*	*13,679*	*15,400*	128	72	54	*4,917*	*2,090*	*2,127*	*279,181*	*134,619*	*144,562*
(3) Khasi States	...	...	...	*2,906*	*1,456*	*1,450*	...	...	...	*152*	*121*	*31*

TABLE XV.

Part I.—Language—*contd.*

DISTRICT OR STATE.	A.—VERNACULARS OF INDIA (VERNACULARS OF ASSAM)—*contd.*											
	Aimol (Kuki).			Anal (Kuki).			Chiru.			Khelma (Sachip) (Kuki.)		
	Persons.	Males.	Females.	Persons.	Males.	Females.	Persons.	Males.	Females.	Persons.	Males.	Females.
	122	123	124	125	126	127	128	129	130	131	132	133
ASSAM	*511*	*265*	*246*	*3,314*	*1,636*	*1,678*	*1,269*	*568*	*701*	*497*	*252*	*245*
(1) British Territory	...	...	...	...	...	...	...	...	...	*497*	*252*	*245*
SURMA VALLEY AND HILL DIVISION	...	...	...	...	...	...	...	...	...	497	252	245
Cachar	...	...	...	...	...	...	...	...	...	367	182	185
Sylhet	...	...	...	...	...	...	...	...	...	...	...	...
Khasi and Jaintia Hills (British)	...	...	...	...	...	...	...	...	...	...	...	...
Naga Hills	...	...	...	...	...	...	...	...	...	130	70	60
Lushai Hills	...	...	...	...	...	...	...	...	...	...	...	...
ASSAM VALLEY DIVISION	...	...	...	...	...	...	...	...	...	...	...	...
Goalpara	...	...	...	...	...	...	...	...	...	...	...	...
Kamrup	...	...	...	...	...	...	...	...	...	...	...	...
Darrang	...	...	...	...	...	...	...	...	...	...	...	...
Nowgong	...	...	...	...	...	...	...	...	...	...	...	...
Sibsagar	...	...	...	...	...	...	...	...	...	...	...	...
Lakhimpur	...	...	...	...	...	...	...	...	...	...	...	...
Garo Hills	...	...	...	...	...	...	...	...	...	...	...	...
SADIYA FRONTIER TRACT	...	...	...	...	...	...	...	...	...	...	...	...
BALIPARA FRONTIER TRACT	...	...	...	...	...	...	...	...	...	...	...	...
(2) Manipur State	*511*	*265*	*246*	*3,314*	*1,636*	*1,678*	*1,269*	*568*	*701*	...	...	...
(3) Khasi States	...	...	...	...	...	...	...	...	...	...	...	...

TABLE XV.

PART I.—LANGUAGE—*contd.*

DISTRICT OR STATE.	A.—VERNACULARS OF INDIA (VERNACULARS OF ASSAM)—*contd.*											
	Kom (Kuki).			Lamgang (Kuki).			Purum (Kuki).			Hmar or Mhar.		
	Persons.	Males.	Females.	Persons.	Males.	Females.	Persons.	Males.	Females.	Persons.	Males.	Females.
	134	135	136	137	138	139	140	141	142	143	144	145
ASSAM	*2,669*	*1,299*	*1,370*	*1,224*	*569*	*655*	*305*	*147*	*158*	*21,583*	*10,035*	*11,548*
(1) British Territory	...	...	...	*17*	*10*	*7*	...	...	...	*15,940*	*7,290*	*8,650*
SURMA VALLEY AND HILL DIVISION	...	...	...	17	10	7	...	...	...	15,940	7,290	8,650
Cachar	...	...	...	17	10	7	...	...	...	...	...	...
Sylhet	...	...	...	...	...	...	...	...	...	...	...	...
Khasi and Jaintia Hills (British)	...	...	...	...	...	...	...	...	...	...	...	...
Naga Hills	...	...	...	...	...	...	...	...	...	...	...	...
Lushai Hills	...	...	...	...	...	...	...	...	...	15,940	7,290	8,650
ASSAM VALLEY DIVISION	...	...	...	...	...	...	...	...	...	...	...	...
Goalpara	...	...	...	...	...	...	...	...	...	...	...	...
Kamrup	...	...	...	...	...	...	...	...	...	...	...	...
Darrang	...	...	...	...	...	...	...	...	...	...	...	...
Nowgong	...	...	...	...	...	...	...	...	...	...	...	...
Sibsagar	...	...	...	...	...	...	...	...	...	...	...	...
Lakhimpur	...	...	...	...	...	...	...	...	...	...	...	...
Garo Hills	...	...	...	...	...	...	...	...	...	...	...	...
SADIYA FRONTIER TRACT	...	...	...	...	...	...	...	...	...	...	...	...
BALIPARA FRONTIER TRACT	...	...	...	...	...	...	...	...	...	...	...	...
(2) Manipur State	*2,669*	*1,299*	*1,370*	*1,207*	*559*	*648*	*305*	*147*	*158*	*5,643*	*2,735*	*2,908*
(3) Khasi States	...	...	...	...	...	...	...	...	...	...	...	...

TABLE XV.

PART I.—LANGUAGE—*contd.*

DISTRICT OR STATE.	A.—VERNACULARS OF INDIA (VERNACULARS OF ASSAM)—*contd.*											
	Vaiphei (Kuki).			Gangte (Kuki).			Kholhang (Khotlang) (Kuki).			Hrangkhol (Kuki).		
	Persons.	Males.	Females.	Persons.	Males.	Females.	Persons.	Males.	Females.	Persons.	Males.	Females.
	146	147	148	149	150	151	152	153	154	155	156	157
ASSAM	*4,624*	*2,268*	*2,356*	*2,455*	*1,218*	*1,237*	*1,697*	*819*	*878*	*1,126*	*563*	*563*
(1) British Territory	*1*	...	*1*	*10*	*6*	*4*	*1,697*	*819*	*878*	*1,126*	*563*	*563*
SURMA VALLEY AND HILL DIVISION	1	...	1	10	6	4	1,697	819	878	1,126	563	563
Cachar	...	...	...	10	6	4	1,690	814	876	1,078	540	538
Sylhet	...	...	...	...	...	...	...	...	...	...	...	...
Khasi and Jaintia Hills (British)	...	...	...	...	...	...	...	...	...	...	...	...
Naga Hills	...	...	...	...	...	...	7	5	2	...	...	...
Lushai Hills	1	...	1	...	...	...	...	...	...	48	23	25
ASSAM VALLEY DIVISION	...	...	...	...	...	...	...	...	...	...	...	...
Goalpara	...	...	...	...	...	...	...	...	...	...	...	...
Kamrup	...	...	...	...	...	...	...	...	...	...	...	...
Darrang	...	...	...	...	...	...	...	...	...	...	...	...
Nowgong	...	...	...	...	...	...	...	...	...	...	...	...
Sibsagar	...	...	...	...	...	...	...	...	...	...	...	...
Lakhimpur	...	...	...	...	...	...	...	...	...	...	...	...
Garo Hills	...	...	...	...	...	...	...	...	...	...	...	...
SADIYA FRONTIER TRACT	...	...	...	...	...	...	...	...	...	...	...	...
BALIPARA FRONTIER TRACT	...	...	...	...	...	...	...	...	...	...	...	...
(2) Manipur State	*4,623*	*2,268*	*2,355*	*2,445*	*1,212*	*1,233*	...	...	...	...	...	...
(3) Khasi States	...	...	...	...	...	...	...	...	...	...	...	...

TABLE XV.

PART I.—LANGUAGE—*contd.*

DISTRICT OR STATE.	A.—VERNACULARS OF INDIA (VERNACULARS OF ASSAM)—*contd.*											
	Beite (Kuki).			Chote (Kuki).			Paite.			Ralte.		
	Persons.	Males.	Females.	Persons.	Males.	Females.	Persons.	Males.	Females.	Persons.	Males.	Females.
	158	159	160	161	162	163	164	165	166	167	168	169
ASSAM	*619*	*297*	*322*	*250*	*135*	*115*	*14,674*	*7,420*	*7,254*	*16,163*	*7,527*	*8,636*
(1) British Territory	*619*	*297*	*322*	...	...	...	*6,634*	*3,336*	*3,298*	*16,047*	*7,476*	*8,571*
SURMA VALLEY AND HILL DIVISION	619	297	322	...	...	...	6,634	3,336	3,298	16,047	7,476	8,571
Cachar	619	297	322	...	...	...	...	...	...	5	5	...
Sylhet	...	...	...	...	...	...	...	...	...	...	...	...
Khasi and Jaintia Hills (British)	...	...	...	...	...	...	...	...	...	...	...	...
Naga Hills	...	...	...	...	...	...	...	...	...	...	...	...
Lushai Hills	...	...	...	...	...	...	6,634	3,336	3,298	16,042	7,471	8,571
ASSAM VALLEY DIVISION	...	...	...	...	...	...	...	...	...	...	...	...
Goalpara	...	...	...	...	...	...	...	...	...	...	...	...
Kamrup	...	...	...	...	...	...	...	...	...	...	...	...
Darrang	...	...	...	...	...	...	...	...	...	...	...	...
Nowgong	...	...	...	...	...	...	...	...	...	...	...	...
Sibsagar	...	...	...	...	...	...	...	...	...	...	...	...
Lakhimpur	...	...	...	...	...	...	...	...	...	...	...	...
Garo Hills	...	...	...	...	...	...	...	...	...	...	...	...
SADIYA FRONTIER TRACT	...	...	...	...	...	...	...	...	...	...	...	...
BALIPARA FRONTIER TRACT	...	...	...	...	...	...	...	...	...	...	...	...
(2) Manipur State	...	...	...	*250*	*135*	*115*	*8,040*	*4,084*	*3,956*	*116*	*51*	*65*
(3) Khasi States	...	...	...	...	...	...	...	...	...	...	...	...

TABLE XV.

PART I.—LANGUAGE—*contd.*

A.—VERNACULARS OF INDIA (VERNACULARS OF ASSAM)—*contd.*

DISTRICT OR STATE.	Sokte (Suhte including Kamhao).			Thado (Kuki).			Changsen (Kuki).			Kuki unspecified.		
	Persons.	Males.	Females.	Persons.	Males.	Females.	Persons.	Males.	Females.	Persons.	Males.	Females.
	170	171	172	173	174	175	176	177	178	179	180	181
ASSAM	*777*	*366*	*411*	*50,080*	*24,292*	*25,788*	*414*	*204*	*210*	*6,154*	*3,092*	*3,062*
(1) British Territory	...	...	...	*3,378*	*1,676*	*1,702*	*414*	*204*	*210*	*5,810*	*2915*	*2,895*
SURMA VALLEY AND HILL DIVISION	...	...	...	3,369	1,667	1,702	414	204	210	5,373	2,672	2,701
Cachar	...	...	...	1,272	608	664	414	204	210	3,344	1,647	1,697
Sylhet	...	...	...	...	...	...	...	...	...	330	159	171
Khasi and Jaintia Hills (British)	...	...	...	...	...	...	...	...	...	1,398	719	679
Naga Hills	...	...	...	2,097	1,059	1,038	...	...	...	117	70	47
Lushai Hills	...	...	...	...	...	...	...	...	...	190	77	113
ASSAM VALLEY DIVISION	...	...	...	9	9	...	...	...	...	437	243	194
Goalpara	...	...	...	...	...	...	...	...	...	...	...	...
Kamrup	...	...	...	...	...	...	...	...	...	...	...	...
Darrang	...	...	...	...	...	...	...	...	...	1	1	...
Nowgong	...	...	...	...	...	...	...	...	...	396	212	184
Sibsagar	...	...	...	9	9	...	...	...	...	5	4	1
Lakhimpur	...	...	...	...	...	...	...	...	...	...	...	...
Garo Hills	...	...	...	...	...	...	...	...	...	35	26	9
SADIYA FRONTIER TRACT	...	...	...	...	...	...	...	...	...	...	...	...
BALIPARA FRONTIER TRACT	...	...	...	...	...	...	...	...	...	...	...	...
(2) Manipur State	*777*	*366*	*411*	*46,702*	*22,616*	*24,086*	...	...	...	*344*	*177*	*167*
(3) Khasi States	...	...	...	...	...	...	...	...	...	...	...	...

TABLE XV.

PART I.—LANGUAGE—*contd.*

DISTRICT OR STATE.	A.—VERNACULARS OF INDIA (VERNACULARS OF ASSAM)—*contd.*											
	Lakher.			Lushei.			Zahao.			Unspecified Chin or Poi.		
	Persons.	Males.	Females.	Persons.	Males.	Females.	Persons.	Males.	Females.	Persons.	Males.	Females.
	182	183	184	185	186	187	188	189	190	191	192	193
ASSAM	*6,186*	*3,004*	*3,182*	*57,597*	*27,017*	*30,580*	*3,886*	*1,845*	*2,041*	*14,191*	*6,935*	*7,256*
(1) British Territory	*6,186*	*3,004*	*3,182*	*57,231*	*26,820*	*30,411*	*3,886*	*1,845*	*2,041*	*14,191*	*6,935*	*7,256*
SURMA VALLEY AND HILL DIVISION	6,186	3,004	3,182	57,200	26,802	30,398	3,886	1,845	2,041	14,191	6,935	7,256
Cachar	...	...	...	412	239	173	...	...	...	...	...	...
Sylhet	...	...	...	32	27	5	...	...	...	...	...	...
Khasi and Jaintia Hills (British)...	...	...	...	7	6	1	...	...	...	...	...	...
Naga Hills	...	...	...	6	4	2	...	...	...	...	...	...
Lushai Hills	6,186	3,004	3,182	56,743	26,526	30,217	3,886	1,845	2,041	14,191	6,935	7,256
ASSAM VALLEY DIVISION	...	...	...	19	13	6	...	...	...	...	...	...
Goalpara	...	...	...	2	...	2	...	...	...	...	...	...
Kamrup	...	...	...	2	2	...	...	...	...	...	...	...
Darrang	...	...	...	4	2	2	...	...	...	...	...	...
Nowgong	...	...	...	...	...	...	...	...	...	...	...	...
Sibsagar	...	...	...	1	1	...	...	...	...	...	...	...
Lakhimpur	...	...	...	9	7	2	...	...	...	...	...	...
Garo Hills	...	...	...	1	1	...	...	...	...	...	...	...
SADIYA FRONTIER TRACT	...	...	...	12	5	7	...	...	...	...	...	...
BALIPARA FRONTIER TRACT	...	...	...	...	...	...	...	...	...	...	...	...
(2) Manipur State	...	...	...	*337*	*171*	*166*	...	...	...	...	...	...
(3) Khasi States	...	...	...	*29*	*26*	*3*	...	...	...	...	...	...

TABLE XV.

PART I—LANGUAGE—*contd.*

DISTRICT OR STATE.	A—VERNACULARS OF INDIA (VERNACULARS OF ASSAM)—*contd.*											
	Kachin or Singpho.			Khamti.			Shan			Bengali.		
	Persons.	Males.	Females.	Persons.	Males.	Females.	Persons.	Females.	Females.	Persons.	Males.	Females.
	194	195	196	197	198	199	200	201	202	203	204	205
ASSAM	*3,049*	*1,659*	*1,383*	*3,858*	*2,097*	*1,761*	*1,855*	*932*	*923*	*3,966,363*	*2,087,060*	*1,879,303*
(1) British Territory	*3,049*	*1,659*	*1,383*	*3,858*	*2,097*	*1,761*	*1,855*	*932*	*923*	*3,960,719*	*2,083,134*	*1,877,588*
SURMA VALLEY AND HILL DIVISION	...	...	...	16	16	...	...	...	...	2,852.483	1,479,033	1,373,450
Cachar	...	...	...	16	16	...	...	...	...	338,772	180,956	157,816
Sylhet	...	...	...	...	...	...	...	...	...	2,509.682	1,295,471	1,214,211
Khasi and Jaintia Hills (British)	...	...	...	...	...	...	...	...	...	2,169	1,432	737
Naga Hills	...	...	...	...	...	...	...	...	...	527	378	149
Lushai Hills...	...	...	...	...	...	...	...	...	...	1,333	796	537
ASSAM VALLEY DIVISION	1,809	1,030	779	1.874	1.074	800	1,855	932	923	1,106.581	603,047	503,534
Goalpara	...	...	...	...	...	...	...	...	...	476.433	253,726	222,707
Kamrup	1	...	1	...	...	...	...	...	...	170.409	96.773	73,639
Darrang	5	3	2	...	...	...	...	...	...	95,115	53,553	42,563
Nowgong	...	...	...	...	...	...	1	1	...	193,349	105,353	87,996
Sibsagar	3	3	...	196	162	34	1,433	719	714	73,351	39,296	34,055
Lakhimpur	1,800	1,024	776	1,688	922	706	420	211	209	77,471	44,354	33,117
Garo Hills	...	...	...	...	...	...	1	1	...	20,453	10,996	9,457
SADIYA FRONTIER TRACT	1.233	629	604	1,897	964	923	...	...	...	1,193	709	484
BALIPARA FRONTIER TRACT	...	...	...	81	48	33	...	...	...	455	275	180
(2) Manipur State	...	...	...	...	...	...	...	...	...	*2,273*	*1,329*	*944*
(3) Khasi States	...	...	...	...	...	...	...	...	...	*3,378*	*2,607*	*771*

TABLE XV.

PART I—LANGUAGE—*contd.*

DISTRICT OR STATE.	A.—VERNACULARS OF INDIA (VERNACULARS OF ASSAM)—*concld.*			A.—VERNACULARS OF INDIA (OUTSIDE ASSAM).					
	Assamese.			Balochi.			Bhotia of Bhutan.		
	Persons.	Males.	Females.	Persons.	Males.	Females.	Persons.	Males.	Females.
	206	207	208	209	210	211	212	213	214
ASSSAM	*1,994,564*	*1,039,207*	*955,357*	*799*	*609*	*197*	*1,155*	*924*	*231*
(1) British Territory	*1,992,846*	*1,038,309*	*954,537*	*799*	*609*	*197*	*1,116*	*906*	*210*
SURMA VALLEY AND HILL DIVISION	4,904	2,915	1,989	35	27	8	1	1	...
Cachar	2,215	1,340	875	...	...	...	1	1	...
Sylhet	1,477	839	638	1	1	...	...	...	...
Khasi and Jaintia Hills (British)	283	175	108	20	16	4	...	...	...
Naga Hills	815	407	318	14	10	4	...	...	...
Lushai Hills	114	74	40	...	...	...	...	...	...
ASSAM VALLEY DIVISION	1,978,823	1,030,404	948,419	763	574	189	1,112	902	210
Goalpara	161,179	83,165	78,014	...	...	...	28	24	4
Kamrup	640,512	331,445	309,067	3	3	...	716	533	183
Darrang	193,089	102,293	90,796	...	...	...	305	285	20
Nowgong	237,406	121,931	115,475	8	6	2	10	10	...
Sibsagar	503,603	266,168	237,435	16	10	6	6	6	...
Lakhimpur	229,461	122,492	106,969	736	555	181	45	42	3
Garo Hills	5,573	2,910	2,663	...	...	...	2	2	...
SADIYA FRONTIER TRACT	8,419	4,551	3,868	1	1	...	2	2	...
BALIPARA FRONTIER TRACT	700	439	261	...	...	...	1	1	...
(2) Manipur State	*125*	*87*	*38*	...	...	...	*37*	*17*	*20*
(3) Khasi States	*1,593*	*811*	*789*	...	...	...	*2*	*1*	*1*

TABLE XV.

Part I.—Language—*contd.*

District or State.	A.—Vernaculars of India (outside Assam)—*contd.*											
	Bhumij.			**Gondi.**			**Gujarati.**			**Gurung.**		
	Persons.	Males.	Females.	Persons.	Males.	Females.	Persons.	Males.	Females.	Persons.	Males.	Females.
	215	216	217	218	219	220	221	222	223	224	225	226
ASSAM	*16,797*	*8,814*	*7,983*	*49,104*	*26,246*	*22,858*	*2,035*	*1,139*	*896*	*762*	*505*	*257*
(1) British Territory	*16,797*	*8,814*	*7,983*	*49,104*	*26,246*	*22,858*	*2,033*	*1,138*	*895*	*711*	*468*	*243*
SURMA VALLEY AND HILL DIVISION	**1,622**	**966**	**656**	**1,586**	**710**	**876**	**386**	**199**	**187**	**501**	**319**	**182**
Cachar	155	75	80	773	423	350	133	82	51	...	...	...
Sylhet	1,467	891	576	808	284	524	252	116	136	...	...	...
Khasi and Jaintia Hills (British)	...	...	...	...	...	...	...	...	...	313	203	110
Naga Hills	...	...	...	5	3	2	1	1	...	56	44	12
Lushai Hills	...	...	...	...	...	...	...	...	...	132	72	60
ASSAM VALLEY DIVISION	**15,157**	**7,838**	**7,319**	**47,320**	**25,426**	**21,894**	**1,647**	**939**	**708**	**202**	**143**	**59**
Goalpara	1	...	1	42	32	10	41	35	6	41	28	13
Kamrup	310	158	152	336	178	158	35	34	1	...	...	...
Darrang	3,225	1,669	1,556	17,631	9,732	7,899	191	111	80	59	30	29
Nowgong	723	363	360	1,336	675	661	393	193	200	23	20	3
Sibsagar	5,500	2,967	2,533	9,973	5,211	4,762	309	155	154	29	20	9
Lakhimpur	5,338	2,681	2,657	18,002	9,598	8,404	670	464	206	50	45	5
Garo Hills	...	...	...	...	...	...	3	2	1	...	...	...
SADIYA FRONTIER TRACT	**18**	**10**	**8**	**197**	**109**	**88**	...	...	...	**7**	**5**	**2**
BALIPARA FRONTIER TRACT	...	...	...	**1**	**1**	...	...	...	...	**1**	**1**	...
(2) Manipur State	...	...	...	...	...	...	...	...	...	*32*	*19*	*13*
(3) Khasi States	...	...	...	...	...	...	*2*	*1*	*1*	*19*	*18*	*1*

TABLE XV.

PART I.—LANGUAGE—*contd.*

DISTRICT OR STATE.	A.—VERNACULARS OF INDIA (OUTSIDE ASSAM)—*contd.*											
	Hindi.			**Ho.**			**Kandhi or Kui.**			**Kharia.**		
	Persons.	Males.	Females.	Persons.	Males.	Females.	Persons.	Males.	Females.	Persons.	Males.	Females.
	227	228	229	230	231	232	233	234	235	236	237	238
ASSAM	*589,841*	*335,880*	*253,959*	*1,729*	*882*	*847*	*6,180*	*3,120*	*3,060*	*14,358*	*7,433*	*6,925*
(1) British Territory	*587,934*	*334,933*	*253,001*	*1,729*	*882*	*847*	*6,180*	*3,120*	*3,060*	*14,358*	*7,433*	*6,925*
SURMA VALLEY AND HILL DIVISION	221,840	117,027	104,813	...	...	...	1,138	471	667	441	229	212
Cachar	103,788	55,117	48,671	...	...	...	298	166	132	...	...	...
Sylhet	116,237	61,098	55,139	...	...	...	840	305	535	434	222	212
Khasi and Jaintia Hills (British)	1,038	836	202	...	...	...	...	...	...	...	...	...
Naga Hills	672	495	177	...	...	...	...	...	...	7	7	...
Lushai Hills	104	81	23	...	...	...	...	...	...	...	...	...
ASSAM VALLEY DIVISION	361,481	214,102	147,379	1,726	879	847	5,003	2,630	2,373	13,896	7,190	6,706
Goalpara	24,759	18,082	6,677	...	...	...	...	...	...	33	19	14
Kamrup	18,891	13,987	4,907	...	...	...	1	1	...	163	81	82
Darrang	50,408	30,206	20,202	30	18	12	870	495	375	3,423	1,755	1,668
Nowgong	29,968	18,147	11,821	50	23	27	402	152	250	202	96	106
Sibsagar	104,225	57,074	47,151	1,517	768	749	635	355	280	3,727	1,925	1,802
Lakhimpur	132,218	75,891	56,327	129	70	59	3,095	1,627	1,468	6,347	3,313	3,034
Garo Hills	859	715	144	...	...	...	...	...	...	...	...	...
SADIYA FRONTIER TRACT	3,453	2,200	1,253	...	...	...	6	3	3	1	1	...
BALIPARA FRONTIER TRACT	400	244	156	3	3	...	33	16	17	21	14	7
(2) Manipur State	*1,049*	*570*	*479*	...	...	...	...	...	...	...	...	...
(3) Khasi States	*1,558*	*1,086*	*472*	...	...	...	...	...	...	...	...	...

TABLE XV.

PART I.—LANGUAGE—*contd.*

A.—VERNACULARS OF INDIA (OUTSIDE ASSAM)—*contd.*

DISTRICT OR STATE.	Korwa.			Kurku.			Kurukh or Oraon.			Limbu.		
	Persons.	Males.	Females.	Persons.	Males.	Females.	Persons.	Males.	Females.	Persons.	Males.	Females.
	339	340	341	342	343	344	345	346	347	348	349	350
ASSAM	*6,825*	*3,555*	*3,270*	*3,742*	*2,028*	*1,714*	*52,516*	*27,898*	*24,618*	*1,176*	*654*	*522*
(1) British Territory	*6,822*	*3,553*	*3,269*	*3,742*	*2,028*	*1,714*	*52,516*	*27,898*	*24,618*	*1,041*	*566*	*475*
SURMA VALLEY AND HILL DIVISION	340	142	198	904	482	422	2,833	1,511	1,322	176	78	98
Cachar	...	...	...	229	109	120	1,604	827	777	4	...	4
Sylhet	335	138	197	659	358	301	1,229	684	545	...	...	...
Khasi and Jaintia Hills (British)	4	3	1	...	...	...	...	...	...	15	15	...
Naga Hills	1	1	...	16	15	1	...	...	...	76	44	32
Lushai Hills	...	...	...	...	...	...	...	...	...	81	19	62
ASSAM VALLEY DIVISION	6,482	3,411	3,071	2,938	1,546	1,392	49,272	26,169	23,103	833	468	365
Goalpara	43	24	19	10	4	6	5,412	2,850	2,562	88	40	39
Kamrup	29	8	21	...	...	...	2,104	1,004	1,100	...	...	...
Darrang	1,877	977	900	601	309	292	13,964	7,331	6,633	579	319	260
Nowgong	305	161	144	653	330	323	1,929	1,022	907	...	...	...
Sibsagar	2,209	1,221	988	820	454	366	6,970	3,778	3,192	84	35	49
Lakhimpur	2,019	1,020	999	855	450	405	18,903	10,203	8,700	72	60	12
Garo Hills	...	...	...	...	...	...	...	...	...	10	6	4
SADIYA FRONTIER TRACT	...	...	...	...	...	...	395	208	187	32	20	12
BALIPARA FRONTIER TRACT	...	...	...	...	...	...	16	10	6	...	...	...
(2) Manipur State	3	2	1	...	...	...	...	...	...	*75*	*39*	*36*
(3) Khasi States	...	...	...	...	...	...	...	...	...	*60*	*49*	*11*

TABLE XV.

PART I.—LANGUAGE—*contd.*

A.—VERNACULARS OF INDIA (OUTSIDE ASSAM)—*contd.*

DISTRICT OR STATE.	Magari.			Marathi.			Mundari.			Naipali (Khas-Kura).		
	Persons.	Males.	Females.	Persons.	Males.	Females.	Persons.	Males.	Females.	Persons.	Males.	Females.
	251	252	253	254	255	256	257	258	259	260	261	262
ASSAM	*2,454*	*1,581*	*873*	*4,327*	*2,433*	*1,894*	*159,156*	*83,509*	*75,654*	*136,106*	*83,449*	*52,657*
(1) British Territory	*2,207*	*1,408*	*799*	*4,315*	*2,422*	*1,893*	*159,156*	*83,509*	*75,654*	*123,788*	*75,093*	*48,695*
SURMA VALLEY AND HILL DIVISION	1,111	781	330	360	186	174	10,152	5,057	5,095	12,558	8,065	4,493
Cachar	5	...	5	123	78	45	4,128	2,100	2,028	1,671	1,012	659
Sylhet	118	63	55	194	83	111	6,020	3,064	3,006	730	490	240
Khasi and Jaintia Hills (British)	743	560	183	5	2	3	1	...	1	6,661	4,600	2,061
Naga Hills	117	86	31	18	3	15	3	3	...	2,590	1,665	925
Lushai Hills	128	72	56	...	...	...	...	...	...	1,906	1,198	708
ASSAM VALLEY DIVISION	963	553	410	3,975	2,256	1,719	148 268	78,011	70,257	103,610	61,855	41,764
Goalpara	96	61	35	76	44	32	1 180	633	547	12,540	7,597	4,943
Kamrup	5	4	1	19	12	7	1,673	829	844	13,437	8,192	5,245
Darrang	773	428	345	1,004	632	372	38,537	20,749	17,788	39,596	22,062	17,534
Nowgong	...	...	...	405	233	173	4,221	2,255	1,966	5,959	3,618	2,341
Sibsagar	52	36	16	1,281	723	558	38 531	19,977	18,554	10,190	6,107	4,083
Lakhimpur	36	23	13	1,189	612	577	64 126	33,568	30,558	19,116	12,480	6,636
Garo Hills	1	1	...	1	1	...	...	...	...	2,782	1,739	1,043
SADIYA FRONTIER TRACT	133	74	59	...	...	...	659	390	269	5,390	3,370	2,020
BALIPARA FRONTIER TRACT	...	...	...	...	...	...	77	44	33	1,221	903	318
(2) Manipur State	*200*	*138*	*62*	*2*	*1*	*1*	...	...	...	*2,705*	*1,603*	*1,102*
(3) Khasi States	*47*	*35*	*12*	...	...	...	...	...	...	*9,613*	*6,753*	*2,860*

TABLE XV.

PART I.—LANGUAGE—*contd.*

A.—VERNACULARS OF INDIA (OUTSIDE ASSAM)—*contd.*

DISTRICT OR STATE.	Oriya.			Panjabi.			Pashto.			Rajasthani.		
	Persons.	Males.	Females.	Persons.	Males.	Females.	Persons.	Males.	Females.	Persons.	Males.	Females.
	263	264	265	266	267	268	269	270	271	272	273	274
ASSAM	*202,737*	*104,874*	*97,863*	*3,587*	*2,823*	*764*	*1,703*	*1,638*	*65*	*16,245*	*11,613*	*4,632*
(1) British Territory	*202,689*	*104,845*	*97,844*	*3,274*	*2,578*	*696*	*1,634*	*1,573*	*61*	*15,854*	*11,376*	*4,478*
SURMA VALLEY AND HILL DIVISION	39,426	19,607	19,819	515	394	121	608	578	30	482	341	141
Cachar	9,611	4,868	4,743	168	127	41	175	165	10	20	8	12
Sylhet	29,701	14,671	15,030	90	71	19	270	265	5	163	144	19
Khasi and Jaintia Hills (British)	17	11	6	179	131	48	27	20	7	169	90	79
Naga Hills	96	56	40	66	55	11	136	128	8	130	99	31
Lushai Hills	1	1	...	12	10	2	...	...	...	...	...	...
ASSAM VALLEY DIVISION	161,568	84,359	77,209	2,733	2,167	566	1,014	983	31	14,839	10,675	4,164
Goalpara	572	362	210	54	40	14	143	139	4	1,120	786	334
Kamrup	1,356	806	550	195	147	48	45	45	...	2,529	1,649	880
Darrang	42,516	22,136	20,380	169	134	35	127	127	...	1,503	1,303	200
Nowgong	7,436	3,833	3,603	183	126	57	70	65	5	1,061	820	241
Sibsagar	55,178	28,409	26,769	530	392	138	162	157	5	3,678	2,687	991
Lakhimpur	54,510	28,813	25,697	1,594	1,322	272	466	449	17	4,941	3,423	1,518
Garo Hills	...	...	...	8	6	2	1	1	...	7	7	...
SADIYA FRONTIER TRACT	1,639	849	790	26	17	9	12	12	...	523	350	173
BALIPARA FRONTIER TRACT	56	30	26	...	...	...	...	...	...	10	10	...
(2) Manipur State	...	...	...	*67*	*47*	*20*	*1*	*1*	...	*308*	*197*	*111*
(3) Khasi States	*48*	*29*	*19*	*246*	*198*	*48*	*68*	*64*	*4*	*83*	*40*	*43*

TABLE XV.

Part I.—Language—*contd.*

District or State.	Santali. Persons.	Santali. Males.	Santali. Females.	Savara. Persons.	Savara. Males.	Savara. Females.	Tamil. Persons.	Tamil. Males.	Tamil. Females.	Telugu. Persons.	Telugu. Males.	Telugu. Females.
	A.—Vernaculars of India (outside Assam)—*contd.*											
	275	276	277	278	279	280	281	282	283	284	285	286
ASSAM	*101,949*	*54,134*	*47,815*	*9,340*	*5,241*	*4,099*	*2,106*	*1,193*	*913*	*30,786*	*16,392*	*14,394*
(1) British Territory	*101,949*	*54,134*	*47,815*	*9,340*	*5,241*	*4,090*	*2,041*	*1,153*	*888*	*30,776*	*16,384*	*14,392*
SURMA VALLEY AND HILL DIVISION	9,725	5,208	4,517	409	206	203	958	585	373	8,310	4,143	4,167
Cachar	3,337	1,736	1,601	...	...	...	146	61	85	2,097	1,068	1,029
Sylhet	6,143	3,234	2,909	...	...	...	811	523	288	6,192	3,061	3,128
Khasi and Jaintia Hills (British)	...	...	...	371	191	180	1	1	...	10	5	5
Naga Hills	173	170	3	...	...	...	...	...	...	11	6	5
Lushai Hills	82	78	4	...	...	...	...	...	...	...	...	...
ASSAM VALLEY DIVISION	92,052	48,781	43,271	8,916	5,024	3,892	1,082	567	515	22,379	12,190	10,189
Goalpara	42,508	22,607	19,901	...	...	...	8	4	4	55	33	22
Kamrup	1,468	813	655	48	25	23	25	16	9	223	138	85
Darrang	8,536	4,469	4,067	2,672	1,552	1,120	145	92	53	3,422	1,853	1,569
Nowgong	1,633	899	734	...	...	...	7	7	...	667	554	310
Sibsagar	19,871	10,453	9,418	2,871	1,555	1,316	293	167	126	9,889	5,170	4,719
Lakhimpur	17,946	9,424	8,522	3,325	1,892	1,433	604	281	323	8,121	4,606	3,515
Garo Hills	...	...	...	...	...	...	...	...	...	2	2	...
SADIYA FRONTIER TRACT	44	30	14	...	...	...	1	1	...	87	51	36
BALIPARA FRONTIER TRACT	128	115	13	15	11	4	...	...	...	...	...	...
(2) Manipur State	...	...	...	...	...	...	*1*	*1*	...	*2*	*2*	...
(3) Khasi States	...	...	...	...	...	...	*64*	*39*	*25*	*9*	*7*	*2*

TABLE XV.

PART I.—LANGUAGE—*contd.*

DISTRICT OR STATE.	A.—VERNACULARS OF INDIA (OUTSIDE ASSAM)—*contd.* Turi. Persons.	Males.	Females.	B.—VERNACULARS OF ASIATIC COUNTRIES BEYOND INDIA. Bhotia of Tibet. Persons.	Males.	Females.	Chinese. Persons.	Males.	Females.
	287	288	289	290	291	292	293	294	295
ASSAM	*7,440*	*3,634*	*3,806*	*790*	*544*	*246*	*532*	*429*	*103*
(1) British Territory	*7,440*	*3,634*	*3,806*	*782*	*539*	*243*	*507*	*408*	*99*
SURMA VALLEY AND HILL DIVISION	837	264	573	70	43	27	52	42	10
Cachar	676	182	494	...	...	...	9	7	2
Sylhet	161	82	79	...	...	...	23	21	2
Khasi and Jaintia Hills (British)	...	...	...	...	...	...	19	13	6
Naga Hills	...	...	...	27	21	6	1	1	...
Lushai Hills	...	...	...	43	22	21	...	...	...
ASSAM VALLEY DIVISION	6,602	3,369	3,233	476	353	123	455	366	89
Goalpara	39	18	21	124	121	3	...	...	...
Kamrup	16	3	13	1	1	...	6	4	2
Darrang	1,263	652	611	92	53	39	132	111	21
Nowgong	190	94	96	...	...	...	25	21	4
Sibsagar	4,103	2,095	2,008	82	65	17	72	60	12
Lakhimpur	992	508	484	161	103	58	220	170	50
Garo Hills	...	...	...	16	10	6	...	...	...
SADIYA FRONTIER TRACT	...	...	...	236	143	93	...	...	...
BALIPARA FRONTIER TRACT	1	1	...	...	...	...	...	...	...
(2) Manipur State	...	...	...	...	...	...	...	...	...
(3) Khasi States	...	...	...	*8*	*5*	*3*	*25*	*21*	*4*

TABLE XV.

PART I.—LANGUAGE—*concld.*

DISTRICT OR STATE.	C.—EUROPEAN LANGUAGES. English. Persons.	English. Males.	English. Females.	Others. Persons.	Others. Males.	Others. Females.	DETAILS OF OTHERS.
	296	297	298	299	300	301	
ASSAM	*3,852*	*2,617*	*1,235*	*1,844*	*1,210*	*634*	A.—Vernaculars of India (outside Assam) :—
							Bhili ... 289+179.
(1) British Territory	*3,615*	*2,500*	*1,115*	*1,629*	*1,041*	*588*	Burmese ... 47+28.
							Garhwali ... 58+18.
							Goanese ... 4+0.
SURMA VALLEY AND HILL DIVISION	1,155	759	396	328	242	86	Kanarese ... 32+50.
Cachar	331	218	113	51	42	9	Kashmiri ... 2+0.
Sylhet	525	393	132	177	130	47	Khambu ... 18+24.
Khasi and Jaintia Hills (British)	229	108	121	41	32	9	Malayalam ... 86+26.
Naga Hills	33	19	14	13	10	3	Malto ... 4+0.
Lushai Hills	37	21	16	46	28	18	Murmi ... 18+12.
							Newari ... 104+72.
							Palaung ... 33+0.
ASSAM VALLEY DIVISION	2,410	1,710	700	1,189	736	453	Rai ... 147+91.
Goalpara	28	21	7	198	128	70	Sindhi ... 14+1.
Kamrup	281	204	77	53	33	20	Tashon ... 14+12.
Darrang	354	244	110	227	147	80	B.—Vernaculars of Asia (beyond India) :—
Nowgong	170	112	58	55	35	20	Arabic ... 67+13.
Sibsagar	567	373	194	350	211	139	Hebrew ... 7+7.
Lakhimpur	1,000	753	247	294	174	120	Persian ... 216+83.
Garo Hills	10	3	7	13	9	4	Turkish ... 0+1.
							Malay ... 4+7.
							C.—European languages :—
SADIYA FRONTIER TRACT	46	27	19	85	48	37	Danish ... 1+2.
							French ... 2+2.
BALIPARA FRONTIER TRACT	4	4	...	27	15	12	German ... 3+2.
							Italian ... 84+11.
							Norwegian ... 0+1.
(2) Manipur State	*31*	*16*	*15*	*60*	*36*	*24*	Polish ... 2+0.
							Portuguese ... 2+1.
							Spanish ... 6+0.
							Swedish ... 5+6.
(3) Khasi States	*206*	*101*	*105*	*155*	*133*	*22*	Welsh ... 13+15.

TABLE XV.

PART II.—BI-LINGUALISM.

AREA OF BI-LINGUALISM.	MOTHER TONGUE—ASSAMESE.								MOTHER TONGUE—BENGALI.							
	Number of persons speaking mother tongue.		Subsidiary languages.						Number of persons speaking mother tongue.		Subsidiary languages.					
			Bengali.		Tibeto-Burmese.		Khasi-Synteng.				Assamese.		Tibeto-Burmese.		Khasi-Synteng.	
	Male.	Female.	Male.	Female.	Male.	Female.	Male.	Female.	Male.	Female.	Male.	Female.	Male.	Female.	Male.	Female.
1	2	3	4	5	6	7	8	9	10	11	12	13	14	15	16	17
Total	*1,039,207*	*955,357*	*15,084*	*5,015*	*982*	*590*	*49*	*7*	*2,087,060*	*1,879,303*	*25,619*	*13,495*	*160*	*39*	*147*	*96*
Cachar	1,360	875	519	320	1	...	...	...	180,958	157,816	16	5	13	12	2	...
Sylhet	829	648	447	303	...	...	3	...	1,296,471	1,214,211	184	61	17	1	68	16
Khasi and Jaintia Hills (British)	175	108	80	36	...	...	10	6	1,433	737	9	1	1	1	37	5
Naga Hills	407	318	18	6	1	9	...	...	378	149	74	20	...	...	...	...
Lushai Hills	74	40	15	10	18	18	...	...	798	537	...	...	26	4	...	...
Goalpara	83,165	78,014	5,864	1,875	307	83	...	...	253,726	222,707	878	339	35	5	...	...
Kamrup	331,445	318,067	2,075	505	667	227	...	...	96,770	73,630	2,964	927	1	...	...	...
Darrang	108,393	90,796	600	150	143	87	...	...	89,553	43,503	4,426	2,378	...	...	...	...
Nowgong	121,931	115,473	616	125	36	96	...	...	105,353	87,006	2,058	846	...	...	...	...
Sibsagar	266,168	237,435	1,009	243	13	1	...	...	39,296	34,053	9,719	6,872	...	...	...	...
Lakhimpur	122,493	106,900	2,261	634	8	2	...	...	44,384	33,117	4,340	2,365	...	...	...	...
Garo Hills	2,910	2,680	1,203	744	186	80	...	...	10,996	9,457	7	3	50	4	...	...
Sadiya Frontier Tract	4,551	3,968	50	17	2	...	...	...	709	434	151	50	2	...	...	...
Balipara Frontier Tract	439	261	6	...	...	...	...	...	275	180	34	9	...	...	...	...
Manipur State	87	38	7	5	...	...	...	...	1,329	944	3	1	16	5	...	...
Khasi States	811	782	179	53	...	...	31	1	2,607	771	26	5	...	...	65	5

TABLE XV.

PART II—BI-LINGUALISM—*concld.*

AREA OF BI-LINGUALISM.	MOTHER TONGUE—TIBETO-BURMESE.								MOTHER TONGUE—KHASI-SYNTENG.							
	Number of persons speaking mother tongue.		Subsidiary languages.						Number of persons speaking mother tongue.		Subsidiary languages.					
			Assamese.		Bengali.		Khasi-Synteng.				Assamese.		Bengali.		Tibeto-Burmese.	
	Male.	Female.	Male.	Female.	Male.	Female.	Male.	Female.	Male.	Female.	Male.	Female.	Male.	Female.	Male.	Female.
	18	19	20	21	22	23	24	25	26	27	28	29	30	31	32	33
Total	*807,190*	*813,904*	*75,695*	*49,928*	*28,027*	*9,379*	*492*	*261*	*113,690*	*120,189*	*190*	*159*	*850*	*548*	*92*	*78*
Cachar	49,643	48,640	16	...	13,022	4,016	...	...	937	800	...	...	101	47	2	...
Sylhet	19,604	17,311	4	2	6,878	3,020	...	...	1,200	1,167	4	...	450	467	1	1
Khasi and Jaintia Hills (British)	10,940	12,880	92	46	47	14	341	223	36,227	38,162	26	16	36	9	58	44
Naga Hills	55,710	57,510	1,202	337	3	...	...	...	9	11	...	1	...	...	...	...
Lushai Hills	56,661	63,642	1	1	273	32	...	...	53	29	...	...	...	...	26	22
Goalpara...	79,540	70,255	5,847	4,099	5,630	1,271	...	...	1	1	1	...	1	...	...	...
Kamrup	55,890	56,251	20,219	17,646	12	...	...	...	351	283	15	10	2	...	...	1
Darrang	32 196	30,075	15,275	10,897	54	6	...	...	61	30	1	1	...	...	...	...
Nowgong	27,666	26,001	5,196	3,254	35	2	...	...	67	113	1	...	...	...	1	...
Sibsagar	38,114	34,356	11,182	7,030	197	30	...	...	26	55	1	1	...	4	...	...
Lakhimpur	27,401	23,633	10,572	6,693	155	16	...	...	94	143	27	8	...	3	...	...
Garo Hills	80,870	79,083	1,492	567	577	96	...	...	162	155	1	1	...	...	4	...
Sadiya Frontier Tract	15,441	15,286	1,277	200	...	...	...	...	4	9	1	3	...	...	...	...
Balipara Frontier Tract	1,033	881	283	168	...	...	...	...	2	2	...	...	...	...	...	...
Manipur State	211,710	226,924	6	3	1,019	79	...	...	1	...	...	...	...	...	...	...
Khasi States	4,671	4,830	31	...	116	16	151	38	74,443	79,182	83	123	260	15	...	5

TABLE XVI.

Religion.

This table shows the population of the province classified according to the main religions. In the interests of economy the sects of Muslims were not sorted for and the sects of Christians were only ascertained under the following heads :—

Christian sects.

Sect.	Males.	Females.
Roman Catholic	8,036	7,020
Roman—Syrian	Nil	Nil
Other Syrians	3	Nil
Other Christians	116,006	118,181
Total	124,045	125,201

The following statement gives details by districts of the 480 persons grouped in the table under the head " Miscellaneous ":—

District.	Religion.	Persons.	Males.	Females.
Cachar	" No Religion " ...	2	2	...
Sylhet	Jew	7	5	2
	" No Religion " ...	5	3	2
Naga Hills	*" Sitters in the Middle "	373	174	199
Kamrup...	Jew	3	3	...
	Zoroastrian (Parsi) ...	1	1	...
Darrang...	Confucian	9	7	2
Nowgong	Confucian	1	1	...
Sibsagar	Jew	8	3	5
Lakhimpur	Confucian	53	45	8
	Zoroastrian (Parsi) ...	6	5	1
	Freethinker ...	3	3	...
Khasi States	" No Religion " ...	7	5	2
	Zoroastrian (Parsi) ...	2	1	1
	Total ...	480	258	222

* This expressive Naga phrase indicates that these persons were animists who became Christians but who were subsequently excommunicated for failure to observe the rules laid down for the conduct of a Christian life.

TABLE XVI.

Religion.

District or State.	Population. Persons.	Population. Males.	Population. Females.	Hindu. Brahmo. Persons.	Hindu. Brahmo. Males.	Hindu. Brahmo. Females.	Hindu. Arya. Persons.	Hindu. Arya. Males.	Hindu. Arya. Females.	Hindu. Other Hindus. Persons.	Hindu. Other Hindus. Males.	Hindu. Other Hindus. Females.	Total Hindu. Persons.	Total Hindu. Males.	Total Hindu. Females.	Sikh. Persons.	Sikh. Males.	Sikh. Females.
1	2	3	4	5	6	7	8	9	10	11	12	13	14	15	16	17	18	19
ASSAM	*9,247,857*	*4,844.133*	*4,403,724*	*448*	*232*	*216*	*12*	*11*	*1*	*5,204,190*	*2,751,414*	*2,452,776*	*5,204,650*	*2,751,657*	*2,452,993*	*2,729*	*1,918*	*811*
(1) British Territory	*8,622,251*	*4,537,206*	*4,085,045*	*266*	*141*	*125*	*12*	*11*	*1*	*4,931,482*	*2,616,492*	*2,314,990*	*4,931,760*	*2,616,644*	*2,315,116*	*2,497*	*1,740*	*757*
SURMA VALLEY AND HILL DIVISION	3,706,047	1,912.144	1,794,903	118	61	57	...	...	...	1,493,838	779,480	714,358	1,493,956	779,541	714,415	232	168	66
Cachar	570,531	301,338	269,193	13	8	5	...	...	...	359,238	189,906	169,332	359,251	189,914	169,337	77	56	21
Sylhet	2,724,342	1,407,645	1,316,697	73	37	36	...	...	...	1,113,354	575,624	537,730	1,113,426	575,661	537,765	72	51	21
Khasi and Jaintia Hills (British Territory).	109,926	55,439	54,487	33	16	17	...	...	...	10,808	7,381	3,427	10,841	7,397	3,444	61	45	16
Naga Hills	178,844	89,536	89,308	...	...	...	...	...	...	6,448	4,236	2,212	6,448	4.236	2.212	5	5	...
Lushai Hills	124.404	59,186	65,218	...	...	...	...	...	...	3,990	2,333	1,657	3,990	2,333	1,657	7	5	2
ASSAM VALLEY DIVISION ...	4,855,711	2,592,144	2,263,567	148	80	68	12	11	1	3,407,831	1,819,716	1,588,115	3,407.991	1,819,807	1,588.184	2,241	1,563	678
Goalpara	882,748	470,273	412,475	28	13	15	1	1	...	385,877	208,362	177,515	385,906	208,376	177,530	36	24	12
Kamrup	976,746	513,345	463,401	35	19	16	...	...	...	709,960	370,669	339,291	709.995	370,688	339.307	89	66	23
Darrang	584 817	317,103	267,714	33	20	13	..	...	...	455,623	246,526	209,097	455.656	246,546	209.110	147	97	50
Nowgong	502,581	298,585	203,996	6	6	1	...	...	...	325,710	172,659	153,051	325,716	172,664	153,063	632	339	293
Sibsagar	933,326	496,288	437,038	5	4	1	3	3	..	841,035	445,658	395,377	841.043	445,670	395,378	304	221	83
Lakhimpur	724,582	389,108	335.474	37	16	21	3	2	1	661,680	360,756	300,924	661,720	360,774	300,946	1,025	810	215
Garo Hills...	180,911	87,442	93,469	4	3	1	...	...	...	27,946	15,086	12,860	27,950	15,089	12,861	8	6	2
SADIYA FRONTIER TRACT...	53,345	28,686	24,659	...	...	...	...	...	...	26,002	14,809	11,193	26,002	14,809	11,193	34	15	19
BALIPARA FRONTIER TRACT	5,148	3,232	1,916	...	...	...	...	...	...	3,811	2,487	1 324	3,811	2,487	1,324	...	...	...
(2) Assam States ...	*625,606*	*306,927*	*318,679*	*182*	*91*	*91*	...	...	...	*272,708*	*134,922*	*137,786*	*272,890*	*135,013*	*137,877*	*232*	*178*	*54*
Manipur	445,606	215,815	229,791	...	...	...	...	...	...	257,255	124,343	132,912	257.255	124,343	132,912	57	36	21
Khasi States	180.000	91,112	88,888	182	91	91	...	...	...	15,453	10,579	4,874	15,635	10,670	4,965	175	142	33

TABLE XVI.

Religion—*concld.*

District or State.	Jain. Persons.	Jain. Males.	Jain. Females.	Buddhist. Persons.	Buddhist. Males.	Buddhist. Females.	Muslim. Persons.	Muslim. Males.	Muslim. Females.	Christian. Persons.	Christian. Males.	Christian. Females.	Tribal. Persons.	Tribal. Males.	Tribal. Females.	Miscellaneous. Persons.	Miscellaneous. Males.	Miscellaneous. Females.
	20	21	22	23	24	25	26	27	28	29	30	31	32	33	34	35	36	37
ASSAM	*2,803*	*2,116*	*687*	*15,045*	*8,552*	*6,493*	*2,780,514*	*1,461,769*	*1,318,759*	*249,246*	*124,045*	*125,201*	*992,390*	*493,755*	*498,635*	*480*	*258*	*222*
(1) British Territory	*2,636*	*2,000*	*636*	*14,955*	*8,565*	*6,390*	*2,755,914*	*1,449,073*	*1,306,841*	*202,586*	*101,640*	*100,946*	*711,432*	*357,292*	*354,140*	*471*	*259*	*212*
SURMA VALLEY AND HILL DIVISION.	375	288	87	1,152	648	504	1,801,738	933,216	868,522	112,932	53,284	59,648	297,295	145,819	151,476	387	184	203
Cachar	96	90	6	58	41	17	196,196	103,718	92,478	4,602	2,427	2,175	10,319	5,160	5,159	2	2	...
Sylhet	248	192	56	40	28	12	1,603,805	828,123	775,682	2,985	1,650	1,335	3,754	1,932	1,822	12	8	4
Khasi and Jaintia Hills (British Territory).	...	...	...	38	30	8	884	708	176	23,314	11,207	12,107	74,763	36,033	38,730	...	...	...
Naga Hills	101	76	25	22	16	6	698	523	175	22,898	11,394	11,504	148,289	73,182	75,107	373	174	199
Lushai Hills	...	...	...	974	513	461	155	146	9	59,123	28,076	31,047	60,155	30,513	30,642	...	...	...
ASSAM VALLEY DIVISION ...	2,237	1,601	636	11,098	6,471	4,627	953,290	515,217	438,073	88,833	47,970	40,863	389,848	199,357	190,491	84	68	16
Goalpara	590	473	117	582	306	276	387,700	205,386	182,323	18,536	9,796	8,740	89,390	45,913	43,477	...	...	...
Kamrup	370	253	117	790	569	221	240,422	128,765	111,657	5,583	3,034	2,549	19,493	9,946	9,547	4	4	...
Darrang	230	197	33	1,186	805	381	67,563	37,589	29,974	15,716	8,453	7,263	44,370	23,469	20,901	9	7	2
Nowgong	300	246	54	33	29	4	177,763	95,597	82,166	5,043	2,615	2,428	53,094	27,094	26,000	1	1	...
Sibsagar	181	128	53	2,612	1,464	1,150	43,007	24,916	18,091	13,231	7,152	6,079	32,034	16,744	15,290	8	3	5
Lakhimpur	556	394	162	5,645	3,182	2,463	25,949	17,541	8,408	14,662	8,156	6,506	14,761	7,998	6,763	66	53	9
Garo Hills	...	...	...	249	126	123	10,047	5,463	4,584	15,850	8,504	7,346	136,707	68,194	68,513	...	...	...
SADIYA FRONTIER TRACT ...	29	16	13	2,551	1,359	1,192	905	579	626	638	331	307	23,496	21,677	11,800	...	...	...
BALIPARA FRONTIER TRACT	5	5	...	154	87	67	73	60	13	293	155	138	812	438	374	...	...	...
(2) Assam States ...	*167*	*116*	*51*	*90*	*57*	*33*	*24,600*	*12,689*	*11,911*	*46,660*	*22,405*	*24,255*	*280,958*	*136,463*	*144,495*	*9*	*6*	*3*
Manipur	164	113	51	61	34	27	22,864	11,329	11,535	10,401	5,110	5,291	154,804	74,880	79,924	...	...	...
Khasi States	3	3	...	29	23	6	1,736	1,360	376	36,259	17,295	18,964	126,154	61,613	64,541	9	6	3

TABLE XVII.

Caste, Tribe or Race.

In the interest of economy the only castes and tribes sorted for at this census were those for which the figures were likely to be necessary for administrative purposes.

The figures given in this table under the head "Castes classed as tea garden cooly castes" and "Castes classed as Hindu Exterior Castes" which were compiled with a view to ascertaining the number of the depressed and backward classes in Assam cannot, for various reasons, be used without considerable adjustment. The matter is dealt with at length in the Appendix to Chapter XII of the Report volume.

The appendices giving details of the Kukis and Lushais contain various anomalies owing to the fact that certain tribes which, in Manipur, would be generally classed as Kukis, would in the Lushai Hills, come under the general term of "Lushai." Thus the Mhars and Paites of Manipur will be found in the Kuki appendix, while the Mhars and Paites who dwell in the Lushai Hills will be found in the Lushai appendix.

The word "Lushai" covers many clans and is the result of incorrect transliteration of the word "Lushei"—the premier clan in the Lushai Hills. In this table, as in Colonel Shakespears' monograph on the Lushei-Kuki clans, Lushai is used to signify all Lushei-Kuki clans dwelling in the Lushai Hills and Lushei for the clan bearing that name.

I have placed Chirus in the Kuki appendix as their language belongs to the Old Kuki sub-group. Some authorities have treated them as a Naga tribe of Manipur and some as an old Kuki clan. In my own mind I have always classed Chirus as a Naga tribe.

Certain castes which are indigenous to Assam have or claim to have the same name as castes from other provinces which appear to have nothing in common with them. Thus the upcountry Mali is quite a different caste from the indigenous Mali (Bhuinmali) of Sylhet. The former appears in the table as Mali (non-indigenous) and the latter will be found in Appendix V under "Hindu Exterior Castes"—a term which is explained in the Appendix to Chapter XII of the Report volume.

TABLE XVII.—Caste, Tribe or Race.

Caste, tribe or race and districts where found.	Males.	Females.
1	2	3
Abor—*Total* ...	**6,954**	**7,088**
Hindu ...	145	95
Tribal ...	6,807	6,993
Christian ...	2	...
Sadiya Frontier Tract—		
Total ...	**6,668**	**6,983**
Hindu ...	2	2
Tribal ...	6,666	6,981
Elsewhere ...	**286**	**105**
Ahir (Hindu) (Goala, Gopi, Yadava)—*Total* ...	**32,056**	**24,342**
Cachar ...	4,066	3,406
Sylhet ...	10,025	8,987
Darrang ...	2,648	2,019
Nowgong ...	1,605	912
Sibsagar ...	5,504	3,887
Lakhimpur ...	5,154	3,944
Elsewhere ...	3,054	1,157
Ahom (Hindu)—*Total*	**129,989**	**119,445**
Darrang ...	2,260	1,915
Nowgong ...	2,206	2,010
Sibsagar ...	79,161	74,191
Lakhimpur ...	43,009	38,444
Sadiya Frontier Tract.	2,624	2,363
Elsewhere ...	727	522
Aka—*Total* ...	**34**	**4**
Tribal ...	32	3
Christian ...	2	1
***Brahman**—*Total* ...	**87,864**	**71,252**
Cachar ...	3,163	2,115
Sylhet ...	23,570	21,176
Goalpara ...	3,907	2,340
Kamrup ...	19,410	18,418
Darrang ...	11,409	9,163
Nowgong ...	5,465	3,987
Sibsagar ...	13,457	10,346
Lakhimpur ...	6,064	3,042
Elsewhere ...	1,419	666
Dafla—*Total* ...	**925**	**675**
Hindu ...	28	11
Tribal ...	891	659
Christian ...	6	5
Darrang—*Tribal* ...	**207**	**102**
Lakhimpur—*Total* ...	**351**	**236**
Hindu ...	27	11
Tribal ...	321	223
Christian ...	3	2
Balipara Frontier Tract—*Total* ...	**366**	**336**
Tribal ...	363	334
Christian ...	3	2
Elsewhere	**1**	**1**
Dhobi (Hindu) (non-indigenous)—*Total* ...	**4,828**	**3,570**
Kamrup ...	1,340	1,060
Sibsagar ...	704	572
Lakhimpur ...	882	680
Elsewhere ...	1,902	1,258
Garo—*Total* ...	**97,611**	**95,862**
Hindu ...	3,201	2,903
Tribal ...	78,826	79,071
Christian ...	15,584	13,888
Khasi and Jaintia Hills (British)—*Total* ...	**1,124**	**1,134**
Hindu ...	1	...
Tribal ...	693	754
Christian ...	430	380
Khasi States—*Total* ...	**2,608**	**2,673**
Tribal ...	2,497	2,578
Christian ...	111	95
Goalpara—*Total* ...	**10,563**	**9,985**
Hindu ...	1,239	1,152
Tribal ...	5,759	5,523
Christian ...	3,565	3,310
Kamrup—*Total* ...	**4,442**	**4,167**
Hindu ...	1,662	1,522
Tribal ...	825	857
Christian ...	1,955	1,788
Garo Hills—*Total* ...	**76,845**	**75,998**
Hindu ...	118	126
Tribal ...	68,152	68,499
Christian ...	8,545	7,373
Elsewhere	**2,029**	**1,905**
Hajong—*Total* ...	**4,020**	**3,575**
Hindu ...	3,936	3,537
Tribal ...	52	38
Christian ...	2	...
Sylhet—*Total* ...	**451**	**520**
Hindu ...	405	488
Tribal ...	46	32
Garo Hills—*Total* ...	**3,499**	**3,043**
Hindu ...	3,497	3,043
Christian ...	2	...
Elsewhere ...	**70**	**12**
Kachari—*Total* ...	**176,281**	**166,038**
Hindu ...	131,585	124,447
Tribal ...	39,380	37,797
Christian ...	5,016	3,792
Cachar—*Total* ...	**9,481**	**9,168**
Hindu ...	9,479	9,166
Tribal ...	1	...
Christian ...	1	...
Goalpara—*Total* ...	**51,774**	**48,093**
Hindu ...	20,250	18,793
Tribal ...	29,806	28,484
Christian ...	1,718	816
Kamrup—*Total* ...	**54,566**	**52,971**
Hindu ...	51,014	49,212
Tribal ...	3,506	3,698
Christian ...	46	61
Darrang—*Total* ...	**29,601**	**27,043**
Hindu ...	21,545	19,676
Tribal ...	4,893	4,533
Christian ...	3,163	2,834
Nowgong—*Total* ...	**6,770**	**6,392**
Hindu ...	5,686	5,343
Tribal ...	1,031	991
Christian ...	53	58
Sibsagar—*Total* ...	**7,969**	**7,210**
Hindu ...	7,852	7,114
Tribal ...	105	84
Christian ...	12	12
Lakhimpur—*Total* ...	**14,857**	**14,104**
Hindu ...	14,846	14,101
Tribal ...	6	...
Christian ...	5	3
Elsewhere	**1,243**	**1,057**
Kayastha (Hindu)—*Total* ...	**76,303**	**59,287**
Cachar ...	6,971	4,208
Sylhet ...	44,894	40,355
Goalpara ...	2,935	1,835
Kamrup ...	4,112	2,896
Darrang ...	2,438	1,439
Nowgong ...	3,303	1,942
Sibsagar ...	4,719	3,222
Lakhimpur ...	4,970	2,292
Elsewhere ...	1,943	1,104
Khamti—*Total* ...	**1,949**	**1,723**
Buddhist ...	1,922	1,722
Tribal ...	13	1
Hindu ...	14	...
Lakhimpur—*Total* ...	**922**	**764**
Buddhist ...	917	763
Tribal ...	3	1
Hindu ...	2	..
Sadiya Frontier Tract—*Total* ...	**963**	**921**
Buddhist ...	962	921
Tribal ...	1	...
Elsewhere	**64**	**38**
†**Khasi**—*Total* ...	**83,717**	**88,240**
Hindu ...	1,127	1,065
Tribal ...	63,689	66,796
Christian ...	18,901	20,379
Sylhet—*Total* ...	**1,211**	**970**
Hindu ...	689	500
Tribal ...	305	274
Christian ...	217	196
Khasi and Jaintia Hills (British)—*Total* ...	**7,976**	**8,195**
Hindu ...	20	11
Tribal ...	6,312	6,832
Christian ...	1,644	1,352
Khasi States—*Total* ...	**73,470**	**77,899**
Hindu ...	83	62
Tribal ...	56,640	59,804
Christian ...	16,747	18,033
Elsewhere	**1,060**	**1,176**
Kuki—*Total* ... (For details *see* Appendix I).	**45,005**	**46,685**
Hindu ...	2,078	2,068
Tribal ...	38,428	40,068
Christian ...	4,499	4,549
Cachar—*Total* ...	**4,378**	**4,389**
Hindu ...	1,980	1,986
Tribal ...	1,750	1,759
Christian ...	648	644
Naga Hills—*Total* ...	**1,196**	**1,145**
Hindu ...	5	4
Tribal ...	1,058	1,113
Christian ...	133	28
Manipur—*Total* ...	**38,277**	**40,069**
Hindu ...	1	...
Tribal ...	35,093	36,728
Christian ...	3,183	3,341
Elsewhere... ...	**1,154**	**1,082**
Kurmi—*Total* ...	**15,332**	**10,999**
Hindu ...	15,329	10,998
Christian ...	3	1
Cachar—*Hindu* ...	1,663	1,540
Sylhet—*Hindu* ...	2,245	1,778
Darrang—*Hindu* ...	1,633	1,283
Sibsagar—*Hindu* ...	4,016	3,099
Lakhimpur—*Hindu* ...	3,278	2,391
Elsewhere ...	2,498	908
Lakher (all in Lushai Hills)—*Total* ...	**2,855**	**3,250**
Tribal ...	2,626	3,012
Christian ...	229	238
Lalung—*Total* ...	**21,607**	**21,841**
Hindu ...	15,729	15,460
Tribal ...	5,759	6,257
Christian ...	119	124
Khasi and Jaintia Hills (British)—*Total* ...	**1,354**	**1,753**
Tribal ...	1,240	1,630
Christian ...	114	123
Khasi States—*Total* ...	**215**	**160**
Hindu ...	3	7
Tribal ...	210	153
Christian ...	2	...
Nowgong—*Total* ...	**19,012**	**18,822**
Hindu ...	14,964	14,683
Tribal ...	4,045	4,138
Christian ...	3	1
Elsewhere ...	**1,026**	**1,106**
Lushai (for details *see* Appendix II)—*Total*	**53,859**	**60,299**
Hindu ...	485	505
Tribal ...	23,636	27,371
Christian ...	29,738	32,423
Lushai Hills—*Total* ...	**53,348**	**59,894**
Hindu ...	446	477
Tribal ...	26,549	27,281
Christian ...	26,353	32,136
Elsewhere ...	**511**	**405**
Mali (Hindu) (non-indigenous)—*Total* ...	**4,545**	**2,451**
Kamrup ...	1,440	1,262
Elsewhere ...	3,105	1,189
‡**Manipuri (Hindu)**—*Total* ...	**158,919**	**165,513**
Cachar ...	22,332	21,718
Sylhet ...	13,742	12,839
Manipur State ...	120,542	130,380
Elsewhere ...	2,303	576
Mech—*Total* ...	**5,032**	**4,184**
Hindu ...	4,183	3,668
Tribal ...	349	333
Christian ...	500	178
Goalpara—*Total* ...	**4,501**	**3,791**
Hindu ...	3,665	3,284
Tribal ...	348	338
Christian ...	488	169
Elsewhere ...	**531**	**393**

* Manipuri Brahmans have been included under Manipuris as what was required was the total number of persons belonging to the Manipuri race.
† Syntengs are given under a separate head.
‡ Including Manipuri Brahmans.

TABLE XVII—Caste, Tribe or Race—*concld.*

Caste, tribe or race and districts where found.	Males.	Females.
1	2	3
Mikir—*Total* ...	**66,045**	**63,752**
Hindu ...	16,053	15,230
Tribal ...	48,155	46,700
Christian ..	1,837	1,822
Cachar—*Total* ...	**1,648**	**1,561**
Hindu ...	1,290	1,274
Tribal ...	85	68
Christian ...	273	219
Khasi and Jaintia Hills (British)—*Total* ...	**7,764**	**8,996**
Hindu ...	2	...
Tribal ...	7,010	8,209
Christian ...	752	787
Khasi States—*Total* ...	**1,680**	**1,452**
Tribal ...	1,623	1,398
Christian ...	57	54
Naga Hills—*Total* ...	**609**	**602**
Hindu ...	127	119
Tribal ...	479	483
Christian ...	3	...
Kamrup—*Total* ...	**5,090**	**5,140**
Hindu ...	2,870	2,756
Tribal ...	2,213	2,381
Christian ...	7	3
Darrang—*Total* ...	**2,255**	**1,943**
Hindu ...	86	55
Tribal ...	2,160	1,881
Christian ...	9	7
Nowgong—*Total* ...	**30,242**	**28,529**
Hindu ...	8,489	8,116
Tribal ...	21,210	19,883
Christian ...	543	530
Sibsagar—*Total* ...	**16,547**	**15,369**
Hindu ...	3,041	2,793
Tribal ..	13,369	12,395
Christian ...	137	182
Elsewhere ...	**210**	**160**
Miri—*Total* ...	**43,669**	**41,369**
Hindu ...	41,004	38,844
Tribal ...	2,640	2,512
Christian ...	25	13
Darrang—*Total* ...	**2,846**	**2,863**
Hindu ...	1,067	1,021
Tribal ...	1,779	1,842
Sibsagar—*Total* ...	**17,817**	**17,036**
Hindu ...	17,283	16,629
Tribal ...	533	407
Christian ...	1	...
Lakhimpur—*Total* ...	**20,003**	**18,971**
Hindu ...	19,739	18,796
Tribal ...	263	175
Christian ...	1	...
Sadiya—*Total* ...	**2,732**	**2,274**
Hindu ...	2,667	2,186
Tribal ...	65	88
Balipara—*Total* ...	**249**	**220**
Hindu ...	228	208
Christian ...	21	12
Elsewhere ...	**22**	**5**
Mishmi—*Total* ...	**1,240**	**994**
Hindu ...	39	27
Tribal ...	1,201	967
Sadiya (all tribal)—*Total* ...	**1,063**	**893**
Elsewhere ...	**177**	**101**
Naga (for details *see* Appendix III)—*Total*	**131,546**	**136,757**
Hindu ...	1,331	1,024
Tribal ...	117,019	122,246
Christian ...	13,196	13,487
Cachar—*Total* ...	**3,357**	**3,564**
Hindu ...	840	881
Tribal ...	2,391	2,549
Christian ...	126	134
Naga Hills—*Total* ...	**82,690**	**84,977**
Hindu ...	12	...
Tribal ...	71,549	73,442
Christian ...	11,129	11,535
Sibsagar—*Total* ...	**1,084**	**711**
Hindu ...	127	65
Tribal ...	837	644
Christian ...	120	2
Lakhimpur—*Total* ...	**2,483**	**2,039**
Hindu ...	332	76
Tribal ...	2,121	1,940
Christian ...	30	23
Sadiya—*Total* ...	**3,248**	**3,213**
Hindu ...	11	...
Tribal ...	3,237	3,213
Manipur State—*Total*	**38,597**	**42,216**
Tribal ...	36,845	40,439
Christian ...	1,752	1,777
Elsewhere ...	**87**	**37**
Nai (Napit, Hajam) (Hindu)—*Total.*	**17,553**	**15,881**
Cachar ...	1,365	1,062
Sylhet ...	10,501	10,060
Kamrup ...	2,909	3,069
Elsewhere ..	2,778	1,690
Nepalis (for details *see* Appendix IV)—*Total.*	**74,946**	**45,341**
Hindu ...	74,910	45,329
Christian ...	36	12
Rabha—*Total* ...	**35,616**	**33,538**
Hindu ...	31,135	29,383
Tribal ...	4,246	3,969
Christian ...	235	186
Goalpara—*Total* ...	**16,356**	**15,242**
Hindu ...	13,616	12,774
Tribal ...	2,728	2,462
Christian ...	12	6
Kamrup—*Total* ...	**10,629**	**10,280**
Hindu ...	9,138	8,784
Tribal ...	1,373	1,382
Christian ...	118	114
Darrang—*Total* ...	**4,248**	**3,911**
Hindu ...	4,147	3,854
Tribal ...	6	3
Christian ...	95	54
Garo Hills—*Total* ...	**3,815**	**3,742**
Hindu ...	3,805	3,736
Tribal ...	6	3
Christian ...	4	3
Elsewhere ...	**568**	**363**
Rajput (Hindu)—*Total.*	**2,521**	**1,573**
Singpho—*Total* ...	**1,562**	**1,346**
Hindu ...	30	23
Tribal ...	666	636
Buddhist ...	856	687
Sadiya ...	632	594
Lakhimpur ...	930	752
Synteng (Pnar)—*Total.*	**29,122**	**31,451**
Hindu ...	17	13
Tribal ...	21,145	22,213
Christian ...	7,960	9,195
Khasi and Jaintia Hills (British)—*Total.*	**28,131**	**29,940**
Hindu ...	...	2
Tribal ...	20,482	21,575
Christian ...	7,649	8,333
Khasi States—*Total* ...	**556**	**1,114**
Hindu ...	...	5
Tribal ...	504	499
Christian ...	52	610
Elsewhere ...	**435**	**397**
Teli (Hindu)—*Total*	**9,678**	**7,600**
Sylhet ...	2,311	2,301
Sibsagar ...	2,221	1,763
Lakhimpur ...	2,180	1,714
Elsewhere ...	2,966	1,822
Tili (Hindu)—*Total*	**11,766**	**11,620**
Sylhet ...	11,051	10,852
Elsewhere ...	715	768
Caste—*Nil*—*Total*...	**1,647**	**869**
* **Castes classed as tea garden cooly castes**—*Total* ...	**681,956**	**604,677**
Hindu ...	653,626	579,886
Tribal ...	28,330	24,791
Cachar—*Total* ...	**78,396**	**73,256**
Hindu ...	77,634	72,571
Tribal ...	762	685
Sylhet—*Total* ...	**90,906**	**84,919**
Hindu ...	90,354	84,418
Tribal ...	552	501
Goalpara—*Total* ...	**29,594**	**22,887**
Hindu ...	22,590	16,673
Tribal ...	7,004	6,214
Kamrup—*Total* ...	**13,317**	**8,765**
Hindu ...	12,769	8,289
Tribal ...	548	476
Darrang—*Total* ...	**107,495**	**94,266**
Hindu ...	93,573	82,156
Tribal ...	13,922	12,110
Nowgong—*Total* ...	**20,043**	**17,192**
Hindu ...	19,800	17,046
Tribal ...	243	146
Sibsagar—*Total* ...	**154,709**	**141,489**
Hindu ...	154,198	141,015
Tribal ...	511	474
Lakhimpur—*Total* ...	**184,410**	**159,697**
Hindu ...	179,622	155,515
Tribal ...	4,788	4,182
Sadiya (all Hindu)—*Total* ...	**2,030**	**1,499**
Elsewhere—*Total* ...	**1,056**	**707**
Hindu ...	1,056	704
Tribal ...	...	3
Castes classed as "**Hindu Exterior Castes**" (exclusive of tea-garden cooly castes) (*See* Appendix V)—*Total* ...	**313,145**	**283,773**
Cachar ...	26,875	22,218
Sylhet ...	168,595	174,425
Goalpara ...	8,244	7,317
Kamrup ...	22,770	20,457
Darrang ...	8,283	7,338
Nowgong ...	24,833	22,388
Sibsagar ...	19,335	17,388
Lakhimpur ...	13,083	11,098
Elsewhere ...	1,627	1,194

* This heading includes Hindu and tribal cooly castes on tea gardens as well as those settled in the villages. It does not, however, include persons (whether on tea gardens or outside) who originally belonged to cooly castes but who have become Christians as the caste of such persons was recorded in many cases as "Indian Christian." Castes which are cooly castes but which appear separately in this table, *e.g.*, Kurmis, have not been included in these figures. The matter is dealt with at length in the appendix to Chapter XII of the Report volume.

APPENDIX I.—Kuki (Details).

Tribe.	Hindu.		Tribal.		Christian.		Distribution by districts and states.		
	Males.	Females.	Males.	Females.	Males.	Females.	Hindu.	Tribal.	Christian.
1	2	3	4	5	6	7	8	9	10
Kuki (Total) ...	*2,078*	*2,083*	*38,428*	*40,053*	*4,499*	*4,549*	Cachar (1,980 + 1,986); Manipur State (1 + 0); Lushai Hills (80 + 83); Naga Hills (5 + 4); Sylhet (5 + 8); Goalpara (1 + 0); Nowgong (6 + 0);	Cachar (1,750 + 1,759); Manipur State (35,[illegible]43 + 36,728); Naga Hills (1,058 + 1,113); Sylhet (110 + 122); Garo Hills (26 + 8); Nowgong (108 + 100); Darrang (0 + 1); Khasi and Jaintia Hills (283 + 222);	Cachar (648 + 644); Manipur State (3,183 + 3,241); Naga Hills (133 + 28); Khasi and Jaintia Hills (431 + 450); Lushai Hills (3 + 1); Nowgong (98 + 85); Sibsagar (3 + 0).
Kuki (unspecified)	367	251	1,832	1,694	543	557	Cachar (293 + 179); Lushai Hills (57 + 60); Naga Hills (5 + 4); Sylhet (5 + 8); Goalpara (1 + 0); Nowgong (6 + 0).	Cachar (1 145 + 1,109); Naga Hills (62 + 38); Sylhet (110 + 122); Garo Hills (26 + 8); Nowgong (108 + 100); Manipur State (98 + 94); Darrang (0 + 1); Khasi and Jaintia Hills (283 + 222).	Cachar (279 + 295); Lushai Hills (3 + 1); Naga Hills (0 + 1); Nowgong (98 + 85); Sibsagar (3 + 0); Khasi and Jaintia Hills (160 + 175).
Aimol... ...	...	...	270	231	...	...	......	Manipur State (270 + 231)	......
Anal ...	...	...	1,243	1,254	358	432	......	Manipur State (1,243 + 1,254).	Manipur State. (358 + 432).
Bieto (Beto) ...	191	219	9	10	361	357	Cachar (191 + 219) ...	Cachar (9 + 10) ...	Khasi and Jaintia Hills (264 + 264); Cachar (97 + 93).
Changsen ...	113	126	79	77	12	7	Cachar (113 + 126) ...	Cachar (79 + 77); ...	Cachar (12 + 7).
Chiru ...	...	...	564	703	...	...	......	Manipur State (564 + 708)	......
Chote ...	...	...	135	133	...	...	......	Manipur State (135 + 133)	......
Gangte ...	...	...	1,106	1,114	125	127	......	Manipur State (1,106 + 1,114).	Cachar (6 + 4); Manipur State (119 + 123).
Hrangkhol (Rangkhol).	556	558	7	5	...	...	Cachar (533 + 533); Lushai Hills (23 + 25).	Cachar (7 + 5) ...	......
Kholhang (Khotlhang).	617	685	38	33	164	160	Cachar (617 + 685) ...	Cachar (33 + 31); Naga Hills (5 + 2).	Cachar (164 + 160).
Kom ...	...	...	1,155	1,257	77	75	......	Manipur State (1,155 + 1,257).	Manipur State (77 + 75).
Lamang (Lamgang)	10	7	557	649	...	...	Cachar (10 + 7) ...	Manipur State (557 + 649)	......
Mhar (Hmar) ...	...	...	1,637	1,681	1,183	1,227	......	Manipur State (1,667 + 1,681).	Manipur State (1,183 + 1,227).
Paite ...	...	...	3,762	3,646	363	292	......	Manipur State (3,762 + 3,646).	Manipur State (363 + 292).
Purum ...	...	...	145	158	...	...	......	Manipur State (145 + 158)	......
Khelma (Sakchip)...	16	8	235	237	1	...	Cachar (16 + 8) ...	Cachar (165 + 177); Naga Hills (70 + 60).	Cachar (1 + 0).
Sokte (Suhte) ...	...	...	330	382	32	40	......	Manipur State (330 + 382)	Manipur State (32 + 40).
Thado ...	208	220	23,261	24,637	1,060	1,058	Cachar (207 + 220); Manipur State (1 + 0).	Cachar (312 + 330); Manipur State (22,028 + 23,274); Naga Hills (921 + 1,013).	Cachar (89 + 85); Manipur State (838 + 946); Naga Hills (133 + 27).
Vaiphei ...	...	...	2,033	2,147	220	217	......	Manipur State (2,033 + 2,147).	Manipur State (213 + 206); Khasi and Jaintia Hills (7 + 11).

APPENDIX II.—LUSHEI-KUKI (DETAILS).

Tribe.	Hindu.		Tribal.		Christian.		Distribution by districts and states.		
	Males.	Females.	Males.	Females.	Males.	Females.	Hindu.	Tribal.	Christian.
1	2	3	4	5	6	7	8	9	10
Lushai (Total) ...	*485*	*505*	*26,636*	*27,371*	*26,738*	*32,423*	Cachar (38 + 27); Lushai Hills (446 + 477); Sadiya Frontier Tract. (0 + 1); Sylhet (1 + 0).	Cachar (9 + 6); Khasi and Jaintia Hills (2 + 1); Lushai Hills (26,549 + 27,281); Naga Hills (4 + 2); Darrang (0 + 2); Manipur State (69 + 77); Sylhet (3 + 2).	Cachar (188 + 141); Khasi and Jaintia Hills (6 + 0; Khasi States (26 + 3); Garo Hills (1 + 0); Lushai Hills (26,353 + 32,136); Sadiya Frontier Tract (4 + 6; Lakhimpur (6 + 0); Kamrup (2 + 1); Manipur State (129 + 133); Sibsagar (1 + 0); Sylhet (22 + 3).
Lushei	484	505	8,993	10,102	13,803	16,383	Cachar (38 + 27); Lushai Hills (445 + 477); Sadiya Frontier Tract (0 + 1); Sylhet (1 + 0).	Cachar (9 + 6); Khasi and Jaintia Hills (2 + 1); Lushai Hills (8,951 + 10,074); Naga Hills (4 + 2); Darrang (0 + 2); Manipur State (24 + 15); Sylhet (3 + 2).	Cachar (188 + 141); Khasi and Jaintia Hills (6 + 0); Khasi States (26 + 3); Garo Hills (1 + 0); Lushai Hills (13,428 + 16,053); Sadiya Frontier Tract (4 + 6); Manipur State (119 + 126); Sibsagar (1 + 0); Lakhimpur (6 + 0); Kamrup (2 + 1); Sylhet (22 + 3).
Fanai	...	...	725	554	853	1,273	......	Lushai Hills (725 + 554)	Lushai Hills (853 + 1,273).
Mhar	...	...	4,237	4,000	4,791	6,061	.. ...	Lushai Hills (4,237 + 4,000)	Lushai Hills (4,791 + 6,061).
Paite	...	...	2,790	2,760	544	549	......	Lushai Hills (2,790 + 2,760)	Lushai Hills (544 + 549).
Poi	1	...	6,506	6,608	2,543	2,818	Lushai Hills (1 + 0) ...	Lushai Hills (6,506 + 6,606)	Lushai Hills (2,543 + 2,818).
Ralte	...	...	3,395	3,347	4,204	5,389	......	Lushai Hills (3,340 + 3,285); Manipur State (45 + 62).	Lushai Hills (4,194 + 5,382); Manipur State (10 + 7).

APPENDIX III.—NAGA (DETAILS).

Tribe.	Hindu.		Tribal.		Christian.		Distribution by districts and states.		
	Males.	Females.	Males.	Females.	Males.	Females.	Hindu.	Tribal.	Christian.
1	2	3	4	5	6	7	8	9	10
Naga (Total) ...	*1,331*	*1,094*	*117,019*	*122,246*	*13,196*	*13,487*	Cachar (840+881); Khasi and Jaintia Hills (1+0); Naga Hills (12+0); Sadiya Frontier Tract (11+0); Lakhimpur (332+76); Darrang (2+1); Nowgong (1+0); Kamrup (1+0); Sibsagar (127+65); Sylhet (1+1); Khasi States (3+0).	Cachar (2,391+2,549); Khasi and Jaintia Hills (5+4); Khasi States (15+3); Naga Hills (71,549+73,442); Lushai Hills (6+11); Goalpara (1+0); Lakhimpur (2,121+1,940); Sadiya Frontier Tract (3,237+3,213); Darrang (6+1); Kamrup (4+0); Manipur State (36,845+40,439); Sibsagar (837+644).	Cachar (128+134); Khasi States (23+1); Garo Hills (1+0); Lushai Hills (5+1); Naga Hills (11,129+11,535); Goalpara (1+1); Lakhimpur (30+23); Nowgong (3+6); Kamrup (6+7); Manipur State (1,752+1,777); Sibsagar (120+2).
Naga* (unspecified)	606	275	6,784	6,590	197	65	Cachar (126+132); Khasi and Jaintia Hills (1+0); Naga Hills (12+0); Sadiya Frontier Tract (11+0); Lakhimpur (315+76); Darrang (2+1); Nowgong (1+0); Kamrup (1+0); Sibsagar (127+65); Sylhet (1+1); Khasi States (3+0).	Cachar (627+761); Khasi and Jaintia Hills (2+0); Lushai Hills (6+11); Naga Hills (38+15); Goalpara (1+0); Sadiya Frontier Tract (3,141+3,209); Lakhimpur (2,121+1,939); Darrang (6+1); Kamrup (4+0); Manipur State (1+0); Sibsagar (837+644).	Cachar (30+29); Khasi States (20+0); Lushai Hills (3+1); Naga Hills (3+10); Goalpara (1+1); Lakhimpur (12+9); Nowgong (3+6); Kamrup (6+7); Sibsagar (119+2).
Angami ...	...	...	24,683	23,972	330	254	......	Khasi and Jaintia Hills (1+0); Khasi States (11+0); Naga Hills (24,405+23,723); Darrang (1+0); Manipur State (264+246); Sadiya Frontier Tract (1+3).	Cachar (2+1); Khasi States (0+1); Garo Hills (1+0); Naga Hills (322+252); Lakhimpur (1+0); Manipur State (3+0); Sibsagar (1+0).
Ao	...	...	9,803	10,714	5,384	6,874	......	Naga Hills (9,800+10,713); Lakhimpur (0+1); Darrang (1+0); Sadiya Frontier Tract (2+0).	Naga Hills (5,384+6,874).
Chang	...	...	279	309	75	11	......	Naga Hills (279+309) ...	Naga Hills (75+11).
Kabui	...	...	8,728	9,843	126	134	......	Naga Hills (15+15); Manipur State (8,711+9,824); Khasi and Jaintia Hills (2+4).	Naga Hills (3+1); Manipur State (123+133).
Kachha† ...	...	...	3,440	3,738	13	5	......	Manipur State (3,440+3,738)	Manipur State (13+5).
Kalyo-Kengyu ...	...	...	312	268	...	...	......	Naga Hills (312+268)	......
Konyak ...	...	...	4,552	4,939	1	1	......	Naga Hills (4,552+4,939)...	Naga Hills (1+1).
Khoirao ...	...	...	1,303	1,362	79	68	......	Manipur State (1,303+1,362)	Manipur State (79+68).
Kwoirong (Quoireng)	...	...	263	289	...	...	......	Manipur State (263+289)...	......
Lhota	...	...	8,274	9,055	683	226	......	Naga Hills (8,269+9,055); Sadiya Frontier Tract (5+0).	Naga Hills (681+223); Manipur State (3+3).
Liyengmai ...	...	...	1,085	1,141	...	...	......	Naga Hills (1,085+1,141)	......
Maram	...	...	1,166	1,340	...	...	......	Manipur State (1,166+1,340).	......
Maring	...	...	2,090	2,138	...	...	......	Manipur State (2090+2,138).	......
Memi (Mao) ...	...	...	8,386	8,320	21	20	......	Naga Hills (646+573); Manipur State (7,740+7,747).	Naga Hills (21+20).
Nsemi or Zemi ...	714	749	4,227	4,314	154	110	Cachar (714+749) ...	Naga Hills (2,463+2,526); Cachar (1,764+1,788).	Naga Hills (58+6); Lushai Hills (2+0); Cachar (94+104).
Phom	...	...	67	69	32	38	......	Naga Hills (67+69) ...	Naga Hills (32+38).
Rengma ...	...	...	2,975	3,121	176	57	......	Naga Hills (2,975+3,121) ...	Naga Hills (176+57).
Sangtam ...	...	...	2,402	2,131	38	37	......	Naga Hills (2,402+2,131) ...	Naga Hills (38+37).
Sema	17	...	14,285	14,783	4,345	4,015	Lakhimpur (17+0) ...	Khasi States (4+3); Naga Hills (14,180+14,779); Manipur State (13+0); Sadiya Frontier Tract (88+1).	Khasi States (3+0); Naga Hills (4,325+4,001); Lakhimpur (17+14).
Tangkhul ...	...	...	11,854	13,763	1,532	1,568	......	Naga Hills (14+8; Manipur State (11,854+13,755).	Manipur State (1,532+1,568).
Yacham (Yimtsungr)	...	...	47	57	10	4	......	Naga Hills (47+57) ...	Naga Hills (10+4).

* Most of the unspecified Nagas occur in the Sadiya Frontier Tract, Lakhimpur and the Cachar plains. Mr. J. P. Mills, I.C.S., Deputy Commissioner of the Naga Hills, informs me that "Rangpang"—itself an inaccurate word—would cover all Sadiya and Lakhimpur Nagas and that practically all Nagas of the Cachar plains are Kabuis.

† Mr. Mills informs me that the term Kachha Naga (though commonly used) is meaningless and that about half of the people recorded as Kachha Naga in Manipur are Zemi and half Liyengmai.

APPENDIX IV.—Nepalis (with details).

Caste.	Hindu. Males.	Hindu. Females.	Christian. Males.	Christian. Females.	Distribution by districts and states. Hindu.	Distribution by districts and states. Christian.
NEPALI CASTES.						
Total ...	74,910	45,329	36	12	Goalpara (6,821+4,306); Kamrup (7,762+4,941); Darrang (16,095+12,024); Nowgong (2,793+1,976); Sibsagar (5,630+3,633); Lakhimpur (11,514+6,040); Garo Hills (1,759+1,050); Sadiya Frontier Tract (3,343+1,766); Lushai Hills (1,301+928); Balipara Froutier Tract (883+300); Naga Hills (1,694+979); Cachar (1,117+705); Manipur State (1,938+1,167); Sylhet (418+228); Khasi States (6,923+2,939); Khasi and Jaintia Hills (4,919+2,348).	Lushai Hills (11+3); Manipur State (2+0); Khasi States (18+9); Khasi and Jaintia Hills (5+0).
Thakuri	2,320	1,379	...	...	Garo Hills (40+24): Cachar (25+4): Lushai Hills (42+15); Balipara Frontier Tract (21+3); Sadiya Frontier Tract (52+20); Manipur State (21+9); Naga Hills (28+11); Nowgong (127+108); Sibsagar (225+155); Khasi and Jaintia Hills (331+167); Khasi States (228+84); Sylhet (50+37); Lakhimpur (340+204); Kamrup (156+124); Goalpara (150+142); Darrang (384+272).	
Chhetri	22,120	15,381	5	...	Garo Hills (406+268); Cachar (217+129); Lushai Hills (231+120); Balipara Frontier Tract (123+31); Sadiya Frontier Tract (516+320); Manipur State (358+211); Naga Hills (267+146); Nowgong (1,536+1,344); Sibsagar (1,601+1,188); Khasi and Jaintia Hills (498+264); Khasi States (1,198+506); Sylhet (73+25); Lakhimpur (3,675+2,231); Kamrup (2,196+1,476); Goalpara (1,732+1,215); Darrang (7,493+6,017).	Khasi States (5+0).
Gurung	3,446	1,681	3	...	Garo Hills (47+24); Cachar (50+30); Lushai Hills (115+89); Balipara Frontier Tract (114+38); Sadiya Frontier Tract (188+97); Manipur State (151+79); Naga Hills (129+77); Nowgong (50+24); Sibsagar (112+50); Khasi and Jaintia Hills (927+412); Khasi States (494+219); Sylhet (13+3); Lakhimpur (482+255); Kamrup (196+93); Goalpara (161+61); Darrang (217+130).	Manipur (2+0); Khasi States (1+0).
Sonowar	2,672	1,942	2	...	Garo Hills (38+34); Cachar (52+15); Lushai Hills (2+2); Balipara Frontier Tract (40+18); Sadiya Frontier Tract (36+78); Manipur State (26+22); Naga Hills (88+47); Nowgong (71+33); Sibsagar (127+129); Khasi and Jaintia Hills (143+93); Khasi States (331+115); Sylhet (8+2); Lakhimpur (646+327); Kamrup (118+74); Goalpara (365+260); Darrang (581+693).	Lushai Hills (1+0); Khasi States (1+0).
Rai	3,905	1,683	2	...	Garo Hills (104+69); Cachar (30+39); Lushai Hills (158+124); Balipara Frontier Tract (93+27); Sadiya Frontier Tract (245+157); Manipur State (163+86); Naga Hills (247+48); Nowgong (186+30); Sibsagar (680+207); Khasi and Jaintia Hills (30+8); Khasi States (174+76); Sylhet (29+3); Lakhimpur (609+357); Kamrup (403+126); Goalpara (399+157); Darrang (455+269).	Lushai Hills (1+0); Khasi and Jaintia Hills (1+0).
Limbu	3,441	1,670	3	...	Garo Hills (70+43); Cachar (23+38); Lushai Hills (146+130); Balipara Frontier Tract (121+43); Sadiya Frontier Tract (137+87); Manipur State (79+58); Naga Hills (122+6); Nowgong (110+18); Sibsagar (168+98); Khasi and Jaintia Hills (67+33); Khasi States (109+57); Sylhet (8+2); Lakhimpur (897+295); Kamrup (381+123); Goalpara (470+219); Darrang (533+420).	Lushai Hills (3+0).
Magar	6,869	3,675	6	...	Garo Hills (58+38); Cachar (31+24); Lushai Hills (75+57); Balipara Frontier Tract (133+82); Sadiya Frontier Tract (470+300); Manipur State (284+160); Naga Hills (156+9); Nowgong (14+0); Sibsagar (296+195); Khasi and Jaintia Hills (1,732+822); Khasi States (1,044+441); Sylhet (43+15); Lakhimpur (538+273); Kamrup (538+262); Goalpara (394+283); Darrang (1,063+715).	Khasi States (6+0).
Ranabhat	172	169	...	...	Garo Hills (14+10); Cachar (3+35): Lushai Hills (37+27); Balipara Frontier Tract (0+1); Sadiya Frontier Tract (1+0); Manipur State (5+2); Naga Hills (10+0); Nowgong (4+1); Sibsagar (3+0); Khasi and Jaintia Hills (16+5); Khasi States (22+23); Sylhet (3+14); Lakhimpur (30+28); Kamrup (4+4); Goalpara (4+2); Darrang (16+17).	
Dura	146	36	—	...	Cachar (12+4); Lushai Hills (1+0); Manipur State (1+0); Sibsagar (10+4); Khasi States (86+1); Sylhet (2+0); Lakhimpur (2+1); Kamrup (5+0); Goalpara (11+0), Darrang (16+16).	
Others	29,919	17,723	15	12	Garo Hills (982+540); Cachar (674+387); Lushai Hills (494+364); Balipara Frontier Tract (236+57); Sadiya Frontier Tract (1,698+707); Manipur State (850+540); Naga Hills (647+635); Nowgong (696+518); Sibsagar (2,506+1,607); Khasi and Jaintia Hills (1,175+554); Khasi States (3,237+1,417); Sylhet (189+127); Lakhimpur (4,295+2,169); Kamrup (2,765+2,659); Goalpara (2,135+1,967); Darrang (5,337+3,475).	Lushai Hills (6+3); Khasi and Jaintia Hills (4+0); Khasi States (5+9).

APPENDIX V.

* Castes (exclusive of tea garden cooly castes) classed as "Hindu Exterior Castes".

				Males.	Females.
* Surma Valley	...	...	...	215,470	196,643
Assam Valley	...	...	...	96,558	86,408
Elsewhere	...	...	...	1,117	722
		Total	...	313,145	283,773

Assam Valley only.

Caste.	Locality.	Male.	Female.
1	2	3	4
NAMASUDRA ...	Total ...	16,966	14,587
	Goalpara ...	4,395	3,701
	Kamrup ...	7,053	6,148
	Darrang ...	214	174
	Nowgong ...	4,382	3,766
	Sibsagar ...	776	699
	Lakhimpur ...	133	97
	Sadiya ...	13	2
KAIBARTTA (Nadiyal, etc.)	Total ...	62,456	56,364
	Goalpara ...	2,077	1,853
	Kamrup ...	10,549	9,690
	Darrang ...	6,263	5,478
	Nowgong ...	14,261	13,233
	Sibsagar ...	17,127	15,396
	Lakhimpur ...	11,726	10,247
	Sadiya ...	450	457
BANIA (Brittial Bania).	Total ...	7,657	6,691
	Goalpara ...	213	168
	Kamrup ...	2,290	2,035
	Darrang ...	1,116	1,009
	Nowgong ...	1,849	1,691
	Sibsagar ...	1,301	1,118
	Lakhimpur ...	887	662
	Sadiya ...	1	8
HIRA	Total ...	8,522	8,106
	Goalpara ...	1,409	1,425
	Kamrup ...	2,701	2,432
	Darrang ...	674	651
	Nowgong ...	3,737	3,597
	Sibsagar ...	10	1
	Lakhimpur ...	1	...
	Sadiya ...	...	...
SWEEPER CASTES	Total ...	957	660
	Goalpara ...	150	160
	Kamrup ...	177	152
	Darrang ...	16	26
	Nowgong ...	111	101
	Sibsagar ...	121	124
	Lakhimpur ...	336	92
	Sadiya ...	46	6

*** Surma Valley only.**

Caste.	Locality.	Male.	Female.
1	2	3	4
MALI (Indigenous) ...	Total ...	20,123	18,512
	Cachar ...	2,135	1,871
	Sylhet ...	17,988	16,641
MUCHI	Total ...	4,559	2,753
	Cachar ...	2,508	1,571
	Sylhet ...	2,051	1,182
DHUPI or DHOBI (Indigenous).	Total ...	11,467	11,054
	Cachar ...	1,023	874
	Sylhet ...	10 444	10,180
DUGLA or DHOLI ...	Total ...	5,121	4,402
	Cachar ...	18	5
	Sylhet ...	5,103	4,397
NAMASUDRA ...	Total ...	71,947	67,019
	Cachar ...	8,164	6,948
	Sylhet ...	63,783	60,071
PATNI	Total ...	27,066	24,342
	Cachar ...	4,912	4,018
	Sylhet ...	22,154	20,324
JHALO and MALO ...	Total ...	6,122	4,704
	Cachar ...	1,048	674
	Sylhet ...	5,074	4,030
YOGI	Total ...	43,888	40,034
	Cachar ...	6,827	6,071
	Sylhet ...	37,061	33,963
MAHARA	Total ...	2,739	2,685
	Cachar ...	18	18
	Sylhet ...	2,721	2,667
SUTRADHAR ...	Total ...	6,496	6,079
	Cachar ...	44	18
	Sylhet ...	6,452	6,061
KAIBARTTA ...	Total ...	15,543	14,711
	Cachar ...	39	30
	Sylhet ...	15,504	14,681
SWEEPER CASTES ...	Total ..	399	348
	Cachar ...	139	120
	Sylhet ...	260	228

* The figures for Cachar and Sylhet are not reliable in the case of certain castes. The matter is dealt with at length in the Appendix to Chapter XII of the Report.

TABLE XVIII.

Variation of population of selected tribes and castes.

In 1921, owing to a misunderstanding of the instructions, Christians belonging to Hill tribes were returned in many cases as "Indian Christian". Furthermore Imperial Table VIII of the 1921 Census—Caste, tribe or race—included only Hindus and Animists and did not include Christians. Hence it is impossible to give the number of Christians belonging to the various Hill tribes for 1921. The same applies also to previous censuses.

As a result the 1931 figures of tribes which have a large number of Christians are not comparable with those of previous years in which the Christians have not been included. In such cases I have given the number of speakers of the tribal language in brackets below the tribal figures.

Owing to the fact that in previous censuses the number of unspecified Kukis was very large, it is useless to give figures for the various Kuki tribes. For example, the number of Thados in Manipur alone is now 47,086 against 29,975 in 1921: this is merely due to the fact that the number of unspecified Kukis in 1921 and earlier years was very large. In fact in the very early censuses all Kukis were lumped together and even in 1901 most of the numerous Naga and Kuki tribes of Manipur appear under the unspecified head of "Naga" or "Kuki".

TABLE XVIII.—VARIATION OF POPULATION

Serial No.	Tribe or caste.	Locality.	Persons. 1931.	1921.	1911.	1901.	1891.	1881.	Variation (Increase + Decrease —). 1921 to 1931.	1911 to 1921.	1901 to 1911.	1891 to 1901.	1881 to 1891.
1	2	3	4	5	6	7	8	9	10	11	12	13	14
1	**Ahom** (Hindu)	Assam Valley.	240,434	215,885	197,444	178,049	153,528	179,314	+23,549	+18,441	+19,395	+24,521	—25,786
2	**Lalung**	Mostly in Nowgong district.											
	Total ...	......	43,448	41,033	39,219	35,513(a)	52,423	47,650	+ 2,415	+ 1,814	+ 3,706	—16,910	+ 4,773
	Hindu ...	......	31,179	3,354	496	...	798	...					
	Tribal ...	......	12,026	37,679	38,723	35,513	51,625	...					
	Christian ...	......	243	...	...	...	...	...					
3	**Mikir**	Principally in Mikir Hills.											
	Total ...	......	129,797	111,629*	106,259	87,043(a)	94,839	77,765	+18,168	+ 5,370	+19,216	— 7,796	+17,074
	Hindu ...	......	31,283	10,977	736	...	504	...					
	Tribal ...	......	94,855	100,653	104,341	87,043	94,335	...					
	Christian ...	......	3,659	...	1,183	...	...	...					
4	**Miri**	Assam Valley.											
	Total ...	......	85,038	68,725	57,792	46,720	37,430	25,636	+16,313	+10,933	+11,072	+ 9,290	+11,794
	Hindu ...	......	79,848	45,424	13,460	24,023	26,574	...					
	Tribal ...	......	5,153	23,301	44,332	22,696	10,856	...					
	Christian ...	......	38	...	...	...	...	...					
5	**Kachari** (including Mech).	Assam Valley and Cachar. Figures for Kamrup and Goalpara given only.											
	Total ...	......	215,696	193,962*	191,773	180,511	173,221	196,689	+21,734	+ 2,189	+11,262	+ 7,290	—23,468
	Hindu ...	......	146,218	107,720	71,475	5,687	6,754	...					
	Tribal ...	......	66,180	86,242	120,298	174,824	166,467	...					
	Christian ...	......	3,298	...	...	...	...	...					
6	**Angami** (including Kezhama).	Almost entirely in Naga Hills.											
	Total ...	......	49,239	51,730(c)*	44,488(b)	28,963	28,499	...	— 2,491	+ 7,242	+15,525	+ 464	...
	Tribal ...	......	48,655	51,730	44,488	28,963	28,499	...					
	Christian ...	......	584	...	...	...	...	...					
			(48,964)†	(48,278)†	(43,740)†	(29,411)†							
7	**Sema**	Almost entirely in Naga Hills.											
	Total ...	......	37,428	33,439*	*32,772(b)	4,668	...	...	+ 3,989	+ 667	+28,104	...	...
	Tribal ...	......	29,068	33,439	32,772	4,668	...	...					
	Christian ...	......	8,360	...	...	...	...	...					
			(38,146)†	(34,853)†	(32,922)†	...	...	...					
8	**Lhota**	Almost entirely in Naga Hills.											
	Total ...	......	18,238	18,399*	19,511	19,250	22,691	...	— 161	— 1,112	+ 259	— 3,432	...
	Tribal ...	......	17,329	18,399	19,511	19,250	22,691	...					
	Christian ...	......	900	...	...	...	...	...					
			(18,264)†	(18,413)†	(19,627)†	...	...	...					
9	**Rengma**	Almost entirely in Naga Hills.											
	Total ...	......	6,329	5,166*	4,370	4,170	7,865(d)	...	+ 1,163	+ 796	+ 200	— 3,695	...
	Tribal ...	......	6,096	5,166	4,370	4,170	...	...					
	Christian ...	......	233	...	...	...	...	...					
			(6,269)†	(5,103)†	(4,367)†	...	...	...					
10	**Tangkhul**	Manipur											
	Total ...	......	28,731	22,828*	27,316*	19,982	...	...	+ 5,903	— 4,488	+ 7,334	...	...
	Tribal ...	......	25,631	22,828	27,316	...	...	...					
	Christian ...	......	3,100	...	...	...	...	...					
			(29,100)†	(23,234)†	(27,285)†	...	...	...					
11	**Kabui**	Manipur											
	Total ...	......	18,831	14,794*	18,447	1,134	...	...	+ 4,037	— 3,653	+17,313	...	...
	Tribal ...	......	18,571	14,794	18,447	1,134	...	...					
	Christian ...	......	260	...	...	...	...	...					
			(18,478)†	(15,647)†	(17,330)†	...	...	...					

* Exclusive of Christians whose numbers are not known.
† Language figures from the language table.
(a) Sudden fall due to ravages of *kala azar*.
(b) Sudden rise due to incorporation of new territory in the Naga Hills district.
(c) Tribal figures appear too high in comparison with language figures.
(d) Including the Rengmas of a part of Sibsagar district who at subsequent Censuses were returned as Naga unspecified.

OF SELECTED TRIBES AND CASTES—*concld.*

Net variation 1881 to 1931.	Males.						Females.						Serial No.
	1931.	1921.	1911.	1901.	1891.	1881.	1931.	1921.	1911.	1901.	1891.	1881.	
15	16	17	18	19	20	21	22	23	24	25	26	27	28
+ 70,120	129,969	112,400	101,961	90,908	78 842	91,485	119,445	103,485	95,483	87,241	74,696	87,829	1
— 4,903	21,007	20,218	19,222	16,760	26,290	23,993	21,841	20,815	19,907	18,753	26,223	23,658	2
+ 52,032	66,045	57,383	54,257	44,100	49,161	39,753	63,752	54,246	52,002	42,943	45,068	38,012	3
+ 59,402	43,069	35,154	29,335	23,773	19,000	13,303	41,360	33,571	28,457	22,947	17,830	12,333	4
+ 16,907	110,841	98,645	94,281	87,268	85,639	98,870	104,855	95,317	97,492	93,943	87,592	99,829	5
...	25,013	26,498	22,538	14,729	14,568	...	24,296	25,232	21,900	14,234	13,931	...	6
...	18,630	16,474	16,325	2,457	...	...	18,798	16,965	16,447	2,211	...	...	7
...	8,957	8,834	9,448	9,026	11,443	...	9,281	9,575	10,063	10,233	11,948	...	8
...	3,151	2,567	2,016	2,116	3,843	...	3,178	2,509	2,354	2,054	4,022	...	9
...	13,460	10,878	12,867	9,400	...	...	15,331	12,250	14,449	10,502	...	...	10
...	9,854	6,906	8,796	527	...	...	9,977	7,288	9,649	607	...	...	11

TABLE XIX.

EUROPEAN AND ALLIED RACES AND ANGLO-INDIANS BY RACE AND AGE.

This table, except for certain alterations in the age groups, corresponds to Table XVI of 1921.

The details of " Others " in Part I are given below :—

No Armenians were enumerated in Assam.

Nationality.	Males.	Females.
1	2	3
United States of America	47	44
Belgian	...	1
Chilean	1	...
Danish	3	4
Dutch	5	2
French	3	3
German	4	3
Italian	83	11
Norwegian	...	1
Polish	1	...
Russian	1	...
Slav	1	...
Swiss	1	...
Swedish	5	5
Spanish	6	...
Total ...	161	74

TABLE XIX.

European and allied races and Anglo-Indians by race and age. Part I.—European and allied races.

District or State.	Total.			British Subjects.																	
				All ages.			0–13.		14–16.		17–23.		24–33.		34–43.		44–53.		54 and over.		
	Total.	Males.	Females.	Total.	Males.	Females.	Males.	Females.	Males.	Females.	Males.	Females.	Males.	Females.	Males.	Females.	Males.	Females.	Males.	Females.
1	2	3	4	5	6	7	8	9	10	11	12	13	14	15	16	17	18	19	20	21
ASSAM	*3,362*	*2,329*	*1,033*	*3,127*	*2,168*	*959*	*158*	*194*	*17*	*9*	*163*	*55*	*865*	*287*	*496*	*251*	*351*	*110*	*118*	*53*
(I) British Territory ...	*3,113*	*2,176*	*937*	*2,961*	*2,093*	*868*	*150*	*176*	*13*	*8*	*153*	*51*	*855*	*272*	*484*	*235*	*338*	*90*	*100*	*36*
SURMA VALLEY AND HILL DIVISION ...	**947**	**642**	**305**	**906**	**618**	**288**	**40**	**48**	**2**	**4**	**37**	**13**	**251**	**86**	**150**	**70**	**98**	**44**	**40**	**23**
Cachar	306	212	94	299	208	91	7	17	...	1	14	4	90	33	52	22	33	10	12	5
Sylhet	379	302	77	374	299	75	13	12	...	1	22	4	140	24	69	17	37	12	18	5
Khasi and Jaintia Hills (British)	198	93	105	177	81	96	13	17	2	2	1	4	14	19	33	22	19	20	9	13
Naga Hills	30	17	13	23	13	10	3	2	...	...	...	...	3	4	3	3	4	1	...	...
Lushai Hills	34	18	16	33	17	16	4	...	...	...	...	1	4	7	3	6	5	1	1	1
ASSAM VALLEY DIVISION ...	**2,127**	**1,510**	**617**	**2,019**	**1,452**	**567**	**109**	**125**	**11**	**4**	**115**	**35**	**596**	**183**	**338**	**165**	**236**	**43**	**57**	**12**
Goalpara	36	23	13	15	14	1	1	...	...	...	...	...	5	...	4	...	3	1	1	...
Kamrup	131	90	41	97	72	25	16	5	7	...	2	5	13	6	17	4	9	3	6	3
Darrang	351	240	111	350	239	111	18	27	3	1	22	8	93	32	57	31	35	9	11	3
Nowgong	99	68	31	90	64	26	6	4	...	1	1	1	25	8	19	11	8	1	5	...
Sibsagar	527	352	175	514	345	169	30	40	...	1	19	7	131	63	91	51	57	14	17	4
Lakhimpur	973	734	239	950	717	233	36	40	1	1	71	14	329	66	140	67	123	14	17	2
Garo Hills	10	3	7	3	1	2	...	...	...	...	...	...	...	...	...	1	1	1	...	...
SADIYA FRONTIER TRACT	**35**	**20**	**15**	**32**	**19**	**13**	**1**	**3**	...	...	**1**	**3**	**6**	**3**	**5**	...	**4**	**3**	**2**	**1**
BALIPARA FRONTIER TRACT	**4**	**4**	...	**4**	**4**	...	...	...	...	...	...	...	**2**	...	**1**	...	...	...	**1**	...
(II) Manipur State	*22*	*11*	*11*	*19*	*10*	*9*	...	*1*	...	...	...	*1*	*5*	*3*	*1*	*1*	*3*	*1*	*1*	*2*
(III) Khasi States	*227*	*142*	*85*	*147*	*65*	*82*	*8*	*17*	*4*	*1*	*10*	*3*	*5*	*19*	*11*	*15*	*10*	*19*	*17*	*15*

TABLE XIX.

EUROPEAN AND ALLIED RACES AND ANGLO-INDIANS BY RACE AND AGE. PART I.—EUROPEAN AND ALLIED RACES—*concld.*

District or State.	Others.																
	All ages.			0—13.		14—16.		17—23.		24—33.		34—43.		44—53.		54 and over.	
	Total.	Males.	Females.	Males.	Females.	Males.	Females.	Males.	Females.	Males.	Females.	Males.	Females.	Males.	Females.	Males.	Females.
1	22	23	24	25	26	27	28	29	30	31	32	33	34	35	36	37	38
ASSAM	*235*	*161*	*74*	*13*	*12*	*2*	...	*30*	*4*	*55*	*17*	*39*	*28*	*13*	*7*	*9*	*6*
(I) British Territory ...	*152*	*83*	*69*	*13*	*12*	*1*	...	*4*	*4*	*22*	*17*	*26*	*24*	*10*	*7*	*7*	*5*
BURMA VALLEY AND HILL DIVISION ...	41	24	17	1	5	...	...	...	...	9	7	7	2	5	2	2	2
Cachar	7	4	3	...	...	...	...	...	...	...	1	4	1	...	...	...	1
Sylhet	5	3	3	...	1	...	...	...	...	2	1	...	...	1	...	...	...
Khasi and Jaintia Hills (British)	21	12	9	...	3	...	...	...	...	4	4	2	...	4	2	2	1
Naga Hills	7	4	3	1	1	...	...	...	...	2	1	1	1	...	...	...	...
Lushai Hills	1	1	...	...	...	...	...	...	...	1	...	...	...	...	...	...	...
ASSAM VALLEY DIVISION	108	58	50	12	7	1	...	4	4	13	10	18	21	5	5	5	2
Goalpara	21	9	12	2	4	...	...	...	2	2	1	3	5	2	...	...	...
Kamrup	34	18	16	3	3	1	...	4	1	3	5	4	3	1	3	2	1
Darrang	1	1	...	...	...	...	...	...	...	...	...	...	...	...	...	1	...
Nowgong	9	4	5	1	...	...	...	...	...	3	2	...	1	...	2	...	...
Sibsagar	13	7	6	3	...	...	...	...	...	...	...	3	5	...	...	1	1
Lakhimpur	23	17	6	3	...	...	...	...	1	3	1	8	4	2	...	1	...
Garo Hills	7	2	5	...	1	...	...	...	...	2	1	...	3	...	...	...	...
SADIYA FRONTIER TRACT	3	1	2	...	1	...	...	...	...	...	...	1	1	...	...	...	...
BALIPARA FRONTIER TRACT	...	...	...	...	...	...	...	...	...	...	...	...	...	...	...	...	...
(II) Manipur State	*3*	*1*	*2*	...	...	...	...	...	...	...	...	*1*	*2*	...	...	...	...
(III) Khasi States	*80*	*77*	*3*	...	...	*1*	...	*26*	...	*33*	...	*12*	*2*	*3*	...	*2*	*1*

TABLE XIX.

PART II.—ANGLO-INDIANS.

District or State.	All Ages. Total.	All Ages. Males.	All Ages. Females.	0–3. Males.	0–3. Females.	4–6. Males.	4–6. Females.	7–13. Males.	7–13. Females.	14–16. Males.	14–16. Females.	17–19. Males.	17–19. Females.	20–29. Males.	20–29. Females.	30–39. Males.	30–39. Females.	40–49. Males.	40–49. Females.	50–59. Males.	50–59. Females.	60–69. Males.	60–69. Females.	70 and over. Males.	70 and over. Females.
1	2	3	4	5	6	7	8	9	10	11	12	13	14	15	16	17	18	19	20	21	22	23	24	25	26
ASSAM	*650*	*409*	*241*	*31*	*26*	*39*	*20*	*84*	*35*	*10*	*18*	*25*	*21*	*65*	*46*	*73*	*33*	*38*	*17*	*24*	*9*	*19*	*15*	*6*	*1*
(I) British Territory ...	*558*	*349*	*209*	*29*	*25*	*25*	*20*	*73*	*39*	*18*	*15*	*22*	*19*	*58*	*41*	*64*	*28*	*33*	*12*	*13*	*7*	*11*	*9*	*3*	*1*
SURMA VALLEY AND HILL DIVISION ...	**263**	**147**	**116**	**16**	**15**	**15**	**14**	**16**	**15**	**1**	**9**	**11**	**10**	**29**	**24**	**27**	**12**	**16**	**7**	**8**	**4**	**6**	**5**	**2**	**1**
Cachar ...	20	7	13	...	...	...	1	...	2	...	2	...	3	1	5	2	...	3	...	1	...	...	...	...	...
Sylhet ...	148	82	66	13	10	9	10	4	5	...	3	7	6	19	17	19	6	7	4	2	1	2	4	...	...
Khasi and Jaintia Hills (British) ...	71	44	27	3	1	3	2	6	5	1	3	4	1	9	2	5	6	3	2	4	3	4	1	2	1
Naga Hills ...	3	2	1	...	...	...	...	...	...	...	...	...	...	...	...	...	...	2	1	...	...	...	...	...	...
Lushai Hills ...	21	12	9	...	4	3	1	6	3	...	1	...	...	...	...	1	...	1	...	1	...	...	...	...	...
ASSAM VALLEY DIVISION ...	**286**	**197**	**89**	**12**	**10**	**10**	**6**	**57**	**15**	**17**	**6**	**10**	**9**	**29**	**16**	**35**	**15**	**16**	**15**	**5**	**3**	**5**	**4**	**1**	...
Goalpara ...	6	4	2	1	...	...	...	...	...	...	...	...	...	...	...	2	1	...	...	...	1	1	...	...	...
Kamrup ...	139	107	32	3	4	7	2	51	5	14	2	2	1	5	3	12	6	10	4	2	1	1	2	...	...
Darrang ...	8	6	2	3	1	...	...	...	...	...	...	...	...	...	...	4	1	...	...	...	...	...	...	...	...
Nowgong ...	65	41	24	4	3	3	2	3	8	1	1	3	4	11	5	11	4	2	1	2	...	1	1	...	...
Sibsagar ...	33	17	16	...	1	...	...	2	4	1	2	2	3	4	4	2	1	3	...	1	1	1	...	1	...
Lakhimpur ...	31	21	10	2	1	...	1	1	...	1	...	2	1	9	4	3	2	1	...	...	...	1	1	...	...
Garo Hills ...	1	1	...	...	...	...	...	...	...	...	...	...	...	...	...	1	...	...	...	...	...	...	...	...	...
SADIYA FRONTIER TRACT ...	**9**	**5**	**4**	**1**	...	...	...	...	**2**	...	...	**1**	...	...	**1**	**2**	**1**	**1**	...	...	...	...	...	...	...
BALIPARA FRONTIER TRACT ...	...	...	...	...	...	...	...	...	...	...	...	...	...	...	...	...	...	...	...	...	...	...	...	...	...
(II) Manipur State ...	*8*	*5*	*3*	...	*1*	...	...	...	...	...	...	*1*	...	*1*	*1*	*2*	*1*	*1*	...	...	...	...	...	...	...
(III) Khasi States ...	*84*	*55*	*29*	*2*	...	*7*	...	*11*	*8*	*1*	*3*	*2*	*2*	*6*	*4*	*7*	*4*	*4*	*5*	*11*	*9*	*1*	*6*	*3*	...

PROVINCIAL TABLE I.

Area and Population of Thanas, Mauzas, etc.

1. This table shows the population of each local unit in every district, State, and subdivision.

The general administrative unit in the plains districts is the thana or police station; where, however, there are smaller administrative units such as the mauzas of the temporarily-settled districts of the Assam Valley, the population of each mauza or part of a mauza has also been shown under the thana in which it falls.

In the hill districts the local unit varies considerably; in some districts there are no convenient local units less than a subdivision; in others, Doloiships, Sardarships, mauzas, etc., are well known administrative units and the population figures of these have been shown.

2. In the districts of Nowgong, Sibsagar and Lakhimpur there are certain areas which have been declared "backward tracts" by notification under section 52A (2) of the Government of India Act, 1919. As a certain amount of confusion has been found to exist regarding the units or parts of units which are included in these tracts the following information may prove to be useful:—

Nowgong and Sibsagar Mikir Hills.

The Mikir Hills "backward tract" is divided between the districts of Nowgong and Sibsagar (Golaghat subdivision). The Nowgong Mikir Hills portion consists mainly of the following mauzas:—Duar Salona, Duar Bamuni, Duar Amla, Namati, Lumding (Mikir, Kuki, Kachari and Town), Langfer, Jamunapar and Rangkhang. Six square miles of Duar Salona and three square miles of Duar Bamuni fall, however, outside the Mikir Hills backward tract. On the other hand 30 square miles of Duar Bagori and 11 square miles of Mauza Garubat fall within the Nowgong Mikir Hills backward tract.

There is thus considerable overlapping between the administrative units of the regularly administered portions of the Nowgong district and the units of the backward tract portion and some simplification of the existing situation appears to be desirable.

The following is the total area and population by religion of those mauzas in Nowgong which fall mainly within the Mikir Hills, *i.e.*, those mauzas marked in the table with an asterisk:—

			Population.	
Nowgong Mikir Hills ...	... Area in square miles	2,345	Total ...	79,898
			Males ...	43,168
			Females ...	36,730

Hindu.		Muslim.		Tribal.	
Total	34,524	Total	8,003	Total ...	35,504
Males	19,195	Males	4,790	Males ...	18,183
Females	15,329	Females ...	3,213	Females ...	17,321

Christian.		Buddhist.		Others.	
Total	1,700	Total	14	Total ...	153
Males	896	Males ...	12	Males ...	92
Females	804	Females ...	2	Females ...	61

and the following is the area and population by religion of the mauzas which fall within the Sibsagar Mikir Hills (Golaghat subdivision):—

			Population.		
Sibsagar Mikir Hills (Golaghat)...	Area in square miles	2,041	Total	...	56,094
			Males	...	30,161
			Females	...	25,933

Hindu.			Muslim.			Tribal.		
Total	...	24,965	Total ...	...	375	Total	...	26,468
Males	...	13,896	Males ...	...	252	Males	...	13,692
Females ...	...	11,069	Females	...	123	Females	...	12,776

Christian.			Buddhist.			Others.		
Total	...	3,531	Total ...	...	749	(All male)	...	6
Males	...	1,900	Males ...	...	415			
Females	...	1,631	Females	...	334			

The total area of the Nowgong and Sibsagar Mikir Hills "backward tract" is thus 4,386 square miles with a total population of 135,992 persons. In this area however are included several mauzas, *e.g.*, Borpathar and Namati, which are really plains areas and are not inhabited by hillmen.

Lakhimpur Frontier Tract.

This small tract has an area of 394 square miles and consists of mauzas Buridihing, Makum Phakial, and the southern portion of Makum which contains the house tax-paying villages of the "Sarkari" Nagas. Over half the total area of the tract is comprised in Buridihing Mauza which is really an undeveloped plains area. The intention of the Local Government is to transfer this mauza to the regularly administered portion of the district as soon as it is sufficiently developed and its communications have been improved. The total population of the Lakhimpur Frontier Tract by sex and religion is as follows :—

Total population.			Hindu.			Muslim.			Tribal.		
Total	...	13,590	Total	...	7,252	Total	...	171	Total	...	3,698
Males	...	8,016	Males	...	4,659	Males	...	144	Males	...	1,838
Females	...	5,574	Females	...	2,593	Females	...	27	Females	...	1,854

Christian.			Buddhist.			Others.		
Total	...	648	Total ...	...	1,817	Total ...	...	10
Males	...	449	Males ...	...	916	Males ...	...	10
Females	...	199	Females	...	901	Females	...	nil.

3. Although all the units of the backward tracts—marked by an asterisk in this table—have been shown under various thanas this must not be taken to mean that they form part of the regular jurisdiction of the thanas concerned. The Code of Criminal Procedure is not in force in the backward tracts which are governed by special rules of their own relating to the administration of justice and these rules regulate the action which the police are permitted to take in these tracts.

PROVINCIAL TABLE I.—Area and Population of Thanas, Mauzas, etc.

Thana, mauza or other local unit.	Area in square miles.	Number of: Towns.	Number of: Villages.	Number of occupied houses.	Population 1931: Persons.	Population 1931: Males.	Population 1931: Females.	Population 1921: Both sexes.	Percentage of variation: 1921 to 1931.	Percentage of variation: 1911 to 1921.	Number of persons per square mile in 1931.
1	2	3	4	5	6	7	8	9	10	11	12
ASSAM	*67,334*	*30*	*35,796*	*1,898,734*	*9,247,857*	*4,844,133*	*4,403,724*	*7,990,246*	+ *15.7*	+ *13.9*	*137*
British Territory	*55,014*	*29*	*33,870*	*1,771,295*	*8,622,251*	*4,537,206*	*4,085,045*	*7,459,128*	+ *15.6*	+ *13.4*	*157*
SURMA VALLEY AND HILL DIVISION ...	*24,170*	*10*	*15,299*	*763,397*	*3,708,047*	*1,913,144*	*1,794,903*	*3,424,010*	+ *8.3*	+ *3.4*	*153*
CACHAR DISTRICT	3,862	2	1,607	122,963	570,531	301,338	269,193	529,301	+ 7.8	+ 6.0	148
Sadr Subdivision	1,451	1	953	84,041	386,695	204,669	182,026	359,376	+ 7.6	+ 6.0	267
Silchar Thana	263	1	240	24,312	117,091	63,004	54,087	109,842	+ 6.1	+ 6.4	440
Lakhipur "	276	...	157	16,306	70,467	37,448	33,019	64,616	+ 9.1	+ 3.5	255
Katigora "	243	...	193	11,921	56,205	29,357	26,848	51,453	+ 7.1	+ 0.2	231
Barkhola "	140	...	79	7,517	32,694	17,909	15,215	33,127	− 1.0	+ 2.1	233
Sonai "	357	...	170	15,166	75,757	39,471	36,286	67,999	+ 11.4	+ 19.5	212
Udharband "	173	...	114	8,816	34,091	18,110	15,971	32,337	+ 5.4	+ 9.0	197
Hailakandi Subdivision	521	1	310	31,235	150,992	79,307	71,635	141,012	+ 7.1	+ 6.2	290
Hailakandi Thana	188	1	210	21,957	108,736	56,935	51,801	102,498	+ 6.1	+ 2.5	578
Katlicherra "	333	...	100	9,278	42,256	22,432	19,824	38,514	+ 9.7	+ 11.6	127
North Cachar Hills Subdivision	1,890	...	339	7,687	32,844	17,302	15,542	28,913	+ 13.6	− 1.7	17
SYLHET DISTRICT	5,478	5	11,717	548,541	2,724,342	1,407,645	1,316,697	2,541,341	+ 7.2	+ 3.7	497
North Sylhet Subdivision	1,090	1	2,551	118,022	580,560	299,355	281,205	538,922	+ 7.7	+ 3.9	533
Sylhet (Sadr) Thana	230	1	504	32,501	159,983	83,365	76,618	143,647	+ 11.4	+ 5.6	696
Gowainghat "	248	...	251	11,615	58,377	32,417	25,960	49,433	+ 18.1	− 5.1	235
Golabganj "	107	...	195	16,082	81,452	40,538	40,914	76,725	+ 6.2	+ 7.9	761
Fenchuganj "	42	...	75	4,841	24,021	12,681	11,340	22,053	+ 8.9	+ 11.9	572
Kanairghat "	153	...	136	14,800	68,835	35,600	33,235	65,781	+ 4.6	− 0.4	450
Jaintiapur "	79	...	89	3,887	17,782	9,536	8,246	15,636	+ 13.7	− 3.3	225
Balaganj "	144	...	673	19,760	97,173	48,687	48,486	94,170	+ 3.2	+ 0.2	657
Biswanath "	83	...	445	14,496	72,937	36,531	36,406	71,453	+ 2.0	+ 3.8	879
South Sylhet (Maulvi Bazar) Subdivision ...	*865*	*1*	*2,032*	*96,126*	*451,364*	*231,457*	*219,907*	*418,022*	+ *8.0*	+ *2.5*	*522*
Maulvi Bazar Thana	129	1	535	20,850	104,331	53,028	51,303	97,098	+ 7.5	− 0.4	809
Kamalganj "	186	...	306	17,004	78,841	40,554	38,287	73,379	+ 7.4	+ 6.2	424
Srimangal "	156	...	316	17,019	68,720	35,450	33,270	66,613	+ 2.9	+ 50.6	441
Rajnagar "	131	...	433	14,400	69,576	35,340	34,236	65,771	+ 5.8	− 22.5	531
Kulaura "	263	...	564	27,036	129,896	67,085	62,811	114,971	+ 13.0	+ 1.9	494

PROVINCIAL TABLE I.—Area and Population of Thanas, Mauzas, etc.—*contd.*

Thana, Mauza or other local unit.	Area in square miles.	Number of Towns.	Number of Villages.	Number of occupied houses.	Population 1931. Persons.	Population 1931. Males.	Population 1931. Females.	Population 1921. Both sexes.	Percentage of variation 1921 to 1931.	Percentage of variation 1911 to 1921.	Number of persons per square mile in 1931.
1	2	3	4	5	6	7	8	9	10	11	12
Habiganj Subdivision	1,003	1	2,630	130,614	632,521	321,900	310,623	592,939	+ 6·7	— ·8	631
Habiganj Thana	90	1	329	19,767	91,835	47,053	44,783	81,323	+ 12·9	— 6·1	1,020
Chunarighat "	191	...	450	20,095	89,850	46,170	43,680	79,144	+ 13·5	— 1·8	470
Baniyachung "	194	...	303	20,401	104,898	53,328	51,570	105,278	— ·4	+ 3·9	541
Ajmiriganj "	82	...	161	7,323	39,101	20,355	18,746	39,704	— 1·5	+ 0·7	477
Madhabpur "	108	...	347	18,626	87,714	44,810	42,904	79,130	+ 10·8	— 0·3	812
Lakhai "	78	...	96	10,710	52,288	25,712	26,576	49,463	+ 5·7	— 1·7	670
Nabiganj "	164	...	459	20,755	105,535	53,857	51,678	100,706	+ 4·8	+ 2·6	644
Bahubal "	87	...	356	13,344	61,330	30,965	30,365	58,198	+ 5·4	— 6·1	706
Sunamganj Subdivision	1,443	1	2,788	95,988	550,263	293,011	257,252	511,193	+ 7·6	+ 6·6	381
Sunamganj Thana	334	1	516	20,016	118,598	63,787	54,811	107,823	+ 10·0	+ 8·1	355
Tahirpur "	110	...	156	5,066	29,400	16,253	13,147	25,450	+ 15·6	+ 3·1	267
Chhatak "	275	...	697	22,299	122,067	64,377	57,690	110,002	+ 11·0	+ 7·5	444
Dirai "	152	...	274	11,784	70,900	37,643	33,257	66,181	+ 7·1	+ 1·0	467
Jagannathpur "	141	...	494	13,964	74,995	39,026	35,969	73,443	+ 2·1	+ 10·5	532
Sulla "	100	...	122	6,036	34,634	18,309	16,325	34,410	+ ·6	+ 2·5	346
Dharamyasha "	331	...	537	16,865	99,640	53,617	46,023	93,877	+ 6·1	+ 7·5	301
Karimganj Subdivision	1,077	1	1,810	107,891	509,634	261,823	247,811	480,265	+ 6·1	+ 3·5	473
Karimganj Thana	258	1	644	36,948	179,735	91,808	87,927	168,066	+ 6·9	— ·24	697
Patharkandi "	273	...	300	16,662	65,620	34,218	31,402	64,385	+ 1·9	+ 23·2	240
Ratabari "	241	...	264	14,275	64,213	34,037	30,176	60,024	+ 7·0	+ 2·2	266
Badarpur "	48	...	99	7,994	38,238	19,504	18,734	35,179	+ 8·7	— 8·1	797
Jaldhup "	257	...	509	33,012	161,634	81,262	80,372	152,011	+ 6·0	+ 4·5	630
KHASI AND JAINTIA HILLS DISTRICT (TOTAL).	6,145	2	2,439	60,349	289,926	146,551	143,375	243,263	+ 19·2	+ 3·5	47
British Territory	*2,445*	*2*	*954*	*22,061*	*109,926*	*55,439*	*54,487*	*96,161*	*+ 14·3*	*— 3·4*	*45*
Khasi States	*3,700*	...	*1,475*	*38,288*	*180,000*	*91,112*	*88,888*	*147,102*	*+ 22·4*	*+ 8·5*	*49*
Shillong Sadr Subdivision (total)	4,039	2	1,653	44,609	208,781	107,407	101,374	170,623	+ 22·4	+ 8·5	52
(1) British Territory	*339*	*2*	*178*	*6,391*	*28,781*	*16,295*	*12,486*	*23,521*	*+ 22·4*	...	*85*
Part of Shillong town	...	1	...	1,180	4,608	3,108	1,500	4,115	+ 12·0	+ 28·1	...
Shillong Cantonment	...	1	...	640	5,236	3,547	1,689	1,734	+ 202·0	+ 26·1	...
British Sardarships and Villages	...	...	178	4,561	18,937	9,640	9,297	17,672	+ 7·1	— 3·9	...

PROVINCIAL TABLE I.—AREA AND POPULATION OF THANAS, MAUZAS, ETC.—contd.

Thana, mauza or other local unit.	Area in square miles.	Number of Towns.	Number of Villages.	Number of occupied houses.	Population 1931. Persons.	Population 1931. Males.	Population 1931. Females.	Population 1921. Both sexes.	Percentage of variation 1921 to 1931.	Percentage of variation 1911 to 1921.	Number of persons per square mile in 1931.
1	2	3	4	5	6	7	8	9	10	11	12
(2) Khasi States	*3,700*	...	*1,475*	*38,988*	*180,000*	*91,112*	*88,888*	*147,103*	+22·4	...	49
Siemships—											
Myllem* (including the part of Shillong town falling within Myllem).	...	...	278	10,158	47,588	24,128	23,460	34,700	+34·3	+13·1	...
Khyrim	...	...	271	9,290	43,558	21,018	22,540	36,833	+18·3	+ 2·5	...
Cherra	...	...	107	2,200	9,738	4,768	4,970	9,454	+ 3·0	+ 2·8	...
Nongstoin	...	...	191	2,443	11,867	5,993	5,874	10,157	+16·7	+ 5·1	...
Maharam	...	...	94	2,925	15,003	7,349	7,654	12,649	+18·6	+21·8	...
Nongkhlaw	...	...	103	3,063	14,278	7,185	7,093	11,743	+21·6	+ 9·8	...
Mariaw	...	...	19	739	3,192	1,582	1,610	2,900	+ 8·8	+15·9	...
Rambrai	...	...	27	646	2,685	1,448	1,237	2,079	+29·1	−23·9	...
Mawiang	...	...	21	591	2,548	1,462	1,086	2,522	+14·0	+19·0	...
Langrin	...	...	17	307	1,344	692	652	1,262	+ 6·4	+ 7·5	...
Nobosohphoh	...	...	17	531	2,546	1,237	1,309	2,146	+18·6	+20·1	...
Mawsynram	...	...	12	454	2,007	970	1,037	1,831	+ 9·6	+10·6	...
Malaisohmat	...	...	8	106	433	120	313	493	−12·2	+ ·0	...
Bhowal	...	...	16	176	757	381	376	629	+20·3	− 6·2	...
Nongspung	...	...	43	752	3,053	1,974	1,079	3,055	+24·1	+30·3	...
Jirang	...	...	13	253	1,458	753	705	1,230	+18·5	− 3·9	...
Lyngdohships—											
Sohiong	...	...	40	710	3,502	1,669	1,833	3,586	− 2·3	+41·5	...
Mawphlang	...	...	11	309	1,730	814	916	1,350	+28·0	+16·3	...
Langiong	...	...	9	305	1,318	651	667	843	+56·3	+10·2	...
Wahadadarship—											
Shella	...	...	43	1,190	4,486	2,305	2,181	4,006	+12·0	− 1·9	...
Sardarships—											
Mawlong	...	...	16	543	2,319	1,214	1,105	1,876	+23·6	− 6·6	...
Mawdon	...	...	6	120	492	242	250	401	+22·7	+ 8·1	...
Dwara Nongtyrmen	...	...	11	156	645	308	337	423	+52·5	+13·4	...
Nonglwai	...	...	3	46	213	89	124	246	−13·4	−40·9	...
Pamsanngut	...	...	4	59	289	141	148	265	+ 9·1	−28·8	...
Road population	...	...	...	...	2,707	2,429	278	...	...	...	...

* The portion of Shillong town falling within Myllem State contains a population of 16,692 persons (males 8,979, females 7,713) with 3,330 occupied houses. In 1921 this portion contained 11,364 persons.

PROVINCIAL TABLE I.—Area and Population of Thanas, Mauzas, etc.—*contd.*

Thana, Mauza or other local unit.	Area in square miles.	Number of Towns.	Number of Villages.	Number of occupied houses.	Population 1931 Persons.	Population 1931 Males.	Population 1931 Females.	Population 1921 Both sexes.	Percentage of variation 1921 to 1931.	Percentage of variation 1911 to 1921.	Number of persons per square mile in 1931.
1	2	3	4	5	6	7	8	9	10	11	12
Jowai Subdivision	2,106	...	776	15,740	81,145	39,144	42,001	72,640	+11·7	−6·7	39
Doloiships—											
Jowai	...	...	60	2,268	12,004	5,584	6,420	10,795	+ 11·3	+ 2·1	...
Nartiang	...	...	65	960	4,294	2,165	2,129	3,833	+ 12·0	− 17·0	...
Raliang	...	...	68	1,563	7,157	3,435	3,722	6,428	+ 11·3	− 20·6	...
Bhoi	...	...	201	2,468	14,880	7,451	7,429	12,239	+ 21·4	+ 5·4	...
Shangpung	...	...	33	781	4,820	2,352	2,468	4,118	+ 17·0	− 0·6	...
Nongtalang	...	...	17	1,083	5,432	2,509	2,923	4,864	+ 11·6	− 10·2	...
Nonglwai (Nongbah)	...	...	22	609	3,269	1,536	1,733	2,827	+ 16·3	+ 3·6	...
Mishut	...	...	2	34	87	43	44	79	+ 10·1	− 20·7	...
Nongjugi	...	...	37	583	2,317	1,131	1,186	2,510	− 7·7	− 10·0	...
Mynso	...	...	6	273	1,268	565	703	1,347	− 6·3	− 10·0	...
Shilliang Myntang	...	...	30	657	2,593	1,277	1,316	2,196	+ 18·1	− 9·4	...
Nongphyllut	...	...	29	449	2,063	1,011	1,052	2,011	+ 2·6	− 9·9	...
Sutnga	...	...	22	644	3,117	1,626	1,491	3,297	− 5·5	− 18·8	...
Nongkhlieh	...	...	8	178	737	374	363	781	− 9·2	− 19·6	...
Narpuh	...	...	17	250	1,236	577	659	1,452	− 14·9	− 24·9	...
Saipator	...	...	30	574	2,776	1,221	1,555	2,294	+ 21·0	− 11·2	...
Lahadong	...	...	9	114	700	312	388	576	+ 21·5	− 13·4	...
Hymbai	...	...	34	663	3,764	1,688	2,076	3,694	+ 1·9	+ 6·4	...
Amwi	...	...	8	416	2,146	1,024	1,122	1,923	+ 11·6	− 6·8	...
Darang	...	...	7	250	1,094	590	504	911	+ 20·1	− 18·7	...
Sardarships—											
Myriang and Langsoh	...	...	86	644	4,143	2,135	2,008	3,543	+ 16·9	− 3·0	...
Saipung	...	...	9	193	1,254	641	613	870	+ 44·1	+ 7·7	...
Survey Camp	...	...	...	...	...	...	...	70	...	...	...
NAGA HILLS DISTRICT	4,293	1	481	47,598	178,844	89,536	89,308	158,801	+12·6	+ 4·8	42
Kohima (Sadr) Subdivision	2,845	1	335	26,311	99,230	50,573	48,657	88,759	+ 11·8	+ ·8	35
Mokokchung Subdivision	1,448	...	146	21,287	79,614	38,963	40,651	70,042	+ 13·7	+ 11·1	55
LUSHAI HILLS DISTRICT	8,092	...	540	22,234	124,404	59,186	65,218	98,406	+26·4	+ 7·9	15
Aijal (Sadr) Subdivision	4,806	...	339	15,996	89,376	42,853	46,523	70,328	+ 27·1	+ 7·9	19
Lungleh Subdivision	3,286	...	201	6,238	35,028	16,633	18,395	28,078	+ 24·8	+ 8·0	11
ASSAM VALLEY DIVISION	*57,084*	*18*	*17,169*	*906,193*	*4,855,711*	*2,592,144*	*2,263,567*	*3,990,203*	*+ 21·7*	*+ 22·9*	*179*
GOALPARA DISTRICT	3,985	3	3,188	157,961	882,748	470,273	412,475	762,523	+15·8	+26·9	222
Dhubri (Sadr) Subdivision	2,888	2	2,197	109,881	620,715	331,690	289,025	551,351	+12·6	+21·4	215
Dhubri Thana	168	2	159	12,920	81,219	44,191	37,028	70,190	+ 15·7	+ 13·2	483
South Salmara "	266	...	208	14,618	91,533	48,212	43,321	88,456	+ 3·5	+ 12·4	330
Golakganj "	182	...	100	15,431	80,989	42,761	38,228	80,319	+ ·8	− 2·0	445
Bilasipara "	375	...	340	14,130	81,476	43,430	38,046	77,792	+ 4·7	+ 30·6	217
Kokrajhar "	506	...	489	15,961	88,567	47,351	41,216	73,147	+ 21·1	...	157
Gossaigaon "	427	...	266	10,901	61,144	33,901	27,243	45,151	+ 35·4	...	143
Bijni "	838	...	400	17,525	98,937	52,802	46,135	81,725	+ 21·1	+ 45·7	130
Mankachar "	59	...	93	7,314	36,820	19,051	17,769	34,563	+ 6·5	+ 21·3	624

CORRECTION SLIP No. 5.

Substitute the following names and figures for those in columns 1 to 8 against the units named Panbari (excluding Gauhati town) and Demoria in column 1 of the Provincial Table 1 at page 281 of Census of India, 1931, Volume III—Assam, Part II—Tables :—

CORRECTION SLIP No. 6.

Substitute the following names and figures for those in columns 1 to 8 against the unit named Dharampur in column 1 of the Provincial Table 1 at page 281 of Census of India, 1931, Volume III—Assam, Part II—Tables :—

Thana, Mauza or other local unit.	Area in square miles.	Number of		Number of occupied houses.	Population, 1931.		
		Towns.	Villages.		Persons.	Males.	Females.
1	2	3	4	5	6	7	8
KAMRUP DISTRICT.							
GAUHATI SUBDIVISION.							
Nalbari Thana.							
Dharampur	21·31	...	24	4,143	21,775	10,599	11,176
Khetri Dharampur	23·69	...	16	1,994	9,217	4,777	4,440

A. G. P. (Edn.) No. 2-680—27-4-1933.

PROVINCIAL TABLE I.—Area and Population of Thanas, Mauzas, etc.—contd.

Thana, mauza or other local unit.	Area in square miles.	Number of Towns.	Number of Villages.	Number of occupied houses.	Population 1931. Persons.	Population 1931. Males.	Population 1931. Females.	Population 1921. Both sexes.	Percentage of variation 1921 to 1931.	Percentage of variation 1911 to 1921.	Number of persons per square mile in 1931.
1	2	3	4	5	6	7	8	9	10	11	12
Goalpara Subdivision	1,097	1	991	48,080	263,083	138,583	123,400	211,172	+ 24·1	+ 34·1	239
Goalpara Thana	230	1	191	9,685	50,665	27,175	23,490	42,180	+ 20·1	+ 18·9	218
Dudnai "	250	...	236	8,845	45,919	22,822	23,097	38,633	+ 18·9	+ 5·2	184
Lakhipur "	268	...	346	12,070	81,850	43,340	38,510	67,431	+ 21·4	+ 57·7	305
North Salmara "	340	...	218	15,430	83,509	44,346	39,163	62,928	+ 32·8	+ 37·5	246
KAMRUP DISTRICT	3,844	3	2,738	189,035	976,746	513,345	463,401	763,571	+ 27·9	+ 14·2	254
Gauhati Subdivision	2,586	2	1,782	131,780	661,491	344,892	316,599	577,056	+ 14·6	+ 9·3	256
Gauhati Thana	*350*	*1*	*154*	*14,170*	*66,514*	*38,868*	*27,646*	*57,484*	+ *15·7*	+ *10·3*	*190*
Gauhati town	2·14	1	...	4,739	21,797	14,506	7,291	16,480	+ 32·3	+ 18·0	10,186
Panbari (excluding Gauhati town)	96·86	...	41	2,433	11,516	6,172	5,344	11,751	− 2·0	+ 16·0	119
Beltola	44	...	35	1,770	7,667	4,154	3,513	8,011	− 7·5	+ 3·4	181
Demoria	140	...	63	2,391	12,365	6,568	5,737	10,403	+ 18·3	+ 1·6	88
Rani (Part)	65	...	15	1,851	9,339	5,509	3,830	6,766	+ 38·0	+ 19·2	144
North Gauhati (Silasundari Ghopa Mauza—Part) ...	2	...	1	796	3,590	1,959	1,631	3,367	+ 6·6	+ 14·3	1,795
Brahmaputra River	...	...	...	...	...	...	...	106	...	...	...
Palasbari Thana	*304*	*1*	*150*	*12,882*	*62,675*	*31,778*	*30,897*	*56,103*	+ *11·7*	+ *5·2*	*206*
Rammaravi (Part)	17	...	21	1,580	7,030	3,606	3,425	7,461	− 5·2	− 0·9	414
Dakhin Rani	80	...	26	985	5,130	2,794	2,336	4,940	+ 3·6	− 2·0	64
Palasbari "small town"	·86	1	...	717	3,454	1,958	1,496	2,733	+ 26·4	+ 6·7	4,103
Chayani excluding Palasbari "small town"	30·44	...	34	1,297	14,617	7,280	7,338	13,899	+ 5·2	+ 5·7	480
Dakhin Saru Bangaar (Part)	51	...	7	251	319	313	6 }	15,433	+ 26·2	{ + 16·5	6
Rampur	26	...	24	3,746	19,145	8,969	10,176 }			+ 16·5	736
Barduar	99	...	48	2,616	12,990	6,860	6,130	11,647	+ 11·5	+ 13·8	131
Chhaygaon Thana	*173*	...	*143*	*6,951*	*34,831*	*19,052*	*15,779*	*25,049*	+ *39·1*	+ *29·4*	*201*
Chhaygaon Pantan	66	...	51	2,402	10,336	6,090	4,546	9,239	+ 18·3	+ 1·8	156
Dakhin Saru Bangaar (Part)	38	...	27	1,966	10,006	5,299	4,707	10,080	− ·7	+ 16·5	263
Pub-Chamaria	60	...	65	2,583	13,897	7,673	6,224	5,730	+ 142·5	+ 24·3	301
Boko Thana	*419*	...	*216*	*8,322*	*44,293*	*23,582*	*20,711*	*33,430*	+ *32·5*	+ *6·8*	*106*
Bangaon-Boko	215	...	97	3,139	16,976	8,784	8,192	15,566	+ 9·3	+ 9·1	79
Luki	107	...	66	2,671	14,523	7,712	6,811	13,062	+ 11·2	+ 15·1	136
Paschim-Chamaria	97	...	53	2,512	12,794	7,086	5,708	4,770	+ 168·2	+ 24·5	132
Nalbari Thana	*285*	...	*337*	*32,739*	*166,617*	*82,669*	*83,948*	*155,206*	+ *7·4*	+ *3·8*	*585*
Upar Barbhag	18	...	46	3,130	24,964	11,694	13,270	22,748	+ 9·7	+ 8·5	1,486
Bamjani	18	...	79	3,214	16,857	8,000	8,857	15,122	+ 11·5	− 0·3	937
Khata	19	...	46	2,463	17,100	8,780	8,320	14,964	+ 14·1	− 1·4	900
Pakowa	23	...	28	3,860	19,985	9,834	10,151	18,197	+ 9·8	+ 6·7	869
Dharampur	45	...	40	6,137	30,988	15,370	15,618	28,065	+ 8·3	+ 4·5	689
Batasgila	32	...	33	2,486	11,974	6,087	5,887	17,036	− ·5	+ 4·3	374
Namati	30	...	28	2,234	12,140	6,100	5,960	12,261	− 1·9	+ 0·7	405
Namberbhag	20	...	28	3,606	18,606	9,386	9,222	18,453	+ ·8	+ 4·5	930
Paschim Basta	25	...	33	1,478	8,003	4,194	3,809	7,245	+ 10·5	+ 4·0	320
Dakhin Basta	30	...	26	1,176	6,004	3,139	2,865	6,372	+ 11·6	+ 6·0	200

PROVINCIAL TABLE I.—AREA AND POPULATION OF THANAS, MAUZAS, ETC.—contd.

Thana, mauza or other local unit.	Area in square miles.	Number of Towns.	Number of Villages.	Number of occupied houses.	Population 1931 Persons.	Population 1931 Males.	Population 1931 Females.	Population 1921 Both sexes.	Percentage of variation 1921 to 1931.	Percentage of variation 1911 to 1921.	Number of persons per square mile in 1931.
1	2	3	4	5	6	7	8	9	10	11	12
Rangia Thana	*662*	...	*402*	*25,030*	*126,914*	*66,230*	*60,684*	*108,477*	*+ 17·0*	*+ 9·1*	*192*
Pub-Borigog	21	...	30	2,149	12,517	6,362	6,155	12,200	+ 2·6	+ 37·4	596
Paschim Borigog	23	...	33	3,107	15,439	7,653	7,786	14,867	+ 3·8	− 12·9	671
Pubrachari Mahal	24	...	18	1,570	8,872	4,661	4,211	14,497	+ 21·6	+ 5·0	370
Kautbaha	31	...	25	1,661	9,245	4,766	4,479			+ 5·0	298
Panduri	34	...	36	2,235	11,291	5,876	5,415	9,948	+ 13·5	− ·16	333
Pub Banbhag	23	...	39	2,123	10,268	5,106	5,162	10,585	− 2·4	+ 3·1	467
Paschim Banbhag	32	...	42	2,071	10,711	5,471	5,240	9,781	+ 9·5	+ 0·9	335
Pub-Baska	175	...	60	3,046	14,107	7,776	6,331	9,519	+ 48·2	+ 11·4	81
Madhya Baska	160	...	63	3,541	16,140	8,727	7,413	9,596	+ 68·2	+ 18·3	101
Betna	130	...	58	3,637	18,334	9,842	8,492	17,146	+ 6·9	+ 34·7	132
Kamalpur Thana	*163*	...	*175*	*13,998*	*73,994*	*38,404*	*35,590*	*68,654*	*+ 7·8*	*+ 10·4*	*454*
Patidarang	32	...	41	2,273	12,307	6,375	5,932	10,244	+ 20·1	+ 20·8	396
Barbangsar	34	...	26	2,096	11,878	6,074	5,804	10,988	+ 8·1	+ 5·6	349
Bilasundari Ghopa (Part)	27	...	22	2,407	11,256	6,305	4,951	9,878	+ 14·0	+ 14·8	417
Karara	17	...	23	1,803	9,921	5,088	4,833	10,466	− 5·2	+ 2·6	584
Madartola	24	...	23	1,923	9,592	4,900	4,692	9,410	+ 1·9	+ 1·4	400
Pubpar	29	...	40	3,495	19,040	9,662	9,378	17,668	+ 7·8	+ 10·0	657
Hajo Thana	*230*	...	*205*	*17,688*	*85,653*	*44,309*	*41,344*	*72,653*	*+ 17·9*	*+ 19·8*	*372*
Hajo	44	...	44	4,333	21,677	11,040	10,637	19,584	+ 10·7	+ 12·5	493
Pub-Bangsar	36·5	...	34	2,961	14,690	7,571	7,119	21,300	+ 18·3	+ 14·3	402
Paschim-Bangsar	34·5	...	23	2,065	10,410	5,192	5,218			+ 14·3	302
Uttar Barkhetri	40	...	40	2,666	13,589	7,279	6,309	12,131	+ 12·0	+ 29·7	340
Dakhin Barkhetri	47	...	43	2,609	12,207	6,777	5,430	8,874	+ 37·6	+ 39·7	260
Ramdia	27	...	23	2,764	13,081	6,450	6,631	10,855	+ 20·5	+ 12·5	494
BARPETA SUBDIVISION	**1,258**	**1**	**950**	**57,255**	**315,255**	**168,453**	**146,802**	**186,515**	**+ 69·0**	**+ 34·1**	**251**
Barpeta Thana	*605*	*1*	*485*	*27,672*	*159,275*	*85,532*	*73,743*	*79,041*	*+101·5*	*+ 71·1*	*263*
Barpeta town	1·49	1	...	2,671	13,777	6,939	6,838	11,730	+ 17·5	+ 26·5	9,246
Barpeta	120·51	...	55	5,067	29,805	15,831	13,974	12,943	+ 130·3	+ 20·5	247
Chenga	55	...	50	3,068	19,415	10,268	9,147	12,856	+ 51·0	+ 312·6	353
Bagribari	205	...	121	6,041	30,792	16,849	13,943	12,336	+ 149·6	+ 312·6	150
Paka	55	...	54	1,289	5,343	3,262	2,081	14,296	+ 40·1	+ 19·1	97
Sarukhetri	57	...	33	3,013	15,966	8,736	7,230			+ 19·1	285
Bhowanipar	58	...	75	4,144	24,759	13,091	11,668	7,431	+ 233·1	+ 73·6	437
Howli	53	...	67	3,579	19,418	10,565	8,853	7,454	+ 160·4	+ 73·6	366
Sorbhog Thana	*490*	...	*283*	*16,189*	*86,753*	*46,943*	*39,810*	*47,008*	*+ 84·5*	*+ 29·9*	*207*
Rupsi	94	...	65	5,410	29,141	15,951	13,190	8,683	+ 235·6	+ 34·6	310
Damka Chakabansi	38	...	49	3,879	20,334	10,043	9,291	15,004	+ 34·5	+ 17·8	535
Bijni	172	...	66	2,032	11,359	6,071	5,288	8,113	+ 40·0	+ 37·1	64
Kharija Bijni	63	...	41	2,311	12,289	6,688	5,670	8,397	+ 46·4	+ 37·1	194
Gobardhona	53	...	33	2,580	13,711	7,440	6,271	6,413	+ 101·3	+ 37·1	259

CORRECTION SLIP No. 4.

Substitute the following names and figures for those in columns 1 to 8 against the unit named Madhya Baska in column 1 of the Provincial Table 1 at page 282 of Census of India, 1931, Volume III—Assam, Part II—Tables:—

Thana, Mauza or other local unit.	Area in square miles.	Number of		Number of occupied houses.	Population, 1931.		
		Towns.	Villages.		Persons.	Males.	Females.
1	2	3	4	5	6	7	8
KAMRUP DISTRICT.							
GAUHATI SUBDIVISION.							
Rangia Thana.							
Madhya Baska	122·65	...	33	2,230	9,825	5,288	4,537
Uttar Baska	37·35	...	29	1,311	6,315	3,439	2,876

No. 45.

Omit correction slip No. 43 and *substitute* the following names and figures for those in columns 1 to 8 against the unit named "Mahabhairab (excluding Tezpur Town)" in column 1 of the Provincial Table 1, page 283 of Census of India, 1931, Volume III—Assam, Part II—Tables:—

Thana, Mauza, or other local unit	Area in sq. miles	Number of—		Name of occupied houses	Population		
		Town	Village		Persons	Male	Female
1	2	3	4	5	6	7	8
Tezpur Town	1·9	1	Nil	2,167	10,381	7,357	3,024
Mahabhairab Mauza excluding Tezpur Town	65·9	..	32	1,485	8,374	4,196	4,178
Bhairabpad Mauza	30·2	..	20	1,587	8,876	4,647	4,229

[Dy. No. $\frac{\text{L. Rev.}}{652}$ of 1941.]

Correction slip No. 20.

Substitute the following names and figures for those in columns 1 to 8 against the units named Chenga and Baguribari in column 1 of the Provincial Table at page 282 of Census of India, 1931, Volume III—Assam, Part II—Tables.—

Thana, mauza or other local unit.	Area in square miles.	Number of		Number of occupied houses.	Population, 1931.		
		Towns.	Villages.		Persons.	Males.	Females.
1	2	3	4	5	6	7	8
KAMRUP DISTRICT.							
BARPETA SUBDIVISION.							
Barpeta Thana—							
Chenga	43·77	...	35	2,250	14,309	7,568	6,741
Baguribari	85·44	...	109	3,856	17,793	9,499	8,294
Baghbar	130·79	...	27	2,003	18,105	10,050	8,055

A. G. P. (Bdn.) No. 26—695—7-4-1934.

Correction slip No. 19.

Substitute the following names and figures for those in columns 1 to 8 against the units named " Sootea " and " Bishnath (part) " in column 1 of the Provincial Table 1 at page 283 of Census of India, 1931, Volume III—Assam, Part II—Tables.

Thana, mauza or other local unit.	Area in square miles.	Number of Towns.	Number of Villages.	Number of occupied houses.	Population, 1931. Persons.	Population, 1931. Males.	Population, 1931. Females.
1	2	3	4	5	6	7	8
DARRANG DISTRICT.							
TEZPUR SUBDIVISION.							
Sootea Thana—							
Sootea	75	...	30	1,819	8,225	4,617	3,608
Bishnath (part)	86	...	37	2,490	12,463	6,941	5,522
Nag-Sankar	85	...	25	2,875	11,673	6,225	5,448

CORRECTION SLIP No. 16.

Substitute the following names and figures for those in columns 1 to 8 against the units named Barpeta thana, Barpeta mauza, Sorbhog thana and Rupsi mauza in column 1 of the Provincial Table I at page 282, of the Census of India, 1931, Volume III—Assam, Part II—Tables and *insert* new mauza Mandia below Barpeta mauza under Barpeta thana.

Thana, mauza or other local unit.	Area in square miles.	Number of—		Number of occupied houses.	Population, 1931.		
		Towns.	Villages.		Persons.	Males.	Females.
1	2	3	4	5	6	7	8
KAMRUP DISTRICT.							
BARPETA SUBDIVISION.							
Barpeta thana ...	629·70	1	492	28,686	163,842	88,043	75,799
Barpeta mauza (excluding town).	45·21	...	54	3,156	18,577	9,487	9,090
Mandia mauza ...	100·00	...	36	2,725	15,795	8,845	6,950
Sorbhog thana ...	395·30	...	276	15,318	82,186	44,432	37,754
Rupsi mauza	69·30	...	78	4,596	24,574	13,440	11,134

PROVINCIAL TABLE I.—Area and Population of Thanas, Mauzas, etc.—*contd.*

Thana, mauza or other local unit.	Area in square miles.	Number of Towns.	Number of Villages.	Number of occupied houses.	Population 1931. Persons.	Population 1931. Males.	Population 1931. Females.	Population 1921. Both sexes.	Percentage of variation 1921 to 1931.	Percentage of variation 1911 to 1931.	Number of persons per square mile in 1931.
1	2	3	4	5	6	7	8	9	10	11	12
Patacharkuchi Thana	*233*	...	*188*	*13,251*	*69,227*	*35,978*	*33,249*	*60,466*	*+ 14·5*	*+ 6·6*	*297*
Chapaguri	70	...	17	1,120	8,320	4,262	4,058	8,319	+ ·01	+ 10·9	119
Sarthe (Dakhin Bajali)	26	...	35	2,336	12,536	6,338	6,198	12,392	+ 1·2	+ 4·3	482
Manikpur	19	...	16	1,790	9,791	4,961	4,830	9,194	+ 7·3	+ 9·3	515
Uttar Bajali	21	...	23	3,003	15,341	7,871	7,470	13,430	+ 14·2	+ 13·2	731
Pub Bajali	17	...	19	1,471	7,120	3,660	3,460	7,900	− 9·9	− 3·2	419
Hastinapur	25	...	41	1,651	[illegible]	4,905	3,671	3,916	+ 119·8	+ 36·3	346
Kakilabari	45	...	38	1,480	7,584	3,951	3,633	5,625	+ 33·4	+ 36·2	167
DARRANG DISTRICT	2,842	3	1,978	129,182	584,817	317,103	267,714	477,188	+ 22·6	+ 27·0	206
Tezpur (Sadr) Subdivision	1,573	1	1,038	78,839	345,168	188,320	156,848	285,969	+ 20·7	+ 38·5	219
Tezpur Thana	*378*	*1*	*282*	*26,442*	*114,637*	*63,067*	*51,570*	*104,230*	*+ 10·0*	*+ 28·2*	*303*
Tezpur Town	1·6	1	...	2,161	10,268	7,297	2,971	7,341	+ 39·9	+ 37·1	6,418
Danshari	56	...	43	5,714	22,519	11,808	10,711	24,743	− 9·0	+ 25·5	402
Bihaguri	89	...	39	2,150	9,756	5,276	4,480	8,372	+ 16·5	+ 17·4	110
Halesvar	75	...	91	6,916	30,625	16,311	14,314	28,321	+ 8·1	+ 53·8	408
Mahabhairab (excluding Tezpur Town) ...	96·4	...	52	3,096	17,363	8,903	8,460	12,171	+ 42·7	+ 31·8	180
Balipara	60	...	58	6,414	24,106	13,472	10,634	23,262	+ 3·6	+ 9·7	402
Dhekiajuli Thana	*398*	...	*256*	*14,596*	*64,317*	*34,921*	*29,396*	*48,315*	*+ 32·9*	*+ 75·4*	*161*
Missamari	42	...	42	2,065	9,981	5,114	4,868	9,767	+ 0·6	+ 44·1	236
Barchola	274	...	148	10,213	42,739	23,438	19,301	28,210	+ 51·5	+ 125·6	156
Bargaon	81	...	66	2,318	11,667	6,3[illegible]7	5,340	10,338	+ 12·9	+ 23·6	144
Chutia (Sootea) Thana	*345*	...	*217*	*18,255*	*79,412*	*43,158*	*36,254*	*63,098*	*+ 25·9*	*+ 22·0*	*230*
Chilabandha	61	...	46	2,915	13,093	7,084	6,009	10,780	+ 21·6	+ 55·4	215
Barbhogia	19	...	20	1,821	[illegible]	4,433	3,858	6,991	+ 18·6	+ 11·8	436
Sootea	68	...	40	4,154	17,340	9,341	7,999	15,370	+ 12·8	+ 5·1	255
Bishnath (Part)	128	...	53	3,050	15,021	8,432	6,589	9,709	+ 54·7	− 39·2	117
Baghmara (Part)	12	...	10	996	4,408	2,363	2,045	2,764	+ 59·5	+ 20·0	367
Sakomatha	57	...	48	5,400	21,200	11,496	9,704	17,466	+ 21·5	+ 210·0	373
Behali Thana	*259*	...	*166*	*12,732*	*54,359*	*29,162*	*25,197*	*47,336*	*+ 14·8*	*+ 32·9*	*210*
Bishnath (Part)	2	...	4	121	553	293	260	1,386	− 60·4	− 76·1	277
Baghmara (Part)	89	...	58	4,245	16,612	8,898	7,734	15,323	+ 8·4	+ 381·7	187
Behali	120	...	65	5,637	24,711	13,346	11,415	21,277	+ 16·1	+ 16·1	206
Halem (Part)	48	...	39	2,729	12,483	6,735	5,748	9,339	+ 33·7	+ 12·9	260
Gohpur Thana	*193*	...	*117*	*6,704*	*32,543*	*18,012*	*14,531*	*22,990*	*+ 41·6*	*+ 124·2*	*169*
Halem (Part)	26	...	29	1,813	8,818	5,009	3,809	5,896	+ 49·6	+ 318·6	339
Kalongpur	81	...	30	1,460	7,460	4,156	3,303	5,198	+ 43·5	+ 33·9	92
Gohpur	86	...	58	3,328	16,266	8,847	7,419	11,896	+ 36·7	+ 83·9	189

PROVINCIAL TABLE I.—AREA AND POPULATION OF THANAS, MAUZAS, ETC.—*contd.*

Thana, mauza or other local unit.	Area in square miles.	Number of Towns.	Number of Villages.	Number of occupied houses.	Population 1931. Persons.	Population 1931. Males.	Population 1931. Females.	Population 1921. Both sexes.	Percentage of variation. 1921 to 1931.	Percentage of variation. 1911 to 1921.	Number of persons per square mile in 1931.
1	2	3	4	5	6	7	8	9	10	11	12
MANGALDAI SUBDIVISION	1,269	1	940	50,353	239,649	128,783	110,866	191,219	+ 25·3	+ 11·6	189
Mangaldai Thana	*373*	*1*	*306*	*18,957*	*97,136*	*50,881*	*46,255*	*82,736*	+ *17·4*	+ *9·7*	*260*
Rangamati	101	...	53	2,226	12,955	6,866	6,089	11,287	+ 14·8	− 1·4	128
Dahi	15	...	19	1,249	6,507	3,276	3,231	5,982	+ 8·4	+ 0·3	434
Chepai (excluding Mangaldai small town)	22·6	...	40	1,635	8,785	4,632	4,153	8,197	+ 7·2	+ 7·2	369
Mangaldai small town	·4	1	...	379	1,806	1,372	434	1,023	+ 65·4	+ 7·2	4,340
Samabari (Part) (Dhula)	57	...	40	3,004	16,457	8,935	7,522	13,403	+ 22·0	+ 65·8	280
Dipila	30	...	50	2,303	11,196	6,063	5,133	7,769	+ 44·3	+ 9·1	387
Lerakuchi (Sarabari Part)	9	...	10	649	2,955	1,092	1,863	3,043	+ 7·0	+ 6·4	368
Rainakuchi	8	...	11	1,073	6,251	3,101	3,150	5,836	+ 7·3	+ 4·6	781
Lokrai	23	...	28	1,752	9,626	4,837	4,789	8,480	+ 13·4	− 0·6	419
Sipajhar	77	...	41	2,242	11,839	6,111	5,728	9,887	+ 19·7	+ 1·0	154
Hindughopa	11	...	15	1,635	8,560	4,040	4,611	7,730	+ 10·7	+ 4·3	778
Udalguri Thana	*260*	...	*167*	*7,721*	*34,173*	*18,902*	*15,271*	*23,111*	+ *47·9*	+ *49·2*	*131*
Ambagaon (Part)	30	...	28	948	5,022	2,774	2,248	3,143	+ 59·8	− 5·4	167
Harsilajhar	130	...	62	2,356	11,362	6,378	4,984	7,560	+ 49·0	+ 7·8	87
Orang	100	...	77	4,417	17,889	9,850	8,039	12,409	+ 44·2	+ 128·7	179
Paneri Thana	*282*	...	*199*	*18,596*	*56,989*	*31,379*	*25,610*	*49,508*	+ *15·1*	+ *11·6*	*202*
Sekhar	113	...	52	6,032	20,438	11,337	9,101	16,285	+ 25·5	+ 31·6	181
Majikuchi	36	...	40	1,311	6,748	3,519	3,229	6,109	+ 10·5	− 12·5	187
Dakua	78	...	40	1,460	7,017	4,223	2,794	5,586	+ 25·6	− 12·6	319
Harisinga	75	...	48	5,083	19,057	10,376	8,681	18,044	+ 5·6	+ 22·6	264
Ambagaon (Part)	36	...	19	705	3,739	1,934	1,805	3,485	+ 7·0	− 11·1	105
Kalaigaon Thana	*159*	...	*168*	*5,625*	*27,967*	*14,867*	*13,100*	*26,545*	+ *5·4*	− *9·9*	*176*
Chinakona	41	...	47	1,446	7,613	4,078	3,535	6,431	+ 18·6	− 15·8	186
Sarabari (Part)	15	...	22	1,062	5,099	2,723	2,376	4,486	+ 13·7	− 14·0	340
Kalaigaon	63	...	47	1,722	7,967	4,315	3,652	8,016	− ·6	+ 5·4	126
Silpota	40	...	47	1,278	6,611	3,293	3,318	6,614	− ·05	− 17·1	165
Samabari (Part)	20	...	5	117	677	358	319	968	− 30·1	− 2·5	34
Dalgaon Thana	*195*	...	*100*	*4,454*	*23,384*	*12,754*	*10,630*	*9,329*	+*150·7*	+ *60·3*	*120*
Dalgaon	195	...	100	4,454	23,384	12,754	10,630	9,329	+ 150·7	+ 60·3	120
NOWGONG DISTRICT	3,896	2	2,323	104,185	562,581	298,585	263,996	398,007	+ 41·3	+ 31·9	144
Sadr Thana	*234*	*1*	*259*	*21,239*	*117,874*	*62,491*	*55,383*	*85,953*	+ *37·1*	+ *47·4*	*504*
Nowgong town	3	1	...	2,207	10,413	6,660	3,753	6,885	+ 51·2	+ 26·7	3,471
Pakhimeria	28	...	40	2,394	13,339	6,747	6,592	11,806	+ 17·4	+ 10·1	476
Kondali	25	...	29	1,474	6,873	3,507	3,366	7,493	− 8·3	+ 4·3	275
Singia Patoni	18	...	34	1,840	9,267	4,619	4,648	8,456	+ 9·6	+ 3·9	515
Nijmhar (excluding Nowgong town)	15	...	25	2,106	10,573	5,631	4,942	7,855	+ 34·6	+ 7·6	705
Hatichang	26	...	27	2,957	16,303	8,262	8,041	14,220	+ 14·6	+ 15·4	632
Kachomari	28	...	39	2,879	14,326	7,456	6,870	11,351	+ 26·2	+ 57·9	513
Juria	92	...	75	5,640	36,781	19,609	17,172	18,327	+ 100·7	+ 527·4	400

PROVINCIAL TABLE I.—AREA AND POPULATION OF THANAS, MAUZAS, ETC.—*contd.*

Thana, Mauza or other local unit.	Area in square miles.	Number of Towns.	Number of Villages.	Number of occupied houses.	Population 1931 Persons.	Population 1931 Males.	Population 1931 Females.	Population 1921 Both sexes.	Percentage of variation 1921 to 1931.	Percentage of variation 1911 to 1921.	Number of persons per square mile in 1931.
1	2	3	4	5	6	7	8	9	10	11	12
Samaguri Thana	*608*	...	*356*	*19,964*	*105,318*	*55,653*	*49,665*	*75,198*	+ *40·1*	+ *50·0*	*173*
Laokhowa	55	...	55	5,976	35,663	19,087	16,576	14,827	+ 140·5	+ 118·8	648
Khatowal	38	...	43	3,604	20,068	10,726	9,342	12,618	+ 47·0	+ 69·0	528
*Duar Salona	207	...	71	3,643	12,116	6,381	5,735	9,747	+ 24·3	+ 4·4	59
Bhelaguri	47	...	65	4,020	17,881	9,327	8,554	16,464	+ 8·7	+ 17·7	380
Chalchali	31	...	46	2,679	13,453	6,999	6,454	14,880	− 9·6	+ 9·6	434
*Duar Bamuni	230	...	76	1,092	6,137	3,130	3,007	5,643	+ 8·8	+ 7·9	27
Lumding Thana	*895*	*1*	*161*	*3,020*	*14,409*	*8,421*	*5,988*	*12,856*	+ *12·1*	+ *31·6*	*16*
*Lumding town	267	1	...	936	3,098	2,101	997	2,654	+ 16·7	+ 14·8	21
*Lumding Mikir			36	479	2,441	1,318	1,123	1,917	+ 27·3	+ 37·9	
*Lumding Kuki and Kachari	628	...	21	335	1,241	629	612	1,006	...	+ 50·0	14
*Langpher			37	475	3,432	2,149	1,283	2,782	+ 23·4	+ 11·7	
*Jamunapar			67	706	4,197	2,224	1,973	4,405	− 4·7	+ 35·1	
Jamunamukh Thana	*935*	...	*627*	*14,785*	*76,785*	*41,284*	*35,501*	*53,931*	+ *42·4*	+ *26·4*	*77*
Garubat	63	...	63	1,965	9,621	5,207	4,414	5,319	+ 80·9	+ 4·7	153
*Rangkhang	350	...	340	3,694	21,870	11,296	10,575	18,968	+ 15·3	+ 10·5	63
Kampur	20	...	26	1,478	9,268	4,845	4,423	7,273	+ 27·4	+ 21·0	463
Kathiatoli	18	...	17	1,406	6,337	3,382	2,955	5,093	+ 24·4	+ 37·1	352
Jamunamukh	38	...	39	2,590	12,203	6,647	5,556	8,871	+ 37·6	+ 59·8	321
*Namati	470	...	143	3,508	17,486	9,908	7,578	8,407	+ 108·0	+ 63·6	37
Kaliabor Thana	*173*	...	*120*	*7,839*	*34,009*	*18,246*	*15,763*	*29,066*	+ *17·0*	+ *21·9*	*197*
Pubtharia	30	...	35	1,078	8,636	4,669	3,967	7,603	+ 13·6	+ 11·7	288
Borbhagia	43	...	36	2,731	11,616	6,183	5,433	9,878	+ 17·6	+ 27·5	270
Chatiai	16	...	16	2,150	9,201	4,877	4,324	8,407	+ 9·4	+ 23·0	575
Duar Bagari	48	...	31	930	4,556	2,517	2,039	3,178	+ 43·4	+ 24·3	94
Raha Thana	*177*	...	*131*	*9,834*	*51,675*	*26,659*	*25,016*	*46,871*	+ *10·2*	+ *12·6*	*293*
Charaibahi	20	...	17	1,630	9,010	4,570	4,440	7,565	+ 19·1	+ 5·8	451
Mikirbhata (Part)	14	...	16	1,053	5,948	3,042	2,906	5,111	+ 16·4	+ 14·2	425
Barapujia	33	...	31	3,007	15,641	7,967	7,674	14,311	+ 9·3	+ 14·1	474
Sahari	85	...	47	2,205	10,599	5,795	4,804	7,193	+ 47·2	+ 10·7	125
Jagiai	25	...	22	2,019	10,477	5,285	5,192	12,685	− 17·4	+ 83·3	419
Laharighat Thana	*213*	...	*229*	*10,277*	*62,269*	*33,719*	*28,550*	*25,495*	+ *144·2*	+ *63·9*	*292*
Bokani	81	...	88	3,199	17,940	9,995	7,945	4,543	+ 294·9	+ 61·2	221
Laharighat	94	...	103	4,846	31,173	16,904	14,269	11,838	+ 163·3	+ 61·2	332
Mikirbhata (Part)	38	...	35	2,232	13,156	6,823	6,333	9,114	+ 44·3	+ 14·2	346
Dhing Thana	*78*	...	*81*	*6,476*	*40,456*	*21,315*	*19,141*	*17,868*	+ *126·4*	+ *114·1*	*519*
Dhing	78	...	81	6,476	40,456	21,315	19,141	17,868	+ 126·4	+ 114·1	519

* The units marked with an asterisk fall with the exception of 6 square miles of Duar Salona and 3 square miles of Duar Bamuni within the "Backward Tract" area of the Nowgong Mikir Hills. *See fly-leaf.*

PROVINCIAL TABLE I.—AREA AND POPULATION OF THANAS, MAUZAS, ETC.—contd.

Thana, Mauza or other local unit.	Area in square miles.	Number of Towns.	Number of Villages.	Number of occupied houses.	Population 1931 Persons.	Population 1931 Males.	Population 1931 Females.	Population 1921 Both sexes.	Percentage of variation 1921 to 1931.	Percentage of variation 1911 to 1921.	Number of persons per square mile in 1931.
1	2	3	4	5	6	7	8	9	10	11	12
Marigaon Thana	*523*	...	*359*	*10,761*	*59,786*	*30,797*	*28,989*	*50,769*	+ *17·8*	+ *20·3*	*114*
Dandua	28	...	29	1,909	9,477	4,921	4,556	8,647	+ 9·6	+ 2·9	370
Nij Tatalia	30	...	36	1,529	8,779	4,398	4,381	7,761	+ 13·1	+ 13·1	225
Gobha	54	...	22	661	3,363	1,773	1,590	3,116	+ 7·9	+ 7·9	62
Mayang	110	...	68	1,978	9,716	5,328	4,388	5,359	+ 81·3	+ 0·8	89
Ghagua	64	...	39	1,161	7,650	3,581	3,069	7,076	+ 8·1	+ 11·3	780
Uttarkhola	74	...	48	2,476	12,995	6,660	6,337	11,690	+ 11·1	+ 15·9	179
*Duar Amla	157	...	121	1,372	7,880	4,030	3,850	7,180	+ 9·7	+ 30·5	50
SIBSAGAR DISTRICT	5,131	4	3,281	204,036	933,326	496,288	437,038	823,107	+13·4	+ 19·1	182
JORHAT SUBDIVISION	1,094	1	867	71,792	327,403	174,069	152,824	301,752	+ 8·5	+ 18·2	299
Jorhat Thana	*311*	*1*	*315*	*32,990*	*147,345*	*78,640*	*68,705*	*136,374*	+ *8·0*	+ *14·9*	*474*
Jorhat town	1·92	1	...	1,818	8,334	5,236	3,098	6,624	+ 25·8	+ 30·7	4,341
Garamur (excluding Jorhat town)	10·08	...	19	1,739	5,892	3,267	2,625	6,059	− 2·9	+ 47·6	585
Katonigaon	20	...	31	3,332	12,524	6,924	5,600	13,473	− 7·0	+ 10·9	626
Charaibahi	23	...	34	2,533	13,265	7,151	6,114	11,163	+ 18·8	+ 13·0	577
Khangia	29	...	36	5,614	22,972	11,643	11,329	21,605	+ 6·3	+ 9·7	792
Chowkhat	20	...	27	1,361	6,900	3,563	3,337	6,090	+ 13·3	+ 10·0	345
Hatighar	16	...	16	1,016	4,897	2,540	2,318	4,875	+ ·5	+ 22·2	306
Hulongapar	61	...	53	5,438	22,560	11,068	10,692	21,391	+ 4·8	+ 8·4	370
Charingaon	20	...	25	3,079	16,466	8,354	8,042	14,787	+ 10·9	+ 11·5	820
Hasuri	29	...	31	2,674	12,992	7,101	5,891	10,721	+ 21·2	+ 23·2	448
Baligaon	53	...	34	2,096	13,224	7,327	5,997	11,433	+ 15·8	+ 30·4	250
Parbatia	28	...	26	1,691	7,379	3,957	3,422	7,972	− 7·4	+ 12·0	264
Teok Thana	*188*	...	*164*	*15,586*	*66,895*	*35,487*	*31,408*	*63,041*	+ *6·1*	+ *27·8*	*356*
Nakachari	49	...	43	5,027	21,528	11,677	9,851	21,877	− 1·6	+ 77·5	439
Lahing	57	...	37	3,557	15,038	7,916	7,122	14,083	+ 6·8	+ 7·4	264
Simaiguri	26	...	30	2,406	13,261	6,930	6,331	11,714	+ 13·2	+ 12·8	510
Teok	37	...	29	3,155	10,710	5,576	5,134	9,318	+ 14·6	+ 19·0	289
Gakhirkhowa	19	...	25	1,461	6,358	3,388	2,970	6,019	+ 5·6	− 7·5	635
Titabar Thana	*236*	...	*210*	*16,172*	*69,018*	*36,956*	*32,062*	*65,348*	+ *5·6*	+ *21·6*	*293*
Amguri Kharikatia	177	...	135	9,905	39,922	21,686	18,236	37,120	+ 7·5	+ 22·5	226
Titabar	38	...	42	4,044	17,916	9,463	8,451	17,208	+ 3·9	+ 21·6	469
Thengal	23	...	33	2,233	11,180	5,808	5,372	10,903	+ 3·0	+ 18·7	486
Majuli Thana	*359*	...	*178*	*7,044*	*44,235*	*23,586*	*20,649*	*36,989*	+*19·6*	+ *10·5*	*123*
Salmara	195	...	68	3,147	21,288	11,080	10,190	17,741	+ 20·0	+ 15·2	109
Kamalabari	164	...	110	3,897	22,947	12,487	10,460	19,248	+ 19·2	+ 6·4	140

* The units marked with an asterisk fall with the exception of 6 square miles of Duar Salona and 3 square miles of Duar Bamuni within the "Backward Tract" area of the Nowgong Mikir Hills. *See* fly-leaf.

CORRECTION SLIP No. 3.

Substitute the following names and figures for those in columns 1 to 8 against the unit named Panidihing in column 1 of the Provincial Table 1 at page 287 of Census of India, 1931, Volume III—Assam, Part II—Tables :—

Thana, Mauza or other local unit.	Area in square miles.	Number of		Number of occupied houses.	Population, 1931.		
		Towns.	Villages.		Persons.	Males.	Females.
1	2	3	4	5	6	7	8
SIBSAGAR DISTRICT.							
SIBSAGAR SUBDIVISION.							
Sibsagar Thana.							
Nitaipukhuri	34·7	...	28	1,535	9,182	4,825	4,357
Panidihing	70·3	...	27	1,161	8,377	4,415	3,962

A. G. P. (Edn.) No. :—690—27-4-1933.

PROVINCIAL TABLE I.—AREA AND POPULATION OF THANAS, MAUZAS, ETC.—*contd.*

Thana, mauza or other local unit.	Area in square miles.	Number of Towns.	Number of Villages.	Number of occupied houses.	Population 1931 Persons.	Population 1931 Males.	Population 1931 Females.	Population 1921 Both sexes.	Percentage of variation 1921 to 1931.	Percentage of variation 1911 to 1921.	Number of persons per square mile in 1931.
1	2	3	4	5	6	7	8	9	10	11	12
SIBSAGAR SUBDIVISION ...	1,012	2	808	72,788	331,052	175,003	156,049	289,291	+14·4	+ 20·5	327
Sibsagar Thana ...	*308*	*1*	*271*	*19,495*	*104,166*	*54,848*	*49,318*	*88,544*	+17·6	+ 20·3	338
Sibsagar town ...	3·75	1	...	1,360	6,123	3,376	2,747	5,320	+ 15·1	− 7·6	1,778
Panidihing ...	95	...	55	2,716	17,559	9,240	8,319	13,951	+ 25·9	+ 87·2	185
Thaura ...	46	...	46	4,068	17,062	9,129	7,933	14,479	+ 17·8	+ 54·0	371
Kowarpur ...	56	...	53	2,452	16,681	8,735	7,946	14,144	+ 17·9	+ 15·9	298
Betbari ...	27	...	21	1,901	11,652	5,881	5,771	10,166	+ 14·6	+ 8·8	432
Bokata ...	38	...	40	2,833	13,827	7,083	6,744	12,418	+ 11·1	+ 12·4	364
Nagar Mahal (excluding Sibsagar town)	3·24	...	7	463	2,497	1,327	1,170	8,430	+ 10·7	+ 20·9	768
Metoka Rongaon ...	14	...	17	1,216	6,838	3,534	3,309				681
Hahchara ...	16	...	16	1,187	6,463	3,404	2,966	5,633	+ 14·7	+ 5·9	462
Solaguri (Part) ...	11	...	13	883	4,983	2,630	2,354	3,961	+ 24·2	+ 19·2	508
Nazira Thana ...	*201*	*1*	*167*	*20,934*	*87,246*	*46,347*	*40,899*	*81,356*	+ 7·2	+ 7·1	434
Nazira "small town" ...	·70	1	...	740	3,485	2,073	1,412	2,633	+ 32·4	− 2·5	4,979
Nazira (excluding Nazira "small town")	15·21	...	17	2,537	10,041	5,250	4,791	9,024	+ 11·3		660
Joktoli ...	18	...	23	1,675	9,206	4,737	4,469	8,637	+ 6·6	− 11·1	511
Athkhel ...	61	...	30	5,154	20,428	10,811	9,617	22,022	− 7·2	+ 27·6	335
Sialkoti ...	54	...	46	3,998	18,671	9,814	8,857	17,950	+ 4·0	+ 4·5	346
Dhopabar ...	43	...	41	5,328	20,651	11,138	9,513	17,638	+ 17·1	+ 35·5	480
Dopdar (Part) ...	9	...	11	1,102	4,765	2,525	2,240	3,444	+ 38·4	− 40·8	529
Amguri Thana ...	*146*	...	*129*	*11,275*	*54,763*	*28,208*	*26,155*	*51,335*	+ 5·9	+ 18·9	372
Gothali bazar ...	24	...	28	2,124	13,413	7,002	6,411	12,889	+ 4·1	+ 22·3	557
Mora bazar ...	25	...	29	2,305	13,401	6,997	6,404	12,215	+ 9·8	+ 14·0	536
Jokaichuk ...	35	...	33	1,879	10,449	6,427	4,022	9,001	+ 16·1	+ 15·6	299
Dopdar (Part) ...	44	...	20	1,631	10,346	5,442	4,904	10,964	− 5·6	+ 18·0	235
Solaguri (Part) ...	17	...	19	1,346	6,760	3,390	3,370	6,277	+ 7·7	+ 12·1	398
Sonari Thana ...	*357*	...	*241*	*21,094*	*85,277*	*45,600*	*39,677*	*68,056*	+25·3	+ 43·5	239
Khalaighogora ...	40	...	35	3,170	13,991	7,273	6,718	10,762	+ 30·0	+ 67·6	350
Mahmara ...	73	...	64	4,232	17,563	9,237	8,326	16,056	+ 9·4	+ 29·3	241
Abhoypur ...	127	...	63	8,160	32,713	17,640	15,073	26,887	+ 21·7	+ 36·2	258
Barhmauli ...	117	...	79	5,132	21,010	11,450	9,560	14,551	+ 44·4		180
GOLAGHAT SUBDIVISION ...	3,025	1	609	59,456	274,781	146,616	128,165	232,154	+18·4	+ 18·4	91
Golaghat Thana ...	*2,360*	*1*	*392*	*35,364*	*163,022*	*87,715*	*75,307*	*131,132*	+24·3	− 1·6	69
Golaghat town ...	1·94	1	...	1,121	4,658	3,013	1,645	3,636	+ 28·3	+ 63·5	2,416
Mowkhoa (excluding Golaghat town)	19·06	...	24	1,583	7,426	3,963	3,463	6,502	+ 14·2	− 6·5	390
Dhekial ...	20	...	22	2,380	11,442	6,027	5,415	9,947	+ 15·0	+ 13·9	572
Khumtai ...	39	...	33	4,106	18,182	9,423	8,759	16,416	+ 10·8	+ 21·7	466
Marangi ...	114	...	50	5,574	21,850	11,941	9,909	16,427	+ 33·0	+ 48·9	192
Athgaon ...	18	...	21	1,438	7,283	4,042	3,241	6,857	+ 6·2	+ 10·8	405
Ghiladhari ...	146	...	42	3,957	16,015	8,439	7,576	16,506	− 3·0	+ 15·5	109
Kacharihat ...	16	...	15	1,290	6,144	3,215	2,929	6,132	+ ·2	+ 0·6	384
Dakhinhengra ...	29	...	25	2,076	12,752	6,743	6,009	11,332	+ 12·5	+ 3·0	440
Mahura ...	99	...	34	1,841	9,233	5,006	4,227	4,030	+ 129·2	+ 34·6	93
*Barpathar ...	596	...	43	6,016	28,300	15,807	12,493	10,716	+ 165·0	+ 72·3	48
*Duarisha Borjan ...	421	...	20	790	5,675	2,937	2,738	8,505	− 33·4	+ 6·7	13
*East Rengma ...	172	...	18	1,139	7,125	3,518	3,607	6,814	+ 5·5		42
*West Rengma ...	283	...	2	206	1,632	826	806	834	+ 95·7	− 53·7	6
*Naga Rengma ...	261	...	7	286	1,266	653	614	1,312	+ ·6·5		5
*Duar Dikharu ...	131	...	6	508	3,008	1,931	1,077	5,337	− 31·1	+ 109·8	20

* The units marked with an asterisk fall within the "Backward Tract" area of the Sibsagar Mikir Hills. *See* fly-leaves.

PROVINCIAL TABLE I.—Area and Population of Thanas, Mauzas, etc.—*contd.*

Thana, Mauza or other local unit.	Area in square miles.	Number of — Towns.	Number of — Villages.	Number of occupied houses.	Population 1931 — Persons.	Population 1931 — Males.	Population 1931 — Females.	Population 1921 — Both sexes.	Percentage of variation 1921 to 1931.	Percentage of variation 1911 to 1921.	Number of persons per square mile in 1931.
1	2	3	4	5	6	7	8	9	10	11	12
Dergaon Thana	*227*	...	*135*	*15,168*	*73,790*	*38,604*	*35,186*	*69,091*	+ *6·8*	+ *44·4*	*325*
Dergaon	23	...	10	3,471	**16,685**	8,720	7,965	13,947	+ 19·6	+ 6·7	725
Missamara	40	...	29	3,340	**14,962**	7,831	7,131	12,365	+ 21·0	— 5·8	374
Ahatguri	106	...	40	1,945	**12,965**	6,848	6,117	10,876	+ 19·2	— 4·0	122
Gurjogonia	18	...	11	1,805	**8,836**	4,616	4,220	8,423	+ 4·9	— 3·2	491
Katodonga	16	...	12	1,423	**6,460**	3,326	3,134	6,447	+ ·2	+ 16·5	404
Rangamati	24	...	31	3,179	**13,882**	7,263	6,610	17,083	— 18·7	+ 63·6	578
Bokakhat Thana	*438*	...	*82*	*6,929*	*37,969*	*20,297*	*17,672*	*31,931*	+ *18·9*	+ *35·8*	*87*
Bokakhat	55	...	38	4,094	**19,003**	10,121	8,879	16,313	+ 16·5 }	+ 49·3	346
Kaziranga	160	...	28	2,611	**10,877**	5,983	4,894	9,034	+ 20·4 }		68
* Duarbagari	194	...	16	1,224	**8,089**	4,190	3,899	6,584	+ 22·9	+ ·7	42
LAKHIMPUR DISTRICT	4,234	4	2,408	172,229	724,582	399,108	325,474	586,577	+ 23·5	+ 30·4	171
Sadr Subdivision (including Lakhimpur Frontier Tract).	2,873	3	1,894	142,558	571,958	317,536	254,422	464,487	+ 23·1	+ 32·2	199
Dibrugarh Thana	*513*	*1*	*358*	*29,159*	*125,792*	*69,261*	*56,531*	*120,117*	+ *4·7*	+ *3·3*	*245*
Dibrugarh town	3·7	1	...	3,682	**18,734**	12,181	6,553	16,007	+ 17·0	+ 9·9	5,059
Dibrugarh (excluding 3·5 square miles of Dibrugarh town)	54·5	...	48	3,300	**12,800**	7,332	5,468	13,471	— 5·0	— 32·8	235
Maukata (excluding ·2 square mile of Dibrugarh town) ...	45·8	...	51	3,226	**14,248**	7,504	6,744	12,419	+ 14·7	+ 18·0	311
Jamira	40	...	36	3,008	**12,929**	6,972	5,957	12,952	— ·2	+ 5·6	323
Larua	154	...	63	2,667	**13,597**	7,144	6,453	12,349	+ 10·1	+ 81·9	88
Rohmoria	125	...	45	2,676	**11,904**	6,391	5,513	10,807	+ 10·2	— 17·7	95
Lahoal	51	...	64	7,800	**28,331**	14,700	13,632	25,858	+ 9·6	+ 16·3	556
Madarkhat	40	...	51	3,110	**13,249**	6,938	6,311	16,274	— 15·6	+ 21·2	331
Dhemaji Thana	*438*	...	*251*	*4,402*	*28,190*	*14,894*	*13,296*	*23,751*	+ *18·7*	+ *83·1*	*64*
Dhemaji	158	...	105	1,811	**11,213**	5,805	5,408	7,752	+ 44·6	— 1·1	71
Bisi	280 }	...	53	1,162	**5,833**	3,164	2,669	16,000 }	+ 6·1	+ 163·4	61
Paik Mahals		...	93	1,429	**11,144**	5,925	5,219				
Moran Thana	*154*	...	*138*	*9,005*	*40,978*	*22,066*	*18,912*	*29,051*	+ *41·1*	+ *46·6*	*266*
Moran	65	...	70	4,951	**21,591**	11,580	10,011	14,651	+ 47·4	+ 46·6	332
Khowang	89	...	68	4,054	**19,387**	10,486	8,901	14,400	+ 34·6	+ 40·6	218
Tinsukia Thana	*526*	*1*	*494*	*36,702*	*143,787*	*78,433*	*65,354*	*103,391*	+ *39·1*	+ *43·6*	*273*
Tinsukia "Small town"	1	1	...	1,272	**5,160**	3,649	1,511	3,080	+ 67·5	+ 56·7	5,160
Rongagora (excluding Tinsukia)	53	...	91	6,656	**24,415**	13,764	10,651	20,004	+ 22·1	+ 54·7	461
Bogdung	162	...	76	7,677	**30,332**	15,947	14,385	29,488	+ 2·0	+ 40·7	187
Chabua Polonga	19	...	16	2,036	**10,243**	5,465	4,778	5,700	+ 77·8	+ 13·0	539
Gherbandi	55	...	112	4,469	**21,725**	11,479	10,246	13,093	+ 65·9	+ 1·0	395
Tipling	157	...	84	7,780	**28,799**	15,736	13,063	7,689	+ 274·1	+ 17·7	183
Tengakhat	78	...	115	6,413	**23,113**	12,393	10,720	24,267	— 4·8	+ 92·0	296

* The units marked with an asterisk fall within the "Backward Tract" area of the Sibsagar Mikir Hills. *See* fly-leaf.

CORRECTION SLIP No. 17.

Substitute **the following names and figures for those in columns 1 to 8 against the units named Doom Dooma (excluding ·1 square mile of Doom Dooma town) and Khowang in column 1 of the Provincial Table I at pages 288 and 289 of Census of India, 1931, Volume III—Assam, Part II—Tables.**

Thana, mauza or other local unit.	Area in square miles.	Number of—		Number of occupied houses.	Population, 1931.		
		Towns.	Villages.		Persons.	Males.	Females.
1	2	3	4	5	6	7	8
LAKHIMPUR DISTRICT SADR SUBDIVISION.							
Doom Dooma Thana :—							
Tingrai	66	...	37	6,892 *	24,384	13,428	10,956
Doom Dooma (excluding ·1 square mile of Doom Dooma town).	70·9	...	28	5,360 *	18,320	9,687	8,633
Moran Thana :—							
Lengri	51·13	...	66	2,094 *	10,834	5,896	4,939
Khowang	37·87	...	70	1,960 *	8,553	4,590	3,963

* The reason for the variation in the figures as compared with those in the Census Table of 1931 is that many blocks, small and non-cadastral villages as also some hamlets with scanty population taken and censused as one village in 1931, have increased in population and having been cadastrally surveyed since were counted separately under new names. Many villages have also increased owing to new survey on traverse, while some have been abolished or amalgamated with others during the Re-settlement operations.

CORRECTION SLIP No. 18.

Substitute the following names and figures for those in columns 1 to 8 against the units named Kamalabari, Telahi, Gohaingaon and Dhakuakhana in column 1 of the Provincial Table I at pages 289 and 290 of Census of India, 1931, Volume III—Assam, Part II—Tables.

Thana, mauza or other local unit.	Area in square miles.	Number of—		Number of occupied houses.	Population, 1931.		
		Towns.	Villages.		Persons.	Males.	Females.
1	2	3	4	5	6	7	8
LAKHIMPUR DISTRICT.							
NORTH LAKHIMPUR SUB-DIVISION.							
North Lakhimpur Thana :—							
Kamalabari	13	...	17	847	4,095	2,199	1,896
Telahi	122	...	47	1,956	11,705	6,315	5,390
Dhakuakhana Thana:—							
Maskhowa	72	...	48	1,643	9,479	5,021	4,458
Dhakuakhana	159	...	34	1,924	13,023	6,786	6,237
Gohaingaon	110	...	26	1,154	8,385	4,410	3,975

CORRECTION SLIP No. 14.

Substitute the following names and figures for those in columns 1 to 8 against the unit named Laluk in column 1 of the Provincial Table I at page 289 of Census of India, 1931, Volume III—Assam, Part II—Tables.

Thana, mauza or other local unit.	Area in square miles.	Number of—		Number of occupied houses.	Population, 1931.		
		Towns.	Villages.		Persons.	Males.	Females.
1	2	3	4	5	6	7	8
LAKHIMPUR DISTRICT.							
NORTH LAKHIMPUR SUBDIVISION.							
Bihpuria thana—							
Bihpuria	52	...	42	1,606	8,445	4,568	3,877
Laluk	120	...	60	2,518	11,467	6,332	5,135

CORRECTION SLIP No. 15.

Substitute the following names and figures for those in columns 1 to 8 against the unit named Jaipur, Gharbandi and Tengakhat in column 1 of the Provincial Table I at pages 288 and 289 of Census of India, 1931, Volume III—Assam, Part II—Tables.

Thana mauza or other local unit.	Area in square miles.	Number of— Towns.	Number of— Villages.	Number of occupied houses.	Population, 1931. Persons.	Population, 1931. Males.	Population, 1931. Females.
1	2	3	4	5	6	7	8
LAKHIMPUR DISTRICT.							
SADR SUBDIVISION.							
Jaipur thana—							
Sessani	53·3	...	58 } *	3,772	17,369	9,408	7,961
Jaipur	109·7	...	89 } *	4,345	17,567	9,593	7,974
Tinsukia thana—							
Kheremia ...	42·19 } *	...	78 } *	2,583	11,621	6,200	5,421
Gharbandi ...	46·41 } *	...	57 } *	4,751	20,623	10,906	9,717
Tengakhat ...	46·00 } *	...	61 } *	3,038	12,594	6,766	5,828

* The reason for the variation in the figures as compared with those in the Census Table of 1931, is that many blocks, small and non-cadastral villages as also some hamlets with scanty population taken and censused as one village in 1931, have increased in population and having been cadastrally surveyed since, were counted separately under new names. Many villages have also increased owing to new survey on traverse, while some have been abolished or amalgamated with others during the Resettlement operations.

No. 29.

Substitute the following names and figures in columns 1 to 8 against the units named Rangagara in column 1 of the Provincial Table I at page 288 of Census of India, 1931. Volume III Assam, Part II-Tables.

Thana, Mauza or other Local unit.	Area in square miles.	Number of Towns.	Number of Villages.	Number o occupied	Population in 1931. Persons.	Males.	Females.
1	2	3	4	5	6	7	8
LAKHIMPUR DISTRICT.							
SADAR SUBDIVISION.							
Tinsukia Thana.							
Tinsukia (excluding Tinsukia town).	15·29	Nil	40	1,835	6,978	4,083	2,895
Rangagara	37·71	Nil	51	4,881	17,437	9,681	7,756

A. G. P. (Edn.) No. 2—695—14-6-1936.

PROVINCIAL TABLE I.—AREA AND POPULATION OF THANAS, MAUZAS, ETC.

THANA, MAUZA OR OTHER LOCAL UNIT.	Area in square miles.	NUMBER OF Towns.	NUMBER OF Villages.	Number of occupied houses.	POPULATION 1931. Persons.	POPULATION 1931. Males.	POPULATION 1931. Females.	POPULATION 1921. Both sexes.	PERCENTAGE OF VARIATION. 1921 to 1931.	PERCENTAGE OF VARIATION. 1911 to 1921.	Number of persons per square mile in 1931.
1	2	3	4	5	6	7	8	9	10	11	12
Digboi Thana	314	...	95	9,267	30,300	20,434	9,866				96
Makum (Part)	81	...	47	17,031	21,696	15,511	6,185				
*Makum-Phakial	50	...	16	337	1,425	759	666				
*Buri Dihing (Part)	183	...	33	1,899	7,179	4,164	3,015				
Margherita Thana	225	...	79	7,643	24,478	15,263	9,215	34,060	+ 60·8	+ 39·7	109
Makum (Part)	64	...	34	6,406	19,492	12,170	7,322				
*Makum (Part)	138	...	30	953	4,183	2,714	1,469				
*Buri Dihing (Part)	23	...	15	104	803	379	424				
Doom Dooma Thana	368	1	231	32,335	116,039	63,333	52,706	105,548	+ 9·9	+ 29·8	315
Doom Dooma (excluding ·1 square mile of Doom Dooma town).	136·9	...	77	12,253	41,704	22,115	19,589	41,291	+ 8·4	+ 31·0	333
Doom Dooma town	0·2	1	...	519	1,910	1,434	476	1,162	+ 63·5	+ 31·0	9,500
Saikhowa	143	...	93	6,323	26,052	14,043	12,009	20,146	+ 29·3	+ 24·9	183
Hapjan (excluding ·1 square mile of Doom Dooma town)	88·9	...	61	13,242	55,383	34,751	20,632	42,949	+ 5·7	+ 31·0	510
Jaipur Thana	334	...	248	14,045	62,894	33,852	28,542	47,684	+ 30·8	+ 90·6	187
Tipling-Phakial	16	...	14	304	2,329	1,294	1,035	10,386	− 70·4	+1,017·9	146
Jaipur-Phakial	2	...	6	166	720	407	313				300
Jaipur	163	...	130	8,117	34,936	19,001	15,935	22,406	+ 48·7	+ 55·2	214
Tingkhong	153	...	98	5,165	24,409	13,150	11,259	13,904	+ 75·6	+ 55·2	160
Hukong Valley Survey Party	...	...	...	...	...	...	...	885	...	...	...
NORTH LAKHIMPUR SUBDIVISION	1,862	1	604	29,671	152,624	81,572	71,052	122,090	+ 25·0	+ 23·7	112
North Lakhimpur Thana	527	1	253	14,821	66,385	35,708	30,677	55,716	+ 19·1	+ 23·4	126
North Lakhimpur small town	1·2	1	...	493	2,120	1,411	709	1,966	+ 7·8	+ 9·0	1,767
Lakhimpur (excluding 1·1 square mile of North-Lakhimpur town).	69·9	...	35	1,396	7,096	3,749	3,347	6,238	+ 13·6	+ 9·9	102
Kadam	198	...	64	3,510	17,142	9,101	8,041	13,853	+ 23·8	+ 15·2	87
Nakari (excluding 0·1 square mile of North-Lakhimpur "small town").	38·9	...	53	2,756	10,416	5,551	4,865	9,750	+ 6·8	− 7·9	268
Kamalabari	11	...	13	757	3,718	1,977	1,741	3,543	+ 4·0	− 14·9	338
Telahi	100	...	46	1,895	10,377	5,662	4,715	8,248	+ 25·8	+ 14·2	104
Naoboicha	100	...	43	4,094	15,516	8,227	7,289	12,119	+ 28·0	+ 144·0	143
Bihpuria Thana	287	...	193	8,131	42,961	23,311	19,650	29,849	+ 43·9	+ 23·4	150
Laluk	172	...	103	4,134	19,912	10,900	9,012	13,808	+ 44·2	+ 3·5	116
Narayanpur	43	...	37	1,566	9,589	5,146	4,443	8,731	+ 9·8	+ 56·4	223
Narayanpur Kherajkhat	23	...	23	974	5,044	2,716	2,329	2,000	+ 10·2	+ 58·4	219
Dhalpur	40	...	31	1,407	8,416	4,550	3,866	4,644	+ 81·2	+ 58·6	172

* Mauzas marked with asterisk fall within the Lakhimpur Frontier Tract which has a total area of 304 square miles. *See* flyleaf.

PROVINCIAL TABLE I.—AREA AND POPULATION OF THANAS, MAUZAS, ETC.—*contd.*

Thana, Mauza or other local unit.	Area in square miles.	Number of Towns.	Number of Villages.	Number of occupied houses.	Population 1931 Persons.	Population 1931 Males.	Population 1931 Females.	Population 1921 Both sexes.	Percentage of variation 1921 to 1931.	Percentage of variation 1911 to 1921.	Number of persons per square mile in 1931.
1	2	3	4	5	6	7	8	9	10	11	12
Dhakuakhana Thana	*548*	...	*158*	*6,719*	*43,278*	*22,553*	*20,725*	*36,525*	*+ 18·5*	*+ 24·6*	*79*
Bardalani	183	...	45	1,847	10,686	5,461	5,225	8,110	+ 21·8	+ 31·6	58
Gohaigaon	144	...	66	2,508	16,235	8,562	7,673	13,397	+ 21·2	+ 17·2	113
Dhakuakhana	221	...	47	2,374	16,357	8,530	7,827	15,018	+ 8·9	+ 28·2	74
GARO HILLS DISTRICT	3,163	...	2,160	39,565	190,911	97,442	93,469	179,140	+ 6·6	+ 12·7	61
Mauza No. I (Hills)	*	...	477	4,670	24,753	12,387	12,366	27,758	− 10·8	+ 19·5	...
" II "	*	...	485	8,498	39,994	20,327	19,667	35,403	+ 13·7	+ 28·4	...
" III "	*	...	493	9,299	39,403	19,764	19,639	36,183	+ 8·9	+ 9·0	...
" IV "	*	...	329	6,278	33,526	16,712	16,814	30,901	+ 8·6	+ 3·7	...
" V (Nibari) plains	*	...	120	3,056	15,864	8,336	7,528	17,486	− 9·3	+ 11·2	...
" VI (Fulbari) "	*	...	53	1,808	9,849	5,237	4,612	9,152	+ 7·6	+ 3·1	...
" VII (Rangapani) "	*	...	51	1,204	5,969	3,193	2,776	5,726	+ 4·2	+ 6·3	...
" VIII (Mahendraganj) "	*	...	54	2,132	10,314	5,398	4,916	10,100	+ 1·5	− 2·0	...
" IX (Ghoshgaon) "	*	...	97	1,917	8,861	4,512	4,349	4,530	+ 95·6	+ 58·4	...
" X (Tura town) "	*	...	1	606	2,358	1,554	804	1,751	+ 34·7	+ 10·4	...
SADIYA FRONTIER TRACT	3,200	1	373	10,607	53,345	28,686	24,659	41,240	+ 29·3	+ 122·5	17
Sadr Subdivision	2,080	1	257	7,656	36,139	19,461	16,678	25,940	+ 39·3	* ...	17
Paighat Subdivision	1,120	...	116	3,041	17,206	9,325	7,881	15,300	+ 12·6	...	15
BALIPARA FRONTIER TRACT	560	...	38	1,008	5,148	3,232	1,916	3,666	+ 40·4	+ 324·8	9
MANIPUR STATE	8,620	1	1,372	80,151	445,606	215,815	229,791	384,016	+ 16·0	+ 10·9	52
Valley Section	*	1	458	57,132	294,767	142,466	152,301	259,614	+ 13·5	+ 16·5	...
Naharup Panah	*	...	93	7,134	31,877	15,836	16,041	28,867	+ 10·4	+ 0·2	...
Ahalup Panah	*	...	[illegible]	10,537	61,674	30,348	31,326	53,960	+ 14·9	+ 17·4	...
Imphal Panah	*	1	21	19,340	95,445	44,634	50,811	87,616	+ 8·9	+ 24·3	...
Khabam Panah	*	...	134	9,572	46,430	23,122	23,308	40,145	+ 15·7	+ 41·8	...
Lailam Panah	*	...	77	9,454	54,417	26,355	28,062	47,060	+ 15·6	+ 0·6	...
Jirighat Panah	*	...	61	1,126	4,924	2,581	2,343	2,257	+ 118·2	+ 91·4	...
Hill Section	*	...	915	32,019	150,839	73,349	77,490	124,402	+ 21·3	+ 0·9	...
Imphal North	*	...	479	19,101	84,197	41,016	43,181	*	...	+ 0·9	...
Imphal South	*	...	436	12,918	66,642	32,333	34,309	*	...	+ 0·9	...

* Separate figures not available.

PROVINCIAL TABLE II.

POPULATION OF DISTRICTS, SUBDIVISIONS AND THANAS BY RELIGION AND LITERACY.

This table shows the population of each district, subdivision and, in the plains of each thana by religion and literacy.

It will be noticed that Dhing thana in Nowgong and Digboi thana in Lakhimpur do not appear in this table. This is due to the fact that these are new thanas constituted during the period the census was taking place. It has been found possible to make the necessary adjustments in Table I to show the areas and populations of these new thanas but it was too late to effect any adjustments in this table.

The division of Hindus into " Brahmans " " Other Hindus " and " depressed classes " is a new feature of this table. The figures for the " depressed " classes given in it cannot, however, for various reasons, *e.g.*, the return of a higher caste name by certain depressed communities, be accepted as accurate but they afford a good indication of the extent of literacy among those classes as compared with the higher classes of Hindu society. The persons included under the head of " depressed classes " in this table represent the castes classed as " exterior castes " *plus* the castes classed as " Tea garden cooly castes " in Imperial Table XVII—Caste, Tribe or Race.

As, however, various adjustments had to be made to the figures in Imperial Table XVII before the correct number of " exterior castes " and of cooly castes could be ascertained, the figures for " depressed classes " in this table which amount to 1,830,000 in all are actually about 148,000 short. Further information regarding the probable numbers of the " depressed " classes of Assam will be found in the Appendix to Chapter XII of the Report volume. The figures for Hindus in this table do not include Brahmos and Aryas whose numbers in Assam are negligible, there being only 448 Brahmos and 12 Aryas. A slight difference will be found in the total of literates and in the total of literates in English as given in this table and in Imperial Table XIII. This is due to the fact that in Imperial Table XIII children under 5 years of age who were returned as literate have been shown as illiterate. Village Census Tables showing the population of each village by sex and religion have been supplied to all district officers.

PROVINCIAL TABLE II.—Population of Districts, Subdivisions, Thanas or other local units by Religion and Literacy.

District, subdivision, thana or other local unit.	Males (M) or Females (F).	Hindus. Brahmans. Number of persons.	Hindus. Brahmans. Number literate.	Hindus. Other Hindus. Number of persons.	Hindus. Other Hindus. Number literate.	Hindus. *Depressed classes. Number of persons.	Hindus. *Depressed classes. Number literate.	Jains. Number of persons.	Jains. Number literate.	Sikhs. Number of persons.	Sikhs. Number literate.
1	2	3	4	5	6	7	8	9	10	11	12
ASSAM	M. ...	87,864	52,154	1,696,779	337,429	966,771	53,579	2,116	1,439	1,918	872
	F. ...	71,952	11,275	1,517,865	35,859	863,659	3,454	687	30	811	70
(1) British Territory ...	M. ...	87,451	51,857	1,563,037	314,558	966,004	53,419	2,000	1,383	1,740	840
	F. ...	71,067	11,176	1,380,918	35,169	863,005	3,437	636	28	757	68
SURMA VALLEY AND HILL DIVISION ...	M. ...	27,414	19,173	368,090	119,188	388,976	34,491	288	227	169	83
	F. ...	23,635	6,461	336,881	20,539	353,909	2,192	87	7	60	5
CACHAR DISTRICT ...	M. ...	3,163	2,223	82,234	22,883	104,509	8,543	20	18	56	29
	F. ...	2,115	868	72,428	3,065	94,789	575	6	2	21	1
Silchar Subdivision ...	M. ...	2,873	1,680	65,412	18,266	78,012	5,832	19	17	10	10
	F. ...	1,601	714	48,036	2,415	70,962	276	6	2	3	...
Barkhola ...	M. ...	168	116	3,336	1,885	7,943	870	...	...	1	1
	F. ...	128	38	3,042	238	7,040	21	...	...	...	...
Silchar ...	M. ...	1,195	931	15,603	4,940	23,346	3,270	16	14	8	8
	F. ...	777	472	12,026	808	21,210	168	5	2	3	...
Lakhipur ...	M. ...	374	158	12,573	4,804	15,598	80	3	3	...	...
	F. ...	216	53	10,207	888	14,540	...	1	...	...	...
Katigora ...	M. ...	234	153	6,864	1,917	9,627	937	...	...	1	1
	F. ...	140	60	6,460	307	9,727	63	...	...	...	...
Sonai ...	M. ...	367	213	18,983	4,268	10,856	650	...	...	...	...
	F. ...	221	46	13,067	615	9,371	24	...	...	...	...
Udharband ...	M. ...	145	109	3,119	1,004	10,902	77	...	...	...	...
	F. ...	112	45	2,365	122	10,675	...	...	...	...	...
Hailakandi Subdivision ...	M. ...	684	471	14,893	3,846	25,039	2,682	1	1	26	5
	F. ...	452	125	13,466	601	22,830	299	...	...	14	...
Hailakandi ...	M. ...	515	359	11,980	3,051	14,072	1,696	1	1	26	5
	F. ...	354	97	10,865	452	13,133	247	...	...	14	...
Katlicherra ...	M. ...	169	112	2,913	795	10,967	986	...	...	...	...
	F. ...	98	28	2,601	149	9,697	52	...	...	...	...
North Cachar Hills Subdivision ...	M. ...	106	71	11,929	711	1,458	29	...	...	20	14
	F. ...	63	29	10,926	49	997	...	...	...	4	1

* These figures cannot be accepted as the correct total for the "depressed classes". See Sylhet.

PROVINCIAL TABLE II.—Population of Districts, Subdivisions, Thanas or other local units by Religion and Literacy—contd.

District, Subdivision, Thana or other Local Unit.	Males (M) or Females (F).	Muslims. Number of persons.	Muslims. Number literate.	Christians. Number of persons.	Christians. Number literate.	Tribal. Number of persons.	Tribal. Number literate.	Others. Number of persons.	Others. Number literate.	Number literate. Aged 4—13.	Number literate. Aged 14—23.	Number literate. Aged 24 and over.	Literate in English.
		13	14	15	16	17	18	19	20	21	22	23	24
ASSAM	M.	1,461,769	139,857	194,045	28,613	493,755	12,565	9,123	1,724	89,199	152,372	383,731	89,430
	F.	1,318,759	17,803	193,901	11,854	498,635	1,573	6,869	174	21,824	29,780	30,488	5,473
(1) **British Territory**	M.	1,449,073	138,559	101,640	21,783	357,299	9,463	8,969	1,655	79,584	145,172	368,754	84,913
	F.	1,306,841	17,617	100,946	7,941	354,140	687	6,735	137	20,748	27,106	27,706	4,756
SURMA VALLEY AND HILL DIVISION	M.	933,918	94,156	53,984	12,577	145,819	4,995	893	910	40,539	69,374	175,187	36,519
	F.	868,590	13,785	59,648	4,134	151,466	387	764	44	13,153	17,058	17,943	2,241
CACHAR DISTRICT	M.	103,718	12,043	2,427	627	5,160	48	51	17	5,500	10,827	29,083	5,960
	F.	92,478	714	2,175	227	5,159	2	22	1	1,551	1,953	1,981	357
Silchar Subdivision	M.	65,015	8,077	1,324	361	2,485	34	19	10	4,117	7,995	22,175	4,299
	F.	57,781	565	1,153	134	2,475	2	9	...	1,215	1,400	1,493	271
Barkhola	M.	5,544	780	69	30	214	8	...	...	311	664	2,002	318
	F.	4,749	28	61	6	207	...	...	...	101	109	121	5
Silchar	M.	21,981	2,810	252	146	447	13	16	7	1,613	3,010	7,895	2,463
	F.	19,306	152	218	75	467	2	6	...	494	507	698	206
Lakhipur	M.	7,794	870	471	83	742	1	3	3	446	1,192	3,750	538
	F.	6,788	45	450	30	704	...	3	...	66	130	214	22
Katigora	M.	12,353	1,749	111	33	188	5	...	...	694	1,097	3,009	343
	F.	11,216	75	16	5	161	...	...	...	174	170	150	6
Sonai	M.	14,278	1,200	124	39	413	5	...	...	914	1,543	4,113	376
	F.	13,116	72	152	8	429	...	...	...	230	263	183	13
Udharband	M.	3,166	569	257	50	481	7	...	...	240	470	1,097	332
	F.	2,546	213	236	13	447	...	...	...	170	166	127	19
Hailkandi Subdivision	M.	38,368	3,885	104	82	236	6	16	3	1,383	2,617	6,981	1,381
	F.	31,582	176	51	27	219	...	11	1	313	485	433	57
Hailakandi	M.	30,131	3,128	67	55	140	4	3	2	1,063	1,987	5,251	1,095
	F.	27,288	160	24	16	122	...	1	1	237	398	339	38
Katlicherra	M.	8,237	757	37	27	96	2	13	1	320	630	1,730	286
	F.	7,294	16	27	11	97	...	10	...	75	87	94	19
North Cachar Hills Subdivision	M.	335	81	999	184	2,439	8	16	4	60	215	827	280
	F.	115	3	971	66	2,465	...	2	...	24	65	56	29

PROVINCIAL TABLE II.—Population of Districts, Subdivisions, Thanas or other local units by religion and literacy—*contd.*

District, subdivision, thana or other local unit.	Males (M) or Females (F).	Hindus. Brahmans. Number of persons.	Hindus. Brahmans. Number literate.	Hindus. Other Hindus. Number of persons.	Hindus. Other Hindus. Number literate.	Hindus. Depressed classes. Number of persons.	Hindus. Depressed classes. Number literate.	Jains. Number of persons.	Jains. Number literate.	Sikhs. Number of persons.	Sikhs. Number literate.
1	2	3	4	5	6	7	8	9	10	11	12
SYLHET DISTRICT	M.	23,570	10,432	273,105	91,737	278,940	25,863	102	159	51	25
	F.	21,176	5,422	257,711	17,040	258,843	1,632	56	4	21	4
North Sylhet Subdivision	M.	*5,655*	*4,092*	*42,431*	*15,528*	*35,239*	*3,067*	*31*	*24*	*26*	*15*
	F.	*5,260*	*1,305*	*38,940*	*3,710*	*30,970*	*194*	*12*	*1*	*9*	...
Sylhet sadr	M.	2,259	1,730	13,741	6,611	9,301	758	24	21	20	10
	F.	1,560	530	11,003	1,915	7,933	57	10	...	9	...
Gowainghat	M.	75	51	3,367	628	4,563	53	1	...	3	3
	F.	46	6	3,217	124	3,827	24	...	...	...	...
Golabganj	M.	612	436	4,912	1,361	4,436	396	...	...	...	...
	F.	633	193	5,038	303	4,108	38	...	...	...	...
Fenchuganj	M.	188	128	1,980	322	2,582	648	6	3	...	...
	F.	164	40	1,864	190	2,061	7	2	1	...	...
Kanairghat	M.	63	50	3,103	545	3,636	243	...	...	...	...
	F.	45	6	3,082	51	3,444	20	...	...	...	...
Jaintiapur	M.	116	85	981	272	1,831	110	...	...	3	3
	F.	110	6	1,063	27	1,307	5	...	...	...	...
Balaganj	M.	1,480	1,040	9,460	3,911	6,390	544	...	...	...	...
	F.	1,587	286	9,816	816	5,797	37	...	...	...	...
Biswanath	M.	830	552	5,078	1,678	2,691	186	...	...	...	...
	F.	805	236	5,007	234	2,573	18	...	...	...	...
South Sylhet Subdivision	M.	*5,394*	*3,780*	*47,991*	*18,588*	*73,823*	*6,826*	*101*	*84*	*4*	...
	F.	*4,769*	*1,257*	*49,456*	*3,530*	*68,607*	*257*	*34*	*3*	...	...
Maulvi Bazar	M.	1,641	1,300	13,560	6,378	8,796	1,478	33	30	...	...
	F.	1,582	398	14,040	1,234	8,534	50	11	1	...	...
Kamalganj	M.	396	202	8,897	2,841	13,334	946	...	...	...	...
	F.	283	81	10,178	396	13,100	40	...	...	...	...
Srimangal	M.	936	671	6,507	2,353	18,018	1,618	58	43	3	...
	F.	736	176	5,804	401	17,914	45	23	2	...	...
Rajnagar	M.	1,058	723	7,306	2,926	8,234	541	...	...	...	...
	F.	994	307	6,061	683	7,582	17	...	...	...	...
Kulaura	M.	1,363	884	11,731	4,090	23,454	2,243	11	11	1	...
	F.	1,194	296	11,413	825	21,707	105	...	...	...	...
Karimganj Subdivision	M.	*3,772*	*2,339*	*49,597*	*15,149*	*69,305*	*8,123*	*33*	*28*	*16*	*7*
	F.	*3,330*	*751*	*46,427*	*2,683*	*66,864*	*724*	*5*	...	*10*	*4*
Karimganj	M.	1,433	1,066	13,195	5,735	22,490	2,491	14	11	7	...
	F.	1,217	297	11,569	1,063	22,353	200	3	...	3	
Badarpur	M.	265	218	4,651	1,894	3,486	273	...	...	7	5
	F.	254	65	4,348	267	3,364	66	...	...	5	3
Patharkandi	M.	367	120	7,216	1,193	13,547	1,413	16	14	1	1
	F.	169	30	6,966	131	14,737	43	2	...	2	3
Ratabari	M.	404	204	8,008	1,600	13,079	1,711	3	3	1	1
	F.	502	22	7,303	153	12,438	368	...	...	...	...
Jaldhup	M.	1,303	734	16,527	5,037	15,673	2,233	...	...	...	...
	F.	1,389	331	16,240	1,086	15,758	130	...	...	...	...

PROVINCIAL TABLE II.—POPULATION OF DISTRICTS, SUBDIVISIONS, THANAS OR OTHER LOCAL UNITS BY RELIGION AND LITERACY—*contd.*

District, subdivision, thana or other local unit.	Males (M) or Females (F).	MUSLIMS.		CHRISTIANS.		TRIBAL.		OTHERS.		NUMBER LITERATE.			LITERATE IN ENGLISH.
		Number of persons.	Number literate.	Number of persons.	Number literate.	Number of persons.	Number literate.	Number of persons.	Number literate.	Aged 4—13.	Aged 14—23.	Aged 24 and over.	
		13	14	15	16	17	18	19	20	21	22	23	24
SYLHET DISTRICT	M. ...	828,123	81,693	1,650	614	1,932	68	73	51	33,354	51,753	131,535	27,892
	F. ...	775,682	12,097	1,335	268	1,822	6	51	25	10,937	13,040	13,321	1,431
North Sylhet Subdivision	*M.* ...	*215,201*	*22,999*	*263*	*108*	*482*	*28*	*28*	*20*	*6,693*	*11,613*	*27,575*	*7,804*
	F. ...	*205,316*	*5,619*	*193*	*59*	*473*	*6*	*32*	*22*	*2,979*	*4,010*	*3,927*	*671*
Sylhet sadr	M. ...	57,876	7,736	163	76	66	6	25	18	2,544	4,803	9,611	4,557
	F. ...	55,899	1,283	114	45	40	1	30	22	937	1,267	1,649	447
Gowainghat	M. ...	24,232	1,396	64	13	239	7	3	2	90	720	1,353	342
	F. ...	19,633	341	22	5	213	...	2	...	128	205	167	24
Golabganj	M. ...	30,839	3,090	9	3	...	...	...	...	677	1,364	3,038	539
	F. ...	30,927	322	8	1	...	...	...	...	226	329	362	1
Fenchuganj	M. ...	8,004	1,307	13	11	...	...	...	...	339	512	1,508	319
	F. ...	7,221	200	8	7	...	...	...	...	150	166	229	11
Kanairghat	M. ...	25,791	3,962	1	1	4	...	...	...	666	947	3,199	404
	F. ...	26,813	1,502	1	1	...	...	...	...	428	780	372	146
Jaintiapur	M. ...	6,353	360	61	2	171	14	...	...	78	209	550	61
	F. ...	6,606	22	40	...	220	5	...	...	8	34	23	...
Balaganj	M.	31,446	3,011	...	...	2	1	...	...	1,386	1,925	5,106	977
	F.	31,296	197	...	...	...	...	...	...	347	466	623	4
Biswanath	M. ...	27,930	2,155	3	2	...	...	...	...	724	1,124	3,065	518
	F. ...	27,931	1,692	...	...	...	...	...	...	755	773	603	38
South Sylhet Subdivision	*M.* ...	*103,501*	*12,638*	*384*	*185*	*244*	*5*	*15*	*12*	*6,025*	*9,845*	*26,248*	*5,067*
	F. ...	*96,282*	*951*	*263*	*56*	*251*	...	*5*	...	*1,665*	*2,002*	*2,387*	*140*
Maulvi Bazar	M. ...	28,678	4,620	31	16	...	...	1	...	2,471	3,383	7,849	1,610
	F. ...	27,102	437	31	10	...	...	3	...	634	706	791	43
Kamalganj	M. ...	16,639	1,531	93	50	4	...	1	1	407	1,274	3,830	613
	F. ...	14,076	57	66	11	4	...	...	...	144	183	260	10
Srimangal	M. ...	9,683	974	111	59	127	4	9	9	606	1,313	3,912	756
	F. ...	8,608	28	63	17	121	...	2	...	143	222	304	26
Rajnagar	M. ...	18,718	1,917	36	14	...	...	...	...	1,043	1,409	3,471	707
	F. ...	17,610	107	19	2	...	...	...	...	856	396	431	17
Kulaura	M. ...	30,285	3,096	123	46	113	1	4	2	1,430	2,464	7,086	1,383
	F. ...	28,286	242	85	10	126	...	...	...	367	500	611	45
Karimganj Subdivision	*M.* ...	*138,486*	*16,800*	*506*	*185*	*98*	*3*	*10*	*6*	*6,401*	*10,501*	*25,738*	*4,765*
	F. ...	*130,628*	*1,369*	*458*	*95*	*85*	...	*4*	*1*	*1,476*	*2,027*	*2,124*	*229*
Karimganj	M. ...	55,724	7,290	81	23	1	...	3	1	2,708	4,270	9,626	2,108
	F. ...	51,606	611	67	27	...	...	...	...	644	748	615	110
Badarpur	M. ...	10,644	1,087	171	60	7	2	7	5	643	790	2,010	603
	F. ...	10,518	233	165	40	...	...	3	1	167	285	222	67
Patharkandi	M. ...	13,059	1,650	96	30	26	...	...	...	406	1,044	3,067	530
	F. ...	11,306	188	87	13	23	...	...	...	68	168	163	22
Ratabari	M. ...	11,800	666	72	23	61	1	...	...	400	954	2,964	341
	F. ...	10,040	19	63	8	61	...	...	...	114	170	102	17
Jaldhup	M. ...	47,210	6,737	88	34	2	...	...	...	2,270	3,434	8,068	1,196
	F. ...	47,003	318	76	7	2	...	1	...	486	686	712	23

PROVINCIAL TABLE II.—Population of Districts, Subdivisions, Thanas or other local units by Religion and Literacy—*contd.*

District, subdivision, thana or other local unit.	Males (M) or Females (F).	Hindus.						Jains.		Sikhs.	
		Brahmans.		Other Hindus.		Depressed classes.					
		Number of persons.	Number literate.	Number of persons.	Number literate.	Number of persons.	Number literate.	Number of persons.	Number literate.	Number of persons.	Number literate.
1	2	3	4	5	6	7	8	9	10	11	12
Sunamganj Subdivision	*M.* ...	*2,954*	*2,138*	*67,663*	*17,573*	*38,315*	*2,914*	*17*	*15*	...	...
	F. ...	*2,633*	*795*	*58,237*	*2,358*	*31,389*	*163*	*3*	...	...	...
Sunamganj	M. ...	677	401	13,140	3,674	6,906	630	12	12	...	...
	F. ...	455	164	10,477	682	5,925	28	1	...	...	...
Tahirpur	M. ...	158	108	3,537	806	1,464	145	...	...	...	...
	F. ...	153	40	3,026	104	1,707	2	...	...	...	...
Chhatak...	M. ...	643	480	8,311	2,903	5,775	377	5	3	...	...
	F. ...	498	331	6,983	236	4,652	65	2	...	...	...
Dirai	M. ...	305	162	11,690	2,960	5,822	451	...	...	...	...
	F. ...	269	64	10,162	327	5,145	14	...	...	...	...
Jagannathpur	M. ...	782	561	7,719	3,061	5,735	363	...	...	...	...
	F. ...	842	212	7,276	637	4,840	10	...	...	...	...
Sulla	M. ...	153	97	8,615	1,435	3,406	297	...	...	...	...
	F. ...	153	36	7,641	60	3,160	13	...	...	...	...
Dharampasha	M. ...	336	341	14,643	2,740	8,067	432	...	...	...	...
	F. ...	364	56	12,672	312	6,060	11	...	...	...	...
Habiganj Subdivision	*M.* ...	*5,795*	*4,083*	*65,423*	*24,899*	*62,267*	*4,932*	*10*	*8*	*5*	*3*
	F. ...	*5,184*	*1,314*	*64,611*	*4,759*	*60,813*	*194*	*2*	...	*2*	...
Habiganj	M. ...	815	608	9,394	4,320	6,081	941	9	8	5	3
	F. ...	595	170	8,665	1,007	6,103	43	2	...	2	...
Chunarighat	M. ...	636	435	8,188	3,002	13,960	512	...	...	...	...
	F. ...	607	180	7,606	536	13,198	35	...	...	...	...
Baniyachung	M. ...	1,110	801	11,946	3,481	8,319	639	...	...	...	...
	F. ...	1,038	288	12,293	704	8,116	15	...	...	...	...
Ajmiriganj	M. ...	214	144	6,351	2,281	3,860	428	1	...	...	...
	F. ...	218	28	5,964	377	3,661	11	...	...	...	...
Madhabpur	M. ...	738	627	7,977	3,343	12,088	798	...	...	...	...
	F. ...	561	195	8,218	655	11,690	23	...	...	...	...
Lakhai..	M. ...	430	362	3,041	1,681	5,323	470	...	...	...	...
	F. ...	454	127	4,231	318	5,021	23	...	...	...	...
Nabiganj	M. ...	1,312	674	11,539	4,491	7,726	811	...	...	...	...
	F. ...	1,203	255	11,499	739	7,407	35	...	...	...	...
Bahubal	M. ...	541	432	6,097	2,400	5,002	343	...	...	...	...
	F. ...	508	131	6,148	423	5,017	9	...	...	...	...
KHASI AND JAINTIA HILLS (British) ...	M. ...	521	389	6,695	2,932	165	20	...	...	45	23
	F. ...	267	148	3,016	318	141	2	...	...	16	...
Shillong Subdivision	*M.* ...	*516*	*384*	*5,969*	*2,815*	*147*	*20*	...	...	*45*	*23*
	F. ...	*267*	*148*	*2,758*	*314*	*135*	*2*	...	...	*16*	...
Jowai Subdivision	*M.* ...	*5*	*5*	*726*	*117*	*18*	...	...	...	...	...
	F. ...	...	...	*258*	*4*	*9*	...	...	...	...	...

PROVINCIAL TABLE II.—Population of Districts, Subdivisions, Thanas or other Local Units by Religion and Literacy—*contd.*

District, Subdivision, Thana or other local Unit.	Males (M) or females (F).	Muslims. Number of persons.	Muslims. Number literate.	Christians. Number of persons.	Christians. Number literate.	Tribal. Number of persons.	Tribal. Number literate.	Others. Number of persons.	Others. Number literate.	Number literate. Aged 4–13.	Number literate. Aged 14–23.	Number literate. Aged 24 and over.	Literate in English
		13	14	15	16	17	18	19	20	21	22	23	24
Sunamganj Subdivision	*M.* ...	*182,927*	*12,188*	*846*	*63*	*781*	*18*	*8*	*7*	*5,899*	*7,999*	*21,018*	*8,768*
	F. ...	*163,962*	*2,370*	*250*	*13*	*746*	...	*9*	*1*	*1,928*	*1,834*	*1,838*	*103*
Sunamganj	M. ...	42,344	3,672	319	34	321	8	...	...	1,316	1,018	4,708	1,203
	F. ...	37,498	477	250	10	300	...	...	...	131	401	411	57
Tahirpur	M. ...	9,946	306	2	1	124	5	3	3	226	286	949	153
	F. ...	6,204	26	1	1	97	...	...	...	68	62	43	3
Chhatak...	M. ...	49,474	3,366	3	3	170	4	6	5	1,066	1,734	4,244	687
	F. ...	46,378	360	2	1	166	...	2	1	214	294	306	7
Dirai	M. ...	19,035	1,313	...	...	...	...	...	...	901	1,039	3,945	423
	F. ...	17,661	381	...	...	...	...	...	...	327	237	223	10
Jagannathpur	M. ...	24,786	3,657	4	...	...	...	...	...	1,206	1,627	3,836	770
	F. ...	23,007	676	6	...	...	...	...	...	553	582	601	16
Sulla	M. ...	6,045	247	...	...	...	...	...	...	306	416	1,254	146
	F. ...	5,371	12	...	...	...	...	...	...	56	46	27	1
Dharampasha	M. ...	30,397	1,439	19	6	166	1	...	...	786	980	3,092	419
	F. ...	26,836	238	17	1	174	...	...	...	180	210	228	9
Habiganj Subdivision	*M.* ...	*188,008*	*17,068*	*152*	*73*	*327*	*14*	*13*	*6*	*8,336*	*11,794*	*30,956*	*6,488*
	F. ...	*179,494*	*2,788*	*141*	*45*	*267*	...	*8*	*1*	*2,889*	*3,167*	*3,045*	*291*
Habiganj	M. ...	30,718	3,406	34	17	6	...	1	1	1,390	2,078	5,006	1,636
	F. ...	29,368	140	46	33	...	...	2	1	300	475	529	83
Chunarighat	M. ...	23,309	2,200	34	34	134	10	5	3	874	1,446	3,966	885
	F. ...	22,211	317	15	9	113	...	...	...	200	331	436	28
Baniyachung	M. ...	31,943	2,105	1	1	...	...	...	...	984	1,476	4,567	811
	F. ...	30,123	218	...	...	...	...	...	...	353	442	430	12
Ajmiriganj	M. ...	9,621	686	...	...	...	...	...	...	435	774	2,310	363
	F. ...	8,663	28	...	...	...	...	...	...	148	158	178	...
Madhabpur	M. ...	23,796	2,713	83	17	159	4	6	2	1,336	1,036	4,001	923
	F. ...	23,170	1,306	77	2	153	...	6	...	771	788	621	125
Lakhai...	M. ...	16,029	943	...	...	...	...	...	...	437	688	2,231	308
	F. ...	16,270	81	...	...	...	...	...	...	132	203	214	7
Nabiganj	M. ...	33,900	3,349	...	...	...	...	...	...	1,575	2,208	5,742	986
	F. ...	31,779	274	...	...	...	...	...	...	436	449	418	21
Bahubal	M. ...	19,391	2,507	6	4	28	...	...	...	1,375	1,198	3,113	658
	F. ...	18,780	425	4	1	21	...	...	...	309	331	259	15
KHASI AND JAINTIA HILLS (British) ...	M. ...	708	246	11,207	2,774	86,032	949	66	40	591	2,171	4,011	1,401
	F. ...	176	32	12,107	1,996	38,736	256	25	14	442	1,153	1,170	339
Shillong Subdivision	*M.* ...	*569*	*236*	*2,135*	*953*	*6,848*	*683*	*66*	*40*	*401*	*1,551*	*3,203*	*1,169*
	F. ...	*157*	*31*	*2,246*	*656*	*6,882*	*192*	*25*	*14*	*244*	*511*	*602*	*258*
Jowai Subdivision	*M.* ...	*139*	*10*	*9,072*	*1,821*	*29,184*	*266*	...	...	*190*	*620*	*1,409*	*232*
	F. ...	*19*	*1*	*9,861*	*1,340*	*31,854*	*63*	...	...	*198*	*642*	*568*	*81*

PROVINCIAL TABLE II.—POPULATION OF DISTRICTS, SUBDIVISIONS, THANAS OR OTHER LOCAL UNITS BY RELIGION AND LITERACY—*contd.*

District, subdivision, thana or other local unit.	Males (M) or females (F).	Hindus. Brahmans. Number of persons.	Hindus. Brahmans. Number literate.	Hindus. Other Hindus. Number of persons.	Hindus. Other Hindus. Number literate.	Hindus. Depressed classes. Number of persons.	Hindus. Depressed classes. Number literate.	Jains. Number of persons.	Jains. Number literate.	Sikhs. Number of persons.	Sikhs. Number literate.
1	2	3	4	5	6	7	8	9	10	11	12
NAGA HILLS DISTRICT ...	M. ...	125	114	3,836	1,073	275	66	76	50	5	3
	F. ...	56	13	2,030	61	126	13	25	1	...	...
Kohima ...	M.	117	106	3,076	851	105	66	70	45	5	3
	F.	55	13	1,766	51	120	13	23	1	...	...
Mokokchung ...	M. ...	8	8	760	212	170	...	6	5	...	...
	F. ...	1	...	264	10	6	...	2	...	...	...
LUSHAI HILLS ...	M. ...	35	16	2,229	623	78	...	...	...	5	3
	F. ...	21	10	1,636	55	...	...	...	...	2	...
Aijal Subdivision ...	*M.* ...	*24*	*9*	*1,538*	*484*	*78*	...	...	...	*4*	*2*
	F. ...	*14*	*7*	*1,103*	*47*	...	...	...	...	*2*	...
Lungleh Subdivision ...	*M.* ...	*11*	*7*	*682*	*139*	...	...	...	...	*1*	*1*
	F. ...	*7*	*3*	*533*	*8*	...	...	...	...	...	...
ASSAM VALLEY DIVISION ...	M. ...	59,819	32,507	1,180,603	193,475	578,994	18,130	1,691	1,148	1,503	749
	F. ...	47,331	4,684	1,033,969	14,499	506,815	1,204	536	21	678	60
GOALPARA DISTRICT ...	M. ...	3,907	2,343	173,621	20,122	30,834	1,545	473	366	24	10
	F. ...	2,310	630	151,185	2,385	23,990	92	117	3	12	4
Dhubri Subdivision ...	*M.* ...	*2,949*	*1,656*	*115,826*	*17,368*	*25,608*	*635*	*378*	*280*	*18*	*8*
	F. ...	*1,642*	*417*	*98,730*	*1,371*	*19,850*	*17*	*109*	*3*	*8*	*4*
Dhubri ...	M.	930	673	11,439	2,055	3,001	110	109	92	7	8
	F.	562	340	9,473	894	1,749	4	16	1	6	4
Golakganj ...	M. ...	380	274	23,485	4,234	1,828	80	46	32	...	...
	F. ...	171	56	21,788	166	1,255	1	6	...	...	...
Gossaingaon ...	M. ...	315	109	10,840	1,098	8,514	30	21	10	...	...
	F. ...	155	10	7,342	39	7,363	2	7	...	...	...
Bijni ...	M. ...	411	106	32,134	2,792	4,230	50	...	...	...	...
	F. ...	312	9	28,369	77	3,635	...	...	...	...	...
Kokrajhar ...	M. ...	222	122	17,013	1,533	3,768	127	9	9	4	...
	F. ...	57	7	12,293	78	2,861	2	3	...	2	3
Bilasipara ...	M. ...	529	350	16,738	3,165	2,143	95	64	41	7	1
	F. ...	299	83	14,007	247	1,561	3	6	...	...	...
South Salmara ...	M. ...	95	70	3,384	934	1,258	92	69	42	...	...
	F. ...	51	9	2,618	113	810	6	43	2	...	...
Mankachar ...	M. ...	67	50	2,793	567	746	30	70	54	...	...
	F. ...	14	3	2,241	37	616	...	29	...	...	...

PROVINCIAL TABLE II.—Population of Districts, Subdivisions, Thanas or other Local Units by Religion and Literacy—*contd.*

District, subdivision, thana or other local unit.	Males (M) or females (F).	Muslims. Number of persons.	Muslims. Number literate.	Christians. Number of persons.	Christians. Number literate.	Tribal. Number of persons.	Tribal. Number literate.	Others. Number of persons.	Others. Number literate.	Number literate. Aged 4—13.	Number literate. Aged 14—23.	Number literate. Aged 24 and over.	Literate in English
		13	14	15	16	17	18	19	20	21	22	23	24
NAGA HILLS DISTRICT	M.	523	135	11,324	820	73,182	652	190	17	327	800	1,743	490
	F.	175	10	11,584	267	75,107	27	205	4	76	173	147	40
Kohima	M.	222	68	1,364	184	45,594	477	20	4	172	411	1,121	327
	F.	113	9	1,255	37	45,310	15	15	...	34	44	61	26
Mokokchung	M.	301	67	9,960	636	27,588	175	170	13	145	349	622	163
	F.	62	1	10,329	230	29,797	12	190	4	42	129	86	14
LUSHAI HILLS	M.	146	39	26,676	7,742	29,513	3,278	513	85	707	3,764	7,315	776
	F.	9	2	32,417	1,376	30,642	97	461	...	147	769	624	71
Aijal Subdivision	M.	*110*	*17*	*20,610*	*6,190*	*20,184*	*2,494*	*5*	*3*	*537*	*3,094*	*5,568*	*638*
	F.	*5*	*1*	*24,959*	*1,056*	*20,740*	*84*	...	...	*112*	*611*	*473*	*52*
Lungleh Subdivision	M.	*36*	*22*	*6,066*	*1,552*	*9,329*	*784*	*508*	*82*	*170*	*670*	*1,747*	*138*
	F.	*4*	*1*	*7,488*	*320*	*9,902*	*13*	*461*	...	*35*	*158*	*152*	*19*
ASSAM VALLEY DIVISION	M.	515,217	44,238	47,970	9,118	139,357	4,451	6,630	1,103	38,793	75,037	191,377	48,134
	F.	438,083	3,820	40,953	3,059	190,491	299	4,712	88	7,538	9,903	10,383	2,498
GOALPARA DISTRICT	M.	205,786	12,872	9,796	1,484	45,912	2,671	320	25	6,736	11,904	31,798	6,025
	F.	182,323	1,030	8,740	495	43,477	174	291	11	1,511	1,673	1,640	347
Dhubri Subdivision	M.	*143,681*	*8,670*	*6,318*	*484*	*36,630*	*1,887*	*282*	*20*	*3,934*	*7,291*	*19,783*	*3,616*
	F.	*128,460*	*612*	*5,499*	*163*	*34,467*	*114*	*260*	*9*	*824*	*927*	*959*	*125*
Dhubri	M.	26,040	2,236	56	21	1,500	188	10	5	913	1,580	3,641	1,340
	F.	23,718	256	47	15	1,124	12	14	8	333	353	437	103
Golakganj	M.	16,976	1,379	19	6	9	...	8	...	734	1,319	3,972	319
	F.	14,978	37	15	...	9	...	6	...	80	95	105	2
Gossaingaon	M.	4,292	239	4,089	339	5,656	593	144	5	276	462	1,300	257
	F.	3,389	8	3,456	123	5,196	62	124	...	82	79	73	7
Bijni	M.	7,623	533	1,457	43	7,017	213	...	...	415	906	2,580	345
	F.	6,257	8	1,200	5	6,362	12	...	...	46	26	89	1
Kokrajhar	M.	8,323	323	522	41	10,446	963	46	2	350	744	2,048	323
	F.	6,853	11	448	7	18,090	28	40	...	34	51	48	6
Bilasipara	M.	31,290	985	138	20	2,519	178	3	3	651	1,143	5,013	651
	F.	19,036	86	130	12	2,385	10	2	1	151	142	144	14
South Salmara	M.	43,272	3,016	3	2	...	...	31	1	377	742	2,040	275
	F.	39,768	124	...	...	...	...	31	...	62	117	86	4
Mankachar	M.	14,917	187	4	3	413	3	41	4	219	706	1,113	164
	F.	14,421	103	3	1	402	...	43	...	46	64	34	...

PROVINCIAL TABLE II.—POPULATION OF DISTRICTS, SUBDIVISIONS, THANAS OR OTHER LOCAL UNITS BY RELIGION AND LITERACY—*contd.*

District, subdivision, thana or other local unit.	Males (M) or females (F).	Hindus. Brahmans. Number of persons.	Hindus. Brahmans. Number literate.	Hindus. Other Hindus. Number of persons.	Hindus. Other Hindus. Number literate.	Hindus. Depressed classes. Number of persons.	Hindus. Depressed classes. Number literate.	Jains. Number of persons.	Jains. Number literate.	Sikhs. Number of persons.	Sikhs. Number literate.
1	2	3	4	5	6	7	8	9	10	11	12
Goalpara Subdivision	*M.* ...	*958*	*687*	*57,795*	*11,764*	*5,236*	*910*	*95*	*66*	*6*	*2*
	F. ...	*698*	*213*	*52,455*	*1,014*	*4,140*	*75*	*8*	...	*4*	...
Goalpara	M. ...	304	306	11,747	3,664	1,891	348	83	80	5	1
	F. ...	226	59	10,377	394	1,418	34	4	...	4	...
Dudnai	M. ...	113	67	12,650	2,346	1,061	196	1	1	1	1
	F. ...	89	11	11,901	142	923	9	...	...	...	...
Lakhipur	M. ...	165	121	10,628	1,305	863	73	11	11	...	...
	F. ...	96	37	9,555	124	577	2	...	...	...	...
North Salmara	M. ...	377	273	22,761	5,430	1,423	293	20	14	...	...
	F. ...	288	106	20,723	354	1,223	30	4	...	...	...
KAMRUP DISTRICT	M. ...	19,410	11,386	315,720	47,268	35,539	3,021	253	178	66	40
	F. ...	18,418	1,239	292,127	3,333	28,746	316	117	4	23	1
Gauhati Subdivision	*M.* ...	*15,885*	*9,601*	*233,520*	*34,138*	*26,425*	*2,334*	*246*	*173*	*56*	*35*
	F. ...	*15,143*	*1,127*	*217,481*	*2,465*	*23,809*	*271*	*117*	*4*	*21*	*1*
Gauhati	M. ...	2,497	1,739	31,136	5,459	6,389	808	83	43	40	31
	F. ...	1,461	454	14,783	997	4,858	306	7	1	17	1
Palasbari	M. ...	1,098	649	23,739	3,770	3,434	174	161	107	...	...
	F. ...	982	86	23,124	211	3,012	5	97	3	...	...
Chhaygaon	M. ...	244	144	10,406	1,107	1,437	218	7	6	...	...
	F. ...	218	6	8,693	57	1,335	13	...	...	...	...
Boko	M. ...	93	69	14,071	1,600	886	148	11	8	...	...
	F. ...	54	3	13,333	107	721	4	1	...	...	...
Nalbari	M. ...	7,669	4,603	60,098	9,285	5,377	450	4	1	3	3
	F. ...	6,578	389	61,435	501	4,003	22	7	...	...	...
* Rangia	M. ...	2,212	1,142	48,469	4,506	3,980	130	...	...	...	...
	F. ...	2,015	69	44,740	178	3,436	6	...	...	...	...
* Kamalpur	M. ...	1,217	713	27,803	3,919	1,221	80	4	3	4	2
	F. ...	1,103	66	25,908	164	1,097	6	3	...	4	...
Hajo	M. ...	867	533	27,438	4,401	3,701	330	7	6	...	...
	F. ...	763	45	25,530	260	3,547	13	3	...	...	...
Barpeta Subdivision	*M.* ...	*3,525*	*1,785*	*82,200*	*13,130*	*9,114*	*687*	*7*	*5*	*10*	*5*
	F. ...	*3,275*	*112*	*74,646*	*868*	*8,937*	*45*	...	...	*2*	...
Barpeta	M. ...	958	546	29,957	7,070	4,697	363	2	2	...	...
	F. ...	830	53	26,633	627	3,246	32	...	...	...	...
Sorbhog	M. ...	563	234	32,775	2,381	2,637	191	5	3	8	5
	F. ...	334	9	30,669	101	1,314	3	...	...	2	...
Patacharkuchi	M. ...	2,004	1,005	20,468	3,679	1,780	133	...	...	2	...
	F. ...	2,113	50	27,345	140	1,377	10	...	...	...	...

* One hundred sixty males and 139 females were subsequently transferred from Rangia to Kamalpur thana. This is shown in Provincial Table I but could not be shown in this table.

PROVINCIAL TABLE II.—Population of Districts, Subdivisions, Thanas or other Local Units by Religion and Literacy—*contd.*

District, subdivision, thana or other local unit.	Males (M) or females (F).	Muslims. Number of persons.	Muslims. Number literate.	Christians. Number of persons.	Christians. Number literate.	Tribal. Number of persons.	Tribal. Number literate.	Others. Number of persons.	Others. Number literate.	Number literate. Aged 6–13.	Number literate. Aged 14–23.	Number literate. Aged 24 and over.	Literate in English.
		13	14	15	16	17	18	19	20	21	22	23	24
Goalpara Subdivision	*M.* ...	*61,705*	*4,202*	*3,478*	*1,000*	*9,282*	*784*	*88*	*5*	*2,802*	*4,613*	*12,015*	*2,409*
	F. ...	*53,863*	*418*	*3,241*	*332*	*9,010*	*60*	*31*	*2*	*687*	*746*	*681*	*152*
Goalpara	M. ...	9,201	900	1,327	483	2,603	74	34	5	755	1,203	2,789	627
	F. ...	7,676	171	1,286	162	2,529	10	31	2	291	288	283	66
Dudnai	M. ...	2,104	198	1,911	507	5,979	705	4	...	634	987	2,622	876
	F. ...	1,030	9	1,788	168	5,807	50	...	...	196	130	133	64
Lakhipur	M. ...	30,609	1,513	205	3	670	4	...	...	420	698	1,911	393
	F. ...	27,336	94	207	1	647	...	...	...	74	91	93	5
North Salmara	M. ...	19,791	1,591	35	8	30	1	...	...	993	1,725	4,900	614
	F. ...	16,961	144	21	1	27	...	...	...	190	237	202	27
KAMRUP DISTRICT	**M.** ...	**128,785**	**10,323**	**3,034**	**1,290**	**9,946**	**826**	**692**	**33**	**10,729**	**19,157**	**43,978**	**9,473**
	F. ...	**111,637**	**786**	**2,549**	**629**	**9,547**	**10**	**287**	**13**	**1,670**	**2,275**	**2,395**	**462**
Gauhati Subdivision	*M.* ...	*56,137*	*6,453*	*2,924*	*1,263*	*9,158*	*273*	*541*	*30*	*8,175*	*14,214*	*31,911*	*7,671*
	F. ...	*49,511*	*547*	*2,472*	*626*	*8,822*	*18*	*223*	*13*	*1,319*	*1,740*	*2,013*	*438*
Gauhati	M. ...	4,893	1,561	439	293	3,377	65	37	21	1,218	3,034	5,880	3,065
	F. ...	2,945	334	390	220	3,358	8	20	13	616	779	829	375
Palasbari	M. ...	1,780	217	379	131	1,681	31	6	3	944	1,328	2,790	579
	F. ...	1,004	13	328	60	1,670	...	...	...	92	115	171	7
Chhaygaon	M. ...	6,623	321	46	9	...	...	...	...	241	376	1,166	134
	F. ...	5,399	5	35	...	...	...	...	...	15	23	43	2
Boko	M. ...	5,023	298	1,617	680	1,060	76	...	...	419	731	1,738	279
	F. ...	4,151	28	1,445	327	1,007	10	...	...	133	176	170	13
Nalbari	M. ...	9,429	1,113	7	4	40	...	9	...	2,700	4,033	6,726	1,386
	F. ...	8,936	63	3	1	37	...	...	...	208	330	363	10
Rangia	M. ...	8,410	945	261	22	2,570	76	489	2	858	1,606	4,339	400
	F. ...	7,819	17	236	2	2,364	...	203	...	64	78	120	6
Kamalpur	M. ...	7,564	1,018	176	135	261	8	4	4	606	1,467	3,711	657
	F. ...	7,003	55	65	16	250	...	...	...	69	103	143	14
Hajo	M. ...	12,166	966	...	...	140	7	...	...	1,069	1,650	3,604	493
	F. ...	11,365	40	...	...	136	...	...	...	71	131	146	6
Barpeta Subdivision	*M.* ...	*72,648*	*3,870*	*110*	*27*	*788*	*52*	*51*	*3*	*2,554*	*4,943*	*12,067*	*1,802*
	F. ...	*62,126*	*239*	*77*	*3*	*725*	*1*	*14*	...	*351*	*535*	*382*	*24*
Barpeta	M. ...	40,877	2,501	1	...	31	...	6	...	1,622	2,721	6,139	1,177
	F. ...	42,991	127	...	...	31	...	1	...	214	317	278	16
Sorbhog	M. ...	20,483	1,152	78	23	361	5	33	2	351	853	2,792	346
	F. ...	17,165	102	46	2	288	...	6	...	17	96	75	8
Patacharkuchi	M. ...	2,286	217	31	4	393	47	12	1	581	1,369	3,136	279
	F. ...	1,970	10	31	1	407	1	7	...	90	123	29	...

PROVINCIAL TABLE II.—Population of Districts, Subdivisions, Thanas or other Local Units by Religion and Literacy—*contd.*

District, subdivision, thana or other local unit.	Males (M) or females (F).	Hindus. Brahmans. Number of persons.	Hindus. Brahmans. Number literate.	Hindus. Other Hindus. Number of persons.	Hindus. Other Hindus. Number literate.	Hindus. Depressed classes. Number of persons.	Hindus. Depressed classes. Number literate.	Jains. Number of persons.	Jains. Number literate.	Sikhs. Number of persons.	Sikhs. Number literate.
1	2	3	4	5	6	7	8	9	10	11	12
DARRANG DISTRICT	M. ...	11,409	4,439	133,261	17,307	101,856	2,900	197	148	97	45
	F. ...	9,162	566	110,441	1,446	89,494	157	33	4	50	1
Tezpur Subdivision	*M.* ...	*8,497*	*3,069*	*70,103*	*11,571*	*74,453*	*2,119*	*120*	*96*	*69*	*32*
	F. ...	*6,879*	*470*	*54,499*	*1,180*	*66,933*	*117*	*10*	*3*	*46*	*1*
Tezpur	M. ...	1,804	948	23,471	5,042	24,128	594	60	45	18	7
	F. ...	1,229	253	18,847	698	20,337	19	6	3	8	...
Dhekiajuli	M. ...	1,253	285	13,636	1,040	13,900	193	16	14	3	2
	F. ...	651	28	9,083	68	14,378	6	...	...	...	...
Chutia (Sootea)	M. ...	2,064	873	18,774	2,637	15,298	899	26	23	7	4
	F. ...	1,780	135	14,889	236	14,096	38	...	...	6	...
Behali	M. ...	2,332	650	6,307	1,029	15,517	278	7	6	17	10
	F. ...	2,203	33	5,164	42	13,743	16	...	...	11	1
Gohpur	M. ...	1,044	300	7,914	1,923	5,622	150	11	9	24	9
	F. ...	817	34	6,576	106	4,351	4	4	...	21	...
Mangaldai Subdivision	*M.* ...	*2,912*	*1,370*	*63,159*	*5,736*	*27,403*	*781*	*77*	*52*	*28*	*13*
	F. ...	*2,283*	*96*	*55,942*	*266*	*22,561*	*40*	*23*	*1*	*4*	...
Mangaldai	M. ...	1,605	947	29,356	3,119	3,240	300	60	38	...	...
	F. ...	1,504	64	27,338	140	2,784	20	19	1	1	...
Kalaigaon	M. ...	288	111	11,497	836	1,364	37	6	4	...	...
	F. ...	217	3	10,435	20	930	...	2	...	...	...
Paneri	M. ...	405	179	13,678	962	13,022	287	3	3	9	8
	F. ...	201	25	11,416	58	11,630	17	...	...	2	...
Udalguri	M. ...	557	104	6,795	607	8,194	128	5	4	19	5
	F. ...	348	14	5,452	30	6,754	3	2	...	1	...
Dalgaon	M. ...	57	29	1,843	212	683	20	3	3	...	...
	F. ...	13	...	1,311	13	454	...	...	...	...	...
NOWGONG DISTRICT	M.	5,465	2,866	123,061	18,834	44,133	3,467	216	160	330	118
	F.	3,987	409	109,630	1,527	39,434	210	54	2	293	14
Nowgong Sadr	M. ...	2,100	1,021	26,359	6,659	6,667	671	40	20	176	37
	F. ...	1,644	184	24,004	540	5,811	53	26	1	158	7
Samaguri	M. ...	773	483	15,750	2,441	11,618	677	23	13	...	...
	F. ...	644	40	13,379	181	11,356	54	8	...	...	...
Kaliabor	M. ...	742	337	9,903	1,576	4,664	311	1	1	3	3
	F. ...	503	58	8,004	130	3,930	10	...	...	2	...
Roha	M. ...	544	340	17,387	2,315	8,068	801	36	26	64	28
	F. ...	404	47	16,335	186	4,926	61	4	...	60	3
Jamunamukh	M. ...	383	227	17,148	2,281	5,306	226	...	...	50	13
	F. ...	344	19	14,440	192	4,880	6	...	...	35	2
Lumding	M. ...	210	122	2,613	647	1,029	95	2	3	67	38
	F. ...	68	22	1,418	115	554	3	3	1	30	2
Lahorighat	M. ...	288	173	15,242	1,506	4,145	260	134	96	...	...
	F. ...	164	18	13,363	82	3,047	11	13	...	...	...
Marigaon	M. ...	416	213	18,620	1,507	5,561	307	1	1	...	...
	F. ...	338	21	17,980	69	4,930	13	...	...	...	...

PROVINCIAL TABLE II.—POPULATION OF DISTRICTS, SUBDIVISIONS, THANAS OR OTHER LOCAL UNITS BY RELIGION AND LITERACY—*contd.*

District, subdivision, thana or other local unit.	Males (M) or females (F).	Muslims. Number of persons.	Muslims. Number literate.	Christians. Number of persons.	Christians. Number literate.	Tribal. Number of persons.	Tribal. Number literate.	Others. Number of persons.	Others. Number literate.	Number literate. Aged 6–13.	Number literate. Aged 14–23.	Number literate. Aged 24 and over.	Literate in English.
		13	14	15	16	17	18	19	20	21	22	23	24
DARRANG DISTRICT	M. ...	37,520	3,259	8,453	820	23,460	230	832	139	3,176	6,919	19,193	4,543
	F. ...	29,074	145	7,203	174	20,901	17	396	14	687	907	930	230
Tezpur Subdivision	*M.* ...	*11,644*	*1,579*	*3,490*	*419*	*19,504*	*166*	*441*	*93*	*2,095*	*4,630*	*12,419*	*3,257*
	F. ...	*8,114*	*76*	*2,790*	*107*	*17,312*	*15*	*265*	*14*	*559*	*720*	*704*	*193*
Tezpur	M. ...	6,337	863	1,375	178	6,775	47	109	57	1,045	1,973	4,783	1,769
	F. ...	4,853	56	1,190	60	6,000	3	41	10	363	388	400	137
Dhekiajuli	M. ...	1,237	203	460	39	4,363	30	23	4	94	347	1,860	350
	F. ...	557	5	411	6	4,006	...	10	2	14	42	47	9
Chutia (Sootea)	M. ...	3,180	315	490	40	3,246	31	95	17	620	1,719	3,114	575
	F. ...	2,431	11	301	13	2,740	6	53	1	125	150	130	16
Behali	M. ...	686	137	550	67	3,557	39	209	10	144	5'6	1,454	315
	F. ...	204	2	436	15	3,287	1	161	1	33	67	63	20
Gohpur	M. ...	234	43	505	86	2,563	29	5	5	293	591	1,078	268
	F. ...	79	2	452	14	2,210	5	...	...	35	74	56	10
Mangaldai Subdivision	*M.* ...	*25,883*	*1,680*	*4,963*	*401*	*3,963*	*64*	*391*	*46*	*1,081*	*2,289*	*6,773*	*1,285*
	F. ...	*21,860*	*69*	*4,473*	*67*	*3,589*	*2*	*131*	...	*128*	*187*	*226*	*38*
Mangaldai	M. ...	15,286	1,075	5	1	1,294	14	35	3	703	1,414	3,200	446
	F. ...	13,208	38	7	1	1,329	2	15	...	77	81	107	6
Kalaigaon	M. ...	600	82	298	7	455	9	9	...	114	208	764	96
	F. ...	716	4	399	...	401	...	...	...	8	7	15	2
Paneri	M. ...	507	137	2,798	233	197	11	200	28	98	374	1,206	446
	F. ...	141	6	2,021	41	109	...	81	...	18	63	66	17
Udalguri	M. ...	477	86	2,179	136	593	20	68	11	40	167	894	212
	F. ...	234	2	1,994	25	451	...	35	...	18	21	25	7
Dalgaon	M. ...	8,755	300	83	5	1,336	10	4	4	37	198	430	86
	F. ...	7,501	19	52	...	1,290	...	...	...	7	15	10	6
NOWGONG DISTRICT	M. ...	95,597	6,837	2,615	400	27,094	300	35	23	4,402	7,907	20,755	3,784
	F. ...	82,165	743	2,428	254	26,000	9	5	2	885	1,187	1,098	180
Nowgong Sadr	M. ...	26,077	2,501	139	84	911	29	4	4	1,784	2,774	6,418	1,380
	F. ...	22,608	400	195	143	934	...	1	1	428	467	422	93
Samaguri	M. ...	20,156	1,572	1,018	90	6,307	64	14	8	706	1,346	3,448	573
	F. ...	17,556	236	904	21	5,916	2	3	...	146	315	173	17
Kaliabor	M. ...	850	130	403	29	1,676	9	6	5	265	575	1,560	343
	F. ...	700	3	330	5	1,526	...	...	...	64	65	66	7
Raha	M. ...	2,761	213	73	15	715	23	1	1	576	953	2,292	333
	F. ...	2,416	16	63	3	799	2	1	...	100	118	100	7
Jamunamukh	M. ...	7,313	686	863	114	10,189	144	3	1	277	700	2,865	326
	F. ...	5,300	17	840	45	9,753	3	1	1	45	109	132	3
Lumding	M. ...	553	183	101	61	3,820	53	7	3	59	317	836	433
	F. ...	186	14	69	35	3,662	1	...	...	47	73	77	47
Laharighat	M. ...	34,978	1,356	1	...	346	1	...	...	477	783	3,143	273
	F. ...	30,793	50	...	...	293	...	...	...	36	61	64	2
Marigaon	M. ...	3,011	198	19	7	3,160	38	...	...	258	400	1,474	306
	F. ...	2,598	7	18	3	3,156	1	...	...	70	50	44	4

PROVINCIAL TABLE II.—POPULATION OF DISTRICTS, SUBDIVISIONS, THANAS OR OTHER LOCAL UNITS BY RELIGION AND LITERACY—*contd.*

District, subdivision, thana or other local unit.	Males (M) or females (F).	Hindus. Brahmans. Number of persons.	Hindus. Brahmans. Number literate.	Hindus. Other Hindus. Number of persons.	Hindus. Other Hindus. Number literate.	Hindus. Depressed classes. Number of persons.	Hindus. Depressed classes. Number literate.	Jains. Number of persons.	Jains. Number literate.	Sikhs. Number of persons.	Sikhs. Number literate.
1	2	3	4	5	6	7	8	9	10	11	12
SIBSAGAR DISTRICT ...	M. ...	13,457	7,869	238,068	40,159	173,533	3,681	128	62	221	100
	F. ...	10,346	1,811	236,678	3,423	158,353	216	53	2	83	10
Jorhat Subdivision ...	*M.* ...	*6,618*	*3,922*	*99,408*	*18,498*	*57,780*	*1,775*	*57*	*30*	*103*	*48*
	F. ...	*5,199*	*659*	*87,007*	*1,371*	*52,410*	*112*	*17*	*2*	*40*	*7*
*Jorhat ...	M. ...	4,344	2,573	42,100	9,276	20,730	800	11	8	64	39
	F. ...	3,360	480	36,073	927	18,661	81	...	...	17	3
*Teok ...	M. ...	1,100	590	20,040	3,636	17,722	405	19	10	16	13
	F. ...	980	100	16,567	181	15,970	9	10	...	5	3
Titabar ...	M. ...	534	346	16,808	2,660	10,553	347	24	9	22	6
	F. ...	386	43	13,467	149	15,306	15	7	2	16	2
Majuli ...	M. ...	731	404	19,900	2,828	2,775	223	3	3	2	...
	F. ...	408	31	17,890	114	2,404	4	...	...	...	...
Sibsagar Subdivision ...	*M.* ...	*3,136*	*1,838*	*95,486*	*17,500*	*61,606*	*1,170*	*35*	*20*	*86*	*42*
	F. ...	*2,326*	*344*	*88,384*	*1,308*	*56,530*	*78*	*14*	...	*34*	*1*
*Sibsagar ...	M. ...	1,310	731	27,436	7,443	11,468	477	7	5	3	2
	F. ...	1,041	198	24,406	701	10,291	56	2	...	3	...
Nazira ...	M. ...	673	425	21,072	3,940	18,702	304	15	5	53	31
	F. ...	306	65	18,336	198	19,067	15	12	...	19	1
*Amguri ...	M. ...	754	437	19,930	3,162	5,393	70	1	1	16	3
	F. ...	627	46	18,003	253	4,939	1	...	...	...	...
Sonari ...	M. ...	490	245	16,140	2,948	20,023	319	12	9	15	6
	F. ...	252	45	14,040	157	23,318	4	...	...	12	...
Golaghat Subdivision ...	*M.* ...	*3,703*	*2,109*	*63,774*	*10,152*	*54,147*	*736*	*36*	*12*	*32*	*19*
	F. ...	*2,821*	*208*	*54,287*	*744*	*49,413*	*26*	*22*	...	*9*	*2*
Golaghat ...	M. ...	1,666	939	38,672	6,560	30,398	375	10	9	23	17
	F. ...	1,070	126	31,962	518	27,677	13	4	...	4	1
Dergaon ...	M. ...	1,793	900	20,646	2,806	12,917	354	23	3	3	...
	F. ...	1,630	75	18,718	191	12,015	9	15	...	2	...
Bokakhat ...	M. ...	244	171	4,456	796	10,637	107	3	...	7	3
	F. ...	112	7	3,607	55	9,721	4	3	...	2	1

* The discrepancy between the total population of these thanas as given in this table and in Provincial Table I is due to the fact that adjustments of portions of Hologapar mauza in Jorhat and Solaguri mauza in Sibsagar were subsequently made. These adjustments have been included in Provincial Table I but could not be shown in this table.

PROVINCIAL TABLE II.—Population of Districts, Subdivisions, Thanas or other Local Units by Religion and Literacy—*contd.*

District, Subdivision, Thana or other Local Unit.	Males (M) or females (F).	Muslims. Number of persons.	Muslims. Number literate.	Christians. Number of persons.	Christians. Number literate.	Tribal. Number of persons.	Tribal. Number literate.	Others. Number of persons.	Others. Number literate.	Number literate. Aged 4—13.	Number literate. Aged 14—23.	Number literate. Aged 24 and over.	Literate in English.
		13	14	15	16	17	18	19	20	21	22	23	24
SIBSAGAR DISTRICT	M. ...	24,916	6,043	7,152	1,329	16,744	291	1,469	233	8,328	16,700	40,731	12,506
	F. ..	18,991	739	6,079	423	15,290	16	1,165	11	1,734	2,042	2,374	600
Jorhat Subdivision	M. ...	7,059	2,007	1,784	439	1,419	17	441	92	3,606	7,037	16 195	5,494
	F. ...	5,154	321	1,412	133	1,256	...	329	6	706	863	1,042	290
Jorhat	M. ...	4,370	1,854	354	228	1,088	5	27	12	2,304	3,543	8,210	3,654
	F. ...	3,309	246	186	79	915	...	14	4	534	509	706	231
Teok	M. ...	1,094	363	336	98	231	2	88	6	630	1,287	3,401	201
	F. ...	706	99	285	37	231	...	21	...	90	119	181	34
Titabor	M. ...	1,563	363	1,094	118	9	...	259	73	403	987	2,469	602
	F. ...	1,189	46	942	17	5	...	203	2	64	106	105	23
Majuli	M. ...	103	27	...	...	111	10	3	1	400	971	2,062	137
	F. ...	51	...	...	...	105	...	1	...	38	39	73	2
Sibsagar Subdivision	M. ...	11,046	2,713	2,397	428	795	27	486	76	3,183	6,003	14,628	4,575
	F. ...	8,710	312	2,067	118	584	...	400	4	712	699	754	207
Sibsagar	M. ...	5,130	1,387	388	121	92	3	17	8	1,090	2,540	5,830	1,967
	F. ...	4,336	246	367	61	60	...	19	3	453	374	377	118
Nazira	M. ...	3,744	944	665	136	446	18	178	29	644	1,409	3,739	1,194
	F. ...	2,948	76	627	31	345	...	129	...	93	137	167	66
Amguri	M. ...	1,040	166	34	13	1	...	8	3	565	1,085	2,233	634
	F. ...	877	17	13	5	...	...	...	...	107	104	110	11
Sonari	M. ...	1,132	307	1,340	150	734	6	283	30	294	901	2,889	600
	F. ...	649	18	1,070	30	180	...	252	1	67	94	150	82
Golaghat Subdivision	M. ...	6,811	1,322	3,041	455	14,530	247	542	65	1,539	3,670	9,908	2,437
	F. ...	5,127	106	2,600	172	13,450	15	436	1	316	480	478	103
Golaghat	M. ...	3,411	886	2,643	367	10,201	200	497	56	906	2,308	6,155	1,080
	F. ...	2,336	86	2,336	141	9,437	14	400	1	316	353	339	69
Dergaon	M. ...	2,800	300	93	20	390	6	11	4	673	1,183	2,326	310
	F. ...	2,455	16	61	11	279	...	12	...	66	101	115	15
Bokakhat	M. ...	380	97	306	66	4,030	22	34	5	63	279	927	267
	F. ...	177	5	201	20	3,734	1	24	...	13	26	25	19

PROVINCIAL TABLE II.—POPULATION OF DISTRICTS, SUBDIVISIONS, THANAS OR OTHER LOCAL UNITS BY RELIGION AND LITERACY—*contd.*

District, subdivision, thana or other local unit.	Males (M) or females (F).	HINDUS.						JAINS.		SIKHS.	
		Brahmans.		Other Hindus.		Depressed Classes.					
		Number of persons.	Number literate.	Number of persons.	Number literate.	Number of persons.	Number literate.	Number of persons.	Number literate.	Number of persons.	Number literate.
1	2	3	4	5	6	7	8	9	10	11	12
LAKHIMPUR DISTRICT	M. ...	6,064	3,514	161,987	33,703	192,705	3,790	394	234	810	423
	F. ...	3,042	610	131,269	2,344	166,613	303	162	6	215	29
Dibrugarh Subdivision	*M.* ...	*4,609*	*2,749*	*110,238*	*25,205*	*171,196*	*3,105*	*312*	*187*	*806*	*419*
	F. ...	*1,957*	*533*	*84,016*	*1,953*	*149,103*	*270*	*146*	*6*	*207*	*29*
Dibrugarh	M. ...	1,686	978	28,455	7,301	33,473	749	99	72	66	39
	F. ...	823	235	23,018	102	28,321	126	53	1	29	6
Tinsukia	M. ...	901	494	21,824	6,477	40,035	603	164	88	103	83
	F. ...	416	92	19,684	399	42,027	32	81	5	27	2
Moran	M. ...	191	118	11,756	2,098	8,017	39	1	1	...	...
	F. ...	81	9	9,253	58	8,671	...	...	...	...	...
Margherita	M. ...	911	624	9,172	2,298	15,376	427	18	13	524	282
	F. ...	263	98	3,073	283	11,030	27	4	...	122	19
Jaipur	M. ...	257	133	12,919	2,548	15,167	434	5	1	9	8
	F. ...	129	28	10,689	107	14,003	24	1	...	6	1
Dhemaji	M. ...	124	78	13,985	1,931	564	42	6	5	...	...
	F. ...	66	10	12,7.8	81	380	4	1	...	...	...
Doom Dooma	M. ...	540	324	12,098	2,862	47,978	791	17	7	104	30
	F. ...	179	63	6,802	174	44,003	57	6	...	23	1
North Lakhimpur Subdivision	*M.* ...	*1,455*	*765*	*51,749*	*8,498*	*21,509*	*685*	*82*	*47*	*4*	*3*
	F. ...	*1,085*	*78*	*47,273*	*391*	*17,510*	*33*	*17*	...	*8*	...
North Lakhimpur	M. ...	469	284	17,828	3,199	14,144	200	26	13	4	3
	F. ...	307	42	16,601	169	11,111	8	2	...	8	...
Dhakuakhana	M. ...	336	202	18,897	2,626	3,886	340	43	26	...	...
	F. ...	280	8	17,567	100	2,410	9	15	...	...	...
Bihpuria	M. ...	650	279	15,024	2,664	4,060	243	13	8	...	...
	F. ...	499	28	12,965	102	3,463	16	...	...	...	...
GARO HILLS DISTRICT	M. ...	107	90	14,686	1,071	394	25	...	...	6	5
	F. ...	36	10	12,639	41	185	...	...	...	2	...
SADIYA FRONTIER TRACT	M. ...	183	144	13,686	1,768	2,310	485	16	3	15	8
	F. ...	92	29	8,130	120	1,971	21	13	...	19	4
BALIPARA FRONTIER TRACT	M. ...	35	33	1,958	847	494	6	5	5	...	...
	F. ...	9	3	998	11	317	...	...	...	...	...

PROVINCIAL TABLE II.—POPULATION OF DISTRICTS, SUBDIVISIONS, THANAS OR OTHER LOCAL UNITS BY RELIGION AND LITERACY—*contd.*

District, subdivision, thana or other local unit.	Males (M) or Females (F).	MUSLIMS.		CHRISTIANS.		TRIBAL.		OTHERS.		NUMBER LITERATE.			LITERATE IN ENGLISH.
		Number of persons.	Number literate.	Number of persons.	Number literate.	Number of persons.	Number literate.	Number of persons.	Number literate.	Aged 4–13.	Aged 14–23.	Aged 24 and over.	
		13	14	15	16	17	18	19	20	21	22	23	24
LAKHIMPUR DISTRICT ...	M. ...	17,541	4,556	8,360	1,637	7,098	72	3,253	646	5,119	11,314	32,141	11,353
	F. ...	8,408	365	6,508	373	6,763	5	2,494	37	951	1,423	1,698	604
Dibrugarh Subdivision ...	M. ...	14,304	3,941	6,528	1,359	6,754	62	2,789	541	3,597	8,566	25,405	10,209
	F.	6,044	817	4,993	325	5,877	2	2,080	85	784	1,200	1,485	589
Dibrugarh ...	M. ...	5,096	1,620	623	400	439	6	176	47	1,307	2,733	7,187	3,748
	F. ...	3,016	202	674	90	351	...	136	12	431	615	638	285
Tinsukia ...	M.	2,417	657	1,597	377	1,196	12	304	50	860	1,943	6,214	2,303
	F. ...	1,126	61	1,317	101	1,053	2	16	5	148	228	315	96
Moran ...	M. ...	469	138	474	64	47	...	221	7	291	458	1,676	330
	F. ...	267	4	419	15	57	...	165	...	16	35	35	21
Margherita ...	M. ...	4,202	936	747	202	2,165	6	1,635	162	169	1,284	3,516	1,725
	F. ...	637	30	387	53	2,023	...	1,283	15	66	233	302	103
Jaipur ...	M. ...	733	209	1,063	97	7,439	28	383	116	390	739	2,444	633
	F. ...	324	10	947	16	2,156	...	288	2	41	50	86	21
Dhemaji ...	M. ...	125	31	...	...	44	...	36	3	287	477	1,327	169
	F. ...	65	...	...	...	4	...	63	...	23	10	34	2
Doom Dooma ...	M. ...	1,133	312	1,764	210	365	...	134	32	203	902	3,041	1,252
	F. ...	390	16	1,317	81	233	...	63	1	60	111	198	79
North Lakhimpur Subdivision ...	M. ...	3,237	615	1,838	278	1,244	10	464	105	1,522	2,748	6,736	1,144
	F. ...	2,364	48	1,515	48	886	3	414	2	167	223	213	15
North Lakhimpur ...	M. ...	1,392	416	1,353	210	469	4	23	7	532	1,041	2,708	708
	F. ...	1,055	47	1,071	33	312	3	10	...	97	105	130	10
Dhakuakhana ...	M. ...	111	31	2	2	469	2	...	...	507	778	1,012	208
	F. ...	60	1	4	1	365	...	...	...	30	60	40	1
Bihpuria ...	M. ...	1,724	108	473	66	317	14	441	18	483	929	2,065	236
	F. ...	1,200	...	440	14	209	...	404	2	40	69	23	4
GARO HILLS DISTRICT ...	M. ...	5,463	349	8,564	2,165	68,194	505	129	10	303	1,136	2,782	451
	F. ...	4,584	12	7,386	711	68,513	60	124	...	100	396	347	65
SADIYA FRONTIER TRACT ...	M. ...	579	143	231	66	11,677	12	1,359	315	237	631	1,876	233
	F. ...	226	10	207	38	11,809	1	1,102	5	63	102	73	26
BALIPARA FRONTIER TRACT ...	M. ...	59	22	155	29	430	2	87	22	16	130	314	37
	F. ...	13	2	138	10	374	...	67	...	4	13	8	1

PROVINCIAL TABLE II. -POPULATION OF DISTRICTS, SUBDIVISIONS, THANAS OR OTHER LOCAL UNITS BY RELIGION AND LITERACY—*contd.*

District, subdivision, thana, or other local unit.	Males (M) or females (F).	HINDUS. Brahmans. Number of persons.	Brahmans. Number literate.	Other Hindus. Number of persons.	Other Hindus. Number literate.	Depressed Classes. Number of persons.	Depressed Classes. Number literate.	JAINS. Number of persons.	JAINS. Number literate.	SIKHS. Number of persons.	SIKHS. Number literate.
1	2	3	4	5	6	7	8	9	10	11	12
(2) Assam States	M. ...	*413*	*297*	*133,749*	*19,874*	*767*	*167*	*116*	*46*	*178*	*39*
	F. ...	*185*	*99*	*136,947*	*690*	*654*	*17*	*51*	*2*	*54*	*2*
Manipur State	M. ...	*15**	*7*	*123,627*	*11,079*	*701*	*149*	*113*	*43*	*36*	*6*
	F. ...	...	...	*132,385*	*345*	*527*	*9*	*51*	*2*	*21*	*1*
Valley Section	M. ...	15	7	122,271	10,843	696	140	107	39	35	6
	F. ...	...	...	131,926	341	527	9	48	2	21	1
Imphal Panah	M. ...	1	...	42,073	7,085	48	5	96	33	21	...
	F. ...	...	...	46,218	198	35	...	44	...	9	...
Naharup Panah	M. ...	14	7	13,283	827	9	...	7	6	14	6
	F. ...	...	...	13,628	14	...	...	3	2	12	1
Ahalup Panah	M. ...	...	...	27,471	1,396	...	...	...	...	...	...
	F. ...	...	...	28,273	72	...	...	...	...	...	...
Laifam Panah	M. ...	...	...	20,558	783	...	...	5	...	...	...
	F. ...	...	...	21,909	33	...	...	1	...	...	...
Khabam Panah	M. ...	...	...	17,867	444	...	...	...	...	...	...
	F. ...	...	...	18,999	11	...	...	...	...	...	...
Jiribam Panah	M. ...	...	...	1,067	330	630	135	...	...	...	...
	F. ...	...	...	905	13	493	9	...	...	...	...
Hill Section	M. ...	...	...	1,356	236	5	2	6	4	1	...
	F. ...	...	...	459	4	...	...	3	...	...	...
Imphal North	M. ...	...	...	1,005	181	5	2	6	4	1	...
	F. ...	...	...	361	4	...	...	3	...	...	...
Imphal South	M. ...	...	...	351	55	...	...	...	...	...	...
	F. ...	...	...	98	...	...	...	...	...	...	...
Khasi States	M. ...	*398*	*290*	*10,115*	*1,795*	*66*	*25*	*3*	*3*	*149*	*36*
	F. ...	*185*	*99*	*4,562*	*345*	*127*	*8*	...	...	*33*	*1*

*Manipuri Brahmans, as explained in the footnote to Imperial Table XVII—Caste Tribe or Race, were classed under Manipuri as what was required for the purpose of that table was the total number of Manipuris of all castes. Hence at the time of compilation Provincial Table II the number of Manipuri Brahmans could not be ascertained without a resort of all the Manipuri slips. The approximate number of Manipuri Brahmans is about 10,000.

PROVINCIAL TABLE II.—Population of Districts, Subdivisions, thanas or other local units by religion and literacy—*concld.*

District, Subdivision, Thana or other local unit.	Males (M) or Females (F).	Muslims. Number of persons.	Muslims. Number literate.	Christians. Number of persons.	Christians. Number literate.	Tribal. Number of persons.	Tribal. Number literate.	Others. Number of persons.	Others. Number literate.	Number literate. Aged 5–13.	Number literate. Aged 14–23.	Number literate. Aged 24 and over.	Literate in English.
		13	14	15	16	17	18	19	20	21	22	23	24
(2) Assam States	M. ...	*12,689*	*1,298*	*22,105*	*6,830*	*136,463*	*3,102*	*154*	*69*	*2,338*	*7,900*	*14,977*	*4,517*
	F. ...	*11,911*	*186*	*21,955*	*4,613*	*141,495*	*886*	*127*	*37*	*1,076*	*2,674*	*2,782*	*717*
Manipur State	M. ...	*11,379*	*983*	*5,110*	*975*	*74,830*	*596*	*34*	*4*	*1,343*	*4,044*	*8,448*	*2,091*
	F. ...	*11,533*	*130*	*5,391*	*173*	*79,954*	*42*	*27*	...	*153*	*244*	*305*	*51*
Valley Section	M. ...	11,298	970	612	212	7,369	228	13	2	1,391	3,594	7,568	1,809
	F. ...	11,526	130	574	55	7,665	13	14	...	133	172	246	45
Imphal Panah	M. ...	1,061	575	73	44	1,240	108	6	2	925	2,546	4,418	1,531
	F. ...	1,118	45	54	13	1,313	3	...	...	68	67	134	31
Naharup Panah	M. ...	408	2	228	101	1,600	78	8	...	93	259	671	85
	F. ...	173	1	146	27	1,771	1	14	...	8	23	15	4
Ahalup Panah	M. ...	1,171	106	159	39	1,214	14	...	...	143	377	1,113	109
	F. ...	1,409	77	158	10	1,439	8	...	...	41	57	69	1
Laifam Panah	M. ...	5,067	116	18	3	716	4	...	...	59	222	626	41
	F. ...	5,323	5	10	...	813	...	...	...	5	13	30	3
Khabam Panah	M. ...	2,707	40	35	10	1,553	17	...	...	24	134	362	29
	F. ...	2,709	2	50	3	1,463	...	...	...	4	2	10	3
Jirighat Panah	M. ...	406	37	133	14	316	12	...	...	48	86	375	21
	F. ...	375	...	114	2	327	1	...	...	7	10	8	4
Hill Section...	M. ...	31	7	4,168	763	67,461	368	31	2	53	450	880	219
	F. ...	9	...	4,717	118	72,289	29	13	...	20	72	59	6
Imphal North	M. ...	11	2	1,340	233	38,018	187	21	2	37	233	371	149
	F. ...	3	...	2,101	41	40,700	22	13	...	16	31	20	2
Imphal South	M. ...	20	5	3,810	510	29,443	181	...	...	15	227	509	70
	F. ...	6	...	3,610	77	31,589	7	...	...	4	41	39	4
Khasi States	M. ...	*1,360*	*313*	*17,295*	*5,855*	*61,613*	*2,506*	*120*	*65*	*1,195*	*3,156*	*6,529*	*2,426*
	F. ...	*376*	*56*	*15,964*	*4,440*	*64,541*	*844*	*100*	*37*	*923*	*2,430*	*2,477*	*666*

PROVINCIAL TABLE III.

TEA GARDEN POPULATION BY SEX AND RELIGION.

Five provincial tables dealing specially with the tea garden population of the province were published in the 1921 volume of tables. At this census, for reasons of economy, it has not been found possible to repeat these tables and the only information I can supply is the actual number of persons censused on tea gardens by sex and religion.

The tea gardens of Assam are all situated in the plains districts of the Assam and Surma Valleys and hence the names of the hill districts do not appear in the table.

The figures include all persons censused on tea gardens; managers, doctors, resident traders, clerks, etc., as well as the actual cooly population are, therefore, all comprised in the table.

PROVINCIAL TABLE III.—POPULATION CENSUSED ON TEA GARDENS BY SEX AND RELIGION.

District.	Number of occupied houses.	Total Population.			Hindu.		Buddhist.		Muslim.		Christian.		Tribal.		Others.	
		Persons.	Males.	Females.	Males.	Females.	Males.	Females.	Males.	Females.	Males.	Females.	Males.	Females.	Males.	Females.
1	2	3	4	5	6	7	8	9	10	11	12	13	14	15	16	17
ASSAM	277,195	979,714	523,326	456,388	499,264	427,438	583	149	15,421	8,840	10,846	8,412	13,770	11,386	483	163
SURMA VALLEY	88,836	325,471	170,267	155,204	160,183	148,049	27	4	7,602	5,086	1,280	963	1,160	1,100	6	2
Cachar Plains	39,257	147,620	77,827	69,793	73,183	66,412	5	2	3,442	2,323	546	401	650	654	1	...
Sylhet	49,579	177,851	92,440	85,411	87,000	81,637	22	2	4,160	2,763	734	562	510	446	5	2
BRAHMAPUTRA VALLEY	188,359	654,243	353,059	301,184	339,081	279,389	506	145	7,819	3,754	9,566	7,449	12,610	10,286	477	161
Goalpara	1,410	5,065	2,836	2,229	2,410	1,838	98	28	31	12	121	174	106	177	...	...
Kamrup	1,965	7,270	4,053	3,217	3,704	2,080	2	1	64	21	276	257	16	17	...	...
Darrang	37,405	133,496	73,071	60,425	60,216	40,180	107	36	1,406	377	7,636	1,096	9,461	7,196	96	51
Nowgong	6,470	23,436	12,451	10,985	10,858	9,078	18	3	436	207	820	606	417	305	3	2
Sibsagar	69,285	234,274	124,159	110,115	116,850	104,974	127	43	3,668	2,370	2,017	1,630	1,393	1,130	106	60
Lakhimpur	72,307	250,348	135,698	114,650	128,235	110,364	154	34	2,130	750	3,633	2,703	1,227	962	269	37
Sadiya Frontier Tract	416	1,403	761	642	741	621	...	...	12	6	5	4	...	...	3	11
Balipara Frontier Tract	16	51	30	21	23	19	...	...	6	2	...	...	...	...	...	...

SHILLONG: Printed and published by the Superintendent, Assam Government Press.
(Census) No 1—660—11-7-1932.